Planning for Retirement Needs

THE AMERICAN COLLEGE PRESS

Huebner School Series

Planning for Retirement Needs

14th Edition

Jamie P. Hopkins • David A. Littell

HS326-14

This publication is designed to provide accurate and authoritative information about the subject covered. While every precaution has been taken in the preparation of this material, the authors, and The American College assume no liability for damages resulting from the use of the information contained in this publication. The American College is not engaged in rendering legal, accounting, or other professional advice. If legal or other expert advice is required, the services of an appropriate professional should be sought.

© 2017 The American College Press
270 S. Bryn Mawr Avenue
Bryn Mawr, PA 19010
(888) AMERCOL (263-7265)
theamericancollege.edu
All rights reserved
ISSN: 1945-2411
ISBN-10: 1-58293-262-X
ISBN-13: 978-1-58293-262-0
Printed in the United States of America

Table of Contents

Note to Students of HS 326 xxiii
Preface xxv
Acknowledgments. xxvii
About the Authors xxix

Pension and Retirement Planning Overview 1.1
Learning Objectives 1.2
The Universe of Retirement Planning Vehicles 1.3
Tax-Advantaged Plans of Private Employers 1.4
Nonqualified Plans 1.7
IRAs 1.8
Other Types of Retirement Plans 1.9
How Tax-Advantaged Plans Benefit Employees 1.10
Case Study: Saving on a Pretax versus an After-tax Basis 1.10
A Penny Saved—More Than a Penny Earned? 1.13
Why Employers Need Tax-Advantaged Retirement Plans 1.14
Attraction and Retention of Employees 1.15
Avoidance or Appeasement of Unions 1.16
Employee Motivation. 1.16
Graceful Transition in Turning over the Workforce 1.16
Social Responsibility. 1.17
Retirement Saving as Part of Successful Compensation Planning 1.17
Why Business Owners Need Tax-Advantaged Retirement Plans 1.18
Tax Shelter for Business Owners 1.18
Liquidity Concerns 1.19
Financial Security Concerns 1.19
Accumulated Earnings Tax Concerns 1.20
Chapter Review 1.21
Key Terms and Concepts 1.21
Chapter 1: Review Questions 1.21
Chapter 1: Review Answers 1.23

The Retirement Field 2.1

v

Learning Objectives 2.2
The Legislative Environment 2.2
Regulatory Agencies 2.7
   The Internal Revenue Service 2.7
   The Department of Labor (DOL) 2.10
   Pension Benefit Guaranty Corporation (PBGC) 2.12
Pensions: Professionals and Organizations 2.14
   Plan Sponsors 2.14
   Prospects—The Candidates for Pensions 2.14
   Service and Financial Groups 2.15
Chapter Review 2.16
   Key Terms and Concepts 2.16
   Chapter 2: Review Questions 2.16
   Chapter 2: Review Answers 2.18

Preliminary Concerns in Retirement Plan Design 3.1
   Learning Objectives 3.2
Identifying Needs and Objectives 3.3
   Understanding the Fact Finder 3.3
   Choosing between a Qualified Plan and the Other Tax-Sheltered Plan 3.6
Choosing Between a Defined-Benefit and a Defined-Contribution Plan 3.7
   Rule Differences 3.8
   Comparing the Defined-Benefit and Defined-Contribution Approaches 3.10
   The Realities of the Marketplace Today 3.12
   Multiple Plans—Combining Defined-Benefit and Defined-Contribution Plans 3.13
Choosing Between a Pension Plan and a Profit-Sharing Plan 3.15
Keogh Plans 3.17
Pension Planning Fact Finder 3.19
Chapter Review 3.23
   Key Terms and Concepts 3.23
   Chapter 3: Review Questions 3.23
   Chapter 3: Review Answers 3.25

Defined-Benefit, Cash-Balance, Target-Benefit, and MPPPs 4.1
   Learning Objectives 4.2

    The Unit-Benefit Formula 4.3
    Other Defined-Benefit Formulas 4.5
    Elements of the Unit-Benefit Formula. 4.7
    Candidates for This Type of Plan 4.9
Cash-Balance Pension Plans **4.11**
    Interest Credit Rate Options 4.13
    Advantages and Disadvantages 4.14
    Legal Issues 4.14
    Candidates for This Type of Plan 4.16
Money-Purchase Pension Plans **4.16**
    Advantages and Disadvantages 4.17
Target-Benefit Pension Plans **4.19**
Chapter Review **4.21**
    Key Terms and Concepts 4.21
    Chapter 4: Review Questions 4.21
    Chapter 4: Review Answers 4.24

Profit-Sharing Plans, 401(k) Plans, Stock Bonus Plans, and ESOPs 5.1
    Learning Objectives 5.2
Profit-Sharing Plans in General. **5.2**
    Contributions. 5.3
    Allocation Formulas. 5.4
Advantages of a Profit-Sharing Plan to the Business and Business Owner **5.5**
    Disadvantages of a Profit-Sharing Plan to the Business and Business Owner 5.6
    Candidates for Profit-Sharing Plans 5.6
Cash or Deferred Arrangements—401(k) Plans. **5.8**
    Special Rules That Apply to 401(k) Plans 5.9
    401(k) Design Considerations 5.17
    Candidates for a 401(k) Plan. 5.25
Stock Bonus Plans and Employee Stock Ownership Plans (ESOPs) **5.27**
    Stock Bonus Plans 5.28
    Employee Stock Ownership Plans 5.29
    Reasons Candidates Choose Stock Bonus Plans and ESOPs 5.30
Case Study: Baker Manufacturing, Inc. **5.31**
Chapter Review **5.32**

Key Terms and Concepts 5.32
Chapter 5: Review Questions 5.32
Chapter 5: Review Answers 5.35

SEPs, SIMPLEs, and 403(b) Plans 6.1
Learning Objectives 6.2
SEPs 6.2
Characteristics of the SEP 6.3
SEP Candidates 6.6
SIMPLEs 6.7
Plan Requirements 6.7
Candidates for the SIMPLE 6.10
403(b) Plans 6.12
Overview of 403(b) Plans 6.12
Eligible Sponsors 6.12
Employee Status 6.13
Funding Vehicles 6.13
Vesting Provisions 6.14
Employee Elections to Defer Salary 6.14
Employer Contributions 6.16
Regulatory and Administrative Aspects 6.17
Loans and Distributions 6.18
Mini-Cases: Tax-Advantaged Retirement Plans 6.18
Case One—Facts 6.18
Case Two—Facts 6.18
Case Three—Facts 6.19
Case Four—Facts 6.19
Chapter Review 6.19
Key Terms and Concepts 6.19
Chapter 6: Mini-Case Answers 6.19
Chapter 6: Review Questions 6.21
Chapter 6: Review Answers 6.23

Coverage, Eligibility, and Participation Rules 7.1
Learning Objectives 7.2

Qualified Plan Coverage Requirements.......................7.4
The Definition of a Highly Compensated Employee......................7.4
The 410(b) Rule.......................7.4
The 401(a)(26) Minimum-Participation Rule......................7.8
Planning Opportunities under the Coverage Rules......................7.9
When Should Participation Begin?.......................7.11
The 2-Year/100 Percent Rule......................7.12
Entry Date......................7.12
Determining Service......................7.13
Case Study: The Matthew Matt Manufacturing Company......................7.16
Aggregation Rules.......................7.17
Controlled-Group Rules......................7.17
Affiliated Service Group Rules......................7.19
The Leasing of Employees......................7.20
Other Tax-Sheltered Retirement Plans.......................7.22
SIMPLEs......................7.23
403(b) Plans......................7.23
Chapter Review.......................7.23
Key Terms and Concepts......................7.23
Chapter 7: Review Questions......................7.24
Chapter 7: Review Answers......................7.26

Designing Benefit Formulas and Employee Contributions......8.1
Learning Objectives......................8.2
Nondiscrimination in Benefits.......................8.2
Nondiscrimination Rules......................8.2
Accrued Benefits......................8.4
Calculating Service......................8.5
Compensation for Benefit-Formula Purposes......................8.6
Amending Benefit Formulas......................8.7
Defined-Contribution Plans.......................8.7
Level Percentage of Compensation......................8.8
Integration with Social Security......................8.8
Cross-testing......................8.11
Types of Plans and Nondiscrimination Approaches......................8.16
Defined-Benefit Plans.......................8.19

    Uniform Percentage of Compensation 8.19
    Integration with Social Security 8.19
    Other Plan-Design Alternatives. 8.22
Voluntary Employee Contributions 8.22
    Nondiscrimination Requirements for Employee Contributions and Employer Matching Contributions. 8.23
Chapter Review 8.24
    Key Terms and Concepts 8.24
    Chapter 8: Review Questions 8.24
    Chapter 8: Review Answers 8.26

Helping Clients Choose the Best Loan, Vesting, and Retirement-Age Provisions 9.1
    Learning Objectives 9.2
Plan Loans. 9.2
Are Plan Loans Appropriate for Your Clients? 9.3
    The Advantages and Disadvantages of Plan Loans 9.3
    Types of Plans. 9.3
Legal Parameters for Plan Loans 9.4
    Loan Availability 9.4
    Restrictions on Amounts and Repayments. 9.5
Vesting 9.6
    Understanding the Vesting System. 9.6
    Vesting Schedules for Defined-Benefit Plans 9.6
    Vesting Schedules for Defined-Contribution Plans. 9.7
    General Vesting Considerations 9.8
    Choosing the Most Appropriate Vesting Schedule. 9.9
    Additional Vesting Rules 9.10
Retirement Ages. 9.12
    Normal Retirement Age. 9.13
    Early Retirement 9.14
    Deferred Retirement 9.15
Top-Heavy Rules. 9.16
    When Is a Plan Top-Heavy? 9.16
    Top-Heavy Provisions 9.17
    Special Top-Heavy Vesting Schedules 9.17

    Minimum Benefits and Contributions for Non-Key Employees 9.18
    Planning Considerations. 9.19
Chapter Review 9.20
    Key Terms and Concepts 9.20
    Chapter 9: Review Questions 9.20
    Chapter 9: Review Answers 9.24

Death and Disability Benefits 10.1
    Learning Objectives 10.2
Death Benefits 10.2
    Mandatory Death Benefits: QPSA and QJSA 10.2
    Incidental Rules for Death Benefits. 10.4
    Incidental Rule for Postretirement Death Benefits 10.6
    Tax Implications of Life Insurance. 10.6
    Death Benefit Plan Design 10.8
Disability Benefits. 10.9
Retirement Plan Beneficiary Designation Planning 10.10
Mini-Cases: Death and Disability Benefits. 10.14
    Case One—Facts 10.14
    Case Two—Facts 10.14
    Case Three—Facts 10.14
Chapter Review 10.15
    Key Terms and Concepts 10.15
    Chapter 10: Mini-Case Answers 10.15
    Chapter 10: Review Questions 10.19
    Chapter 10: Review Answers 10.21

Plan Funding and Investing 11.1
    Learning Objectives 11.2
Plan Funding Requirements 11.2
    Funding Defined-Benefit Plans. 11.3
    Funding Requirements for Other Types of Plans 11.7
Funding Vehicles 11.9
    Trusts. 11.9
    Common Trust Funds 11.11

    Split-Funded Plans 11.11
Insurance-Funded Plans 11.12
Establishing Investment Guidelines 11.13
    Why Establish Investment Guidelines? 11.13
    Who Establishes Investment Guidelines? 11.14
    Funding Policy and Plan Objectives 11.14
    Investment Responsibilities 11.15
    Investment Policy 11.16
    Investment Goals 11.16
    Monitoring Investment Management 11.17
    Reviewing Investment Guidelines 11.17
Investment Considerations 11.17
    Investment Considerations Specific to Pension Investing 11.17
    Unrelated Business Income Tax 11.18
    Diversification Requirements for Defined-Contribution Plans 11.19
Investment Classes 11.19
    Hedge Funds and Private Equity 11.25
Chapter Review 11.26
    Key Terms and Concepts 11.26
    Chapter 11: Review Questions 11.26
    Chapter 11: Review Answers 11.28

Fiduciary Responsibility **12.1**
    Learning Objectives 12.2
Scope of Fiduciary Rules 12.2
    Plans Subject to ERISA 12.3
    Individuals Considered Fiduciaries under ERISA 12.4
    Plan Assets 12.5
Affirmative Fiduciary Obligations 12.6
    Exclusive-Benefit Rule 12.6
    Prudence 12.8
    Diversification of Investments 12.9
    Conformance with Documents 12.9
    Participant Fee Disclosure 12.10
Limitations: The Individual Account Plan Exception **12.12**
    General Requirements 12.12

Participants Failing to Exercise Control	12.14
Limitations on Relief	12.15

Prohibited Transactions 12.15
    Prohibited-Transaction Exemptions 12.17
    Common Problems 12.19
    Eligible Investment Advice 12.19
    Fee Disclosure 12.20

Fiduciary Liability 12.22
    Limiting Liability 12.23
    Bonding 12.24
    Expanded Fiduciary Role 12.25

Chapter Review 12.27
    Key Terms and Concepts 12.27
    Chapter 12: Review Questions 12.27
    Chapter 12: Review Answers 12.29

Plan Installation and Administration 13.1
    Learning Objectives 13.2

Setting up a Corporate Plan 13.3

Annual Administration of a Corporate Plan 13.8
    Annual Report 13.9
    Participant Communications 13.12
    Special Issues Applicable to Keogh Plans 13.16

Additional Administrative Issues 13.17
    Divorce 13.17
    Compliance Problems 13.19

Chapter Review 13.23
    Key Terms and Concepts 13.23
    Chapter 13: Review Questions 13.23
    Chapter 13: Review Answers 13.25

Retirement Plan Termination 14.1
    Learning Objectives 14.2

To Terminate or Not to Terminate 14.3
    Why Plan Termination? 14.3

    Alternatives to Plan Termination 14.3
    Limitations on Plan Termination 14.5
Terminating a Defined-Contribution Plan 14.6
    Submitting the Plan to the IRS 14.7
Terminating a Defined-Benefit Plan 14.7
    Plans Covered under the PBGC Insurance Program 14.8
    Plans Not Covered under the PBGC Insurance Program 14.9
    Reversion of Excess Plan Assets 14.9
Distributions From a Terminating Plan 14.10
Terminations by Operation of Law 14.11
    Partial Plan Termination 14.12
    Profit-Sharing Plans 14.13
    Involuntary Terminations of Defined-Benefit Plans 14.14
    Abandoned Plan Program 14.14
Chapter Review 14.15
    Key Terms and Concepts 14.15
    Chapter 14: Review Questions 14.15
    Chapter 14: Review Answers 14.17

Nonqualified Retirement Plans: An Overview 15.1
    Learning Objectives 15.2
Nonqualified Versus Qualified Plans 15.4
    Case Study: The Smallco Company 15.5
Tax Considerations 15.5
    Economic Benefit Doctrine 15.6
    Code Sec. 409A 15.6
    Code Sec. 83 . . . . 15.10
    Code Sec. 3121(v)(2) 15.11
Choosing a Nonqualified Plan 15.13
    Determining the Company's Needs 15.13
    Choosing the Right Type of Plan 15.15
Design Considerations 15.18
    Forfeiture Provisions 15.18
    Protecting the Executive 15.19
    Other Features in Plan Design 15.20
Plan Funding 15.22

Funded Plans 15.22
Unfunded Plans. 15.23
Informally Funded Plans 15.23
Income Tax Effects on the Employer. 15.23
"Funding" Nonqualified Plans with Life Insurance 15.24
Benefit Security **15.26**
Rabbi Trust 15.26
Secular Trusts 15.28
Surety Bonds **15.29**
The Installation of Nonqualified Plans **15.29**
ERISA Considerations. 15.29
Installation Process. 15.31
Sec. 457 Plans. **15.31**
457(b) Eligible Plans 15.32
457(f) Ineligible Plans 15.34
Executive-Bonus Life Insurance Plans. **15.35**
Implementation of Sec. 162 Plans 15.36
Double-Bonus Plans. 15.36
Chapter Review **15.37**
Key Terms and Concepts 15.37
Chapter 15: Review Questions 15.37
Chapter 15: Review Answers 15.40

Equity-Based Compensation Plans: And Overview 16.1
Learning Objectives 16.2
Reasons for Equity-Based Compensation. **16.2**
Assessing the Closely Held Business. **16.4**
Valuation 16.4
Mechanism for Repurchasing Stock. 16.5
Performance Criteria. 16.5
Extent of Employee's Economic Risk. 16.6
Federal Tax Consequences. 16.6
Corporate Structure 16.7
Other Legal and Accounting Considerations **16.9**
Other Preliminary Concerns **16.9**
Creating a Plan or Program. 16.9

Accounting Considerations	16.10
Public Corporations	16.11
Stock Option Plans	**16.13**
What Is an Option?	16.13
Nonqualified Stock Options (NQSOs)	16.14
Incentive Stock Options (ISOs)	16.19
Tax Withholding and Employment Taxes	16.21
Choosing and Designing a Plan	16.21
Exercising NQSOs and ISOs	16.23
Gifting Opportunities	16.25
Employee Stock Purchase Plans	**16.27**
Tax Consequences	16.29
Qualification Requirements	16.30
Planning	16.31
Other Forms of Equity-Based Compensation	**16.31**
Restricted Stock	16.32
Stock Appreciation Right	16.34
Chapter Review	**16.35**
Key Terms and Concepts	16.35
Chapter 16: Review Questions	16.35
Chapter 16: Answers	16.37

Individual Retirement Plans—Part I ... 17.1

Learning Objectives	17.2
Overview of Individual Retirement Plans	**17.2**
Contribution Limits	**17.3**
Spousal IRAs	17.4
Catch-up Election	17.5
Timing of Contributions	17.5
Excess Contributions	17.5
Recharacterization	17.5
Traditional IRAs	**17.6**
Eligibility for Deductible Contributions	17.6
Rollover Contributions	17.10
Tax Treatment of Distributions	17.11
Roth IRAs	**17.12**

Rollovers and Conversions 17.13
Tax Treatment of Roth IRA Distributions 17.14
Chapter Review 17.15
Key Terms and Concepts 17.15
Chapter 17: Review Questions 17.15
Chapter 17: Review Answers 17.18

Individual Retirement Plans—Part II 18.1
Learning Objectives 18.2
Funding Vehicles 18.2
Individual Retirement Accounts (IRAs) 18.2
Individual Retirement Annuities (IRA Annuities) 18.3
Types of Investments 18.3
Investment Restrictions. 18.4
IRAs Used with SEPs and SIMPLEs 18.6
IRAs and the Financial Services Professional 18.6
Should Your Client Make an IRA or Roth IRA Contribution? 18.7
Easier Access to IRA funds. 18.9
Choosing the Roth IRA over the Nondeductible IRA 18.11
Choosing the Roth IRA over the Deductible IRA 18.12
IRA-to-Roth IRA Conversions 18.14
Deemed IRAs 18.16
Chapter Review 18.17
Key Terms and Concepts 18.17
Chapter 18: Review Questions 18.17
Chapter 18: Review Answers 18.19

Social Security 19.1
Learning Objectives 19.2
Background/History 19.2
Extent of Coverage 19.3
Breadth of Coverage 19.5
Funding 19.6
Eligibility for Benefits 19.7
Currently Insured 19.8

Disability Insured... 19.8
Types of Benefits Clients Receive............................ **19.9**
    Retirement Benefits... 19.9
    Survivors Benefits... 19.10
    Disability Benefits... 19.11
    Eligibility for Dual OASDI Benefits......................... 19.11
    Termination of Benefits.................................... 19.11
Amount of Benefits Clients Can Expect...................... **19.12**
    Calculation of AIME....................................... 19.12
    Determination of PIA and Monthly Benefits.................. 19.14
    Other Factors Affecting Benefits........................... 19.16
Requesting Information and Filing for Benefits............. **19.18**
Taxation of Social Security Benefits....................... **19.19**
When to Take Early Retirement Benefits.................... **19.21**
    Threshold Issues.. 19.22
Chapter Review.. **19.25**
    Key Terms and Concepts................................... 19.25
    Chapter 19: Review Questions.............................. 19.25
    Chapter 19: Review Answers................................ 19.27

Introduction to Individual Retirement Planning............ 20.1
    Learning Objectives.. 20.2
The Role of the Retirement Planner......................... **20.3**
    Does the Retirement Planner Have an Impossible Task?...... 20.4
    Retirement Resources...................................... 20.6
    Steps in the Retirement Planning Process................... 20.7
Critical Issues That Affect Retirement Planning............ **20.9**
    Issue One: Employer Sponsored Retirement Plan Availability.... 20.10
    Issue Two: Women and Retirement.......................... 20.10
    Issue Three: The Need for Education and Planners........... 20.12
    Issue Four: The Changing Face of Retirement................ 20.13
    Issue Five: Baby Boomers and Retirement.................... 20.14
    Issue Six: Roadblocks to Retirement Saving.................. 20.15
    Issue Seven: Retirement Objectives......................... 20.16
The Retirement Ladder: Sources of Retirement Income...... **20.16**
Chapter Review.. **20.19**

Key Terms and Concepts	20.19
Chapter 20: Review Questions	20.19
Chapter 20: Review Answers	20.21

Retirement Needs Analysis: The Assumptions 21.1
Learning Objectives	21.2
Assumption One: Retirement Age	**21.2**
Reasons Clients Choose Early Retirement (Or Have It Thrust Upon Them)	21.3
Reasons Clients Should View Early Retirement Skeptically	21.5
Other Considerations	21.7
Assumption Two: Life Expectancy	**21.8**
Assumption Three: Expected Standard of Living During Retirement	**21.9**
Late-Career Clients	21.9
Mid-Career Clients	21.9
Early-Career Clients	21.9
The Replacement-Ratio Method	21.10
The Expense Method	21.15
Assumption Four: Expected Inflation Before and During Retirement	**21.18**
Illustrating the Effect of Increases in Inflation and Standards of Living	21.19
Assumption Five: Total Return on Investments	**21.20**
Retirement Investment Strategies	21.20
Chapter Review	**21.24**
Key Terms and Concepts	21.24
Chapter 21: Review Questions	21.24
Chapter 21: Review Answers	21.25

Developing Retirement Savings and the Building Blocks of a Retirement Income Plan 22.1
Learning Objectives	22.2
Products for the Systematic Withdrawal Approach	**22.18**
Chapter Review	**22.25**
Key Terms and Concepts	22.25
Chapter 22: Review Questions	22.25
Chapter 22: Review Answers	22.27

Additional Retirement Planning Issues 23.1
    Learning Objectives 23.2
Choosing to Move 23.2
    Tax Implications of Selling a Home 23.3
    Planning for a Move 23.3
    Relocation Out of State 23.6
Planning for Clients Remaining in Their Homes 23.7
    Creating Income from the Home 23.8
Medicare and Retiree Health Care 23.12
    Eligibility for Medicare 23.12
    Part A Benefits 23.14
    Part B Benefits 23.16
    Part D Drug Benefits 23.16
Additional Coverage for Those Eligible for Medicare 23.18
    Medicare Supplement (Medigap) Insurance 23.18
    Managed Care Option under Medicare 23.19
    Employer-Provided Health Benefits 23.21
Medical Coverage Before Eligibility for Medicare 23.21
    COBRA Coverage 23.21
    Other Options 23.22
Long-Term Care Insurance 23.23
    The Need for Long-Term Care 23.23
    Characteristics of Individual Policies 23.24
    Deductibility of Premiums and Taxation of Benefits 23.29
Advance Directives 23.30
Chapter Review 23.32
    Key Terms and Concepts 23.32
    Chapter 23: Review Questions 23.32
    Chapter 23: Review Answers 23.35

Distributions from Retirement Plans—Part I 24.1
    Learning Objectives 24.2
Tax Treatment 24.3
    Tax Treatment in General 24.3
    Estate Taxation of Pension Accumulations 24.3
    Sec. 72(t) Penalty Tax 24.4

Nontaxable Distributions. 24.11
IRA Distributions 24.11
Roth IRAs and Roth Accounts 24.15
Exclusion of Income for Charitable Contributions 24.18
Rollovers **24.19**
Distributions from Qualified, Governmental 457, and 403(b) Plans 24.20
Distributions from IRAs 24.22
Rollovers by Beneficiaries. 24.23
Waivers for the 60-Day Rollover Requirement 24.24
Lump-Sum Distributions **24.25**
Net Unrealized Appreciation 24.26
Taking Advantage of the NUA Rule. 24.27
Minimum-Distribution Rules **24.28**
General 24.28
Required Minimum Distributions at the Required Beginning Date 24.29
Preretirement Death Benefits 24.37
Beneficiary Issues. 24.38
Additional Rules 24.39
Planning 24.41
Chapter Review **24.43**
Key Terms and Concepts 24.43
Chapter 24: Review Questions 24.43
Chapter 24: Review Answers 24.47

Distributions from Retirement Plans—Part II 25.1
Learning Objectives 25.2
Choosing a Distribution Option. **25.2**
Distribution Options Available from the Plan 25.3
Reasons to Consider a Longevity Annuity 25.7
IRAs. 25.12
403(b) Plans 25.13
Putting It All Together **25.13**
Qualified Plans 25.14
IRAs. 25.15
Working with Clients 25.17
Mini-Cases: Distributions From Retirement Plans **25.23**

    Case One—Facts 25.23
    Case Two—Facts 25.23
    Case Three—Facts 25.24
Chapter Review **25.24**
    Key Terms and Concepts 25.24
    Chapter 25: Answers to Mini-Cases 25.24
    Chapter 25: Review Questions 25.30
    Chapter 25: Review Answers 25.32
Appendix A: Post-ERISA Legislation **A.1**
Appendix B: Pension Acronyms **B.3**
Appendix C: Average Life Expectancies **C.3**
Appendix D: Annuity Tables **D.1**
Index **Index.1**

Note to Students of HS 326

For those of you reading this book in conjunction with The American College's HS 326 course, please note the following:

Due to the constant law and regulatory changes that can affect the content of this course, all students of The American College taking HS 326 are required to check the HS 326 American College Online course delivered through Blackboard to see if there have been any changes to the content. Content changes identified on Blackboard may have an impact on the exam for HS 326.

In addition, if you find any errors in the book or course materials please contact Professor Jamie Hopkins at jamie.hopkins@theamericancollege.edu. If any mistakes are found we will publish an errata sheet on Blackboard.

Preface

This book represents a radical departure from traditional pension literature by focusing primarily on the practical application of the retirement material in a financial services practice. To this end, it includes a feature titled "Your Financial Services Practice" as well as a shorter counterpart called the "Planning Note." In addition, the book is replete with examples and case studies intended to demonstrate how the pension concepts apply in real-world situations. This new practitioner-oriented approach came about for a variety of reasons, perhaps the most important of which is that student feedback indicated a need for change in this direction.

This book is geared to those with little or no experience in the retirement field. The material focuses on the basics that a financial services professional needs to know and deals sparingly with the retirement concepts that are not germane. For example, stock plans are not discussed in great detail because they are not typically a part of the typical financial services professional's practice. In addition, the amount of detail on any given topic depends on the topic's relevance to our audience. Determining the appropriate plan for the small business is covered in great detail, for example, whereas funding defined-benefit plans (which is handled by the plan's actuary) is covered only briefly. While the material is applicable to the large-, medium-, and small-plan markets, the emphasis is on the small-plan market, where the financial services professional does most of his or her business.

Almost all general statements that one can make about pension material are subject to qualification or exception. If the qualifying remark or exception is of significant magnitude, we have put it into the text as a parenthetical expression. If the qualifying statement or exception would serve to confuse the larger issue, however, we have omitted it so you will not get caught up in the minutia and miss the major point.

It is our sincere hope that this practitioner-oriented approach will speak to your interests and provide both a practical and educational treatment of retirement planning for the business and the business owner as well as for the individual. For those interested in learning more about the topics discussed in other course materials and books prepared by The American College, related courses includes the following:

Acknowledgments

The authors would like to acknowledge the help of many individuals who were instrumental in the development of current/former editions of this textbook.

- Current and former faculty members who participated in the drafting of this text, including William J. Ruckstuhl, Edward E. Graves, Don A. Taylor, Burton T. Beam, Jr., Ted Kurlowicz, and John J. McFadden
- The College's editing team, especially Corinne Myers and Jane Hassinger
- Stephen Rosen of Stephen H. Rosen & Associates for his actuarial guidance and examples

About the Authors

Jamie Patrick Hopkins, Esq., MBA, LLM, CLU®, RICP®, is Associate Professor of Taxation at The American College of Financial Services in the Retirement Income Program and is Co-director of the New York Life Center for Retirement Income. He also holds the Larry R. Pike Chair in Insurance and Investments at The College. Teaching courses in retirement, estate planning, and life insurance, he has educated thousands of financial services professionals and continues to move the needle for retirement income planning.

Professor Hopkins is recognized as one of the leading retirement planning experts in the United States and, in 2015, was selected by InvestmentNews for its list of the top 40 financial services professionals under the age of 40. Professor Hopkins has also contributed numerous articles for periodicals including Villanova Law Review, Nebraska Law Review, and Hastings Science & Technology Law Journal, and has authored articles published by the American Bar Association and the Pennsylvania Bar Association.

Professor Hopkins received his Bachelor of Arts degree in political science at Davidson College. He then attended Villanova University School of Law, where he obtained his JD and graduated with honors. He later received his MBA from the Villanova University School of Business. Professor Hopkins also holds an LLM from Temple University and two financial planning designations from The American College: the Chartered Life Underwriter® (CLU®) and Retirement Certified Professional® (RICP®).

David A. Littell, JD, ChFC®, holds the Joseph E. Boettner Chair in Research at The American College of Financial Services where he teaches and develops courses and textbooks for both graduate and certificate programs dealing with planning for retirement needs and understanding the older client. He is the co-creator of the Retirement Income Certified Professional® (RICP®) designation and coordinates its course curriculum. As Co-director of The American College New York Life Center for Retirement Income, Professor Littell manages the Center's website containing over 300 educational videos. He also designs original research projects and interacts with media to promote industry and consumer articles on retirement income planning.

Professor Littell speaks regularly to financial advisors on the topics of pensions, retirement planning, and working with older clients. He also co-authored several books associated with The College's courses, including *Planning for Retirement Needs, Financial Decision Making at Retirement*, and *The Practitioner's Guide to Advanced Pension Topics*. He has published numerous articles for such periodicals as the *Journal of Financial Service Professionals, FOCUS, Compensation and Benefits Management*, and *Benefits Quarterly*. In 1997, Professor Littell won an Article Award from the Certified Financial Planner® (CFP®) Board of Standards. He also has served on several CFP® item-writing committees for the CFP® Board of Examiners.

Professor Littell received a Bachelor of Arts in Psychology degree from Northwestern University and earned a Juris Doctorate at the Boston University School of Law. He also received the Chartered Financial Consultant® (ChFC®) designation from The American College of Financial Services.

The American College

The American College® is an independent, nonprofit, accredited institution founded in 1927 that offers professional certification and graduate-degree distance education to men and women seeking career growth in financial services.

The Solomon S. Huebner School® of The American College administers the Chartered Life Underwriter (CLU®); the Chartered Financial Consultant (ChFC®); the Chartered Special Needs Consultant (ChSNC™); the Chartered Leadership Fellow® (CLF®); the Retirement Income Certified Professional (RICP®); and the Financial Services Certified Professional (FSCP®) professional designation programs. In addition, The College offers a prep program for the CFP® certification.[1]

The Richard D. Irwin Graduate School® of The American College offers a Master of Science in Financial Services (MSFS) degree, a Master of Science in Management (MSM), a one-year program with an emphasis in leadership, and a PhD in Financial and Retirement Planning. Additionally, it offers the Chartered Advisor in Philanthropy® (CAP®) and several graduate-level certificates that concentrate on specific subject areas.

The American College is accredited by **The Middle States Commission on Higher Education**, 3624 Market Street, Philadelphia, PA 19104 at telephone number 267.284.5000.

The Middle States Commission on Higher Education is a regional accrediting agency recognized by the U.S. Department of Education and the Commission on Recognition of Postsecondary Accreditation. Middle States accreditation is an expression of confidence in an institution's mission and goals, performance, and resources. It attests that in the judgment of the Commission on Higher Education, based on the results of an internal institutional self-study and an evaluation by a team of outside peer observers assigned by the Commission, an institution is guided by well-defined and appropriate goals; that it has established conditions and procedures under which its goals can be realized; that it is accomplishing them substantially; that it is so organized, staffed, and supported that it can be expected to continue to do so; and that it meets the standards of the Middle States Association. The American College has been accredited since 1978.

The American College does not discriminate on the basis of race, religion, sex, handicap, or national and ethnic origin in its admissions policies, educational programs and activities, or employment policies.

The American College is located at 270 S. Bryn Mawr Avenue, Bryn Mawr, PA 19010. The toll-free number of the Office of Professional Education is (888) 263-7265; the fax number is (610) 526-1465; and the home page address is theamericancollege.edu.

---

1. Certified Financial Planner Board of Standards, Inc., owns the certification marks CFP®, CERTIFIED FINANCIAL PLANNER™, and CFP (with flame logo)®, which it awards to individuals who successfully complete initial and ongoing certification requirements.

Chapter 1

Pension and Retirement Planning Overview

Learning Objectives

An understanding of the material in this chapter should enable the student to

LO 1.1 Identify why tax-advantaged retirement plans are a beneficial retirement-saving vehicle for employees.

LO 1.2 Explain how tax-advantaged retirement plans benefit employers.

LO 1.3 Explain how tax-advantaged plans benefit business owners.

Retirement planning continues to be an important marketplace for the financial services professional. Public consciousness regarding the need for retirement planning has never been higher. The baby-boom generation (1946–1964) is marching toward retirement age (the first baby-boomers reached age 65 in 2011 and in 2016 the first baby-boomers reached age 70.5); and employer sponsored retirement plan benefits are more visible to consumers as employers promote the advantages of employee involvement in 401(k) and 403(b) plans. But this is only part of the story. The retirement market is where the money is; $25 trillion in assets (which is up from $19.7 trillion in 2012), including plans sponsored by private employers, government plans, IRAs, and annuities.[1] At the end of 2016, IRAs have $7.8 trillion in assets, as compared to $7 trillion in defined contribution plans. Also, Americans are aging. As of the year 2014, one out of every eight Americans was over age 65 and, by the year 2040,[2] that figure will increase to one out of five. In 2017, there are roughly 48 million people in the U.S. age 65 or older and by 2060 it is estimated that there will be closer to 100 million older persons, more than double today's number. Considering these demographics, the potential for the growth of the retirement market is nothing short of tremendous.

For financial services professionals, the retirement market offers many attractive and lucrative opportunities to serve clients, including:

- setting up qualified plans or other tax-advantaged retirement plans for corporations and other for-profit business entities
- setting up retirement programs for nonprofit organizations
- designing retirement programs that meet the owner-employee's tax and savings objectives
- modifying existing retirement programs to maximize tax-shelter potential, either by changing the existing plan or by instituting multiple plans

---

1. Investment Company Institute News Release, Quarterly Retirement Market Data, Third Quarter, 2016.
2. United States Department of Health and Human Services, Administration for Community Living, Administration on Aging, *Aging Statistics*, available at https://aoa.acl.gov/Aging_Statistics/Index.aspx.

- supplementing existing retirement programs with 401(k) plans
- updating existing 401(k) and other plans to conform with changing organizational needs
- updating existing plans to conform with legislative changes
- advising clients about investment strategies that are appropriate for retirement programs
- selling investment products that are appropriate for retirement programs
- planning for the purchase of life insurance in tax-sheltered plans
- setting up nonqualified plans for executives
- selling IRAs and Roth IRAs to clients
- planning for a client's retirement
- planning for the best disposition of a client's retirement benefits

Many financial services professionals choose to specialize in pensions. Others, however, complement their existing practice by providing one or more of these services under the umbrella of comprehensive financial planning. Whether you choose to specialize or offer a number of these services to clients as part of a comprehensive package, the information in this book should open up a world of opportunity.

THE UNIVERSE OF RETIREMENT PLANNING VEHICLES

LO 1.1   Identify why tax-advantaged retirement plans are a beneficial retirement saving vehicle for employees.

Entering the world of employer and individually sponsored retirement vehicles means exposure to a new vocabulary. Learning and remembering this terminology is facilitated through the careful organization and categorization of the material. You will find that many plans share similar features and have only occasional or slight differences. Additionally, the charts and tables throughout the book will help you remember the material.

Tax-Advantaged Plans of Private Employers

tax-advantaged retirement plans

qualified plans

One way to organize this discussion is to look at the types of **tax-advantaged retirement plans** that can be sponsored by for-profit and nonprofit employers. Most of these are employer-sponsored plans, referred to as **qualified plans**. Qualified plans, subject to Code Sec. 401(a), include defined-benefit pension plans, cash-balance plans, money-purchase pension plans, target-benefit plans, profit-sharing plans, 401(k) plans, stock bonus plans, and ESOPs.

All qualified plans are subject to a number of basic requirements, and each type of plan has its own special characteristics. Two other types of tax-advantaged plans available to for-profit entities, that are not qualified plans because they are not subject to the same ERISA Code Sec. 401(a) rules, are referred to as SEPs (simplified employee pensions) and SIMPLEs (savings incentive match plans for employees). Eleven types of tax-exempt entities can also sponsor qualified plans, SEPs, and SIMPLEs. In addition, public school systems and those nonprofit organizations qualifying for Code Sec. 501(c)(3) tax-exempt status can sponsor 403(b) plans that are also referred to as tax-sheltered annuities. These 11 types of tax-advantaged plans make up the bulk of the retirement market because of their tax advantages, business applications, and special appeal to the business owner.

Universe of Qualified Plans
1. Defined-benefit pension plan
2. Cash-balance pension plan
3. Money-purchase pension plan
4. Target-benefit pension plan
5. Profit-sharing plan
6. 401(k) plan
7. Stock bonus plan
8. ESOP (employee stock ownership plan)

All of the employer-sponsored tax-advantaged plans share some characteristics. First, they all provide for deferred compensation. The compensation may be part of an employee's salary that is held for retirement (as in a salary reduction 401(k) plan, SIMPLE, or 403(b) plan), a share of the profits (as in a profit-sharing plan), an employer-provided amount equal to a percentage of salary (as in a money-purchase plan), or the promise of a monthly salary substitute after retirement (as in a defined-benefit plan). In all tax-advantaged plans, the sponsor is required to make contributions to a trust, an insurance contract, or, in the case of a SEP or SIMPLE, an IRA account. Such amounts are held and invested, and distributed only at a later time according to the rules applicable to that plan.

Other Tax-Advantaged Plans Available to Private Employers
- SEPs (simplified employee pensions)
- SIMPLEs (savings incentive match plans for employees)
- 403(b) plans (limited to 501(c)(3) organizations and public school systems)

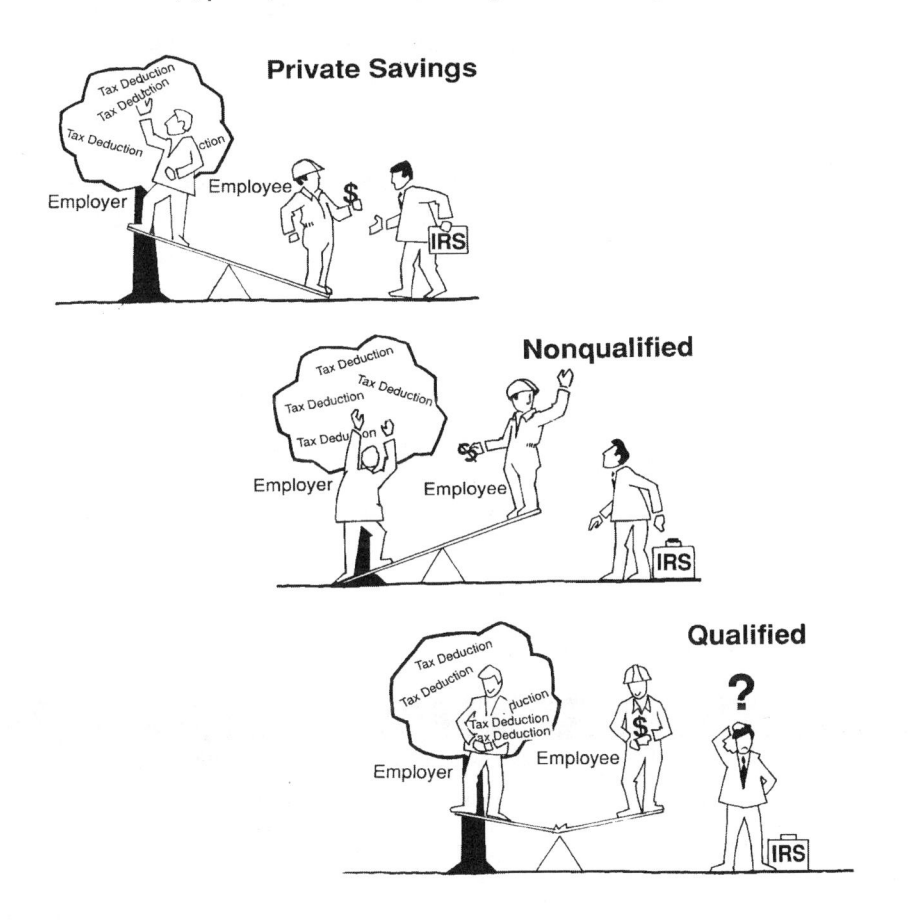

Private Savings

Nonqualified

Qualified

There are four key special tax rules for tax-advantaged retirement plans. First, the employer receives a tax deduction at the time employer contributions are made to the plan, even though employees do not have to pay income tax until benefits are paid to them. Under the normal rules that apply to the taxation of compensation, the employer is eligible for a tax deduction only when employees are determined to have taxable income. For example, in a nonqualified plan for executives, the taxation of compensation can be deferred, but it is accompanied with the cost of deferring the employer's deduction until when taxes are paid by the employee. The normal taxation rules are like a seesaw—the employer on one end can be elevated (receive a tax deduction) only if the employee at the other end is touching the ground (paying taxes). Conversely, the employee can be elevated (avoid paying taxes) only if the employer is on the ground (not receiving a tax deduction). These "laws of tax physics" are suspended, however, if the employer is willing to satisfy the requirements of one of the tax-advantaged retirement plans.

A second unique tax advantage is that income on assets held in a trust or an insurance product is not taxed. Retirement investments earn interest and appreciate without being subject to taxation in the year any gain occurs. Although such amounts are not taxed at this level, income is taxed as it is paid out as part of an employee's benefits.

A third advantage has to do with taxation of distributions. As we have discussed, benefits are not taxed until they are distributed from the plan. Unlike nonqualified plans, the participant in a qualified plan can make an election as to the form of payment at the time benefits are to begin.

The fourth advantage is the ability to roll benefits into other tax-deferred vehicles when the participant becomes eligible to receive the benefit. This typically means that the individual can defer paying taxes until the time that he or she intends to spend the funds.

Tax Treatment of Tax-Advantaged Retirement Plans
- Employer deduction with contribution
- No tax on trust account
- Employee taxed on benefits distributed
- Ability to roll distributions into other tax-deferred plans

Nonqualified versus Tax-Advantaged Plans

Issue	Nonqualified Plan	Tax-Advantaged Plan
Employer's tax deduction	Deducted at the time employees have taxable income	Deducted at the time contributions are made to the plan
Tax treatment of earnings	Earnings on assets held to pay benefits are taxed as income to the employer	Earnings are not taxed at the trust level
Back-end tax advantages	Plan can be designed to defer taxes until benefits are distributed; law does not allow rollovers to other tax-deferred plans	Taxes are paid at the time of distribution unless benefits are rolled into another tax-advantaged plan
Coverage	Can limit plan to certain key executives	Must cover a portion of rank-and-file employees
Administrative costs	Lower—few administrative requirements	Higher—significant reporting and administrative obligations

Qualified plans have some additional special tax rules and benefits that are not available in or applicable to all other plans. Currently, only qualified plans allow a portion of the plan's assets to be invested in life insurance. When a qualified plan provides for death benefits paid from the proceeds of a life insurance contract, such amounts are excludible from income to the extent the payment is purely for life insurance. In addition, certain distributions from qualified plans may be eligible for special tax treatment.

In exchange for these tax advantages, the law imposes a large number of requirements on tax advantaged plans. Although the rules are different for each type of plan, there are many similarities. Before we get into the details, it is helpful to get a feeling for what types of requirements are involved.

- *Broad employee participation*—In order for the owners and managers to participate in the tax benefits, the plan must cover a significant number of rank-and-file employees.
- *Vesting*—To make sure that long-service employees who leave prior to the plan's normal retirement age receive some benefits, an employee must be vested in some benefits after he or she has reached a specified number of years of employment. Some types of plans require immediate vesting.
- *Employee communications*—All plans must describe to employees what the terms and conditions of the plan are and to what benefits a participant will be entitled.
- *Nondiscrimination*—All plans have rules regarding the relationship between the level of benefits provided for highly compensated employees and the level of benefits provided to the rank and file.
- *Prefunded*—As previously mentioned, all plans require that assets be contributed to a funding vehicle—once assets are in the plan, they are no longer owned by the employer sponsoring the plan. These assets can be used only to pay plan benefits.
- *Plan document*—Plans need to be clearly stated in writing.

Nonqualified Plans

nonqualified plan

Another very different type of employer-sponsored retirement planning vehicle is the nonqualified plan. This term usually refers to deferred-compensation plans other than the tax-advantaged plans described above. **Nonqualified plans** differ in almost every way from their tax-advantaged counterparts. Unlike tax-advantaged plans, nonqualified plans are generally for only a few key people. There are few design restrictions regarding the benefit structure, vesting requirements, or coverage. In most cases, nonqualified plans do not have separate assets.

The employer either pays benefits out of general corporate assets or sets up a side account. Sometimes a trust is set up, but assets must be available to pay the claims of creditors in order to avoid current taxation.

In exchange for the added flexibility in plan design, the tax rules are not as advantageous to nonqualified plans. A nonqualified plan can be designed to defer the payment of income taxes by the employee until benefits are paid out; however, the employer's tax deduction is deferred to the time of payout as well. This is a disincentive to the corporation because cash payments or qualified plan contributions for the executive would be currently deductible. Because the loss of the tax deduction does not affect nonprofit or governmental entities, Congress has established special limits on the amount of deferred compensation to employees of such entities under Code Sec. 457. Another difference between tax-advantaged and nonqualified plans is that benefits in nonqualified plans are not as secure. In a nonqualified arrangement, if the entity has financial difficulty, money set aside to pay benefits can be attached by creditors.

Nonqualified Plans
- Can limit to executives
- Few design restrictions
- Employer deduction matched to employee income
- Limited benefit security for participants

IRAS

individual retirement account (IRA)

The final type of plan discussed is the **individual retirement account (IRA)**. As its name implies, this type of plan is generally established not by the employer but by individuals. Although most of the text focuses on employer-sponsored plans, an understanding of both IRAs and Roth IRAs is crucial to this discussion. At times, a business owner or employee will be faced with the choice of participating in a company-sponsored plan or establishing an IRA or Roth IRA. (In some cases, an individual can choose to participate in both). Understanding the connection between employer-sponsored plans and IRAs is crucial for the following reasons:

1. Many working individuals will have the option of making a $5,500 contribution (2017 indexed limit) to a Roth IRA, and some will have the option of choosing instead to make a deductible contribution to a traditional IRA.

2. The IRA is the funding vehicle for the employer-sponsored SEP and SIMPLE. This means that most rules applicable to IRAs will apply to those plans as well.

3. A significant portion of qualified plan and 403(b) benefits paid to terminated employees are rolled over into IRAs. Participants will also have the option to convert to a Roth IRA.

Other Types of Retirement Plans

The focus of this book is on the type of retirement plans that can be sponsored by private employers. It is important to mention several other types of plans that cover a large number of employees and share many of the same characteristics as the types of plans discussed in this text. These include government plans and multiemployer plans.

Federal Government Plans

Federal Civilian employees are eligible for both promised benefits under a Federal defined-benefit type retirement plan and can also participate in a salary deferral plan referred to as the Thrift Saving Plan. The defined-benefit program for those hired before 1984 is the Civil Service Retirement System (CSRS). Under that program the benefit formula is quite generous and employees contribute 7 percent of pay. Employees under this system do not pay Social Security taxes and do not receive Social Security benefits. Federal employees hired after December 31, 1983 are generally in the Federal Employee Retirement System (FERS). Employees in this program do pay Social Security taxes and receive benefits. FERS employees make a smaller contribution to the FERS system, just .8 percent of pay, and the benefit structure is more modest.

Military retired pay is completely different than either FERS or CSRS. Generally, an individual who retires with 20 or more years of service is immediately eligible for lifetime retirement pay. The benefit structure is calculated based on the average-high-three-year-salary and years of service. Retiree pay goes all the way up to 100 percent of base pay for 40 years of service. Military employees pay Social Security taxes and are eligible for benefits.

The Thrift Savings Plan operates essentially as the federal government's 401(k) plan. It allows for salary deferral contributions and participant investment direction. All federal civilian and military employees are eligible to make salary deferral contributions. FERS civilian employees are eligible for a government matching contribution. Military and civilian employees under CSRS are not eligible for the matching contribution.

State and Local Government Plans

Unlike private sector pensions that are subject solely to federal regulation, state and local government plans created under state law, and must comply with state and local requirements, as well as government accounting and reporting standards. State and local government plans must also satisfy Federal tax qualification and age discrimination requirements. However, many of the ERISA provisions concerning funding requirements, fiduciary requirements and other ERISA provisions do not apply.

State and local governments can elect out of the Social Security system, and some have. In this case, employees are generally required to make larger required contributions and the plans provide more generous benefits.

Government entities are generally not eligible to sponsor 401(k) or 403(b) plans (except for public school systems). If these entities want to offer a salary deferral plan, the only option is a 457 plan, which for government entities operates like a 401(k) plan. Unlike 457 plans sponsored by nonprofit organizations, a government sponsored plan is funded with an irrevocable trust, and benefits can be rolled over at termination of employment to an IRA or other tax-advantaged retirement plan.

HOW TAX-ADVANTAGED PLANS BENEFIT EMPLOYEES

LO 1.2   Explain how tax-advantaged retirement plans benefit employers.

Tax-advantaged retirement plans make up the bulk of the retirement planning market because of their significant benefits to employees, employers, and business owners. Tax-sheltered plans play a vital role in the retirement security of American workers. In private industry, retirement benefits were available to 50 percent of workers in small establishments, 79 percent of workers in medium-size establishments (those employing between 100 and 499 workers), and 86 percent of workers in large establishments. Along with Social Security and individual savings, employer-provided pensions have an important effect on the retirement security of Americans.

In addition, employer-provided savings plans—such as 401(k) plans and SIMPLEs—help employees save even more for retirement by providing an easy payroll deduction savings vehicle with tax advantages for the employee. Savings plans have significantly changed the retirement planning landscape. In 2014, approximately 52 million American workers were active 401(k) participants (according to the Investment Company Institute).

Case Study: Saving on a Pretax versus an After-tax Basis

To demonstrate how saving on a tax-deferred basis affects retirement accumulations, let's take the example of William Whitecollar (aged 40), who earns $100,000 and has a marginal state and federal income tax rate of 30 percent. Whitecollar's employer offers him the opportunity to receive an additional $5,000 annually in cash or have that amount contributed to a 401(k) plan on a pretax basis. All invested money earns a 6 percent rate of return.

Under the qualified plan, Whitecollar will save $5,300 by the end of the first year.

Amount contributed	$5,000
plus 6 percent interest	$300
Amount saved after one year	$5,300

If Whitecollar invested the cash he received for retirement (individual savings approach), he would have less saved. The culprit would be the individual taxes that Whitecollar (30 percent) would have to pay on the cash and interest earnings. If Whitecollar paid taxes (30 percent) on this total amount ($5,300) after year one he would have accumulated $3,710.

Now let's look at what happens if Whitecollar saves outside of a tax-qualified retirement plan in an annually taxable account. First, Whitecollar will not be able to invest as much because taxes will be taken out immediately. Leaving only $3,500 to invest. As such, the investment returns will be less year one because there is less money to invest. Additionally, taxes will be paid on the investment returns for year 1, assuming its an annually taxable investment. In the end, Whitecollar will have $3,647 in after-tax savings at the end of year 1. Using a tax-advantaged savings vehicle saved Whitecollar an additional $63 in one year, which represents over an additional 1 percent return for that year.

	Whitecollar
Amount of bonus	$ 5,000.00
minus individual taxes	1,500.00
Amount actually saved	3,500.00
plus 6 percent interest	210.00
Subtotal	3,710.00
minus taxes on interest earned	63.00
Amount saved after one year	$3,647.00

Table 1-1
After-tax Comparison of Retirement Savings Methods*

Participant	Qualified	Individual Savings
Whitecollar at age 65	$207,047	$166,240

*Certain underlying assumptions were made that may affect the actual amount received. The assumptions do not, however, significantly affect the disparity between the savings methods.

Table 1-1 shows the growth of Whitecollar's retirement savings, both inside and outside of the plan, from ages 40 to 65. With the qualified plan, the number shown assumes accumulation to age 65, and then distribution of the entire amount to Whitecollar with taxation at a 30 percent rate. This assumption allows us to compare after-tax figures at one point in time. However, it doesn't fully represent what will happen. Most taxpayers will continue to take advantage of additional tax-deferred growth by withdrawing funds over time as they are needed. While after one year, the difference in assets is only $63 in after-tax real dollars ($3,710 compared to $3,647), the difference in assets would continue to compound over the years.

With this assumption, Whitecollar saves $40,807 more in the qualified plan than he would if he saved on an after-tax basis. This shows us an important trend, but unfortunately, quantifying the tax situation is actually a lot more complicated than it first seems. The comparison of before-tax and after-tax savings depends on how long the pension amount is held in the tax-deferred vehicle and how slowly or quickly it is distributed from the plan. In most cases, the participant takes the benefit slowly over a long period of time. The longer the deferral period, the greater the advantage to using the qualified plan. Also, the comparison is affected by the type of investments the individual chooses when saving on an after-tax basis. The previous example assumes that all earnings would be taxed each year, which would be the case if the individual invested in bonds. The tax situation is quite different if assets are invested in equities, with qualified dividends and capital gains taxed at a lower rate, and the tax on capital appreciation is deferred until the assets are sold. Because the tax situation has become more difficult to quantify today, it is important to look at other reasons why the advantaged plan has value for the participant.

YOUR FINANCIAL SERVICES PRACTICE: INVESTING THE SPREAD

In the William Whitecollar example, at the end of one year, Whitecollar would have $5,300 to invest in a qualified plan and $3,647 to invest using the private savings approach. The $1,653 difference (the spread) represents a significant opportunity to the client. In effect, Whitecollar gets to invest the money that would have been lost in taxation. This is analogous to getting an interest free loan from Uncle Sam which lasts until the time that Whitecollar takes a distribution of the assets during retirement. This "loan" is larger the higher the individual's tax rate, meaning that the tax advantage is the greatest for those in the top tax bracket.

Clients with an understanding of the time value of money should have a greater appreciation of tax-advantaged retirement plans when they view the opportunity as an interest free loan from the government. If this approach doesn't work, clients familiar with poker or other gaming will appreciate the value of betting with "house money."

A Penny Saved—More Than a Penny Earned?

An individual could accumulate funds in ways other than through a qualified plan, but clearly there are advantages to an employer-sponsored pension program. First, we will discuss employer-provided benefits, and then separately, we will discuss the opportunity to save additional amounts on a pretax basis in 401(k) plans, SIMPLEs, and 403(b) plans.

When the employer fully funds the plan, as in a defined-benefit or profit-sharing plan, the employee is developing assets to provide for retirement without any direct cost. Because the value of this benefit can be significant, it is crucial for prospective employees to carefully evaluate and compare company retirement programs.

Because the employer makes contributions, they are not part of discretionary income and the participant does not feel the same sense of sacrifice that can accompany trying to save a portion of salary. Because of federal ERISA law, these benefits are extremely secure. Assets are held in an irrevocable trust (they no longer can be used by the employer), must be invested according to strict fiduciary scrutiny, and generally offer significant flexibility in the timing and form of benefit payments. Plan participants can benefit from professional management of the trust fund and additional return due to lower investment costs than if each individual was saving separately.

If the plan allows for additional salary deferrals, a participant can benefit simply from a forced savings program through payroll deduction. Also, by saving on a steady ongoing basis, the participant can buy into the investments on a regular basis, which can reduce risk (this investment strategy is commonly referred to as dollar cost averaging). Employee contributions are often matched by the employer. An employer match can be viewed as an instant return on the employee's investment. Finally, some plans offer investment alternatives that are not available individually—for example, a guaranteed investment option that provides for a stated rate of return for a specified time period.

Today, participants in savings plans also benefit from the retirement planning and investment education that they receive from the plan sponsor and related service providers. Employees often attend seminars, receive written information, utilize software to help them with their retirement planning, and use toll-free numbers for additional information and guidance.

Furthermore, there are several other advantages for participating in employer-sponsored retirement plans versus investing on an individual basis:

- Some plans offer participant loans, giving participants a ready source of credit.
- Qualified plans may offer asset protection from the claims of creditors.

- Investment costs may be lower than with individual investors.

YOUR FINANCIAL SERVICES PRACTICE: INTEGRATING RETIREMENT PLANS AND RETIREMENT PLANNING

In today's retirement plan market, the employer sponsored retirement plan and the individual retirement planning considerations of the participants have become more integrated. With so many 401(k) and other types of plans that allow employee contributions, retirement planning has become more of a partnership between the employer and the employees. Employees are sharing some of the cost, but the employer is also providing investment education, retirement planning education, software and other planning tools and, in some cases, even individual retirement and investment advice. This integration creates a tremendous opportunity for financial services professionals competing in the employer sponsored retirement planning market. Financial advisors are uniquely trained and prepared to help meet the employer's objectives and help employees with their individual retirement planning concerns.

WHY EMPLOYERS NEED TAX-ADVANTAGED RETIREMENT PLANS

In addition to meeting the retirement needs of employees, why do employers implement a retirement program? Unlike participation in the public retirement program—Social Security—participation in a tax-advantaged or nonqualified retirement program is voluntary. Administrative and funding costs represent a major expenditure (the average cost of providing retirement benefits for private industry is 3.9 percent of total payroll, based on 2016 Bureau of Labor Statistics data). However, government provided defined benefit plans were much more expensive, costing almost 10 percent of total compensation. So, what is the bottom-line payoff for employers?

The payoff comes in the way retirement plans solve a number of operational problems. Although these solutions do not show up on the balance sheet, the following are key ingredients in a company's fiscal success:

- attraction and retention of employees
- avoidance or appeasement of unions
- employee motivation
- graceful transition in turning over the workforce
- social responsibility

- retirement saving as part of successful compensation planning

Attraction and Retention of Employees

Managers contend that the compelling reason for the salary levels and other employee benefits they offer is the local and industry standards. The same logic holds true for private pension programs. In other words, if the local pay scale calls for X amount in salary to attract and retain employees, it also calls for a certain level of retirement benefits. Further, if industry standards in insurance, for example, mandate a certain level of commissions, they also mandate a certain level of retirement benefits. Employers who ignore what the competition is doing with retirement programs soon become noncompetitive with regards to employee compensation.

By meeting competitive standards, retirement programs play an important role in attracting and retaining key employees. An attractive retirement program has a special appeal for employees whose current income needs are being satisfied. Those employees whose skills and knowledge command a high salary are particularly interested in a qualified plan as a means of sheltering their earnings from taxes. These highly compensated employees are usually desired by both employers and their competitors, and the right retirement plan may be the deciding factor in determining which employment opportunity is best.

Retirement plans may also attract older employees who are not as highly marketable because they are specifically seeking a job with retirement benefits. As such, a robust and well developed retirement plan can make a job and employer more attractive to potential employees. For example, many capable employees have flocked to federal and state government jobs—even though the salary levels are not equal to those in the private sector—because of their attractive retirement benefits (for example, up to 75 percent of final salary) and their unique plan design (early retirement after 20 years of service).

Perhaps the most important role of retirement plans is not to attract but to retain employees. Well-designed and properly implemented retirement plans can be the primary reason for staying with a particular company. Benefit formulas can be structured to account for length of service, and benefits can be vested to make it economically desirable for employees to remain with the company instead of joining a competitor. In this age of job-hopping and multiple careers, a soundly structured pension program can be the employer's best recourse against the loss of experienced personnel.

Avoidance or Appeasement of Unions

In 1948, the courts determined that because pensions constitute wages, they are a condition of employment and therefore are negotiable for collective-bargaining purposes.[3] Since then, retirement plans and unions have developed a special relationship.

On one hand, retirement plans have been used to stifle or limit the growth of unions. The implementation of a retirement system or the embellishment of an existing system is believed by some managers to be a viable method of forestalling the establishment of a union. While federal law prohibits employers from "union busting," it does not prohibit the employer from competing with unions in trying to meet employee needs. What better way to demonstrate that the employer is looking out for the employee's best interests than to establish a system of retirement benefits?

On the other hand, in unionized companies, retirement benefits and other elements of plan design are always one of the hottest bargaining chips. In these companies, private retirement plans have become a necessary way of life rather than an option. In addition, the laws for regulation and design of some union retirement plans (collectively bargained plans in which more than one employer is required to contribute) have evolved differently from the laws for nonunion plans. (The laws for the so-called multiemployer pension plans are beyond the scope of this book. For more information, see Code Sec. 414(f)).

Employee Motivation

Employee motivation is another reason employers need private retirement plans. Numerous studies have shown that profit-sharing plans and stock ownership plans increase employee identification with the corporation and provide an incentive to increase productivity. A highly visible retirement plan can do wonders for employee morale, improve workers' attitudes toward authority in the work environment, and may be the best management tool available for turning the corner on important projects or getting through crucial times.

Graceful Transition in Turning over the Workforce

superannuated employee

Employers face a common problem when dealing with employees who outlast their usefulness. Such employees have been with the company "forever" and are highly compensated, but their current productivity does not warrant their high salary. These employees are sometimes

---

3. *Inland Steel Company v. National Labor Relations Board,* 170 F.2d 247.

called **superannuated employees**. Because it is not considered valid business practice to dismiss long-time employees who are not economically productive (for whatever reason) and because personal affection and respect may keep an employer from demoting these employees, an alternative solution is necessary. The alternative is the proper use of pension or other retirement plans. Sound plan structure can make early retirement attractive. In addition, "golden handshakes"—special packages that make early retirement even more appealing—can be offered. If handled properly, a potentially uncomfortable situation can be turned into a mutually beneficial solution through the use of the private retirement program.

Social Responsibility

Some employers implement private retirement programs because of their social desirability. These employers want to provide economic security for retired workers despite the lower profit margin that will result. Although retired workers traditionally rely on Social Security, private savings, and a company pension, some employers feel the need to improve the company pension because they fear for the future existence of Social Security (at least in its current state) and they recognize that we have become a society of spenders and not savers. Furthermore, the needs of the aged are increasingly entering into the social consciousness, and many employers feel obliged to do their part by instituting forced savings through a retirement program.

Less altruistically, fear of negative public relations stemming from the perception that an employer did not "take care of" employees can stimulate a social conscience, resulting in the development of an improved retirement program. Companies often go to painstaking lengths to be known as a good place to work, and few employers want former employees to be destitute after retirement.

Retirement Saving as Part of Successful Compensation Planning

One question often raised by clients is: "Why not pay retirement benefits out as current compensation and let employees fend for themselves when it comes to saving for retirement?" After all, the funds used to provide for retirement and the funds used to pay salary are both part of the same compensation package. Enlightened employers, however, feel that by committing a certain part of salary to retirement purposes, they not only allow their employees to benefit from the aforementioned tax advantages of a qualified plan, but also provide employees with the most effective compensation package possible. In other words, they maintain a system that meets their employees' financial security needs for both today and tomorrow in the most tax-efficient manner available.

WHY BUSINESS OWNERS NEED TAX-ADVANTAGED RETIREMENT PLANS

LO 1.3   **Explain how tax-advantaged plans benefit business owners.**

Small business owners establish retirement plans for different reasons. These include the following:

- tax sheltering as much income as possible
- solving liquidity problems that occur at retirement or death
- sheltering their assets from legal liability and bankruptcy
- avoiding taxes on excess accumulated earnings

Tax Shelter for Business Owners

Qualified plans and other tax-advantaged plans represent one of the best tax shelters available. We have already shown how much more an employee can save for retirement on a pretax versus an after-tax basis. Remember that, in the small-business environment, employers are also employees. Owners of closely held businesses, members of professional corporations, partners, and the self-employed frequently set up retirement plans with the tax sheltering of personal income as their primary motivation. These markets consist of upscale clients who want the greatest possible tax savings from the qualified-plan tax shelter (and who, consequently, make the biggest contributions toward their retirement). Retirement plans are one of the few tax shelters still remaining today. Because their rules are clear, their degree of tax risk is quite low, making them an attractive tax shelter that is not likely to go away.

> **YOUR FINANCIAL SERVICES PRACTICE: COST OF COVERING EMPLOYEES**
>
> When the business owner compares saving for retirement through a tax-sheltered vehicle versus after-tax savings, the owner may view required contributions for other employees in the qualified environment as a drain on his or her own savings account. For example, if only 50 percent of the contribution to the plan is for the owner's benefit, the owner may feel that he or she is better off taking the entire contribution amount, paying taxes, and saving outside the plan. This is a legitimate concern and may stop some business owners from establishing a plan. However, when working with these clients, be sure to fully consider the following:
>
> - In almost all cases, contributions for the other employees have some value to the business. If contributions to the plan are not made, the employer may have to pay additional cash benefits to employees. Also, other reasons for establishing a plan

(discussed above) will come into play, such as employee attraction and retention.
- If the contributions do have some value to the owner, consider quantifying that value when making the mathematical comparison of the qualified plan versus after-tax savings. For example, take a small business owner who has $50,000 to save. If the amount is contributed to a qualified plan, assume that he or she will get $30,000 and the employees will get the remaining $20,000. If the owner feels that the contribution for the employees has a value to the business of $10,000, then compare a $40,000 contribution to the plan versus $40,000 saved in an after-tax environment.
- An experienced pension professional may be able to suggest creative ways to limit the cost of benefits for other employees. Salary deferral plans, such as 401(k) plans, and cross-tested profit-sharing plans can often be used to accomplish this goal. Also, with the right census, a defined-benefit plan can work as well.

Liquidity Concerns

In addition to functioning as a stable tax shelter, tax-advantaged plans solve liquidity problems that often occur at retirement or death. Small-business owners typically have a difficult time building business or personal liquidity. They are self-achievers and often feel psychologically compelled to reinvest money in their "baby." A common profile of a business owner is someone who initially finds success by investing in himself or herself and the business and who continues to do so throughout his or her lifetime. Because his or her "money personality" tends to be more that of a spender than of a saver, the savings that occur through a qualified plan may represent the business owner's only available cash at retirement or death. Thus, the qualified plan (along with, for example, a buy-sell agreement) may be essential to the continuation of the business after the owner's death or retirement.

Financial Security Concerns

A third reason that business owners are well served by a tax-advantaged retirement plan is that the plan may provide them with certain creditor protections. The clearest situation is the debtor who has filed for protection under federal bankruptcy law. The Bankruptcy Abuse Protection and Consumer Protection Act of 2005[4] provides sweeping protection for all assets held in tax-advantaged plans. Specifically, assets in qualified plans, SEPs, SIMPLEs, 403(b) plans, and 457 plans are exempt from the bankruptcy estate so they cannot be attached by bankruptcy creditors.

Regarding IRAs and Roth IRAs, the maximum amount of the exemption is limited to an aggregate IRA account value of $1 million. However, this million-dollar limit does not apply to

---

4. Sec. 522 of the Bankruptcy Code, 11 U.S.C. Sec. 522.

SEP or SIMPLE IRAs, or to amounts that are rolled over from qualified plans, 403(b) plans, or 457 plans. Because of this exception to the $1 million limit, advisors should encourage clients to maintain rollover IRAs and Roth IRAs separate from newly established IRAs and Roth IRAs.

Outside of federal bankruptcy (for example, state law insolvency or enforcement proceeding), pension assets may still have creditor protection, but unfortunately, the situation is not as clear. ERISA has an anti-alienation clause[5] that does provide protection for qualified plans. However, this provision does not apply to plans that only cover owners and are therefore considered non-ERISA plans. Other notable exceptions include: 1) payments under a qualified domestic relations order to divide property and attachment for child support, and 2) federal tax levies and judgments. Also, courts have held that pension assets may be subject to attachment for federal criminal penalties or restitution.[6] IRAs are more complex as they are not eligible for ERISA's anti-alienation provision. Many states, however, do provide protection for IRAs and Roth IRAs. Some protect all assets while others cap benefits to a particular dollar limit. Some states also treat inherited IRAs differently than other IRAs and Roth IRAs.

Unfortunately, the complexity in this area makes it difficult to provide advice, and clients concerned about this issue need to consult an attorney. However, the broad bankruptcy protection and the relatively broad ERISA and state law provisions protecting IRAs do provide asset protection for many retirement plans, providing one more reason for the business owner to establish an employer-sponsored retirement plan.

Accumulated Earnings Tax Concerns

accumulated earnings tax

Qualified plan contributions sometimes offer one other advantage to the small corporation—lowering the business's exposure to the **accumulated earnings tax**. This tax is essentially a penalty tax for C corporations that attempt to reduce the shareholders' tax burden by accumulating earnings instead of paying them out to shareholders. The tax rate on improper accumulations for years beginning after 2017 is 20 percent of such accumulations that exceed at a minimum $250,000 ($150,000 for a personal services corporation). Any amounts contributed to a qualified plan will reduce the exposure to the accumulated earnings tax. (For a discussion of the accumulated earnings tax, see Code Secs. 531 through 537).

---

5. ERISA Sec. 206(d)(1), see 29 U.S.C. Sec. 1056, et al.
6. *United States v. Novak*, 476 F.3d 1041 (9th Cir. 2007).

CHAPTER REVIEW

Key Terms and Concepts

tax-advantaged retirement plans
qualified plans
nonqualified plan

individual retirement account (IRA)
superannuated employee
accumulated earnings tax

Chapter 1: Review Questions

Review questions are based on the learning objectives in this chapter. Thus, a [1.3] at the end of a question means that the question is based on learning objective 3. If there are multiple objectives, they are all listed.

1. Name all the qualified plans as well as the other tax-advantaged retirement plans (11 plans in total). [1.1]

2. What are the tax advantages shared among all tax-advantaged plans, and what makes qualified plans different from the other tax-advantaged plans? [1.1]

3. In exchange for special tax advantages, what common requirements do all tax-advantaged retirement plans share? [1.1]

4. Describe the basic differences between tax-advantaged retirement plans and nonqualified plans. [1.1]

5. Scopes is the owner of Monkey Business, Inc., a small business that trains monkeys for work in films. Scopes would like to save $15,000 a year for retirement. Scopes pays federal and state taxes at the 36 percent marginal rate. [1.1]

    a. Explain to Scopes why he might save more for retirement under a tax-advantaged retirement plan than by taking the $15,000 as extra income and investing it on his own.

    b. Calculate the amount that Scopes will have saved after one year under the qualified plan and individual savings approaches, assuming the amount saved earns a 5 percent return and the earnings are taxable when he saves outside of the plan.

6. Why has the tax comparison between saving in tax-advantaged plans versus saving on an after-tax basis become more complicated in today's tax environment? [1.1]

7. Identify benefits (other than tax advantages) of participating in an employer-sponsored retirement plan. [1.1]

8. RAMCO is a relatively small nonunionized company with 60 "younger" employees. RAMCO is in the competitive computer software market and will soon face a major project of updating its technology to be competitive with the new generation of computers. How can a qualified plan help RAMCO? [1.2]

9. What special personal needs does a qualified plan serve for the owner of the business? [1.3]

Chapter 1: Review Answers

1. Tax-advantaged retirement plans include eight kinds of qualified plans—defined-benefit pension plans, cash-balance plans, money-purchase pension plans, target-benefit plans, profit-sharing plans, 401(k) plans, stock-bonus plans, and ESOPs—as well as SEPs (simplified employee pensions) and SIMPLEs (savings incentive match plans for employees). Public school systems and those nonprofit organizations qualifying for Code Sec. 501(c)(3) tax-exempt status can also sponsor 403(b) plans (also referred to as tax-sheltered annuities).

2. In all tax-advantaged plans, the employer receives a deduction for contributions, while employees do not have to pay income taxes until benefits are distributed. Furthermore, plan assets that accumulate in a trust or an insurance product are not subject to tax, even though such earnings are taxed as distributed to employees. Also, benefits can generally be rolled over to an IRA or other tax-deferred plan until they are needed. What makes qualified plans different from the other plans is that only qualified plans allow a portion of the plan's assets to be invested in life insurance. In addition, a lump-sum distribution from a qualified plan may be eligible for special tax treatment that is not available from other plans.

3. All tax-advantaged plans share some basic characteristics. First, for the owners and managers to participate in the tax benefits, the plan must cover a significant number of rank-and-file employees. Second, an employee must be vested in some benefits after he or she has reached a specified number of years of employment. (Some types of plans require immediate vesting). Third, employees must be notified of the terms and conditions of the plan and to what benefits a participant will be entitled. Fourth, plans have nondiscrimination requirements regarding the relationship between the level of benefits provided for highly compensated employees and the level of benefits provided to the rank-and-file. Fifth, all plans require that assets be contributed to a funding vehicle—once assets are in the plan they are no longer owned by the employer sponsoring the plan. These assets can be used only to pay plan benefits. Sixth, the terms of the plan must be stated clearly in writing.

4. Nonqualified plans differ in almost every way from their tax-advantaged counterparts. Unlike tax-advantaged plans, nonqualified plans are generally for only a few key people. There are few design restrictions regarding the benefit structure, vesting requirements, or coverage. In most cases, nonqualified plans do not have separate assets. The employer either pays benefits out of general corporate assets or sets up a side account. Sometimes a trust is set up, but assets must be available to pay the claims of creditors in order to avoid current taxation. In exchange for the added flexibility in plan design, the tax rules are not as kind to a nonqualified plan. A plan can

generally be designed to defer the employee's payment of income taxes until benefits are paid out, but the employer's tax deduction is deferred to the time of payout as well. Another difference between tax-advantaged and nonqualified plans is that benefits are not as secure. With a nonqualified arrangement, if the entity has financial difficulty, any money set aside to pay benefits can generally be attached by creditors.

5. Explain to Scopes that the individual savings approach is not as lucrative because the retirement funds are saved after paying personal income taxes at 36 percent, and the earnings on retirement savings can be invested only after they, too, are taxed (unless a tax-sheltered vehicle is used). With the tax-advantaged plan, all taxes are deferred until the time of distribution, which means that he is saving the entire amount and will only pay taxes much later when he needs the assets. The deferral of taxes should result, in most cases, in a larger accumulation than savings after tax.

	Qualified	Personal Savings	
Amount of savings	$15,000	$15,000	
Less taxes	0	5,400	(36%)
Amount actually invested	$15,000	$9,600	
Plus interest earned on amount invested at 5%	750	480	
Less taxes on interest earned	0	173*	(36%)
Amount saved after one year	$15,750	$9,907*	
After-Tax Comparison Year 1	$10,080	$9,907	(36%)
* All figures have been rounded to the nearest dollar.			

6. The tax comparison is difficult for two reasons. First, it underestimates the value of tax deferral if you assume that the pension is distributed and taxed all at once. Most participants take distributions over a long period of time. Also, the cost of investing on an after-tax basis depends in part on the type of investments. For example, if after-tax investments are in equities, dividends are taxed at a rate that is generally lower than the individual's marginal tax rate. Moreover, the tax on capital appreciation is deferred until the assets are sold; again, the tax is at a lower rate.

7. When the employer funds the plan fully, as in a defined-benefit plan or profit-sharing plan, the employee has no choice (to receive cash) and the contributions are not part of discretionary income. Because of federal ERISA law, these assets are held in an irrevocable trust, must be invested according to strict fiduciary scrutiny, and generally offer significant flexibility in the timing and form of payment of benefit payments. If the plan allows for additional salary deferrals, the individual can benefit simply from a forced savings program through payroll deduction. If employee contributions are matched by the employer, the participant has an instant return on the investment.

Participants can also benefit from some investment options not available to them in the market, as well as the education and advice that they receive as plan participants.

8. A qualified plan will help RAMCO in all of the following ways:
    - RAMCO will be able to attract and retain key employees who have valuable technical skills and knowledge of the new generation of computers, because high-salaried employees are generally interested in the income tax sheltering that a qualified plan provides.
    - A qualified plan will help RAMCO avoid unionization because the workers will not feel the need to start a union in order to have their retirement needs met.
    - By instituting a qualified plan related to profits or stock ownership, RAMCO can help increase productivity and employee enthusiasm for its upcoming project.
    - Even though its current concern may not be to promote a graceful transition in the workforce, RAMCO will eventually want younger employees. When the now-younger employees are approaching retirement, RAMCO will be glad that these high-salaried employees can move out and be replaced by lower-paid younger employees who grew up using computers.
    - RAMCO will establish a reputation in the community as a good place to work. In addition, RAMCO will meet its social responsibility of providing a comfortable retirement for long-service employees.
    - RAMCO will provide employees with the most effective compensation package possible.

9. In addition to the reasons that larger businesses establish retirement plans, owners of small businesses have several other reasons for establishing plans including creating a tax shelter, building a liquid asset, building retirement security, and, for C corporations, avoiding the effect of the accumulated earnings test.

Chapter 2
The Retirement Field

Learning Objectives

An understanding of the material in this chapter should enable the student to

- **LO 2.1** Explain how ERISA changed the retirement planning landscape, as well as the major trends in post-ERISA legislation.
- **LO 2.2** Identify the agencies involved in the regulation of tax-advantaged retirement plans and the role of each of these agencies.
- **LO 2.3** Describe the types of entities that sponsor retirement plans and the professionals that service these plans.

Success in finding clients, planning for clients, and servicing clients starts with an understanding of the boundaries, players, and equipment involved in the retirement field. The retirement field's boundaries are the rules set up by federal legislation and government agencies. The players include your clients, potential clients, support-service companies, and even the inner workings of your own organization. The equipment is the information sources that are available to provide answers when experience fails to provide them. This chapter takes you on a tour of the retirement field and introduces you to the regulatory environment, pension players, and information sources that will become an integral part of your financial services practice.

Because the multifaceted pension industry is largely an outgrowth of the regulatory process, we will explore this complex area first (including the relationship between the financial services professional and the industry-shaping laws) and review the functions of the regulatory agencies. Then, we will discuss the pension prospects—who is involved and to what extent—and the service and financial organizations that serve them, with special emphasis on the insurance industry. We will end by reviewing the sources for pension information—those that provide answers to a client's questions and those that analyze current trends and put pensions in perspective.

THE LEGISLATIVE ENVIRONMENT

LO 2.1 Explain how ERISA changed the pension landscape, as well as the major trends in post-ERISA legislation.

Employee Retirement Income Security Act (ERISA)

The passage of the **Employee Retirement Income Security Act (ERISA)** in 1974 marked the beginning of the current retirement-plan era.8 ERISA represented an intensified commitment by the federal government to oversee the retirement market (especially plans that cover nonhighly compensated employees). Leery of broken retirement promises and plans being used as tax shelters for the wealthy, the federal government decided to protect the retirement interests of all plan participants and implemented ERISA to establish equitable standards and curtail perceived abuses. The text of ERISA has become the pensioner's bible. ERISA's commandments forbid discrimination in favor of the prohibited group (highly compensated employees), restrictive vesting schedules that keep longtime participants from receiving benefits, and inadequate plan funding, which leads to bankrupt plans. In addition, ERISA requires reporting and disclosure of information about retirement plans to the Internal Revenue Service (IRS), the Department of Labor (DOL), the Pension Benefit Guaranty Corporation (PBGC), and plan participants. In fact, ERISA forces information to be widely disseminated, thereby causing such administrative nightmares that it has become affectionately known as the "full employment in pensions act."

ERISA is composed of four sections known as titles. The purpose of the first title is to protect an employee's right to collect benefits. To accomplish this, Title I requires employers to report plan information to the federal government and disclose information to participants (reporting and disclosure rules), restricts unlimited employer discretion regarding vesting and plan participation (employers cannot discriminately choose whom to cover), implements plan funding standards (employers must set aside sufficient assets to fulfill retirement promises), and lists fiduciary responsibilities (the responsibilities and liabilities of those in charge). Title II amends the Internal Revenue Code, setting forth the necessary requirements for special tax treatment (the plan qualification rules). Title III creates the regulatory and administrative framework necessary for ERISA's ongoing implementation. Responsibilities are divided between the IRS and the DOL, with the IRS having primary jurisdiction for much of the initial and operational administration of pension plans. Title IV establishes the Pension Benefit Guaranty Corporation, an agency that insures certain pension benefits. The PBGC collects premiums from covered plans (defined-benefit plans only; defined-contribution plans are not insured) and insures a minimum level of benefits for employees if the plan is terminated with insufficient funds.

Four Titles of ERISA
- Title I—Amends the labor law to ensure the employee's right to collect promised benefits
- Title II—Amends the Internal Revenue Code to condition tax benefits on meeting certain minimum standards
- Title III—Creates a regulatory framework for ongoing implementation
- Title IV—Establishes the Pension Benefit Guaranty Corporation to insure benefit payments from defined-benefit pension plans

The enforcement strategies provided by ERISA are interesting. To enforce Title I of ERISA, plan participants, the DOL, and plan fiduciaries can sue to force the payment of appropriate benefits and to require plan representatives to fulfill their jobs. Also, to encourage compliance, errant plan officials can be held personally liable for losses to the plan, fined for certain errors, and in some cases even held criminally liable. It is interesting to note that courts have generally interpreted ERISA's enforcement provisions to prohibit monetary punitive damages for ERISA claims. Even though ERISA does provide for the award of attorney's fees, the inability to receive punitive damages has probably limited the number of private suits under ERISA over the years.

The strategy for encouraging compliance under the Internal Revenue Code is quite different. Here, both the plan sponsor and the plan participants enjoy special tax treatment in exchange for compliance with the law. Failure to comply can enable the IRS to remove the plan's tax-advantaged status. Because this penalty can harm participants (who are not responsible for ensuring plan compliance), plan disqualification is rarely enforced. In lieu of this terminal penalty, the IRS often negotiates a monetary penalty (payable by the sponsor) and requires the employer fix any plan defects.[1] Additionally, disqualification is not the sole punishment contemplated under the Code. Some plan defects result in a penalty tax. Examples of this will be seen throughout the text.

Unfortunately (or fortunately, depending upon your perspective), ERISA was just the beginning of what has seemed like an endless stream of legislation further regulating private pension plans. From 1974 until today, the only constant has been change. There have been many post-ERISA changes. (For those interested in a detailed description of the changes over the years, see the first appendix). For the newcomer to the pension field, the presentation in the appendix may seem overwhelming and confusing. Therefore, an overview of some of the major areas of congressional involvement and a description of the legislative trends over the years appear below.

- *Taxation of pension benefits*—At the time of ERISA, pension benefits were subject to many significant income and estate tax benefits. Over the years, the special tax advantages have been repealed one by one. For example, at one time, pension benefits were not subject to estate taxes. Today, all pension assets that remain after the participant's death are included in the taxable estate. Similarly, many of the special income tax rules have been repealed and, in most cases, pension income is treated as ordinary income (although some rules have been grandfathered).

---

1. The IRS currently has several formal programs for substituting plan disqualification with a monetary penalty. The programs can apply upon an IRS audit or can be voluntarily entered into by employers who discover that qualification violations have occurred.

- *IRAs*—Over the years, IRA rules have swayed with the political breeze. At the time of ERISA, deductible IRA contributions were limited, then IRAs were opened up to virtually everyone, and then, once again, deductible contributions were limited to those who do not participate in an employer-sponsored retirement plan or have relatively low income. However, more recently, law changes have expanded the use of the IRA with the introduction of the Roth IRA, an increase in the maximum contribution limits, and an increase in the phaseout ranges.

- *Maximum deductible contributions*—Through the 1980s and 90s, the trend was to lower the maximum deductible contribution for highly compensated employees. This was done to raise tax revenue, and maybe also out of a perception that plans inappropriately benefited the highly compensated. Contributions were limited by lowering the maximum allowable contribution for each employee; freezing cost-of-living adjustments on contribution limits; limiting the amount of compensation that can be taken into account; imposing limits on employee contributions; and aggregating plans. This trend had a significant effect on executive compensation and benefit planning, making supplemental executive nonqualified deferred-compensation plans a more and more important part of the retirement planning package. In 2001, there was a significant departure from this trend, with increases in allowable contributions for each participant, the compensation cap, and the maximum deductible contributions. These changes were intended to increase retirement savings and to encourage small businesses to establish retirement plans.

- *Limiting tax deferral*—Tax revenue is also lost the longer pension assets remain in a tax-deferred environment. To speed up the taxation of benefits, Code Sec. 401(a)(9) was introduced in 1986, requiring that distributions from all tax-sheltered plans begin at age 70½ (or, in some cases, at actual retirement, if later). These minimum-distribution rules affect any retiree receiving qualified plan, 403(b), or IRA distributions.

- *Parity*—Over the years, the trend has been toward giving all types of business entities equal access to retirement plan vehicles. With a few minor exceptions, C corporations, S corporations, sole proprietorships, partnerships, and even limited liability companies (LLCs) are all on the same footing.

- *Small business plans*—Apparently, based on the perception that retirement plans of small businesses have treated rank-and-file employees unfairly, today a special set of rules, referred to as the top-heavy requirements, applies to the plans of many small businesses. These rules require special minimum contribution and vesting requirements for certain top-heavy plans. Again, the law change in 2001 altered this trend somewhat, simplifying the top-heavy rules and giving the owner the opportunity to accumulate more in a retirement plan.

- *Affiliation requirements*—Over the years, Congress has enacted a series of complex rules requiring the aggregation of related employers to ensure that businesses cannot avoid pension coverage requirements by operating separate entities, and to eliminate "double dipping" under the maximum deduction rules. These rules have successfully eliminated loopholes and at the same time have complicated matters for both multinational corporations operating multiple divisions and for the small entrepreneur involved in several businesses.

- *Funding*—ERISA imposed minimum funding requirements for defined-benefit pension plans and established the PBGC. This organization ensures that employees in privately sponsored defined-benefit plans will receive at least some of the benefits promised by the plan. At times, the PBGC has run deficits, and in response, a number of law changes have required both larger employer contributions and higher PBGC premiums.

- *Employee Stock Ownership Plans (ESOPs)*—To encourage employee stock ownership, in 1981 the Economic Recovery Tax Act (ERTA) provided for a new type of retirement plan vehicle with numerous special tax advantages referred to as an ESOP. Today, some of these provisions have been repealed, but ESOPs still provide significant tax advantages, as well as a plan mechanism to purchase stock on a leveraged basis—providing a viable buyer for the small-business owner looking to sell or retire. In fact, ESOP coverage was expanded by the 1996 Small Business Jobs Protection Act that allowed an S corporation to sponsor an ESOP.

- *Simplification*—One legislative trend that had been consistent from the time of ERISA until 1996 was that each new law made the pension world more complex. However, beginning in 1996, law changes began a trend toward simplification as an attempt to make it easier for the small employer to maintain a tax-advantaged plan. The 1996 law simplified the definition of highly compensated employee and the distribution rules; it eliminated several complex aggregation requirements; and it introduced the SIMPLE, a savings plan alternative to the 401(k) plan with fewer administrative requirements. The 2001 tax law contained additional simplification provisions, making plans (especially 401(k) plans) easier to administer.

One more recent law, the Pension Protection Act (PPA) of 2006, is worth noting, since it was the most extensive pension legislation since ERISA. The legislation did not really change recent legislative trends but reinforced them. A large part of the law relates to the funding status of defined benefit plans. The law revised the minimum funding requirements and imposed increased accelerated funding for most plans. The law also created additional requirements and new consequences for seriously underfunded plans.

The law included other provisions that protect plan participants. Plan benefits become more portable by requiring more accelerated vesting for most plans. Also, defined contribution plans that invest in employer securities must give most participants the option to elect alternative investments in their accounts.

Another important feature of the PPA was that it made many of the increased pension limits from previous laws permanent. The law tries to improve the pension system by validating the cash balance design, encouraging the practice of allowing automatic enrollment in 401(k) plans, and providing a mechanism to allow participants to receive appropriate investment advice.

REGULATORY AGENCIES

LO 2.2 **Identify the agencies involved in the regulation of tax-advantaged retirement plans and the role of each of these agencies.**

Legislation makes up only part of the regulatory picture. The other part, the administration of the qualified-plan system (and, to a lesser extent, the nonqualified-plan system), is carried out by the Internal Revenue Service, the department that is required to interpret the laws, explain legal fine points, and oversee the day-to-day operations of retirement plans.

The Internal Revenue Service

The IRS regulatory responsibilities are wide ranging, including providing determination letters, auditing plans and providing regulatory guidance.

Initial Plan Qualification

In order for an employer to receive favorable tax treatment, the pension plan must meet the qualification requirements. Plan sponsors may, and usually do, request an IRS advance determination letter. Employers send in the plan and appropriate forms requesting IRS approval; the IRS agent checks the plan to see if it meets the guidelines (over time the IRS has developed elaborate rules regarding what provisions may and may not be included); and, if necessary, the IRS and employer enter into negotiations over points at issue. If the plan meets IRS standards, a favorable advance-determination letter—which assures the employer that the plan is qualified and that the first year's contributions will be deductible—is issued. Although the program is voluntary, most employers take advantage of getting "preapproval" that plan contributions are eligible for special tax treatment.

IRS Regulatory Responsibility
- Qualification letter program
- Audit existing plans
- Interpret legislation

Ongoing Auditing

The IRS monitors retirement plans after initial qualification through periodic planned IRS audits. The purpose of IRS surveillance is to make sure changes in facts or circumstances have not affected plan qualification and plans are used as retirement vehicles rather than as a tax shelter for the prohibited group. Plans chosen for audit are selected from information supplied in the annual 5500 filings, which includes the type and structure of the plan, plan assets, plan liabilities, plan income, and plan funding. In addition, information regarding plan changes, actuarial methods, and distributions to participants and their beneficiaries is required.

The IRS has developed another ongoing enforcement strategy that encourages employers to step forward voluntarily when plan problems are discovered. In exchange for voluntary compliance, the employer is subject to much smaller penalties—usually a set fee—instead of the much larger penalties that could occur if the IRS found the problem upon the plan's audit. There are a number of different programs that have been coordinated under the Employee Plans Compliance Resolution System (EPCRS). These programs encourage voluntary correction of problems and, in many cases, reward employers for taking reasonable steps to keep their plans in compliance with the law.

YOUR FINANCIAL SERVICES PRACTICE: QUALITY SERVICES PROTECT CLIENTS

Because the IRS correction program rewards plans that adopt appropriate administrative procedures, quality service providers can help minimize plan problems. One step is to provide employers with periodic updates of important developments in the field and action required. In addition, performing periodic audits can ensure that
- the plan continues to meet the employer's objectives
- the document has been properly updated to reflect law changes
- the plan's eligibility, vesting, and other provisions are being properly administered
- required nondiscrimination and other required tests are being properly performed
- reporting requirements are being satisfied

Interpretation

One of the major responsibilities of the IRS is to issue numerous communications that further explain the existing laws of the Internal Revenue Code. These communications include the following:

final regulations

- *Final regulations* explain and interpret the various sections of the Internal Revenue Code and deal with legal fine points that are not specifically addressed in the Code. **Final regulations** are legally enforceable, and the IRS is bound by them. Originally published in the Internal Revenue Bulletin and the Federal Register, the final regulations are later bound together with other regulations in a set of Internal Revenue Regulations. Final regulations can also be found in many of the loose-leaf services (discussed later).

proposed regulations

- *Proposed regulations* are sometimes issued right after major legislation to guide practitioners on complex provisions of new laws. Unlike final regulations, **proposed regulations** will have no legal effect unless they specifically state that they can be relied upon by taxpayers. Still, they are an indication of the IRS's current thinking and are widely followed. Proposed regulations can be changed before they are finalized—often as the result of negative feedback at public hearings during the open comment period.

temporary regulations

- *Temporary regulations* may be issued as an alternative to final regulations, or can be issued simultaneously with proposed regulations. They are binding until they are superseded or withdrawn. This allows individual and corporate taxpayers to rely on the regulations without fear of incurring a Sec. 6661 penalty for substantially understating income tax liability, a protection that is not available to proposed regulations. A great deal of time can pass between when a regulation is proposed and when it becomes final, and **temporary regulations** are relied on heavily in the interim.

revenue rulings

- *Revenue rulings* are the IRS's interpretations of the provisions of the Internal Revenue Code and regulations as they apply to the factual situations presented by taxpayers. **Revenue rulings** are replete with valuable examples that clarify complex legal issues and may be used as precedents, thus giving you and your clients a sense of security if you are venturing into an area to which the rulings apply.

private letter rulings

- *Private letter rulings* interpret the law in light of a specific set of circumstances and indicate whether the IRS believes the action to be acceptable. **Private letter rulings** address only the specific facts presented to the IRS and, because of this, a taxpayer cannot rely upon the guidance provided. Still, they are an important form of guidance, because they address real-life cases that might be similar to your client's situation. (*Planning Note:* If the IRS's position regarding a situation your client is entering into is unclear, you should recommend that the client consider getting a private letter ruling. For a fee, the IRS will issue a ruling that will be binding in the client's situation. However, private letter rulings can be very expensive to obtain and take over a year for the IRS to finalize).

- *Publications* include general reviews of retirement topics provided by the IRS. Using understandable terms (no legalese), these publications cover a variety of topics. (*Planning Note:* Publications are written to provide a general overview of the tax law on certain subjects. The publications on Keogh plans and qualified retirement plans make good mailers for your clients).

The Department of Labor (DOL)

Through the Employee Benefits Security Administration (EBSA), the DOL's regulatory responsibilities focus on protecting plan participant's through the enforcement of reporting and disclosure rules and policing plan investments.

DOL Regulatory Responsibilities
- Protect participants through enforcement of the reporting and disclosure rules
- Oversee plan investments
- Govern actions of fiduciaries
- Interpret legislation

Reporting and Disclosure Rules

The DOL's first duty is to ensure compliance with the reporting and disclosure rules. The most important disclosure requirement is that the plan provide summary plan descriptions (SPDs) to participants. Failure to comply with this or other reporting and disclosure requirements can result in fines and, in some egregious cases, imprisonment.

Prohibited Transactions

The DOL's second duty is to oversee plan investments. To ensure that no self-dealing or conflict of interest is involved, ERISA provides that plans cannot have certain dealings with parties who have close relationships with the plan or the company (referred to as parties in interest). Such behavior is referred to as a prohibited transaction. (The responsibility for overseeing prohibited transactions is shared by the IRS, as a separate but similar set of rules governing prohibited transactions is also part of the tax law). The IRS in the late 1970s, shared some of its responsibilities with the DOL, allowing the DOL to regulate IRAs with regards to prohibited transactions. For now, understand that the goal of the rules is to keep the plan's interests separate from the sponsoring entity's interests, and to ensure that no persons benefit unduly because of their close relationship to the plan. Also, note that the statutory scheme prohibits a broad range of behaviors, carves out a number of statutory exemptions, and gives the DOL the authority to issue others.

Fiduciaries

fiduciary

In conjunction with its responsibility to monitor plan investments, the DOL governs the actions of those in charge of running the retirement plans—fiduciaries. A **fiduciary** is a person or corporation that exercises any discretionary authority or control over the management of the plan or plan assets, renders investment advice for a fee, or has any discretionary authority or responsibility in the administration of the plan. Every plan has at least one named fiduciary who is responsible and accountable for operating the plan. Fiduciaries (named or otherwise) invest plan assets (subject to the rules on prohibited transactions), ensure that plan documents conform to the law, administer plans, and make major decisions regarding plan operation.

The DOL has the means to ensure that fiduciaries uphold their responsibilities; it may sue plan fiduciaries and require a restitution to the plan for any losses that result from breach of fiduciary duty. (In addition, under the tax provisions overseen by the IRS, a fiduciary may be responsible for excise taxes for violation of the prohibited-transaction provisions). In doing its job of overseeing the fiduciary responsibility rules and the prohibited-transaction rules, the DOL (and, in a subordinate role, the IRS) acts like a police officer on the beat, carefully checking to see that the laws protecting plan participants are not broken.

Interpretation

As we have just seen, like the IRS, the DOL issues numerous communications that create pension rules and explain existing laws. Many of these items parallel IRS publications. The DOL issues final regulations, temporary regulations, and proposed regulations, which perform the same functions as their IRS counterparts. In addition, the DOL issues advisory opinions that are similar to the private letter rulings issued by the IRS. As with IRS private letter rulings, your clients can inquire about the acceptability of their acts or transactions, and only the parties actually involved can safely rely on the opinion. Owing to the DOL's unique responsibilities, not all of its communications are similar to those of the IRS. The DOL issues important communications called prohibited-transaction exemptions (PTEs). These exemptions can either be on a class basis (for example, "All banks with FDIC insurance are exempt from . . .") or on a particular transaction basis. (*Planning Note:* The prohibited-transaction exemption is an avenue your client can travel to get approval before taking an investment action that falls into the prohibited-transaction gray area. For example, if your client is a party in interest, he or she can get an exemption from the restrictions on prohibited transactions by applying for a PTE).

Pension Benefit Guaranty Corporation (PBGC)

Pension Benefit Guaranty Corporation (PBGC)

The **Pension Benefit Guaranty Corporation (PBGC)** was established under Title IV of ERISA as a quasi-governmental corporation. Both the IRS and the Department of Labor are involved to a certain extent with the PBGC, because its board of directors includes the Secretaries of Labor, Treasury, and Commerce. Even though the organization has access to federal government resources, the federal government is not generally liable for any of its obligations or liabilities. This is meaningful because the PBGC's primary responsibility is to insure participants in and beneficiaries of employee benefit plans against the loss of benefits arising from complete or partial termination of the plan. PBGC insurance coverage applies to most defined-benefit plans of private employers. Coverage generally excludes: plans maintained solely for substantial owners; professional service employers (such as doctors and lawyers) that have always had fewer than 26 active participants; church groups; federal, state, or local government.[2] The program does not apply to defined-contribution plans.

PBGC Regulatory Responsibility
- Administer insurance program for defined-benefit plans
- Oversee termination of covered plans
- Interpret legislation

The PBGC operates by collecting compulsory premiums, which are $69 (for plan years beginning in 2017) per participant per plan year (and possibly substantially more if the plan is

---

2. For a complete list of characteristics that prohibit the PBGC from covering a plan, see ERISA Section 4021(b).

underfunded, with a maximum of $517 per participant for the variable portion of the premium). For such premiums, the PBGC guarantees to pay certain benefits promised under the plan in the event that the plan has insufficient assets. From a retirement planning perspective, it is important to note that the PBGC does not guarantee all benefits. Most notable is that guaranteed benefits are subject to a monthly ceiling which depends upon the age of the participant at the time benefits begin (2017 indexed limit). The limit for a 65-year-old receiving a straight-life annuity is $5,369.32. The monthly guarantee for 2017 for a 50 percent joint-and-survivor annuity is $4,832.39 per month for a 65-year-old.

In conjunction with its duty to insure benefit payments, the PBGC has the power to investigate anyone who has violated or is about to violate any of the plan termination insurance provisions. It can also initiate a lawsuit in federal court to enforce the provisions of Title IV. To help the PBGC identify problems, certain events that would indicate that the plan is in financial difficulty must be reported to the PBGC.

The PBGC has another enforcement tool. If a PBGC investigation reveals that a plan is not funded according to legal standards, or that the plan is unable to meet its benefit payments, or if there is a possible long-run loss that will get out of hand unless the plan is terminated, the PBGC may require the plan to be involuntarily terminated to help reduce PBGC's potential losses. The PBGC can also cut its losses by tapping up to 30 percent of the net worth of employers whose plans have terminated, leaving the PBGC liable for payments.

Another function of the PBGC is overseeing plan terminations initiated by the plan sponsor. Today, an employer can terminate a defined-benefit plan covered by the PBGC insurance program only in limited circumstances. Essentially, the plan must either have sufficient assets to pay all benefits (referred to as a voluntary termination), or the company must virtually be facing liquidation (called a distress termination). When the employer terminates such a plan, it is required to give advance notification to employees and submit the proper forms to the PBGC.

As is the case with the IRS and the DOL's Office of Pension and Welfare Benefit Plans, the PBGC issues various communications that serve as sources of information for the financial services professional: PBGC regulations, news releases, opinion letters, publications, and multiemployer bulletins.

Table 2-1
Review of the Regulatory Environment for Qualified Plans

IRS	DOL	PBGC
Initial plan qualification	Summary plan descriptions	Insure defined-benefit plans
Ongoing auditing through 5500 forms	Oversee fiduciaries and plan investments	Oversee plan fund solvency
Legal interpretation	Legal interpretation	Legal interpretation

PENSIONS: PROFESSIONALS AND ORGANIZATIONS

LO 2.3   Describe the types of entities that sponsor retirement plans and the professionals that service these plans.

While the regulatory environment has a significant impact on the retirement market, these federal laws and agencies are nonetheless only the rules and umpires. Employers sponsoring pension plans plus the expanding service and investment industry are the pension professionals and organizations.

Plan Sponsors

Retirement plan sponsors constitute one of the most important financial markets today. And because demographics indicate an aging population, which means increased savings for retirement, the plan sponsors' market is possibly the most important financial market of tomorrow. Sponsors of retirement plans include corporations, partnerships, and self-employed individuals. According to the Bureau of Labor Statistics, larger employers are most likely to sponsor plans. For example, 75 percent of employees working for companies of 500 or more employees are currently participating in retirement plans, while only 32 percent of those working at companies with fewer than 50 employees are covered. Those who do adopt plans contribute, on average, 3.9 percent of payroll.

Prospects—The Candidates for Pensions

Small employers maintain retirement plans less frequently than larger employers. This demonstrates both an opportunity and a weakness in the market. While too few small employers offer plans, there is a tremendous opportunity to develop and set up plans for these employers. This includes small businesses, self-employed individuals as well as those who have a second income as an independent contractor. The small plan market also includes nonprofit organizations.

With larger organizations, the opportunities are more likely to be in the take-over business. Sponsors may be dissatisfied with their current service providers, because of lack of service or knowledge. A proactive advisor who ensures that the plan continues to meet employer objectives, offers suggestions that will make employees more satisfied, and keeps a careful eye on compliance issues will be very successful in this market. In many cases, the financial services professional is the quarterback coordinating the efforts of a number of service providers.

YOUR FINANCIAL SERVICES PRACTICE: RETIREMENT PROSPECTING

Prospecting techniques in the retirement market differ from those in the personal selling market. While prospecting in the retirement market does include the traditional methods of direct mail, preapproach letters combined with phone calls for appointments, and the use of existing clients as referred leads, other unique methods are available. These include (1) developing accountants and attorneys—professionals who are in touch with employers' financial ability to provide retirement benefits—into centers of influence, (2) creating working relationships with banks interested in trust business that complements pension insurance sales, (3) obtaining pension consultants or actuarial firms as referral sources, (4) working with casualty and insurance brokers in the commercial and industrial market whose clients are probably also pension prospects, and (5) obtaining lists of pension prospects in your area. Because plans must file annual forms with the government which are accessible to the public, it is possible to obtain information about ongoing plans in your area. The data is available through the Department of Labor, but several companies offer services that help to sort through the information. One source is Judy Diamond Associates at www.freeerisa.com. Another source is Pension Data Resources, Inc., at www.pensionplanet.com.

Service and Financial Groups

third-party administrators (TPAs)

The pension market is replete with organizations that design and implement plans; provide consulting, record-keeping, legal, and actuarial services; furnish employee communications; and oversee plan administration. In short, those in charge of pensions, if desired, can easily farm out the entire process to **third-party administrators (TPAs)**. The same is true regarding the management of the pension plan assets. For those plan administrators who would rather do some or all of their work in house, there are a variety of computer services, many offered by small, specialized companies.

The organizations that provide plan services include consulting houses, actuarial firms, insurance companies, administrative consultants, mutual fund companies and software companies. In the financial market, there are trust companies, commercial banks, investment houses, asset-management groups, mutual fund companies and insurance companies. The major service and financial groups have no particular areas of concentration, but rather offer a myriad of services. For example, consulting houses do not just do consulting, plan installation, and administration, they may also offer computer services and investment facilities. Computer software companies may offer consulting services as well as create software.

master and prototype plans

Many financial services organizations sponsor **master and prototype plans**, standardized plans approved and qualified in concept by the Internal Revenue Service, which are then adopted by their customer organizations. The master and prototype plans offer an employer fewer choices in plan design and, thus, can be installed very easily. The use of a master or prototype plan simplifies the task for the financial services professional by setting up an easily understood framework with which to work, known as an adoption agreement. An adoption agreement resembles a smörgåsbord in many ways—for example, you choose one out of five benefit formulas, one out of three vesting tables, and so on—which simplifies the plan design process and saves time.

CHAPTER REVIEW

Key Terms and Concepts

Employee Retirement Income Security Act (ERISA)
final regulations
proposed regulations
temporary regulations
revenue rulings
private letter rulings
fiduciary
Pension Benefit Guaranty Corporation (PBGC)
third-party administrators (TPAs)
master and prototype plans

Chapter 2: Review Questions

Review questions are based on the learning objectives in this chapter. Thus, a [2.3] at the end of a question means that the question is based on learning objective 3. If there are multiple objectives, they are all listed.

1. What were the major reforms instituted by the Employee Retirement Income Security Act of 1974 (ERISA)? [2.1]

2. What have been the post-ERISA legislative trends with regard to the following areas? [2.1]
    a. maximum deductible contributions
    b. limiting tax deferral
    c. parity between various business entities
    d. funding
    e. simplification

3. What does the financial services professional need to do whenever there is new legislation in the retirement area? [2.1]

4. What is the role of the Internal Revenue Service with regard to the retirement market? [2.2]

5. What are the various types of guidance issued by the IRS to help explain existing and proposed laws or regulations? [2.2]

6. What is the role of the Department of Labor in the pension process? [2.2]

7. What are the types of organizations involved in providing consulting and investment services to retirement plans? [2.3]

Chapter 2: Review Answers

1. ERISA has four distinct Titles. The first protects an employee's right to collect benefits. Title II amended the Internal Revenue Code, setting forth the necessary requirements for special tax treatment. Title III created the regulatory and administrative framework necessary for ERISA's ongoing implementation. Title IV established the Pension Benefit Guaranty Corporation, an agency that insures pension benefits.

2. a. Maximum deductible contributions—Throughout the 1980s and 1990s, the trend was to lower the maximum deductible contribution for highly compensated employees. However, the 2001 tax law changed direction by allowing larger contributions for individual employees. This change in direction was intended to encourage small businesses to establish plans and to encourage a higher level of qualified plan savings.

    b. Limiting tax deferral—Code Section 401(a)(9) was introduced in 1986, requiring that distributions from all tax-sheltered plans begin at age 70 ½ (or, in some cases at actual retirement, if later). These minimum-distribution rules affect any retiree receiving qualified plan, 403(b), or IRA distributions.

    c. Parity—Over the years, the trend has been toward giving all types of business entities equal access to retirement plan vehicles. With a few minor exceptions, today C corporations, S corporations, sole proprietorships, partnerships, and even limited liability companies (LLCs) are all on the same footing.

    d. Funding—Over the years, a number of law changes increased required employer contributions and PBGC insurance premiums to shore up the financial status of the PBGC.

    e. Simplification—After years of more and more complexity, in 1996 there was true pension simplification. Administration of 401(k) plans became easier after this law change. The simplification trend continued in 2001 with several rules that simplified administration of 401(k) plans.

3. Legislative changes require a lot of effort by the financial services professional. After studying the new law, clients have to be informed of the changes and notified of the effect of the new law on their particular plan design. Many law changes also require plan amendments. Even though new laws require a lot of work, they can also provide for new opportunities to help clients meet their particular needs.

4. The IRS plays the most prominent role of all the bureaucratic agencies: It (1) supervises the creation of new retirement plans (in pension parlance, initial plan qualification), (2)

monitors and audits the operation of existing plans, and (3) interprets federal legislation, especially with regard to the tax consequences of certain pension plan designs.

5. The IRS issues final regulations that help explain and interpret various code sections. These final regulations are similar to law as they bind both the IRS and the public. In addition, the IRS issues proposed regulations that do not always become finalized and enforceable. Furthermore, the IRS might release temporary regulations. The IRS also has revenue rulings which are similar to court cases that determine the law surrounding an IRS related issue. Lastly, the IRS can issue private letter rulings that are only binding to one party and other explanatory documents that have no direct legal authority but to help provide additional explanations and examples.

6. Through its office of Employee Benefit Security Administration (EBSA), the DOL (1) ensures that plan participants are adequately informed through enforcement of some of the reporting and disclosure rules, (2) polices the investment of plan assets, (3) monitors the actions of those in charge of the pension plans (fiduciaries), and (4) interprets legislation.

7. The organizations that provide plan services include consulting houses, actuarial firms, insurance companies, administrative consultants, and software companies. In the financial market, there are trust companies, commercial banks, investment houses, asset-management groups, and insurance companies.

Chapter 3

Preliminary Concerns in Retirement Plan Design

Learning Objectives

An understanding of the material in this chapter should enable the student to

- **LO 3.1** Describe the fact-finding process for helping an employer select the appropriate tax-advantaged retirement plan.
- **LO 3.2** Identify the rule differences between defined-benefit and defined-contribution plans.
- **LO 3.3** Compare the defined-benefit with the defined-contribution plan approach.
- **LO 3.4** Compare plans in the pension category with those in the profit-sharing category.
- **LO 3.5** Define the term "Keogh" plan and calculate the maximum allowable deduction under a defined-contribution plan.

One of the most promising and lucrative opportunities in the retirement market is the chance to design a client's retirement program. Financial services professionals who act as consultants in this area provide a valuable service that not only leads to the sale of retirement-plan products, but also to the investment of their client's retirement assets. Furthermore, financial services professionals who bring technical expertise to the retirement-decision process gain the confidence of clients and may be entrusted with additional sales opportunities in other business areas. Conversely, financial services professionals who desire only to manage plan assets or sell investment products find themselves at a competitive disadvantage if they cannot offer the technical expertise expected.

For these reasons, it is essential that financial services professionals learn how to select the most appropriate retirement plan or plans for their clients. The study of this process starts with the selection of the most appropriate tax-advantaged plan for your client. Next, a thorough review of the issues involved in investing plan assets precedes a brief discussion of the various administrative issues involved with maintaining retirement plans. Before moving on to individual retirement planning, we discuss supplemental nonqualified plans, generally for executives, and the role of individual retirement plans.

In order to choose the best retirement plan, you must identify the client's needs and objectives, understand the various plan options, and match the client's needs and objectives with the proper tax-advantaged retirement plan or plans.

IDENTIFYING NEEDS AND OBJECTIVES

LO 3.1   **Describe the fact-finding process for helping an employer select the appropriate tax-advantaged retirement plan.**

When advising a client on retirement-plan choices, your initial step is to focus the client on the important issues he or she faces, both personally and professionally. In addition, you need to discern the organization's needs and objectives that are relevant to plan selection. The device used to accomplish these steps is a pension planning fact finder. We have provided a seven-step fact finder as an example; other tools can be used as well. A fact finder allows you to

- guide the client toward focusing on important issues
- gather the information necessary for you to make insightful recommendations
- provide a systematic approach for solving the client's retirement puzzle
- serve as a due diligence checklist that will ensure the selection of the most appropriate plan
- record your dealings with the client for liability protection

Understanding the Fact Finder

Even basic information about the company will impact the plan design. For example, the type of entity may limit the type of plan that can be established. Another key issue is whether or not the entity has any related entities. Under the rules that apply to tax-advantaged retirement plans, certain related employers have to be aggregated to determine whether a plan satisfies coverage requirements. Because the rules are quite complex it is best to write down all related companies that fit the description in the fact finder, and then have a qualified tax expert carefully analyze the aggregation issues.

Step 1 of the fact finder helps you begin to identify organizational needs, laying the foundation for proper plan choice. The important comparative analysis that is started in step 2 (involving the interplay between these factors) requires additional discussion with the client to establish the relative desirability of each objective. For example, when an employer seeks to attract and retain key employees, avoid an annual financial commitment to fund the plan, and provide tax shelter for top executives, you must gauge which need is most important and to what degree the other needs will have to be subordinated in order to choose the best plan for your client.

Step 3 lists the primary and secondary reasons for establishing the plan, and is a culmination of steps 1 and 2. It forces your client to set priorities on the motives for establishing the plan.

Motives can be disparate even in similarly structured organizations, but several generalizations about motives can be made:

- Large organizations typically want to meet the needs of the business while getting the most for the employees out of a given expenditure.
- Small organizations, such as closely held businesses, are particularly concerned with providing tax shelter and extensive retirement benefits to owners and key employees.
- Some organizations (both large and small) desire to adequately provide for rank-and-file employees; others want to favor key employees and will only grudgingly meet the minimum statutory requirements for other employees; and still others fall somewhere between these two polar viewpoints.
- Some organizations establish plans to attract and retain key employees or to motivate employees, and they want the most cost-effective system to meet those goals.
- Some organizations are interested in resolving problems with older, unproductive employees and in creating a graceful transition out of the workforce.
- In today's world, more and more employers want to form a retirement savings partnership with employees and want employer contributions to primarily match employee contributions.

The first three steps provide insight into the best type of plan for the client. Steps 4 and 5 (discussing cost objectives and cash flow) are, however, perhaps the most important determinants of the type of plan the client will adopt. The price tag the client can comfortably live with is sometimes a product of the client's objectives (what he or she wants to provide) and sometimes a product of the economics of the situation (what he or she can afford). What clients can afford will vary according to what they want and what they consider a cost-effective price. When considering cost objectives, the organization's ability to make the economic commitment year in and year out should be carefully studied. Some industries have fluctuating profits that ebb and flow with certain uncontrollable economic conditions, while others are fairly stable. In other words, it is not just a question of how much, but also how consistently a certain payment level can be maintained or how much flexibility is needed in order to meet benefit commitments. Carefully examine the following issues before deciding on a price range:

- annual variations in profits
- future cash needs for capital expansion
- potential changes in the prospect's industry over the next 5 years
- length of time until the principals retire
- tax-shelter needs of owner-employees

Step 6 (distinguishing between personal and organizational goals) helps you to better understand the priorities laid out in step 3 and the cost objectives laid out in step 4 by differentiating between the client's personal needs and corporate objectives. You may find that, in the small-plan market, the client's personal needs are of the utmost importance and, as the size of the company grows, the organizational needs become more central to the decision-making process.

Step 7 (analyzing the company's census) is perhaps the most important step in the fact-finding process. A thorough understanding of the ages and salary levels of the people who will be covered by the plan is essential in establishing the best possible plan design. For example, if all the members of the firm are "older" (by pension standards, over age 45), then it may be desirable to put in a defined-benefit plan that accounts for past service (discussed later). If, however, salary levels are low and employees are young, a defined-contribution plan, such as a 401(k) plan, may be desirable. The employee census also can have an impact on cost. For example, in a defined-benefit plan the cost of funding a benefit for an older participant can be quite high, as there is a short time to fund the retirement benefit.

Step 8 is also crucial. Under the plan rules, certain related employers have to be aggregated for purposes of determining whether a plan satisfies coverage requirements. The rules are quite complex; therefore, it is best to ask broad questions that will enable a qualified tax professional to analyze the ownership relationships to determine whether aggregation issues exist.

YOUR FINANCIAL SERVICES PRACTICE: INFORMATION GATHERING

The pension planning fact finder is just the jumping-off point in your quest to identify your client's needs and objectives. The initial interview should be followed by open communication lines that allow the client's concerns to be more clearly developed over time. The following points typify what can happen in this intervening time:

- Frequently, the person you speak with will not correctly represent the desires of the entire body of authority within the organization. The company will need time to sort out its collective feelings and develop a response. Try not to get involved in the infighting that may occur, and try to remain as diplomatic and neutral as possible.
- The company's attorney or accountant should be brought into the process in the early stages. A common problem is that the attorney or accountant may resent playing the subordinate role (even though he or she may know little about pension plans). Once again, the solution is diplomacy.

Choosing between a Qualified Plan and the Other Tax-Sheltered Plan

Employers in private industry can choose between qualified plans, SEPs, and SIMPLEs. The nonprofit employer, a 501(c)(3) organization, can choose any of these plans and also has the option of sponsoring a 403(b) tax-sheltered annuity plan.

Establishing and maintaining a qualified plan requires a significant amount of documentation, government reporting, and employee communication. For the small business, these requirements can be quite onerous. SEPs and SIMPLEs are intended to provide the small business with some less complicated options. Plan documents are less complicated, and there are fewer IRS reporting requirements. Simplicity translates into lower administrative expenses and less time spent operating the plan. However, in exchange for simplicity, the plan designs are more rigid, offering less flexibility than qualified plans in most regards. The important differences include:

- *Coverage.* While the qualified plan rules provide significant flexibility in the number and makeup of the employees covered by the plan, the SEP and SIMPLE eligibility requirements are set in stone.
- *Vesting.* Contributions must be fully and immediately vested in the contributions to SEPs and SIMPLEs, while qualified plans can have a vesting schedule.
- *Contributions.* In some cases in a qualified plan, benefits or contributions can be different for different classes of employees. This is not the case in SEPs and SIMPLEs, where all participants must receive essentially the same level of benefits.
- *Maximum contributions.* In most regards, the limits are lower for SEPs and SIMPLEs than for qualified plans.

The SEP is the appropriate plan option when the employer is going to fund all of the plan benefits. In a SEP, as in a profit-sharing plan, the employer can make contributions annually (or more often) on a discretionary basis. When the employer wants to allow employees the opportunity to make additional contributions on a pretax basis (making it similar to a 401(k) plan), then the SIMPLE is the appropriate choice.

The 403(b) tax-sheltered annuity is a unique retirement planning vehicle. Only tax-exempt 501(c)(3) organizations and public school systems are allowed to sponsor such plans. At one time, there were relatively few rules governing these plans. However, over time, the situation has evolved, and more and more of the rules that apply to qualified plans now also apply to 403(b) plans.

CHOOSING BETWEEN A DEFINED-BENEFIT AND A DEFINED-CONTRIBUTION PLAN

LO 3.2   Identify the rule differences between defined-benefit and defined-contribution plans.

defined-benefit plan

Assuming the employer is going to choose from among the qualified plan options, the first consideration is whether the employer wants a defined-benefit or defined-contribution plan. All qualified plans fall into one of those two categories and each category represents a different philosophy of retirement planning. This philosophy is reflected in the definition of each term. A **defined-benefit plan** specifies the benefits each employee receives at retirement. In most plans, the benefit is stated as a percentage of preretirement salary, which is payable for the participant's remaining life. Under a defined-benefit plan, the contributions required by the employer vary depending upon what is needed to pay the promised benefit, and the amount of annual funding is determined each year by the plan's actuary.

In many ways, the defined-benefit plan looks like an insurance solution to the retirement problem. As such, the defined-benefit plan insures against the risk of lost income due to the inability to work any longer in retirement. Another retirement risk is that chance an individual will outlive his or her money. The traditional defined-benefit plan addresses both of these issues. The benefit amount is tied to what will be lost—employment income. To address the issue of longevity, in the traditional plan, the benefit is payable for the retired employee's entire life. It is interesting to note that this plan design is due in part to the fact that the first defined-benefit plans were funded with insurance products, although today many "self-fund" the promised benefits.

defined-contribution plan

In a **defined-contribution plan,** on the other hand, employer contributions are allocated to the accounts of individual employees. This approach is similar to a personal savings approach in which an individual opens a bank account and makes regular contributions, and the account grows based on the rate of investment return. Because of this characteristic, defined-contribution plans are sometimes called individual account plans. One way to look at these dissimilar approaches is to say that defined-benefit plans provide a fixed predetermined benefit that has an uncertain cost to the employer, whereas defined-contribution plans have a predetermined cost to the employer and provide a variable benefit to employees (based upon the rate of return).

All qualified plans fall into either the defined-benefit or the defined-contribution category. The names of the various qualified plans and the categories into which they fall are listed below. Note, however, that two types of plans are referred to as hybrid plans. First is the cash-balance plan, which is a defined-benefit plan that has some of the characteristics of a plan using the defined-contribution approach. Second is the target-benefit plan, which is a defined-contribution plan that has some of the characteristics of a defined-benefit plan. These distinctions will become more clear when the plans are discussed in more detail. Also note that the SEP, the SIMPLE, and the 403(b) tax-sheltered annuity plan all use a defined-contribution approach and share the same strengths and limitations of other defined-contribution plans (in comparison to the defined-benefit approach).

Qualified Plan Categories

Defined-Benefit Plans
- Defined-benefit pension plan
- Cash-balance pension plan

Defined-Contribution Plans
- Money-purchase pension plan
- Target-benefit pension plan
- Profit-sharing plan
- 401(k) plan
- Stock bonus plan
- ESOP

Rule Differences

Because of their vastly different natures, there are a number of important rule differences that apply to defined-benefit and defined-contribution plans. First, there are differences to how the maximum contribution and benefit rules of Code Sec. 415 apply. Code Sec. 415(b) limits the maximum annual benefit that can be provided in a defined-benefit plan. The rule allows payment of a life annuity beginning at age 65 in the amount of the lesser of 100 percent of the highest consecutive 3-year average compensation or $215,000 (as indexed in 2017, with no actuarial reductions if benefits begin as early as age 62). If payments begin before age 62, the dollar limit is reduced to reflect early commencement. The dollar limit is also increased to reflect commencement after age 65. If the form of payment is other than a life annuity, the benefit generally must be actuarially adjusted.

Compensation under Code Sec. 415 includes taxable wage income as well as salary deferral contributions to all types of tax-sheltered plans and pretax contributions to cafeteria plans and fringe benefit programs. Compensation cannot exceed the cap stated in Code Sec. 401(a)(17). In 2017, the compensation cap is $270,000.

In a defined-contribution plan, the maximum contribution each year is limited under Code Sec. 415(c). The rule states the maximum annual additions for any participant for the year cannot exceed the lesser of $54,000 (indexed for 2017) or 100 percent of salary. Annual additions include all employer contributions, employee contributions (of any type), and forfeitures that are allocated to the participant's account. There is one exception: catchup salary deferral contributions, $6,000 for 2017 (indexed), made for those individuals over age 50 are not counted under the limit. This enables those over age 50 to have a maximum allocation of $60,000 for 2017.

All defined-contribution plans of related employers are added together to determine whether the annual additions limit of Code Sec. 415(c) has been satisfied. Similarly, defined-benefit plans are aggregated to determine whether Code Sec. 415(b) has been satisfied. This means if an individual participated in two defined-contribution plans of a single or related employers, the maximum annual addition for 2017 would be the lesser of 100 percent of compensation or $54,000. Related employers generally means aggregated under the controlled group, affiliated service group, or leased employees rules, except that under the parent-subsidiary rules, aggregation exists if the parent owns more than 50 percent of the subsidiary (instead of the 80 percent or more rule that normally applies).

The next rule difference has to do with the PBGC. The PBGC insurance program guarantees certain benefit payments from most privately sponsored defined-benefit plans (with the exception of certain small plans). In a defined-benefit plan, the amount of assets never exactly matches the promised benefits, and the PBGC program is there to provide assistance if the company is in financial trouble and the plan does not have sufficient assets to pay the promised benefits. This program does not cover defined-contribution plans because the plan's assets always match the promised benefits owed to participants.

minimum-participation rule

Another important rule difference is that defined-benefit plans are subject to a special coverage provision referred to as the **minimum-participation rule**. Defined-contribution plans are not subject to this rule.

Another distinction is the way the maximum deductible contribution is calculated. In defined-contribution plans, the maximum deductible contribution is 25 percent of the aggregate compensation of all covered participants. In a defined-benefit plan, the limit is based on actuarial calculations and is not limited to a specific percentage of compensation.

Table 3-1
Rule Differences (2017)

Defined-Benefit Plans	Defined-Contribution Plans
Maximum annual benefit limited to lesser of 100% of average compensation or $215,000	Maximum annual additions limited to the lesser of 100% of compensation or $54,000
Subject to the PBGC insurance program	Exempt from the PBGC insurance program
Satisfy Sec. 401(a)(26) minimum participation rule	Not subject to the minimum participation rule
Deductible contribution based on actuarial calculations	Deductible contribution limited to 25% of aggregate compensation
5-year cliff or 7-year graded vesting	3-year cliff or 6-year graded vesting

Today, defined-contribution plans are required to have more accelerated vesting schedules than defined-benefit plans. Defined-contribution plans must use a vesting schedule as favorable as either a 3-year cliff (participants become fully vested after 3 years of service) or a 6-year graded schedule (participants must be 20 percent vested after 2 years and earn an additional 20 percent for each additional year of service). Defined-benefit plans can choose a more extended schedule—either 5-year cliff vesting or 7-year graded vesting.

Comparing the Defined-Benefit and Defined-Contribution Approaches

LO 3.3 Compare the defined-benefit with the defined-contribution plan approach.

Because defined-benefit plans typically describe benefits as a percentage of final-average compensation, benefits can be geared to replace a specified percentage of salary for the long-service employee. Also, defined-benefit plans can provide benefits based on past service (that is, years worked before the plan was initiated), while defined-contribution plans cannot. This means that benefits can accumulate more quickly for the older employee in a defined-benefit plan. Such plans reward those employees who continue employment until retirement, because benefits are usually tied to both length of service and final income.

In defined-benefit plans, the burden of providing an adequate retirement income is placed solely on the employer, because the employer promises to fund the plan sufficiently to pay promised benefits. This means the risk of the investment experience is on the employer; contributions will increase if investment experience is worse than expected and will decrease if performance is better than expected. Even though the employer is responsible to make required contributions, it is important to note that there is generally some funding flexibility in defined-benefit plans. There is, typically, some range (as determined with the help of an actuary) from the required minimum to the maximum allowable deductible contribution.

Also, defined-benefit plans generally provide for a built-in "preretirement" inflation factor by tying benefit payments to salary levels received just prior to retirement. However, defined-benefit plans generally do not increase automatically for inflation occurring after retirement—although it is not unusual for an employer to provide periodic ad hoc benefit increases for retirees. This makes the defined-benefit plan unique, because defined-contribution plans cannot imitate this inflation protection.

Tying benefits to final-average salary does have one down side. When a participant changes jobs, the benefit can be reduced significantly because of the loss of the highest years of salary in the calculation. This means the benefit is not as portable as in a defined-contribution plan where benefits accrue more ratably over the years. This lack of portability ties the employee to the employer, which has a benefit for the employer who offers the defined-benefit plan.

For these reasons, employers looking to (1) maximize benefits for older workers, (2) give long-term employees (including key people) a secure and specified retirement income, and (3) tie employees to the company through the benefit program will be interested in the defined-benefit plan. Still, the defined-benefit plan is only an option if the company is in the financial position and competitive posture to be able to meet the financial obligation of maintaining this type of plan.

Plans in the defined-contribution category are significantly different. From the perspective of both the employer and the employee, such plans look and feel more like deferred-compensation plans. A specified amount is set aside for the employee's benefit, which is paid out at termination of employment (as long as the participant is "vested") or, in some cases, even earlier.

This means that defined-contribution plans do not provide a retirement benefit that is closely tied to the individual's retirement needs (as in a defined-benefit plan). This does not mean that defined-contribution plans will not provide adequate retirement income; it is just much harder to pinpoint the benefit. Also, in a very real way, the employee is at more risk because the benefit is tied to the plan's investment return. In other words, if stock market prices fall drastically, it is the employee who must worry in a defined-contribution plan and the employer who must worry in a defined-benefit plan.

With a defined-contribution plan, the employer's cost is determinable and will not vary with the plan's investment return. Also, these plans cost less to administer as there are fewer administrative functions. The cost is higher with a defined-benefit plan primarily because the sponsor needs to hire an actuary to determine the cost of providing benefits. The actuary has to make multiple calculations as required by funding, accounting, and PBGC rules.

Employees can more easily follow the growth of their benefits with a defined-contribution plan and can more readily appreciate the value of the cost of the plan to the employer. Defined benefits can have great value, but the cost of the benefit to the employer is not as transparent.

Defined-contribution plans may also allow employees to direct the investments in their individual accounts. As well, the participant's benefit is stated as a single account balance and lump-sum distributions are generally allowed—which is not always the case in a defined-benefit plan.

A defined-contribution account balance is more portable should an employee switch jobs. The lump-sum value can be rolled over to an IRA or to the new employer's plan. Because the benefit grows with annual contributions and investment experience, a participant is not penalized by changing employers, as can be the case with a defined-benefit plan.

**Table 3-2
Types of Plans Compared**

Defined-Benefit Plans	Defined-Contribution Plans
Defines the benefit	Defines the employer's contribution
Contributions not attributed to specified employees	All contributions allocated to individual employee accounts
Employer assumes risk of preretirement inflation, investment performance, and adequacy of retirement income	Employee assumes risk of preretirement inflation, investment performance, and adequacy of retirement income
Can provide benefits based on past service	Cannot provide benefits for past service
Costly to administer	Lower administrative costs
Can be difficult to communicate both the amount of benefits and the value of benefit (amount it costs the employer)	Easy to communicate the amount of employer contributions and the "bank-account" type accumulation
Unpredictable costs	Predictable costs

Easily determinable costs appeal to employers whose financial positions dictate caution (typically organizations with volatile cash flow). In addition, key employees tend to feel more comfortable with individual accounts, portable benefits, and the lump-sum distributions traditionally offered under defined-contribution plans. As a result of employer and key-employee appeal, defined-contribution plans have become a hot ticket for financial services professionals in the pension field.

The Realities of the Marketplace Today

A look at the contrast between the defined-benefit and the defined-contribution approach would not be complete without a discussion of the realities of today's marketplace. Even though the defined-benefit approach still has a variety of strengths and unique benefits, few small businesses today are maintaining defined-benefit plans. In March 2016, the Bureau of Labor Statistics released information on how many companies offered defined contribution as compared to defined benefit plans. A significantly higher percentage of workers had access (58 percent) and participated in a defined contribution plan (40 percent of population) than had access (27 percent) to a defined benefit plan and participated (23 percent of population).[1] However, this creates a take-up rate in a defined benefit plan of roughly 85 percent while only 69 percent of defined contribution potential workers take up the plan and participate.

This does not mean, however, that defined-benefit plans are not an important part of the retirement planning landscape. The same study revealed that in 2016, 43 percent of employers in private industry with 500 or more employees offer defined-benefit plans. Also, in the small-plan marketplace, the pension industry has begun to recognize that defined-benefit plans could play an important role for the older business owner who has not accumulated enough for retirement, has a strong cash flow, and is looking for a significant tax shelter.

Nevertheless, defined-contribution products have become the bread-and-butter sale for those who deal in qualified deferred compensation. The defined-contribution approach appears to appeal both to senior managers, who are looking for simplicity and contribution certainty, and to employees, who like that they can more easily understand the plan and appreciate that benefits are more portable. According to the Bureau of Labor Statistics in 2016, 36 percent of employees in companies with 1–99 employees participate in defined-contributions plans. For companies with 100–499 employees, the number increases to 59 percent and in companies with more than 500 employees, the number increases to 76 percent.

Multiple Plans—Combining Defined-Benefit and Defined-Contribution Plans

Defined-benefit plans and defined-contribution plans are not mutually exclusive, and two or more plans can be set up for any one employer. If defined-benefit and defined-contribution plans are used together, restrictions apply to the overall deduction limits.

Today, a combination of both a defined-benefit and a defined-contribution plan is typically used in larger companies to provide a comprehensive benefits package. A combination of both a defined-benefit and a defined-contribution plan may be appropriate in the small-plan marketplace as well, when the business owner is looking to maximize benefits and deductible

---

1. BLS, *National Compensation Survey: Employee Benefits in the United States.* March 2016. https://www.bls.gov/ncs/ebs/benefits/2016/ownership/civilian/table02a.pdf.

contributions. Theoretically, a plan sponsor could contribute the maximum Code Sec. 415(c) amount to a defined-contribution plan on behalf of the owner and fund the Code Sec. 415(b) maximum allowable benefit in a defined-benefit plan for the owner as well. In practice, this may be beneficial in some cases, but this type of arrangement could run up against the maximum deductible contribution limits. When a sponsor maintains both a defined-benefit and a defined-contribution plan for the same group of employees, the maximum deductible contribution will generally be the greater of the cost of funding the defined-benefit plan or 25 percent of aggregate compensation. There are several important exceptions. First, if the defined-benefit plan is subject to the PBGC insurance program this combined limit does not apply. Also, when applying the combined limit, the first 6 percent contributed to the defined-contribution plan is not counted (essentially making the limit 31 percent of compensation). In addition, employees can make salary deferral contributions (including catch-up contributions for those age 50 or older) as long as total contributions do not exceed the Code Sec. 415(c) maximum allocation limits.

Partially due to these exceptions, a combination of a defined-benefit plan and a 401(k)/profit-sharing plan can also work quite well for the small business owner (at least 45 years old to get a significant deduction for the defined-benefit plan) with the goals of maximizing retirement benefits and maximizing tax deductions.

> **EXAMPLE**
>
> Betty, age 50, has an office organization business called EZ Order, Inc. She is 100 percent owner of the corporation and her annual W-2 pay is $215,000. Her goal is to maximize her retirement benefits. She plans to retire in 12 years when she is 62. A traditional defined-benefit plan established in 2017 will provide Betty with an annual benefit of $215,000 at age 62, assuming that she participates in the plan for at least 10 years and sustains a 3-year average salary of at least $215,000. The actuary working for Betty's business estimates that she can contribute $135,000 per year to the defined-benefit plan. In addition, she can contribute 6 percent of pay ($12,900) to the profit-sharing plan and maximize her salary deferral of $24,000 ($18,000 plus the $6,000 catchup). So the total annual contribution for EZ Order, Inc. will be $171,900 ($135,000 + $12,900 + $24,000). Future contributions to the defined-benefit plan will depend on the performance of the plan assets, as well as the amount of Betty's W-2 income.

Instead of adopting two separate plans, under Code Sec. 414(x) employers with no more than 500 employees can adopt a combination defined-benefit plan and 401(k) plan referred to as a DB(k) plan. The plan uses a single plan document, trust and annual Form 5500 filing. The defined-benefit portion of the plan can use a traditional defined-benefit formula or a cash-balance benefit structure.

This approach requires that the defined-benefit portion provide minimum benefits and that the 401(k) portion contain a specified matching contribution. In exchange, the plan is exempt from the top-heavy rules and does not have to meet certain nondiscrimination requirements.

CHOOSING BETWEEN A PENSION PLAN AND A PROFIT-SHARING PLAN

LO 3.4   **Compare plans in the pension category with those in the profit-sharing category.**

All qualified plans fall into either the defined-benefit or defined-contribution categories. Similarly, all plans are also classified as either pension plans or profit-sharing plans. As you can see in the chart below, both types of defined-benefit plans, along with target-benefit and money-purchase plans, are categorized as pension plans. All other defined-contribution plans are profit-sharing plans.

Qualified Plan Categories

Pension Plans	Profit-Sharing Plans
• Defined-benefit pension plan	• Profit-sharing plan
• Cash-balance pension plan	• 401(k) plan
• Money-purchase pension plan	• Stock bonus plan
• Target-benefit pension plan	• ESOP

pension plan category

profit-sharing plan category

The most important difference between a plan in the **pension plan category** and one in the profit-sharing plan category concerns the employer's commitment to the plan. Under a pension plan, the organization is legally required to make annual payments to the plan because the plan's main purpose is to provide a retirement benefit. Under a profit-sharing-type plan, however, an organization is not required to make annual contributions. The reasoning here seems to be that **profit-sharing plans** are not necessarily intended to provide retirement benefits as much as to provide a sharing of profits on a tax-deferred basis.

Consistent with this rationale, the law generally allows that profit-sharing-type plans may be written to permit distributions during employment. These are often referred to as in-service distributions. The plan can distribute funds accumulated under the plan after a fixed number of years, the attainment of a stated age, or upon the prior occurrence of some event such as layoff, illness, financial hardship, disability, retirement, death, or severance of employment. The IRS has interpreted "a fixed number of years" to mean that:

- Distributions can be made of any contributions that have been held in the plan for 2 years or more.
- Any participant who has 5 or more years of plan participation can receive a distribution of his or her entire account balance.

Note that salary deferral contributions to 401(k) plans are subject to special, more restrictive in-service withdrawal limitations.

Since pension plans are meant to provide retirement income, the rules generally require that benefits cannot begin until termination of employment. However, plans are allowed to begin payments when a participant attains normal retirement age, even if the participant does not retire. To ensure that plans don't take advantage of this exception, the IRS has issued rules establishing the earliest allowable normal retirement age in a pension plan. The rules provide that a normal retirement age of 62 or later is always acceptable, and that an age earlier than 55 is presumed to be unreasonable, unless the sponsor can demonstrate that the normal retirement age is reasonably representative of the typical retirement age for the industry in which the covered workforce is employed. The rules give some deference to an employer's judgment in applying this same "industry" standard to retirement between ages 55 and 62.

A final distinction between pension and profit-sharing plans concerns the ability of these plans to invest in company stock. Plans in the pension category can invest only up to 10 percent of plan assets in employer stock. Plans in the profit-sharing category, on the other hand, have no restrictions; all plan assets can be used to purchase employer stock (although this is seldom the case). The following table summarizes plan differences.

Table 3-3
Differences between Pension and Profit-Sharing Plans

Characteristic	Pension Plan	Profit-Sharing Plan
Employer commitment to annual funding	Yes	No
Withdrawal flexibility for employees	In-service withdrawals restricted	In-service withdrawals freely permitted
Investment in company stock	Limited to 10%	Unlimited

KEOGH PLANS

LO 3.5   Define the term "Keogh" plan and calculate the maximum allowable deduction under a defined-contribution plan.

Keogh plans

In addition to categorizing plans either as defined-benefit or defined-contribution, or as pension or profit-sharing, qualified plans are categorized by the type of business organization they serve. Today, all types of businesses choose from among the same group of qualified plans. Historically, that was not always true. At one time, plans for partnerships and self-employed persons were governed by separate statutory provisions, and plans for such organizations were referred to as **Keogh plans**. Unfortunately, the name still sticks—generally creating more confusion than information. Today, a sole proprietor does not establish a Keogh plan; he or she establishes a profit-sharing, defined-benefit, or other plan from the array of tax-advantaged retirement plans. And, except as described below, the rules for sole proprietorships and partnerships are entirely the same as for corporate entities, and the same considerations regarding plan choice and design apply.

There is, however, one remaining distinction between plans of sole proprietorships and partnerships[2] and corporate plans: The self-employed person's contribution or benefit is based on net earnings instead of salary. This creates some complications because net earnings can be determined only after taking into account all appropriate business deductions, including the deduction for the retirement contribution—thus, the amount of net earnings and the amount of the deduction are dependent on each other.

If a defined-benefit plan is used, an actuary is needed to straighten out the confusion and to determine the plan contribution amount itself. In a profit-sharing plan, this means that a sole proprietor or partner can only contribute 20 percent of Schedule C earnings (not 25 percent of compensation as with a corporate plan). Further complicating matters is the fact that self-employed individuals get a deduction for income tax purposes equal to one-half of their Social Security self-employment tax on their federal tax return. Also, the contribution amounts still cannot exceed the Code Sec. 415(c) annual limit or take into consideration earnings in excess of the compensation cap. To ensure compliance with this rule it is useful to follow the formula in the Keogh Deduction Work Sheet to calculate the maximum contribution in a defined-contribution plan.

---

2.   Limited-liability companies that are taxed as partnerships are subject to the same limitations as those that apply to partnerships.

Table 3-4
Keogh Deduction Work Sheet

Step I: Self-employed person's work sheet			Value
	1	Plan contribution as a decimal (for example, 25% would be 0.25)	
	2	Rate in Line 1 plus 1, shown as a decimal (for example, 0.25 plus 1 would be 1.25)	
	3	Divide Line 1 by Line 2. This is the self-employed contribution rate. (For example, 0.25 ÷ 1.25 = .20)	
Step II: Figure the deduction			
	1	Enter the self-employed contribution rate from Line 3 of Step I.	
	2	Enter the amount of net earnings that the business owner has from Schedule C (Form 1040) or Schedule F (Form 1040).	$
	3	Enter the deduction for self-employment tax from the front page of Form 1040.	$
	4	Subtract Line 3 from Line 2 and enter the amount.	$
	5	Multiply Line 4 by Line 1.	$
	6	Multiply $270,000 (2017 compensation cap) by Line 1.	$
	7	Enter the smaller of line 5 or 6.	$
	8	Enter the smaller of line 7 or $54,000 (the maximum allocation allowed for 2017).	$
Total			$

ADDITIONAL PRELIMINARY CONCERNS

Before we study the menu of qualified plans, it should be noted that choosing the best retirement plan is not as simple as picking one type of plan from the menu. The plan's design must also be considered in order to make the proper choice. This is because qualified plans are principally differentiated by only one design feature—their benefit formulas. The many other design choices, however, also affect your plan choice. To put it another way, plan choice is a function of plan design, and plan design is a function of plan choice.

A second consideration when choosing a qualified plan is the makeup of the entire benefits package. For example, if there is a nonqualified plan for key employees, the choice of a qualified plan for all employees should be dovetailed with the nonqualified plan to reach the desired result. When group life and group disability plans are involved, other considerations arise. As a general rule, the choice of a retirement plan should reflect the fact that it is only one part of a benefits package. Special care should be taken to ensure that benefits are not duplicated under the different employee benefit plans.

PENSION PLANNING FACT FINDER

Client's Name				
Address				
Phone Numbers				
Key Contacts	Name			
	Title		Phone No.	
	Name			
	Title		Phone No.	
	Name			
	Title		Phone No.	
	Attorney		Phone No.	
	Accountant		Phone No.	
Employer Identification Number				
Fiscal Year				
Accounting Method (Circle One)		Cash	Accrual	
Business Structure (Circle One)		C Corp.	S Corp.	Municipal Corp.
		Partnership	Limited Liability Company	Sole Proprietorship
		Exempt Organization	Professional Corp.	Government Agency
State of Incorporation or Domicile				
Date of Incorporation or Establishment				
Were there any predecessor entities? (Circle One)		Yes	No	
Describe Relationship				
Affiliated Entities Identify (1) other entities that the owner of this entity own in full or in part, (2) other entities that this entity owns in full or in part, (3) other entities that own this entity in full or in part, and (4) other entities that work with this entity to provide a single product or service. Describe in detail the chain of ownership and how the entities work together.	1.			
	2.			
	3.			
	4.			
Name				
Address				
Phone No.				
Describe Relationship				

Step 1: Set retirement priorities.

Listed below are some typical concerns that organizations have when instituting a retirement program. Grade each of these concerns by scoring 1 for very valuable, 2 for valuable, 3 for moderately valuable, and 4 for least valuable.

1. To what extent is it important to use a qualified plan as a tax shelter for owner-employees and key employees? [1] [2] [3] [4]
2. To what extent is it important to maximize benefits for long-service employees by including service prior to the inception of the plan? [1] [2] [3] [4]
3. To what extent is it important to place the risk of investing plan assets with the employee? [1] [2] [3] [4]
4. To what extent is it important to institute a plan that is easily communicated to employees? [1] [2] [3] [4]
5. To what extent is it important to institute a plan that is administratively convenient? [1] [2] [3] [4]
6. To what extent is it important to institute a plan that has predictable costs? [1] [2] [3] [4]
7. To what extent is it important to avoid an annual financial commitment? [1] [2] [3] [4]
8. To what extent is it important to allow employees (including owner-employees) to withdraw funds? [1] [2] [3] [4]
9. To what extent is it important to minimize plan costs by limiting benefits for lower-paid employees? [1] [2] [3] [4]
10. To what extent is it important to create a market for employer stock? [1] [2] [3] [4]
11. To what extent is it important that the plan be able to borrow to purchase employer stock? [1] [2] [3] [4]
12. To what extent is it important to attract key employees? [1] [2] [3] [4]
13. To what extent is it important to retain experienced personnel? [1] [2] [3] [4]
14. To what extent is it important to motivate the workforce? [1] [2] [3] [4]
15. To what extent is it important to encourage the retirement of superannuated employees? [1] [2] [3] [4]
16. To what extent is it important to give participants the opportunity to save additional amounts on a pretax basis? [1] [2] [3] [4]
17. To what extent is it important that employer contributions be made only for employees who elect to contribute? [1] [2] [3] [4]
18. To what extent is it important that benefits for those who terminate prior to retirement be portable? [1] [2] [3] [4]
19. To what extent is it important for participants with a salary deferral option to be able to choose between tax-deferred and tax-free withdrawals? [1] [2] [3] [4]

Step 2: Discuss with the client the interplay between various factors in step 1. For example:

		Yes / No
1.	Does the desire to provide tax shelter for owner-employees and key employees outweigh the need to cut costs attributable to lower-paid employees?	[Y] [N]
2.	Does the desire to provide tax shelter for owner-employees and key employees outweigh the need to have an easily communicated and administratively convenient plan?	[Y] [N]
3.	Does the need to provide tax shelter for owner-employees and key employees outweigh the need to have predictable costs and payment flexibility?	[Y] [N]
4.	Is it more important to retain employees than to attract employees?	[Y] [N]
5.	Is it more important to motivate employees than to attract or retain them?	[Y] [N]
6.	Is it more important to provide an adequate retirement standard of living than to cut plan costs?	[Y] [N]
7.	Is it more important to provide an adequate retirement standard of living than to have predictable costs?	[Y] [N]
8.	Is it more important to provide an adequate standard of living during retirement than to avoid an annual commitment to funding the plan?	[Y] [N]
9.	Is it more important to provide an adequate standard of living during retirement than to allow employees (including owner-employees) to withdraw funds?	[Y] [N]
10.	Is it more important to provide an adequate standard of living during retirement than to have administrative convenience and an easily communicated plan?	[Y] [N]
11.	Is it more important that contributions go only to employees who elect to participate than to provide retirement benefits to all workers?	[Y] [N]

Additional Comments

Step 3: List the primary reason(s) for establishing the plan and the secondary reason(s) for establishing the plan.

Primary	1.
	2.
	3.
Secondary	1.
	2.
	3.

Step 4: Discuss the employer's cost objectives. Discuss the price range that is desired both now and in the future.

Step 5:

(A) What are the current and future cash-flow situations?

1. for the company
2. for the industry in general

(B) Attach balance sheets from the last 3 years.

(C) Attach appropriate profit and loss statements.

Step 6:   Distinguish between the personal needs that the plan will satisfy for the principals and the organizational goals that are sought.

Step 7:   Analyze the company's census (list of employees).

1. What percentage of employees can be expected to turn over before retirement?

    _____% leave before they complete one year of service

    _____% leave between their first and second years of service

    _____% leave between their second and third years of service

    _____% leave between their third and fourth years of service

    _____% leave between their fourth and fifth years of service

    _____% leave between their fifth and sixth years of service

    _____% leave between their sixth and seventh years of service

    _____% leave with more than seven years of service

    _____% are "lifers" with the company

2. What groups of employees exist?

    _____ salaried employees

    _____ hourly paid employees

    _____ collective-bargaining unit employees

    _____ leased employees

3. To what extent are part-time employees used?

    _____ part-time employees are used

    _____ no part-time employees are used

    _____ part-time employees work less than 500 hours

    _____ part-time employees work between 500 and 999 hours

    _____ part-time employees work 1000 or more hours

4. How many offices (profit centers) are there?

    _____ number of different locations

5. What benefit programs do chief competitors offer?

6. Attach employee census.

7. Attach other group benefit plans.

Step 8: Identify other related employers and the relationship to this one. The list should include any entities with interrelated ownership and other entities that work together with this one to produce a product. Describe in detail the chain of ownership and how the entities work together.

CHAPTER REVIEW

Key Terms and Concepts

defined-benefit plan
defined-contribution plan
minimum-participation rule
pension plan category
profit-sharing plan category
Keogh plans

Chapter 3: Review Questions

Review questions are based on the learning objectives in this chapter. Thus, a [3.3] at the end of a question means that the question is based on learning objective 3. If there are multiple objectives, they are all listed

1. June Jones is thinking of installing a retirement plan for her budding flower business. June has indicated that she knows nothing about retirement plans and would like to speak with her financial advisor on the issue. What steps should the advisor take to help June focus on the important issues facing both her and the business and to gather the appropriate information that would enable the advisor to make recommendations? [3.1]

2. What are two typical stumbling blocks that financial services professionals face when helping to plan a client's retirement program? [3.1]

3. Answer these client questions about Code Sec. 415. [3.2]

    a. Can a defined-benefit plan pay the owner $215,000 (2017 indexed limit) a year for life beginning at age 60?

    b. I've heard that in 2017, an owner aged 50 or older can actually receive an allocation in a 401(k) plan of $60,000. Is this correct?

c. Is it true that, if an individual works for a company and participates in two defined-contribution plans with that employer, up to $54,000 (2017 indexed limit) can be allocated to the participant in each plan?

4. Sam Doyle, owner of Doyle's Furniture, Inc., has requested a qualified plan that (1) provides an adequate pension for his employees, regardless of what the stock market does, (2) takes care of employees who have been with him for a long time, (3) provides a pension that reflects his employees' salaries at retirement, and (4) ties his long-service employees to the company. Should Doyle's Furniture, Inc., use a defined-benefit or a defined-contribution plan? Explain. [3.3]

5. What advantages are available to the employer under a defined-contribution plan? [3.2]

6. Indicate whether the following statements describe a defined-benefit plan or a defined-contribution plan: [3.3]

    a. Benefits accrue based on all years of salary.
    b. Benefit costs are less predictable.
    c. Administrative costs are lower.
    d. Plan assets are allocated to individual accounts for each participant.
    e. Annual additions for any participant cannot exceed the limits of Code Sec. 415(c).
    f. It can provide benefits based on past service.

7. Under what circumstances is it desirable to use a combination defined-benefit plan and defined-contribution plan? [3.3]

8. What are three basic differences between plans that fall into the pension family and plans that fall into the profit-sharing family? [3.4]

9. Faye is a sole proprietor with a qualified profit-sharing plan that enables her to contribute 25 percent of earned income. Faye's net earnings from schedule C are $100,000. Faye's deduction for one-half of her self-employment tax is $7,650 (15.3 percent in 2017). What is the maximum deduction that Faye is allowed to take under her profit-sharing plan for the year? [3.5]

Chapter 3: Review Answers

1. The financial advisor should sit down with June and walk her through a pension planning fact finder. The fact finder contains a list of the most common retirement concerns that face people like her. This list includes questions that ask June to prioritize her personal tax needs, her desires to underwrite benefits for other employees, and other typical retirement issues. Once the issues have been prioritized, June should be asked to discuss the interplay among each of the factors. For example, do June's tax and retirement needs outweigh the need to avoid the cost of including rank-and-file employees in a qualified plan? After this comparative analysis, June should once again be asked to prioritize her retirement concerns, this time in list form. She should be concerned with costs, and at this juncture, cost concerns should be addressed. The advisor will then distinguish between June's personal needs that the plan will satisfy and the organizational goals that will be accomplished. This is especially important if other principals are involved because the advisor can begin to see what issues will ultimately be considered important by all principals, not just by June. Finally, the advisor must analyze the flower shop's employee data. After taking all of these steps and garnering as much information as possible, the advisor is then in a position to make insightful recommendations.

2. Frequently, the person you speak with will not correctly represent the desires of the entire body of authority within the organization. Also, the company's attorney or accountant may resent playing the subordinate role (even though he or she may know little about pension plans). For both problems, the solution is diplomacy.

3. a. No, the maximum benefit ($215,000 in 2017) must be actuarially reduced if pay-outs begin before age 62.

    b. Yes, the Code Sec. 415(c) limit in 2017 is $54,000. However, catch-up contributions to a 401(k) plan are not included. This means that an owner age 50 or older making a salary deferral election can receive an allocation of $60,000.

    c. No, the Code Sec. 415(c) annual addition limitation applies to all the defined-contribution plans of an employer. If the plans were sponsored by two unrelated employers the answer may be different.

4. Doyle's Furniture, Inc., should use a defined-benefit retirement plan. Under a defined-benefit approach, the company, not the employees, runs the risk of investing contributions. This allows Doyle's employees to have a benefit that is not subject to the stock market; but it also means that, if investment performance is poor, the company must come up with extra funding to provide the promised benefit.

A second reason a defined-benefit approach is preferable is because defined-benefit plans can fund for past service, whereas defined-contribution plans cannot. This enables Doyle to take care of employees who have been with him for a long time because service worked for the employer prior to the inception of the plan can be counted.

A third reason for using a defined-benefit approach is because defined-benefit plans can gear retirement payments to salary levels used just prior to retirement. Defined-contribution plans, on the other hand, can only provide benefits based on the entire career earnings, which are less than the final years' earnings of an employee. In addition, salary levels at retirement will account for any inflation that took place during the employee's career, whereas a career-average salary will not fully account for preretirement inflation.

A final reason that a defined-benefit plan would be preferable is that long-service employees will lose benefits if they change employers. Under a defined-benefit plan, the benefit builds more quickly at the end of the person's career, when he or she has many years of service and the highest salary. Changing jobs means that benefits are calculated based on a lower salary.

5. Defined-contribution plans have more easily determinable costs, participants more easily appreciate the value of the benefits, the benefits are more portable, and participants generally have the option to receive a lump-sum distribution. These factors are appealing to both the employer and the employee, and for these reasons most new plans set up today are of the defined-contribution type.

6.
   a. defined-contribution plan
   b. defined-benefit plan
   c. defined-contribution plan
   d. defined-contribution plan
   e. defined-contribution plan
   f. defined-benefit plan

7. Combination defined-benefit and defined-contribution plans are most commonly used by larger employers looking for a very comprehensive retirement package. In addition, for the older small business owner looking to maximize benefits and deductible contributions using tax sheltered plans, a defined-benefit and 401(k) profit-sharing plan combination can be extremely effective.

8. The three differences are: (1) In a pension plan, the employer is committed to annual funding; in a profit-sharing plan, the employer is not. (2) A profit-sharing-type plan can allow for in-service distributions; a pension plan cannot (unless participant is aged 62 or older). (3) In a pension plan, only 10 percent of the plan's assets can be invested in employer securities; in a profit-sharing plan, up to 100 percent of the plan's assets can be invested in employer securities.

9. To determine Faye's maximum deduction for the year, you must first determine her contribution rate as follows:

(1)	List the plan contribution as a decimal	0.25
(2)	Add 1 to the rate in line 1 and show this as a decimal	1.25
(3)	Divide line 1 by line 2.	.20

Once you know what percentage Faye can contribute, you can then determine her maximum deduction:

(1)	Self-employment contribution rate	.20
(2)	Net earning from Schedule C	$100,000
(3)	Deduction for self-employment tax	$ 7,650
(4)	Subtract step 3 from step 2	$ 92,350
(5)	Multiply step 4 by step 1	$18,470
(6)	Multiply $270,000 by line 1	$ 54,000
(7)	Enter the smaller of line 5 or 6	$ 18,470
(8)	Enter smaller of 7 or $54,000	$ 18,470

Thus, we have determined that Faye's deduction will be $18,470.

Chapter 4

Defined-Benefit, Cash-Balance, Target-Benefit, and MPPPs

Learning Objectives

An understanding of the material in this chapter should enable the student to

- **LO 4.1** Identify the types of benefit formulas available in a defined-benefit plan.
- **LO 4.2** Identify the key components in a unit-benefit formula. Also identify the appropriate candidate for a defined-benefit plan.
- **LO 4.3** Describe the basic features of a cash-balance plan. Also describe why large employers choose to convert traditional defined-benefit plans to a cash-balance arrangement
- **LO 4.4** Describe the features of a money-purchase plan and why this plan design is not often chosen today
- **LO 4.5** Explain how a target-benefit plan is different than a defined-benefit plan, and why this plan design has fallen out of favor.

In order to help your client choose the best retirement plan, you first need to examine the menu of tax-advantaged plans. Considering the full range of qualified plans, you will assess each plan's strengths and weaknesses, focus on the objectives that each plan serves for your client, and discuss the typical candidates for each type of plan.

The various types of qualified plans are explained in part by the characteristics of the categories they fall under (defined-benefit versus defined-contribution, and pension versus profit-sharing) and in part by their benefit or contribution formula. Let's take a closer look at the various types of retirement plans and their benefit (contribution) formulas.

DEFINED-BENEFIT PENSION PLANS

A defined-benefit pension plan falls within both the defined-benefit and pension categories. Knowing this means you already know that defined-benefit plans have the following characteristics:

- The maximum benefit that a person can receive each year is limited by Code Sec. 415(b).
- Assets are not allocated to individual accounts.
- The employer assumes responsibility for preretirement inflation, income adequacy, and investment results.
- The benefit formula can be designed to consider past service.

- The older business owner can provide the maximum tax-shelter potential available under a qualified plan.
- They are more costly to administer than defined-contribution plans because, among other things, they require the services of an actuary.
- The benefit formula and value of the benefit may be more difficult to communicate than in defined-contribution plans.
- The employer's future costs are not precisely known.
- Annual employer contributions are required.
- Participants may not take in-service withdrawals prior to age 62.
- Investment in the sponsoring company' stock is limited to 10 percent of the plan's assets.

Let's take a closer look at defined-benefit pension plans from a design standpoint by examining the various types of benefit formulas that are used.

The Unit-Benefit Formula

unit-benefit formula

The most frequently used defined-benefit formula is the **unit-benefit formula** (also known as the percentage-of-earnings-per-year-of-service formula). This formula uses both service and salary in determining the participant's pension benefit. A unit-benefit formula might read this way: "Each plan participant will receive a monthly pension commencing at normal retirement date and paid in the form of a life annuity equal to 1.5 percent of final-average monthly salary multiplied by years of service. Service is limited to a maximum of 30 years."

EXAMPLE

Larry Novenstern is retiring after 25 years of service with his employer. Larry's final-average monthly salary is $5,000. To determine Larry's benefit, multiply 1.5 percent by the $5,000 final-average monthly salary by 25 (the number of years of service). Larry's monthly retirement benefit will be equal to $1,875 paid in the form of a life annuity. (Note that if a different distribution option is chosen, the benefit will be the actuarial equivalent of the life annuity).

income-replacement ratio

The unit-benefit formula is the most frequently used benefit formula because it best serves a variety of employer goals.

- The goal of retaining and rewarding experienced personnel is achieved because the pension benefit is based, in part, on the years of service an employee works for an employer.
- The goal of rewarding owner-employees and key employees is achieved because the pension benefit is based, in part, on salary, which is higher for owner-employees and key employees.
- The goal of providing the desired income-replacement ratio can be achieved through proper design of the benefit formula. The **income-replacement ratio** represents the amount of an employee's gross income that will be replaced under the retirement plan. Employers believe that there is no need to replace 100 percent of an employee's final-average salary in order to provide the desired standard of living at retirement for several reasons:
  - Social Security benefits and private savings will fund part of the needed retirement benefit.
  - The preretirement standard of living can be maintained at retirement on a lower income because the employee pays less in taxes in the retirement years (such as no Social Security taxes).
  - The preretirement standard of living can be maintained at retirement on a lower income because the employee has reduced living expenses (no work-related expenses such as transportation and clothing; self-supporting children; paid-up home mortgage; and so on).

For these reasons, employers generally choose an income replacement of between 40 and 60 percent of final-average salary for employees who have spent their career with the employer, and something less for employees who have not spent as long with the employer.

EXAMPLE

The Cooper Corporation would like to provide a 60 percent income-replacement ratio for long-service employees and would like to provide a proportionately reduced income-replacement ratio for shorter-service employees. In order to accomplish these goals, the Cooper Corporation should choose a benefit formula that reads: Each plan participant will receive a monthly pension commencing at normal retirement date and paid in the form of a life annuity equal to 2 percent of final-average monthly salary multiplied by years of service. Service is limited to a maximum of 30 years.

Under this benefit formula, the long-service employees will be provided with a 60 percent income-replacement ratio, and employees with fewer than 30 years of service will be provided with an equitably reduced income-replacement ratio. In addition, by placing the years-of-service cap at 30 years, the Cooper Corporation will never have to fund for benefits higher than 60 percent of average monthly salary.

Through the use of this benefit formula, the Cooper Corporation has achieved several goals:

- The goal of providing for a graceful transition in the workforce is achieved because the use of a years-of-service cap (in the example above, 30 years) discourages employment beyond the stated period. If the employer desires a more rapid turnover of older employees, a lower service cap can be used. If the employer wants to retain experienced personnel, however, a longer service cap may be used, or the employer may choose not to cap service at all.

- The goal of providing the most cost-effective defined-benefit plan possible is achieved because the unit-benefit formula is more cost-effective than other types of defined-benefit formulas. Cost-effectiveness can be defined in this case as getting the most value for each pension dollar by achieving employer goals at the least possible cost. To the extent permitted by law, the employer can reward employees with long service and/or high compensation and avoid paying disproportionate benefits for other employees.

The reason that unit-benefit formulas are the most cost-effective means of spending defined-benefit dollars can be best understood by examining the alternative defined-benefit formulas.

Other Defined-Benefit Formulas

LO 4.1   **Identify the types of benefit formulas available in a defined-benefit plan.**

flat-percentage-of-earnings formula

Under an alternative defined-benefit formula called the **flat-percentage-of-earnings formula** (on IRS forms, it is called a fixed-benefit formula), the benefit is related solely to salary and does not reflect an employee's service.

> **EXAMPLE**
>
> Such a benefit formula may read: "Each plan participant will receive a monthly pension benefit equal to 40 percent of the final-average monthly salary commencing at normal retirement date and paid in the form of a life annuity."

This formula is generally not cost-effective, however, because it provides a disproportionate benefit to employees hired later in their careers, which is costly to fund. At one time, these formulas were quite popular with small businesses when the owner was significantly older than the rank-and-file employees. The owner could accrue a full benefit over a short period of time while benefits for other employees accrued over a much longer period of time. Realizing that this was discriminatory, the IRS passed regulations that now require a flat-percentage-of-earnings formula to have a 25-year minimum period of service in order for the participants to receive the full benefits promised. For those with less than 25 years of service, the benefit will be proportionately reduced.

> **EXAMPLE**
>
> Use the 40 percent retirement benefit from the previous example and apply a pro rata reduction for those with less than 25 years of service. If Debbie had final-average compensation of $100,000 and 10 years of service, her benefit would be $16,000 (40 percent of $100,000 multiplied by 10/25).

flat-amount-per-year-of-service formula

A second alternative to the unit-benefit formula is a formula that relates the pension benefit solely to service but does not reflect an employee's salary. This type of formula, called a **flat-amount-per-year-of-service formula**, might read: "Each plan participant will receive a monthly pension benefit commencing at normal retirement date and paid in the form of a life annuity equal to $10 for every year worked."

Flat-amount-per-year-of-service formulas are relatively uncommon except in union-negotiated plans. When used in union plans, a flat-amount-per-year-of-service formula may relate the benefit to the actual hours a participant worked. For example, participants working 1,000 hours might receive half as much as participants working 2,000 hours.

Table 4-1
Defined-Benefit Plan Formulas*

Formula	Example
Unit-benefit	2% of FAC* times years of service
Flat-percentage of-earnings	50% of FAC*
Flat-amount-per-year of service	$30 per month times years of service
Flat-amount	$450 per month
*Final-average compensation	

flat-amount formula

A third alternative to the unit-benefit formula is the **flat-amount formula** (called a flat-benefit formula on IRS forms). The flat-amount formula provides the same monthly benefit for each participant. This formula treats all employees alike and does not account for differences in earnings or service. A flat-amount formula might read: "Each plan participant will receive a $200-per-month pension benefit commencing at normal retirement date and paid in the form of a life annuity." As with the flat-amount-per-year-of-service formula, this formula is found primarily in union plans. (See Table 4-1 for examples of the four types of benefit formulas).

Elements of the Unit-Benefit Formula

LO 4.2   **Identify the key components in a unit-benefit formula. Also identify the appropriate candidate for a defined-benefit plan.**

We will take a closer look at the specific elements of the unit-benefit formula because it is the most common. If a plan has a unit-benefit formula, that formula may read as follows:

> **EXAMPLE**
>
> **A participant will be entitled to a life annuity, beginning at the normal retirement age, in the amount of 1.5 percent of final-average compensation times years of service. Normal retirement age is the later of age 65 or 5 years of plan participation.**

Each of the factors in this benefit formula affects the ultimate value of the benefit. These factors include the definition of compensation under the plan, the definition of final-average compensation, the definition of years of service, the form of benefit, and the age at which benefits can begin. Each of these factors is discussed more fully below.

The Definition of Compensation

One of the most important elements of the defined-benefit formula is the amount of compensation used in the benefit formula. This is a function of both the definition of compensation and the definition of final-average compensation. The most comprehensive definition of compensation includes all wages that are included in taxable income, plus any pretax salary deferrals under a 401(k) (or 403(b)) plan or SIMPLE. A less comprehensive definition can be selected, but must undergo scrutiny under rules that prohibit discrimination in favor of highly compensated employees. As a way to keep plan costs both predictable and under control, many employers choose base salary as the definition of compensation—excluding any extra pay such as bonuses, overtime, or commissions. Under the nondiscrimination rules, this definition would be a problem only if the rank-and-file employees received significant additional pay while the highly compensated did not.

final-average compensation

Just as meaningful is how **final-average compensation** is defined. Benefits could simply be based on the participant's final year (or highest year) of compensation—but this, too, could result in both higher and more unpredictable plan costs. It is more common to choose a definition such as the average of the final 3 (or 5) years' salary, or the average of the highest 3 (or 5) years' consecutive salary. Averaging the highest few years of salary serves the dual purpose of leveling off any abnormal years of compensation while providing a benefit that is tied to the individual's highest salary (providing preretirement inflation protection). As with all types of qualified plans, compensation is capped at $270,000 (as indexed for 2017), meaning that compensation used for a particular year in the formula cannot exceed that year's compensation cap.

Service

Another important element of the defined-benefit formula is the definition of service. Many times years of service in the benefit formula only include years of active plan participation in which the participant earns a minimum of 1,000 hours of service. However, years of service could also include years of service prior to eligibility for the plan and/or service with the employer prior to plan inception. This type of service is commonly called past service.

past service

This ability to provide for **past service** in the benefit structure is unique to defined-benefit plans. This feature can be particularly important to clients who are setting up a new plan for the benefit of long-service employees or to maximize the plan's tax-shelter potential for owner-employees and key employees. A plan that takes into consideration past service can provide the same benefit accrual for prior years or provide a smaller rate of accrual.

Form of Benefit

In a defined-benefit plan, the form of payment specified in the benefit formula is an essential characteristic of the plan benefit. The most common form of payment is a life annuity (meaning that payments continue only for as long as the participant lives). However, some plans will use a different form, such as a life annuity with a certain period of payments (typically 5 to 10 years)—meaning that the benefit will be payable for the longer of either life or the specified time period.

normal form of benefit payment

The plan will also offer a number of other optional forms of payment, for example, a lump sum, or other types of annuities. The **normal form of payment** has a direct effect on the value of alternative forms of payment, since the payments under these options will be actuarially equivalent to the normal form. So, for example, the lump sum benefit in the case of a normal form which is a life annuity would be somewhat smaller than the lump sum payment in the case of a plan that had a life annuity with a 10-year certain payment as the normal form. This second annuity would cost more to purchase because of the 10-year certain feature.

Finally, note that providing a benefit as a life annuity is very different from a defined-contribution plan, where the benefit is based on the account balance. With a defined-contribution plan, if the participant elects to receive a life annuity, the amount of the benefit payment will be based on the annuity that can be "purchased" with the single-sum amount. Another way of saying this is that in the defined-contribution plan, the normal form of payment is a single-sum amount.

Normal Retirement Age

Because defined-benefit plans generally provide benefits in the form of a life annuity, another factor that directly affects the value of the benefit is the date at which benefits can begin, referred to as the normal retirement age. The earlier the retirement age, the longer the payout period and the more valuable (and costly) the benefit.

Elements of the Unit-Benefit Formula	
Compensation	Base pay, taxable income, or some other nondiscriminatory definition
Final-average compensation	Typically takes the average of the highest 3–5 years of compensation
Years of service	Can count years of participation or years of service, even service prior to the plan set-up
Form of benefit	Typically a life annuity, or a life annuity with period certain
Normal retirement age	Typically 65 but can be age 62 or younger

Candidates for This Type of Plan

Unlike defined-contribution plans, defined-benefit plans can be designed to ensure that benefits replace a specified portion of the participant's preretirement income. But this type of plan comes with a fairly high price tag. Although there may be mitigating factors, such as integration of the plans with Social Security and lower costs owing to better-than-expected investment return, defined-benefit plans remain expensive to fund. Also, the actuarial calculations involved make them costly to administer.

For the older business owner, the defined-benefit pension plan is a way to shelter larger amounts than can generally be contributed to a defined-contribution plan. This is because the time to fund for the benefit is short and the annual contributions required to fund the plan will be more significant. At the same time, the older business owner can create a significant retirement benefit over a short period of time, because past service can be factored into the retirement computation.

> **YOUR FINANCIAL SERVICES PRACTICE: DEFINED-BENEFIT PLANS FOR THE SMALL BUSINESS OWNER**
>
> The defined-benefit plan may be a great fit for the business owner in his or her late 40s or early 50s, who has not accumulated sufficient assets for retirement. Unlike defined-contribution plans, there is no specific annual dollar limit (currently $54,000 in 2017) for contributions to defined-benefit plans. The law allows for the funding of a life annuity beginning at age 62 in the amount of the lesser of 100 percent of the final 3 years of salary or $215,000 (as indexed in 2017). Without specific facts, it is hard to identify the exact contribution amount required. But clearly for the 50-year-old owner who establishes a plan providing the maximum benefit, the cost could easily exceed $100,000 a year, significantly more than the maximum contribution to the defined-contribution plan.
>
> A better way of looking at the issue may be to determine how much the individual needs to accumulate for retirement. If that amount exceeds the amount that can be accumulated—assuming $54,000 (2017) annual contributions plus investment return—over the remaining period to retirement, then a defined-benefit plan may be appropriate. Remember that with a defined-benefit plan, as long as certain requirements are met, the plan can pay out the present value of a $215,000 (2017) life annuity. The exact value depends on interest rates at the time of the distribution. Also, the maximum amount is indexed for inflation and will continue to increase over time. Given these uncertainties, it is still likely that the present value would be almost $3.4 million.

The Fact Finder

Candidates for defined-benefit pension plans fill out step 1 of the fact finder by grading the following as "very valuable:"

- To what extent is it important to use a qualified plan as a tax shelter for owner-employees and key employees?

- To what extent is it important to maximize benefits for long-service employees by including service prior to the inception of the plan?
- Candidates for a defined-benefit pension plan frequently grade these goals as "least valuable":
- placing the investment risk with the employee
- avoiding an annual financial commitment
- instituting a plan that has predictable costs
- instituting a plan that is administratively convenient
- instituting a plan that is easily communicated to employees

In addition, defined-benefit pension plan candidates fill out step 2 of the fact finder by answering "yes" to these questions: Is it more important to provide an adequate retirement standard of living than to cut plan costs? Is it more important to provide an adequate retirement standard of living than to have predictable costs? Is it more important to provide an adequate standard of living during retirement than to have administrative convenience and an easily communicated plan?

YOUR FINANCIAL SERVICES PRACTICE: GETTING MORE OUT OF DEFINED-BENEFIT PLANS FOR LITTLE OR NO COST

Because of the relative complexity of the defined-benefit plan, employees will not appreciate the plan without significant communication. Ways to improve the employee's appreciation of the plan would be to issue frequent and informative benefit statements rework the summary plan description set up periodic meetings to review benefits demonstrate how favorably an employee's defined-benefit plan compares with other retirement plans provide general retirement planning seminars showing how the defined-benefit plan fits into planning publicize the percentage of employee payroll used to fund the defined-benefit plan and the approximate cost of funding each participant's benefit

CASH-BALANCE PENSION PLANS

LO 4.3   Describe the basic features of a cash-balance plan. Also describe why large employers choose to convert traditional defined-benefit plans to a cash-balance arrangement

The cash-balance concept, first introduced in 1984, has been used primarily by large, and in some cases midsize, corporations as an alternative to the traditional defined-benefit plan. In fact, many of the cash-balance plans in existence today started as traditional defined-benefit plans that were later amended into cash-balance arrangements. The cash-balance plan is generally motivated by two factors: first, the selection of a benefit design that mirrors the defined-contribution approach, and second, cost savings.

cash-balance plan

The **cash-balance plan** is often referred to as a hybrid plan because it is a defined-benefit plan that is designed to look like a defined-contribution plan. As a defined-benefit plan, it is subject to minimum funding requirements and the PBGC insurance program. At the same time, the defined-contribution-like design means an easy-to-explain account balance type of plan.

The heart of the cash-balance plan is the benefit structure. As in the defined-contribution plan, the benefit is stated as an account balance that increases with contributions and investment experience. However, in a cash-balance plan the account is hypothetical. Annual credits (referred to as pay credits) are a bookkeeping credit only—no actual contributions are allocated to participants' accounts. Investment credits are also hypothetical and are based either on a rate specified in the plan or on an external index referenced in the plan. To the participants, however, this plan looks like a traditional defined-contribution "account balance" plan. When an individual terminates employment, the benefit payout is based on the value of the participant's hypothetical account. The following example illustrates how a cash-balance formula might appear.

> **EXAMPLE**
>
> The participant is entitled to a single-sum benefit that is based on a pay credit of 5 percent of compensation each year. The credited amounts will accumulate with interest. Interest will be credited annually using the 30-year Treasury rate as of the valuation date.

Most typically, the contribution credit is stated as a percentage of the individual's current year's pay (for example, 5 percent of salary), or as a formula that considers both salary and years of service to reward those with longer service. For example, a formula can assign credits of 3 percent of salary for those with less than 5 years of service, 6 percent for those with 10 or more years of service, and 9 percent for 20-year veterans. Credits given for investment experience can be stated as a fixed, predetermined rate, a floating rate (based on some external index outside the control of the employer), or a combination of a fixed and floating rate, such as the rate of 30-year Treasury bonds. Also, because this is a defined-benefit plan, contribution and interest credits can be made for past years of service.

From the employer's perspective, this plan is still a defined-benefit plan. Contributions are required in the amount necessary to satisfy the minimum funding requirements. Under these rules, the employer has a degree of flexibility in determining the required contribution. Also, as in any defined-benefit plan, the employer is ultimately responsible for making contributions necessary to pay promised benefits—meaning that the sponsor is "on the hook" for the plan's investment experience. If trust assets earn a higher rate of return, then expected future contributions are reduced, and vice versa.

From the employee's perspective, the cash-balance design looks mostly like a defined-contribution plan. The only similarity to the defined-benefit approach is that benefits are guaranteed by the PBGC and the investment credits are not affected adversely by downturns in the market. In other ways, the cash-balance plan mirrors the strengths and weaknesses of the defined-contribution plan. Benefits accrue (depending on the formula) more evenly over the participant's career, meaning that benefits are more portable than a traditional defined-benefit plan, which is beneficial for today's mobile workforce. The cash-balance plan shares some of the disadvantages of the defined-contribution approach. Benefits do not replace a specified percentage of preretirement income, and because benefits are not based on final salary, the benefit is not inflation adjusted up to the time benefits begin.

Interest Credit Rate Options

In September of 2014, the IRS issued final regulations entitled "Additional Rules Regarding Hybrid Retirement Plans." These rules could have a major impact on cash balance type of plans that use a lump sum-based benefit formula. The new regulations made significant changes to the allowable interest credits that can be credited to a cash balance participant's 'hypothetical account.' Language in the 2006 Pension Protection act allowed for the use of any interest crediting rate that was not in excess of a market rate of return. However, this ambiguity created uncertainty for plans. The new rules were designed to clear up some of this confusion.

The new regulations allow for a maximum fixed rate of 6 percent, up from 5 percent in previous years. In addition, the regulations changed the permitted floor interest credits rates based off of certain government fixed income rates. However, most importantly was that the new regulations allow for variable returns based on the actual returns realized by investments. Plans can now allow participants to be credited with an interest credit based off of the actual rate of return of plan assets or even a subset of plan assets.

At first glance this appears to make a cash-balance plan nothing more than a defined contribution plan by eliminating the certainty of returns for the employee. However, a maximum cumulative floor of 3 percent is allowed, meaning that overtime the hypothetical account balance would see at least percent interest credits attributed to the hypothetical account. This change allows the plan to shift some of the annual risks away from the employer and onto the employee by allowing for variable interest credits. This means that benefits could actually be reduced due to market performance year to year, but would never fall below a cumulative percent interest credit overtime if the plan used the maximum guaranteed floor amount. For example, if you have five years of 5 percent returns on the assets, the credit amount could be 5 percent each year. However, if you averaged 2 percent for the entire plan life, the beneficiary would ultimately be credited with the higher 3 percent cumulative required interest rate. Additionally, there is a preservation of capital rule that keeps the cumulative return from ever dropping below 0 percent returns for any cash balance plan. The plans will still not allow the participants to choose their own interest credit rates or investment options. Ultimately, these rules will not go into effect until 2016 so further changes could occur.

Advantages and Disadvantages

The fact that the cash-balance plan looks like a defined-contribution plan makes the plan easier for participants to understand. But the more interesting question is, looking at the plan as a defined-contribution substitute does it offer anything that a defined-contribution plan does not? The answer is yes. A cash-balance plan formula can establish credits for past service; in some circumstances, this is a big advantage over the defined-contribution plan.

From the participant's perspective, an actual defined-contribution plan will often result in a larger accumulation than the cash-balance plan. In an account plan, assets are generally invested with a long-term investment horizon. Participants sharing in the investment experience of a long-term stock-oriented portfolio will usually be better off than if they are credited with a small but steady rate of return. In a defined-contribution plan, benefits are fully funded at all times and are outside the reach of the employer's creditors. However, if a cash-balance plan is matched with a defined-contribution plan, such as a 401(k) plan, the participant has both the security of the fixed return in the cash-balance arrangement and the upside potential of the asset growth in the defined-contribution plan.

From the employer's perspective, the cash-balance approach offers some flexibility in funding (as compared to a money-purchase pension plan with a fixed contribution) and also the potential for cost savings. If plan assets, on average, outperform the promised rate of return, the employer will benefit through lower required contributions.

Legal Issues

Cash-balance plans have had a short but rough history. The earliest cash-balance plans were overfunded, large-company, defined-benefit plans that were converted to cash-balance arrangements. The conversion allowed the sponsor to switch to a defined-contribution type approach and seamlessly use the excess assets to fund future benefit promises. Under a cash-balance conversion, the former defined-benefit promise usually is frozen at the current accrued benefit level, and the benefit is stated as its single-sum equivalent. Benefits accruing after the change simply increase the total account balance.

Several large employers who converted traditional defined-benefit plans to cash-balance plans received bad publicity afterward. There were two primary issues: (1) a lack of communication—employees did not understand the change and (2) older employees were not fully informed that their overall benefits would be lower than they were under the old plan. In response, other employers converting to the cash-balance approach protected older employees by grandfathering the old benefit formula or giving them a larger annual credit under the new formula. Congress responded to the controversy by amending ERISA to require full disclosure to participants of any plan amendment that reduces future benefit accruals.

On another legal front, employees have argued that cash-balance plans inherently discriminate against older workers. This issue was settled by the Pension Protection Act of 2006, which clarified that a cash-balance plan that provides an accrued benefit based on an accumulated account balance can demonstrate nondiscrimination if all participants with the same salary and years of service are similarly situated—regardless of age. For example, if all participants receive a pay credit of 5 percent of compensation, the plan will satisfy the nondiscrimination requirement.

The Pension Protection Act of 2006 added other new rules. Cash-balance plans must fully vest participants once they have attained 3 years of service. This is in contrast to the 5-year cliff vesting or 7-year graded vesting options available for other defined-benefit plans. Also, investment credits cannot exceed a "market rate of return." The rules, however, do allow a plan to provide for a reasonable minimum guaranteed rate of return, or for a rate of return that is equal to the greater of a fixed or variable rate of return. Also, the investment credit cannot be less than zero.

The Pension Protection Act also addressed several other issues that had been litigated in the past. First, a lump-sum benefit payment from a cash-balance plan can simply equal the hypothetical account balance. The plan does not have to look to the interest rate used to calculate lump-sum benefits in traditional defined-benefit plans.

The law also clarifies the process for converting traditional defined- benefit plans into cash-balance formulas. Each participant's benefits after the conversion must equal the sum of the pre-conversion benefit under the prior plan formula and the post-conversion benefit under the hybrid formula. In addition, a special conversion rule preserves the value of early retirement subsidies associated with benefits accrued under the prior formula.

Candidates for This Type of Plan

The Pension Protection Act has eliminated much of the legal uncertainty surrounding cash-balance arrangements. In doing so, employers continue to convert traditional defined-benefit plans into cash-balance arrangements. Clearly the funding obligation for cash-balance plans is less volatile than with traditional defined-benefit plans as both pay credits, and investment credits are relatively predictable. An employer with an underfunded defined-benefit plan may use the conversion as a way to reduce the employer's future cost. With this type of plan the employer benefits if the average return on investments exceeds the relatively conservative rate of return typically promised to participants.

The cash-balance design is finding it's place as a new plan—especially in the small-plan market—for one important reason: the maximum contribution on behalf of the owner can exceed the Code Sec. 415(c) dollar limitation. For older business owners looking to shelter a significant amount of income, the cash-balance arrangement becomes an alternative to a traditional defined-benefit plan design. With this design, the sponsor can (as long as the nondiscrimination rules are satisfied) make large contributions for the owner-employees while providing contributions as a level percentage of compensation for rank-and-file employees. The down side to the cash-balance plan will be that this approach has many of the headaches of a defined-benefit plan: PBGC premiums, administrative costs, and satisfaction of the minimum funding requirements. However, the minimum-funding rules do allow for more funding flexibility than with a traditional money-purchase or target-benefit plan.

MONEY-PURCHASE PENSION PLANS

A money-purchase pension plan falls within both the defined-contribution and pension categories. Knowing this means you already know that money-purchase pension plans have the following characteristics:

- The maximum annual additions for individual participants are limited by Code Sec. 415(c).
- Participants in the plan have individual accounts that are similar to bank accounts.
- Participants assume the risk of preretirement inflation, investment performance, and adequacy of retirement income.
- The plan cannot provide for past service.

- Administrative costs are relatively low.
- The plan is easily communicated to employees.
- The plan has predictable employer costs.
- The employer is required to fund the plan annually.
- Participants may not take in-service withdrawals prior to age 62.
- The employer can deduct up to 25 percent of compensation.
- Investments in company stock are limited to 10 percent of the plan's assets.

LO 4.4   **Describe the features of a money-purchase plan and why this plan design is not often chosen today**

money-purchase pension plan

Under a **money-purchase pension plan**, the company's annual contributions are based on a percentage of each participant's compensation. For example, the money-purchase contribution formula may provide that annual contributions will equal 10 percent of compensation for each participant (if Karen Lamb earns $40,000, the annual contribution placed in her account is $4,000). Money-purchase plan benefits for each employee are the amounts that can be provided by the sums contributed to the employee's individual account plus investment earnings. For example, if Karen Lamb worked for 20 years and her salary remained at $40,000, at retirement she would have $80,000 plus accumulated interest of $58,876 (assuming a 5 percent annual rate) in her account. The term money-purchase arose because the participant's account is traditionally used to purchase an annuity that provides monthly retirement benefits.

A money-purchase plan is used to provide a fixed contribution and, therefore, gives employees the sense that it is a substantial and permanent retirement plan. Typically, these organizations provide between 3 and 12 percent of compensation as the annual contribution. Self-employed people provide another market for money-purchase plans (they like the money-purchase plan's simplicity). For example, a self-employed person may express a desire to tax-shelter 15 percent of his or her earned income for retirement.

Advantages and Disadvantages

Money-purchase pension plans can be likened to the station wagons of the retirement fleet because of their dependable annual contributions and simple, basic design. The major advantages of money-purchase pension plans are the predictable costs for the employer (because contributions are based on employee compensation, the employer contribution is basically a percentage of payroll), administrative ease, and understandability for the employees.

Corporate objectives, such as competitiveness, attraction, and retention of key employees, can be met within the money-purchase framework without being prohibitively expensive for the employer.

One major drawback of a money-purchase plan (or, for that matter, any defined contribution plan) is that contributions are based on the participant's salary for each year of his or her career, rather than on the salary at retirement. Given a stable inflationary environment, this may not have a negative effect on the adequacy of retirement income. If inflation spirals in the years prior to retirement, however, the chances of achieving an adequate income-replacement ratio are diminished. Take, for example, someone who earned an average middle-class income and whose career spanned the 1950s, 1960s, and 1970s. In 1950, this person earned $2,000 and received a 10 percent money-purchase contribution of $200. In 1960, the employee earned $12,000 and received a 10 percent money-purchase contribution of $1,200. In 1970, the employee earned $24,000 and received a $2,400 contribution. During the 1970s, double-digit inflation hit, and salary levels increased to account for the increased cost of living. If the participant retired in 1980, he or she would be at a disadvantage because only part of the plan contributions would account for the inflationary period right before retirement. What's more, most of the annual contributions would be based on deflated salaries that accrued before the inflationary spiral. If a defined-benefit plan were chosen that calculated benefits based on final average compensation, the participant would have received some inflation protection through the operation of the benefit formula.

A second drawback, also applicable to all defined-contribution plans, is the inability to provide an adequate retirement program for older participants. Those who enter money-purchase pension plans later in their careers have less time to accumulate sufficient assets. However, money-purchase pension plans can work, given the right set of circumstances.

EXAMPLE 1

New employee Bill Nelson is 55 years old and has no other retirement funds except Social Security. Nelson earns $50,000 annually and plans to retire at age 65. The money-purchase pension formula calls for 10 percent of salary to be deposited in Nelson's account each year. The account earns 10 percent annually. Under this accumulation scheme, Nelson will have $79,687 at age 65. Even after combining this with Social Security, Nelson's income will not be adequate to continue his preretirement standard of living.

EXAMPLE 2

New employee Gloria Benson is 35 years old and has no other retirement funds except Social Security. Benson earns $50,000 annually and plans to retire at age 65. The money-purchase formula calls for 10 percent of salary to be deposited in Benson's account each year. The account earns 10 percent annually. Under this accumulation scheme, $822,470 will be amassed at retirement. Combined with Social Security, Benson's income is likely to be adequate during the retirement years to maintain the same standard of living.

Candidates for money-purchase plans are businesses with

- a steady cash flow
- young, well-paid key employees
- a stable workforce (low turnover)
- the need for easily communicated employee benefits

Money-purchase candidates disclose on the fact finder that it is less important to provide an adequate retirement standard of living than to have predictable costs, and that it is more important to have administrative convenience and an easily communicated plan than to provide an adequate retirement standard of living.

TARGET-BENEFIT PENSION PLANS

LO 4.5   Explain how a target-benefit plan is different than a defined-benefit plan, and why this plan design has fallen out of favor.

target-benefit pension plan

A **target-benefit pension plan** is a close cousin to the money-purchase pension plan. It is a defined-contribution plan in the pension category, and all of the characteristics described above that apply to the money-purchase plan apply to the target plan as well. What makes the structure of a target-benefit plan unique is that contributions are determined in a way that is similar to a defined-benefit plan. For that reason we often refer to a target plan as a hybrid plan design—it is a defined-contribution plan that in some ways looks like a defined-benefit plan.

A defined-benefit plan has a specified benefit formula and the actuary then determines the required contribution to fund the targeted benefit. Similarly, a target-benefit pension plan identifies a targeted benefit at retirement, and contributions are made in the amount necessary to fund the targeted amount. The plan specifies the actuarial method and interest rates used to determine annual contributions so that the amount of contribution can be clearly determined. Unlike a defined-benefit plan, however, the contribution amounts will not change each year based on the value of the plan's assets. Contributions only change to reflect new plan participants and increases in the compensation of existing plan participants. For the sake of convenience and simplicity, the plan is often equipped with a chart indicating contribution levels; an actuary is seldom needed after the plan's inception (see figure).

Figure 4-1
Target-Benefit Pension Plans

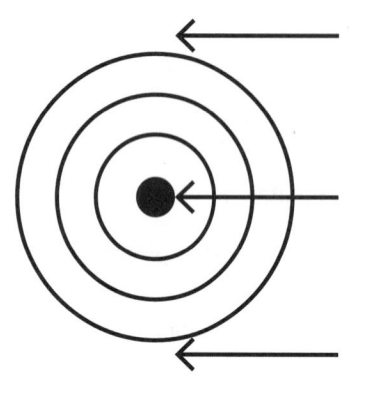

If the investment assumption is lower than the actual investment experience, the total benefit will exceed the

Target Benefit

If an investment assumption is overly optimistic, the actual amount will fall short of the target.

What is fundamentally different about target plans and defined-benefit plans is that with a target plan the contributions are allocated to the participant's account. The participant's benefit will be the value of the account balance and not the promised monthly retirement benefit. The account balance should approximate the amount needed to provide the targeted retirement benefit, but it will be more or less based on the plan's actual investment experience.

Table 4-2 Hybrid Plans: Mirrors of Each Other	
Target- Benefit Pension Plan	**Cash-Balance Pension Plan**
Defined-contribution plan	Defined-benefit plan
Not subject to PBGC	Subject to PBGC
Participant entitled to vested account balance	Participant entitled to promised benefit regardless of actual plan assets
Feels like a defined-benefit plan because contributions target a monthly benefit at retirement	Feels like a defined-contribution plan because promised benefit is based on an accumulated hypothetical account balance
Contribution is fixed based on the contribution formula	Contribution is variable based on the actuarial determination

The scheme allows the employer to provide a benefit that attempts to replace a specified portion of the participant's salary without taking on the same risk as a defined-benefit plan. The target-benefit design also can be a good way to provide larger contributions for older, more highly compensated employees. For the business owner with mostly younger employees, this plan design is a way to direct a large percentage of the contribution to the business owner. The plan design, however, is not popular today, since similar results can be had with a profit-sharing plan using an age-weighted or cross-tested contribution formula. The profit-sharing approach is more flexible because the employer is never required to make specific contributions.

CHAPTER REVIEW

Key Terms and Concepts

unit-benefit formula
income-replacement ratio
flat-percentage-of-earnings formula
flat-amount-per-year-of-service formula
flat-amount formula

final-average compensation
past service
normal form of benefit payment
cash-balance plan
money-purchase pension plan
target-benefit pension plan

Chapter 4: Review Questions

Review questions are based on the learning objectives in this chapter. Thus, a [4.3] at the end of a question means that the question is based on learning objective 3. If there are multiple objectives, they are all listed.

1. Ralph Camdon, the owner of a local tour bus company, would like to establish a defined-benefit plan that helps to retain and reward experienced personnel, that rewards owner-employees and key employees who have high salaries, and that provides an income-replacement ratio of 60 percent for "career" employees. [4.1]

    a. What type of benefit formula should Ralph use in his plan? Explain.

    b. Give an example of how the benefit formula should be written.

2. In what situations are flat-amount-per-year-of-service formulas typically used? [4.1]

3. Describe a flat-amount formula. [4.1]

4. Answer the following: [4.2]

a. Explain how the definitions of compensation and final-average compensation affect the participant's benefit.
b. If the normal form of benefit is a life annuity, does this have the same value if the normal form of benefit is a life annuity with 10-year certain payments?
c. Does a life annuity payable at a normal retirement age of 65 have the same value as a life annuity payable at age 62?

5. Why would an employer choose to account for past service in the defined-benefit plan? [4.2]

6. What can the defined-benefit plan offer the older small business owner that a defined-contribution plan cannot? [4.2]

7. Explain the following about cash-balance plans: [4.3]
   a. Is the cash-balance plan a defined-benefit or defined-contribution type of plan?
   b. What makes the cash-balance benefit formula different from a traditional defined-benefit plan?
   c. Why do employers with traditional defined-benefit plans choose to amend them into cash-balance plans?

8. What are the major advantages and disadvantages of a money-purchase plan? [4.4]

9. Dr. Debbie Dwyer runs her own veterinary clinic, Pet Care, Inc. Dr. Dwyer is 56 years old and has never set up a qualified plan for her practice. Dr. Dwyer has two younger employees whom she would like to include in a retirement plan, but she cannot afford to pay too much. In fact, Dr. Dwyer can afford to save only 20 percent of her $100,000 salary. What type of pension plan should Dr. Dwyer adopt? Explain. [4.5]

10. Indicate what type of plan from the pension category you would recommend in each of the following situations: [4.5]
    a. Candidate Able owns a business that has a steady cash flow, young, well-paid key employees, and a low turnover rate. Able's objectives are to adopt a plan that has predictable costs, has a clearly stated contribution for employee security, is administratively convenient, and is easily communicated to employees.
    b. Candidate Baker wants to have a plan that provides for a contribution for himself that is well in excess of the Code Sec. 415(c) annual addition limit. He would like to provide a benefit structure that is similar to the account plan approach of a defined-contribution plan.

c. Candidate Charley has indicated that the following objectives are very important: (1) maximizing benefits for older owner-employees and key employees, (2) maximizing benefits for older employees, (3) maximizing benefits for long-service employees, and (4) providing a predictable pension in retirement that replaces a percentage of the participant's salary.

Chapter 4: Review Answers

1. a. Ralph should use a unit-benefit formula. The unit-benefit formula accommodates Ralph's objective to retain and reward experienced personnel because a unit benefit is based in part on the years an employee works for the employer. The unit-benefit formula also meets Ralph's goal of rewarding owner-employees and key employees who have high salaries because the pension benefit is based, in part, on salary. Finally, the unit-benefit formula meets Ralph's need to provide a specific income-replacement ratio for employees (see b)..

   b. A formula that meets Ralph's needs reads: Each plan participant will receive a monthly pension commencing at the normal retirement date and paid in the form of a life annuity equal to 2 percent of final-average monthly salary multiplied by years of service. Service is limited to a maximum of 30 years. (Note: Ralph would probably want to integrate this formula with Social Security in order to limit the costs of providing benefits to lower-paid employees. Integration is discussed later in the course).

2. A flat-amount-per-year-of-service formula is most typically found in a union setting.

3. In a flat-amount formula, all participants receive the same benefit regardless of their salary or years of service.

4. a. In any benefit formula that is tied to compensation, participants must read the definitions of compensation and final-average compensation carefully. Defining compensation as base salary may result in a much different benefit than if all taxable compensation is considered. Similarly, if final-average salary is the highest 3 years of compensation, the benefit will be larger than if it is the highest 5 years of compensation.

   b. No. A life annuity with 10 years certain is a more valuable benefit than the life annuity only.

   c. No. A life annuity payable at 65 is less valuable than a life annuity payable at 62.

5. Using past service is a way to provide larger benefits for long-service employees. It can also be used in small tax-sheltered plans to increase the benefit (and deductible contribution) for the business owner.

6. The defined-benefit plan can offer the older business owner the opportunity to accumulate a large amount in a short period of time. In a defined-contribution plan,

this is not true, since annual contributions for the owner are limited to the Code Section 415(c) limit.

7. a. The cash-balance plan is a defined-benefit plan that looks like a defined-contribution plan to employees. As a defined-benefit plan, it is subject to the flexible contribution requirements that apply to such plans, and it is subject to the PBGC insurance program.

   b. In a traditional defined-benefit formula, the benefit is stated as a life annuity in an amount that is generally expressed as a percentage of the participant's final salary. In a cash-balance plan, the plan still promises a benefit; but in this case, the promise is stated as a single sum, which is the total of employer contribution credits and interest credits (using a stated rate in the plan).

   c. If the employer currently maintains a defined-benefit plan and perceives that employees would prefer a defined-contribution-type plan, the employer will consider the cash-balance option. The plan is simply amended so that participants have an opening "account balance" based on the old benefit, then future additions are added each year.

8. A money-purchase pension plan may be the right choice for a company with a steady cash flow, relatively young employees, and a need for a fixed contribution level that is easily communicated to employees. Drawbacks include the inability to protect against preretirement inflation and the inability to accumulate adequate benefits for older participants who have only been in the plan for a short time. Probably the most serious drawback is the annual required contribution, which is why many employers today choose the profit-sharing plan instead.

9. Dr. Dwyer should consider a target-benefit plan. A target-benefit plan permits a speedy accumulation of substantial retirement benefits for her, while at the same time minimizing costs for lower-paid employees. This occurs because there is less time to "fund" Dr. Dwyer's benefit than there is to fund the younger employees' benefits. Therefore, contributions will be high for Dr. Dwyer and low for other employees. A second factor in Dr. Dwyer's choice is that she can only afford to contribute $20,000. If she wanted to contribute a much larger amount, a defined-benefit plan would have best served her needs because the plan would have allowed annual funding for her in excess of the Code Sec. 415(c) annual addition limitation that applies to defined-contribution plans. Note that an age-weighted or cross-tested profit-sharing plan (discussed in the next chapter) might even be more appropriate than the target-benefit plan because she can benefit from the same age disparity but would also have the benefit of discretionary contributions.

10. a. money-purchase plan
    b. cash-balance plan
    c. defined-benefit plan

Chapter 5

Profit-Sharing Plans, 401(k) Plans, Stock Bonus Plans, and ESOPs

Learning Objectives

An understanding of the material in this chapter should enable the student to

- **LO 5.1** **Describe the characteristics of a profit-sharing plan that make it a popular plan design.**
- **LO 5.2** **Identify the features available in a 401(k) plan.**
- **LO 5.3** **Describe the special rules that apply to 401(k) plans.**
- **LO 5.4** **Identify the design features that will help maximize participation in a 401(k) plan.**
- **LO 5.5** **Describe the special rules that apply to stock bonus plans and ESOPs and what objectives they can meet.**

Let's turn our attention to qualified plans that are not necessarily intended to provide a pension at retirement. Unlike pension plans, profit-sharing plans, 401(k) plans, stock bonus plans, and employee stock ownership plans (ESOPs) are often designed to distribute organizational earnings on a tax-sheltered basis with only a partial regard to meeting retirement needs. Historically, these plans have been considered more of a tax shelter for deferred income than a retirement system that will provide an adequate pension in the retirement years. More recently, however, these plans have become an important tool for employers to meet the need for an adequate pension in the following ways:

- They have become part of a comprehensive retirement package that combines these plans with other plans to fund for retirement needs.
- They have become "pension-like" in their actual application (for example, regular reoccurring substantial contributions, even if the employer has no profits).

PROFIT-SHARING PLANS IN GENERAL

LO 5.1 **Describe the characteristics of a profit-sharing plan that make it a popular plan design.**

A profit-sharing plan is a defined-contribution plan that also falls within the profit-sharing category. (*Planning Note:* Do not be confused by the fact that profit sharing is both a category of plan and a type of plan.) Before we begin to discuss the specifics of this plan, we already know the following:

- Employer contributions are discretionary.

- The plan allows for in-service withdrawals.
- The plan can conceivably invest up to 100 percent of its assets in the sponsoring company's stock.
- The maximum deductible employer contribution is 25 percent of compensation.
- The maximum annual contribution that an employee can receive is the lesser of 100 percent of salary or $54,000 (as indexed for 2017).
- Participants in the plan have individual accounts that are similar to bank accounts.
- The employee assumes the risk of preretirement inflation, investment performance, and adequacy of retirement income.
- Administrative costs are relatively low.
- The plan is easily communicated to employees.

There are two essential parts to a profit-sharing plan. The first is the determination of the annual contribution. The other is the allocation formula, which determines how contributions are allocated among the participants. Let's take a closer look.

Contributions

From the employer's perspective, one of the primary strengths of a profit-sharing plan is that the employer can make contributions on a discretionary basis. In addition, since 1987, an employer can make a contribution to a plan whether or not there are profits. However, there is one limitation: contributions must be "substantial and recurring." If there is a "complete discontinuance" of contributions, the IRS could determine that the plan has been terminated. The result of a deemed plan termination would be all participants would become immediately vested.

Most plans written today specify that the board of directors makes the decision each year as to whether to make contributions and/or how much to contribute. Whether a company actually contributes more in a good financial year is a business decision. However, if the employer is trying to use the plan to motivate participants, there should be a clear relationship between the company's performance and contributions made to the plan.

Another way to address the issue of employee motivation is to write the plan to require a specified contribution. One way to do this is to state the required contribution as a specified percentage of profits or some other objective formula stated in the plan. This approach is appropriate when the employer wants employees to feel they have a clear and determinable stake in the company's performance. Another way is to stipulate that a certain percentage of each participant's salary will be contributed each year. For example, the company will contribute 10 percent of a participant's compensation. This type of contribution requirement allows the employer to use the profit-sharing plan in the same manner as a money-purchase pension plan, in which the corporate goal is typically to provide an adequate pension benefit, not to provide a vehicle for employees to share in company profits.

Allocation Formulas

The heart of a profit-sharing plan is the allocation formula which is method of allocating the employer contribution among the participants. This formula must be definite and predetermined. Historically, the most common allocation formula allocates the total contribution so each participant receives a contribution that is the same percentage of compensation (for example, 3 percent or 5 percent). This allocation formula in the plan document would read something like

> "Employer contributions made for the year will be allocated, as of the last day of each plan year, to each participant's account in the proportion that the participants compensation bears to the total compensation of all eligible participants for the plan year."

Under this type of allocation formula, for example, if the employer contributed $10,000, total payroll was $100,000, and Alexander earned $25,000, he would have an allocation of $2,500 ($10,000 × $25,000/$100,000). If Barbara earned $30,000, her allocation would be $3,000 ($10,000 × $30,000/$100,000). As you can see, the employer contributed 10 percent of payroll and each participant received an allocation of 10 percent of his or her compensation.

> **YOUR FINANCIAL SERVICES PRACTICE: GETTING THE MOST MILEAGE OUT OF THE PLAN**
>
> Employers never enjoy spending money on retirement benefits that employees do not appreciate. Because a profit-sharing plan typically does not require a specified employer contribution, it may be difficult to get employees to appreciate the value of the plan. To get the most out of the plan, the employer should consider taking the following steps:
> - Clearly communicate the amount of the contribution and how it was derived.
> - Make regular and reoccurring contributions, if at all possible.
> - Provide clear and comprehensive benefit statements.
> - Identify circumstances that would result in larger employer contributions.

This allocation formula has been popular, in part because it is clear that it satisfies the requirement of Code Sec. 401(a)(4), which requires that contributions or benefits do not discriminate in favor of highly compensated employees. Other ways to allocate contributions include integration with Social Security and newer methods, such as age-weighting and cross-testing. As you will see, these allocation formulas add a whole new dimension to the profit-sharing plan, allowing this simple, versatile plan to skew contributions to older (and, not coincidentally, more highly compensated) business owners. Allocation formulas also can be designed to meet any number of other compensation objectives.

> **YOUR FINANCIAL SERVICES PRACTICE: SWITCHING INVESTMENT CARRIERS**
>
> Frequently, when you are prospecting in the retirement field, you will encounter an established plan that is invested with a competitor. The emergence of new ideas, like cross-testing or age-weighting, can be a useful weapon in fighting the uphill battle of converting already-spoken-for assets. Even if the new design does not fit the needs of these prospective clients, at the very least you will be regarded as someone who is in touch with current trends and who is on the cutting edge of your profession. Future dealings can stem from this favorable impression.

ADVANTAGES OF A PROFIT-SHARING PLAN TO THE BUSINESS AND BUSINESS OWNER

Even though the profit-sharing plan does not provide the most secure benefit to employees, it is an extremely flexible vehicle that is a very popular choice. Some of the organizational objectives these plans serve are:

discretionary contributions

- *allowing* **discretionary contributions**—The board of directors can simply decide how much, if any, to contribute each year.
- *permitting withdrawal flexibility*—Plans can be designed to allow employees to withdraw funds from participant accounts as early as 2 years after they were contributed by the employer.
- *controlling benefit costs*—Organizations find that adopting a profit-sharing plan is a fiscally responsible move. The organization will not be saddled with cash-flow problems caused by mandatory contributions. Flexibility is especially important for employers with fluctuating profits.
- *improving productivity*—Another cost advantage is profit sharing's correlation to productivity. Many believe these plans help to increase employee identification with

the employer and provide an incentive to employees. This increased productivity can be viewed as a way to maximize the cost-effectiveness of the employer's contributions. The old saying "You have to spend more to get more" applies here, however.

- *providing legal discrimination in favor of older owner-employees*—The profit-sharing plan can be set up to give (allocate) the majority of the profits to older, high-salaried owner-employees. When used in this manner, the profit-sharing plan makes an excellent tax shelter for the older business owner. This approach also lowers contributions for rank-and-file employees.

Disadvantages of a Profit-Sharing Plan to the Business and Business Owner

A profit-sharing plan is an extremely versatile vehicle for a small business. However, as compared to other types of plans, there are a few disadvantages. The primary one is that rank-and-file employees might perceive the plan as a hollow benefit if discretionary contributions are not made or if the lion's share of profits goes to the business owner. As discussed above, this problem can be mitigated through good communication with employees.

> **Profit-Sharing Plans: A Summary of the Rules**
> - *Contributions*—discretionary unless otherwise specified in the plan
> - *Allocation formula*—must have a definite and predetermined formula for allocating the contribution among participants. Allocating based on compensation or integration with Social Security is common, with other formulas possible as long as the plan can satisfy a nondiscrimination test.
> - *In-service withdrawals*—if allowed by the plan, benefits can be distributed to active participants as long as the participants have met the plan's conditions
> - *Maximum contribution*—like other defined contribution plans, the maximum contribution is 25 percent of the payroll of all participants
> - *Employer securities*—like other profit-sharing type plans, the plan can invest more than 10 percent of its assets in employer securities
> - *Other provisions*—subject to eligibility and vesting requirements that apply to qualified plans

Candidates for Profit-Sharing Plans

Because of the profit-sharing plan's incredible versatility, a large number of companies are candidates for profit-sharing plans. These include businesses with

- cash-flow problems

- less economic stability (for example, new businesses and capital-intensive businesses)
- young, well-paid key employees
- no desire to ensure the adequacy of an employee's retirement income

Candidates for profit-sharing plans fill out the fact finder typically by grading the following as "very valuable":

- placing the investment risk on the employee
- avoiding an annual financial commitment
- allowing employees (including owner-employees) to withdraw funds. (If this is the case, design the plan to allow withdrawals after 2 years; if this is not the case, a profit-sharing plan may still be implemented but withdrawal restrictions should be incorporated.)
- motivating the workforce

Candidates for a profit-sharing plan typically grade the following goals as "least valuable":

- maximizing benefits for long-service employees by accounting for past service
- providing a specified replacement ratio

Profit-sharing candidates typically answer "yes" to the fact finder question: Is it more important to motivate employees than to attract or retain them? And they typically answer "no" to these fact finder questions: Is it more important to provide an adequate retirement standard of living than to allow employees (including owner-employees) to withdraw funds? Is it more important to provide an adequate retirement standard of living than to have predictable costs?

Candidates for a profit-sharing plan usually put contribution flexibility at the head of their priority list, usually opt for a low income-replacement ratio, and typically come from an organization or industry with an unstable cash-flow history.

With the flexibility in allocation formulas available today, profit-sharing candidates also include those businesses interested in providing a lion's share of the benefits for the key employees while minimizing the cost of benefits for the rank-and-file employee. This can be done quite effectively using the age-weighted and cross-tested allocation formulas. At one time, employers with this goal looked either to the defined-benefit plan or the target-benefit plan. Today, the profit-sharing plan allows for similar skewing of the contribution to the targeted group while maintaining the flexibility of the profit-sharing plan.

YOUR FINANCIAL SERVICES PRACTICE: KEY-PERSON LIFE INSURANCE IN PROFIT-SHARING PLANS

Life insurance in a profit-sharing plan can meet a unique need. In addition to using life insurance to fund participant's accounts, life insurance can be purchased on the client's key people (owner-employees, key employees, and officers) as a general asset of the profit-sharing trust. The profit-sharing trust is permitted to make this purchase because it has an insurable interest in the client's key people. This insurable interest stems from the fact that company profits are generally required to fund the profit-sharing trust and that these people are primarily responsible for these company profits. Here's how it works:

- Insurance contracts are purchased out of unallocated assets given to the trust by the organization.
- The insurance contracts are owned by the trust, which pays the premiums and is also the named beneficiary.
- Because the contracts are not allocated to participant accounts, the percentage limitation applied under the incidental death benefit rules is not applicable.
- Upon the death of the insured, the insurance proceeds are paid to the trust and are then typically allocated among participants on the basis of each participant's account balance.

CASH OR DEFERRED ARRANGEMENTS—401(k) PLANS

LO 5.2   Identify the features available in a 401(k) plan.

cash or deferred arrangement (CODA)

An option that is available under a profit-sharing plan or stock bonus plan is the **cash or deferred arrangement (CODA)**. A plan with a CODA, referred to as a 401(k) plan, allows a plan participant to defer taxation on a portion of regular salary or bonuses simply by electing to have such amounts contributed to the plan instead of receiving them in cash. As a variation of a profit-sharing or stock bonus plan we already know the following:

- The maximum annual contribution that an employee can receive is the lesser of 100 percent of salary or $54,000 (as indexed for 2017).
- The employer can deduct up to 25 percent of compensation.
- Employer contributions can be discretionary or a stated amount.
- The plan can provide for in-service withdrawals.

- The plan can invest up to 100 percent of its assets in the sponsoring company's stock.

A 401(k) plan can be simple or quite complex. Occasionally, a plan will only offer the salary deferral feature, but in many cases the employer will also provide a matching contribution and, in some cases, an additional profit-sharing type contribution. The plan may give employees the option to elect "Roth" tax treatment on their salary deferrals. Older plans may also give participants the option to make after-tax contributions. Here are a list of common 401(k) features.

- **Salary deferrals**—Participants choose to defer salary on a pretax basis. The employer can also allow a "Roth" election, in which case salary deferrals are made after-tax but qualifying distributions will be entirely tax-free.
- **Employer matching contributions**—The employer makes matching contributions only for those participants that elect to make salary deferrals. Most employers elect a stated matching contribution, however, the match can be made on a discretionary basis as well.
- **Employee profit-sharing contributions**—The employer makes contributions for all eligible employees. As with a profit-sharing plan, in most cases these contributions are made on a discretionary basis. These are also referred to as nonelective contributions as they are not contingent upon the employee making a salary deferral contribution.
- **Employee after-tax contributions**—Employees make contributions on an after-tax basis and earnings are tax-deferred. Plans established before the 401(k) plan type was enacted (called "thrift plans") often continue to offer after-tax contributions as an option. Employee after-tax contributions could become more popular again as the IRS in 2014 eased the ability to roll these amounts over to a Roth IRA. Employee after-tax contributions count towards the annual 415(c) limit but not towards the basic limit on salary deferrals. As such, the use of after tax contributions can be the only way for many people to max out their contributions each year in a 401(k). After-tax contributions receive tax-deferred growth and can now be separated out from other amounts at the time of distribution and rolled into a Roth IRA.

In addition to these design options, there are a number of special rules that apply to 401(k) plans. Below we discuss the special rules, 401(k) design considerations and which employers are appropriate candidates for a 401(k) plan.

Special Rules That Apply to 401(k) Plans

LO 5.3 Describe the special rules that apply to 401(k) plans.

The 401(k) salary deferral feature is subject to a number of special rules:

- Salary deferral contributions are subject to an annual limit.
- 401(k) salary deferrals are immediately 100 percent vested and cannot be forfeited.
- In-service withdrawals can be made only if an individual has attained age 59½ or has a financial hardship.
- A nondiscrimination test called the actual deferral percentage (ADP) test applies to salary deferral amounts.
- Plans with matching contributions and/or after-tax contributions are subject to the actual contribution percentage (ACP) test.

Salary Deferral Limitations

automatic enrollment

The heart of the 401(k) plan is the salary deferral feature. In most plans, participants are allowed to make salary deferral elections from their regular paycheck. Often the deferral amount is expressed as a percentage of pay or as a specified dollar amount. Occasionally, the plan will also allow for salary deferral elections of extraordinary pay, like bonuses. Another option is for the employer to provide for **automatic enrollment** in which a specified amount is withdrawn from each paycheck unless the individual elects out of the deferral option. More and more employers are choosing automatic enrollment because it often has a positive effect on the plan's participation rate.

Regardless of the methodology for making the salary reduction, salary deferral amounts can never exceed a specified limit for a calendar year. For 2017, the limit is $18,000. In addition, the maximum salary deferral is increased for those individuals who have attained age 50 by the end of the current year. For 2017, the additional allowable contribution is $6,000.

It is important to understand that this maximum salary deferral limit to a 401(k) plan is both a plan limit and an individual limit. As a plan limit, each plan must ensure that participants do not exceed the salary deferral limits. It is also a limit that applies to the individual. It is a somewhat unusual rule in that an individual is subject to one deferral limit aggregating all salary deferral contributions to any 401(k) plan, Code Sec. 403(b) annuity, simplified employee pension (SEP), or savings incentive match plan for employees (SIMPLE) regardless of who the employer is. This means that the limit applies across plans and even across unrelated employers.

EXAMPLE

Ina Thrifty, aged 52, is a doctor doing research for Drug Co., which maintains a 401(k) plan. For 2017, Ina plans to make the maximum $24,000 salary deferral contribution

($18,000 plus the $6,000 catch-up). Ina is also in a group medical practice (which is unrelated to Drug Co.). The practice also has a 401(k) plan. Unfortunately, Ina cannot make any salary deferral contributions to that plan because the maximum deferral limit applies to all plans in which she participates. Ina may have another option; the Code Sec. 415(c) limit ($54,000) does not apply across unrelated employers which means that Ina could establish a profit-sharing plan or a SEP for her medical practice.

Vesting

Technically, amounts contributed to the plan under a salary deferral election are considered employer contributions—even though they are made at the election of the participant. Still, such amounts are treated somewhat differently from how other employer contributions are treated. Normally, employer contributions can be subject to a vesting schedule, meaning that if the employee leaves the company before working for a designated period of time, some or all benefits are forfeited. In a 401(k) plan this means that employer matching contributions and nonelective profit-sharing contributions can be subject to vesting provisions. However, the portion of the participant's account that is made up of employee salary deferrals (and investment experience thereon) must be 100 percent nonforfeitable (vested) at all times.

In-service Withdrawals

financial hardship

A regular profit-sharing plan can allow employees the option of withdrawing the entire account upon 5 years of plan participation or withdrawing contributions 2 years after they are made. However, under a 401(k) plan, withdrawals from the salary deferral account are restricted.[1] The plan must provide that no distributions from the salary deferral account will be made before separation from service unless the employee either has attained age 59½ or has incurred a financial hardship (referred to as a hardship withdrawal). A **financial hardship** is defined as a financial need that is "necessary in light of immediate and heavy financial needs of the participant or his or her beneficiary" at a time when no other resources are reasonably available to meet this need.

The regulations provide a safe harbor method for determining hardship so plan administrators do not have to make difficult hardship determinations on a case-by-case basis. Under the safe harbor rules, the following specific circumstances constitute hardships:

- medical expenses

---

1. Similar to the vesting rules, the participant's profit-sharing and matching contribution accounts can be subject to the normal withdrawal rules that apply to profit-sharing plans.

- purchase of a principal residence for the participant
- payment of up to 12 months of tuition and related expenses for postsecondary education for a participant, his or her spouse, children, or dependents
- payment of amounts necessary to prevent the eviction of the participant from his or her principal residence or from foreclosure on his or her mortgage
- payments for burial or funeral expenses for the participant's deceased parent, spouse, children, or dependents.
- expenses for the repair of damage to the participant's principal residence

The rules also provide a safe harbor method for determining whether "other resources are reasonably available to meet the need." An employee will be deemed to lack "other reasonable resources" if the following conditions are met:

- The employee must obtain all distributions other than hardship distributions and all nontaxable loans available under all plans maintained by the employer.
- The plan must provide that the employee's elective deferral contributions and nondeductible contributions will be suspended for 6 months after the distribution.

EXAMPLE

Employee Aileen makes elective contributions from January 2017 to June 2017 to her company's 401(k) plan. In June 2017, Aileen takes a hardship distribution from the plan. Aileen cannot make elective deferral contributions to her 401(k) plan until January 2018 (after the 6-month waiting period has elapsed).

Most employers choose to adopt both safe harbor provisions so they do not have to examine an employee's financial condition. Regardless of whether the general approach or the safe harbor method is elected, distributions are limited to the amount necessary to meet the financial need. This amount can include amounts necessary to pay taxes on the withdrawal. Generally, only the portion of the salary deferral account that represents employee salary deferral contributions can be withdrawn; earnings cannot. However, withdrawals under more liberal provisions can be allowed from the profit-sharing or matching contribution accounts.

A plan does not have to allow for hardship withdrawals, and some employers choose instead to allow loans because loans can be made without tax consequences. A hardship withdrawal will generally be taxed as ordinary income, as well as be subject to the Section 72(t) 10 percent penalty tax for those who have not yet attained age 59½.

Actual Deferral Percentage Test

actual deferral percentage (ADP) test

401(k) plans are subject to a special nondiscrimination test known as the **actual deferral percentage (ADP) test**, which

- compares the salary deferrals of highly compensated employees and nonhighly compensated employees,
- only allows highly compensated employees to make salary deferrals up to the salary deferral limit if nonhighly compensated employees contribute sufficient amounts, and
- forces employers to design the 401(k) plan so it attracts participation by lower-paid employees.

More specifically, in order to pass the ADP test, the plan must satisfy one of two tests:

- the 125 percent requirement—Under this requirement, the average of the actual deferral percentages (ADPs) for highly compensated employees for the current year cannot be more than 125 percent of the average ADPs for nonhighly compensated employees in the previous year.
- the 200 percent/2 percent difference requirement—Under this requirement, the average of the ADPs for highly compensated employees for the current year cannot be more than 200 percent of the average ADPs for nonhighly compensated employees in the previous year, and the difference between the deferral percentages for the two groups cannot be more than 2 percent.

highly compensated employees (HCEs)

The first step in performing the ADP test is to determine the **highly compensated employees (HCEs)**. Highly compensated employees include

- individuals who are 5-percent owners during the current or previous year and
- individuals who earned over the earnings limit in the preceding year. In 2016 and 2017, the earnings limit is $120,000. For someone to be highly compensated in 2017, that person would have to have made $120,000 in 2016 (the previous year).

Note that even though the Code refers to 5-percent owners, regulations define a 5-percent owner as an individual owning more than 5-percent of the outstanding value of the stock of the corporation[2]. Also, under the dollar limit category, if more than 20 percent of the workforce

---

2. Treas. Reg. §1.414(q)-1T

earns more than the dollar limit, the employer has the option to elect to limit the group to the top-paid group, The top-paid group is simply the 20 percent of the workforce that is most highly paid. For example, if the employer has 100 employees the 20 most highly paid are in the top-paid group.

The second step is determining the ADP for each employee who is eligible to participate in the plan. The ADP is the individual's salary deferral contribution for the year divided by compensation earned for the year. Employees who are eligible for the plan but choose not to make salary deferrals have an ADP of zero. The third step is determining the average for the nonhighly compensated group for the previous year.

Finally, once the average of the ADPs for the nonhighly compensated employees for the prior year is determined, the maximum average of the ADPs for the highly compensated employees for the current year can be determined. In general, if the ADP for the nonhighly compensated group is less than 2 percent, the 200 percent limit applies. If the ADP for the nonhighly compensated group is at least 2 percent and not more than 8 percent, the 2 percent spread limit applies. If the ADP for the nonhighly compensated group is 9 percent or more, the 1.25 percent limit applies (see Table 5–1).

Table 5-1
Maximum ADP Limits for Highly Compensated Employees

ADP of Nonhighly Compensated Group	ADP Limit
1%	2%
2%	4%
3%	5%
4%	6%
5%	7%
6%	8%
7%	9%
8%	10%
9%	11.25%
10%	12.50%
11%	13.75%
12%	15%
13%	16.25%
14%	17.50%
15%	18.75%
16%	20%

Case Study: Medical Group Professional Corporation

Now that we have laid out the rules, let's examine the application of the ADP test in a case study. The Medical Group Professional Corporation has a 401(k) plan and wants to know what the maximum deferral percentage for HCEs will be for 2017. At the end of 2016, the census data are as follows:

Employees	Salary	Percentage Contributed
Dr. Ben Casey (CEO/75% owner)	$80,000	8%
Dr. Roberta Stone (V.P./25% owner)	80,000	8%
Dr. Mel Practice	150,000	6%
Dr. Frank Burns (treasurer)	20,000	5%
Dr. Ruth Rosenhauser	125,000	8%
Dr. Julius Miller	40,000	8%
Nancy Doe	40,000	5%
Joe Jones	25,000	5%
Sally Crowe	25,000	5%
Jack Dixon	20,000	5%

The first step in the ADP test is to determine who falls into the highly compensated group and who is not a member of that group.

- Dr. Ben Casey and Dr. Roberta Stone are highly compensated employees because they are more-than-5-percent owners.

- Dr. Mel Practice and Dr. Ruth Rosenhauser are highly compensated employees because they receive annual compensation in excess of $115,000 (the indexed number in the look-back year—2014).

- Dr. Frank Burns, Dr. Julius Miller, Nancy Doe, Joe Jones, Sally Crowe, and Jack Dixon are nonhighly compensated employees.

After determining the deferral percentage for each employee, the next step is to perform the ADP test for the nonhighly compensated group.

Nonhighly Compensated	Percentage Contributed
Dr. Frank Burns	5.0%
Dr. Julius Miller	8.0%
Nancy Doe	5.0%
Joe Jones	5.0%
Sally Crowe	5.0%
Jack Dixon	5.0%
Average Percent Deferred	5.5%

Since the average ADP for the nonhighly compensated group is 5.5 percent for 2016, in 2017 the maximum average ADP for the highly compensated group will be 7.5 percent. Looking at the 2016 data, the average of the ADPs for the highly compensated is on track, and probably will not have to be adjusted in 2017 to satisfy the test.

Highly Compensated	Percentage Contributed
Dr. Ben Casey	8.0%
Dr. Roberta Stone	8.0%
Dr. Mel Practice	6.0%
Dr. Ruth Rosenhauser	8.0%
Average Percent Deferred	7.5%

Actual Contribution Percentage Test

actual contribution percentage (ACP) test

If a 401(k) plan has matching contributions, after-tax employee contributions, or both, the plan generally must satisfy another nondiscrimination test referred to as the **actual contribution percentage (ACP) test**. This test is essentially the same mathematical test as the ADP test, but in this case the deferral percentage for each participant is based on matching and after-tax contributions. For a plan with a simple matching formula (such as a 50 percent match up to 6 percent of compensation deferred) the results of the ACP test will mirror the ADP test results. However, for plans that allow after-tax contributions or have a more complex matching formula (such as one that provide a larger contribution for participants with more years of service), the results of the ACP test can be very different than under the ADP test.

401(k) Plans: Contribution Limits for 2017

- Salary deferral limit—Salary deferral contributions made at the election of the participant are limited to $18,000. The limit is increased to $24,000 for participants over age 50. Note that this limit applies to all salary deferral plans (including

- SIMPLEs and 403(b) plans) to which a participant contributes, even with an unrelated employer.
- <u>Maximum allocation</u>—As with other defined-contribution plans, the maximum allocation to a single participant (counting all types of contributions except catch-up salary deferrals for those over age 50) cannot exceed the lesser of 100 percent of compensation or $54,000 (2017). If the individual participates in 401(k) Plans: Contribution Limits for 2017 other defined-contribution plans sponsored by the same (or related) employer, then both plans are aggregated in determining the $54,000 limit.
- <u>Employer deduction limit</u>—The employer's deductible contribution is limited to 25 percent of all covered payroll. This limit rarely affects an individual participant because it is an aggregate limit. Also, salary deferral contributions are not counted when determining the 25 percent limit.
- <u>Nondiscrimination tests</u>—The nondiscrimination tests that apply to salary deferral contributions (the ADP test) and to matching employer contributions (ACP test) can, in some cases, result in lowering the allowable contribution for one or more highly compensated employees. These tests have no effect on nonhighly compensated employees. The tests can also be avoided in some cases by using a safe harbor contribution.

401(k) Design Considerations

LO 5.4 Identify the design features that will help maximize participation in a 401(k) plan.

Part of the challenge of maintaining a 401(k) plan is satisfying the special ADP and ACP nondiscrimination tests. This generally requires getting a large percentage of the nonhighly compensated employees to participate. Features such as automatic enrollment, and an employer matching contribution can go a long way toward meeting this goal. The employer also has some options with regard to testing methods and can choose from several correction methods if the nondiscrimination tests are not satisfied. An employer willing to make a "safe-harbor" contribution may be able to avoid the tests entirely. There are a number of other ways to influence the participation level, including the design of the plan's eligibility provision, participant's access to their accounts, and participant investment direction.

Matching Contributions

Most 401(k) plans contain a matching contribution to encourage employee participation. The matching contribution is generally, but not always, a fixed amount. For example, the sponsor might agree to contribute 50 cents to the plan for each dollar the employee saves, up to the first 6 percent of compensation that the participant saves. In this example, the maximum employer match is 3 percent of compensation. The presumption is that a 50 percent match will be enough of an enticement to encourage participants to contribute at least 6 percent. One way to characterize the match is as an instant return on the participant's savings.

There are essentially unlimited options when designing a matching contribution. The first step is clarifying the employer's objectives and budget. Besides encouraging contributions, another common goal is to create a retirement planning partnership between the employer and the participants.

As in the example above, many employers choose a level matching contribution for all participants. Because of budget concerns, some employers will choose a match that is less than 50 percent. Other employers will choose a lower matching amount (for example, 25 percent) but choose to match a higher deferral percentage (for example, up to 10 percent of salary deferred) to encourage higher savings rates.

Another common matching design is a graded schedule. For example, the employer contributes 50 cents for each dollar saved by the plan participant, up to 4 percent of covered earnings, plus 25 cents for each dollar saved over 4 percent, but not more than 8 percent of covered earnings. Some employers use a graded schedule to reward long service. For example, providing a 50 percent match for employees with up to 5 years of service and a 75 percent match with those with 5 or more years of service.

Matching contributions can also be made on a discretionary basis. This may be appealing to the employer, but may not have the effect of encouraging participation. Another option is to provide a small, guaranteed matching contribution, which can be made larger at the employer's discretion. During the recession of 2008, some employers did switch from a stated match to a discretionary matching approach. Most who did this indicated the intention to return to a fixed match when the economy improved.

In addition to considering the matching amount, the sponsor also has to choose vesting provisions for the company matching contribution. As with other types of defined-contribution employer contributions, the plan can adopt a 3-year cliff vesting or 6-year graded vesting schedule. A vesting schedule with a match can be a disincentive to participate for those individuals uncertain of whether they will satisfy the vesting provisions. For this reason, some employers adopt immediate full vesting with matching contributions. If the match is used to satisfy the "safe harbor" contribution rules, then immediate full vesting may be required.

Automatic Enrollment

Another way to encourage plan participation is to have an automatic enrollment provision. This design feature provides that all eligible employees automatically make the default salary deferral election unless they opt out of the plan via an affirmative election or elect a different deferral amount. Studies have shown that this type of provision can significantly improve plan participation.

Since the Pension Protection Act of 2006 resolved a number of legal uncertainties, automatic enrollment has become a popular plan feature. Under the Act, a plan that has automatic enrollment must provide participants with a notice explaining the participant's right to elect out of the plan or to change the rate of contribution, the time periods for making elections, and how contributions will be invested in the absence of any contrary direction by the participant.

401(k) Eligibility Provisions

An eligible, nonhighly compensated employee who does not make salary deferrals will have a zero deferral percentage. This negative impact on the ADP test can be eliminated by excluding that person from the plan. Since the qualified plan coverage requirements do not require that all employees are covered, carefully choosing the eligibility provisions becomes an important design consideration with 401(k) plans. The sponsor will want to consider carving those nonhighly compensated employees unlikely to contribute. The only caveat is that the plan must cover enough employees to satisfy the minimum coverage requirements of Code Sec. 410(b).

Roth 401(k)

Roth 401(k) plans can include a plan feature that allows participants to establish a designated Roth account by making a Roth election on some or all of their salary deferral contributions. If an employee makes a Roth election, salary deferrals will be made on an after-tax basis and qualified distributions will be tax-free, similar to a Roth IRA. This means that the participant would have the option to forgo tax deferral in exchange for tax-free treatment upon distribution.

Plan participants who like the tax treatment of the Roth IRA may be very interested in having this feature added to their own 401(k) plan for two reasons. First, the 401(k) plan salary deferral limit ($18,000 in 2017) is significantly higher than the Roth IRA limit ($5,500 in 2017). Second, a designated Roth account does not have the income phaseout rules that apply for eligibility for a Roth IRA. Individuals at all income levels can contribute to a designated Roth account.

designated Roth accounts

At the same time, employers should have a clear mandate from employees that they want this feature because it will add administrative complexity to the plan. The plan will have to keep separate bookkeeping for **designated Roth accounts**.

YOUR FINANCIAL SERVICES PRACTICE: DO 401(k) PLANS OFFER ROTH ELECTIONS?

A January, 2015 Aon Hewitt survey found that about half (51 percent) of 401(k) plans offer a Roth election option. The employers who do not offer this option cite a lack of employee demand and administrative complexity as the primary reasons for not including this feature in the plan. However, the trend continues to be adding the Roth election, as 29 percent of those that do not offer the feature today indicated that were considering adding the feature in the next year.

From the 401(k) plan's perspective, Roth 401(k) contributions are characterized as salary deferral contributions. Salary deferral limits, nonforfeitability rules, distribution restrictions, and nondiscrimination testing rules remain the same (and apply to both pretax and Roth salary deferrals in aggregate). Because participants can only elect Roth treatment on salary deferral contributions, the election does not affect employer matching or profit-sharing contributions.

Another way to build a Roth account in a 401(k) plan is through a conversion. Plans that have a Roth contribution option also have the option to offer participants the option to convert other accounts in a 401(k) plan into a designated Roth account. Similar to a Roth IRA conversion, the conversion is subject to ordinary income tax—but not the 10 percent early withdrawal penalty tax. Under the American Taxpayer Relief Act of 2012, a participant can elect to convert any type of 401(k) contributions into a Roth account. Future guidance may, however, provide some limits on the number of conversions or limits on the types of accounts that can be converted. An amount is only eligible for an in-plan Roth rollover if it is an amount that would be eligible under law to be distributed from the plan and would also be an eligible rollover distribution (meaning that it could be rolled over to an IRA). It is important to note that with this type of conversion (unlike a Roth IRA conversion) the participant will not be allowed to later undo the transaction through a recharacterization.

Qualifying distributions from Roth 401(k) plans will generally be subject to the same tax-free treatment as Roth IRAs. However, Roth accounts are subject to several rules that do not apply to Roth IRAs including:

- Nonqualified distributions from a Roth account are subject to a pro rata tax rule.

- The 5-year rule (for determining whether a distribution is qualified) applies to each 401(k) plan with a Roth account.
- Roth accounts in a 401(k) plan are subject to the requirement minimum-distribution rules.

These tax differences are generally not of serious concern because a participant receiving a Roth 401(k) distribution is allowed to roll it to a Roth IRA. Once an amount is rolled over, it is subject to the Roth IRA tax rules.

YOUR FINANCIAL SERVICES PRACTICE: MAXIMIZING SALARY DEFERRAL CONTRIBUTIONS

If your client is looking to maximize salary deferral contributions consider making the Roth election. If for example, a client contributes $24,000 on a tax-deferred basis, the after-tax cost is lowered because of the deduction, but a portion of the account is owned by the government. If for example the client is paying taxes at a 25 percent rate, the client really only owns $18,000 ($24,000 less $6,000 in taxes). On the other hand, with the Roth election, the client has prepaid the tax liability and all $24,000 to spend in retirement.

Access to Funds

Employees may be reluctant to make salary deferrals unless they can access funds in case of an emergency. Participant loan programs are quite common in 401(k) plans because they allow at least limited access without tax consequences. Another way for employees to access funds is through hardship withdrawals. Most 401(k) plans allow either loans or hardship withdrawals, and in some cases both options.

A third option is to make employer profit-sharing or matching contributions available to participants as in-service withdrawals. These accounts are subject to the more liberal profit-sharing in-service withdrawal rules, meaning that the plan can give participants access to these funds without having to demonstrate a financial hardship. As with hardship withdrawals, these distributions will be subject to income taxes and in some cases the 10 percent early withdrawal penalty tax.

Investment Direction

Because employees perceive salary deferrals as "their own money," most 401(k) plans give participants the right to direct the investment of at least the salary deferral account. This trend is extremely widespread, and it is rare to find a 401(k) plan that is designed otherwise. Characteristics of participant investment direction programs include the following:

- The plan offers a limited number of investment alternatives chosen by the plan's fiduciaries. Care is taken to provide options that allow participants to build an appropriate retirement portfolio, regardless of their risk tolerance.
- The plan provides investment information and retirement plan education to participants.
- The plan provides a default investment option for those who do not make affirmative investment decisions.
- Plans will generally comply with the ERISA 404(c) provisions that limit the liability of fiduciaries for the investment decisions of participants.

Testing Alternatives and Correction

Under the ADP nondiscrimination test, the determination of the maximum average ADP for the highly compensated employee group is tied to the nonhighly compensated average ADP from the previous year (referred to as prior year testing). Prior year testing allows the plan administrator to know where the highly compensated employees stand at the beginning of the year, giving the administrator the opportunity to appropriately limit contributions by the highly compensated so the test is satisfied. Treasury Regulations also give the plan sponsor the option to elect current-year testing. Some employers do make this election, since an improvement in the deferral percentage of the nonhighly compensated employees has a more immediate impact on how much the highly compensated can defer. This may be particularly true in the first year of plan operation, because under prior year testing the ADP for the nonhighly compensated group is deemed to be 3 percent.

One way to help ensure that the ADP test is satisfied is to limit the salary deferral contributions of the highly compensated. This is easier to accomplish with prior year testing, but even with current year testing a preliminary test early in the year can estimate how much the highly compensated are likely to be able to contribute.

Even with careful planning, plans do sometimes fail the ADP and ACP tests. The employer has to correct the failure by the end of following year to avoid plan disqualification. Correction is a complex subject , but generally the employer can choose one of three correction approaches. One is to return contributions to the highly compensated. The regulations prescribe how to apportion the excess to specific highly compensated employee. When contributions are returned, any earnings attributable to the contributions must also be returned. Another option is to make additional contributions for nonhighly compensated employees. For these contributions to be treated as salary deferrals, they need to be fully vested and be subject to the withdrawal restrictions that apply to salary deferrals. A third option is to recharacterize excess contributions as after-tax contributions.

YOUR FINANCIAL SERVICES PRACTICE: 401(k) PLANS AND RETIREMENT SECURITY

The 401(k) plan is the sole retirement plan for many companies today. This means that these plans are exceedingly important to the retirement security of the plan participants. Here are a number of simple design considerations that can help maximize the effectiveness of the 401(k) plan as a retirement savings vehicle.

- Add an automatic enrollment feature: This simple step has been shown to increase plan participation, especially for lower income employees.
- Redesign the matching contribution: Review the current matching contribution to determine if a change could encourage additional employee savings. For example, add a 25 percent match on salary deferrals above the current limit.
- Provide participants with retirement planning education and software: Giving participants the tools to help them plan properly can go a long way to providing retirement security.
- Give participants the option to make a Roth election: A Roth account gives participants the ability to achieve tax diversification—allowing them to be better prepared for the uncertainty of future taxes.
- Provide participants with information about lifetime income: A simple change that helps the participants know whether their 401(k) account balance is sufficient is to add information about how much lifetime income the account balance will generate. This can be based on an annuity purchase price or using a 4 percent withdrawal rate.
- Contribute unused vacation pay: IRS guidance has offered a number of ways to allow employees to add the cash value of unused vacation pay as additional salary deferrals.
- Offer annuities as distribution options: Some 401(k) plans only offer lump-sum distributions or installment payments. Offering life annuities gives participants the option to elect guaranteed income for life.

Safe Harbor Contributions

Another alternative for complying with the ADP and ACP tests is to avoid them entirely by making what are referred to as 401(k) safe harbor contributions. If an employer makes safe harbor contributions either to the 401(k) plan or other defined contribution plan of the sponsor, the plan does not have to satisfy the ADP test, and is also deemed to have satisfied the top-heavy requirements that normally apply. In most cases, plans with a safe harbor contribution also avoid the ACP nondiscrimination test that applies to matching contributions. Choosing the safe harbor approach can be especially useful in the small plan market where passing the test may be difficult because of the small size of the group. A new nonhighly compensated employee, for example, that chooses not to participate may result in a limitation in the salary deferrals for the highly compensated.

Until 2008, there were two types of 401(k) safe harbor contributions. A third was added for plans that offer automatic enrollment. Let's first review the traditional safe-harbor designs. One of the options is to make a nonelective contribution for all eligible nonhighly compensated employees (NHCEs) in the amount of 3 percent of compensation. As an alternative, the employer can make a matching contribution for NHCEs. The basic matching contribution is 100 percent of the first 3 percent of compensation that the participant elects to defer. In addition, a 50-percent match is made on the next 2 percent of compensation deferred.

> **EXAMPLE**
>
> Employee Candice elects to defer 8 percent of her $100,000 compensation. The company contributes the basic safe harbor matching contribution. Candice will receive a $4,000 matching contribution, 100 percent of the first 3 percent deferred, and 50 percent of the next 2 percent deferred.

The sponsor can choose a different matching contribution (referred to as an enhanced match) as long as the enhanced formula provides an aggregate amount of matching contributions at least equal to the aggregate amount of matching contributions that would have been provided under the basic matching formula. For example, the sponsor could choose instead to match 100 percent of the first 4 percent of compensation.

With these safe harbor options, contributions must be made for all eligible employees, regardless of how many hours they work during the year, and all contributions must be fully vested. Technically, these contributions are also subject to the hardship withdrawal provisions that apply to salary deferral contributions.

The third safe harbor design, referred to as a qualified automatic contribution arrangement (QACA), only applies to plans that provide for automatic enrollment. To qualify for the automatic enrollment feature the plan can allow automatic deferrals of up to 10 percent of compensation, but as a minimum must require an automatic deferral of 3 percent of compensation for the first year of eligibility; 4 percent during the second year; 5 percent during the third year; and 6 percent during the fourth year and thereafter. A qualifying automatic enrollment plan that makes a safe-harbor contribution will not have to satisfy the ADP or ACP test or satisfy top-heavy testing. The employer has the option to make a 3 percent nonelective contribution for each eligible nonhighly compensated employee or a 100-percent matching contribution on up to one percent of salary deferred and a 50-percent match on up to the next 5 percent deferred. Under the matching approach the maximum match is 3.5 percent of compensation, a bit lower than the 4 percent in a plan with a regular safe harbor match. Also, the vesting rules for a QACA are somewhat more liberal than the immediate vesting required for the other safe harbor designs. The plan can require 2 years of service before a participant becomes fully vested in his or her safe harbor contribution account.

Coordinating with Other Employee Benefit Plans

Many employee benefit plans (including pension plans, group life insurance, and disability insurance) calculate benefits based on the participant's compensation. For example, in a group life insurance plan, the employee's beneficiaries may be entitled to a benefit of two times compensation. When an employer installs a 401(k) plan, benefits under other plans may be reduced if, for example, the definition of compensation only includes taxable income. Sometimes the employer forgets to review the effect of salary deferrals on other employee benefits, and benefits are accidentally reduced. The advisor should be sure to discuss this issue with the employer when the plan is installed.

Note that salary deferral elections do not adversely affect Social Security benefits. Salary deferrals are considered wages for calculating benefits (as well as for determining Social Security taxes).

A popular use of 401(k) plans is to include them as one of the available benefits under a cafeteria plan. In fact, the 401(k) plan is the only type of qualified plan that can be part of a cafeteria plan. The term cafeteria plan stems from the fact that these plans allow employees to pick from a menu of benefit choices. More specifically, the benefit dollars in a cafeteria plan are flexible; employees can take them in cash, allocate them to pay for certain welfare benefits (such as life insurance, health insurance, or child care), place them in a 401(k) plan, or do a combination of any of these three. To the extent that an employee elects to spend benefit dollars on tax-advantaged benefits like a 401(k) plan, there is no current taxation. For this reason, employees may wish to contribute to 401(k) plans in lieu of other benefits available in the cafeteria plan (such as group life insurance in excess of $50,000) that are taxable.

Candidates for a 401(k) Plan

stand-alone plan

401(k) plans are extremely versatile, making them appropriate for a wide number of employers and objectives. A plan can be as simple as a **stand-alone plan** (a plan that allows only pretax salary deferrals) for an organization that cannot afford a comprehensive retirement program.

The stand-alone plan can be expanded and enhanced in the future as the sponsor's financial strength grows. It can also be established as a supplement to other retirement plans.

Many employers also choose to use matching contributions to satisfy a range of objectives. The primary goal is usually to encourage participation which will also help to improve the chances of satisfying the nondiscrimination tests. The match can also encourage long service by providing an escalating contribution based on years of service. Since matching contributions can be partially or completely discretionary, the employer can use the match as an incentive by making larger contributions in years of substantial profits.

When the 401(k) plan is the only plan sponsored by the employer, the employer may also make profit-sharing contributions for eligible employees as well. The design of the profit-sharing allocation formula has the same flexibility as in a traditional profit-sharing plan.

Candidates for the 401(k) plan will have many of the same objectives as those employers that choose a profit-sharing plan. However, the 401(k) candidate will also fill out the fact finder by grading the following as "very valuable":

- giving participants the opportunity to save additional amounts on a pretax basis
- providing employer contributions only for those employees electing to contribute

An employer that identifies as an objective giving participants the choice between tax-deferred salary deferrals and tax-free withdrawals should consider giving participants a Roth election in the 401(k) plan.

YOUR FINANCIAL SERVICES PRACTICE: DESIGNING 401(k) PLANS FOR THE SMALL BUSINESS

Small business owners establishing qualified plans are generally concerned about limiting the cost of benefits for nonhighly compensated employees. A 401(k) plan can be a good plan design to meet this concern. Salary deferrals (up to $24,000 for those over age 50) can be made with no direct cost for the other employees. However, since the plan must address the ADP test, the employer may choose to make a safe-harbor contribution to avoid the test. This means, for example, that for a 3 percent contribution for all employees, the owner can make the maximum salary deferral, and receive the additional 3 percent contribution. For the business owner looking to save more, a profit-sharing allocation formula using cross-testing can be chosen to bring the owner up to the maximum $54,000 allocation ($60,000 for the owner over age 50).

STOCK BONUS PLANS AND EMPLOYEE STOCK OWNERSHIP PLANS (ESOPs)

LO 5.5 Describe the special rules that apply to stock bonus plans and ESOPs and what objectives they can meet.

Stock bonus plans and ESOPs are variations of profit-sharing plans and are similar in many ways:

stock bonus plans

- **Stock bonus plans**, ESOPs, and profit-sharing plans are all defined-contribution plans and all fall into the profit-sharing (not pension) category.
- Unless required under the terms of the plan, contributions can be made on a discretionary basis.
- The plan will have a predetermined allocation formula.
- The maximum deductible contribution limit is generally 25 percent of payroll (ESOPs may be eligible to a larger deduction).
- Contributions for all three types of plans are usually, but are not legally required to be, based on profits.

Stock bonus plans and ESOPs differ from profit-sharing plans, however, in three important ways:

- Both stock bonus plans and ESOPs typically invest plan assets primarily in the employer's stock (in fact, an ESOP is required to invest primarily in employer stock). Profit-sharing plans, on the other hand, are usually structured to diversify investments and do not concentrate investments in employer stock (even though they are legally permitted to do so).
- Both stock bonus plans and ESOPs are chosen because they provide a market for employer stock. If the stock is purchased from the company, the purchase generates capital for the corporation and helps finance a company's growth. Profit-sharing plans, however, are not viewed as a way to finance company operations but are more concerned with providing tax-favored deferred compensation that can be used for retirement purposes.
- Stock bonus plans and ESOPs are required to allow distributions to participants in the form of employer stock. Profit-sharing plans can allow this option, but often do not. This creates a distinct advantage for participants in a stock bonus plan or an ESOP

because they receive a tax break inasmuch as the unrealized appreciation (gain in value) is not taxed until the stock is sold.

Stock Bonus Plans

Stock bonus plans have existed for a long time, since well before the Code provisions that permitted ESOPs. The design features of a stock bonus plan are:

- Employer contributions to the plan may be made in cash or directly in the form of employer securities, newly issued or otherwise.
- Cash contributions and shares of stock are allocated to participants' accounts under a formula that must meet the same nondiscrimination requirements as the allocation formula in a profit-sharing plan.
- A stock bonus plan can also include a 401(k) salary deferral feature.
- Distributions must be available in the form of employer stock, although the plan can give participant's the option to receive cash of equal value.

A stock bonus plan involves an investment risk to the employee that is much greater than the risk connected with a regular defined-contribution plan that has diversified investments. However, if the company's stock is publicly traded, the plan will be subject to the diversification requirements that apply to defined-contribution plans. Generally, participants with 3-years of vesting service have to be given the option to choose to diversify their accounts.

Because of the risks and other unique aspects of stock bonus plans, there are three additional special rules for these plans.

- *Accelerated distributions:* Distributions from a stock bonus plan or ESOP must occur no later than one year after the end of the fifth plan year after the employee's separation from service, or no later than one year after retirement, disability, or death. The distribution must be in the form of substantial equal annual (or more frequent) payments over a period not longer than 5 years (except for certain large accounts).[3]
- *Put option:* A participant that receives stock not traded on an established market must have the right to require that the employer repurchase the securities under a fair valuation formula. This option must be available for a minimum of 60 days following

---

3. Code Sec. 409(o).

distribution, and, if the option is not exercised in that period, for an additional 60-day period in the following year. The participant must be paid over no more than 5 years.[4]

- *Voting rights:* If the employer stock is publicly traded, participants must be permitted to vote on all issues. For closely held stock, participants must generally be given the right to vote on stock held for them in the plan on corporate issues requiring more than a majority of the outstanding common shares. Under most state corporate laws, very few issues require more than a majority vote, so this requirement may not be burdensome.[5]

Employee Stock Ownership Plans

leveraged ESOP

ESOPs enjoy the same advantages as stock bonus plans. A **leveraged ESOP** is unique because of the ability of the plan to borrow by purchasing shares of stock either from existing shareholders or directly from the company (either treasury or newly issued shares). The company then makes tax-deductible contributions to the ESOP to repay the loan, meaning both principal and interest are deductible.

ESOPs can be used to:

- create a market to purchase shares of a departing shareholder,
- allow the company to borrow money at a low cost, or
- provide employees with an additional employee benefit.

The most obvious use of an ESOP is with a C corporation; however, ESOPs can also be adopted by S corporations. This creates a tax advantage for the S corporation, since the general pass-through rules do not apply to profits attributable to the ownership share of the ESOP. For example if the ESOP owns 50 percent of the stock, 50 percent of the profits are not subject to income tax.

There are a number of ways to structure an ESOP loan but with one common approach: the plan trustee acquires a loan from the bank and uses the borrowed funds to purchase employer stock. Generally, the employer guarantees repayment of the loan, and the purchased stock is held as collateral. The result is that the plan receives the full proceeds of the bank loan immediately and pays the loan off with the employer's tax-deductible contributions to the ESOP. The collateralized stock is placed in a suspense account. The employer makes annual

---

4. Code Sec. 409(h).
5. Code Secs. 409(e), 401(a)(22).

(deductible) contributions to the plan, which are used to pay back the bank. As the loan is paid off, the stock is released from the suspense account.

ESOPs are subject to a number of special tax rules. First of all, the accelerated distributions, put option, and voting rights rules that apply to stock bonus plans also apply to ESOPs. In addition, the following rules also apply:

- *Investment in employer stock*: An ESOP must be invested primarily in employer securities. The term primarily has not been interpreted by the government, but it appears that there is less investment flexibility in an ESOP than in a regular profit-sharing plan.
- *Allocation formula*: An ESOP's contribution allocation formula may not be integrated with Social Security, since plan allocations must be based on total compensation.
- *Deductibility of contributions*: Contributions are generally limited to 25 percent of the compensation of employees covered under the plan. However, a special rule provides that contributions used to repay interest are deductible without any percentage limit.
- *Diversification requirement*: A special diversification requirement applies to ESOPs. Participants who have reached age 55 with 10 years of service are entitled to an annual election requiring the employer to diversify investment in the participant's account. For a 5-year period after becoming eligible for this election, the participant can elect annually to diversify 25 percent of the account balance. In the final year, diversification of 50 percent of the account balance can be elected.
- *Deferral of gain for shareholder sales*: To encourage shareholder sales of employer stock to ESOPs, the shareholder may elect nonrecognition of gain on the sale if the ESOP owns 30 percent of the company stock after the sale, the seller held the stock for three years, and the seller acquires replacement securities of another domestic corporation. There are also restrictions on allocation of stock by the ESOP to the accounts of the seller, a related party, or a more-than-25-percent owner of the employer.

Reasons Candidates Choose Stock Bonus Plans and ESOPs

One major advantage of stock bonus plans and ESOPs is that they give employees a stake in the company through stock ownership. This neatly fits most employers' goals of employee motivation and retention. A second major advantage is the previously mentioned delayed taxation of gain on stock distributions. Enhanced cash flow is a third advantage. Cash flow is enhanced because the employer makes a cashless contribution to the retirement plan. A fourth—and perhaps most important—advantage of stock ownership plans is that they help to create a market for employer stock. The leveraging advantage associated with ESOPs is also enticing to organizations.

From the participant's perspective, the major disadvantage of stock ownership plans is the possibility of the employer's stock falling drastically in value and, therefore, cutting the availability of retirement funds. However, the diversification rules that apply to defined-contribution plans of companies with publicly traded stock as well as the ESOP diversification rules provide some protection for participants. From the employer's perspective, one disadvantage for the closely held company is the significant cost to repurchase shares of terminating employees. Also, the cost of setting up an ESOP can be substantial. Current shareholders can be negatively affected as well. Any time the ESOP is funded with new shares of stock, the stock of existing owners is diluted.

YOUR FINANCIAL SERVICES PRACTICE: FUNDING STOCK BUY-BACKS

Closely-held companies that sponsor stock bonus plans and ESOPs are required to satisfy the put option requirement. Special arrangements must be made in advance for the corporation to buy back stock from a terminated employee or from a deceased employee's estate without creating a cash-flow crunch. One common funding approach is corporate-owned life insurance. Life insurance contracts on plan participants, held by the employer as key person insurance—owned, paid for, and payable to the employer—can provide funds in the form of either cash values accessible at the employee's retirement, or funds available at the employee's death to reimburse the employer for its outlays.

Candidates for ESOPs and stock bonus plans are similar to candidates for profit-sharing plans and generally fill out the fact finder in a similar manner. But, unlike the typical profit-sharing candidate, ESOP and stock bonus plan candidates rate as "very valuable" fact-finder item "creating a market for employer stock." Also, ESOP candidates rate as "very valuable" fact finder item "leveraging the purchase of employer stock."

CASE STUDY: BAKER MANUFACTURING, INC.

Bill Baker is the president of Baker Manufacturing, Inc., a firm that produces parts for personal computers. Baker Manufacturing has a defined-benefit pension plan for its 40 employees. Bill wants to improve rank-and-file productivity and morale. Business is excellent, but to meet increased sales orders, Bill needs to get more out of his employees. To make matters worse, two of Bill's experienced line workers have just left to work for a competitor. In addition, several of Bill's people have approached him regarding tax-sheltering part of their salary (Bill is also interested). Bill would like to do something extra, but cash flow is a problem. He feels he may need to hold onto profits in case the never-ending new generations of computers require different manufacturing equipment. How would an ESOP help to solve Bill's problems? Would a 401(k) plan offer a solution? An employee stock ownership plan (ESOP) would be helpful in solving Bill's problems; it would allow him to do something extra without creating cash-flow problems because his ESOP would be leveraged. In addition, employee morale would be improved by the extra benefit provided. Employees would be encouraged not to leave because of their ties to the company's fortunes through the stock itself, and through the amount of stock contributions, which are based on company profits. And, because company profits would be more important to the employees than ever, productivity would likely increase. Bill and his executives could also enjoy the tax advantages of taking distributions of highly productive company stock when they terminate.

A cash or deferred arrangement (401(k) plan) would also be helpful because it would provide something extra for only a minor cost. The executives who wanted to shelter income from taxes would have the opportunity to convert some of their salary into pretax savings (up to the $18,000 maximum in 2017). If Bill provides a matching contribution, the organization's cost would rise slightly, but the paybacks would be increased productivity, better morale, and retention of employees.

CHAPTER REVIEW

Key Terms and Concepts

discretionary contributions
cash or deferred arrangement (CODA)
automatic enrollment
financial hardship
actual deferral percentage (ADP) test
highly compensated employees (HCEs)

actual contribution percentage (ACP) test
Roth 401(k)
designated Roth accounts
stand-alone plan
stock bonus plans
leveraged ESOP

Chapter 5: Review Questions

Review questions are based on the learning objectives in this chapter. Thus, a [5.3] at the end of a question means that the question is based on learning objective 3. If there are multiple objectives, they are all listed

1. Umbrella, Inc., is a business with a cash flow that literally fluctuates with the weather. Umbrella, Inc., would like a qualified plan, despite its erratic cash flow. In addition, the owners of this small business would like to be able to withdraw their funds if they decide to expand the business. What type of qualified plan should Umbrella, Inc., have? Explain. [5.1]

2. Describe the concern about the discretionary nature of the profit-sharing plan and the strategies necessary to ensure that the plan is successful. [5.1]

3. What is an allocation formula? [5.1]

4. Accountants, Inc., has decided to adopt a profit-sharing plan that allocates profits in excess of $10,000 to participants by the ratio that the compensation for a participant bears to the compensation of all participants. Anne with $100,000 in compensation, Bob with $70,000 in compensation, and Cassie with $30,000 in compensation are the plan's only participants. How much will be contributed to each participant's account if Accountants, Inc., has a $30,000 profit? [5.1]

5. In addition to discretionary contributions and withdrawal flexibility, name several other strengths of a profit-sharing plan. [5.1]

6. How can life insurance be used by a profit-sharing trust to protect plan participants from an economic downturn in the event of the death of a key profit maker? [5.1]

7. Describe the types of contributions that can be made to a 401(k) plan. [5.2]

8. What is the maximum salary deferral in a 401(k) plan? [5.3]

9. Dr. Jones, age 47, works for Mega Hospital and makes a $18,000 salary deferral election to the plan in 2017. If Dr. Jones also has a medical practice that includes a 401(k) plan, what is the maximum salary deferral he can make in that plan? [5.3]

10. Under what circumstances may withdrawals be made from a 401(k) plan? [5.3]

11. ABCO, Inc. has adopted a 401(k) plan whose participants, their compensation, and their percentage contributed are as follows: [5.2]

Eligible Employee	2014 Compensation	Percent of Compensation Contributed
Abner Anderson (CEO/75% owner)	$150,000	8%
Barbara Bellows (VP/25% owner)	80,000	8%
Cindy Clark (sec/treasurer)	60,000	5%
Don Davidson	40,000	5%
Ellen Ewer	30,000	9%
Frank Fern	20,000	5%
Gary Grant	20,000	5%

In 2017, what will be the maximum deferral percentage for highly compensated employees under the actual deferral percentage test? Explain.

12. How might automatic enrollment help the participation rate in a 401(k) plan? [5.4]

13. What is the effect of making a safe-harbor contribution to a 401(k) plan? [5.4]

14. Why would employees be interested in a Roth 401(k) feature? [5.4]

15. Describe the advantage ESOPs have with regard to borrowing to fund the plan. [5.5]

16. How can an employer use life insurance to fund the repurchase obligation in an ESOP? [5.5]

Chapter 5: Review Answers

1. Umbrella, Inc., should adopt a profit-sharing plan. A profit-sharing plan suits the company's needs because it can be designed to work around the cash-flow problem by structuring the plan's contribution formula so the company makes contributions only in the year it has substantial profits. For example, a portion of profits in excess of $50,000 will be contributed to the plan.

   A second advantage that a profit-sharing plan holds for Umbrella, Inc., is the ability for participants to withdraw funds from their accounts as early as 2 years after they were contributed by the employer. By adopting this feature in the plan, the owners of Umbrella, Inc., will have access to most of their retirement funds when it comes time to expand the business.

2. Because of the discretionary nature of a profit-sharing plan, it may be difficult to get employees to appreciate the value of the plan. To get the most out of the plan, the employer should clearly communicate the amount of the contribution and how it was derived, identify circumstances that would result in larger employer contributions, and be sure to provide clear and regular benefit statements to participants.

3. An allocation formula is the method for determining how much of the total contribution is allocated to specific participants.

4. To calculate how much will be allocated to each participant, you must calculate the percentage for each employee multiplied by the total contribution of $20,000 ($30,000 less $10,000) as follows:

   Step 1. Find the percentage of contributions to which each participant is entitled.

Anne	$100,000 / $200,000	= 50% of total
Bob	$70,000 / $200,000	= 35% of total
Cassie	$30,000 / $200,000	= 15% of total

   Step 2. Multiply the percentage of the allocation by the amount of profits to determine the amount allocated to each participant's account. In this case, the amount of profits is $20,000 ($30,000 profit less the $10,000 of profit that is not to be allocated).

Anne	50%	of $20,000	= $10,000
Bob	35%	of $20,000	= $ 7,000
Cassie	15%	of $20,000	= $ 3,000
			$20,000

5. Profit-sharing plans promote fiscal responsibility because the employer is not tied to a set contribution. Profit-sharing plans can be used to improve productivity by linking contribution levels to the company's performance. Also, some employers will choose an allocation formula in the plan that directs a large portion of the contribution to the owners.

6. A profit-sharing plan can invest a portion of the plan's assets in key person life insurance. If the key person dies, the plan receives the proceeds of the policy, which is then allocated to the participants.

7. The four types of 401(k) contributions are employee salary deferrals, employee after-tax contributions, employer-matching contributions, and employer profit-sharing-type contributions.

8. For 2017, the maximum salary deferral is $18,000 for individuals under the age of 50 and $24,000 for individuals who are aged 50 or older.

9. Dr. Jones will not be able to make any salary deferral contributions to the 401(k) plan because the salary deferral limit applies to all 403(b) plans, 401(k) plans, and SIMPLEs in which an individual participates.

10. Salary deferral contributions can only be withdrawn upon termination of employment, attainment of age 59½, or for a financial hardship. The plan could provide for more liberal in-service withdrawals for other types of employer contributions.

11. The first step toward determining whether ABCO will pass the actual deferral percentage test is to determine who falls into the highly compensated group.

    - Abner Anderson is a highly compensated employee because he falls into both categories—he's a more than 5 percent owner and he earns more than $120,000 (the limit in 2016).

    - Barbara Bellows is also a highly compensated employee because she is a more than 5 percent owner. It does not matter that Barbara's earnings are below the $120,000 limit.

    - The rest of the employees are not highly compensated employees because they do not meet any of the definitions. Note that for a company this size, the top 20 percent election is not meaningful. Under that rule, if, for example, there were 10 employees and four made more than $120,000, only the two highest-paid employees would be considered highly compensated if the company made the election.

The second step necessary to perform the ADP test is to determine the average deferral percentage for the nonhighly compensated group for 2016.

Highly Compensated	Percentage	Nonhighly Compensated	Percentage
Abner Anderson	8%	Cindy Clark	5%
Barbara Bellows	8%	Don Davidson	5%
		Ellen Ewer	9%
		Frank Fern	5%
		Gary Grant	5%
average deferral	8%	average deferral	5.8%

The final step is to calculate the maximum salary deferral for the highly compensated employees for 2017. This is based on the higher of the two numbers from performing the two tests.

> Test 1: Under the first test, the maximum deferral percentage for the nonhighly compensated employees is 5.8% x 1.25 = 7.25%.

> Test 2: Under the second test, the maximum deferral percentage for the highly compensated employees cannot be more than the lesser of (a) 200 percent of the deferral percentage for nonhighly compensated employees (5.8% x 2 = 11.6%) or (b) the deferral percentage for all nonhighly compensated employees plus 2 percentage points (5.8% + 2% = 7.8%).

Therefore, the maximum deferral percentage for the highly compensated group for 2017 is 7.8 percent. Looking at the deferral percentage for the highly compensated group for 2016 (8 percent), the plan administrator will have to require that the highly compensated group lower their contribution rates for 2017.

12. Forcing employees to elect out of the plan means that those who choose inaction will become participants in the plan.

13. The plan does not have to perform the ADP nondiscrimination test.

14. Similar to the Roth IRA, Roth 401(k) contributions can result in the tax-free accumulation of earnings. In some ways the Roth 401(k) is better than a Roth IRA since

the contribution limits are substantially higher with a Roth 401(k) and all individuals, regardless of income, can make Roth 401(k) salary deferrals.

15. An ESOP can borrow to purchase a large block of stock at one time and the employer pays the loan off with the employer's tax-deductible contributions to the ESOP.

16. Life insurance on the lives of the key employees gives the plan a source of funding to purchase stock from terminating or deceased employees.

Chapter 6

SEPs, SIMPLEs, and 403(b) Plans

Learning Objectives

An understanding of the material in this chapter should enable the student to

- **LO 6.1** Compare simplified employee pensions (SEPs) to qualified plans and identify when a SEP is a good alternative to a profit-sharing plan.
- **LO 6.2** Describe the SIMPLE plan and discuss when its use would be appropriate.
- **LO 6.3** Describe a 403(b) plan with regard to how it can be funded, the applicable legal requirements, and the determination of an individual's maximum contribution.

Three types of tax-advantaged retirement plans are not qualified plans covered under Code Sec. 401(a). What is meaningful about these plans is that each has its own unique set of rules. Who can sponsor each type of plan, how much can be contributed, who must participate, vesting provisions, and how contributions are allocated are different from these aspects of qualified plans—and different from each other. You will also see that in some instances, some of the qualified plan rules do apply.

To determine whether the SEP, the SIMPLE, or the 403(b) plan is more appropriate for your client than any of the qualified plan alternatives, fully explore each type of plan and compare them with qualified plans. At times, the comparisons might be somewhat confusing if you are not yet familiar with all of the rules that apply to qualified plans.

SEPs

LO 6.1 Compare simplified employee pensions (SEPs) to qualified plans and identify when a SEP is a good alternative to a profit-sharing plan.

simplified employee pension (SEP)

A **simplified employee pension (SEP)** is a retirement plan that uses an individual retirement account (IRA) or an individual retirement annuity (IRA annuity) as the receptacle for contributions. As its name implies, this type of plan is simpler than a qualified retirement plan, making it, in many cases, attractive to the small business owner.

The documentation, reporting, and disclosure requirements are less cumbersome than for a qualified plan. Trust accounting is also eliminated because separate IRAs are established for each participant and all contributions are made directly to each participant's IRA. Because contributions must be nonforfeitable, the participant's benefit at any time is simply the IRA account balance.

The SEP is often a good choice for the small business because of the reduced administrative tasks and expenses. However, the SEP still has its complications, and the prospective sponsor needs to go in with a clear understanding of the ongoing responsibilities of maintaining such a plan. Also note that there is a trade-off under the tax rules: in exchange for simplicity is the loss of flexibility. For example, under a SEP, all employees meeting specified requirements must be covered under the plan; the allocation formula may not contain an age-weighting factor (unlike the profit-sharing plans); and benefits must be fully vested at all times. These requirements are reviewed in more depth below.

Characteristics of the SEP

From a design perspective, the SEP is quite similar to the profit-sharing plan. The employer may, on a discretionary basis, make contributions, which are allocated to participants' accounts. The maximum deductible contribution is the same as for a profit-sharing plan.

Technically, SEPs are subject to the rules contained in Code Sec. 408(k)—in contrast to qualified plans, which are subject to Code Sec. 401(a) and related provisions. Code Sec. 408(k) provides some requirements that are unique to SEPs, borrows some of the qualified plan requirements, and states that the investment and distribution provisions for IRAs also apply to SEPs. To learn these rules, it is helpful to group them in these categories.

Requirements Unique to SEPs

Coverage Requirements. SEP coverage requirements are very different than those that apply to qualified retirement plans. The rules require that contributions be made for all employees who have met all three of the following requirements:

- attained age 21
- performed services for the employer for at least 3 of the immediately preceding 5 years
- earned the required minimum compensation from your business for the year ($600 in 201)

From a planning perspective, this set of requirements means that the employer can exclude employees with less than 3 years of service, but must cover all employees—including part-time employees earning more than the compensation limit—who have 3 or more years of service. This provision works well for the employer with numerous short-term employees, but is more problematic for the employer with a number of long-term part-time employees. However, it is also important to remember that a plan can choose to use less restrictive requirements for participation in the plan, such as attainment of age 18 or 90 days of service.

The rigid coverage rules can also cause problems for companies with related subsidiary companies and for small groups of individuals who own two or more companies. If, in either case, the affiliation constitutes a "controlled group of corporations,"[1] the employees of all the related companies must all be covered under the same plan. This rule generally eliminates the SEP as a viable alternative in the larger corporate setting. The most dangerous problem is that a small employer who is unaware of this rule will establish a plan for one company and forget to cover employees in related companies.

Allocation Formula. Even though the contribution limits are the same for a SEP as a profit-sharing plan, the options for the SEP allocation formula is more limited. The allocation formula must either allocate contributions as a level percentage of compensation or be integrated with Social Security using the same method as for other defined-contribution plans. This means that unlike the profit-sharing plan, the allocation formula cannot use age-weighting or cross-testing to skew contributions to older, more highly compensated employees.

Vesting. All contributions to a SEP, either by the employer directly or as an employee contribution (by deferral election), must be immediately and 100 percent vested. From the employer's perspective, this requirement is more onerous than for qualified plans, but remember that employees can be excluded from the plan until they have completed 3 years of employment.

Employee Elective Deferrals. Before 1997, an employer could establish a SEP that allowed employees the opportunity to make pretax contributions in the same way as in a 401(k) plan (often referred to as a SARSEP). In 1996, the Small Business Job Protection Act replaced the SARSEP with the SIMPLE and prohibited new SARSEPs. However, employers were allowed to continue to sponsor plans that were in effect as of December 31, 1996. The SARSEP was never a very popular plan, but there are still a few remaining SARSEPs in existence today. In a SARSEP, employees can elect to defer up to the same deferral amount allowed in a 401(k) plan. Like the 401(k) plan, the SARSEP is subject to a nondiscrimination rule similar to the ADP test. SARSEPs

---

1. The determination of whether a controlled group of corporations exists is governed by Code Secs. 414(b) and (c). The area is quite complex, but as a rule of thumb, a controlled group exists when one company owns 80 percent or more of another corporation or the same five or fewer individuals have controlling interest in two or more businesses. The rules also apply to partnerships and sole proprietorships. In the small business setting, a common example would be one individual owning two separate businesses.

also are subject to several requirements that do not apply to 401(k) plans, each of which makes the plan less attractive than a 401(k) plan:

- Only an employer with 25 or fewer employees can sponsor a SARSEP.
- At least 50 percent of all eligible employees must participate in the SARSEP.
- The employer may not make matching contributions to encourage employees to contribute to the plan.

Timing of Distribution. Participants must be given the opportunity to withdraw the account balance at any time. This is entirely different from the situation with qualified pension plans, which do not allow distributions until termination of employment, and with qualified profit-sharing plans, in which the employer can choose whether or not to allow in-service withdrawals.

Documentation and Reporting. The supporting plan document is much simpler than with a qualified plan. The IRS supplies Form 5305(SEP) and service providers, such as banks and insurance companies, may also sponsor a SEP prototype document and receive IRS approval. If the IRS form or the prototype document is used, the plan does not have to file Form 5500 annually as long as participants receive (1) either a copy of the plan or a summary of the plan, (2) some general information about SEPs, and (3) annual notice of contributions made on their behalf. When working with SEPs, note that these alternative document and disclosure requirements must be followed exactly or the plan sponsor will be required to file annual Form 5500 reports and meet all other ERISA disclosure requirements.

Qualified Plan Rules That Apply to SEPs

Maximum Contributions. The maximum employer contribution to the SEP is the same as for a profit-sharing plan, that is, 25 percent of the compensation of all employees eligible to participate in the plan. All profit-sharing plans and SEPs sponsored by the same company are aggregated under this rule. The Code Sec. 415(c) maximum allocation limit also applies to the allocation of contributions to each participant. Similarly, the compensation cap that applies to qualified plans also applies to SEPs.

Top-heavy Rules. The same rules that apply to qualified plans apply to SEPs. Although most SEPs will be top-heavy (benefits for key employees will generally equal or exceed 60 percent of total benefits), the top-heavy rules do not have much effect on the SEP. SEPs are already required to have 100 percent immediate vesting, and the minimum contribution requirement for nonkey employees does not have much effect because of the special nondiscrimination rules that apply.

IRA Rules That Apply to SEPs

Investment Restrictions. Because contributions are held in IRA accounts, the limitations that apply to individually sponsored IRAs also apply to SEPs. These rules prohibit investment in life insurance and in collectibles (except for U.S. government gold coins). Similarly, loans cannot be made from a SEP.

Taxation of Distributions. Distributions are taxed in the same way as distributions from IRAs. Distributions are treated as ordinary income and are not eligible for special lump-sum averaging. The penalties for early withdrawals and large distributions apply (as they do with qualified plans). Most distributions can also be rolled over to either an IRA or other tax-advantaged retirement plan to avoid current taxation.

SEP Candidates

Candidates for SEPs fill out the pension planning fact finder by grading as "very valuable" the items regarding the avoidance of an annual financial commitment and by instituting a plan that is administratively convenient. SEP candidates say "no" to the following questions in step 2 of the fact finder: Is it more important to provide an adequate retirement standard of living than to avoid an annual commitment? Is it more important to provide an adequate retirement standard of living than to have administrative convenience and an easily communicated plan?

> ### SEP: A Summary of the Rules
> - Employer contributions—similar to a profit-sharing plan, contributions are discretionary, with a maximum deductible contribution of 25 percent of compensation
> - Allocations—must allocate based on compensation or integrated with Social Security and cannot exceed the Sec. 415(c) maximum allocation rules
> - Eligibility—must cover all employees aged 21 with 3 years earning more than the current year's dollar limit in the last 5 years
> - Vesting—full and immediate vesting required
> - Withdrawal restrictions—withdrawals can be made at any time
> - Investment restrictions—like other IRAs, cannot invest in life insurance or most collectibles
> - Salary deferral contributions—not allowed except in grandfathered SARSEP started before 1997
> - Taxation—like other IRAs, subject to ordinary income tax upon distribution

The SEP is a good choice for the small employer with these goals in mind. The coverage rules are easier to work with than those for a qualified plan; shorter-term employees (less than 3 years) can be excluded from the plan, eliminating cost and administrative burdens. However, the SEP is not the right approach when the employer has many long-term part-time employees, because they will have to be covered under the plan. The lack of flexibility in the coverage and vesting requirements typically eliminates larger employers as SEP candidates.

Any employer considering a profit-sharing plan should also consider a SEP, because the maximum deduction limits (25 percent of compensation) and the ability to make discretionary employer contributions are the same. Assuming the coverage requirements discussed above do not cause any problems, the SEP is usually the better choice. The employer should avoid the more complex profit-sharing plan unless the employer really values one or more of the features only available in a profit-sharing plan, including:

- age-weighted or cross-tested allocation formulas that skew contributions to older, more highly compensated employees
- investments in life insurance
- limits on plan withdrawals
- participant loans
- deferred vesting

SIMPLEs

LO 6.2 Describe the SIMPLE plan and discuss when its use would be appropriate.

savings incentive match plan for employees (SIMPLE)

Since 1997, employers have had another plan option that allows pretax salary deferrals, referred to as the **savings incentive match plan for employees (SIMPLE)**.

Plan Requirements

Like SEPs and SARSEPs, the SIMPLE plan is funded with individual retirement accounts, which means that the following requirements apply to the SIMPLE:

- Participants must be fully vested in all benefits at all times.
- Assets cannot be invested in life insurance or collectibles.
- No participant loans are allowed.

Eligible Employers

Any type of business entity can establish a SIMPLE; however, the business cannot have more than 100 employees (only counting those employees who earned $5,000 or more of compensation). If the employer grows beyond the 100-employee limit, the law does allow the employer to sponsor the plan for an additional 2-year grace period. Also note that to be eligible, the sponsoring employer cannot maintain any other qualified plan, 403(b), or SEP at the same time it maintains the SIMPLE.

Salary Deferral Contributions

In a SIMPLE, all eligible employees have the opportunity to make elective pretax contributions of up to $12,500 (indexed for 2017). As with the 401(k) plan, participants who have attained age 50 before the end of the year can make additional contributions to a SIMPLE. For 2017, the additional amount is $3,000 resulting in a maximum employee contribution of $15,500 for those age 50 or older.

Employer Contributions

Unlike the 401(k) plan (or the old SARSEP), there is no nondiscrimination testing, meaning that highly compensated employees can make contributions without regard to the salary deferral elections of the nonhighly compensated employees.

However, in exchange, the SIMPLE has a mandatory employer contribution requirement. This contribution can be made in one of two ways:

1. The employer can make a dollar-for-dollar matching contribution on the first 3 percent of compensation that the individual elects to defer, or
2. The employer can make a 2 percent nonelective contribution for all eligible employees.

If the employer elects the matching contribution, there is one other option. Periodically, the employer can elect a lower match as long as

- the matching contribution is not less than one percent of compensation
- participants are notified of the lower contribution within a reasonable time before the 60-day election period that comes before the beginning of the year

The employer can elect the lower percentage for up to 2 years in any 5-year period, which can even include the first 2 years that the plan is in force.

The employer contribution amount just described is both the minimum required and the maximum employer contribution allowed. In other words, if the employer elects the matching contribution, 3 percent is the maximum match, and nonelective contributions are not allowed. If the employer elects the nonelective contribution, then the 2 percent contribution is the maximum, and matching contributions are not allowed.

Eligibility Requirements

The SIMPLE has eligibility requirements that are different from both the SEP and the qualified plan. The plan must cover any employee who earned $5,000 in any 2 previous years and is reasonably expected to earn $5,000 again in the current year. Employees subject to a collectively bargained agreement can be excluded. Eligible employees must be given the right to make the salary deferral and receive either an employer matching or nonelective contribution. For determining eligibility, compensation is essentially taxable income plus pretax salary deferrals. For a self-employed person, compensation is net earnings (not reduced by salary deferral elections). SIMPLEs can be maintained only on a calendar-year basis, and all employees become eligible to participate as of January 1.

Plan Operations

The sponsoring employer must notify participants that they have the 60-day election period just prior to the calendar year to make a salary deferral election or modify a previous election for the following year. The employee who does make a salary deferral election must be given the option to stop making deferrals at any time during the year. The sponsor can require that the participant wait until the following year to elect back into the plan, or may have a more liberal election modification provision—for example, allowing participants to modify their election at any time.

Every year, prior to the 60-day election period, the trustee must prepare and the employer must distribute a summary plan description (SPD) that includes employer-identifying data, a description of eligibility under the plan, benefits provided, terms of the salary election, and description of the procedures for and effects (tax results) of making a withdrawal. Also, 30 days after the calendar year ends, the trustee must give participants a statement of the year's activity and the closing account balance.[2]

---

2. Code Sec. 408(l).

> **YOUR FINANCIAL SERVICES PRACTICE: MARKETING SIMPLEs**
>
> Some financial services professionals choose not to get involved in selling the highly technical qualified plan. These professionals may still want to consider marketing the SIMPLE. With individual IRA accounts (no trust fund), no annual reporting, and no distribution paperwork, the SIMPLE poses little time-consuming administration. With a SIMPLE, the professional is likely to establish a direct relationship with all the participants, providing an ever-expanding group of individual clients.

The clear and precise disclosure requirements are accompanied by clear penalties for failure to comply. The trustee is fined $50 a day for late distribution of participant statements or the annual summary plan description. The employer is fined $50 a day for late notification to participants of their right to make salary deferral elections.[3] The disclosure requirements and penalty system were probably deemed necessary because there is no direct incentive for the employer to encourage SIMPLE participation (unlike the 401(k) plan, in which highly compensated contribution levels are tied to nonhighly compensated contributions under the ADP nondiscrimination test)s.

Like SEPs, the plan cannot put any limitations on participant withdrawals. This means that participants have access to funds at any time to spend them or roll them over into another IRA. To discourage participants from spending their SIMPLE accounts, a special tax rule assesses a 25 percent penalty tax (in addition to ordinary income taxes) for amounts withdrawn within 2 years of the date of participation. Other early withdrawals may be subject to the special 10 percent excise tax.

Administrative costs for a SIMPLE should be quite low. At the present time, no annual reporting with the IRS or DOL is required. Also, unlike the 401(k) plan, no ADP test or other nondiscrimination tests must be performed.

Candidates for the SIMPLE

The candidate for the SIMPLE will be the employer looking for a plan that allows participants the right to make pretax contributions and who wants to develop a plan that creates a retirement planning partnership between the employer and employee. The candidate must have 100 or fewer employers and also be looking for a plan with the lowest possible administrative hassle and cost.

The employer considering the SIMPLE will be choosing between the 401(k) plan and the SIMPLE. Feature by feature, the advantage almost always goes to the 401(k) plan. The 401(k)

---

3. Code Sec. 6693(c)(1).

plan is better for maximizing contributions and skewing employer contributions to a targeted group of employees—which are typically two common goals of small plan sponsors. In addition, a 401(k) plan is much more flexible. The plan can be limited to part of the workforce as long as the minimum coverage requirements are met, and matching and profit-sharing contributions can be designed to meet a variety of goals. Finally, employer contributions can increase or decrease over time.

This is not to say, however, that the SIMPLE IRA is not a good retirement plan. It is most likely to appeal to the employer who has never maintained a plan before and who is looking for a low-cost plan with few administrative headaches. With little expense, the employer can have a plan that looks to the employees just like a 401(k) plan. Also, the employer does not have to be concerned about how many employees choose to make salary deferrals because the plan does not have to satisfy a nondiscrimination test.

There are several other advantages that the SIMPLE has over the 401(k) plan regarding the IRA funding vehicle. Participants can withdraw their funds at any time or even change investment vehicles. If money is withdrawn to pay educational expenses, the 10 percent early withdrawal penalty tax will not apply. Also, an employer can terminate the plan quite simply without having to be concerned about making distributions from the trust.

SIMPLE: A Summary of the Rules

- <u>Limits on sponsorship</u>—any type of employer as long as there is no other plan and 100 or fewer employers
- <u>Salary deferral contributions</u>—eligible participants can defer $12,500 (in 2017)
- <u>Catch-up election</u>—participants over age 50 can defer an additional $3,000 (in 2017)
- <u>Employer contributions</u>—sponsor must contribute either a specified matching or nonelective contribution (but not both)
- <u>Eligibility</u>—must cover all employees with 2 years of $5,000 or more of compensation
- <u>Vesting</u>—full and immediate vesting required
- <u>Withdrawal restrictions</u>—eligible for withdrawal at any time, but subject to special 25 percent penalty tax in first 2 years of participation
- <u>Investment restrictions</u>—like other IRAs, cannot invest in life insurance or most collectibles
- <u>Taxation</u>—like other IRAs, subject to ordinary income tax upon distribution

403(b) PLANs

Overview of 403(b) Plans

LO 6.3 Describe a 403(b) plan with regard to how it can be funded, the applicable legal requirements, and the determination of an individual's maximum contribution.

403(b) plans

The plans we have studied up to this point are not limited to any particular type of industry. For the most part, they are available to any organization. In contrast to other retirement plans, **403(b) plans** can be sold only to tax-exempt organizations and public schools. Despite these limitations, 403(b) plans represent a separate and lucrative opportunity for financial services professionals, particularly those who sell annuity products. A 403(b) plan, which is also referred to as a tax-sheltered annuity (TSA) or a tax-deferred annuity (TDA), is similar to a 401(k) plan. Like the 401(k) plan, the 403(b) plan

- permits an employee to defer tax on income by allowing before-tax contributions to be made to the employee's individual account
- allows the employer to make matching or nonelective contributions
- can be used in conjunction with, or in lieu of, most other retirement plans

However, 403(b) plans are distinguishable from 401(k) plans both in the market they serve and in their makeup. In this section, we will discuss the distinct market that 403(b) plans serve and analyze the fundamental makeup of a 403(b) plan.

Eligible Sponsors

Sec. 501(c)(3) organizations

A 403(b) program can only be sponsored by either **Sec. 501(c)(3) organizations** (employers that are exempt from tax under Code Sec. 501(c)(3)) or educational institutions of a state or political subdivision of a state. These can include public school districts, community colleges, state colleges, and state universities. Tax-exempt organizations under Code Sec. 501(c)(3) include entities organized and operated exclusively for religious, charitable, scientific, public safety testing, literary, or educational purposes. A state or local government or any of its agencies or instrumentalities can be a qualified employer, but only with regard to employees who perform (or have performed) service, directly or indirectly, for an educational organization. An educational organization is defined as one that maintains a regular faculty and curriculum and has a regularly enrolled body of students in attendance at the place where its educational activities are conducted.

Employee Status

Contributions to a 403(b) annuity plan can only be made on behalf of individuals who are current, former, or retired employees of an eligible employer. This includes employees who receive wages, bonuses, or other compensation reported on Form W-2, but does not include independent contractors. For example, physicians on a hospital staff are often treated as independent contractors, and therefore could not be covered by the hospital's 403(b) plan. Clergy members are an exception. Even though they are generally considered self-employed for purposes of applying Social Security taxes, the employer may establish a 403(b) account on behalf of a clergy member.

Funding Vehicles

Funding a 403(b) annuity plan can be done either by purchasing an annuity contract from an insurance company or by purchasing shares in a mutual fund. Neither the Code nor the Regulations define what type of annuity contracts can be provided. Therefore, contracts with a wide variety of features may be used. They may be single-premium or annual-premium, provide for fixed variable annuity payments, begin immediately or provide deferred payments, and either include or omit a refund provision. The other funding alternative is contributions to custodial accounts invested in regulated investment company stock, whether or not shares are redeemable—more commonly referred to as a mutual fund.

Even though there is some flexibility in the investment vehicles, there is certainly less flexibility than in qualified retirement plans. In qualified plans, assets can be invested directly in stocks, bonds, money instruments, or even more exotic investment alternatives. This distinction is probably less important than it first seems because 403(b) plans are most similar to 401(k) plans. Most 401(k) plans provide individual investment direction, giving participants the option to choose between a number of mutual funds or annuity options. Some 401(k) plans, however, actually offer individual brokerage accounts, which would not be allowed in a 403(b) plan.

At one time, a 403(b) plan could also invest in life insurance as long as death benefits satisfied the same incidental death benefit requirements that apply to qualified plans. Today, life insurance is no longer an allowable investment; however, policies issued in a plan before September 24, 2007 can still be maintained.

Vesting Provisions

Similar to 401(k) plans, salary deferral contributions must be fully vested at all times. Employer contributions can be subject to the vesting schedules available for defined-contribution plans.

Employee Elections to Defer Salary

Tax-sheltered annuity contracts must be purchased by an eligible employer. However, the premiums paid by the employer may either constitute additional compensation for the employee or be indirectly paid by the employee as a reduction in salary. Amounts contributed under salary reduction are excludible from gross income (for federal tax purposes).

Plans that offer salary deferral contributions must offer the opportunity to all employees (regardless of age or years of service), unless such employees are covered under another salary deferral type plan.[4] In addition, the employer may not require a minimum contribution level beyond a de minimis contribution of $200. Nonresident aliens, students who work for their schools, and employees who normally work less than 20 hours per week are excluded from this requirement.

The agreement to defer salary must be legally binding and irrevocable for amounts earned while the agreement is in effect. An individual can change the election prospectively during the year (as often as the plan allows) or end the agreement for amounts not yet earned.

Maximum Deferral Limit

The maximum salary reduction contribution made by an individual is subject to the same dollar limitations that apply to 401(k) plans. For 2017, the dollar limit is $18,000. Also, as with the 401(k) plan, additional contributions can be made by individuals who have attained age 50 by the end of the current year. For 2017, the additional allowable contribution is $6,000 resulting in a maximum contribution of $24,000 for a participant age 50 or older.

Also remember that the dollar limit applies to all contributions made by the individual to any 403(b) plan, 401(k) plan, simplified employee pension (SEP), or savings incentive match plan for employees (SIMPLE). This is true even if the individual is covered by plans of unrelated employers. For example, a 40-year-old participant deferring $8,000 in a 403(b) plan for 2017 would be able to defer only a maximum of $10,000 under a 401(k) arrangement for 2017.

---

4. Including a Code Sec. 457 plan, a Code Sec. 401(k) plan, a SIMPLE, or another Code Sec. 403(b) annuity plan.

On top of the normal limit (including the additional contribution allowed by participants over age 50), another special "catch-up" election applies to 403(b) plans. Individuals who have completed at least 15 years of service with most qualified sponsors[5] are eligible for the catch-up election. The otherwise applicable limit ($18,000 for 2017) is increased for such eligible individuals by the smallest of the following amounts:

- $3,000 (which makes the limit $21,000 for 2017)
- $15,000, reduced by increases to the regular limit the individual was allowed during earlier years because of this rule
- $5,000 times the number of years of service with the organization, minus the total elective deferrals made under the plan for the individual during earlier years.

In one way, 403(b) plans are less complicated than 401(k) plans. They are not subject to the ADP (average deferral percentage) test that applies to 401(k) plans. This means that highly compensated employees are not at risk of having contributions reduced as could happen in a 401(k) plan.

Roth 403(b)

As with 401(k) plans, 403(b) plans can include a plan feature that allows participants to establish a designated Roth account by making a Roth election on some or all of their salary deferral contributions. If an employee makes a Roth election, salary deferrals will be made on an after-tax basis and qualified distributions will be tax-free, similar to a Roth IRA. This means that the participant would have the option to forgo tax deferral in exchange for tax-free treatment upon distribution.

From the 403(b) plan's perspective, salary deferrals subject to a Roth election continue to be treated as salary deferral contributions. Salary deferral limits, nonforfeitability rules, and distribution restrictions remain the same (and apply to both pretax and Roth salary deferrals in aggregate). Because participants can only elect Roth treatment on salary deferral contributions, the election does not affect employer matching or nonelective contributions.

Another way to build a Roth account in a 403(b) plan is through a conversion. Plans with a Roth contribution option can offer participants the option to convert other accounts in the 403(b) plan into a designated Roth account. Similar to a Roth IRA conversion, the conversion is subject to ordinary income tax—but not the 10 percent early withdrawal penalty tax. It is important to

---

5. Including an educational organization, hospital, home health service agency, health and welfare service agency, church, or convention or association of churches (or associated organization).

note that with this type of conversion (unlike a Roth IRA conversion) the participant will not be allowed to later undo the transaction through a recharacterization.

Automatic Enrollment

The Pension Protection Act of 2006 provisions that allow automatic enrollment in 401(k) plans also apply to 403(b) plans that are subject to ERISA. These plans can provide for automatic enrollment at a specified salary deferral level and allow eligible employees the option to elect out of (or change) the salary deferral election. The PPA provisions specifically preempt state garnishment laws that often prohibit payroll deductions without consent. However, many 403(b) plans (including government sponsored and church plans) are exempt from ERISA. These employers will have the same concerns that existed prior to PPA, that is, existing state garnishment laws and the fiduciary responsibility of investing employee contributions.

Employer Contributions

As in a 401(k) plan, employer contributions can be made as matching contributions based on employee elections to defer compensation. When matching contributions are made they are subject to the actual contribution percentage (ACP) test that applies to qualified retirement plans. As an alternative (or in addition to matching contributions), the sponsor can make contributions on a nonelective basis, as in a profit-sharing plan or money-purchase pension plan. Typically, such plans provide contributions as a uniform percentage of compensation; however, some flexibility is available in determining the allocation formula. When nonelective employer contributions are made, the nondiscrimination requirements of Code Sec. 401(a)(4) will apply to the amount allocated to such contributions.

The Code Sec. 415 limitations that apply to qualified defined-contribution plans also apply to Code Sec. 403(b) annuity plans. The annual amount that can be credited to a participant's account, including employer contributions, employee contributions, and forfeitures, cannot exceed the lesser of 100 percent of the employee's compensation from the employer or $54,000 (indexed for 2017).

> **YOUR FINANCIAL SERVICES PRACTICE: WORKING WITH NONPROFIT ORGANIZATIONS**
>
> Nonprofit organizations can be an excellent market for the retirement plan advisor. Small organizations may not have plans, while others have 403(b) plans that need to be updated. Especially with smaller organizations, the plan may not have been brought into compliance with IRS regulations or considered some of the new opportunities available such as offering auto enrollment or Roth accounts. Plan sponsors may want

to improve services available to participants as well. The advisor with a background working with for-profit corporations with their 401(k) plans will need to beware of the rule differences between 401(k) and 403(b) plans. It is also important to become familiar with the culture differences between corporations and nonprofit organizations. One great way to do that is to volunteer for an organization of your choice.

Regulatory and Administrative Aspects

Generally, the reporting and disclosure requirements applicable to 403(b) plans are similar to those applicable to qualified plans. However, as with qualified plans, 403(b) plans of governmental units and churches that have not elected to come under ERISA are exempt from these requirements, unless mutual funds, rather than annuity contracts. Also, for other plan sponsors, if the 403(b) plan is purely of the salary reduction type and does not include any direct employer contributions, the reporting, disclosure, and other regulatory requirements are greatly reduced.

Regardless of whether the plan is subject to ERISA, recent regulations require that tax-sheltered annuities must be issued and maintained pursuant to a written plan of the employer. A plan must contain all the material terms and conditions for eligibility, benefits, applicable limitations, the contracts available under the plan, and the time and form under which benefit payments are made. A plan may assign administrative responsibility to persons other than the employer (for example, the insurance companies maintaining the annuity contracts) and the plan can incorporate by reference other documents, including annuity contracts or custodial accounts.

403(b) plans that are subject to ERISA are subject to the following additional requirements:

- *Coverage requirements:* The employer contribution feature has to satisfy the provisions of Code Sec. 410(b).
- *Matching contributions*: The employer contribution must satisfy the actual contribution percentage (ACP) test that applies to 401(k) plans.
- *Nonelective employer contributions*: The allocation of employer contributions must satisfy the nondiscrimination requirements of Code Sec. 401(a)(4).
- *Timing of contributions*: Employee salary deferral contributions must be submitted by the 15th day of the month following the month when the employee would have otherwise received the contribution. Employer contributions can be made up to the due date of the employer's tax return (plus extensions) for the tax year ending with or within the plan year.

- *Joint-and-survivor requirements*: The plan will be subject to the qualified joint-and-survivor rules. The plan may, however, be eligible for the exception that applies to profit-sharing plans.

Loans and Distributions

Similar to 401(k) plans, 403(b) plan benefits are generally distributed at the time of termination of employment. In a plan funded with annuity contracts, the salary deferral portion of the participant's account can only be withdrawn in-service if the participant has attained age 59½ or suffers a financial hardship. When the plan is funded with mutual fund custodial accounts, then the in-service withdrawal restrictions apply to the entire account (including salary deferrals as well as employer contributions). Distributions are generally subject to ordinary income tax treatment and the 10 percent early withdrawal Sec. 72(t) penalty tax.

As an alternative to a distribution, loans can be made from 403(b) plans. The maximum amount that can be borrowed without creating a taxable event is the same as with qualified plans. ERISA-subjected 403(b) plans will have to satisfy the ERISA requirements concerning availability, adequate security, and interest rates that apply to qualified plans.

MINI-CASES: TAX-ADVANTAGED RETIREMENT PLANS

Case One—Facts

Survey, Inc., wishes to establish a qualified plan for its employees. The company is relatively new, and profits fluctuate wildly. The employer would like to reward employees when the company does well and is somewhat concerned that the company has no retirement plan, which might make it difficult to attract experienced people to work there. The company is also concerned about the costs of maintaining the plan.

Case Two—Facts

Near Retirement, Inc., is a closely held company whose original owners are about to retire. The company has a defined-benefit pension plan, which has already served the purpose of providing benefits for the current owners. Assume that the owners do not have family members interested in the business, that the employees have worked for the company for a long time, and that the employees are potential buyers of the company.

Case Three—Facts

Stable, Inc., has had a modest money-purchase pension plan for a long time. Participation in the plan precludes employees from participating in a tax-deferred IRA. The company realizes that the plan is not adequate but has little additional money to provide retirement benefits.

Case Four—Facts

Teeny-Tiny Corp. has four employees. The owner realizes that competing employers are sponsoring 401(k) plans. To compete with the other employers, the owner would like a similar plan, but is not willing to pay the administrative expenses associated with that type of plan.

CHAPTER REVIEW

Key Terms and Concepts

simplified employee pension (SEP)
savings incentive match plan for employees (SIMPLE)

403(b) plans
Sec. 501(c)(3) organizations

Chapter 6: Mini-Case Answers

Case One Answer

Survey, Inc. clearly sees the value of maintaining a retirement plan. Because its profits vary, the company would probably not want a plan that has a significant fixed cost; instead it would want to choose a plan that allows for discretionary contributions, such as a pro it-sharing plan or a SEP. Since the company wants to minimize administrative costs, the SEP is a logical choice. However, some employers do not like the fact that SEP benefits must be fully vested at all times and that employees have access to withdrawals.

If the company is concerned about having a plan that is competitive with other employers, it should also consider a 401(k) plan. Remember that a 401(k) is not required to have a fixed employer matching contribution, although such a feature is quite common. The matching contribution could be discretionary or quite modest. To minimize the cost, the administrative expenses can be shared with the plan participants. Also, administrative costs have been dropping due to increased competition and "cookie cutter" products. If the employer is willing to make the 3 percent matching contribution each year, then the SIMPLE IRA plan should also be considered.

This company is not a good candidate for any of the plans in the pension category because of the ongoing funding obligation for these type of plans.

Case Two Answer

This is an interesting case study. One solution really stands out: to establish an ESOP as a mechanism to sell the company to the current employees. The ESOP can borrow to purchase the stock of the retiring owners. If the current owners meet certain rules, they may even be able to delay the payment of capital gains on the sale. The company can make regular payments to the ESOP, which can be used to pay back the loan, at which time stock held in a suspense account can be allocated to the participants. As the loan is retired, the participants of the plan earn more and more shares of stock.

Even though the ESOP is a good choice for a new plan, what should happen to the current defined-benefit plan? Since the company will have to make contributions to the ESOP to retire the loan, the company will be concerned about also having to make required contributions to the defined-benefit plan. One alternative is simply to terminate the defined-benefit plan. If the plan is well funded and currently has excess assets, another alternative is to amend the plan into a cash-balance plan. It is possible in this way to use up the excess assets to fund the future benefit accruals under the cash-balance arrangement.

Case Three Answer

This is a classic case for terminating the money-purchase plan and establishing a 401(k) plan. This plan is not providing an adequate retirement benefit and is actually getting in the way of the participants helping themselves. The modest benefits of participating in the money-purchase plan are offset by the potential loss of the deductible IRA contribution. If the company switches to a 401(k) plan, employees can save up to $18,000 (as indexed in 2017) on a pretax basis. The employer can continue to make the same type of contributions to the 401(k) plan or may choose instead to spend its budget on matching contributions for only those employees who choose to contribute.

When the employer's budget is small, the 401(k) plan should always be compared with the SIMPLE IRA. The SIMPLE IRA has many more design limitations, but it is less expensive and easier to administer. Even though employees can contribute only up to $12,500 (for 2017, that is still a lot more than in an IRA.)

Case Four Answer

This company is the perfect candidate for the SIMPLE IRA. From the employee's perspective, this plan looks like a 401(k) plan, but from the employer's perspective, it is less expensive to maintain. Remember, with the SIMPLE, the basic employer contribution is a dollar-for-dollar matching contribution (up to 3 percent of pay) for employees who elect to make salary deferrals.

Chapter 6: Review Questions

Review questions are based on the learning objectives in this chapter. Thus, a [6.3] at the end of a question means that the question is based on learning objective 3. If there are multiple objectives, they are all listed.

1. Describe a simplified employee pension (SEP) plan's similarities to the qualified plan and IRA, as well as the SEP's unique design characteristics. [6.1]

2. What are the major advantages and disadvantages of a SEP? [6.1]

3. In the following situations, identify whether a SEP is appropriate and, if not, what other type of plan the sponsor should consider. [6.1]

    a. Candidate Growthco, Inc., has indicated that it would like to have the option to avoid contributions in certain plan years. Growthco wants to motivate employees, but it is hesitant to use stock ownership as an incentive because the owners want to control all stock.

    b. Candidate Smallco, Inc., has five employees and has indicated that it would like to institute a plan that is administratively convenient and allows the company to skip contributions.

    c. Candidate TAMCO, Inc., would like to provide a plan that encourages participants to save for their own retirement. and that allows for discretionary employer contributions. TAMCO would like to accomplish this objective in the most tax-efficient manner possible.

    d. The owner of candidate Transition, Inc., would like to retire and sell the company to the employees. Transition, Inc., employees do not have sufficient funds to purchase the stock outright.

4. Technology, Inc., maintains a SEP. Determine whether the following employees are eligible to participate in the plan as of January 1, 2017. [6.1]

a. Sally, aged 45, was hired August 15, 2012, on a full-time basis. Sally earns $65,000 a year.

b. Rich works part-time on an on-and-off basis. He earned $3,000 in 2011, nothing in 2012, $2,500 in 2013, and $1,500 in 2014.

5. Describe the major characteristics of the SIMPLE plan. [6.2]

6. What are the contribution options that the employer has in a SIMPLE? [6.2]

7. What employers are most likely to choose the SIMPLE? [6.2]

8. Identify the market in which 403(b) plans can be used. [6.3]

9. The benefits administrator of Mercy Hospital has asked you to determine which of the following employees could be allowed to participate in the hospital's 403(b) plan. [6.3]

a. Dr. Smith, who heads up the hospital's radiology department and is a full-time employee of the hospital

b. Dr. Jones, who has admitting privileges at the hospital and is considered an independent contractor

c. Gary Green, who is called in by the hospital every summer to clean out the boilers

d. Joy Cheerful, who works part-time (500 hours per year) distributing magazines to patients

10. List the two methods that can be used to fund a 403(b) plan. [6.3]

11. What are the withdrawal restrictions that apply to 403(b) plans? [6.3]

Chapter 6: Review Answers

1. A SEP is similar to a profit-sharing plan in that contributions are discretionary and the maximum deductible contribution is 25 percent of compensation. It is similar to other qualified plans because the annual additions limit applies and the plan is subject to the top-heavy limitations. Because SEPs are funded with IRA accounts, they are subject to the full and immediate vesting rules, investment restrictions, withdrawal limitations, and tax treatment that apply to other IRAs. The eligibility rules are unique to SEPs, as is the requirement that contributions can only be allocated on a compensation-to-compensation or integrated basis.

2. A SEP has many of the same advantages of a discretionary profit-sharing plan with less administrative hassle. If the employer has many part-time, long-service employees, or wants to limit the plan to one group of employees, then the profit-sharing eligibility rules may be preferred. Also, many employers do not want to give participants full and immediate vesting or immediate access to the retirement account. The SEP, however, has immediate full vesting and the employer contribution can only be allocated as a level percentage of compensation or integrated with Social Security.

3. a. Either a profit-sharing plan or a SEP looks like an appropriate choice. What is chosen will depend on the coverage, vesting, and withdrawal issues.

    b. Because of the interest in administrative ease, the SEP seems preferable to a profit-sharing plan in this case.

    c. Because of the employer's interest in a salary deferral option, a SEP is not a good choice. The employer should consider a 401(k) plan. A SIMPLE is not appropriate because the employer wants discretionary contributions.

    d. Because of the interest in purchasing stock using leveraging, an ESOP is the right choice.

4. Both Sally and Rich are eligible. Each earns more than $600 (as indexed for 2017) in 3 of the 5 calendar years prior to the year in question.

5. A SIMPLE can only be sponsored by an employer that does not sponsor another type of retirement plan and does not have more than 100 employees. It has to be available to those employees who earn at least $5,000 in 2 calendar years, and eligible employees must be given the right to defer up to $12,500 (2017 limit) of compensation. The employer either has to make a 2 percent nonelective contribution for all eligible contributions or a dollar-for-dollar matching contribution up to 3 percent of compensation. No other contributions are allowed, and all contributions

must be fully vested. SIMPLEs are funded with IRAs so that the investment restrictions, access to funds, and other considerations that apply to SEPs also apply to SIMPLEs.

6. An employer is required to make a contribution every year. The contribution can be a 2 percent contribution for all eligible employees or a matching contribution. The matching contribution must be a dollar-for-dollar match, with a maximum contribution of 3 percent of compensation. With the matching contribution, the employer does have some flexibility. The match can be reduced to as low as one percent of compensation in any 2 of 5 years.

7. The SIMPLE is especially effective for employers looking for their first retirement plan that offers participants the option to make pretax salary deferrals. The plan can work much better than a 401(k) plan if only a small percentage of the workforce intends to make salary deferral contributions.

8. A 403(b) plan can be used in public school districts and 501(c)(3) nonprofit organizations.

9. a. Dr. Smith is eligible because he would be considered a hospital employee and not an independent contractor.

   b. Dr. Jones is an independent contractor and as such is not an employee of the hospital; therefore, he is not eligible for the plan.

   c. Gary Green would also be considered ineligible because of independent contractor status.

   d. Joy Cheerful could be made eligible because she is an employee.

10. A 403(b) plan can only be funded with annuity contracts or mutual fund custodial accounts.

11. In a plan funded with annuity contracts, salary deferral contributions can only be withdrawn in-service if the participant has attained age 59½ or suffers a financial hardship. When the plan is funded with mutual fund custodial accounts, then the in-service withdrawal restrictions apply to all types of contributions.

Chapter 7

Coverage, Eligibility, and Participation Rules

Learning Objectives

An understanding of the material in this chapter should enable the student to

- **LO 7.1** Explain how the adoption agreement can help facilitate the plan design process.
- **LO 7.2** Determine whether a qualified plan satisfies the minimum-coverage requirements of Code Sec. 410(b) and the minimum-participation rule of Code Sec. 401(a)(26).
- **LO 7.3** Identify planning opportunities under the minimum-coverage rules.
- **LO 7.4** Explain the rules for determining when participation must begin.
- **LO 7.5** Describe the impact of the controlled group, affiliated service group, and leased employee rules on tax-advantaged retirement plans.

Perhaps the most challenging assignment in the retirement field is advising a client about how his or her plan should be designed. In order to design a plan effectively, the financial services professional must

- acquire expertise about the qualification rules
- ascertain the client's objectives
- choose plan provisions that meet the qualification rules and accomplish employer objectives

In addition, both the client's objectives and the qualification rules are constantly evolving and require financial services professionals to monitor client needs and to know the latest laws and regulations. In this chapter and the following three chapters, we will define and explore the various plan-design features. The emphasis is on the qualification rules that apply to qualified plans and the ways in which plan design can be used to meet your client's objectives. The last part of the chapter reviews the different rules that apply to other tax-sheltered plans. Let's start, however, with a brief overview of the plan-design process.

THE PLAN-DESIGN PROCESS

The first step toward effective plan design has already been taken. The fact finder that you set up to choose the best retirement plan can also be used to help you properly design the plan. However, the plan design is dictated not only by the client's objectives but also by the laws and regulations regarding plan qualification. In other words, picking the specific provisions that will constitute the client's plan consists of weighing what the Internal Revenue Code permits against the client's objectives and pocketbook. Take, as an example, the first design feature we consider—which employees should be eligible for the plan. The coverage rules are quite complex. In this case, complexity allows a great deal of freedom in plan design, but it also requires intimate knowledge of the boundaries of the law.

LO 7.1 **Explain how the adoption agreement can help facilitate the plan design process.**

adoption agreement

The plan-design process is simplified for insurance agents and other financial services professionals by the use of master and prototype plan documents. With these documents, most of the plan language is standardized and the employer has limited design alternatives, which are contained in a document referred to as the **adoption agreement**. The adoption-agreement approach helps the advisor by organizing the design process. The document is relatively simple to follow because it lists the design features and provides several alternatives under each one (for example, the various vesting schedules and the alternative design choices available for early, normal, and deferred retirement). Employers (with your help) then pick from the menu of options that is provided.

The adoption agreement simplifies plan design by directing and limiting available design options, but it also locks out from consideration some important but nonstandard design choices that might meet a unique employer need. Generally, if employers desire this specialized treatment, they should pay the additional fees to have an attorney, consulting firm, or insurance company home office design the plan (called an individually designed plan). On the other hand, employers willing to buy an "off-the-rack" plan probably can save on fees and yet meet their goals and objectives through the use of the standard design options contained in your company's adoption agreement.

You can see that to properly advise the client, the advisor needs to have an in-depth understanding of the rules. Knowing the options in the adoption agreement is not enough. The advisor must know the limits of the law, so the client will be able to decide when it is time to establish a plan that does not fall within the prototype options.

YOUR FINANCIAL SERVICES PRACTICE: EFFECTIVE PLAN DESIGN

Any design decision you make in one area of the adoption agreement should be consistent with design decisions you make in other areas of the adoption agreement. For example, if the objective of minimizing costs for short-service employees motivates the employer to choose restrictive age and service requirements, then this objective would lead the employer to choose a long vesting schedule and require a year of service before the employee earns a benefit accrual for the year. However, remember the words of Alfred North Whitehead: "Seek simplicity and distrust it." There may be reasons to stray from design consistency to meet a unique employer objective.

QUALIFIED PLAN COVERAGE REQUIREMENTS

LO 7.2 Determine whether a qualified plan satisfies the minimum-coverage requirements of Code Sec. 410(b) and the minimum-participation rule of Code Sec. 401(a)(26).

The first major design decision that faces you and your client is to decide which employees to cover under the retirement plan. This decision is directed by extensive and complicated laws and regulations. As a payback for providing valuable tax advantages for tax-advantaged retirement plans (and consequently losing revenue), the legislature requires that retirement plans must cover a broad spectrum of employees and not just a group of highly compensated employees (who are defined by statute).

All qualified plans are governed by the same qualified plan coverage rules, except that defined-benefit-type plans are subject to an additional coverage requirement. In this section, we review the qualified plan rules. SEPs, SIMPLEs, and 403(b) plans are each subject to separate eligibility requirements, which are discussed at the end of the chapter.

The Definition of a Highly Compensated Employee

Understanding the coverage requirements begins with the identification of the employees who are considered highly compensated employees (HCE). We first encountered the highly compensated group when discussing the 401(k) actual deferral percentage test. As you may recall, highly compensated employees include individuals who are 5-percent owners during the current or previous year and individuals who earned $120,000 (indexed for 2017). Under the second category, the employer can elect to limit the group to only those individuals whose earnings put them in the top 20 percent of all employees.

The 410(b) Rule

Sec. 410(b) of the Internal Revenue Code specifies who must be covered under a qualified plan. The rules are meaningful any time the employer decides not to cover all employees under the plan. The employer may want to exclude one class of workers, such as hourly employees, or employees who are part-time or have short service. In other cases, the employer may want to set up two or more plans, each covering a different group of employees. Essentially, a plan can cover any portion of the workforce, as long as it satisfies one of three tests under Sec. 410(b): the percentage test, the ratio test, or the average-benefit test.

excludible employees

When performing any of these tests, note that certain classes of employees can always be excluded from testing. These include collectively bargained employees, employees who have worked less than one year, certain part-time employees (those who work less than 1,000 hours per year), and employees younger than age 21 (discussed in more detail later in this chapter). These employees are referred to as **excludible employees**. Essentially, this means a plan can always exclude those employees defined as excludible, as well as any additional employees as allowed under one of the three coverage tests.

Also, be aware that when testing a 401(k) plan, an individual eligible to make a salary deferral election is considered a participant in the plan, regardless of whether he or she makes the election to make a salary deferral. For other plans, this is not the case. Subject to several exceptions, a participant must actually receive a contribution (or benefit accrual in a defined-benefit plan) in order to be considered a participant for that year.

The Percentage Test

percentage test

A plan will satisfy Sec. 410(b) if it benefits at least 70 percent of employees who are not highly compensated employees. As just described, employees who are not eligible for participation in the plan because they do not meet the age and service requirements or who are covered by a collective-bargaining agreement (discussed later in the chapter) are not counted for purposes of this test, known as a **percentage test**.

> **EXAMPLE**
>
> The law firm of Block, Meyers, and Andrews has 24 employees. Because four of these employees work part-time and have not met the minimum-service requirements for participation in the plan (discussed later in the chapter), the percentage test would apply only to the remaining 20 employees. Of these employees, 12 fall within the statutory definition of highly compensated and eight do not. Six of the eight employees who are not highly compensated belong to the Manhattan office (the one covered by the plan) and two belong to the Teaneck, New Jersey, office (which does not have a plan). Under the percentage test, the plan must benefit at least 70 percent of the eight

employees who are not highly compensated (note that employees from both offices are counted). That is, six employees (six out of eight is 75 percent) must be benefited. Because the law firm's Manhattan plan benefits six of the nonhighly compensated employees, the plan passes the percentage test.

The Ratio Test

ratio test

The **ratio test** requires a plan to benefit a percentage of nonhighly compensated employees equal to at least 70 percent of the percentage of highly compensated employees benefited under the plan. Again, employees who are not eligible for participation in the plan because they do not meet the age and service requirements or are covered by a collective-bargaining agreement are not counted for purposes of the ratio test.

> **EXAMPLE**
>
> The Thunder Company has 120 employees on its payroll. Because 20 of these have not yet met the plan's minimum age and service requirements, the ratio test would apply to only 100 employees. Thirty of the remaining employees are highly compensated, and 15 of the 30 highly compensated employees actually participate in the plan (the additional 15 are part of a separate group that does not have a plan). Seventy of the remaining employees are nonhighly compensated, and 40 of the 70 nonhighly compensated employees participate in the plan (the additional 30 are part of the separate group that does not have a plan).
>
> Because 50 percent (15 out of 30) of the highly compensated employees participate in the plan, the ratio test requires that at least 35 percent of the nonhighly compensated employees (70% × 50% = 35%) must benefit under the plan. In other words, at least 25 (35% × 70 = 24.5) nonhighly compensated employees must benefit under the plan. Because Thunder Company has 40 nonhighly compensated employees benefiting under the plan, the plan satisfies the ratio test.

Average-Benefit Test

average-benefit percentage test

Another way to satisfy the minimum-coverage requirements is to satisfy the **average-benefits percentage test**. This is a complex analysis that has three separate parts. Here we will summarize these rules and explain when they are generally applied, but will not get into all of the details.

The first requirement under the average-benefits test is that the plan has to cover employees who represent a reasonable classification of employees—which means that the eligibility requirements (specifying who qualifies for participation and who does not) must use some objective means of classification, such as job classification, nature of compensation (salaried or hourly), or geographic location. The second part of the test is a complicated percentage test. Suffice it to say that the percentage of nonhighly compensated employees required to be covered under this section is generally quite small. The third part of the test is the average-benefit-percentage test. This portion is satisfied if the average-benefit percentage for nonhighly compensated employees is at least 70 percent of the average-benefit percentage of the highly compensated employees. This requirement is different from the others in that it counts benefits earned in any qualified plan sponsored by the employer.

In operation, note that the administrator will test the plan under the less complicated percentage and ratio tests before tackling the more complex average-percentage test. The reason for this test is to provide relief for the larger employer that wants to cover most employees under some qualified plan, but chooses to cover them under two or more separate plans. The employer might want to do this because it has different geographic locations or has workers with very different types of jobs. Although the math is complex, the bottom line is that the employer can generally have such an arrangement as long as, overall, the benefits for nonhighly compensated employees under all of the plans are at least 70 percent of the benefits provided to the highly compensated under all of the plans.

For the small employer sponsoring one plan, the average-benefit test will not result in lower required participation than the ratio test. All of the nonhighly compensated employees who are excluded from the plan are counted as having zero benefits when determining whether the average-percentage test has been satisfied. In other words, the small employer sponsoring one plan will have to satisfy the percentage or ratio test. The average-benefit test will be of no help.

Three Minimum-Coverage Tests

- <u>Percentage test</u>—the plan covers at least 70 percent of nonhighly compensated employees
- <u>Ratio test</u>—the percentage of nonhighly compensated employees covered is at least 70 percent of the percentage of HCEs covered under the plan
- <u>Average-benefit test</u>—the group covered represents a reasonable classification, a complex minimum percentage test is satisfied, and the benefits of nonhighly compensated employees average at least 70 percent of the benefits provided to HCEs, looking at all of the sponsor's retirement plans

Separate Lines of Business

separate lines of business

If an employer has separate lines of business, the 410(b) tests may be applied separately in each line of business. In order to qualify for this favorable treatment, the separate lines of business must be operated for bona fide business reasons and must have at least 50 employees. The IRS has issued complex regulations for determining whether a **separate line of business** exists. Because of the difficulty of demonstrating compliance, most employers will look to the separate-lines-of-business rules only as a last resort—when trying to ensure that each plan meets the coverage requirements.

Coverage of Employees in Comparable Plans

For various reasons an employer may want to establish two or more plans for separate groups of employees. The sponsor may have different business locations, or have acquired the retirement plan of a subsidiary. If one or more of the plans cannot satisfy the coverage rules on their own, Sec. 410(b) allows the plans to be aggregated and tested together, as long as their total combined benefits do not discriminate in favor of the highly compensated. Chapter 8 clarifies the nondiscrimination requirements.

The 401(a)(26) Minimum-Participation Rule

401(a)(26) minimum-participation rule

Defined-benefit plans must satisfy a second coverage requirement under Code Sec. 401(a)(26), referred to as the **401(a)(26) minimum-participation rule**. Under this rule, an employer's plan is not qualified unless it covers (1) 50 employees or (2) 40 percent of the employer's employees, whichever is lesser. However, a special rule applies when there are two employees; in this case, both employees must be covered.

This rule does not count employees who are not eligible because of the age and service requirements or who are part of a group covered by a collective-bargaining agreement. The effect of this rule is that employers with more than 125 employees cannot maintain a plan covering fewer than 50 participants, and if the employer has fewer than 125 employees, then the 40 percent limit applies. The result is that smaller employers are limited to a maximum of two separate plans (in order to meet the 40-percent rule).

Apparently, the justification to have an additional eligibility requirement for defined-benefit plans is because Congress is concerned that small employers would establish defined-benefit plans that only covered the companies' owners and would cover other employees under a separate defined-contribution plan with less value. The minimum-participation requirement eliminates this possibility.

Planning Opportunities under the Coverage Rules

LO 7.3   Identify planning opportunities under the minimum-coverage rules.

As we have seen, the qualified plan coverage rules provide a significant amount of flexibility. This allows the employer to meet a range of objectives. Some employers will see the value of covering all employees, while some will want to save costs by excluding certain employees. Others will want to provide a different level of benefits for different classes of employees. And some small employers will simply want to maximize retirement benefits for owners and key employees and limit the expense of providing benefits for the rank-and-file employees. Here, we will discuss some of the tools that can be used to satisfy these objectives.

Advantages of Covering Employees

Covering employees does have an associated cost, and an employer may be tempted to limit coverage as much as possible. Before taking this action, the employer should appreciate that there can be real value to covering employees. This is not an idealistic plea for the underdog or merely an opportunity to increase commissions for the financial advisor—there are sound business reasons to cover employees.

First, an employee who is not covered by the plan resents being excluded and will eventually seek employment elsewhere. Even if the employer spent only 40 work-hours training that individual, 80 work-hours have been lost because the training process must be repeated with the replacement. The cycle is also apt to repeat itself several times. What's more, the most important asset a small business can have is experienced rank-and-file employees. There is little room for inexperienced, unproductive, or counterproductive people in any organization, and—especially in small businesses—retirement plans go a long way toward coaxing employees to remain long enough to become experienced, productive workers.

The second reason to cover the rank-and-file in a small business is to encourage loyalty and team spirit. For small businesses, it is crucial that their employees be not only experienced but also committed to the welfare of the business. The result is that the principal reasons to encourage a retirement umbrella that covers all employees is that the business is best served by this arrangement and that it is cost-effective to include nonkey employees.

Excluding Employees

If the employer does want to limit coverage, the rules allow the employer to exclude a portion of the workforce. As discussed in this chapter, the rules allow the employer to exclude the following employees:

- All employees who have not satisfied minimum age and service requirements or who are subject to a collective bargaining agreement (often referred to as excludibles) can be excluded without issue.
- If the plan covers all of the highly compensated employees, up to 30 percent of the (nonexcludible) nonhighly compensated employees can also be excluded.
- Any HCE can be excluded from coverage.
- If the plan excludes some of the highly compensated employees, even more than 30 percent of the nonhighly compensated employees can be excluded.

Also note that if the employer excludes all highly compensated employees, the plan can cover any group of nonhighly compensated employees without regard to either coverage rule. This strategy will not work for many small employers, but occasionally the employer may be satisfied to provide executive benefits through a nonqualified plan. This approach can make sense if the employer wants to cover a very small percentage of the rank-and-file employees.

More typically, at least some highly compensated are covered. But as you can see in the example below, the coverage tests (specifically the ratio test) allow the exclusion of a significant number of rank-and-file employees when some of the highly compensated employees are excluded from the plan. This rule can be effective for small businesses when some highly compensated employees are not interested in participating in the plan because they are very young, very old, or not interested for other reasons.

EXAMPLE

Loophole, Inc., has 10 employees (who are not excludibles). Two are highly compensated and eight are not. If the employer establishes a defined-contribution plan that covers one highly compensated employee, only 35 percent, or three, of the nonhighly compensated employees have to be covered. This is because, under the ratio test, 70 percent of the percentage of highly compensated employees covered (50 percent) equals 35 percent.

One important limitation applies to the rules as described. The Age Discrimination in Employment Act (ADEA) prohibits discrimination against individuals aged 40 and older. To avoid problems under this act (and possibly other state laws), a plan provision excluding a group of employees from a qualified plan should be based on a reasonable (and real) job classification. For example, the plan may exclude hourly employees, secretaries, associate attorneys, or other job classifications. It is a good idea to seek the advice of a labor or employment lawyer when addressing this specific issue. Also, remember that defined-benefit plans have to satisfy the minimum participation rule.

Other Planning Strategies

When the employer wants to limit costs for rank-and-file employees, there are a number of other strategies, which include the following:

- *Delay participation.* As described below, the rules allow the employer to defer participation up to 6 months after attaining the eligibility requirements. Taking advantage of these rules eliminates the costs of covering some short-term employees.
- *Minimize the benefit.* In the next chapter, we discuss another way to limit costs—to cover many employees but limit the benefit for rank-and-file employees. This can be accomplished by using a defined-benefit plan, target-benefit plan, or cross-tested profit-sharing plan when the owners are older than the rank-and-file employees.
- *Divide into separate employers.* One strategy that generally will not work is to establish a plan for the key employees, and then create a separate business entity for the rank-and-file employees. As discussed below, in most cases these separate entities will be treated as a single employer, and this creates a problem under the aggregation rules

WHEN SHOULD PARTICIPATION BEGIN?

LO 7.4   Explain the rules for determining when participation must begin.

Once you and your client have decided on the employees who should and must be covered, the next step is to decide when an employee's participation should begin. In general, participation can be delayed for certain employees on the basis of their ages and their years of service with the company.

There are several reasons to delay participation as long as legally possible. For one thing, employees do not start earning benefits until they become plan participants (except in defined-benefit plans, which may count service with the employer prior to the participation date for benefit purposes). Also, by delaying participation, the client's organization can save retirement dollars attributable to turnover. A second cost-saving feature of delayed participation involves the administrative and record-keeping duties associated with tracking employees who leave. Because turnover is highest for employees in their first few years of employment and for younger employees, it makes sense from an administrative standpoint to delay their participation in the plan. Besides, if the retirement plan is funded with individual insurance policies, the employer loses out on funds that provide death benefits and the commissions paid for benefits for employees who leave (the front-end load).

There are, on the other hand, some good reasons to begin participation immediately. These include the maximization of contributions for employees by not delaying coverage and attracting specialized employees by making the plan highly competitive. These specialized employees (such as a computer professional or a high-powered salesperson) usually possess desired skills or profit-making ability, and any delay in participation may make the plan's benefit package less appealing to them.

21-and-one rule

If your client's circumstances warrant immediate participation, then the plan should be designed appropriately. But even under such circumstances, the client must still adhere to the statutory participation rules. In general, any employee who is not excluded from the plan based upon employment classification must become a participant no later than the first entry date after the employee meets the plan's age and service requirements. The maximum age and service requirements are age 21 and one year of service (commonly referred to as the **21-and-one rule**). After an employee becomes 21 and has completed one year of service, he or she is entitled to join the plan on the next plan entry date.

The 2-Year/100 Percent Rule

2-year/100 percent rule

There is one exception that applies to the general 21-and-one rule, and that is a special provision that allows up to a 2-year service requirement if the employee is immediately 100 percent vested upon becoming a participant (called the **2-year/100 percent rule**). This method is desirable if the company's vesting schedules are already as liberal as the 2-year/100 percent schedule and your client desires to delay participation as long as possible. If your client wants both a more restrictive vesting schedule and to delay participation, however, you will have to determine which carries more weight—the maximum-service requirement or the restrictive vesting schedules.

Entry Date

The last component associated with plan participation is the selection of an entry date for employees to become participants in the plan. An employee who meets the plan's minimum age and service requirements, and who is otherwise eligible to participate in the plan, must be allowed to participate no later than the earlier of (1) the first day of the first plan year beginning after the date the employee met the age and service requirements, or (2) the date 6 months after these conditions are met. In other words, entry dates can delay participation up to 6 months after the 21-and-one or 2-year/100 percent hurdles are jumped. For clients who want to delay participation as long as possible, semiannual entry dates should be set up, typically January 1 and July 1. This way, the employer can maximize the pre-participation period. Other typical entry dates include the plan's anniversary date (this can be used only if the age requirement is not more than 20 ½ and the service requirement is 6 months or less), quarterly entry dates, monthly entry dates, and daily entry dates.

Determining Service

The term year of service has a special meaning for purposes of meeting the one-year-of-service or 2-years-of-service eligibility requirements. An employee who works 1,000 hours during the initial 12-month period after being employed will earn a year of service. For example, Larry is hired on October 5, 2016. If Larry has worked at least 1,000 hours or more by October 4, 2017, he has acquired a year of service. Note that Larry does not receive a year of service after he worked his 1,000th hour, but rather on his first anniversary of employment.

The phrase an hour of service also has a special meaning; it includes not only the hours an employee works, but also any hours for which an employee is entitled to be paid, such as for vacations, holidays, and sick time. One way to compute the hours for purposes of the 1,000-hour requirement is to count each hour an employee works for which he or she is entitled to be paid (the standard-hours counting method).

Because the standard-hours counting method can be administratively cumbersome, the IRC permits alternative counting methods—called equivalencies—to be used. However, in choosing an equivalency, the employer pays a premium of extra hours for using this administratively convenient system. Therefore, another aspect of plan design is to help your client choose the best alternative. Equivalencies include the following:

- The elapsed-time method, which does not look at hours of service worked because service is measured from date of employment to date of severance. For example, if Barbara starts working on January 18, she would have one year of service on the following January 18, regardless of how many hours she actually worked.

- The hours-worked-including-overtime method, which looks at the actual hours worked including overtime but excluding nonworked hours such as vacations, holidays, and sick time. If this test is used, an employee needs to work only 870 hours to earn a year of service.

- The hours-worked-excluding-overtime method, which looks at the actual hours worked, excluding overtime, vacations, holidays, and sick time. If this test is used, an employee needs only 750 hours for a year of service.
- The time-period or pay-period method, which looks at the days, weeks, semimonthly pay periods, months, or shifts actually worked by the employee and applies the following equivalencies:
- The hours-worked-excluding-overtime method, which looks at the actual hours worked, excluding overtime, vacations, holidays, and sick time. If this test is used, an employee needs only 750 hours for a year of service.
- The time-period or pay-period method, which looks at the days, weeks, semimonthly pay periods, months, or shifts actually worked by the employee and applies the following equivalencies:
    - a credit of 10 hours of service per day if the employee worked one hour in any day
    - a credit of 45 hours of service per week if the employee worked one hour in any week
    - a credit of 95 hours of service per semimonthly pay period if the employee worked one hour in any pay period
    - a credit of 190 hours per month if the employee worked one hour in any month
    - a credit of the number of hours per shift if the employee worked one hour in any shift
- The equivalencies-based-on-earnings method, which calculates the hours worked on the basis of the employee's earnings. For example, if the employee is paid hourly, the equivalency can be determined by dividing the employee's total earnings by the hourly wage. (If the hourly wage changed over a period, the employer should look at the actual hourly wage, the lowest hourly wage during the period, or the lowest hourly wage paid to employees in the same or similar job classification during that period.) If the employee's earnings are not based on hourly rates, the hourly rate is calculated by translating the employee's salary into an hourly rate—for example, by dividing annual salary by a 40-hour week or 8-hour day.

Your Financial Services Practice: The Eligibility and Participation Rules In A Sample Adoption Agreement

The following sample illustrates how the rules might appear in a typical adoption agreement (note that terms with the first letter capitalized are defined in the plan):

Section B: Eligibility (refers to Section 2 of the plan)

1. The Age and Service requirements for participation in the Plan are
   a. attainment of age ___ (not to exceed 21)
   b. completion of ___ year(s) of service (not to exceed one year, unless the Plan provides full and immediate vesting (Section G). (If the Plan provides for full and immediate vesting, it is not to exceed 2 years.)
2. The Plan's entry date will be (check one)

   ( ) daily

      ( ) the Friday in any calendar week

      ( ) the first day of any calendar month

      ( ) quarterly (Jan. 1, April 1, July 1, Oct. 1)

      ( ) semiannually (Jan. 1, July 1)

      ( ) annually (Jan. 1) (Note: If the entry date is annually then the age requirement in Section

        B(1)(a) cannot exceed 20 ½ and the service requirement in Section B(1)(b) cannot be more than 6 months.)

3. Hours of service shall be determined on the basis of the method selected below. The method selected shall be applied to all employees covered under the Plan

   (check one)

      ( ) On the basis of actual hours for which an employee is paid or entitled to payment

      ( ) On the basis of days worked. An employee shall be credited with 10 hours of service if, under Section 19 of the Plan, such employee would be credited with at least one hour of service during the day.

      ( ) On the basis of weeks worked. An employee shall be credited with 45 hours of service if, under Section 19 of the Plan, such employee would be credited with at least one hour of service during the week.

      ( ) On the basis of semimonthly payroll periods. An employee shall be credited with 95 hours of service if, under Section 19 of the Plan, such employee would be credited with at least one hour of service during the semimonthly payroll period.

      ( ) On the basis of months worked. An employee shall be credited with 190 hours of service if, under Section 19 of the Plan, such

employee would be credited with at least one hour of service during the month.

The choice of an equivalency boils down to two disparate considerations. The first is administrative convenience. By coordinating the hours of service with payroll's records, the employer may be able to use an existing computer or accounting system and eliminate duplication of work efforts. The second and more important concern when choosing an hour-of-service definition is to permanently exclude part-time employees from the plan. This can result in substantial savings for your client. If your client wants to exclude part-time employees, as is usually the case, then it is likely that the standard-hours counting method should be used in lieu of any equivalency (note that all equivalency methods generously define the hours used). To make sure part-time employees do not slip in under these rules—and complicate administration of the plan—the employer may want to establish a policy that limits the number of hours part-time employees can work.

Case Study: The Matthew Matt Manufacturing Company

The Matthew Matt Manufacturing Company, makers of wrestling mats, employs 75 full-time employees and 15 part-time employees. Owner Matthew Matt is establishing a qualified plan and is trying to determine the appropriate eligibility and participation provisions. He desires to minimize costs, encourage rank-and-file employees to stay (experienced mat makers are hard to find), and exclude part-time employees from the plan. In addition, Matthew tells you that a competitive wrestling mat company is forming in the area. The relevant questions the financial services professional must address are these:

- Should participation be delayed and, if so, for how long?
- What definition of hour of service should be used?
- What entry date should be used?

In answer to the first question, Matthew Matt should delay participation as a cost-saving measure. When a plan is installed in an existing business, however, the employer must take into account the service already acquired (preplan service) for eligibility purposes. In this case, to placate employees who might jump to the competitor, the plan will count preplan service.

How long Matthew delays participation—which could be for one or 2 years, the statutory maximums—would depend on his decision about vesting and his perception of the competitive threat.

Because Matthew wants to exclude part-time employees to the fullest possible extent, the company will choose the most restrictive method for determining whether the

1,000-hours-of-service requirement has been met. This is generally the standard-hours counting method. However, if Matthew uses his part-time employees seasonally (for 2 months during wrestling season) and needs them for overtime during that period, then the most restrictive method might be the hours-worked-excluding-overtime method. This method looks at the actual hours worked and excludes overtime, the Christmas holidays (which fall in wrestling season), sick time, and the like.

When choosing an entry date, considerations such as administrative convenience and employee morale also come into play. Because employee morale is most important in light of the threat of competition, it will probably be desirable to choose a less restrictive entry date that matches administrative pay practices—monthly, for example.

AGGREGATION RULES

LO 7.5 Describe the impact of the controlled group, affiliated service group, and leased employee rules on tax-advantaged retirement plans.

To avoid the coverage requirements, some employers try to segregate their management employees from the rank-and-file employees by creating a related or subsidiary corporation. To close this loophole, the Code contains what are referred to as the controlled-group rules that require aggregation of employers that have a sufficient amount of common ownership, and the affiliated service groups rules for other situations in which related businesses work together to provide goods or services to the public. When either aggregation rule applies, the employers are treated as one employer for virtually all of the qualified plan rules. Both rules apply to corporations and "trades and businesses," including partnerships, proprietorships, estates, and trusts. Note that the affiliation rules also apply to SEPs, SIMPLEs, and 403(b) plans. Regulations provide guidance for determining ownership interests in these kinds of entities.

A third type of affiliation relates to situations in which individuals are "leased" on a long-term, full-time basis. In some cases, such individuals are treated as working for the recipient for purposes of the coverage requirements. Each of these rules is covered more fully below.

Controlled-Group Rules

controlled group

There are three types of controlled groups: parent-subsidiary controlled group, brother-sister controlled group, and combined groups. A parent-subsidiary **controlled group** exists whenever one entity (referred to as the parent company) owns at least 80 percent of one (or more) of the other entities. Additional entities may be brought into the group if a chain of common ownership exists. Other entities included in the chain must be at least 80 percent owned by one or more (in combination) of the other entities within the chain.

EXAMPLE

Corporation A owns 80 percent of Corporations B and C, and Corporations B and C each own 40 percent of Corporation D. Because Corporation D is 80 percent owned by entities within the group, Corporation D is part of the parent-subsidiary controlled group that includes all four corporations.

A brother-sister controlled group exists whenever the same five (or fewer) owners of two or more entities own 80 percent or more of each entity, and more than 50 percent of each entity when counting only identical ownership. Identical ownership is tested by counting each person's ownership to the extent that it is identical in each entity. For example, if an individual owns 10 percent of Corporation A and 20 percent of Corporation B, he or she has a 10 percent identical ownership interest with respect to each corporation. The identical ownership interests of each of the five (or fewer) individuals is added together to determine whether the 50-percent test has been satisfied, as shown in Table 7-1 for these shareholders.

Table 7-1
Identical Ownership

Shareholder	Corporation X	Corporation Y	Identical Ownership
Joe	20%	12%	12%
Sally	60%	14%	14%
Ralph	20%	74%	20%
Total	100%	100%	46%

Under these assumed facts, the 80 percent ownership test has been met, because three individuals who have ownership in each entity own 100 percent of both businesses. However, the 50-percent-identical-ownership-interest test has not been satisfied (only 46 percent identical ownership). Therefore, this group does not constitute a controlled group.

Several operational rules are extremely important when determining brother-sister controlled group status. First, when performing the 80-percent test, only shareholders owning interests in each potential member of the group are counted; any shareholder who does not own stock in all of the companies being considered is ignored.

> **EXAMPLE**
> A owns 100 percent of Alpha and 50 percent of Beta and B owns 50 percent of Beta. Since A is the only individual with an ownership interest in both companies, no controlled group exists, as A does not own at least 80 percent of both companies.

Another key consideration is the stock attribution rule that applies to stock owned by certain family members. First, a spouse is generally deemed to own an interest owned directly or indirectly by or for his or her spouse. However, attribution is not required if the spouses are separated or divorced, or in situations in which an individual has no direct ownership interests in the entity owned by his or her spouse and is not an employee, director, or otherwise involved in the management of the company.

An individual is considered to own an interest owned by the individual's children who are under age 21. Also, children under age 21 are attributed ownership interests of parents. Because of this attribution rule, if a husband and wife each own 100 percent of their own businesses and they have a child under age 21, the child is deemed to own both businesses. Therefore, a controlled group will exist even if the spousal exception would otherwise apply.

In addition, when a person owns more than 50 percent of an entity, he or she is deemed to own any interest owned in that entity by his or her adult children, grandchildren, parents, and grandparents.

Types of Controlled Groups
- Parent-subsidiary
- Brother-sister
- Combined

The last type of controlled group is the combined group under common control. A combined group exists if an entity is both a common parent in a parent-subsidiary group and a member of a brother-sister group. If this is the case, the two related controlled groups are treated as one controlled group.

Affiliated Service Group Rules

affiliated service group

In 1980, Congress enacted the first **affiliated service group** rules. Small business corporations had managed to divide management and the rank-and-file into separate entities and avoid the controlled-group rules. The rules have been expanded several times over the years to address new avoidance schemes. Today, the law is quite complex, and the details are beyond the scope of this book. However, when working with clients, there are several threshold issues that help advisors to identify when affiliation problems might be present. Except for management services affiliation (discussed below), affiliated groups exist only when all three of the following elements are present:

- two or more business entities work together to provide one service or product to the public
- at least one of the entities is a service organization
- at least some common ownership exists between the two entities

A service organization is an organization for which capital is not a material income-producing factor. Generally capital is deemed a material income-producing factor if a substantial portion of gross income is attributable to substantial investments in such things as plant and inventory. Organizations in the fields of health, law, engineering, actuarial science, consulting, and insurance are always treated as service organizations.

The affiliation rules come into play regularly in the medical world, where there are partnerships between doctors and hospitals that provide services in outpatient clinics, MRI testing centers, and other cooperative medical centers. In these cases, there must be a careful analysis to see if the MRI testing center, for example, is affiliated with the doctor's medical practice or with the hospital.

Management services affiliation is defined by a much broader rule, which essentially prohibits an executive of any size company from separating him or herself from the company for the purpose of establishing his or her own retirement plan.

A management-affiliated group consists of

- an organization whose principal business is performing, on a regular and continuing basis, management functions for one organization (management organization), and
- the organization for which such functions are so performed (recipient organization).

The Leasing of Employees

Instead of hiring employees directly, a business may lease employees from a third party for a number of legitimate reasons. Unfortunately, at one time, leasing of employees was also used as a way to circumvent the minimum-coverage requirements. The employer would lease rank-and-file employees and then exclude them from plan eligibility. Code Sec. 414(n) was enacted to eliminate such practices by requiring that individuals leased on a full-time, ongoing basis would be treated as employees for purposes of the coverage requirements.

leased employee

A **leased employee** is a person who provides services to the recipient and meets all three of the following requirements:

- The services are provided pursuant to an agreement between the recipient and a leasing organization.
- The services are provided on a substantially full-time basis for a period of at least one year.
- The individual's services are performed under the primary direction or control of the service recipient.

Services are deemed to be substantially full time for a year if the individual is credited with 1,500 or more hours of service (this number is reduced if employees generally work fewer than 40 hours per week).

Even if an individual is a leased employee under the above conditions, he or she will not be treated as an employee of the recipient if leased employees constitute no more than 20 percent of the recipient's nonhighly compensated workforce and the leasing entity maintains a safe harbor plan. A safe harbor plan must be a money-purchase plan with a nonintegrated contribution rate of at least 10 percent of compensation and must provide for immediate eligibility and 100 percent immediate vesting.

The objective of the leased employee rule is to ensure that a company cannot avoid covering a large number of employees by leasing them versus hiring them directly. On the other hand, if the employer leases only a few individuals, the minimum-coverage rules have enough latitude to allow the leased employees to be excluded from the qualified plan—or, in the alternative, the leased individuals can be ignored if the leasing organization maintains a safe harbor qualified plan. In this way, the leased employee rules work fairly well to eliminate abusive situations without penalizing the average employer.

YOUR FINANCIAL SERVICES PRACTICE: AVOIDING HIDDEN AGGREGATION PROBLEMS

One common problem the financial services professional faces when setting up a retirement plan is finding out important information at the last minute or after the fact. For example, an employer who is interested in setting up a plan for the ABC Company may also own the XYZ Company, but fails to mention this important information. Because it is possible that the employees of both ABC and XYZ must be considered for the purposes of the coverage requirements, it is important to question the employer about additional holdings, other key employees' additional holdings, and the corporation's additional holdings. (See Step 8 in the fact finder in chapter 3.) In the small-company context, the minimum-coverage rules are unforgiving, and an employer who misses a controlled-group issue may very well end up with one or more disqualified plans. The problem is even worse with a SEP or SIMPLE where the coverage rules have no flexibility at all. This is a complex area of the law, and the role of the pension advisor should be to identify affiliation issues and then encourage the client to pursue a final determination from a qualified tax attorney.

Finally, note that the controlled-group rules, affiliated service rules, and leased employee rules were written to eliminate most situations in which entities were artificially separated so a qualified plan would cover only some of the employees. Be careful when looking at any arrangement that "smells bad." The rules are fairly comprehensive—most such schemes are prohibited. This is one area of the law where if it looks too good to be true, it probably is!

OTHER TAX-SHELTERED RETIREMENT PLANS

While the eligibility and participation requirements for qualified plans are quite flexible, this is not the case for **SEPs** and SIMPLEs. The rules here are rather rigid. The same eligibility requirements that apply to qualified plans apply to 403(b) plans, as well as an additional requirement that applies to salary deferral elections. Also note that the aggregation rules discussed in this chapter apply when performing the coverage tests for 403(b) plans, SEPs, and SIMPLEs.

As described in chapter 6, any individual (not subject to a collective bargaining agreement) who is aged 21 and has earned $600 (The indexed amount for earnings in the previous year for 2016 and 2017.) In 2018, to determine if someone is eligible you will look at what they made in 2017, and see if that was at least $600 in 2017. in 3 of the 5 previous plan years must be a participant as of the first day of the following plan year. Take, for example, an individual who meets the compensation requirement in 2015, 2016, and 2017 (by receiving compensation of at least $600 in each year) and works for a company that maintains a SEP on a calendar-year basis. That person must have become a participant as of January 1, 2018.

Under these inflexible requirements, all long-term employees—even part-timers—must be covered under the plan. This causes problems for larger employers that may want to establish separate plans for different groups of employees and employers with a significant number of part-time employees. Finally, note that nothing in the SEP rules stops an employer from establishing less restrictive eligibility requirements.

SIMPLEs

Similar to SEPs, SIMPLEs have totally inflexible coverage requirements. The rules, however, are different from both the qualified plan and the SEP requirements. The SIMPLE must cover any employee (including those under age 21) who earned $5,000 in any two previous calendar years and is reasonably expected to earn $5,000 again in the current year. Employees subject to a collectively bargained agreement can be excluded. SIMPLEs can be maintained only on a calendar-year basis. All employees become eligible to participate as of the January 1 after they have earned $5,000 in two prior years. Essentially, SEPs have a 3-year waiting period, while SIMPLEs have a 2-year waiting period.

403(b) Plans

All 403(b) plans are subject to a special eligibility provision. With regard to the opportunity to make salary deferral elections, all full-time employees who can contribute $200 or more must be given the option to make a salary deferral election. Exceptions are made for employees who normally work fewer than 20 hours per week and employees eligible to make salary deferral elections to other types of plans, including 401(k) and 457 plans. If a 403(b) plan includes employer contributions (that are not related to a salary reduction agreement), the plan must generally satisfy the 410(b) requirement discussed earlier in this chapter. However, church plans and government sponsored plans are exempt from this requirement.

CHAPTER REVIEW

Key Terms and Concepts

adoption agreement
excludible employees
percentage test
ratio test
average-benefit percentage test
separate lines of business
401(a)(26) minimum-participation rule

21-and-one rule
2-year/100 percent rule
controlled group
affiliated service group
leased employee

Chapter 7: Review Questions

Review questions are based on the learning objectives in this chapter. Thus, a [7.3] at the end of a question means that the question is based on learning objective 3. If there are multiple objectives, they are all listed.

1. List two planning tools that can be used in the plan-design process. [7.1]

2. Which of the following employees of the Off the Books Company (a business accounting computer software firm) are considered highly compensated employees in 2017, assuming the company makes the election to limit highly compensated to those in the top 20 percent group? [7.2]

	2016 Salary
Al Abernathy (96% stock owner/president)	$200,000
Becky Brooks (4% stock owner/vice president)	150,000
Charlie Carr (secretary)	125,000
Dick Dawson (treasurer)	60,000
Ellen Elko	30,000
Fran Forcey	25,000
Greg Gillespie	25,000
Hanna Hill	20,000
Isabel Ingram	20,000
James Jordan	20,000

3. Describe the three ways to satisfy the minimum-coverage requirements of IRC Sec. 410(b). [7.2]

4. What do the separate-line-of-business rules allow an employer to do, and what are the basic requirements necessary to satisfy the separate-line-of-business rules? [7.2]

5. Explain the 401(a)(26) nondiscrimination rule and the types of plans subject to this rule. [7.2]

6. Dr. Ebenezer Smith would like to cover the minimum amount of employees in his office's qualified plan. What factors should be brought to his attention regarding the effects of avoiding coverage of rank-and-file employees? [7.3]

7. Discuss the opportunities available for limiting participation under a qualified plan. [7.3]

8. The B&W architectural firm is thinking of amending its qualified plan. [7.4]

    a. List the pros and cons of delaying participation in the plan for as long as possible.

b. If the B&W firm chooses to have an entry date that occurs only once annually (January 1), what maximum age and service requirements can be used?

9. a. What are the various methods that can be used to count hours of service in a qualified plan? [7.4]

b. What are the design considerations underlying the selection of an hour-of-service provision?

10. What happens when two companies are treated as one under the controlled group or affiliated service group rules? [7.5]

11. Does an individual who is considered a leased employee have to be covered by the recipient company's retirement plan? [7.5]

12. In addition to their involvement in the Off the Books Company, Al Abernathy and Becky Brooks (see question 2) are 50 percent co-owners and the only employees of By the Numbers, Inc., a consulting firm that advises companies about their accounting systems. Answer the following questions about the treatment of these businesses under the nondiscrimination rules: [7.5]

a. Will Off the Books and By the Numbers be aggregated for purposes of the nondiscrimination tests?

b. Assuming that Off the Books has a defined-contribution plan that covers all of its 10 employees and that By the Numbers has no plan, will the Off the Books plan pass the 410(b) nondiscrimination requirements?

c. Assuming that By the Numbers has a defined-contribution plan that covers its two employees and Off the Books does not have a plan, will the By the Numbers plan pass the 410(b) nondiscrimination requirements?

d. What effect does the separate-line-of-business exception have on the answer in part (c) above?

13. Describe the coverage rules that apply to SEPs, SIMPLEs, and 403(b) plans. [7.5]

Chapter 7: Review Answers

1. The design process is facilitated by the use of a detailed fact finder and the adoption agreement that makes up the optional part of a prototype plan.

2. Highly compensated employees include individuals who are 5 percent owners during the current or previous year and individuals who earned more than the dollar limit in the previous year. For 2016, the "previous year" in our problem, the limit was $120,000. Moreover, under the $120,000 rule, the employer can—and in the example did—elect to limit the group to only those individuals whose earnings put them in the top 20 percent of all employees. Because this group has 10 employees, only the two highest paid (Al Abernathy and Becky Brooks) are in the top 20 percent group.

    - Al Abernathy is a highly compensated employee because he is a more-than-5-percent owner.
    - Becky Brooks is a highly compensated employee because she earns over $120,000 in annual compensation from the employer and her earnings put her in the top 20 percent group.
    - Charlie Carr is not a highly compensated employee because, even though he earns more than $120,000, he is not in the top 20 percent group. He is the third highest paid employee in a group of 10 employees. It does not matter that he is an officer.
    - The rest of the employees do not fit the definition of a highly compensated employee.

3. The three ways are: percentage test, ratio test, and average-benefits test.

4. If an employer has qualifying separate lines of business, the 410(b) test performed is counting only the employees of the separate line of business. To qualify, the line of business must be operated for bona fide business reasons and must have at least 50 employees.

5. Every defined-benefit plan must cover the lesser of 50 employees or 40 percent of the entire workforce. However, if there are only two employees, both must be covered.

6. Even though the law allows an employer to exclude some employees from a qualified plan, the decision to include or exclude employees is more of a business decision. Exclusion could result in dissatisfied employees who do not stay with the company for long.

7. The law provides that short-term employees, part-time employees, and HCEs can be excluded from the plan. Also, up to an additional 30 percent of the nonhighly compensated workforce can be excluded, as long as the Age Discrimination in Employment law is not violated.

8. a. The benefits to the architectural firm of delaying participation are (1) to save retirement dollars attributable to turnover, (2) to save administrative and record-keeping costs, (3) to save front-end load costs if insurance policies are used to fund the plan, and (4) to help the firm's plan pass nondiscrimination tests because employees who have not met the minimum age and service requirements are not required to be counted for nondiscrimination purposes.

    The architectural firm may want to avoid delay in plan participation because immediate participation allows employees to maximize retirement benefits, and it helps to attract key employees by making the plan highly competitive. In this case, B&W should consider what is best for the firm, keeping in mind these factors, as well as its hiring practices and objectives.

    b. If an annual entry date is chosen, the age requirement cannot be more than 20 ½, and the service requirement cannot be more than 6 months.

9. a. In addition to counting actual hours worked, there is the elapsed-time method, hours-worked-excluding-overtime method, and a number of pay-period methods.

    b. When picking a counting method, the employer will be concerned about administrative convenience as well as choosing a method that does not include part-time employees who could have been excluded under another counting method.

10. The employees of both companies are counted when performing the coverage requirements—even if the plan only covers one of the companies.

11. Under the leased employee rules, the leased employee generally has to be counted as an employee when determining whether the plan satisfies the coverage requirements. Leased employees do not actually need to be covered unless they are needed to satisfy the coverage requirements. Leased employees can be disregarded entirely if no more than 20 percent of the recipient company's nonhighly compensated employees are leased and the leasing entity maintains a safe harbor plan.

12. a. All businesses under common control are treated as a single employer in determining whether the proper number of employees are covered under the plan. Off the Books and By the Numbers would be considered under common

control because they are a brother-sister group. This is because Al and Becky each have ownership interests in both companies—together they own 100 percent of both companies (satisfying the 80 percent test), and they have an identical ownership interest of 54 percent (satisfying the 50 percent test). Remember, under the 50 percent test, Al's identical ownership is 50 percent (the lesser of his 95 percent ownership in Off the Books and his 50 percent ownership interest in By the Numbers), and Becky's identical ownership interest is 4 percent (the lesser of her 50 percent interest in By the Numbers and her 4 percent interest in Off the Books). Because both ownership tests are satisfied, the companies have to be aggregated (considered together) to determine whether the coverage tests are satisfied.

b. The Off the Books plan will satisfy the 410(b) nondiscrimination requirement, even though it is aggregated with By the Numbers, Inc., because it passes the percentage test. To pass the percentage test, at least 70 percent of the nonhighly compensated employees have to be covered. In fact, because all Off the Books employees are covered and none of the By the Numbers employees are nonhighly compensated, 100 percent of the nonhighly compensated employees are covered (more than the 70 percent required). Because the plan is a defined-contribution plan, it is not required to satisfy the 401(a)(26) minimum-participation test. Therefore, all of the coverage requirements have been met.

c. The By the Numbers plan will not satisfy the 410(b) nondiscrimination requirements. Because the two plans must be aggregated, the seven nonhighly compensated employees from Off the Books must be counted. This means that zero percent of the nonhighly compensated employees are covered, hence neither the percentage nor the ratio test is satisfied. Finally, the average-benefit-percentage test is not satisfied; because the nonhighly compensated employees receive no benefits, the average-benefit percentage for nonhighly compensated employees cannot be at least 70 percent of the average-benefit percentage of highly compensated employees.

d. The separate-line-of-business exception does not apply because a separate line of business must have at least 50 employees. Therefore, this escape route is closed to small businesses such as those involved in this case.

13. SEPs must cover employees who have attained age 21 and who have earned $600 in 3 of the 5 previous calendar years. SIMPLEs must cover any employee who earned $5,000 in 2 previous calendar years and is reasonably expected to earn $5,000 in the current year. If a 403(b) plan includes employer contributions, the plan must satisfy IRC

Sec. 410(b). In addition, the ability to make salary deferrals must be given to any full-time employee who is willing to contribute $200 or more to the plan.

Chapter 8

Designing Benefit Formulas and Employee Contributions

Learning Objectives

An understanding of the material in this chapter should enable the student to

- **LO 8.1** Identify the rules that relate to the service and compensation that can be considered in a plan's benefit formula.
- **LO 8.2** Explain the strategies for satisfying the nondiscrimination rules for defined-contribution plans.
- **LO 8.3** Explain the strategies for satisfying the nondiscrimination rules for defined-benefit plans.
- **LO 8.4** Discuss the past and current role of voluntary employee after-tax contributions and describe the nondiscrimination rules that apply to these types of contributions.

NONDISCRIMINATION IN BENEFITS

LO 8.1 Identify the rules that relate to the service and compensation that can be considered in a plan's benefit formula.

When designing the benefit structure in a qualified plan or 403(b) plan, the rules provide for a substantial degree of discretion. The primary limitation is Code Sec. 401(a)(4), which provides that benefits cannot discriminate in favor of highly compensated employees. In this context, the definition of highly compensated is the same as described in previous chapters. In this chapter, we will review the nondiscrimination rules and explore their boundaries. First, we will give an overview of the nondiscrimination rules. Next, we will review some concepts relevant to a discussion of nondiscrimination, and then discuss the specific impact on defined-contribution and defined-benefit plans. Finally, we will compare these rules to the allocation rules that apply to SEPs and SIMPLEs.

Nondiscrimination Rules

Sec. 401(a)(4) nondiscrimination rule

Qualified plans (and 403(b) plans that include employer nonelective contributions) must be designed to satisfy the **Sec. 401(a)(4) nondiscrimination rule** that a plan cannot discriminate in favor of highly compensated employees (HCEs) with regard to benefits or contributions. The only exception applies to employee contributions and employer matching contributions. As discussed in Chapter 5, pretax salary deferral contributions are subject to a special nondiscrimination rule referred to as the ADP test. Employee after-tax and matching contributions are subject to the ACP nondiscrimination test.

The requirements of 401(a)(4) are satisfied if either the contributions or the benefits are nondiscriminatory. Under the statutory language, a plan will be deemed nondiscriminatory if contributions or benefits bear a uniform relationship to compensation. For instance, if in a defined-contribution plan contributions are allocated so all participants receive 3 percent of the current year's total compensation, the plan is not discriminatory. If the plan is a defined-benefit plan and each participant earns an accrued benefit of 2 percent of compensation for the current year of service, the plan is also deemed nondiscriminatory.

The more interesting question is to what extent the plan can deviate from the uniform percentage-of-compensation rule without being considered discriminatory. Since the enactment of ERISA, one form of discrimination has been allowed: the plan can have benefits that integrate with Social Security. Essentially, this allows a plan to discriminate in favor of the highly compensated employees to make up for the fact that the Social Security system discriminates against them. However, for many years it was unclear what else could be done, because no regulations clarified the general statutory language. Due to the lack of guidance, designing any other type of formula was risky. Since 1993, when the IRS issued almost 200 pages of final regulations, the situation has changed drastically. The regulations are quite helpful, because they

- establish objective criteria for determining whether a plan violates the nondiscrimination requirement
- clarify that a plan can demonstrate it is not discriminatory by showing that its contributions or benefits are not discriminatory
- establish several safe harbor methods for determining whether the plan satisfies the nondiscrimination standards
- create general tests for testing a plan that chooses not to adopt one of the design safe harbors

With regulations that contain clear, objective rules, a plan can determine at any time whether or not it is in compliance with the nondiscrimination standards, and if the employer is willing to do some testing, the plan design can be quite creative.

After reviewing some preliminary issues, we will more fully discuss exactly what these regulations allow defined-contribution and defined-benefit plans to do.

Accrued Benefits

accrued benefit

projected benefit

One key concept under the nondiscrimination rules is that discrimination is tested based on the benefit provided for that year, not the overall benefit provided under the plan. When discussing the total benefit that a participant has earned under a plan up to the present time, this amount is referred to as the participant's **accrued benefit**. This is in contrast to describing the benefit that is expected to be paid out if the participant continues in employment until normal retirement age, which is referred to as the **projected benefit**. The amount earned for the current year is simply referred to as the accrued benefit for the year.

In a defined-contribution plan, the participant's accrued benefit at any point is his or her present account balance. The accrual for the specific year is the amount contributed to the plan on the employee's behalf for that year. In a defined-benefit plan, the concept is the same. The accrued benefit is the benefit earned to date, using current salary and years of service. The accrued benefit earned for the year is the additional benefit that has been earned based upon the current year's salary and service.

A number of complex rules apply to the way benefits accrue under a plan. This is due to the fact that before ERISA was enacted, a participant would often be entitled to no benefit until he or she hit normal retirement age after, say, 30 years of employment. In this case, the entire benefit was essentially earned in the final year. This was called backloading the benefit. ERISA imposed rules to prohibit backloading. For example, under the rules, a plan's benefit formula could not be written to say that an individual earns a benefit of one percent of final-average compensation times years of service for the first 10 years of service and 2 percent of final-average compensation for service in excess of 10 years. This would be a prohibited backloading.

Permissible methods of determining a participant's accrued benefit are complex and are well-understood by pension actuaries who work with defined-benefit plans. However, we will simply discuss the most predominant method of accruing benefits today. If you were to see a different benefit accrual method, you might want to discuss the issue with the plan's actuary. As discussed in Chapter 4, the most common benefit formula in a defined-benefit plan is the unit-benefit formula. In most cases, under this formula, the accrued benefit is determined by applying the formula based on current salary and service.

EXAMPLE

The Average Corporation has a retirement benefit formula of 1.5 percent of final-average compensation times years of service. Normal retirement age is 65. Joe started employment at age 30. At age 40, after 10 years of service, Joe's accrued benefit is 15 percent of his final-average compensation, based on his salary history to date. He has accrued a benefit of 1.5 percent of final-average compensation for the current year. His projected retirement benefit is 45 percent of final-average compensation because he will have earned 30 years of service if he continues working until normal retirement age.

Calculating Service

In Chapter 4, we began to discuss the implications of the definition of service for purposes of determining the participant's benefit in a defined-benefit plan. There is one additional concern that is important to consider. Similar to the eligibility and vesting rules, there are minimum service requirements for determining whether the participant is entitled to earn a year of service under the plan. In a defined-benefit plan, a participant is not typically credited with a year of service if he or she has 1,000 hours of service (as is the requirement with the eligibility and vesting rules). In a defined-benefit plan, a year of service can be defined for benefit purposes in a variety of ways, as long as the definition of a year of service

- is applied on a reasonable and consistent basis
- does not require more hours of service than are customarily rendered during a work year in the industry involved
- accrues benefits for less than full-time service on at least a pro rata basis
- gives participants with 1,000 hours at least a partial year of service. (For certain industries that customarily work for seasonal or nontraditional years, 1,000 hours must constitute a full year of service.)

This last requirement means that, unlike the rules that apply to eligibility and vesting, the plan can actually require up to 2,000 hours of service before a full benefit accrual is credited.

In a defined-contribution plan, contributions must be made for participants who earn 1,000 hours of service for the year. This means an individual can become eligible to participate, receive an allocation for one year, and, if he or she then goes part-time, may not be eligible for contributions in subsequent years. There is an exception. Participants who terminate employment before the last day of the year can be excluded from receiving a contribution for the year, even if they have earned 1,000 hours of service. However, if such persons are excluded, they are also not considered participants under the minimum-coverage requirements. Therefore, having a last-day requirement means the employer could have trouble passing the coverage tests if a significant number of employees terminate employment before the end of the year.

In either a defined-contribution or a defined-benefit plan, hours of service may be determined by using the standard-hours counting method (each hour actually worked is counted, plus hours for which the employee is entitled to be paid, such as vacations and holidays) or by using one of the equivalency methods discussed earlier. The definition of hour of service for contribution or benefit purposes can be different from the definitions used for eligibility or vesting purposes.

Compensation for Benefit-Formula Purposes

When looking at the plan's benefit or contribution formula, benefits are based, in part, on how the plan defines compensation. The definition of compensation can include or exclude overtime, bonuses, and other nonrecurring compensation. In the small-plan market, the plan should be designed with a liberal definition of compensation in order to maximize the amount of contributions or benefits (tax shelter) that can be made. In larger, nonintegrated plans, employers typically ask you to use the definition of compensation that best suits the company's goals. If a restrictive definition is chosen, the definition will have to satisfy IRS nondiscrimination regulations. For example, if executives are the only employees who receive bonuses and rank-and-file employees are the only ones who work overtime, a definition of compensation that includes bonuses but not overtime will be considered discriminatory. Many plans choose an inclusive definition of compensation to avoid the nondiscrimination issue.

A second rule that relates to compensation is that the annual compensation considered in the benefit or contribution formula is limited to the compensation cap, which is indexed for inflation. In 2017, compensation is capped at $270,000.

> **EXAMPLE**
>
> George Yungle earns $400,000 in 2017. He notices that the company is contributing 10 percent of compensation for all participants in 2017 to the company's profit-sharing plan. When he looks at his benefit statement, he sees that only $27,000 has been allocated to his account. When he asks the benefit department about this, they inform him that, under the law, compensation cannot exceed the compensation cap of $270,000 (as indexed for 2017).

Amending Benefit Formulas

The process of plan amendment is typically thought of in conjunction with changes mandated by legislative reform and changes necessitated by unforeseen business developments. Some employers may also want to gradually increase benefits for a variety of reasons, including the following:

- A gradual benefit upgrade may satisfy the employer's benefit objective of consistently improving the employee benefits package. Some employers feel that periodic movement in the employee benefits package is necessary in order to retain employees.
- Employers may be skeptical of funding unknown plan costs and may desire to ease into the plan commitment slowly.
- An employer with erratic cash flow may set up a manageable benefit formula that will gradually be increased as cash flow stabilizes, as opposed to adopting a discretionary profit-sharing plan.

The primary legal restriction on plan amendments is the anti-cutback rule. Essentially, the rule provides that benefits that have already accrued cannot be taken away from the participant. Several years ago, the anti-cutback rules were expanded to include other aspects of the participant's benefit, such as the form of benefit payment. Congress considered the form of payment to be an essential part of the benefit promise. For example, if the plan allows benefits to be paid as a life annuity or as a single sum, the plan cannot be amended to take away the single-sum form of payment.

The anti-cutback rules do not, however, prohibit amending the benefit formula on a prospective basis. This applies both to the actual benefit formula and the form of payments.

DEFINED-CONTRIBUTION PLANS

LO 8.2　Explain the strategies for satisfying the nondiscrimination rules for defined-contribution plans.

The nondiscrimination rules apply (with the exception of the target-benefit plan) in essentially the same manner for all types of defined-contribution plans. First, we will discuss three major allocation approaches that are currently used: contributions as a level percentage of compensation, integration with Social Security, and cross-testing. Then, we will apply these concepts to specific types of plans.

Level Percentage of Compensation

As mentioned above, the nondiscrimination regulations offer several methods for determining whether the plan satisfies the nondiscrimination rules. One method is to satisfy a safe harbor test that is completely design based. That is, if the plan design fits within the specified safe harbor design, the plan will be deemed to satisfy the nondiscrimination test. To satisfy the basic defined-contribution plan design safe harbor, the plan must

- have a uniform normal retirement age and vesting schedule applicable to all employees, and
- group all employer contributions and forfeitures for the plan year under a single, uniform formula that allocates the same percentage of compensation or the same dollar amount to every participant

integration with Social Security

The **integration with Social Security** formula is often chosen. In larger companies, a plan that provides the same benefits to everyone is easy to administer and explain. If larger benefits are to be provided to executives, they are provided in a nonqualified environment. Small employers also choose this approach, sometimes for the same reason, although other times simply because this allocation formula is offered as an option in a prototype plan and the owner (and unfortunately sometimes the advisor) does not fully understand other options. In today's qualified plan environment, the small employer should, even in a simple profit-sharing plan, make an informed choice between the level percentage of pay, integration with Social Security, and cross-testing methods.

Integration with Social Security

Nondiscrimination regulations also provide that the benefit structure can be integrated with Social Security. Under this approach, the employer essentially gets to make larger contributions for those individuals who earn more than the taxable wage base. This is allowed because, under the Social Security system, the employer does not make contributions (pay taxes) on earnings in excess of the wage base. In this way, Social Security actually discriminates against the highly compensated. This disparity can be made up, to a degree, under a qualified plan using the methods described below.

Both money-purchase and profit-sharing plans can use this method, although if an employer sponsors both types of plans, only one plan can have a fully integrated formula. If a defined-contribution plan formula is integrated with Social Security, contributions may be higher (as a percentage of compensation) for those employees who earn more than a specified integration level. If the integration level is set at the current taxable wage base ($127,200 for 2017), HCEs may receive up to 5.7 percent of compensation in excess of the taxable wage base, as long as the employer makes contributions that equal at least 5.7 percent of total compensation.

EXAMPLE

Justin, Inc., establishes a money-purchase pension plan that provides for a contribution of 5.7 percent of compensation plus 5.7 percent of compensation in excess of the taxable wage base. Justin, the owner, earns $300,000. The contribution made on his behalf for 2017 is $23,455.50. This is 5.7 percent of $270,000 (the maximum allowable compensation for 2017, or $15,390) plus 5.7 percent of $142,800 ($270,000 minus $127,200), which equals $8,139.60.

If the employer cannot afford to contribute at least 5.7 percent of compensation across the board, the maximum disparity will be reduced. Under the rules, the integrated portion cannot exceed the contribution that is based on total compensation. This means that if 4 percent is contributed based on total salary, an additional 4 percent can be contributed based on compensation in excess of the integration level.

Under the rules, the integration level cannot exceed the taxable wage base. The integration level can be lower, but this generally reduces the maximum disparity allowed. Table 8-1 shows the required reductions. The reason for the reduction is to remove the advantage of setting the integration level just above the compensation level of the highest rank-and-file employee.

EXAMPLE

Bakery, Inc.'s rank-and-file workers earn a maximum of $30,000. The owner, Mr. Crueller, earns $270,000 for 2017. He might want to consider setting the level at $30,000 (instead of the taxable wage base) to maximize the integrated contribution on his own behalf.

Table 8-1
Maximum Integration Disparity Using Different Integration Levels

Integration Level	Maximum Disparity Allowed
Taxable Wage Base (TWB)	5.7%
Below the TWB but at least 80% of the TWB	5.4%
Below 80% of the TWB but at least 20% of the TWB.	4.3%
Below 20% of the TWB	5.7%*

Note that the maximum disparity bounces back to 5.7 percent with a very low integration level. This is because, at very low levels, the rank-and-file employees will also be receiving a contribution based on salary above the integration level.

Even though the required reductions are supposed to remove the advantage of lowering the integration level, it may be worth running the numbers to see what happens in a particular situation. Let's look at our example above. Because $30,000 is between 20 percent and 80 percent (30,000/127,200 = 23.5%) of the taxable wage base (25.3 percent), the maximum disparity is reduced to 4.3 percent. Comparing the two integration levels, the maximum integrated portion using the $30,000 integration level is $10,320 ($270,000 − $30,000 × 4.3 percent), while in 2017 the maximum integrated portion using the taxable wage base is $8,139.6 ($270,000 − $127,200 × 5.7 percent). In this case, there is more than a $2,000 difference, but that is only for this year. If next year the rank-and-file employees' salaries change and the integration level needs to be modified, the amendment process could cost more than the savings involved. In most cases, the "game is not worth the hunt," and the integration level should simply be set at the then-current taxable wage base.

Choosing the Integrated Formula

An integrated formula is an appropriate method for skewing contributions toward highly compensated employees. However, the maximum excess amount that a highly compensated employee can get is only $10,500 (see the Justin, Inc., example above). This means if the business owner wants the maximum allocation allowed under Code Sec. 415(c), other employees would have to get a contribution of slightly more than 16 percent of compensation calculated as follows: $54,000 − $10,500 = $43,500, $43,500/$270,000 = 16.11 percent compensation.

Today, if the business owner's goal is to maximize disparity, he or she should consider the cross-tested allocation formula described below. However, as you will see, these are complex plans that have some extra administrative costs. As an alternative, the integrated plan provides some disparity without much complication. A plan may be adopted by using a standardized prototype plan document. This means that the inexpensive standardized plans sponsored by many insurance companies and other service providers can be adopted at little expense. Also, a plan can be designed to fit within the safe harbor, ensuring ongoing satisfaction of the nondiscrimination regulations without annual testing.

The compensation cap has created another reason for using an integrated formula. Some small-business owners are perfectly happy to establish a plan that allocates the same percentage of compensation for each participant (such as 3, 4, or 5 percent of compensation). However, if the owner earns more than the $270,000 (indexed for 2017) compensation cap, the contribution on behalf of the owner with this type of formula will actually result in a smaller amount (as a percentage of pay) than for other employees.

EXAMPLE

Mr. Nice Guy wants to contribute 5 percent of compensation for each employee. If he earns $350,000, because of compensation cap the contribution on his behalf will only be approximately 3.5 percent of compensation!

For this reason, the same business owner might consider the integrated formula simply to make up for the loss associated with the compensation cap.

Cross-testing

cross-testing

new comparability

If the employer does not want to use a contribution or allocation formula that fits within one of the design safe harbors, virtually any other formula can be adopted as long as, on an annual basis, the plan can demonstrate compliance with the general nondiscrimination test. This can be done in one of two ways: either by testing contributions made to the plan on behalf of each participant or testing benefits that can be provided from contributions and forfeitures made for the year. Testing benefits in a defined-contribution plan is referred to as **cross-testing**. It requires the conversion of allocations into equivalent life annuity benefit amounts by using the methodology described in the regulations. Once these allocations have been converted, the general test is then performed, using benefit accrual rates based on those annuity amounts expressed as a percentage of compensation. This strategy of satisfying the nondiscrimination rules is also referred to as **new comparability**.

In the most practical of terms, the regulations allow discrimination in favor of older workers because it takes a larger contribution to buy a specific benefit for an older worker than it does to buy the same benefit for a younger worker. This is a powerful concept, and the regulations are quite flexible. An employer that decides to go the cross-testing route must understand the following:

- *Mathematical test*—The administrator must perform a test on an annual basis to demonstrate compliance with the nondiscrimination rules.

- *Retroactive compliance*—Even if the test is not satisfied, the plan can be amended, increasing benefits for the nonhighly compensated employees to the extent necessary to satisfy the test.

- *Additional expense*—Plan documents, IRS determination letters, and annual administration are somewhat higher for a cross-tested plan.

- *Minimum contribution*—In most cases, when cross-testing is used, the regulations require a 5 percent minimum gateway contribution for rank-and-file employees.

age-weighted formula

The simplest method to satisfy the general test is to allocate the contributions and forfeitures in such a way that, after conversion to a monthly benefit accrual at retirement, the rate of accrual is the same for each participant. In this way, the general nondiscrimination test is always satisfied, without further testing. This type of allocation formula is referred to as an **age-weighted formula**. Let's look at an example that demonstrates how age weighting works.

EXAMPLE

A plan has three participants. Susan, aged 50, earns $150,000 per year. Her employees, Ralph and Paula, ages 35 and 28, respectively, each earn $30,000 per year. Also, assume the employer wants to contribute $49,000. Use the following steps to determine the appropriate allocation formula that will result in a uniform benefit accrual for each participant:

- First, determine how much would have to be contributed for the year to provide a monthly benefit at age 65 equal to one percent of each participant's compensation. One percent of Susan's $150,000 annual ($12,500 monthly) compensation is $125. One percent of Ralph's and Paula's $30,000 annual ($2,500 monthly) compensation is $25.
- Next, assume it costs $95.38 (see Table 8-2) at age 65 to provide a benefit of $1 per month payable for life. Susan would then need $125 × $95.38 = $11,922; Ralph and Paula each would need $25 × $95.38 = $2,384 at age 65 to provide a benefit of one percent of their pay.
- Assuming plan assets earn 8.5 percent, a single contribution of $3,506 today would accumulate after 15 years to the $11,922 Susan would need at age 65 ($11,922 × .2941; see Table 8-3). Similarly, a single contribution of $206 today would accumulate after 30 years to the $2,384 Ralph will need at age 65, and a single contribution of $117 today would accumulate after 37 years to the $2,384 Paula will need at age 65.
- Under the age-weighted profit-sharing plan, the actual contribution is discretionary. The contribution will be allocated to participants in proportion to the $3,506, $206, and $117 amounts calculated above. Susan receives 91.57 percent of the total contribution, Ralph receives 5.39 percent of the contribution, and Paula receives the remaining 3.04 percent of the contribution.
- If the employer contributed enough to provide a one-percent benefit accrual for each participant the contribution would be $3,829 ($3,506 + $206 + $117). Since a $49,000 contribution is more than 12 times this amount, the contribution for each employee in this case hypothetically would support a monthly benefit at retirement of approximately 12 percent of compensation. (Table 8-4)

In this example, age weighting results in a high percentage of the total contribution because the owner is significantly older than the other employees. In many cases, the plan will pass the annual nondiscrimination test because each participant is receiving the same benefit accrual. However, even under this design, nonhighly compensated participants will generally need to receive an allocation of 5 percent of compensation in order to satisfy the regulations.

Table 8-2
Annuity Purchase Factors

1984 UP Mortality Table 8.5% Interest

Age	Amount to Purchase $1 Monthly Annuity	Age	Amount to Purchase $1 Monthly Annuity
55	$115	63	$99
56	113	64	97
57	111	65	95
58	109	66	93
59	107.83	67	90
60	105.88	68	88
61	103	69	86
62	101	70	84

Table 8-3
Discount Factor

8.5% Interest

Years before Retirement Age	Discount Factor	Years before Retirement Age	Discount Factor
1	0.921659	23	0.153150
2	0.849455	24	0.141152
3	0.782908	25	0.130094
4	0.721574	26	0.119902
5	0.665045	27	0.110509
6	0.612945	28	0.101851
7	0.564926	29	0.093872
8	0.520669	30	0.086518
9	0.479880	31	0.079740
10	0.442285	32	0.073493
11	0.407636	33	0.067736
12	0.375702	34	0.062429
13	0.346269	35	0.057539
14	0.319142	36	0.053031

Table 8-3
Discount Factor

8.5% Interest

Years before Retirement Age	Discount Factor	Years before Retirement Age	Discount Factor
15	0.294140	37	0.048876
16	0.271097	38	0.045047
17	0.249859	39	0.041518
18	0.230285	40	0.038266
19	0.212244	41	0.035268
20	0.195616	42	0.032505
21	0.180292	43	0.029959
22	0.166167	44	0.027612

The age-weighted example is an excellent place to begin the discussion of cross-testing because it illustrates the concept behind the rules. The major problem with the age-weighted formula is that it is contingent upon having the perfect employee census. Even a single older employee can destroy the intended result. In addition, age weighting is hard to explain and might cause employee dissatisfaction. In the following example, Paula might have difficulty understanding why Ralph is entitled to a $2,641 allocation, while she receives only $1,489, because they each earn the same salary.

Table 8-4
Age-Weighted Allocation Method

Name	Age	Monthly Earnings	1% Monthly Annuity	Single Sum at 65	Present Value	Allocation Percentage	Allocation of $49,000
Susan	50	$12,500	$125	$11,922	$3,506	91.57%	$44,869
Ralph	35	2,500	25	2,384	206	5.39	2,641
Paula	28	2,500	25	2,384	117	3.04	1,489

For these reasons, the age-weighted allocation approach is not popular. As the pension industry has grown to understand the general nondiscrimination test, the opportunities it provides have become clear. When working with the general nondiscrimination test, the employer can essentially start with any plan allocation formula, which is then tested against the general nondiscrimination test. This design approach is much more satisfying because the employer can first create a design that meets its goals and then analyze whether the design satisfies the test.

For the small employer, one common objective is to allocate the maximum allowed under Code Sec. 415(c) and the minimum required for other employees. The regulations require a 5 percent of compensation allocation to nonhighly compensated employees in most cases in a cross-tested plan. With this objective in mind, the next step is to translate the projected contributions into an accrued benefit for each employee, which is tested under the general nondiscrimination test. If the plan passes, then the design can be adopted. If not, then the contribution level for the nonhighly compensated can be raised, or the contribution for the owners can be lowered, until the test is satisfied.

The actual mechanics of cross-testing are quite complex and are beyond the scope of this book. However, note that the following objectives can generally be accomplished with a cross-tested plan:

- *Skewing contributions*—When the average age of the business owners is 10 years or more older than the nonhighly compensated employees, cross-testing will allow the plan to establish an allocation formula in which the owners receive the maximum Code Sec. 415(c) allocation, while the rank-and-file employees receive substantially less—possibly as low as 5 percent of compensation.

- *Older nonhighly compensated employees*—Unlike age-weighting, cross-testing works even with several older nonhighly compensated employees—as long as the average age of the owners is somewhat greater than the average age of the nonhighly compensated employees.

- *Design flexibility*—One other substantial advantage is the design flexibility allowed under the general test. Often an employer will want to make a larger contribution for a specific group of employees (for example, longer service employees or salespersons). Before these regulations, an employer had little flexibility. Now the opportunities for creative plan designs that meet a number of planning objectives are almost limitless. For example, the employer may decide to contribute 5 percent of pay for new employees, 6 percent for employees with 5 or more years of service, and 7 percent for employees with 10 or more years of service.

Any employer considering a plan with a cross-tested allocation formula must be advised of certain disadvantages. The plan needs to be tested for discrimination on an annual basis. Gathering accurate employee data, especially age information, can be a daunting task. Preliminary testing (at the beginning of the year) and final testing will have to be performed. The plan design may have to change on an annual basis if census data or employee salaries change. For example, the plan may satisfy the rules in year one with a 5 percent allocation for NHCEs, while the next year a 6 percent allocation may be required. A design change must be accompanied by a properly timed plan amendment. Plan document charges, filing for an

IRS determination letter, and the ongoing administration costs are typically a bit higher than with other types of defined-contribution plans. The additional costs will typically not stop the employer if the savings under the cross-tested plan (compared to an age-weighted or integrated plan) are substantial.

Types of Plans and Nondiscrimination Approaches

Now that we have looked at the nondiscrimination rules in general, let's examine the types of choices employers commonly make with specific types of plans.

Profit-Sharing Plans

Profit-sharing plan allocation formulas are designed using a wide range of approaches. Many employers use one of the safe harbor designs, either allocating as a level percentage of compensation or using a formula integrated with Social Security. Employers interested in age-weighting or cross-testing are choosing the versatile profit-sharing plan. Discretionary contributions, in-service withdrawals, and the ability to circumvent the qualified joint-and-survivor annuity rules (see Chapter 10) are meaningful qualities for the small-business owner in today's business environment.

401(k) Plans

Remember that 401(k) plans are profit-sharing plans. If the 401(k) plan has a profit-sharing-type contribution, an allocation could be designed that takes advantage of the cross-testing flexibility. 401(k) nondiscrimination testing can be confusing because of the different types of contributions allowed and the nondiscrimination rules that apply to different types of contributions. Let's review.

- Employee salary deferral contributions—Nondiscrimination is tested solely through the actual deferral percentage ADP test. The 401(a)(4) rules do not apply.
- Employer-matching contributions—Nondiscrimination is tested solely through the actual contribution percentage ACP test (which is discussed later in this chapter). The 401(a)(4) rules do not apply.
- Employee after-tax contributions—Nondiscrimination is tested solely through the ACP test.
- Employer profit-sharing contributions—Only these types of contributions must satisfy the 401(a)(4) nondiscrimination rules discussed in this section.

Perhaps the most powerful plan design for a defined contribution plan is the use of a safe harbor 401(k) feature in combination with a cross-tested/new comparability feature. Such a design provides the following advantages:

- The 401(k) feature can be maximized by HCEs without regard to the level of deferrals for NHCEs;
- Assuming that the 3 percent nonelective contribution is used to satisfy the safe harbor (see Chapter 5), it can also be used to satisfy the top-heavy minimum for nonkey employees;
- Assuming that the 3-percent nonelective contribution is used to satisfy the safe harbor (see Chapter 10), it can also be applied to the gateway contribution for NHCEs described earlier;
- The cost of the plan for NHCEs can be minimized because only a portion of the total benefit for the HCEs is provided through the profit-sharing allocation. For example, for 2017, a HCE could defer $18,000 using the 401(k) feature so that the profit-sharing allocation only needs to be $36,000 in order to provide the HCE with the maximum total allocation of $54,000.

403(b) Plans

403(b) plans, like 401(k) plans, must be analyzed feature by feature. These plans are subject to the following discrimination requirements:

- *Employee salary deferral contributions*—Unlike in the 401(k) plan, salary deferrals in a 403(b) plan are not subject to any nondiscrimination requirements.
- *Employer-matching contributions*—If the 403(b) plan has a matching contribution, these contributions do have to satisfy the ACP test (which is discussed later in this chapter). The 401(a)(4) rules do not apply.
- *Employer nonelective contributions*—If the 403(b) plan has an employer contribution for all eligible employees, these types of contributions must satisfy the 401(a)(4) nondiscrimination rules discussed in this section. Like profit-sharing plans, the 403(b) plan can use either of the design safe harbors: level percentage of compensation or integration with Social Security. The allocation formula also can take advantage of the cross-testing or age-weighted approaches.

Money-Purchase Pension Plans

Even though a money-purchase pension plan can take advantage of cross-testing, most employers that choose this allocation approach have chosen profit-sharing plans because contributions are discretionary. Money-purchase plans more typically contain contributions that are a level percentage of compensation or that are integrated with Social Security.

Target-Benefit Pension Plans

The contribution formula established under a target-benefit plan could be tested under the general nondiscrimination test. However, the regulations provide a separate design safe harbor for such plans, and employers that establish such a plan will probably want to take advantage of the design safe harbor.

Several threshold issues determine whether a target plan is suited for a particular employer. First, a target plan, like the age-weighted profit-sharing plan, will not work with even a single older NHCE. Second, because the target plan is a pension plan, the employer must be willing to commit to a timely annual contribution. Third, unlike a defined-benefit plan, the annual contribution is a fixed amount. Finally, the employer must be willing to live with pension plan requirements (including no in-service distributions and the qualified joint-and-survivor annuity requirements).

Because today an age-weighted profit-sharing plan could be designed to give similar results as in the target-benefit plan, the employer is more likely to choose either the age-weighted or more flexible cross-tested profit-sharing plan. Most employers today are simply not willing to make a commitment to a fixed annual contribution. And for those few who are willing to commit to annual contributions, a defined-benefit plan is often the better choice, due to the flexibility of annual contributions and the ability (in the right circumstances) for the employer to contribute more on the key employees' behalf than in a defined-contribution plan.

SEPs

As you learned in Chapter 6, the contribution to a SEP either must be allocated as a level percentage of compensation or integrated with Social Security (in the manner described above). The SEP cannot use a cross-tested or age-weighted allocation formula.

SIMPLEs

Contributions to a SIMPLE are subject to even more rigid rules. If the employer makes a profit-sharing-type contribution, all eligible participants must receive 2 percent of compensation. If, instead, the employer makes a matching contribution, the match is fixed as a dollar-for-dollar match, up to the first 3 percent of compensation deferred.

DEFINED-BENEFIT PLANS

LO 8.3   **Explain the strategies for satisfying the nondiscrimination rules for defined-benefit plans.**

The nondiscrimination rules provide design safe harbors for defined-benefit pension plans that include level benefits and those that integrate with Social Security. Again, if the employer wants to establish a plan that does not fit within the safe harbor, the formula can be defined in any way, as long as the plan can demonstrate nondiscrimination on an annual basis. Each of these three alternatives is discussed below.

Uniform Percentage of Compensation

There are actually three design-based safe harbors for defined-benefit plans under the regulations. For all three, the plan must have the same benefit formula (and form of payment) for all participants and a uniform retirement age. Most important, the benefit formula must provide, at the normal retirement age—for all participants with the same years of service—either the same dollar benefit or the same percentage of average annual compensation. Also, the plan cannot require mandatory employee contributions.

All of the following designs can satisfy the safe harbors:

- *Unit credit plans*—As long as the above requirements are met, the plan can use a standard unit credit plan that accrues the benefit each year based on the plan's benefit formula.
- *Fractional accruals*—A unit-benefit formula or a flat percentage of pay (with a 25-years-of-service requirement) that accrues benefits using the fractional accrual method can also satisfy the design safe harbor.
- *Fully insured plans*—As long as the above requirements are met and the plan satisfies the definition of a fully insured plan under Code Sec. 412(i), the plan satisfies the nondiscrimination requirements.

In addition, any of these approaches will still satisfy the design safe harbor if the plan is integrated with Social Security as described below.

Integration with Social Security

Similar to the defined-contribution plan, the defined-benefit formula can be designed to provide a greater percentage of benefits for highly paid employees than for rank-and-file employees. Even though the rules are conceptually similar to defined-contribution plans, the integration-level approach for defined-benefit plans applies somewhat differently.

The rules also allow for an integration approach in which a benefit is described and then a portion of an individual's Social Security benefit is subtracted from the total (referred to as offset integration). At one time, this was the most common integration approach in defined-benefit plans. However, because under current law this approach rarely works as well as the integration-level approach and is, therefore, not used very often, it will not be discussed here.

The integration-level approach is called excess integration. Here's how an excess plan works:

- The plan has a specified integration level, which is generally the IRS's covered compensation table.
- The benefit formula provides the participant an additional benefit for final average compensation earned above the integration level.
- The additional or "excess" benefit cannot exceed either of the following limits:
  - The excess benefit percentage for each year of service cannot be more than the lesser of 0.75 percent of final average compensation or the percentage of final average compensation based on total compensation. For example, if the plan's formula provides a benefit of .5 percent of total final average compensation, the maximum excess percentage that can be provided is only .5 percent.
  - An excess benefit can only be provided on a maximum of 35 years of service, meaning that the maximum excess benefit can not exceed 26.25 percent of compensation (.75 multiplied by 35).

covered compensation

The integration level in a defined-benefit plan is almost always covered compensation, which is the average of the taxable wages for the individual participant using the 35-year period ending with the year that the employee reaches his or her Social Security full retirement age. The table below provides a portion of a **covered compensation** table for 2016. The concept of covered compensation is confusing for two reasons. First, as you can see in the table, covered compensation is different for participants of different ages, because the average of taxable wage bases depends on the years worked. Older workers will have lower covered compensation levels than younger workers, because the taxable wage bases over their final 35 years of work are lower than those for younger workers using more current years. Second, every year the table for covered compensation changes as cost-of-living increases apply. This means that the covered compensation amount keeps increasing as an individual gets older. To satisfy the integration rules, the plan must define final-average compensation as at least the 3 highest years of compensation.

EXAMPLE

The ABC Corporation has a defined-benefit plan with an integrated benefit formula. The formula provides participants with an annual benefit of one percent of final-average compensation (defined as the average of the highest 3 years of compensation) plus an additional .75 percent of compensation earned in excess of an individual's covered compensation, multiplied by years of service. The additional integrated portion of the benefit is capped at 35 years of service. This benefit formula complies with the integration rules. The excess benefit does not exceed the lesser of .75 percent per year of service or 1 percent (the benefit provided on final average compensation) and the excess is only provided on the first 35 years of benefit service. Let's calculate a benefit for Joe who retires at age 65 in 2017 (born in 1951) with 30 years of benefit service and a final-average salary of $90,000. Joe's covered compensation is $77,880. Joe's annual benefit is ($90,000 × .01 x 30) + ($12,120 × .0075 x 30) = ($27,000 + $2,727) $29,727.

Table 8-5
2017 Covered Compensation

Calendar Year of Birth	Calendar Year of Social Security Retirement Age	2017 Covered Compensation ($)
1951	2017	77,880
1952	2018	80,496
1953	2019	83,052
1954	2020	85,560
1955	2022	90,372
1956	2023	92,724
1957	2024	94,980
1958	2025	97,152
1959	2026	99,264
1960	2027	101,304
1961	2028	103,296
1962	2029	105,204
1963	2030	107,088
1964	2031	108,924
1965	2032	110,700
1966	2033	112,380
1967	2034	113,940
1968	2035	115,392

Other Plan-Design Alternatives

If the employer with a defined-benefit plan wants to establish a benefit formula that does not satisfy any of the safe harbor designs, the plan will have to satisfy the general nondiscrimination tests. Two types of plans are likely to have plan designs that do not satisfy the safe harbors. The first group includes plans that historically have had nonconforming benefit formulas. In other words, the sponsor adopted a formula in the past that today does not satisfy the nondiscrimination safe harbors. If the plan is still meeting the objectives of both employer and employees, the sponsor may choose not to bring the formula into compliance, but instead to go through the testing process.

The second group will be employers that choose to provide different benefit levels for different groups of employees in one plan. The employer might, for example, want to provide different benefit levels for employees of certain classes, in different geographic locations, or in different subsidiaries. The employer here has two choices: either establish one plan with different benefit levels and go through annual nondiscrimination testing, or establish separate plans for each group, with each plan having its own benefit structure. Separate plans may be easier if each plan will be able to satisfy the minimum-coverage requirements of Code Sec. 410(b) as well as the minimum-participation test.

VOLUNTARY EMPLOYEE CONTRIBUTIONS

LO 8.4 Discuss the past and current role of voluntary employee after-tax contributions and describe the nondiscrimination rules that apply to these types of contributions.

voluntary after-tax employee contribution

Today, in most cases, qualified plan benefits are funded by employer contributions, with the exception of pretax elective salary deferral contributions that participants make to 401(k) plans, 403(b) plans, and SIMPLEs. However, qualified plans are technically allowed to provide for another type of contribution, the **voluntary after-tax employee contribution**.

Prior to 1987, this feature was quite common in qualified plans because up to 10 percent of compensation could be contributed by any employee without having to consider any of the other contribution limits and without regard to which employees elected to make contributions. This feature was often used primarily by the business owner and other highly compensated employees.

Beginning in 1987, however, many of these provisions were eliminated due to new nondiscrimination requirements and a new rule requiring that all such contributions count toward calculating annual additions under the Code Sec. 415(c) limit. Because of this, most plans eliminated contributions after 1986; however, plans may still have contributions that were made prior to this date. This is important to note when dealing with a client who is receiving a pension distribution. The principal amount of employee contributions is treated as basis, and is not subject to income tax. Earnings are subject to the same taxation rules that apply to other pension distributions.

The only place where after-tax contributions are common today are in 401(k) plans, where employees are sometimes given the opportunity to make contributions on a pretax or after-tax basis. Some employees prefer after-tax contributions because they can be withdrawn more easily than pretax contributions, which are subject to the special withdrawal requirements discussed in Chapter 5. They are most common in large company plans that have been in existence for many years.

Nondiscrimination Requirements for Employee Contributions and Employer Matching Contributions

Plans that provide for voluntary employee after-tax contributions must satisfy a nondiscrimination test that is similar to the actual deferral percentage (ADP) test called the actual contribution percentage (ACP) test. This test considers after-tax contributions along with matching employer contributions. Under the ACP test, instead of comparing the salary deferrals as a percentage of compensation, we are comparing the matching and after-tax contributions as a percentage of compensation.

In operation, the test is virtually the same as the ADP test. In order to pass the ACP nondiscrimination test for employer matching contributions and employee contributions, one of two requirements must be satisfied:

1. The 1.25 requirement. Under this requirement, the contribution percentage for all highly compensated employees for the current year cannot be more than 125 percent of the contribution percentage for nonhighly compensated employees for the previous year.

2. The 200 percent/2 percent difference requirement. Under this requirement, the contribution percentage for highly compensated employees for the current year cannot be more than 200 percent of the contribution percentage (in the previous year) for nonhighly compensated employees, and the difference between the two groups must be 2 percent or less.

CHAPTER REVIEW

Key Terms and Concepts

Sec. 401(a)(4) nondiscrimination rule
accrued benefit
projected benefit
integration with Social Security
cross-testing
new comparability
age-weighted formula
covered compensation
voluntary after-tax employee
   contribution

Chapter 8: Review Questions

Review questions are based on the learning objectives in this chapter. Thus, an [8.3] at the end of a question means that the question is based on learning objective 3. If there are multiple objectives, they are all listed.

1. Does allocating 3 percent of compensation to each participant in a profit-sharing plan satisfy the 401(a)(4) nondiscrimination requirements? [8.1]

2. Answer the following questions regarding accrued benefits: [8.1]

    a. What does the term accrued benefit mean in a defined-contribution plan?

    b. What does the term accrued benefit mean in a defined-benefit plan?

    c. What does the term projected benefit mean in a defined-benefit plan?

3. In a defined-benefit plan, what are the maximum number of hours of service an employer can require in order to credit a participant with a full year of service for benefit purposes? If the maximum number of hours is required, what happens if the participant earns only 1,000 hours of service? [8.1]

4. Describe the compensation cap and its effect on the benefits of highly compensated employees. [8.1]

5. Answer the following questions regarding Social Security integration in defined-contribution plans:

    a. If the employer contributes 8 percent of total compensation for each participant, how much more can be contributed for employees who earn more than the taxable wage base (assuming this is the integration level)?

b. If the employer contributes 3 percent of total compensation for each participant, how much more can be contributed for employees who earn more than the taxable wage base (assuming this is the integration level)?

c. If the employer contributes 8 percent of total compensation for each participant, how much more can be contributed for employees who earn more than $110,000 in 2017 (assuming this is the integration level)? [8.2]

6. Describe what cross-testing is and how it can be used to channel a larger percentage of the employer's contribution to the older, highly compensated employees. [8.2]

7. What is the major limitation with an age-weighted contribution formula? [8.2]

8. What are the strengths and limitations of the cross-tested formula? [8.2]

9. What type of defined-contribution plan is most often used with the age-weighted or cross-tested contribution formula? [8.2]

10. Describe the nondiscrimination requirements that apply to 401(k) plans. [8.2]

11. Describe the types of allocation formulas that can be contained in a SEP. [8.2]

12. Weese has a final-average salary of $100,000 and has worked for his employer for 20 years. Weese's covered compensation is $77,880, and the plan's benefit formula provides for one percent of final-average compensation plus .75 percent of final-average salary in excess of covered compensation multiplied by years of service (limited to 35 years of service). Does the plan satisfy the integration rules, and what is Weese's benefit under the plan? [8.3]

13. Explain the nondiscrimination requirements for employer matching contributions and employee contributions. [8.4]

Chapter 8: Review Answers

1. Yes, providing a level percentage of compensation for each participant is considered nondiscriminatory under Sec. 401(a)(4).

2. a. In a defined-contribution plan, the accrued benefit is the participant's account balance.

   b. In a defined-benefit plan, the accrued benefit is the participant's currently earned benefit using compensation and years of service to date.

   c. In a defined-benefit plan, the projected benefit is the benefit expected at normal retirement age, assuming the individual continues in service until that time. The projected benefit is generally calculated by using current salaries.

3. As long as the average work year is at least 2,000 hours, an employer can require a maximum of 2,000 hours of service before a participant is credited with a full year of service for benefit purposes. If this is done, participants with 1,000 hours of service must be given credit for at least one half-year of service.

4. The compensation cap limits the compensation that can be used under the plan's benefit or allocation formula. It limits benefits for those who earn more than the cap ($270,000 for 2017).

5. a. When the integration level is the taxable wage base and the contribution based on total compensation is 5.7 percent or more, the maximum contribution for wages earned in excess of the taxable wage base is 5.7 percent.

   b. When the integration level is the taxable wage base and the contribution based on total compensation is 3 percent, the maximum contribution for wages earned in excess of the taxable wage base is 3 percent.

   c. When the integration level is set under the taxable wage base, the maximum contribution in excess of the taxable wage base has to be reduced. In 2017, the taxable wage base is $127,200. A $110,000 integration level is more than 80 percent of the taxable wage base (110,000/127,200 = 86.47%), meaning that the maximum contribution on wages in excess of the integration level is 5.4 percent.

6. Cross-testing in a defined-contribution plan means converting the contributions to equivalent annuity benefits at retirement. This method results in larger allowable contributions for older participants because they have a shorter time to retirement and the annuity purchase price would be higher than for a younger participant.

7. Even one older nonhighly compensated employee can disrupt the plan design.

8. The strength is its flexibility and the ability to make larger contributions for the older business owners. The limitations are usually related to administrative complexity and cost. It is also possible that, if the owners are young and the rest of the workforce is older, that a cross-tested formula will not result in larger contributions for the owners. Another limitation is that the maximum contribution for any one participant is the Sec. 415(c) annual addition limit that applies to defined-contribution plan.

9. A profit-sharing plan, because of the ability to make discretionary contributions.

10. A 401(k) plan is subject to three possible nondiscrimination tests. The salary deferrals must satisfy the ADP test, the employer matching contributions and after-tax contributions must satisfy the ACP test, and profit-sharing contributions must satisfy the 401(a)(4) nondiscrimination test.

11. SEP must either allocate contributions as a level percentage of compensation or allocate with a formula that is integrated with Social Security.

12. The plan satisfies the integration rules because the excess benefit percentage does not exceed either limit. The excess benefit is .75 percent and the maximum total excess benefit equals 26.25 percent. Furthermore, the benefit based on total compensation is one percent, greater than the .75 percent excess amount. Weese's benefit is $23,318, calculated as follows:

.01	x	$100,000	x	20	=	$ 20,000
.0075	x	$22,120	x	20	=	$ 3,318
						$ 23,318

13. Plans with voluntary contributions must perform the ACP nondiscrimination test, which is quite similar to the ADP nondiscrimination test that applies to salary reduction contributions in a 401(k) plan. If the plan also calls for employer matching contributions, voluntary after-tax contributions and matching contributions are both counted in the nondiscrimination test.

Chapter 9

Helping Clients Choose the Best Loan, Vesting, and Retirement-Age Provisions

Learning Objectives

An understanding of the material in this chapter should enable you to

- **LO 9.1** Describe the reasons for including participant loans in a client's plan and the legal requirements that apply.
- **LO 9.2** Explain the vesting requirements applicable to qualified retirement plans.
- **LO 9.3** Identify the design considerations associated with choosing normal, early, and deferred retirement provisions.
- **LO 9.4** Determine when a plan is top-heavy, and describe the additional restrictions that apply to a top-heavy plan.

Three of the most important decisions in designing a plan are:
- deciding whether the plan should permit loans
- choosing the plan's vesting schedules
- choosing the plan's retirement-age provisions

Decisions in these areas significantly affect the makeup of the plan's participants, the makeup of the employer's work force, and the employer's costs.

PLAN LOANS

Most types of retirement plans may allow participants the opportunity to borrow from the plan. Loans provide access to funds without tax consequences. However, loans also add administrative expense and may undermine retirement planning objectives. The decision whether or not to have a loan provision depends upon the type of plan, plan objectives, and the legal restrictions upon plan loans. An informed decision must address the following two important concerns:
- Are plan loans appropriate?
- What legal restrictions will apply?

ARE PLAN LOANS APPROPRIATE FOR YOUR CLIENTS?

The Advantages and Disadvantages of Plan Loans

LO 9.1   **Describe the reasons for including participant loans in a client's plan and the legal requirements that apply.**

The primary reason to include a participant loan program in the plan is to give participants access to sheltered funds when the need arises without causing a taxable distribution. Several good reasons for not allowing plan loans also exist. First, a loan provision in the plan may be inconsistent with the employer's objective of providing retirement security. Second, loan provisions are labor intensive and costly to administer. Furthermore, if a loan is defaulted:

- There is an immediate tax liability to the participant, because the defaulted loan is treated as a current distribution.
- The participant may incur a 10 percent penalty if the distribution occurs prior to age 59½.

Despite their pitfalls, loan provisions are very popular for the following reasons:

- Business owners are eligible for plan loans to the same extent as other employees.
- Administrative problems with plan loans can be minimized by using a program that would only permit loans under a stipulated number of circumstances, such as for college education payments, purchase of a home, or demonstrated financial hardship.
- Administrative problems can also be mitigated by placing a $1,000 minimum on the amount of any loan, thus eliminating pesky small loans.
- Problems with loan defaults can be eliminated if the employer requires both payroll deduction for loan repayments and complete repayment upon termination of employment. If the participant defaults, benefits payable are reduced by the outstanding balance (resulting in a taxable distribution of the amount of default).

Types of Plans

The degree to which a loan provision is considered desirable depends in part on the type of plan involved. 401(k) and 403(b) plans are most likely to include a loan provision, since they give participants who may otherwise be reluctant to contribute access to their funds. Since other retirement plans are funded with employer contributions, they are less likely to include loan provisions. However, in other defined-contribution plans, loans can be used to meet certain goals. For example, a money-purchase plan is not allowed to have in-service withdrawals. So a loan provision is a way to allow "use" of plan assets during employment. Profit-sharing plans can allow in-service withdrawals, but the loan is a way to get access without tax consequences.

Defined-benefit and cash balance pension plans seldom contain loan provisions. Since there is no account balance in a defined-benefit plan, the plan would have to obtain other security from the participant, which would be very cumbersome. Employee stock ownership plans (ESOPs) and stock bonus plans generally do not have loans as they may not have sufficient cash investments to support a loan provision. Finally, note that plan loans are prohibited in SEPs, SIMPLEs, and IRAs.

Table 9-1
Desirability of Plan Loans

Plan	Consideration
401(k) plans	A loan provision entices participation so the ADP and ACP tests can be passed.
403(b) plans	A loan provision entices participation so the ACP test can be passed.
Money-purchase and target-benefit pension plans	A loan provision can get around the restriction against in-service withdrawals.
Profit-sharing plans	A loan provision allows for tax-free access to benefits.
Defined-benefit and cash-balance plans	A loan provision is rarely chosen because of administrative complexity.
ESOP and stock bonus plans	A loan provision may not be feasible if plan does not have sufficient nonstock liquid assets.
SEP, SIMPLE, IRA	No loans are permitted.

LEGAL PARAMETERS FOR PLAN LOANS

Plans designed to permit loans must adhere to certain requirements that govern the availability, amount, duration, interest, security, and repayment of the loan.

Loan Availability

Loan provisions are optional; however, if included in the plan, they must be available to all participants on a reasonably equivalent basis and must not be available to highly compensated employees in an amount greater than the amount made available to other employees. In addition, loans must

- be adequately secured
- be made in accordance with specific plan provisions
- bear a reasonable rate of interest (market rate for similar loans)

Almost all plans use the participant's accrued benefit as security. Only one-half of the account balance can be used for security. Other security can be appropriate, but most plans will want to avoid this because of the administrative complexities. If the participant defaults on the loan, the benefit will be reduced in the amount of the outstanding principal (and accrued interest). If this happens, the participant has a taxable distribution subject to ordinary income tax and the 10 percent early distribution excise tax, if he or she has not attained age 59½.

Another issue that arises with loans is that, in plans subject to the qualified joint-and-survivor annuity requirements, both spouses must sign off on the loan. This is because a loan default can reduce the participant's benefit, which affects the spousal rights to that benefit as well.

Restrictions on Amounts and Repayments

In addition to rules on loan availability, there are limits on the amount each participant can borrow. The limit is $50,000 or one-half of the vested account balance, whichever is less. Under the tax rules, a participant may borrow up to $10,000, even if this amount is more than one-half of the vested benefit. However, in practice, employers typically do not allow loans in excess of the 50 percent limit, because DOL regulations allow only one half of the vested account balance to be used as collateral. Allowing loans in excess of that amount would require additional security—which complicates plan administration.

A participant's loan must be repayable by its terms within 5 years. The loan must be repaid using a level amortization method and payments must be made at least quarterly. To limit the use of ongoing maximum loans, the $50,000 loan limit is reduced by the highest outstanding loan balance during the one-year period ending the day before the loan date.

EXAMPLE

Bill Smith borrows $50,000 from his qualified plan and pays off the loan on a level amortization basis over 5 years. At the end of 5 years, when the loan is repaid, Bill wants to take out another loan. The maximum amount available for this second loan is limited by the highest outstanding principal balance in the last year of the first loan.

Interest on a plan loan is treated as consumer interest that is not deductible by the employee as an itemized deduction unless the loan is secured by a principal residence. Because plans generally do not want to make loans on this basis, the tax deduction is rarely available. In addition, deductions are not allowed in any case if the loan is (1) made to a key employee, as defined by the Code's rules for top-heavy plans or (2) made to any participant in a 401(k) or 403(b) plan.

VESTING

LO 9.2 **Explain the vesting requirements applicable to qualified retirement plans.**

Another important design decision is choosing a plan's vesting schedule. The vesting schedule can have some impact on plan costs, but more importantly it should be consistent with the plan's objectives.

Understanding the Vesting System

vesting schedules

The vesting concept is perhaps best understood in light of its history. Before the passage of the Employee Retirement Income Security Act (ERISA) in 1974, it was accepted practice in some companies to offer retirement benefits only to employees who retired from the company after completing long periods of service (for example, 30 years). The result was a system that ignored the retirement needs of many, bound others in an unwanted fashion to their company, and shortchanged employees whose service was long but not long enough. Partly as a result of a television documentary and subsequent congressional hearings that publicized horror stories of long-service employees left penniless during retirement, Congress recognized the injustices of this situation and enacted ERISA, which ensured that employees would receive some retirement benefits if they terminated employment prior to reaching normal retirement age. ERISA established rules for determining how much service is required before benefits become nonforfeitable. These rules were called **vesting schedules**. Subsequent to ERISA, the rules have been changed several times, with each law mandating less and less required service before full vesting occurs. Today the vesting schedules allowed for defined-contribution and defined-benefit plans are somewhat different.

Vesting Schedules for Defined-Benefit Plans

In a defined-benefit plan an employer is required to choose a vesting schedule that is at least as favorable as one of two statutory schedules: the 5-year cliff vesting or the 3-through-7-year graded vesting. The 5-year cliff vesting is a schedule under which an employee who terminates employment prior to the completion of 5 years of service will be entitled to no benefit (zero percent vested). After 5 years of service, the employee becomes fully entitled to (100 percent vested in) the benefit that has accrued on his or her behalf. Five-year cliff vesting is easy to remember if you visualize an employee climbing a cliff for 5 years and finally becoming entitled to the benefits upon reaching the top. The cliff vesting schedule is as follows:

5-Year Cliff Vesting

Years of Service	Percentage Vested
0–4	0
5 or more	100

The other statutory vesting schedule, known as the 3-through-7-year graded schedule, requires no vesting until the third year of service has been completed; at that point, the vested portion of the accrued benefit increases 20 percent for each year served.

3-through-7-Year Graded Vesting

Years of Service	Percentage Vested
0–2	0
3	20
4	40
5	60
6	80
7 or more	100

An employer is allowed to choose a more liberal vesting schedule than either of the statutory vesting schedules. For example, an employer could establish a 2-year cliff vesting schedule or a 4-year graded schedule, where the participant earned an additional 25 percent vesting for each year of service. Also note that top-heavy defined-benefit plans (described further in chapter 10) will be subject to more accelerated vesting schedules that apply to defined-contribution plans. This is often the case for small businesses.

Vesting Schedules for Defined-Contribution Plans

In order to facilitate portability of benefits in defined-contribution plans, the Pension Protection Act of 2006 required more accelerated vesting schedules for defined-contribution plans. Defined-contribution plans are required to choose a vesting schedule that is at least as favorable as 3-year cliff vesting or 2-through-6-year graded vesting. With 3-year cliff vesting an employee who terminates employment prior to the completion of 3 years of service will be entitled to no benefit. After 3 years of service, the employee becomes fully entitled to the benefit that has accrued on his or her behalf.

3-Year Cliff Vesting	
Years of Service	Percentage Vested
0–2	0
3 or more	100

The 2-through-6-year graded schedule requires no vesting until the second year of service has been completed; at that point, the vested portion of the accrued benefit increases 20 percent for each year served. After 6 years the participant is fully vested.

2-through-6-Year Graded Vesting	
Years of Service	Percentage Vested
0–1	0
2	20
3	40
4	60
5	80
6 or more	100

General Vesting Considerations

The vesting schedules just described apply when a participant terminates employment on a voluntary or involuntary basis. If the participant continues working until the plan's normal retirement age, he must be fully vested regardless of the years of service earned. Plans may also choose to fully vest at attainment of an early retirement age, upon disability, or at death. Also remember that the participant's benefit attributable to employee after-tax contributions or employee pretax salary deferral elections in a 401(k) plan must be 100-percent vested at all times.

In today's pension environment, there are numerous other situations in which benefits must be fully vested at all times. All of them are summarized below. As you can see, Congress keeps whittling away at deferred vesting. This is probably because anything less than full and immediate vesting limits benefit "portability"—an important concern to a mobile workforce that changes jobs frequently.

- SEPs and SIMPLEs—Contributions to a SEP or SIMPLE must be fully vested at all times.
- Plan termination—Benefits must become fully vested upon a full or partial plan termination.
- Safe harbor 401(k) plans—Contributions to a 401(k) SIMPLE and contributions made to satisfy the 401(k) safe harbor provisions must be fully vested.

- Two-year eligibility rule—In exchange for the ability to exclude employees for 2 years (instead of one), contributions must be fully vested.

Choosing the Most Appropriate Vesting Schedule

forfeiture

reallocated forfeiture

The various vesting schedule choices and their exceptions obviously have design implications you must consider in helping your clients make the best choice. To the employer, the major advantage of choosing a restrictive vesting schedule is that it may be able to cut costs attributable to employee turnover. When employees terminate employment prior to being fully vested, the nonvested portion of the accrued benefit (referred to as a **forfeiture**) can be used to reduce future employer contributions. For example, if five employees terminate employment with the National Furniture Company, each with a $4,000 forfeited benefit, National's contribution for next year is reduced by $20,000. The employer also has the choice in any defined-contribution plan to use forfeitures as an additional contribution for remaining employees (in pension parlance, this is referred to as reallocated forfeitures). **Reallocated forfeitures** do not result in a direct cost savings, but they do allow the employer to provide bigger benefits for long-term highly compensated employees at no extra cost.

The forfeitures that are reallocated to employees are added to other contributions, and the aggregate amount cannot exceed the Code Sec. 415 maximum contribution limit. If the plan's benefit formula is already designed to reach this limit, then forfeitures should not be reallocated.

Another advantage of choosing a restrictive vesting schedule is that it helps retain employees. Many employees are convinced that it is economically desirable to delay a job change until they become fully vested (this may not always be the case in reality) and, consequently, stick it out at a company until the vesting requirements are fulfilled. When employers have spent time training employees and having them become acclimated, a restrictive vesting schedule that encourages employees to stay around after they have reached a productive level may pay back the organization for the time it invested.

In contrast to these reasons for adopting a restrictive schedule, there are some good reasons to adopt a more liberal schedule or to have immediate and full vesting:

- to foster employee morale
- to remain competitive in attracting employees

- to meet the design needs of the small employer who desires few encumbrances to participation for the "employee family"

YOUR FINANCIAL SERVICES PRACTICE: WHEN TO REALLOCATE FORFEITURES

If a defined-contribution plan is drafted to reallocate forfeitures to the remaining employees, a decision has to be made as to when the forfeitures will occur. One option is to wait until the participant has been gone for 5 years (five one-year breaks in service). This option ensures that the contributions are still available if a terminated employee returns to service and earns the right to such amounts. When the plan does not allow the distribution of benefits before the normal retirement date, the employer should always elect this option. However, if the employer allows immediate payment at termination of employment, the employer may wish to allocate forfeitures on the valuation date immediately following termination. This eliminates both the administrative expense and the confusion involved in maintaining many small accounts for terminated employees. This option makes sense if terminated employees generally do not return to service. If this option is elected, the employer must understand that additional contributions might have to be made if terminees return to service within 5 years.

Additional Vesting Rules

The choice of a vesting schedule is only the first in a series of vesting-design choices. The vesting schedule raises several questions that need to be answered through plan design:

- What years of service must be counted for vesting-schedule purposes?
- What happens if an employee leaves employment and then returns?

Vesting-Service Considerations

When determining vesting service, an employee must be credited with a year of service if he or she earns 1,000 or more hours of service in a 12-month period. For vesting purposes, the 12-month period can be measured from the date of hire or based on some other 12-month period. Many employers choose the plan year as the measuring period to simplify administration. Hours of service can be determined by using the standard-hours counting method (each hour actually worked is counted, plus hours for which an employee is entitled to be paid, such as vacations and holidays) or by using any one of the equivalency methods discussed in chapter 7.

In addition to designing these definitions, you can design the plan to exclude certain years of service.

- Years of service earned prior to age 18 can be excluded. (Generally, it is a good idea to exclude vesting service prior to age 18, because turnover is higher among younger employees, and the employer could save on future expenditures because of forfeitures.)
- Years of service before the plan went into effect can be excluded.
- Certain years of service prior to a break in service can be excluded (discussed below).

There are, however, circumstances where the plan cannot be designed to cut service for vesting purposes.

- Service prior to eligibility (past age 18) will be counted even if the employee was not a participant in the plan.
- Service for a different component of the employer, even though the employee was not covered by the plan, must be counted. For example, Sally Jerkins is a 15-year member of the Oakland office, which does not have a pension plan. Her company transfers her to the San Diego office, which does have one. Sally will be 100 percent vested when she transfers to San Diego under the plan's cliff vesting schedule because of her 15 years of service.
- Service with any member of a controlled group of corporations, with a commonly controlled business, or with an affiliated service group must be counted for vesting purposes. For example, George Gray is a 15-year employee of Modern Kitchens, which is under a controlled group with Total Home Concepts. Modern Kitchens has no plan; Total Home has one. When George is hired by Total Home, his years of service from Modern Kitchens will apply for vesting purposes.
- Service with a predecessor employer if the successor employer maintains the predecessor's plan must be counted. In other words, if an employee's company changes hands and the new owners maintain the same plan, service with the old owner counts for vesting purposes.

Breaks in Service

In some limited circumstances, the rules allow a plan to disregard certain years of vesting service during which a participant has had sporadic employment. The employer establishing the plan can take advantage of these rules or choose to disregard them.

break in service

For any of the rules to apply, the participant must first incur a **break in service**. A break in service is a year (using the same measuring period used for determining vesting) in which the individual does not complete more than 500 hours of service. If there is a break in service, there are three rules that may be applicable. Under the first rule, pre-break service may be disregarded until an individual is reemployed and completes a full year of service. For administrative purposes, this is probably a good idea, in case the reemployment does not last.

The second and most useful rule applies only to defined-contribution plans. Under this rule, if an individual has five consecutive breaks in service, the nonvested portion of the benefit earned prior to the break can be permanently forfeited.

> **EXAMPLE**
>
> Ralph terminates employment with a $2,000 account balance. He is 50 percent vested and so he is eligible to receive a benefit of $1,000. He returns to the same employer 7 years later. Regardless of how much post-break service he earns, Ralph cannot earn back the $1,000 benefit that he forfeited.

Most defined-contribution plans should consider adopting this provision. Otherwise, it is possible to have to make up contributions (or hold the forfeitures in a separate account) virtually forever.

Under the third rule, pre-break and post-break service do not have to be aggregated for an individual who is zero percent vested and who then incurs five consecutive one-year breaks in service. This rule is not adopted as regularly as the others because it adds administrative complexity and rarely applies. The employer who has a revolving workforce might want to consider adopting this vesting requirement.

RETIREMENT AGES

LO 9.3 Identify the design considerations associated with choosing normal, early, and deferred retirement provisions.

The choice of the plan's retirement age should be motivated primarily by business reasons, not tax or plan cost considerations. The employer should carefully consider at what age it wants to encourage employees to retire. The employer has to be concerned about the orderly retirement of older, highly compensated employees, while it does not want to inadvertently encourage its older, more experienced employees to leave and go to competitors. Such issues determine the success or failure of an organization and are much more important than plan cost or tax considerations.

Effective plan design concerning retirement age boils down to the following four questions:
- What should the normal retirement age be?
- Should there be early retirement, and if so, when should it start?
- Should early retirement be subsidized?
- What provisions should be made for deferred retirement?

Normal Retirement Age

normal retirement age

When you are designing the retirement plan, you typically define a **normal retirement age**—that is, the age specified in the plan at which the employee has the right to retire. The term right to retire means the employee can retire without the employer's consent and will receive his or her full benefit under the plan. In general, an employer and his or her advisor can choose any age up to 65 as the normal retirement age. Age 62 is another common choice for normal retirement because that is the earliest age at which a retiring worker can receive reduced Social Security benefits. In addition, the retirement age may be lower, if it is common for individuals in that industry to retire at a younger age. For example, a relatively young age can be chosen if it is the age at which employees customarily retire, such as in professional sports. As mentioned in chapter 3, plans in the pension category (including defined-benefit, cash-balance, money-purchase, and target-benefit plans) are subject to some limitations in choosing the minimum normal retirement age. The rules provide that a normal retirement age of 62 or later is always acceptable, and that an age earlier than 55 is presumed to be unreasonable, unless the sponsor can demonstrate that the normal retirement age is reasonably representative of the typical retirement age for the industry in which the covered workforce is employed. The rules give some deference to an employer's judgment in applying this same "industry" standard to a retirement between ages 55 and 62.

Under certain circumstances, the normal retirement age can be greater than 65. This usually occurs in new defined-benefit plans that have a number of older employees, which makes the start-up funding cost prohibitive, or in existing plans that frequently hire people 55 or older. In these cases, the employer should take advantage of an exception to the general rule: For an employee who commences participation in the plan within 5 years of the plan's normal retirement age, the plan can delay actual retirement until the employee's fifth anniversary.

For example, a 62-year-old hiree can have a normal retirement age of 67, not 65 as do other employees in the plan.

Early Retirement

An employer can include an early retirement provision that provides for the payment of retirement benefits earlier than normal retirement age. Typical early retirement ages are 55, 60, and 62. Early retirement provisions need to be written carefully to ensure that participant behavior matches the employer's objectives.

early retirement provision

Age is not the only determinant of early retirement (especially in defined-benefit plans); both age and service can dictate the early retirement age. One typical **early-retirement provision** requires age 55 and 10 years of service (in pension parlance, this is known as 55 and 10). The service requirement is valuable for employers who want to ensure enough time to fund the benefit (for example, when life insurance is used to fund the plan). Hence, if cash flow is a problem, a years-of-service requirement is desirable.

If the employer's industry is prone to superannuated employees or if the industry requires physical skills that employees may lack later in their careers, an early-retirement option is a good idea. In addition, an early-retirement option allows for a graceful change in management and the attraction of key employees who consider early retirement a valuable lifestyle choice. However, if the employer fears that certain key employees will take jobs with competitors in order to acquire a second pension check, or if a majority of the organization's business skills and knowledge are centered in a few key people whose loss would devastate the organization, early retirement is probably not a good idea.

The early-retirement benefit can be either subsidized or nonsubsidized. If it is subsidized, the actuarial reductions for early retirement (that is, the percentage reductions taken from the normal-retirement-age benefit to reflect the longer payout period) do not reflect the true cost of providing the benefit, and the difference represents an increased employer cost. For small plans whose owner-employees are looking for tax savings, a subsidized early-retirement program will garner bigger deductions and should be strongly considered as a planning alternative. For medium-sized and large plans, some subsidy may be called for—if, for example, the employer desires to eliminate older employees—but a substantial subsidy can be prohibitively expensive.

Employers who want to offer early retirement (say for competitive reasons), but are not delighted with the prospect of losing experienced employees, should consider nonsubsidized early retirement. If early retirement is not subsidized, the actuarial reduction will reflect as closely as possible the true experience of the early-retirement costs.

Deferred Retirement

deferred retirement

A plan should always be designed to accommodate the possibility of **deferred retirement**—retirement after the normal retirement age. Note that the Federal Age Discrimination in Employment Act prohibits involuntary retirement (except for some executives and employees in high policymaking positions). Also, Helping Clients Choose the Best Loan, Vesting, and it is desirable from a business standpoint to make provisions that allow, or even encourage, productive employees to remain on the team. Under the age discrimination law, the employer must continue to make contributions in a defined-contribution plan if a deferred retirement is chosen. In a defined-benefit plan, benefits cannot stop accruing at a specified age; however, the plan can contain a maximum number of years of service for determining benefits under the plan. For example, the benefit formula could be stated as two percent of final-average compensation times years of service, with service limited to 30 years.

> **YOUR FINANCIAL SERVICES PRACTICE: THE RETIREMENT-AGE RULES IN A SAMPLE ADOPTION AGREEMENT**
>
> Regardless of what the employer chooses with regard to early, normal, and deferred retirement, these decisions are reflected in the plan's definition section, which contains detailed descriptions of the terms early retirement, normal retirement, and deferred retirement, and it often spells out the actuarial reductions attributable to early retirement. In addition to containing choices with regard to the plan's definition section, the adoption agreement also includes sections for choosing early, normal, and deferred retirement provisions.
>
> The following sample illustrates how the early retirement age sections might appear in a typical adoption agreement:
>
> Section T: Early Retirement Age (refers to Section 20 of the Plan)
>   (1) Retirement Prior to Normal Retirement Age (Section S) *(check one)*
>   ( ) will not be permitted
>   ( ) will be permitted upon attaining age ___ and completing ___ years of
>   ( ) service
>   ( ) participation

TOP-HEAVY RULES

LO 9.4 Determine when a plan is top-heavy, and describe the additional restrictions that apply to a top-heavy plan.

In chapter 1, it was implied that retirement plans were a tug-of-war. On one side of the rope are the government regulations regarding eligibility, coverage, and vesting. On the other side, pulling equally hard, are financial services professionals looking to gain tax shelter and retirement protection for their business owner clients without overspending for the rank and file. The government's intervention stems from a spread-the-wealth philosophy and the desire to get the most for its money when it comes to allowing tax advantages for retirement plans.

The anchor of the government's tug-of-war team is the top-heavy rules, aimed specifically at small employers such as professional corporations and closely held businesses. The rationale for the strict scrutiny of small organizations is that employers and owners of these organizations are more prone to the temptation to shape the organization's retirement plan primarily to shelter taxes for themselves and key employees. As financial services professionals would be the first to attest, the government's suspicion is well-founded. (Clients that fall into the small-plan category are almost invariably interested in tax shelter first and retirement needs second.)

When Is a Plan Top-Heavy?

A defined-contribution plan is top-heavy if more than 60 percent of the account balances of all employees are allocated to key employees. A defined-benefit plan is top-heavy if more than 60 percent of the present value of the accrued benefits for all participants is accrued for key employees.

key employee

An individual is a **key employee** if at any time during the prior year he or she has been any of the following:

- an officer receiving annual compensation in excess of $175,000 (as indexed for 2017). If there are 30 or fewer employees, no more than three officers are treated as key employees. If there are 31 to 500 employees, no more than 10 percent of the employees are treated as officers. And, if there are more than 500 employees, no more than 50 officers are key employees
- a person who owns more than 5 percent of the company
- a person who is more than a 1 percent owner with annual compensation of more than $150,000

The top-heavy test is applied once a year on the determination date. Except for the first year of the plan, the determination date is the last day of the preceding plan year. In the calculation, distributions made within one year of the determination date are counted when determining account balances. However, the accounts of former employees who have not performed any services for the employer during the one-year period ending on the determination date are excluded from the calculation.

Separate plans of the same or related employers are generally aggregated for purposes of top-heavy testing. There is required aggregation of every plan that covers a key employee or that allows a key-employee plan to meet the applicable nondiscrimination and minimum-participation standards. Other plans that are not required to be aggregated may be added on a permissive basis. All these complicating factors demonstrate that the top-heavy determination should be made with the help of a qualified plan administrator.

Top-Heavy Provisions

Plan documents must contain top-heavy language. The plan document must specify that if the plan is or ever becomes top-heavy, certain special rules will become effective. The plan must satisfy the following top-heavy requirements:

- special vesting rules
- minimum benefits for non-key employees
- a special limit for situations where both a defined-benefit and a defined-contribution plan are present

If these rules are satisfied, a top-heavy plan will continue to remain qualified.

Special Top-Heavy Vesting Schedules

Today the vesting rules that apply to defined-contribution plans and the special top-heavy vesting provisions are the same. This means that the top-heavy vesting requirements only apply to top-heavy defined-benefit plans. A defined-benefit plan that is top-heavy must use a vesting schedule just as favorable as one of the two schedules in the tables below.

3-Year Cliff Vesting	
Years of Service	Percentage Vested
0–2	0
3 or more	100

6-Year Graded Schedule	
Years of Service	Percentage Vested
0–1	0
2	20
3	40
4	60
5	80
6	100

Minimum Benefits and Contributions for Non-Key Employees

A top-heavy plan must provide minimum benefits or contributions for non-key employees. For defined-benefit plans, the benefit for each non-key employee must be at least 2 percent of compensation multiplied by the number of the employee's years of service in which the plan is top-heavy up to a maximum of 10 years (maximum 20 percent benefit accrual). This 2 percent minimum annual accrual is typically larger than the typical plan benefit for non-key employees, especially if a plan is integrated with Social Security benefits. This means that the top-heavy requirements can result in additional costs for the employer in a defined benefit plan.

For a defined-contribution plan, the minimum employer contribution is generally 3 percent of compensation for non-key employees. If the plan provides less than a 3 percent contribution for any key employee, then the highest contribution percentage for any key employee is substituted. For example, if an employer with a profit-sharing plan made no contribution for any key employee, then no top-heavy contribution is required for non-key employees. If the employer contributed 1 percent of compensation for a key employee, then the required minimum contribution for non-key employees is 1 percent.

In a defined-contribution plan that allocates contributions as a level percentage of compensation, the top-heavy minimum contribution requirements have no effect on plan design or cost. However, if the contribution formula is integrated with Social Security or with any other design that results in larger contributions (as a percentage of compensation) for key employees, the top-heavy minimum will affect plan design. For example, in an integrated profit-sharing plan, the plan typically allocates the first 3 percent of compensation on a pro rata basis, to ensure that the top-heavy minimum is satisfied. Only after 3 percent is allocated does the formula address Social Security integration.

If a non-key employee participates in both a defined-benefit and a defined-contribution plan, the employer is not required to provide the non-key employee with both the minimum benefit and minimum contribution. However, since the defined-benefit minimum is the more valuable benefit, if the sponsor chooses to make the top-heavy contribution to the defined-contribution plan (instead of the defined-benefit plan), the contribution must be 5 percent of compensation for each non-key employee.

Planning Considerations

Although larger plans (covering over 100 employees) are rarely top-heavy, top-heavy contingency language must be included in the plan's boilerplate language. Most plans of small businesses (covering 25 or fewer employees) become top-heavy within a few years of formation. For plans that are likely to be top-heavy, instead of providing the top-heavy language as a contingency, these plans are typically designed to satisfy the top-heavy provisions.

The top-heavy rules can cause special difficulty for the small 401(k) plan. The problem is that elective salary deferral contributions count toward determining top-heavy status, which means that even a plan that only contains salary deferral contributions can become top-heavy. Also, because salary deferral contributions are treated as employer contributions, if any key employee defers 3 percent of compensation, the sponsor has to make a top-heavy contribution of 3 percent for non-key employees. It is important to communicate this possibility to employers so they are not surprised by this information at the end of the year. Remember, this would not happen in a traditional profit-sharing plan because a contribution of zero for the key employees means no required contribution for the non-key employees.

The problem can even occur if the company makes matching contributions. Matching contributions do count toward satisfying the top-heavy minimum, but there could still be an additional required contribution for those non-key employees who are not eligible for the matching contributions. A way to solve the top-heavy problem in a 401(k) plan is to make a safe harbor contribution (see chapter 5). If either the matching or nonelective safe harbor contribution is made to the plan, the plan is exempt from the top-heavy rules.

Sometimes, small employers that establish SEPs have very little administrative help. They may not be aware that the top-heavy rules apply to SEPs. Top-heavy status is a problem with a SEP mainly if the plan has a contribution formula integrated with Social Security. SIMPLE IRAs are not required to satisfy the top-heavy rules.

CHAPTER REVIEW

Key Terms and Concepts

vesting schedules
forfeiture
reallocated forfeiture
break in service

normal retirement age
early retirement provision
deferred retirement
key employee

Chapter 9: Review Questions

Review questions are based on the learning objectives in this chapter. Thus, a [9.3] at the end of a question means that the question is based on learning objective 3. If there are multiple objectives, they are all listed

1. What are the advantages and disadvantages of designing a plan to include a loan provision? [9.1]

2. To what extent does the type of plan involved affect planning for a loan provision in [1]
   a. 401(k) plans
   b. 403(b) plans
   c. defined-contribution pension plans
   d. profit-sharing plans
   e. defined-benefit plans
   f. stock plans
   g. SEPs and SIMPLEs

3. How can a loan provision help a financial services professional to overcome the client's objection that plan funds are being "locked up"? [9.1]

4. The New City Heating Supply Company (an S corporation) has a qualified money-purchase plan that allows employees to take loans up to the maximum legal limit. What is the maximum loan that can be taken by the following employees? [9.1]

Employee	Vested Account Balance	Percentage of Corporate Ownership
a. Mary Wood	$ 17,000	0
b. Peter Muhlenberg	$160,000	0
c. Donna Dickenson	$200,000	50

5. Which of the following sets of vesting schedules can be used in a defined-benefit plan? [9.2]

   a.
Years of service	Percentage vested
0–9	0
10	100

   b.
Years of service	Percentage vested
1	50%
2	60
3	70
4	80
5	90
6	100

   c.
Years of service	Percentage vested
0–4	0%
5	50
6	100

6. What is the difference between defined-benefit and a defined-contribution plans under the vesting rules? [9.2]

7. Under what conditions should an employer choose a restrictive vesting schedule for the plan? Under what conditions should the employer choose a liberal vesting schedule for the plan? [9.2]

8. Identify the following periods of service that must be included and those that can be excluded for vesting purposes: [9.2]

   a. service prior to eligibility earned by a 20-year-old participant
   b. service earned by a 16-year-old employee
   c. service for a subsidiary of the employer, even though the subsidiary did not have a qualified plan
   d. years of service before the effective date of the plan

9. Identify the three break-in-service rules that may allow the employer to disregard prior service for vesting purposes. [9.2]

10. When should a post-65 normal retirement age be considered? [9.3]

11. What are the advantages and disadvantages of [9.3]
    a. including an early retirement provision in a plan
    b. subsidizing an early retirement benefit

12. Can an employer stop making contributions in a defined-contribution plan once the participant attains age 65, which is the plan's normal retirement age? [9.3]

13. In a defined benefit plan, how can the employer effectively limit the benefits for older, long-service employees without violating age discrimination law? [9.3]

14. a. What is the purpose of the top-heavy rules?
    b. What size organizations do these rules affect the most? [9.5]

15. At the end of the prior year, the Trophy Shop money-purchase plan had the following participants:

Employee	Percentage of Stock Owned	Salary	Account Balance
Allen (president)	95%	$85,000	$100,000
McFadden (VP/treasurer)	3	170,000	60,000
McGill	2	50,000	40,000
Melone	0	45,000	12,000
Rosenbloom	0	35,000	8,000

    a. Identify the employees who would be considered key employees for top-heavy testing purposes.
    b. Is the Trophy Shop plan top-heavy? Explain. [9.5]

16. Which of the following vesting provisions would satisfy the top-heavy vesting requirements? [9.5]
    a. The participant becomes fully vested after 4 years of service.
    b. The participant becomes fully vested after 2 years of service.
    c. The participant becomes 50 percent vested after 3 years and 100 percent vested after 6 years.

17. What is the minimum required top-heavy contribution if an employer has a top-heavy profit-sharing plan and no contributions are made for any key employees for the year? [9.5]

18. What is the minimum required top-heavy contribution if an employer has a top-heavy 401(k) plan that only contains employee salary deferrals and at least one key employee makes a 5 percent salary deferral to the plan? [9.5]

Chapter 9: Review Answers

1. The advantages of including a loan provision are that (1) it provides a safety valve for those concerned about losing access to contributions, (2) business owners can have plan loans, and (3) there are mechanisms to minimize administrative problems. The disadvantages of including a loan provision include the fact that (1) the loan provision may be inconsistent with the employee's objective of providing retirement security and (2) the loan may default, which would put additional administrative responsibilities on the administrator.

2. Loans are quite common to 401(k) and 403(b) plans because they provide tax-free access to participants' salary deferral contributions. Loans are less common in plans funded totally with employer contributions. Still, they may be available simply as an additional benefit or as an alternative to in-service withdrawals. Defined-benefit plans rarely have loan provisions because there are no participant accounts; ESOPs do not because of the investment restrictions. SEPs and SIMPLEs are not allowed to have participant loans.

3. Plan loans unlock funds by making them currently available to employees. Plan sponsors who are hesitant to set up a plan because they are reluctant to "put money away" may find the loan provision mitigates this fear.

4. The maximum loan limit is the lesser of $50,000 or one-half of the vested account balance. Although the tax rules provide an exception that allows a participant to borrow up to $10,000 (even if this exceeds one-half of the vested account balance), plans generally do not use the exception, as the labor regulations only allow one-half of the vested account to be used as collateral for the loan.

    a. The maximum loan for Woods under most plans is $8,500. If the plan were to allow Woods to take $10,000, it would have to have the loan secured with property in addition to Woods's account balance.

    b. The maximum loan for Muhlenberg is $50,000 (which equals the lesser of $50,000 or one-half of his account balance).

    c. The maximum loan for Dickenson is $50,000. Prior to 2002, loans could not be made to owners of S corporations. This restriction no longer applies.

5. An employer is required to choose a vesting schedule for a defined-benefit plan that is equal to or more liberal than one of two statutory vesting schedules. The first statutory vesting schedule (a) is a 5-year cliff vesting schedule under which the employee is zero percent vested until 5 years of service are completed, at which time the employee

becomes 100 percent vested. The second statutory vesting schedule (b) is a 3-through-7-year graded vesting schedule, under which the participant becomes 20 percent vested after 3 years of service and receives an additional 20 percent vesting for each subsequent year of service.

   a. The first schedule cannot be used in a defined-benefit plan because it exceeds the maximum cliff period of 5 years.

   b. The second schedule can be used in a defined-benefit plan because it is at least as "liberal" as the 3-through-7-year graded schedule. Note that in each year of service, an employee is as well off or better off under the graded schedule presented.

   c. The third schedule cannot be used in a qualified plan even though the participant becomes 100 percent vested more quickly than in the 3-through-7-year graded vesting schedule. The reason the third schedule is not as liberal as the 3-through-7-year schedule is that a participant with 3, 4, and 5 years of service is "worse off" than is statutorily permitted under a graded schedule.

6. Today, defined-benefit plans can require longer periods of service under the vesting rules than defined-contribution plans. Defined-benefit plans can use 5-year cliff vesting or 3-to-7-year graded vesting, while defined contribution plans must use 3-year cliff vesting or 2-to-6-year graded vesting.

7. a. Restrictive vesting schedules may reduce benefit costs if a significant number of employees terminate employment before becoming fully vested. Also, a restrictive vesting schedule acts as a "golden handcuff," tying the employee to the company until benefits become vested.

    b. More liberal vesting schedules are often used to create a competitive advantage by providing a better plan than a competitor.

8. a. Service prior to eligibility earned by a 20-year-old participant must be counted for vesting purposes.

    b. Service earned by a 16-year-old employee need not be counted for vesting purposes.

    c. Service for a subsidiary of the employer, even though the subsidiary did not have a qualified plan, must be counted for vesting purposes.

    d. Years of service before the effective date of the plan need not be counted for vesting purposes.

9. Prior vesting service can be disregarded under three break-in-service (a year with fewer than 500 hours of service) rules. First, pre-break service can be disregarded until an individual is reemployed and completes a full year of service. Second, in a defined-contribution plan, if a participant has five consecutive breaks in service, the nonvested portion of the benefit earned prior to the breaks can be permanently forfeited. The third, but less useful, rule applies only to participants who are zero percent vested. If such a participant has five consecutive breaks in service, pre-break service can be disregarded entirely.

10. To give the employer time to fund benefits for older employees, it would make sense to make the normal retirement age the later of age 65 or 5 years of participation.

11. a. The advantages of putting an early retirement provision in the plan is that it enables employees who are superannuated or physically worn out to gracefully retire. The disadvantages of putting an early retirement provision in the plan is that certain key employees will leave and take a job with a competitor.

    b. Subsidizing an early retirement benefit gives employees an incentive to retire at the early retirement age. This can be a disadvantage if the employer does not want to encourage early retirement. It is also expensive to provide a subsidized benefit.

12. The Age Discrimination in Employment Act requires that contributions continue to defined-contribution plans regardless of the participant's age.

13. The defined-benefit plan cannot limit the benefit formula based on age, but it can limit the years of service taken into consideration under the benefit formula. This makes sense from a plan design perspective. If, for example, the employer wants to replace 50 percent of final average compensation for long-service employees, it could design a formula of 2 percent of final average compensation multiplied by years of service, with service limited to 25 years.

14. a. The purpose of the top-heavy rules is to ensure that small organizations do not make the plan exclusively a tax shelter for the business owners.

    b. Top-heavy rules typically affect small businesses.

15. a. An individual is a key employee if at any time during the prior year he or she has been any of the following:

    - an officer receiving annual compensation in excess of $175,000 (as indexed for 2017)

- a person who owns more than 5 percent of the company
- a person who is more than a one-percent owner with annual compensation of more than $150,000

Allen is a key employee because she was a 5-percent owner at the end of the previous year. In addition, McFadden is also a key employee because she is an officer earning more than the required dollar limit. McGill, Melone, and Rosenbloom, however, are not key employees because they do not meet any of the definitions.

b. To determine whether the Trophy Shop plan is top-heavy, we must check whether more than 60 percent of the aggregate account balances belong to key employees. The key employees are Allen ($100,000) and McFadden ($60,000), and combined they hold $160,000 of the plan's assets. The non-key employees are McGill ($40,000), Melone ($12,000), and Rosenbloom ($8,000); combined they hold $60,000 of the plan's assets. Because the $160,000 in assets held by key employees is 72 percent of the total plan assets ($220,000), the plan is top-heavy.

16. a. No, this schedule does not satisfy the top-heavy provisions. It is not as beneficial as 3-year cliff vesting.

b. Yes, this schedule satisfies the top-heavy vesting rules. It is more beneficial than 3-year cliff vesting.

c. No, this schedule does not satisfy the top-heavy vesting rules. It is not as favorable as 6-year graded vesting.

17. The required contribution is zero because the highest rate of contribution for any key employee is zero.

18. Because salary deferrals are treated as employer contributions, the employer would have to contribute 3 percent of compensation for each non-key employee. The owners would be very unhappy with that situation if they were unaware of this possibility.

Chapter 10

Death and Disability Benefits

Learning Objectives

An understanding of the material in this chapter should enable you to

- **LO 10.1** Explain the death-benefit requirements that apply to qualified plans.
- **LO 10.2** Understand how the incidental death-benefit requirements limit the amount of life insurance in a qualified plan.
- **LO 10.3** Describe why preretirement death benefits are typically provided outside of the qualified retirement plan.
- **LO 10.4** Describe common disability provisions found in qualified retirement plans.
- **LO 10.5** Understand the importance of choosing the correct retirement plan beneficiary.

The primary purpose of a qualified retirement plan is to provide retirement benefits to employees. The retirement plan, however, can be used to meet the insurance needs of participants by providing both death and disability coverage in the preretirement period.

DEATH BENEFITS

LO 10.1 Explain the death-benefit requirements that apply to qualified plans.

Qualified retirement plans have a number of alternatives regarding the provision of preretirement death benefits. There is a minimum required benefit for certain married participants and a maximum benefit when the plan wants to provide a large benefit through the purchase of life insurance. There is a wide range of options in between. The design of the plan's death benefits will depend on the company's objective, as well as on the other benefit programs that provide for preretirement death benefits.

Mandatory Death Benefits: QPSA and QJSA

There are two mandatory death benefits. For a participant that dies prior to retirement, the plan must provide a spousal benefit called a qualified preretirement survivor annuity (QPSA). For participants receiving retirement benefits, the normal form of distribution from the retirement plan for a married participant must be a qualified joint-and-survivor annuity (QJSA). The legislative motive behind both of these rules is to protect the spouse's right to a piece of the participant's retirement income.

qualified preretirement survivor annuity (QPSA)

The **qualified preretirement survivor annuity (QPSA)** (pronounced "quip-sa") is defined differently for defined-benefit and defined-contribution plans. In both cases, however, the QPSA is required to be provided only for married participants who were married for one year before the participant's death (plans sometimes waive the one-year requirement for administrative convenience). For a defined-benefit plan, the amount of the survivor annuity is basically equal to the amount that would have been paid under the qualified joint-and-survivor annuity (below). To determine this amount, the plan administrator assumes that the participant retired the day before death, or if the participant was not yet able to retire, left the company the day prior to death, survived until the plan's earliest retirement age, and then retired with an immediate joint-and-survivor annuity. For a defined-contribution plan, the qualified preretirement survivor annuity is an annuity for the life of the surviving spouse that is at least actuarially equivalent to 50 percent of the vested account balance of the participant as of the date of death.

The QPSA need not be an employer-sponsored benefit; the employer has the choice of requiring employee contributions to fund this benefit or, conversely, reducing the normal benefit actuarially. If the second choice is made, the employee generally has the option of electing out of the QPSA benefit any time after age 35. A written confirmation of the spouse's consent to the election out is required. Many employers choose to pay for the cost of providing the QPSA in order to avoid the administrative and legal problems that could result from the administration of the spousal consent forms.

qualified joint-and-survivor annuity (QJSA)

The **qualified joint-and-survivor annuity (QJSA)** must be the normal form of benefit distribution offered to a married participant at retirement. A QJSA is an annuity for the life of the participant, with a survivor annuity for the life of the spouse which is not less than 50 percent (and not more than 100 percent) of the amount of the annuity payable during the joint lives of the participant and his or her spouse. The participant and his or her spouse may waive the right to a QJSA and QPSA provided certain requirements are satisfied. In general, these conditions include providing the participant with a written explanation of the terms and conditions of the survivor annuity, the right to make, and the effect of, a waiver of the annuity, the right of the spouse to waive the survivor annuity, and the right of the participant to revoke the waiver. In addition, the spouse must provide written consent to the waiver, witnessed by a plan representative or a notary public, which acknowledges the effect of the waiver.

The Pension Protection Act of 2006 has amended the QJSA rules somewhat. Participants now have to be given the option to elect a qualified optional survivor annuity. A qualified optional survivor annuity is an annuity for the life of the participant with a survivor annuity for the life of the spouse which is equal to 75 percent (if the survivor portion under the QJSA is less than 75 percent) or 50 percent (if the survival portion under the QJSA is greater than or equal to 75 percent) of the survival portion under the QJSA.

> **YOUR FINANCIAL SERVICES PRACTICE: PROVIDING MINIMUM DEATH BENEFITS IN QUALIFIED PLANS**
>
> Especially in larger defined-benefit plans, the employer will typically provide death benefits outside of the pension plan, and if given a choice will not provide death benefits in the plan. However, by law the employer must provide the QPSA benefit for eligible married participants. In this case, it is not uncommon for the plan to provide the QPSA for married participants and no death benefit for unmarried participants—a situation that the unmarried participants may feel is unfair.
>
> The same strategy could be used in defined-contribution plans, but because individual accounts have accrued for each participant, most employers choose to pay out the entire account balance as a preretirement death benefit for both married and unmarried participants.

These rules apply to all qualified plans; however, plans in the profit-sharing category (including stock bonus plans, ESOPs, and 401(k) plans) are exempt from the QJSA requirement if certain criteria are met. Most advisors encourage employers to take advantage of this exception in order to simplify plan administration. In order to qualify, the plan must not allow any life annuity options and must not accept direct transfers of plan benefits from other plans subject to the QJSA requirements. Finally, the plan must provide that if a married participant dies prior to retirement, the spouse must be entitled to receive 100 percent of the participant's plan benefit, unless the spouse elects to waive the benefit.

Incidental Rules for Death Benefits

LO 10.2   Understand how the incidental death-benefit requirements limit the amount of life insurance in a qualified plan.

Death benefits under a retirement plan must be incidental because Uncle Sam is providing tax advantages to the qualified plan for retirement needs, not insurance needs. The word incidental, however, may be somewhat of a misnomer, since a fairly substantial incidental death benefit can be provided through the use of life insurance in a qualified plan. The incidental death benefit rule is a qualification requirement, meaning that failing to satisfy the rule can result in plan disqualification.

The rules described below apply to qualified plans, which are allowed to invest in life insurance. The rules do not apply to SEPs, SIMPLEs, and 403(b) plans because these types of plans cannot have investments in life insurance.

Preretirement Death Benefits

LO 10.3 Describe why preretirement death benefits are typically provided outside of the qualified retirement plan.

For defined-contribution plans, to satisfy the incidental benefit requirement, the aggregate premiums paid over the entire life of the plan must either be

- less than 50 percent of aggregate employer contributions for permanent insurance or
- no greater than 25 percent of aggregate employer contributions for other types of insurance.

EXAMPLE

Tim Rivers has an account that includes $100,000 of employer contributions. If he uses variable, universal, or term insurance, the aggregate premiums that can be used to pay for Tim's life insurance total a maximum of $25,000. If he has a whole life policy, the aggregate premiums that can be used to pay for his life insurance total a maximum of $50,000.

The IRS has defined permanent life insurance as insurance on which the premium does not increase and the death benefit does not decrease. Ordinary life insurance and whole life insurance are examples of permanent insurance. Term insurance clearly is not permanent insurance and is subject to the 25-percent limit. The IRS has also indicated that universal life insurance and variable life insurance are subject to the lower 25-percent limit.

In a defined-benefit plan, the plan can meet the incidental benefits requirement using the 25 percent/50 percent test or the 100-to-1 ratio test. Under this test, the death benefit is limited to a maximum of 100 times the expected monthly benefit or, if greater, the reserve for the pension benefit. For example, if the expected monthly benefit is $1,500, then the total death benefit could be $150,000 or the reserve (at the date of death) if greater.

Exceptions

There are several exceptions to the incidental death benefit rule. First, the limitation does not apply to life insurance bought with after-tax employee contributions. Second, the incidental limitations do not apply to profit-sharing plans if 1) the plan permits in-service withdrawals (for example, after 2 years) and 2) life insurance is purchased with funds that could be withdrawn. If the plan has a 401(k) feature, this exception would not apply to the salary deferral account because of the in-service withdrawal restrictions on this portion of the account.

> **YOUR FINANCIAL SERVICES PRACTICE: LIFE INSURANCE IN A PROFIT-SHARING PLAN**
>
> With the incidental death benefit exception that applies to profit-sharing plans, a small business owner with a significant life insurance need may consider purchasing the policy within the plan. Another unique feature of profit-sharing plans is that the plan can allow for the purchase of second-to-die policies. If all participants are given investment direction and have the option to purchase life insurance in their own accounts, the owner can purchase a policy even if the owner is the only participant taking advantage of the option.
>
> This approach may be appropriate when the owner's only source of funds to purchase the policy is the profit-sharing plan. It's not uncommon to fund the policy in the plan for a number of years, but eventually attempt to remove the policy from the plan. The policy can be sold to the owner or distributed as part of a benefit distribution and transferred to an irrevocable life insurance trust.

Incidental Rule for Postretirement Death Benefits

We have been looking at limitations on the amount of death benefits that can be provided if a participant dies prior to retirement. However, there are also limitations on the amount of death benefits that can be provided after retirement. These rules have become part of the required minimum-distribution rules. Conceptually, the rules require that the amount of benefits paid to beneficiaries is incidental to the retirement benefits paid to participants. To do this, the rules impose very specific minimum payout requirements during the participant's lifetime.

Tax Implications of Life Insurance

Table 2001

As discussed in chapter 1, employees are generally not taxed on the benefits promised from, or the contributions made to, a qualified plan. Taxation occurs at the time benefits are received. The one exception is when life insurance is purchased in a plan to provide death benefits. In this case, the current cost of the "pure insurance" protection is subject to taxation. The cost attributable to this pure life protection will be the rates supplied by the IRS table found in Notice 2001-10 referred to as Table 2001 (below). Prior to **Table 2001**, the PS 58 table was used and the cost of insurance that is included in income is still referred to by many as PS 58 costs.

Table 10-1
IRS Table 2001: One-Year Term Premiums for $1,000 of Life Insurance Protection

Attained Age	Section 79 Extended and Interpolated Annual Rates	Attained Age	Section 79 Extended and Interpolated Annual Rates	Attained Age	Section 79 Extended and Interpolated Annual Rates
0	0.70	35	0.99	70	20.62
1	0.41	36	1.01	71	20.72
2	0.27	37	1.04	72	25.07
3	0.19	38	1.06	73	27.57
4	0.13	39	1.07	74	30.18
5	0.13	40	1.10	75	33.05
6	0.14	41	1.13	76	36.33
7	0.15	42	1.20	77	40.17
8	0.16	43	1.29	78	44.33
9	0.16	44	1.40	79	49.23
10	0.16	45	1.53	80	54.56
11	0.19	46	1.67	81	60.51
12	0.24	47	1.83	82	66.74
13	0.28	48	1.98	83	73.07
14	0.33	49	2.13	84	80.35
15	0.38	50	2.30	85	88.76
16	0.52	51	2.52	86	99.16
17	0.57	52	2.81	87	110.40
18	0.59	53	3.20	88	121.85
19	0.61	54	3.65	89	133.40
20	0.62	55	4.15	90	144.30
21	0.62	56	4.68	91	155.80
22	0.64	57	5.20	92	168.75
23	0.66	58	5.66	93	186.44
24	0.68	59	6.06	94	206.70
25	0.71	60	6.51	95	228.35
26	0.73	61	7.11	96	250.01
27	0.76	62	7.96	97	265.09
28	0.80	63	9.08	98	270.11
29	0.83	64	10.41	99	281.05
30	0.87	65	11.90		
31	0.90	66	13.51		
32	0.93	67	15.20		
33	0.96	68	16.92		
34	0.982	69	18.70		

EXAMPLE

Joe, a 55-year-old participant in a 401(k) plan has made the election to invest in a life insurance policy with a death benefit of $250,000. Joe will have taxable income for the year based on the Table 2001 rate. The annual cost for $1,000 of coverage for a 55-year-old is $4.15. The total cost is $4.15 x 250 (he has $250,000 of coverage) or $1,037.50. That is the amount included in Joe's taxable income for the year.

Any amounts currently taxed to the participant according to this rule (along with any employee after-tax contributions or employer contributions on which the employee has paid tax) are considered part of an employee's cost basis. When the employee takes retirement distributions from the plan, he or she will not be required to pay taxes on the portion of the distribution attributable to cost basis. In other words, the pure life insurance protection will not be taxed twice.

For a self-employed person with a Keogh plan or a 5 percent owner in an S corporation, the rules are applied differently. The portion of employer contribution that is allocable to the cost of pure insurance protection for the self-employed individual is treated as a nondeductible contribution. Also, at the time of payment, the taxable insurance costs are not recovered tax free by the business owner.

Death Benefit Plan Design

There are innumerable reasons to include life insurance in an employee benefits package, including competitiveness, attraction and retention of employees, and other advantages for the business owner. By including life insurance protection in a benefit package, business owners are able to (1) receive favorable group rates for themselves and their employees, (2) shift a nondeductible personal expense to the company, and (3) if necessary, gain favorable underwriting for ratable or uninsurable individuals (which potentially means life insurance protection without physical exams or medical questions).

Essentially, the most important question facing the financial services professional is not whether death benefits should be provided, but rather what vehicle should provide them. Is it in the employer's best interest to provide the majority of death benefits in a group insurance plan or in a retirement plan? What system will provide the lowest employee and employer cost for the desired benefit level?

Many employers choose to provide the death benefits outside of the qualified plan. One reason is that the benefit structure, especially in defined-benefit plans, does not provide an appropriate amount of insurance. In defined-benefit plans, the death benefit is tied to the participant's benefit (for example, 100 times the monthly retirement benefit). This means the death benefit would be quite small in the early years, when the participant may need the insurance protection the most. Insurance in a defined-contribution plan poses a different problem. Premiums are taken from the participant's account and can have the effect of reducing the ultimate retirement benefits provided. There are also tax reasons that motivate employers to choose to provide death benefits outside the qualified plan. Code Sec. 79 provides a $50,000 exemption (the premiums paid for the first $50,000 of term insurance covering an employee are not taxable), which further eases the tax bite. Also, the tax treatment of insurance proceeds is more favorable outside of the plan, where in most cases the entire death benefit is not taxable.

For these reasons, most mid-size and large organizations provide death benefits outside of the qualified plan. For small organizations, however, providing the death benefit in the qualified plan may be more administratively convenient, be better serviced by the life agent, and do double duty for the retirement dollar by offering a tax-favored way of providing permanent life insurance. Small business owners also sometimes use qualified plan assets to purchase life insurance for estate planning purposes. If the individual has a life insurance need, the most available assets to pay the premiums may well be in the qualified plan. One popular planning device is to purchase a second-to-die life insurance policy in a profit-sharing plan (pension plans cannot hold second-to-die policies). However, this is a very complicated subject which is outside the scope of this text (it is even somewhat unclear what the IRS's position is on this matter).

DISABILITY BENEFITS

LO 10.4   Describe common disability provisions found in qualified retirement plans.

Similar to the issue of death benefits, many employers provide disability benefits, although the question is how to provide the benefits. Most large companies that maintain separate short-term and long-term disability plans do not provide disability income benefits in their retirement programs. If there is an existing disability income program, the financial services professional needs to be concerned primarily with the coordination of the retirement plan and the disability income plan.

Most plans do have some provisions for disability. The most common provision is to fully vest participants if they have to terminate due to a disability. It is also fairly common, especially in a defined-contribution plan, to allow payouts at the time of the disability.

Less common, and much more expensive, is to continue accruing benefit service while the participant is out on disability. Because most company-provided long-term disability benefits will stop at age 65, this is a way to continue building an adequate retirement benefit for the disabled person.

EXAMPLE

The Northeast Corporation has a defined-benefit plan that provides a monthly life annuity at age 65 in the amount of 2 percent of final average compensation multiplied by years of service. The company also provides a long-term disability program that pays a disability benefit to a disabled worker until age 65. To ensure that the disabled worker has an adequate retirement benefit, the plan counts service (until age 65) for those individuals out on disability.

No matter what form the disability benefit takes, there are two additional decisions about plan design that must be considered. First, the plan must contain a definition of disability. One simple, but restrictive, option is to define disability as eligibility for Social Security disability benefits. If the company also has a disability insurance program, another option is to define disability as eligibility for benefits under that plan. Both of these options simplify administration by putting the task of determination and verification on an outside organization.

Second, consider whether or not the retirement plan's disability benefit should have age and service requirements. Reasons to include these requirements are to permit enough time to properly fund the benefit and to limit the benefit to long-service employees. In addition, if there are age and service provisions, the question of whether the disability was attributable to a preexisting condition is also sidestepped. The main reason for not having age and service requirements for disability is the negative impression it can create among employees.

RETIREMENT PLAN BENEFICIARY DESIGNATION PLANNING

LO 10.5 Understand the importance of choosing the correct retirement plan beneficiary.

In this chapter we have been discussing the pre- and post-death benefits offered inside of a qualified plan. However, many of these death benefits and the overall value of the retirement plan could be seriously jeopardized by not paying close attention to the beneficiary designation. Many people are unaware that the beneficiary designation, QPSA, and QJSA rules control over an individual's estate planning documents, such as a will. Additionally, documents such as a premarital agreement or prenuptial will have no legal impact on ERISA controlled beneficiary designations or spousal rights. Beneficiary designations can have a big impact on taxes, creditor protections, wealth transfer, and estate planning. As such, choosing the right beneficiary designation is crucial to ensuring the value of the retirement plan is transferred to the proper beneficiaries in accordance with the plan participant's wishes upon his or her death.

Beneficiary designations fulfill a very important role as they allow the retirement plan participant to state the individual (natural person or otherwise) that will receive any remaining benefits upon the participant's death. Again, this designation controls over any estate planning documents or state law, as long as the retirement account was under the control of ERISA because ERISA contains a state preemption clause in Section 514(a). The reason for the state preemption law is to take away some of the confusion that would arise if each state dealt with federally created retirement accounts differently. However, there are local state, church, and government plans that are exempt from ERISA. The distribution of plan assets in non-ERISA plans could be impacted by state laws, contracts, wills and other planning mechanisms. Retirement assets in an ERISA covered retirement plan would pass outside of state probate in accordance with the beneficiary designation. The form, style, and requirements of the beneficiary designation are controlled by each ERISA plan document.

While proper transfer of the death benefit is the most important reason to name the proper beneficiary, there could be other reasons as well. First, because a death beneficiary would take the benefit outside of probate, this could significantly cut down on expenses for the deceased participant's estate and reduce the time it would take for the beneficiary to take control over the assets. This could be incredibly important if the money will be needed by the surviving spouse or family members for support immediately following the deceased's death. Secondly, since 2007, nonspousal beneficiaries are allowed to do a direct tax free trustee-to-trustee rollover under Code Section 402(c)(11) of an interest in the inherited plan to an "inherited IRA." However, if the assets were first distributed to an estate and then distributed out to the deceased's heirs, this ability would be lost. Rolling the plan into an inherited IRA could have a variety of benefits as the inherited IRA can often offer more favorable benefits, distributions, and features. Additionally, the inherited plan needs to be distributed in accordance with the required minimum-distribution rules discussed in a later chapter, providing for additional tax deferred growth to the beneficiary that would not be achieved by leaving the retirement plan to the participant's estate. After 2010, eligible ERISA retirement plans are now required to offer nonspouse beneficiaries a trustee-to-trustee transfer. These rules also apply to spousal beneficiaries.

In addition, choosing the right beneficiary could open up access to in-service withdrawals from plan assets. Some plans permit a payment from the plan to meet a participant's needs before retirement. For instance, upon a stated hardship or financial emergency, a plan can pay out before all of the plan's retirement conditions are fully met. However, in some cases the beneficiary could have an impact, as a plan is allowed pay out if the reasons for the hardship conditions concerned the primary beneficiary, someone with "an unconditional right to all or a portion of the participant's account balance under the plan upon the death of the participant."[1] The distribution allowable under this hardship expense must meet all other hardship requirements but could be used for medical, tuition, or funeral expenses of the primary beneficiary.

Most entities and people can be listed as a beneficiary. Spouses, children, friends, parents, trusts, and charities can all be listed as a beneficiary of a retirement plan. In addition, contingent beneficiaries are allowed. In some cases, a beneficiary can even make a contingent beneficiary designation if the participant did not designate a contingent beneficiary and the plan lacked any default provision on the topic.[2] Beneficiaries are also allowed to disclaim any benefits that they do not want.

In many cases, the spouse has a survivor right to some portion of the plan benefits regardless of the beneficiary designation selected unless the surviving spouse waived his or her rights. However, spouses are also a common beneficiary designation. Spousal beneficiaries can inherit the account under preferential RMD rules in many cases and often need the accounts for retirement or other income upon the death of the participant spouse. However, children can also be a good beneficiary designation as it can allow a way to pass along tax-deferred benefits as a legacy or to provide for children after the sudden loss of a parent. However, if a trust is used to house the assets for multiple beneficiaries, there can be many complications. While a trust can be a beneficiary, the retirement account cannot be held inside of a living trust. Additionally, trusts owe income taxes, trustees often charge fees, access to the money can be limited, and the RMD rules can be unfavorable, especially for multiple beneficiaries. If a trust is used as a beneficiary, the trustee of the trust should be listed as the beneficiary and in existence at the time the beneficiary designation is made. However, there are times when trusts can function as a proper beneficiary. If the deceased participant wants to control the assets even after death with a qualified-terminable interest property (QTIP) trust they could use a trust to accomplish this goal. In addition, if the deceased participant was worried about the spending habits, ability to manage the assets, or creditor situation of the beneficiaries a trust might serve as a better vehicle than leaving the retirement account directly to the beneficiary. This is even more important since inherited IRAs are not considered retirement accounts and all of the assets are available to the inherited account owner's creditors. Ultimately, trusts are usually not the best beneficiary for a retirement plan due to increased levels of complexity and costs.

---

1. See IRS Notice 2007-7, 2007-5 Internal Revenue Bulletin 395 (Jan. 29, 2007) at Q & A-5(a). Available at http://www.irs.gov/pub/irs-irbs/irb07-05.pdf.
2. See Letter Ruling 199936052 (June 16, 1999).

It is important to review all beneficiary designations and any default beneficiary designation language inside of the plan documents. A plan usually has default beneficiary provision that pays out the benefits to the deceased's estate or executor. It is crucial to review the designations overtime, to ensure the benefits will be transferred in accordance with the plan participants wishes. For instance, major life events such as the birth of a new child, divorce, or marriage could have a significant impact on the planning considerations of the participant. While ERISA plans must include some survivor benefit for the spouse, it can be waived (QJSA). Failure to review and update the beneficiary designations could have seriously detrimental results as divorce will not automatically terminate a beneficiary designation and marriage does not always add the new spouse as an immediate beneficiary, meaning that an ex-spouse of 15 years could collect the benefit over the participant's desired heirs if the designation was not timely and properly updated.

While minor children can be listed as beneficiary, it does create serious challenges. While state laws vary as to the age of a minor, a child is often treated as minor until age 18 and is not deemed legally competent to enter into contracts or manage his or her own assets. As such, a trust, conservator, custodian, or guardian often has to accept payment on behalf of the minor child.

Two other issues that can arise with beneficiary designations are short-term survivorship and simultaneous death situations. This most frequently occurs when a husband and wife die in a common accident. As such, it can be difficult for the plan administrator to determine the proper beneficiary as one needs to be alive in order to take the benefit. As such, the order of death needs to be determined. Sometimes no one knows the order of death, in those cases there are state laws on this issue that presume the beneficiary pre-deceased the participant in the event of a simultaneous death. However, if the order of death is known, even by an hour, that order controls. This can cause the plan assets to pass through an extra estate before getting to the intended contingent beneficiaries, the children in many cases. If the beneficiary dies before the participant the account would transfer to the contingent beneficiary or under the default provisions if no contingent was listed. As such, it is important to make sure a contingent beneficiary is listed. In some cases, a charity can serve as a final contingent beneficiary to ensure that the funds do not escheat back to the state government.

Ultimately, the beneficiary designation is an important decision that should be made only after careful consideration and examination of the plan documents and benefits. Unfortunately, many people do not put much thought into the designation. Beneficiary designations should be coordinated with the participant's estate planning, wealth transfer, creditor protection and other goals. Additionally, the beneficiary designation should be reviewed periodically to ensure that the designation still matches the participant's desires and to ensure that the plan provider still has the correct documents, as they can get lost or destroyed by accident. Remember, the beneficiary designation for ERISA covered plans controls over state law, contracts, wills, and other agreements, so make sure that the participant understands the importance of the decision.

MINI-CASES: DEATH AND DISABILITY BENEFITS

In each of the following, fact patterns design the benefit structure, eligibility, vesting, and benefit provisions of the plan in a way that satisfies the employer's objectives.

Case One—Facts

Fast Fun, Inc., is a growing company that manufactures go-carts. The company has decided to adopt a 401(k) plan as its only qualified plan. Fast Fun has 150 employees, and the turnover in the shop is significant. A large number of employees have relatively low wages, and making salary-deferral contributions will be somewhat of a hardship for them. Because this is the company's only plan, the sponsor is prepared to contribute a minimum of 3 percent of compensation each year and possibly, in a good year, a lot more.

Case Two—Facts

Professional Corp. is a group of three owner-physicians and six other support staff. The doctors have decided to establish a profit-sharing plan. They want a plan that has flexible contributions and skews contributions as much toward the doctors as possible. Review plan design options for these doctors.

Case Three—Facts

New Nonprofit, Inc., has been in existence for 4 years. The company has 12 employees and has decided to set up its first pension plan. Because New Nonprofit wants a plan that allows employees to make pretax contributions and creates a retirement savings partnership between the employee and employer, the company considered the 403(b) plan, the 401(k) plan, and the SIMPLE. It chose the SIMPLE because it had the lowest cost and administrative burden, and it met the company's benefit budget (3 percent of payroll). New Nonprofit wants its plan to satisfy its current employees and to keep the company competitive when hiring new employees.

CHAPTER REVIEW

Key Terms and Concepts

qualified preretirement survivor annuity (QPSA)

qualified joint-and-survivor annuity (QJSA)

Table 2001

Chapter 10: Mini-Case Answers

Case One Answer

Contributions

In a 401(k) plan, the sponsor has to decide whether to make matching contributions and/or profit-sharing contributions (for all eligible employees). Because there is a large group of lower-paid employees who will need incentives to make salary-deferral contributions, the employer will probably want to make a generous matching contribution. One option is a 50-cent matching contribution for each dollar that the participant contributes up to 6 percent of salary contributed. This means that the maximum contribution the employer will make is 3 percent of compensation. If lower-paid employees simply cannot afford a 6 percent deferral (to obtain the 3 percent match), the employer could consider a dollar-for-dollar match on the first 3 percent of salary deferred. One determinative issue here is how much will the highly compensated employees want to defer and what rank-and-file deferral percentage is necessary to support that level of participation. If this does not encourage enough participation, the sponsor may consider a safe-harbor contribution to avoid having to perform the ADP nondiscrimination test. This plan also seems like a good candidate for automatic enrollment as a way to increase the participation rate.

Any additional employer contributions should probably be made as profit-sharing contributions (as opposed to additional matching contributions). The profit-sharing contributions are totally discretionary, and lower-paid employees who cannot afford to make salary-deferral contributions will still be eligible to earn a benefit. In this way, the plan can both act as a more traditional pension plan and provide a profit-sharing incentive (assuming the employer really does make larger contributions in good years). The plan would probably adopt a compensation-to-compensation allocation formula so all employees will receive the same percentage of compensation.

Eligibility

The considerations for determining the appropriate eligibility provisions for a 401(k) plan are somewhat different than for other plans. With the 401(k) plan, nonhighly compensated employees who are eligible but do not contribute bring down the amount that highly compensated employees can contribute under the ADP test. In this case, with a large number of lower-paid employees and a high turnover rate, the employer will probably want to limit eligibility in a number of ways. First, the employer will want to eliminate employees who are allowed to be excluded by law. This includes short-term employees (by requiring a full year of service for eligibility), part-time employees (by requiring 1,000 hours of service), and employees who have not yet attained age 21. Second, the employer may want to identify and exclude a class of employees that is unlikely to make salary-deferral contributions. This is allowed as long as the plan can still pass the coverage requirements (remember that up to 30 percent of the nonhighly compensated employees can generally be excluded).

Vesting

In a 401(k) plan, employee salary-deferral contributions must be fully vested, but employer-matching contributions and profit-sharing contributions can be subject to a vesting schedule. Because this employer has a high turnover rate, a vesting schedule, such as 3-year cliff vesting, could encourage employees to stay at least that long to be eligible for that benefit. Second, even if the vesting schedule does not change employee behavior, it will save the employer some money. Forfeited matching contributions are typically used toward meeting the employer's matching contribution requirement for the remaining employees. Forfeited profit-sharing contributions are typically allocated among remaining employees, which does not reduce costs but does boost benefits for the longer-service employees.

Benefit Payouts and Forms of Benefit

In a 401(k) plan, vested benefits are typically available for distribution within a short time after termination of employment. It is not uncommon for a plan to offer only a lump-sum payment option. Some employers also offer installment payments. A new plan will typically not offer annuities because this will mean the plan will have to allow for qualified joint-and-survivor benefits. Because terminated employees have immediate access to benefits, the concepts of normal retirement, early retirement, or death benefits become somewhat less important. Here, the primary reason to include such benefits is to fully vest those who otherwise have not satisfied the vesting schedule. The law requires that benefits become fully vested at normal retirement age; the most common age is 65. The sponsor may also want to fully vest participants who die or become disabled before completing the 3 years of service.

Case Two Answer

Contributions

This employer wants the option to vary contributions but will most likely make significant contributions each year. The doctors will want to allocate a large percentage of the contribution to themselves. Assuming that the doctors as a group are somewhat older than the other employees, a cross-tested allocation formula can quite possibly result in the doctors receiving 70 percent or more of the total contribution. The design process here is to determine the objectives and then to test the formula (using software) under the general nondiscrimination test.

Note that if the doctors want to reward some employees more than others, the allocation formula can be designed with a number of different allocation groups. For example, one group can receive a maximum of 5 percent of compensation, another can receive 8 percent, and the doctors can receive the maximum allocation allowed under Code Sec. 415(c). The minimum contribution for any participant is likely to be 5 percent, the amount generally required under the nondiscrimination regulations.

Eligibility

Because this employer is interested in limiting the costs of benefits for employees, the first inclination is to create eligibility requirements that eliminate as many employees as possible. However, when a plan is using a cross-tested allocation formula, there are advantages to bringing in young, less highly paid employees. Under cross-testing, any contributions for young employees convert to significant retirement benefits (because of the length of the accumulation period). These high benefits support a higher level of benefits for the doctors. For this reason, all employees in this case will become eligible immediately.

Vesting

Because one main goal in this case is to limit costs, either 3-year cliff vesting or 6-year graded vesting is appropriate, depending on employee turnover patterns.

Other Considerations

The benefit considerations here are similar to those in the 401(k) plan. In a small defined-contribution plan of any type, most sponsors will want to give participants the opportunity to withdraw benefits shortly after termination of employment. In addition, the doctors will definitely want benefits to vest upon a premature disability and/or a preretirement death. As with the 401(k) plan, forms of distribution will probably be limited to lump-sum payments and installments to avoid the effects of the qualified joint-and-survivor annuity rules.

One more important issue in a small profit-sharing plan like this is whether the plan allows for individual investment direction. In 401(k) plans, employee investment direction has become almost universal. In defined-contribution plans funded solely by the employer, on the other hand, employee investment direction is less common. The three doctors in this plan, however, may have extremely different financial goals. This case looks like a good candidate for self-directed accounts, similar to a self-directed IRA, in which the participant can choose essentially from among any legal investment choice.

Case Three Answer

The SIMPLE has rigid design constraints and the employer has only a few options. A SIMPLE must cover all employees who have earned at least $5,000 in any 2 prior years. The employer can choose to cover employees sooner or lower the $5,000 requirement. New Nonprofit, Inc., is choosing to cover all employees to make the company better able to compete for good employees.

The next decision is the employer contribution—a matching contribution or a nonelective contribution. Because New Nonprofit wants to create a partnership with the participants, the matching approach is better.

In most other respects, the plan design is fixed. Benefits must be fully vested. Participants can withdraw benefits (subject to income tax) or move plan assets to another investment advisor (maintaining either a SIMPLE IRA or other IRA). Employees can contribute up to $12,500 (as indexed for 2017) without regard to the other benefit limitations that apply to qualified plans.

One final interesting issue is communication with employees. In a SIMPLE, participants must be given notice of their rights to make salary deferrals, but unlike in a 401(k) plan, there are no extensive ERISA education requirements. Because New Nonprofit, Inc., wants to get as much value for its plan as possible, it will want to communicate it fully and may want to provide more generic retirement planning education in conjunction with the rollout of the plan. Even for this small organization with a small budget, there are still options, such as buying video educational programs, accessing information from the Internet, and obtaining free information from the IRS and Department of Labor.

Chapter 10: Review Questions

Review questions are based on the learning objectives in this chapter. Thus, a [10.3] at the end of a question means that the question is based on learning objective 3. If there are multiple objectives, they are all listed.

1. Answer these typical questions about mandatory death benefits that would be asked by prospective plan sponsors. [10.1]

    a. We would prefer not to provide a preretirement death benefit in our defined-benefit plan because we have a life insurance program for employees outside of the plan. What death benefits are we obliged to provide in the plan?

    b. Does the provision of the QJSA have any cost for the sponsor?

    c. We are setting up a profit-sharing plan and want to simplify administration of the plan. What do you suggest with regard to benefit payment options?

2. The owner of Dance Corp. wants to purchase a large amount of universal life insurance with her own profit-sharing account. Is there any way to solve the incidental death benefit problem? [10.2]

3. An employee, aged 50, in a profit-sharing plan has chosen to invest a portion of his account balance to purchase life insurance. If the participant purchases $100,000 of whole life insurance, what is the cost of insurance that has to be included into income? [10.2]

4. What are the different considerations applicable to providing preretirement death benefits in the small-plan market as opposed to the medium- and large-plan market? [10.3]

5. Your client, a small professional corporation, is unsure whether to include death benefits in its employee benefits package. What are the reasons for and against providing death benefits through a qualified retirement plan? [10.3]

6. What types of plan provisions are appropriate for addressing the situation in which a participant becomes disabled? [10.4]

7. Describe the considerations necessary for choosing a definition of disability in a qualified plan. [10.4]

8. Johnny has always been single and accumulated nearly $2 million in his 401(k) account at Big Farm Corp. over his work career. Johnny never filled out a beneficiary designation form when he originally started with the company. Joe decides to set up

a revocable living trust and places all of his property into the trust and lists his best friend Joe as the beneficiary, with the intention of leaving all of his assets to Joe. Soon after setting up the trust Johnny dies. [10.5]

a. Will the 401(k) assets likely be paid out to Joe?

b. What if Johnny had a will stating all of his property goes to Joe? Are there any downsides to this transfer?

Chapter 10: Review Answers

1. a. You must provide a preretirement death benefit for those married participants who have been married for one year. You do not have to provide preretirement death benefits for other participants. You could choose to charge participants for this benefit. This is typically done by reducing the retirement benefit by a small amount. The problem with this approach is that you will have to give married participants the option to opt out of the benefit. Most employers in this case choose to provide the benefit at no cost to married participants in order to avoid the waiver procedure. For most groups, this will not be an expensive benefit because few participants will die prior to retirement. Be aware that if you only provide the death benefit for married participants, your unmarried employees may feel that this is unfair.

    b. If the employer makes the QJSA the actuarial equivalent to the stated form of payment in the benefit structure, then this benefit does not have a direct cost.

    c. For simplicity, avoid administering the QJSA form of benefit at retirement. Most participants elect a lump-sum benefit anyway, and administering the benefit at retirement requires giving out QJSA notices and getting waiver signatures from both participants and their spouses. The plan should avoid all annuity forms of payment, pay out 100 percent of the preretirement death benefit to the spouse, and prohibit the transfer of assets into the plan that would be subject to the QJSA requirements. The simplest distribution provision would be to only offer a single sum form of payment.

2. Generally only 25 percent of aggregate contributions can be used to purchase life insurance in a qualified plan. However, if a profit-sharing plan allows for in-service withdrawals, the entire portion of the account that is eligible for withdrawal can be used to purchase life insurance in the plan.

3. The cost of insurance that must be included in income is the Table 2001 amount for a 50-year-old. The table amount for $1,000 of coverage is $2.30. For $100,000 of coverage the amount included in income is $230.

4. When designing a plan for a small professional corporation, the insurance needs of the principal individuals control the death benefit design. In medium and large companies, the retirement plan's insurance benefits are decided by competition and other market factors.

5. The advantages of including death benefits in a qualified plan are (1) competitiveness, (2) attraction and retention of employees, and (3) the ability of the business owner to receive group rates, shift a personal expense to the company, and gain favorable underwriting. On the other side, it may be difficult to get an appropriate level of benefits to meet the needs, and there are more tax-efficient ways outside of the plan to provide for life insurance.

6. Common provisions include fully vesting the participant in his or her benefit, allowing a payout at the time of disability, and providing for service under the plan during the time that the participant is on disability.

7. Two typical options would be to mirror the company's disability plan or match the Social Security definition.

8. a. The 401(k) assets will not pass to Joe. First, the 401(k) cannot be held inside of a revocable living trust so that beneficiary designation has no impact. Secondly, the distribution of the 401(k) benefits upon Johnny's death will pass via the beneficiary designation in the plan. Since Johnny did not specify a specific beneficiary, the plan documents would control. Typically, the plan would have a provision to pay out to Johnny's estate, even in absence of a provision it would likely pass to his estate in this scenario. Because Joe is not related to Johnny, it is unlikely Joe would ever see any of this money. If Johnny left behind no surviving relatives that could inherit under the state succession laws, the property would eventually go to the State.

   b. The outcome would be different if Johnny had a will that left all of his property to Joe. The 401(k) would still have been transferred via the default provision in the plan to the estate, but then the will would have controlled this property as it then would be probate property. The downsides to the transfer would be the loss of the ability to do a direct rollover into an inherited IRA, possible probate delays, and additional fees. The stretch IRA possibility will be lost as the account will have to be distributed within five years or over the deceased remaining life expectancy. Instead of allowing the 401(k) to pass to Johnny's estate, Johnny should have listed Joe as his beneficiary, skipping the entire probate process.

Chapter 11

Plan Funding and Investing

Learning Objectives

An understanding of the material in this chapter should enable the student to

- **LO 11.1** Describe the funding requirements that apply to a qualified plan.
- **LO 11.2** Identify the various funding instruments, and describe in detail how a trust operates.
- **LO 11.3** Know what should be included in investment guidelines and how they protect fiduciaries.
- **LO 11.4** Describe investment characteristics that are relevant in pension investing.

This chapter and the next provide an overview of the issues surrounding plan funding and investing. In this chapter, three important issues are addressed. First is a review of the plan funding requirements. For defined-benefit plans, this topic is involved, while for other types of plans, the issue is straightforward. The next topic is a review of the various funding vehicles that are used in conjunction with tax-advantaged retirement plans. This discussion will familiarize you with the parties responsible for plan investing. The third topic addresses the legal constraints surrounding the investment of plan assets, who is legally responsible for making investment decisions, what investment limitations apply, and the potential liability for failing to meet fiduciary standards.

The following chapter focuses entirely on plan investing. There we discuss choosing an appropriate investment policy; then, we look at various investment options. The materials first cover typical investment classes and their role in the investment mix, and then go into specialized insurance products that have been developed to meet specific needs.

PLAN FUNDING REQUIREMENTS

LO 11.1 Describe the funding requirements that apply to a qualified plan.

The financial services professional needs to be acquainted with the plan funding requirements, much as the home buyer needs to be familiar with the plumbing and heating systems of a potential purchase. In other words, a passing knowledge of some of the buzzwords and the general implications can help you avoid an unpleasant experience. And although a detailed understanding of the complex requirements and their underlying actuarial voodoo is unnecessary, you should understand enough to be able to school your client in the basics and to deal effectively with a consulting actuary.

terminal funding approach

Once a tax-advantaged retirement plan is in place, the employer must fund it in order to meet the benefit obligations promised under the plan. At one time, it was possible for the employer to wait until the employee retired and monthly retirement obligations became due before providing for the employee's benefit. This pay-as-you-go system (also called a **terminal funding approach**) is no longer possible since the passage of ERISA, requiring the current funding of future pension liabilities. Instead, retirement benefits must be prefunded according to the minimum funding standards that were set out in ERISA.

Under the minimum funding standards, employers are required to (1) set aside funds irrevocably (meaning the pension money is beyond the reach of the employer or the employer's creditors), (2) place the funds with a trustee, custodian, or insurance company, and (3) fund their retirement obligations in advance. Advance funding basically means the employer must pay the retirement liability according to specific rules.

Funding Defined-Benefit Plans

This section explores the funding of defined-benefit plans. First we explore some of the conceptual issues. Next we review the required minimum contribution rules and finally address the maximum deductible contribution limits that apply to defined-benefit plans.

Actuarial Assumptions and Methods

Defined-benefit plans do not focus on contributions, but on the promised benefits that will be paid. Assuming that the employer will cover the costs through annual payments, the amount for each year and the spread of these costs over future years is inherently indefinite. In order to provide a means of determining these costs, an actuarial cost method based on actuarial assumptions must be used.

All qualified defined-benefit plans subject to the funding provisions of ERISA must provide advance funding over the working lives of the participants, using an actuarial cost method and assumptions. The ERISA funding requirements apply generally to all qualified defined-benefit plans of private employers. Certain government and church plans are exempted from coverage, as well as certain types of plans having no employer contributions. Also, fully insured plans are treated under special rules.

actuarial cost method

An **actuarial cost method** is a method of determining an annual employer contribution for a given set of plan benefits and a given group of employees. The method produces a schedule of annual contributions aimed at providing a plan fund sufficient to make all benefit payments when they come due without any further contributions by the employer. The Pension Protection Act of 2006 dramatically changed the minimum funding rules for defined-benefit plans and provides for a single actuarial cost method with a limit on the interest and mortality assumptions that may be used.

actuarial assumptions

Actuarial assumptions refer to assumptions about future investment return and the character of the employee group that are made in order to determine the annual contribution.

> **EXAMPLE**
>
> Actuarial assumptions include investment return and mortality. An investment return assumption of 10 percent is an assumption that current amounts deposited into the plan will earn 10 percent annually. For a given amount needed in the future, a 10 percent assumption therefore will require a smaller annual employer contribution than a 5-percent assumption. Similarly, a high mortality assumption assumes that a larger-than-average number of employees will die before receiving benefits. The higher this mortality assumption, the lower the amount of the annual contribution to the plan.

Choosing an Actuarial Cost Method

Before the Pension Protection Act of 2006 (PPA), the initial choice of an actuarial cost method was affected by the employer's concerns as to how plan costs would be spread over future years. Think of an actuarial cost method as a budget, a means of spreading the cost of the plan over future years. Certain methods will often produce a lower initial cost than other methods and might be chosen if the employer wishes to minimize costs at the plan's inception with the expectation of increased funding in later years. Sometimes this deferral of funding led to underfunding of plans in declining industries, hence the passage of PPA-mandated minimum funding requirements to ensure that plan sponsors would meet their commitments to provide benefits under defined-benefit plans.

PPA overhauled the funding requirements for defined-benefit plans. Today, the minimum required contribution is determined using a solvency-based measure versus the two-tier approach involving long-term funding and solvency under pre-PPA law. In other words, pre-PPA funding looks at benefits projected into the future and allows the spreading of those future benefits over future years. PPA looks at the year-by-year solvency of the plan; in other words, whether the plan assets are sufficient in the current year to satisfy the accrued benefits for all participants.

Minimum Funding Requirements

funding target

The minimum funding standards of the Code and corresponding ERISA provisions provide the legal structure for enforcing the advance funding requirement that applies to qualified pension plans.

The rules found in Code Sec. 430 require the calculation of the **funding target**. The funding target is the present value of all benefits accrued or earned under the plan as of the beginning of the plan year, as determined under the plan document's benefit accrual rules. If the value of the plan's assets is less than the funding target, the minimum required contribution for the year is the sum of:

- the target normal cost of the plan for the plan year
- the shortfall amortization charge
- the waiver amortization charge

The target normal cost, except for plans in at-risk status (see below), is generally the present value of benefits expected to accrue under the plan during the plan year. The amortization charges refer to amounts that are required to cover shortfalls in funding in prior years; generally shortfalls must be amortized (paid in level installments) over a 7-year period. There is also a provision under which the IRS can "waive" a portion of the required minimum funding amount for a given year, subject to payment over a specified future period—the waiver amortization charge in the above list refers to this.

In recent years, there have been a number of concerns about underfunded plans, both with respect to the risks to participants and also the potential liability of the PBGC. The funding rules include provisions to bring underfunded plans into a funded status as quickly as possible. The at-risk rules do not apply to plans with 500 or fewer participants.

The at-risk rules are complex, but in general a plan is deemed to be at risk if it met less than 80 percent of its funding target for the preceding year or 70 percent of its funding target using certain at-risk assumptions. If the plan is at risk, its funding target and normal cost are determined under special assumptions that will accelerate its funding.

The Fully Insured Life Insurance Option

fully insured

In a defined-benefit plan, the required employer contributions vary over time due to changes in the performance of plan assets. Some employers would prefer fixed costs and can sleep better knowing their liabilities. There is relief for these employers if the plan is fully funded with life insurance policies or annuity contracts. Under a plan that is funded by individual insurance contracts, it is the insurance company's actuary who selects the assumptions and the actuarial cost method. The premium based on that actuary's assumptions is the actual contribution due. Additionally, **fully insured** plans (plans funded in their entirety by level-premium annuities or retirement-income contracts) are exempt from the minimum funding standards (and their corresponding administrative costs, such as actuarial fees) if (1) the insurance contract provides for level premiums from participation until retirement, (2) the benefits under the plan are equal to the benefits provided under the contract, (3) the benefits are guaranteed by a licensed insurance company, (4) premiums are paid on time, (5) there are no rights under the contract subject to a security interest, and (6) there are no policy loans. Because fully insured plans are described in Code Sec. 412(e), they are sometimes referred to as 412(e) plans.

Maximum Deductible Contributions

While the minimum funding standards create a funding floor for defined-benefit plans, the maximum deduction rules create a ceiling. The deduction limit is the greater of

- the minimum funding amount under the rules of Code Sec. 430 described above, or
- the excess of plan assets over the funding target plus the target's normal cost for the plan year and the "cushion" amount for the plan year

The rules for the cushion amount are, in effect, designed to encourage plan sponsors to overfund or generously fund the plan. For example, the cushion amount takes into account expected future benefit increases.

The employer can contribute any amount between the minimum funding requirement and the maximum deductible contribution. This is one of the reasons why a defined-benefit plan can be relatively flexible for the employer. In many cases there will be a relatively comfortable range of contributions that can be adjusted according to the employer's specific financial situation.

Funding Notice Requirements for Defined Benefit Plans

In 2015 the Department of Labor finalized a rule proposed back in 2010 in order to implement the annual funding notice requirements in ERISA Sec. 101(f). Under the rules, the plan administrator must provide a plan funding notice to the PBGC, each participant, each beneficiary, and to any labor organizational representing those individuals. The funding document must show the funding levels of the plan, the value of its assets, the total amount of assets compared to liabilities, and a statement regarding all of the people receiving benefits, entitled to future benefits, and active participants under the plan. There are other requirements for multi-employer plans that are not discussed here. Large plans must provide the notice to all parties within 120 days of the end of the plan year. Small plans have until the due date of the plan's 5500 form filing, with extensions.

Funding Requirements for Other Types of Plans

Minimum Required Contribution

Although the minimum funding requirements are most complex for the defined-benefit plan, it is important to note that the requirements do apply to other pension plans as well. This includes the two types of defined-contribution plans that are also pension plans—target-benefit and money-purchase pension plans. The minimum required contribution is the amount required under the plan's contribution formula each year. Failure to meet the required contribution subjects the plan to the 10 percent excise tax on funding deficiencies that applies to defined-benefit plans.

The minimum funding requirements do not apply to profit-sharing plans, stock bonus plans, ESOPs, SEPs, SIMPLEs, or 403(b) plans. Technically, this means that the 10 percent excise tax will not apply for failure to make contributions. However, if the plan document calls for a required annual contribution in one of these types of plans, the employer will have to make the contribution. Otherwise, the plan will face disqualification because the employer failed to follow the terms of the plan.

Maximum Deductible Contribution

When a plan has a specified contribution, this amount essentially constitutes the minimum and maximum allowable contributions. For discretionary profit-sharing plans, stock bonus plans, employee stock ownership plans, or SEPs, the maximum contribution is subject to the limitations discussed previously. That is, no individual can receive an annual allocation in excess of the Code Sec. 415(c) limit and the total employer contribution cannot exceed 25 percent of compensation of all participating employees.

To more fully understand the maximum contribution rules, let's examine a number of examples. The first illustrates the maximum contribution limits when the plan only covers the owner of the company. The example illustrates the interaction between the 25-percent-deduction rule and the Sec. 415(c) maximum allocation rule.

> **EXAMPLE**
>
> Sylvia is incorporated, she has no other employees, and for 2017 she has $100,000 of compensation. The maximum contribution on her behalf to her profit-sharing plan for 2017 is $25,000 (25 percent of $100,000). Now let's assume that her compensation is $270,000. The maximum contribution would then be $54,000, the Sec. 415(c) maximum allocation limit for 2017.

As you can see with a single participant, the maximum deductible contribution limit of 25 percent of compensation can be the prevailing limit. However, note that this deduction limit is an aggregate limit, and when there are a number of employees, the amount allocated to specific individuals can exceed 25 percent of compensation.

There is another way to exceed the 25 percent deduction limit. Salary deferral contributions to a 401(k) plan are not counted toward the 25 percent limit. This means that an owner, without employees, can establish a one-person 401(k) plan and can contribute both 25 percent as a profit-sharing contribution plus make salary deferral contributions.

> **EXAMPLE**
>
> Esther, who is incorporated, has compensation of $100,000. If she establishes a 401(k) plan, she can contribute $25,000 (25 percent of compensation) as a profit-sharing contribution as well as $18,000 under the salary deferral feature (for 2017).

If Esther, in this example, is age 50 or older, she can make an additional catch-up election of $6,000 in 2017. This additional contribution is allowed, even if the total allocation exceeds the Code Sec. 415(c) annual allocation limit, because catch-up elections are not counted as allocations under the 415(c) limit.

The one-person 401(k) plan is a method for making larger contributions for the individual with a modest level of compensation. For many individuals in this situation, the profit-sharing plan or SEP will work just as well, especially if they are not in the financial position to contribute more than 25 percent of compensation (20 percent if the entity is unincorporated).

As the above example illustrates, the 401(k) plan for the sole proprietor (often referred to as a solo 401(k) plan) can be an excellent way for an client with modest income to get a large deductible contribution. This is because salary deferrals and catch-up contributions can be made in addition to the employer's contribution of up to 25 percent of compensation (20 percent if the entity is unincorporated).

This strategy may be helpful for a second wage earner in a family with relatively low earnings and the ability to save a lot or an older person with lower expenses that is trying to contribute as much as possible.

There is one additional reason to use the solo 401(k). A solo 401(k) can allow for Roth elections. This may be appealing to the owner who earns too much to contribute to a Roth IRA, or wants to save more than the current $5,500 Roth IRA contribution limit.

FUNDING VEHICLES

LO 11.2   Identify the various funding instruments, and describe in detail how a trust operates.

funding instrument

A qualified plan must use a **funding instrument** that must be a trust, custodial account, or group insurance contract. This section discusses these various funding instruments and how they work, as well as the typical parties involved in the investment of plan assets. The rules are different for the other tax-advantaged retirement plans.

SEPs and SIMPLEs must use individual retirement accounts and annuities, while 403(b) plans must use annuity contracts or mutual fund custodial accounts.

Trusts

Trusts are the most popular funding vehicles for qualified plans. The trust approach allows for tremendous flexibility in both investments and benefit design.

A trust used for a qualified plan is based on the same principles of trust law as trusts used for other purposes. This means the grantor of the trust is the plan's sponsor; the grantor transfers the res (the plan assets) to trustees of the trust; and the trust makes payments as specified to the beneficiaries of the trust (the plan participants and their beneficiaries).

Like all trusts, a trust used for a qualified plan contains a trust agreement, which is set up primarily to control the receipt, investment, and disbursement of funds. A typical trust agreement spells out the following particulars:

- the irrevocability of trust assets
- the trustee's investment powers (the investment discretion of a trustee varies from plan to plan; in some cases, the employer wants to maintain full control; in others, the trustee or investment manager has almost unchecked discretion)
- the allocation of fiduciary responsibility to a named fiduciary (who is responsible for the plan and becomes the target of legal action when required)
- the payments of benefits and plan expenses
- the rights and duties in case of plan termination

If the plan is large enough, the trustees may also keep records of employer and employee contributions, each participant's salary and service, and account and benefit information. In smaller plans, this function is handled outside the trust agreement by the employer, third-party plan administrator, or consulting company.

An essential part of the trusteed plan is the plan trustees, who may be corporate (banks and trust companies) and/or individuals related to the business.

Functions of Plan Trustees
- Accept and invest employer contributions
- Pay benefits to plan participants
- Provide periodic accounting to the employer of investments, receipts, disbursements, and other transactions that involve plan assets
- Maintain administrative records, if appropriate

It is important to remember that, when carrying out these duties, trustees have a fiduciary relationship to plan participants. As discussed further in the next section, the fiduciaries must act in the best interest of the plan participants. Thus, a business owner who is also a plan trustee cannot act in his or her own self-interest. Also, the trustee must act prudently, as compared to other plan trustees, meaning that a business executive should think carefully before choosing to become a plan trustee.

In large plans, sometimes the trustee acts primarily as custodian of plan assets, while the fund is invested by several investment managers. Investment managers will also be plan fiduciaries, subject to essentially the same standard of care in handling plan investments. Similarly, in smaller plans, the executives will act as trustees, while one or more corporate investment managers is responsible for investing. Regardless of the arrangement, in all cases, those responsible for investing plan assets are responsible to act in accordance with the plan documents and in accordance with the funding and investment policies (discussed further in the next chapter), which are established by the employer or a committee made up of executives of the employer.

In lieu of a trust agreement, the funding vehicle can also be a custodial account with a bank (or other person as authorized by IRS regulations under Code Sec. 401(f)) as custodian. With the custodial-account approach, the custodian is the record keeper, with others actually investing plan assets.

Common Trust Funds

common trust fund

Generally, the assets of one trust cannot be commingled or pooled with the assets of other trusts; a separate accounting and segregation of trust assets is usually required. However, an exception to this rule applies to common trust funds. **Common trust funds**, which are sponsored and operated by banks and trust companies, permit the pooling of funds from all participating trusts (typically many small-plan sponsors). The trust buys units of a common fund, which either increase or decrease in value depending on investment return. The common trust fund was developed because relatively small trust fund plans could not adequately diversify their investment portfolios on their own. In addition to eliminating the diversification problem, common trust funds also provide the potential for higher return (because of their size, they can attract expert investment advice), lower brokerage fees, and liquidity of funds to meet cash requirements.

Split-Funded Plans

split-funded plan

A **split-funded plan** refers to a plan that uses a trust fund arrangement, but chooses to invest a portion of plan assets in insurance and annuity contracts. Insurance products can include individual insurance and annuity contracts or group funding products that are available. This approach can be used to take advantage of the flexibility of the trust approach while also taking advantage of the guarantees of insurance products, the ability to provide significant death benefits through the plan, or simply the yields available in a group product.

Split funded plans are common in a number of contexts including:

- A defined-benefit plan provides an incidental death benefit for all participants on a nondiscriminatory basis. In this case the trustee purchases separate permanent contracts on the life of each participant with plan assets. With this approach the trustee applies for the insurance, pays the premiums when due, is custodian of the individual contracts, and has legal ownership of the insurance contract. The participant, however, selects the death beneficiary.

- A defined-contribution plan offers life insurance as a participant-directed investment alternative. If the participant elects life insurance coverage, premiums are paid out of the participant's account balance.

- A qualified plan trust purchases, as a plan investment, life insurance on key employees of the sponsoring employer. Key person life insurance can protect the trust from reductions in future contributions that would result at the death of the key person whose efforts produce the profits on which contributions are based.

- The plan purchases guaranteed investment products (GICs) or other group investment products to partially fund the plan or as a participant investment option.

INSURANCE-FUNDED PLANS

A pension plan under which retirement benefits are provided completely by annuity or insurance contracts does not have to maintain a trust fund. This applies to both individual and group products. However, to avoid the trust requirement, the terms of the plan must be incorporated in the policy. This is not practical with individual policies and, therefore, individual policies are generally issued under a trust fund agreement, with the trustee as owner of the policies. With a group policy, it is more common for the master contract to be the sole investment vehicle.

Insurance-funded plans are common in a number of contexts including:

- a fully insured defined-benefit plan under Code Sec. 412(e). These plans can be funded with any combination of life insurance and annuity products.

- a group variable annuity product that can be used to fund 401(k) and other qualified plans.

As we saw in the discussion of trusteed plans, split-funded plans, and insurance-funded plans, the pension plan can be funded with any combination of trust fund and insurance product investments. What will distinguish the insurance product is not the type of documentation, but the strength of the investment contracts.

ESTABLISHING INVESTMENT GUIDELINES

LO 11.3   Know what should be included in investment guidelines and how they protect fiduciaries.

Determining appropriate investments for a retirement plan begin with identifying objectives. ERISA specifically requires that every plan have a funding policy which establishes procedures for establishing and carrying out a funding program consistent with the plan's objectives and ERISA requirements. Once the objectives are determined, the next step is creating investment guidelines that become a road map for investment decisions. Here we discuss these issues.

Why Establish Investment Guidelines?

investment guidelines

Now that you are familiar with ERISA's fiduciary requirements, you can see that the rules are relatively complex and that fiduciaries have a strong incentive to meet their obligations. The first, and probably most important, tool for ensuring compliance is clearly written plan investment guidelines. Essentially, **investment guidelines** are written instructions that provide structure for those involved in investing plan assets. These are crucial for the following reasons:

- *to satisfy fiduciary obligations*—Investment guidelines help to establish procedures. They clarify who is responsible for what, when various tasks need to be completed, and how performance will be evaluated. They encourage a disciplined approach to fiduciary management and help to establish a paper trail.

- *to be the first line of defense*—If the Department of Labor (DOL) or plan participants question the investment performance, courts will look for a rationale for the investments chosen. The investment guidelines should be the fiduciary's most powerful shield.

- *to avoid investing in a vacuum*—An investment decision simply cannot be made or properly evaluated in a vacuum. A Treasury bill is a great investment when the main concern is protecting principal, but a terrible investment for long-term capital growth. Appropriate investment decisions must follow clear objectives.

For all of these reasons, it is extremely important to establish clear investment guidelines that tie the investment policy into the plan's objectives, clarify who is responsible for the various decisions surrounding the investment of plan assets, specify investment guidelines and goals, and establish procedures for reviewing both the investment performance and the plan's investment guidelines.

Who Establishes Investment Guidelines?

ERISA requires every plan to have a named fiduciary and a plan administrator that are responsible for the operation of the plan. Many companies appoint a benefits committee to fulfill both roles. In a very small company the committee may consist of simply the owner or owners. In larger organizations it may include the chief financial officer, the human resources director, and others. A crucial part of the benefits committee's work is making decisions about plan assets. In large companies the benefits committee will sometimes delegate this responsibility to a separate investment committee.

Regardless of who is making the investment decisions, it is important to understand that ERISA holds all fiduciaries, regardless to the size of the firm or the individual's background, to a professional standard. So the decision makers need to act professionally in all situations. This means meeting regularly, deliberating, and write down conclusions. The responsibilities include:

- writing an investment policy statement
- selecting, evaluating, and removing any investment managers
- monitoring the activities of all service providers to the plan
- reviewing investment management fees paid by the plan
- ensuring that proper financial reporting occurs

Funding Policy and Plan Objectives

funding policy

Every plan is required to establish a funding policy—procedures for establishing and carrying out a funding program consistent with the plan's objectives and ERISA requirements. A **funding policy** addresses the level and timing of contributions necessary to fund benefit obligations throughout the life of a retirement plan.

In a defined-benefit plan, the policy should address the minimum funding requirements, provide a process for reviewing the policy periodically, and most important, require documentation of actions taken and reasons for those actions.

The funding policy and the investment guidelines are driven by the plan's objectives. In a defined-benefit plan, the primary objective is to provide sufficient funds to pay both current and future benefit obligations. In addition, there is the goal of minimizing long-term total required contributions. And, in most cases, there will be concern about the variability in annual contributions. The second and third objectives are generally at odds with one another, because minimizing costs over the long haul requires taking some risks. With risk usually comes volatility in the investment return, and, thus, a degree of variability in the required contributions. How important this is to a particular plan depends, in part, on how well-funded the plan is—the more well-funded plan has a higher tolerance for volatility. Also, the tolerance for volatility depends upon whether the sponsoring entity is cyclical in nature.

In a defined-contribution plan, the funding policy is simpler. If the plan calls for a specified contribution, the policy simply addresses the timing of contributions. With discretionary contributions in a profit-sharing plan, the employer establishes a policy for determining how and when contributions are to be made. Also, in a defined-contribution plan, there should be less conflict with the plan's objectives because the employer's contribution is not tied to the plan's investment performance. The employer does not have to be concerned about the long-term cost of funding the plan or short-term variability. The only objective is to provide for the retirement needs of the participants.

However, because participants will be of different ages and have different needs and risk profiles, many defined-contribution plans pass the investment decisions on to the participants. In such plans, the objective at the trust level is somewhat different. Here the goal is to offer participants a number of sufficiently diverse investment vehicles—each with different risk and return characteristics—so each participant will be able to assemble a portfolio that will meet his or her individual investment needs. Also, to assist participants in the formation of appropriate investment objectives, the trustees will have to provide them with suitable education.

Investment Responsibilities

Investment guidelines should identify all of the parties involved in the investment of plan assets and should address each individual's specific investment responsibilities. To do this requires, first, a review of the plan and trust documents. These documents offer more detail on accountability issues than most people realize. Commonly, the document provides that either the employer or an investment committee is responsible for establishing and periodically reviewing the investment policy. The employer often retains the responsibility of choosing and monitoring the trustee and any investment managers. Trustees are responsible for investing plan assets in accordance with the stated investment goals and reporting to the employer or investment committee, unless some or all of this responsibility is passed on to one or more investment managers. The trustees will always account for, and report on the status of, plan assets. In some cases, there may also be consultants who help with the selection and monitoring of investment managers.

Investment Policy

investment policy

The plan's **investment policy** should identify the appropriate degree of risk and yield for the trust and the importance of yield in relation to safety of principal and the plan's cash-flow needs. These decisions must be made in relation to the plan's objectives and the investment objectives. When trying to determine the plan's objectives, it is helpful to ask the following questions:

- Are there other resources available to pay benefits if investment performance is bad in the short run?
- What is the appropriate investment horizon?
- What is an acceptable level of risk?
- What is the minimum level of investment return necessary to accomplish the goals?

These questions are relevant to the plan trustees when they are responsible for investment decisions, as well as to plan participants in cases where they have investment control.

Investment Goals

The next step is to establish concrete performance objectives for monitoring investment performance. It is almost always more sensible to establish investment goals that are tied to appropriate benchmarks as opposed to specific rates of return. If more than one investment manager is involved, a specific set of investment guidelines should be established for each manager and cover the following:

- permissible categories of investments
- asset allocation ranges among different investment classes
- appropriate investments within categories (such as specified bond quality)
- diversification concerns, such as maximum holding in specific investments, limits on small capitalization stocks, and limits on any particular sector
- policies regarding proxy voting
- limitations based on fiduciary rules, prohibited transactions, etc.

Monitoring Investment Management

Another part of the investment policy includes procedures for monitoring investment management. The safest course of action is to track performance on a continual basis, and to meet with investment managers on a quarterly, semiannual, or annual basis. Investment performance should be evaluated over relatively long periods, although significant deviation in short-term performance can be a warning sign. Performance can be evaluated against peer groups as well as against benchmarks.

Reviewing Investment Guidelines

The final part of the investment procedure should be a plan for an annual review of the investment guidelines to ensure that they are still appropriate. Again, it is important to keep accurate records of any meetings that discuss, reconfirm, or change the guidelines.

INVESTMENT CONSIDERATIONS

Almost every investment option available to an individual investor is available to a pension plan sponsor. In fact, pension funds can be invested in such a large number of products that it is impossible to cover them all fully in this text. Instead, in the rest of this chapter, we will concentrate on several objectives: identifying certain basic investment characteristics, clarifying the role of major asset classes in the asset mix, and finally, reviewing several of the products that the insurance industry typically markets to pension funds.

Investment Considerations Specific to Pension Investing

LO 11.4 Describe investment characteristics that are relevant in pension investing.

Let's start by looking at several aspects that need to be considered before selecting investments. One factor is the investment's tax treatment. Because qualified plans and other tax-advantaged plans are tax exempt (at the trust level), investments that also have special tax advantages are generally not appropriate for the plan. This is because the investor pays a premium for the tax advantage. For example, tax-free municipal bonds have a lower investment return than comparable taxable bonds. Because the trust does not benefit from the special tax treatment, these types of investments should generally be avoided.

Another concern is investment liquidity. This refers to the ability to convert the investment to cash in a short period of time. An adequate portion of the pension assets needs to be sufficiently liquid so benefit payments can be made without the need to sell long-term investments at a bad price.

A third consideration is the investment's stability. A stable investment has little fluctuation in value. For example, money market accounts and Treasury bills have almost no variability. As mentioned above, stability of the investments can affect the short-term variability of plan contributions to a defined-benefit plan. The downside of investments with little variability is that they also have low rates of return.

Unrelated Business Income Tax

When considering plan investments, qualified plans must be concerned about the unrelated business income tax (UBIT). If a qualified plan is deemed to operate an unrelated trade or business, any earnings (reduced by deductions allowed in connection with such business) will be taxable income to the trust, which reduces the return on the investment by the amount of the tax. If there is UBIT, the trust must also file a tax return and the UBIT is reported on the annual Form 5500.

For a qualified plan, operating any trade or business on a regular basis, either directly or as a partner in a partnership, will be considered operating an unrelated business. This broad language means that a plan participating in any limited partnership has to carefully evaluate whether the investment could generate UBIT.

The primary objective of this rule is to eliminate a source of unfair competition for taxable enterprises. A distinction must be made between operating a business (which would result in unfair competition) and a passive investment (which would not). A "trade or business" generally includes any activity carried on for the production of income from the sale of goods or performance of services.

From a practical perspective, this issue is most likely to arise when a pension trust is considering an investment in a limited partnership. In this case, it would be appropriate for the investment to provide a legal opinion about the UBIT issue in the prospectus. If the issue is not addressed, the plan should seek legal counsel to determine whether the investment could result in UBIT.

In addition to the UBIT determined above, a percentage of the plan's unrelated debt-financed income is also to be taxed as UBIT. Such income is taxed to the extent that the plan acquires income-producing assets by means of debt financing. There are exceptions; an important one is that debt-financed property does not include property whose use is substantially related to the trust's exempt purpose. This exception generally exempts ESOP debt-financed purchases from the tax. Again, this is a complicated area that requires careful investigation if the plan is considering a debt-financed investment.

Diversification Requirements for Defined-Contribution Plans

The Pension Protection Act of 2006 created a diversification requirement for defined-contribution plans which requires plans that invest in certain stock of the sponsoring employer to permit participants to diversify investments. The rule only applies to stock that is publicly traded. The right to choose alternative investments applies at all times to employee contributions invested in employer securities. With employer contributions, participants who have earned 3 years of service (as measured under the plan's vesting rules) must be permitted to direct such amounts to alternative investments.

The diversification requirements do not apply to an ESOP as long as it is a separate plan and does not have salary deferral or a matching contribution account. The reason that ESOPs are excluded is that they are subject to a separate diversification requirement. The requirements also do not apply to plans that only cover owners that are exempt from ERISA.

A plan subject to the diversification requirements is required to give participants a choice of at least three additional investment options. Each investment alternative must have materially different risk and return characteristics. Plan sponsors must allow diversification elections at least quarterly (on the same basis as the opportunity to make other investment changes, except as provided in regulations or securities laws).

INVESTMENT CLASSES

Cash Equivalents

cash equivalents

To satisfy the need to make other investment transactions and to have readily accessible money to pay benefits, plans generally invest some of a plan's assets in instruments that are known as **cash equivalents**. Typically, cash equivalents have either no specified maturity date or one that is one year or less in the future.

A number of different investments are considered cash equivalents. The investment with the least risk of default is the U.S. Treasury bill (T-bill). These obligations of the U.S. government have maturity dates of 90 days, 180 days, or one year when issued, and are backed by the full taxing authority of the government. They can be readily sold and converted to cash at a modest cost. Other federal government agencies also issue short-term marketable obligations. These are available with a range of maturity dates, and generally pay a slightly higher interest rate than T-bills.

Another category, bank deposits, includes savings accounts and certificates of deposit (CDs) at banks, savings and loans, and credit unions. Savings accounts face minimal risk and are subject to few restrictions on withdrawals. CDs, which are deposits for a specified period of time (such as 3, 6, or 12 months), generally impose a loss of a portion of the interest earnings as a penalty for a withdrawal before maturity, although some banks have eliminated this penalty or reduced it to a minimal amount. Banks also sell negotiable CDs with a minimum denomination of $100,000 or greater. However, trades in negotiable CDs have a minimum denomination of $1 million. Several New York-based CD dealers handle most secondary market trading. The first $250,000 in principal of a negotiable CD is covered by FDIC insurance (2017). Unfortunately, this means that most of the principal of high-denomination CDs ($1 million or more) is uninsured. Despite the lack of FDIC insurance guarantee, negotiable CDs are considered essentially as safe as commercial paper. Hence, the yields on these two instruments are nearly identical.

Money market deposit accounts (MMDAs) and money market mutual funds (MMMFs) are other popular cash equivalents. Both MMDAs and MMMFs hold portfolios of short-term obligations of the federal government and its agencies, of state and local governments, and of businesses. The securities are, in most cases, completely liquid without penalty. Money market instruments pay a yield slightly lower than the underlying investments (to account for management fees), but also allow greater diversification, protecting the plan from default risk.

Other investments that have the characteristics of cash equivalents include short-term obligations of state and local governments and of businesses and the long-term debt obligations of governments, businesses, and nonprofit institutions that are to mature within one year.

Bonds

Bond owners are creditors of the issuing institution, whether it is a government, business, or nonprofit organization. This status grants the investors the legal right to enforce their claims to interest income and principal repayment as contained in the agreement that specifies the terms and conditions of the debt issue. In the case of business debt instruments, debt claims have priority over any claims of its owners.

Bond issues of state and local governments (both of which are referred to as municipals) and of businesses typically are quality rated by Standard and Poor's Corporation (S&P) and/or Moody's Investors Service. These ratings express the likelihood that the issuer will default on the timely payment of interest or principal. Based on a financial analysis of the issuer, a letter grade is assigned to each bond issue. Bonds rated at the top of the B grade (BBB for S&P, Baa for Moody's) or higher are considered to be investment quality. Lower ratings are assigned for bonds assessed as speculative. The lower the quality rating, the greater the risk of default and the higher the interest rate (return) that the investor can expect to earn.

Government Bonds. Governmental debt includes securities of the federal, state, and local governments. Some federal bonds are backed by the full faith and credit of the U.S. government. For example, all U.S. Treasury obligations have such backing. Other U.S. government bonds issued by federal agencies or organizations, such as the Tennessee Valley Authority or the U.S. Postal Service, are not direct obligations of the U.S. Treasury. These bonds, known collectively as agency bonds, provide investors with a return greater than that available on U.S. Treasury bonds. A few of these agency bonds have guarantees that effectively place the full faith and credit of the U.S. Treasury behind the bonds.

Some state and local government bonds, known as general obligations, are backed by the taxing power of the state or local government. Others, usually issued by agencies of a state or local government, are known as revenue bonds. They are backed by the revenues earned from such ventures as turnpikes, airports, and sewer and water systems. Without the taxing authority behind them, these revenue bonds are viewed as riskier and pay investors a somewhat higher interest rate than do general obligation bonds.

Maturities of governmental debt instruments vary from more than one year to 30 years. Bonds with maturities of 10 years or less are often referred to as being of intermediate-term duration and have somewhat less risk than longer-term bonds. If such a risk difference does exist, intermediate-term obligations would pay a slightly lower rate than would longer duration bonds.

Corporate Bonds. Businesses are major contributors to the supply of debt securities available in the marketplace. These securities, either notes if intermediate term or bonds if long term, have various characteristics, which are detailed in the indenture. Some of the more frequently encountered characteristics include the following:

- *secured*—a promise backed by specific assets as further protection to the bondholder should the corporation default on payment of interest or principal
- *debenture*—an unsecured promise, based only on the issuer's general credit status, to pay interest and principal
- *callable*—an option exercisable at the issuer's discretion to redeem the bond prior to its maturity date at a specified price

- *convertible*—an option exercisable by the bondholder to exchange the bond for a predetermined number of common or preferred shares

For bonds of the same quality rating, these features affect the interest rate available to the investor. If the feature provides a benefit to the bondholder, such as being secured or convertible, a lower interest rate is paid. If the feature provides a benefit to the issuer, such as the flexibility of not having specific assets pledged as collateral (debenture) or the presence of a call feature, the interest rate is higher.

When plan assets are invested by the trustee, bonds are often used to ensure that the plan will have sufficient cash to pay expected benefits as they arise. For example, if a defined-benefit plan expects to pay out monthly benefits to current beneficiaries in the amount of $50,000 a month, bonds are purchased in the amount necessary to generate a stream of interest payments in this amount. Also, bonds are used simply because they provide more stable returns than equities and higher returns than the cash equivalents mentioned above.

Equity Securities

Equity investments represent an ownership position in a business. As such, they represent a higher short-term risk for the investor than do debt investments, but they also offer higher potential long-term return. Because most retirement plans have long-term investment goals, equity investments play a significant role in the asset mix. At the end of 2009, assets held in equities in U.S. defined benefit plans were approximately 45 percent of total plan assets. This is down somewhat from previous years; for example, in 2005, 62 percent of assets were held in equities.

Investors in common stock have the ultimate ownership rights in the corporation. They elect the board of directors that oversees the management of the firm. Each common share receives an equal portion of the dividends distributed, as well as any liquidation proceeds. If the firm is unsuccessful, losses will occur that can lead to cessation of any dividend payments and, if losses continue, to eradication of the common equity ownership and eventual bankruptcy.

Current income distributed as dividends to shareholders is at the sole discretion of the board of directors. The board is under no legal obligation to make dividend payments and may instead retain the profits within the business. Only by threatening to elect, or actually electing, a new board can common shareholders force a dividend payment, regardless of the profitability of the business.

The owners of common stock also vote on major issues, such as mergers, name changes, sale of a major part of the business, or liquidation. Finally, common stockholders sometimes have a preemptive right, which is the right to maintain their relative voting power by purchasing shares of any new issues of common stock of the corporation.

Mutual Funds

An open-end investment company, popularly called a mutual fund, continually sells and redeems its shares at net asset value, that is, the value of the fund's assets divided by the number of outstanding shares. Mutual funds acquire a portfolio of securities in which each of the fund's shares represents a proportionate interest in the total portfolio. As sales and redemptions of the fund's shares take place, the size of the fund's total portfolio changes, increasing when additional shares are sold and decreasing when shares are redeemed.

Mutual funds can be differentiated on the basis of their portfolio objectives. These major categories include

- *money market mutual funds*—These funds own a portfolio of short-term interest-bearing securities. As mentioned earlier, investors use them as an alternative to cash.
- *bond funds*—These companies own a portfolio of bonds. Subcategories include some that invest only in U.S. government issues, municipal issues, corporate issues, or low-quality (junk) bonds. Further subcategories can be short-term (up to 4 or 5 years), intermediate-term (5 to 10 years), or long-term (10 or more years in duration) bond funds.
- *common stock companies*—These companies hold a portfolio of common stocks and perhaps a small number of preferred stocks. Subcategories include those that invest primarily in conservative (defensive) stocks, growth stocks, aggressive growth stocks, or foreign stocks.
- *mixed portfolio companies*—These companies own a portfolio of bonds, stocks, and other investment instruments. Subcategories include balanced companies and income companies.

Another way to distinguish funds is to look at whether they are actively managed (securities chosen individually by management) or passively managed. A common passive strategy includes those funds referred to as index funds. An index fund owns a portfolio that replicates a major market index, such as the S&P 500. Passive strategies generally result in lower management fees.

In addition to the fees charged by the management of the fund, funds have various acquisition fees. In many cases, fees that would apply to individual investors are waived for the pension fund. If fees exist, they must be carefully evaluated.

Mutual funds are more and more frequently used in pension plans. With small plans, assets may be too small to be handled by an investment manager. Like the common trust fund (described in the previous chapter), mutual funds provide an easy way to achieve diversification. Mutual funds also provide liquidity and ease of entry and exit. As mutual fund return data is published and studied, it simplifies evaluation of investment performance.

When participants in defined-contribution plans are given investment choices, mutual funds (and other look-through investments such as common trust funds and insurance contracts) are becoming the primary form of investment. These types of investments allow participants to build individualized portfolios while still taking advantage of professional management and asset diversification. In addition, these look-through investments are required in order to take advantage of the fiduciary liability relief described in the previous chapter.

Stable Value Funds

stable value funds

A class of investments referred to as **stable value funds** are commonly offered to participants as an investment option in defined-contribution plans. While these are quite popular; there has been a recent downward trend in their use, according to one study, 27 percent of 401(k) assets were allocated to stable value funds at the end of 2009 but only 21 percent by the end of 2012.[1] For Aon Hewitt, the stable value fund continued its decline in use with only 11.9 percent at the end of 2014, a drop of 3.5 percent from the end of 2013.

Stable value funds allow participants to make transactions at "book" value regardless of the market value of the underlying assets. Book (or contract) value means that the value of the account is tied to contributions, plus accrued interest, reduced by previous withdrawals or transfers. Participants' ability to transact at book value is called "benefit responsiveness," and is a characteristic shared by all stable value products. This gives these products the liquidity and certainty of money market funds. However, returns tend to be more comparable to those of high-quality, intermediate-term bond funds—but with lower volatility.

guaranteed investment contracts (GICs)

The first generation of stable value products were the insurance company **guaranteed investment contracts (GICs)**. They feature a guaranteed rate of return, guaranteed principal, a specified maturity date and the ability of plan participants to make allocations to and from the

---

1. Hewitt 401(k) Index™, Asset Allocation for December 2009 - 2014 Year End 401(k) Index Observations. Available at http://www.aon.com/human-capital-consulting/thought-leadership/outsourcing/401k_index/401k-index-2014-year-end.jsp.

funds at book value. Traditional GICs are guaranteed by insurance companies and backed by the insurer's general account.

separate account GIC

A variation known as a **separate account GIC** offers a guarantee supported by one or more fixed income separate accounts instead of the insurance company's general account. This innovation enabled plans to credit higher rates to plan participants with funds invested in fixed income strategies not limited by regulatory constraints that affect general account assets. With separate account GICs, crediting rates are reset periodically and market value gains and losses of the portfolio are smoothed over a period of years.

synthetic GIC

The most recent development is the synthetic GIC. While **synthetic GIC** contracts vary, generally they are different from insured GICs in two ways. First, the stable value investments are held directly by the qualified plan trust. Second, the plan obtains a book value guarantee (called a wrap contract) from another financial institution. These agreements impose limitations on how the funds under the book value guarantee can be invested.

Hedge Funds and Private Equity

From 2001 through 2010, large defined-benefit plans have increased their investments into both hedge funds and private equity. Nearly ninety percent of plans with at least $1 billion in total assets invest in private equity. In 2001, only about 10 percent of firms with $1 billion in assets invested in Hedge funds. By the end of 2010, nearly 60 percent of such plans had Hedge fund investments. However, the total average allocation of plan assets into hedge funds remained small, with just around 5 percent of plan assets. Private equity saw a higher allocation of plan assets with nearly 9 percent.

CHAPTER REVIEW

Key Terms and Concepts

terminal funding approach
actuarial cost method
actuarial assumptions
funding target
fully insured
funding instrument
common trust fund
split-funded plan
investment guidelines

funding policy
investment policy
cash equivalents
stable value funds
guaranteed investment contracts (GICs)
separate account GIC
synthetic GIC

Chapter 11: Review Questions

Review questions are based on the learning objectives in this chapter. Thus, an [11.3] at the end of a question means that the question is based on learning objective 3. If there are multiple objectives, they are all listed.

1. What is an actuarial cost method and what is the role of actuarial assumptions. [11.1]

2. Discuss the current minimum funding requirements. [11.1]

3. Describe the terms of a qualified plan trust. [11.2]

4. Describe the other funding vehicles available to the qualified plan. [11.2]

5. Why is it so important to establish investment guidelines? [11.3]

6. Name the common objectives of a defined-benefit plan. [11.3]

7. Name the common objectives of a defined-contribution plan. [11.3]

8. What is the primary objective that the trustees must satisfy when plan participants have investment options? [11.3]

9. What questions are helpful to ask when determining the plan's investment policy? [11.3]

10. Name the specific areas that should be addressed when identifying investment goals. [11.3]

11. What types of investments must a pension plan look at carefully in order to be sure that they do not result in unrelated business taxable income? [11.4]

12. Describe how the diversification requirements that apply to defined contribution plans apply differently to employee and employer contributions. [11.4]

13. Explain the role that cash equivalencies, bonds, and stocks have in the pension portfolio. [11.4]

Chapter 11: Review Answers

1. An actuarial cost method is a method of determining an annual employer contribution for a given set of plan benefits and a given group of employees. Actuarial assumptions refer to assumptions about future investment return and the character of the employee group that are made in order to determine the annual contribution.

2. The current minimum funding rules require contributions that cover the current year's benefit accrual (target normal cost) and any funding shortfall, which is calculated by comparing the plan's assets and the present value of promised benefits at the beginning of the year. Any shortfall has to be made up with level amortization payments over 7 years.

3. An irrevocable trust, valid under state law, clarifies the investment powers of the trustees, the allocation of fiduciary responsibility, the payment of benefits and plan expenses, and the rights and duties upon plan termination.

4. Life insurance and annuity contracts can also act as the plan's funding instruments.

5. Investment guidelines help to establish the fiduciaries' obligations. They are also the appropriate first step in making investment decisions—that is, determining the fund's goals and objectives. They can also provide protection for the fiduciaries when their actions are questioned.

6. The common objectives of a defined-benefit investment plan usually include the accumulation of sufficient assets to pay benefits and the minimizing of the long-term cost and variability in annual costs. Sometimes these objectives are at odds with each other.

7. The single investment objective in a defined-contribution plan is to invest for the long-term retirement needs of the plan participants.

8. With self-directed defined-contribution plans, the primary objective is to provide investment alternatives appropriate to meet the diverse needs of participants with different ages, risk tolerances, and investment goals.

9. When establishing investment guidelines, it is helpful to ask such questions as: What is the minimum level of return necessary to accomplish the goal? What is an acceptable level of risk in relation to the whole portfolio? What is the appropriate time horizon?

10. Considerations when identifying investment goals should include permissible categories of investments, limits on asset quality, asset allocation ranges,

diversification concerns, policies on proxy voting of stock, and other limits due to legal restrictions.

11. Plans invest in cash equivalents to satisfy the need to make other investment transactions and to have readily accessible money to pay benefits. Bonds are often used to ensure that the plan will have sufficient cash to pay expected benefits as they arise. Also, bonds are used simply because they provide more stable returns than equities and higher returns than the cash equivalents mentioned above. Because investment in equities generally results in higher returns over the long haul, equities typically represent more than half of the assets held by the plan.

12. Any time the plan is deemed to be operating a business or invests in debt-financed property, a tax opinion about whether the investment generates UBIT should be sought. The issue comes up most often for pension plans regarding investments in limited partnerships.

13. With employee contributions, employees have the right to choose alternative investments at all times. With employer contributions, participants who have earned 3 years of service must be permitted to direct such amounts to alternative investments.

Chapter 12

Fiduciary Responsibility

Learning Objectives

An understanding of the material in this chapter should enable the student to

- **LO 12.1** Identify the scope of the fiduciary rules that apply to retirement plans.
- **LO 12.2** Describe the affirmative duties of plan fiduciaries involved in the investment of plan assets.
- **LO 12.3** Explain the individual account plan exception that limits fiduciary liability when participants make investment decisions.
- **LO 12.4** Identify what the prohibited transaction rules are intended to accomplish and how they work.
- **LO 12.5** Describe the impact of failing to satisfy the fiduciary rules and ways to protect the plan and fiduciaries.

SCOPE OF FIDUCIARY RULES

LO 12.1 Identify the scope of the fiduciary rules that apply to retirement plans.

Fiduciaries are generally those individuals or entities who manage an employee benefit plan and its assets. Employers often hire outside professionals, sometimes called third-party service providers, or use an internal administrative committee or human resources department to manage some or all of a plan's day-to-day operations. Even if an employer hires third-party service providers or uses internal administrative committees to manage the plan, it still has fiduciary responsibilities.

Fiduciary status is based on the functions the person performs for the plan, not just the person's title. A plan must have at least one fiduciary, a person or an entity, named in the written plan, or through a process described in the plan.[1] The "named fiduciary" can be identified by office or by name.[2] For some plans, it may be an administrative committee or a company's board of directors.

---

1. *CSA 401(k) Plan v. Pension Professionals, Inc.*, 195 F. 3d 1135 (9th Cir. 1999) (stating that a plan must have at least one fiduciary named in the written plan).
2. ERISA Sec. 402(a) & 29 U.S.C. Sec. 1102 (A named fiduciary must be named in the plan document or by a qualified person through specific ERISA guidelines).

Fiduciaries and their decisions are subject to the scrutiny of the fiduciary rules. In this chapter we clarify who is subject to these rules, what the fiduciaries' obligations are, and the liability imposed on fiduciaries. There are many important issues affecting financial services professionals discussed in this chapter including:

- service provider fee disclosure
- participant fee disclosure
- limiting fiduciary liability through employee investment direction
- choosing a default investment alternative

Plans Subject to ERISA

The fiduciary provisions of Title I of ERISA generally apply to both pension and welfare benefit plans. ERISA defines a pension plan as any plan, fund, or program which is established or maintained by an employer or by an employee organization (such as a labor union), or by both, to the extent that it (1) provides retirement income to employees, or (2) results in a deferral of income by employees for periods extending to the termination of covered employment or beyond.[3] This definition includes plans regardless of their tax qualified status including pension, profit-sharing, stock bonus, and similar qualified plans as well as SEPs and SIMPLEs, and many 403(b) plans. (403(b) plans that do not include employer contributions are generally exempt.) It also can include some nonqualified deferred-compensation plans, however unfunded excess benefit plans and unfunded plans maintained for a select group of management and highly compensated employees are exempt from Title I of ERISA.[4]

Other plans that are exempt are those that only cover a business owner (owning 100 percent of the entity) and his or her spouse or only covers partners and their spouses. ERISA also exempts governmental and church plans. Generally, a governmental plan means a plan established or maintained for its employees by the government of the United States, by the government of any state or political subdivision thereof, or by any agency or instrumentality of the foregoing.[5]

---

3. See 29 U.S.C. 1002 (defining the term pension plan).
4. See ERISA Sec. 3(36) (29 U.S.C. Sec. 1002(36)) (defining an unfunded excess benefit plan as "a plan maintained by an employer solely for the purpose of providing benefits for certain employees in excess of the limitations on contributions and benefits imposed by Sec. 415 of Title 26 on plans to which that section applies without regard to whether the plan is funded. To the extent that a separable part of a plan (as determined by the Secretary of Labor) maintained by an employer is maintained for such purpose, that part shall be treated as a separate plan which is an excess benefit plan.")
5. See ERISA Sec. 4(b) (29 USC Sec. 1003(b) (Exceptions for certain plans) (setting forth a list of plans not covered by the subsection regarding fiduciary provisions of Title I of ERISA.))

Individuals Considered Fiduciaries under ERISA

Under ERISA Sec. 3(21), a person is a fiduciary with respect to a plan to the extent that he or she

- has any discretionary authority or discretionary responsibility in the administration of such plan,
- exercises any authority or control respecting management of the plan or disposition of the plan's assets, or
- renders investment advice for a fee or other compensation.[6]

fiduciaries

Practically speaking, **fiduciaries** will include the sponsoring company, plan trustees, investment managers, and officers of the company who participate in the selection of trustees and/or investment managers.

Service providers, such as accountants, lawyers, and administrative firms, are generally not identified as fiduciaries.[7] Even individuals who sell investments to the plan are generally not considered fiduciaries. According to Department of Labor (DOL) regulations, rendering investment advice for a fee means[8]

- the exercise of discretionary control over the purchase or sale of securities or
- the provision of investment advice on a regular basis on the purchase and sale of assets, with such advice being the primary basis for the investment of plan assets

This definition of investment advice is rather limited and in 2010, the DOL issued proposed regulations[9] (which are not yet effective), that would expand the definition by eliminating the "advice on a regular basis" requirement and expands the term advice to include appraisals. The proposed regulations specifically include registered investment advisors (RIAs) and their agents as fiduciaries. The proposed regulations also identify several common plan activities that do not rise to the level of fiduciary status:

- recommendations by a seller of security to the plan and the buyer should know that the seller is not necessarily offering impartial advice
- the provision of investment education to plan participants

---

6. See 29 U.S.C. Sec. 1002 (21) (defining fiduciary).
7. DOL Reg. §2509.75-5.
8. DOL Reg. §2510.3-21 (29 CFR Sec. 2510.3–21).
9. DOL Prop. Reg. §2510.3-21.

- making available a menu of investment alternatives and providing information to assist in the selection of specific funds
- providing general financial information and data to assist a plan fiduciary's selection of securities

The last two items both require a written disclosure that the person is not undertaking to provide impartial investment advice. However, the DOL withdrew the proposed regulations but they are expected to repropose the regulations in the near feature.

Also, it is important to note that the definition of fiduciary is a functional one and determining whether someone is a fiduciary is based on the facts and circumstances (regardless of whether the individual is specifically identified as a fiduciary). Even commissioned insurance agents have been determined to have been fiduciaries when the agent's advice has been determined to be the primary basis for the investment of plan assets.

It is important to note that even though the employer will almost always be considered a fiduciary, some decisions made by the employer about the plan are considered business decisions and not fiduciary actions. For example, the decisions to establish a plan, to include certain features in a plan, to amend a plan, and to terminate a plan are business decisions not governed by ERISA.

Plan Assets

As the fiduciary responsibility rules only apply to assets of the plan, it becomes critical to be able to identify which assets are considered plan assets. This issue can arise when a plan invests in another entity. Generally, a plan's assets include its investments and any "amounts (other than union dues) that a participant or beneficiary pays to an employer, or amounts that a participant has withheld from his wages by an employer, for contribution or repayment of a participant loan to the plan, as of the earliest date on which such contributions or repayments can reasonably be segregated from the employer's general assets," but do not include any of the underlying assets of the entity.[10]

However, if the plan's investment is in an equity interest of an entity that is neither a publicly-offered security nor a security issued by an investment company registered under the Investment Company Act of 1940, its assets generally include both the equity interest and an undivided interest in each of the underlying assets of the entity. Still there are exceptions if the

---

10. See 29 CFR 2510.3–101 (defining plan assets—investment assets); see also 29 CFR 2510.3–101 (defining plan assets—employee contributions).

entity is an operating company, or equity participation in the entity by benefit plan investors is not significant.

Another concern relates to plans that contains employee salary deferrals (such as a 401(k) plan, SIMPLE, or 403(b) plan).[11] Under these plans as soon as an individual has earned the salary that is being deferred, the amount becomes a plan asset. Out of concern that the employer will use these assets, DOL segregation of plan assets regulations require that salary deferrals have to be segregated from the employer's general assets as of the earliest date that it is reasonably feasible but never later than the 15th day of the month following the month of the salary deferral. The rules imply that a reasonable date can be quite soon after the election is made. To provide additional clarity, DOL regulations[12] have established a 7-business-day safe harbor period for employers with fewer than 100 participants to submit employee contributions.

AFFIRMATIVE FIDUCIARY OBLIGATIONS

LO 12.2 Describe the affirmative duties of plan fiduciaries involved in the investment of plan assets.

Fiduciaries involved in the investment of plan assets are required to make decisions within the framework of five rules:

- the exclusive-benefit rule
- the prudent-fiduciary rule
- the diversification requirement
- the requirement that investment decisions conform with plan and trust documents
- the participant fee disclosure rules for participant-directed individual account plans

Each of these rules is described in more detail below.

Exclusive-Benefit Rule

exclusive-benefit rule

Fiduciaries are required to discharge their duties solely in the interest of the plan's participants and beneficiaries for the exclusive purpose of providing benefits and defraying reasonable expenses. This **exclusive-benefit rule** means the fiduciary must act first and foremost in the

---

11. See 29 CFR 2510.3–101.
12. Labor Reg. 2510.3-102(a).

plan participant's interest.[13] If an investment decision has a collateral benefit for the employer, the fiduciary or other party, the fiduciary will have a difficult decision. If a fiduciary sees the possibility of a conflict of loyalty between the plan participants and another party (employer), according to the DOL,[14] he or she should seek the advice of a competent, independent advisor, and possibly elect not to participate in the decision.

While the law does not specify a permissible level of fees, it does require that fees are "reasonable." This requires that fiduciaries carefully review fees when selecting service providers as well as monitoring fees on an ongoing basis. In comparing estimates from service providers, the fiduciary needs to be careful to compare "apples to apples" which is not always easy as quotes can cover a range of services. Also, some fees are not direct, but are paid to service providers through investment vehicles, such as mutual funds. For example, mutual funds often charge fees to pay brokers and other salespersons for promoting the fund and providing other services. There also may be sales and other related charges for investments offered by a service provider.

Plan expenses may be paid by the employer, the plan, or both. In addition, for expenses paid by the plan, they may be allocated to participants' accounts in a variety of ways. In any case, the plan document should specify how fees are paid.

YOUR FINANCIAL SERVICES PRACTICE: EXCESSIVE FEES LITIGATION

Since 2006, a tremendous amount of class action complaints have been brought against fiduciaries claiming breach of fiduciary duty related to fees and expenses. One of the first cases to come to judgment is *Tibble v. Edison Int'l*.[15] In this case, the court ruled that fiduciaries breached their duty by offering more expensive retail share classes of certain mutual funds rather than the cheaper institutional share classes as investment alternatives in the 401(k) plan. The court found that under the facts of this case, there was no advantage offered by the more expensive retail funds, and there was no evidence that the fiduciaries considered offering the less expensive institutional funds. This case should be a wake-up call for both fiduciaries and the financial services profession about the importance of evaluating fees.

---

13. See ERISA Sec. (404(a)(1) (29 U.S.S. Sec. 1104(a)(1)).
14. DOL Adv. Op. Lty. No. 84-09A and DOL reg. 2550.408b-2(e).
15. 2010 WL 2757153 (C.D. Cal. July 8, 2010).

Prudence

prudent-fiduciary rule

According to the **prudent-fiduciary rule**, fiduciaries must act with the care, skill, prudence, and diligence (under prevailing circumstances) that a prudent person acting in a like capacity and familiar with such matters would use in the conduct of an enterprise of a like character and with like aims.[16] Note that this standard compares, for example, plan trustees with other experienced plan trustees. With regard to the choice of prudent investments, DOL regulations[17] refer to six factors that should be considered:

1. the role of the investment as part of the plan's overall portfolio;
2. whether the investment is reasonably designed as part of the portfolio;
3. the risk of loss and opportunity for gain;
4. the diversification of the portfolio;
5. the liquidity and current return relative to the anticipated cash flow requirements of the plan;
6. and, the projected return of the portfolio relative to the funding objectives of the plan.

In a recent case, *Tibble v. Edison Int'l.*,[18] the court said that fiduciaries act prudently if at the time they engaged in the challenged transactions, the fiduciaries employed the appropriate methods to investigate the merits of the investment. Thus, the prudence test focuses on the conduct of the fiduciaries when making the investment decision and not on the resulting performance of the investment. Also, the challenged decision is judged at the time it was made, rather than with the benefit of hindsight.

The Tibble court also pointed out that a fiduciary may secure independent advice from counsel or a financial advisor when making investment decisions, and indeed must do so where he lacks the requisite education, experience, and skill. Also, even though securing independent advice is evidence of a thorough investigation, the fiduciary must investigate the expert's qualifications, provide accurate information to the expert, and ensure that reliance on the expert's advice is reasonably justified under the circumstances.

---

16. 29 U.S.C. Sec. 1104(B).
17. Reg. 29 CFR 2550.404a-1(b).
18. *Tibble v. Edison Int'l.*, 2010 WL 2757153 (C.D. Cal. July 8, 2010).

Diversification of Investments

diversification requirement

The **diversification requirement**[19] means that trustees have the duty to diversify the plan's investments to minimize the risk of large losses, unless it is clearly prudent not to do so under the plan. According to the legislative history of ERISA,[20] "clearly prudent" language was intended to mean that if a fiduciary were sued for failing to diversify investments, once the plaintiff demonstrated that assets were not diversified, the defendant fiduciary would have the burden of proof to demonstrate why his or her actions were appropriate. Apparently, the diversification referred to here means both diversification among asset classes and diversification within a single asset class.

Conformance with Documents

Fiduciaries are required to operate the plan in accordance with the document and instruments that govern the plan.[21] Trust instruments spell out the types of investments that are allowed, whether any types of investments are prohibited, and who is responsible for making the decisions. Problems in this area do arise when trustees and others make investment decisions without carefully consulting relevant documents. If the plan has a funding policy, an investment policy, or both (discussed further below), these documents must be carefully followed as well.

> **YOUR FINANCIAL SERVICES PRACTICE: EDUCATING FIDUCIARIES**
>
> At the DOL Employee Benefits Security Administration website (www.dol.gov/ebsa) there are a number of interesting items about fiduciaries of small retirement plans. In 2002 a DOL working group on fiduciary education and training discussed the lack of sophistication among small-plan fiduciaries and the serious need for education of nonprofessional fiduciaries. In the small-plan market the primary educator is the financial services professional. This is a valuable and important role. Fulfilling it well can mean satisfied clients and a competitive edge in the market. The DOL website does contain some documents that your clients may want to read—most notably the booklet entitled, "Meeting Your Responsibilities."

---

19. See 29 U.S.C. Sec 1104 (C).
20. Conference Committee Report to ERISA, H.R. Rep. No. 93-1280.
21. See 29 U.S.C. Sec. 1104 (D).

Participant Fee Disclosure

Recent DOL regulations require the disclosure of certain plan and investment-related information, including fee and expense information, to all participants and beneficiaries in participant-directed individual account plans (for example, 401(k) plans).[22] To some extent, these participant fee disclosures are already required for plans that elect to comply with the ERISA §404(c). Additionally, these rules do not apply to IRAs, SEPs, SIMPLE Plans, or non-ERISA employer-sponsored plans (that is, where a business owner and his spouse are the only two participants). However, these disclosure requirements are more comprehensive and explicit than under 404(c) and apply to all participant-directed plans even if the fiduciaries do not take advantage of the 404(c) limitation. Also, failure to meet these requirements can result in a finding that the responsible fiduciaries have breached their fiduciary obligations. On May 7, 2012, the DOL issued Field Assistance Bulletin 2012–02 to help answer questions regarding the Sec. 404(a) participant fee disclosure regulations.

The general plan information required to be disclosed up front and then again annually includes

- information about the structure and mechanics of the plan, including how participants provide investment instructions and a current list of investment options offered in the plan
- fees for general plan administrative services (for example, accounting and recordkeeping services) that are charged to the individual accounts of participants
- fees and expenses for individual participant actions, such as taking a participant loan or fees for processing a qualified domestic relations order (QDRO)

In addition, participants must receive statements, at least quarterly, showing the dollar amount of the plan-related fees and expenses actually charged to or deducted from their individual accounts, along with a description of the services for which the charge or deduction was made. The administrator must also disclose investment-related information. For investment options that do not have a fixed rate of return (for example, mutual funds), items that must be disclosed include

- historical investment performance returns for 1-, 5-, and 10-year periods
- the name of an appropriate broad-based securities market index and historical returns over the same 1-, 5-, and 10-year periods

---

22. See 29 CFR 2550.404(a)-5.

- total annual operating expenses expressed as both a percentage of assets and as a dollar amount for each $1,000 invested
- shareholder-type fees or restrictions on the participant's ability to purchase or withdraw from the investment

Disclosures for investment options that have a fixed or stated rate of return include

- the annual rate of return and the terms of the investment must be disclosed
- shareholder-type fees or restrictions on the participant's ability to purchase or withdraw from the investment

The disclosure rules also require giving participants a web address that offers additional information about investment options as well as providing participants a glossary of investment terms. Finally, the rules require that information be furnished in a chart or similar format designed to facilitate a comparison of each investment option available under the plan. The DOL has created a sample of such a model.

YOUR FINANCIAL SERVICES PRACTICE: ANSWERING CLIENT'S FIDUCIARY QUESTIONS

Advisors should be ready to address the concerns of potential clients. The Department of Labor and the SEC developed the following set of questions to assist plan fiduciaries in evaluating the objectivity of the recommendations provided, or the fiduciary status of a pension advisor. These should be of interest both to the employer and advisor communities.

- Are you registered with the SEC or a state securities regulator as an investment advisor?
- Do you or a related company have relationships with money managers that you recommend, consider for recommendation, or otherwise mention to the plan?
- Do you or a related company receive any payments from money managers you recommend, consider for recommendation, or otherwise mention to the plan for our consideration?
- Do you have any policies or procedures to address conflicts of interest or to prevent these payments or relationships from being a factor when you provide advice to your clients?
- If you allow plans to pay your consulting fees using the plan's brokerage commissions, do you monitor the amount of commissions paid and alert plans when consulting fees have been paid in full?
- If you allow plans to pay your consulting fees using the plan's brokerage commissions, what steps do you take to ensure that the plan receives best execution for its securities trades?

- Do you have any arrangements with broker-dealers under which you or a related company will benefit if money managers place trades for their clients with such broker-dealers?
- If you are hired, will you acknowledge in writing that you have a fiduciary obligation as an investment advisor to the plan while providing the consulting services we are seeking?
- Do you consider yourself a fiduciary under ERISA with respect to the recommendations you provide the plan?

LIMITATIONS: THE INDIVIDUAL ACCOUNT PLAN EXCEPTION

LO 12.3   Explain the individual account plan exception that limits fiduciary liability when participants make investment decisions.

Because qualified plans of the defined-contribution type allocate dollars to the separate accounts of participants, the sponsoring employer has the option either to direct the trustees to invest plan assets or to give participants some choice over the investment of individual accounts. Because SEPs and SIMPLEs are funded with individual IRAs, participants almost always have investment options. Similarly, 403(b) plans almost always give participants investment choices.

ERISA Sec. 404(c) (individual account plan exception)

If a defined-contribution plan, SEP, SIMPLE, or 403(b) plan gives individual participants options with regard to the investment of their own plan benefits, it makes sense that the fiduciaries should not be responsible for the participant's investment decisions. **ERISA Sec. 404(c) (individual account plan exception)** grants such fiduciary relief by providing that in the case of a participant exercising independent investment direction over his or her own account, no fiduciary will be liable for losses that arise from such participant direction.

General Requirements

In order to qualify for this relief, the plan must conform to strict DOL requirements. The DOL's general rule is that the plan must provide an opportunity for a participant or beneficiary to exercise control over the assets in his or her account and offer the individual an opportunity to choose from a broad range of investment alternatives.

More specifically, the rules require the following:

- *Notice of 404(c) status*—Participants must be notified that the plan is seeking to qualify for the fiduciary relief provided under ERISA Sec. 404(c).

- *Adequate information*—The participant must also be provided with specific information regarding each investment option. The central item is a description of the investment alternative and a general description of the risk and return characteristics of that investment. Participants must also be informed about procedures for making investment elections, any expenses involved, and to whom to go for additional information.

- *Exercise of control*—The participant must be given a reasonable opportunity to forward investment instructions to the fiduciary either in writing or otherwise (as long as the participant can request a written confirmation).

- *Diversification*—To meet diversification requirements, the investment options generally must be look-through investments, such as mutual funds, pooled separate accounts, or guaranteed-investment contracts.

- *Number of investment options*—Participants must have the opportunity to choose from at least three core investment alternatives, each with materially different risk and return characteristics. Also, in the aggregate, the options must offer a balanced mix appropriate for a participant and, when combined with the other investments, have the effect of minimizing risks.

- *Employer stock*—Securities of the plan sponsor can also be an investment option; however, this cannot be one of the three core options.

- *Election frequency*—The opportunity to change investment elections with respect to each investment alternative must be appropriate in light of market volatility. At a minimum, the three core investment alternatives must offer the opportunity to change investment choice at least quarterly.

- *Prospectus for investors*—Immediately following a participant's or beneficiary's initial investment in a particular option, he or she will be given a copy of the most recent prospectus provided to the plan.

- *Information upon request*—Upon request, the participant has the right to receive additional information about each investment alternative, including copies of the prospectus, description of operating expenses (as a percentage of net assets), and other detailed financial information about each option.

Participants Failing to Exercise Control

qualified default investment alternative

A fiduciary generally is not eligible for ERISA 404(c) relief unless the participant actually exercises control over the investment of his or her account. In some cases, especially with plans that provide for automatic enrollment, some participants fail to provide investment instructions. To encourage plans to provide for automatic enrollment, the Pension Protection Act of 2006 created an exception to protect fiduciaries in such cases. Under the exception, a participant failing to provide investment direction will be deemed to have exercised control over assets in his or her account (allowing the fiduciaries protection under 404(c)) if the plan invests in a **qualified default investment alternative**. In addition, participants must be notified about

- the circumstances under which assets will be invested in a qualified default investment alternative
- the investment objectives of the default investment alternative, how assets are invested and how that may change over time
- the right to direct investments out of the default investment alternative

Regulations have offered guidance on what can be treated as a qualified default investment alternative. The regulations attempt to provide specific guidance while giving the fiduciaries a range of possible investment alternatives. The default investment must be diversified and managed by either a professional investment manager or an investment company registered under the Investment Company Act of 1940. More specifically a qualified default investment alternative can include any of the following:

- a life-cycle or target retirement date fund, designed to provide varying degrees of long-term appreciation and capital preservation through a mix of equity and fixed income investment options based on the participant's age, target retirement date, or life expectancy
- a balanced fund, designed to provide both long-term appreciation and capital preservation through a mix of equity and fixed income investments, consistent with a target level of risk appropriate for all of the plan's participants
- an investment management service that invests the participant's account among the plan's investment options to achieve a mix of long-term appreciation and capital preservation, based on the participant's age, target retirement date, or life expectancy

Limitations on Relief

Note that a plan offering individual investment options is not required to satisfy the requirements of ERISA 404(c). If the rules are not satisfied, then the fiduciary could still be liable if the participant makes an imprudent investment choice. Meeting the requirements is the best way to protect the plan fiduciaries. However, if a plan sponsor decides that meeting the requirements in the DOL regulations is impractical, yet still wants to give participants investment choices, the next best line of protection is adequate fiduciary insurance and employer indemnification. Also, in this case, employee investment education and communication can also serve to minimize risk.

If all the rules are satisfied, then ERISA Sec. 404(c) indicates that the fiduciary will not be liable for a breach of duty because of the participants' exercise of control over investment decisions. In other words, the fiduciary is not responsible for the results of the participant's asset allocation decision.

> **EXAMPLE**
>
> Emily, aged 60, decides to invest all of her 401(k) account in an aggressive growth stock mutual fund, shunning the four other, less risky alternatives. In the following year, the value of her account drops by 20 percent. Under Sec. 404(c), the fiduciary should not be liable for Emily's loss because it was her decision.

Still, Sec. 404(c) does not get the fiduciary completely off the hook. Fiduciaries are obligated to ensure that participant investment choices do not constitute prohibited transactions. Further, investment choices must conform to other fiduciary obligations, such as compliance with plan documents. Most important, fiduciaries are never granted relief from the obligation to prudently select the available options. In the example above, if the aggressive growth fund available to Emily has had inferior performance—as compared to similar aggressive growth funds—then the fiduciary may have a liability problem.

PROHIBITED TRANSACTIONS

LO 12.4 Identify what the prohibited transaction rules are intended to accomplish and how they work.

prohibited transactions

A large number of transactions are **prohibited transactions** because they are deemed by their nature to be contrary to the interest of plan participants. Their common denominator is that they include transactions involving the plan and those parties close to the plan or employer (referred to as parties in interest). More specifically, these individuals are defined as any individuals in the following eight categories:

1. all plan fiduciaries, as well as plan counsel to, and employees of, the plan
2. plan service providers
3. sponsoring employers
4. employee organizations (for example, unions) whose members are covered
5. 50-percent owners of an employer or an employee organization described in paragraphs (3) or (4)
6. relatives of individuals described in paragraphs (1), (2), (3), or (5)
7. organizations (including corporations, partnerships, and trusts) that are owned by persons described in paragraphs (1), (2), (3), (4), or (5)
8. employees, officers, directors, and 10-percent owners of the sponsoring employer or others described in paragraph (2), (3), (4), (5), and (7)

parties in interest

There are several different categories of prohibited transactions. The first category prohibits a fiduciary from causing the plan to engage in a transaction if the fiduciary knows or should know that such transaction constitutes a direct or indirect

- sale, exchange, or leasing of any property between the plan and a **party in interest**
- lending of money or other extension of credit between the plan and a party in interest
- furnishing of goods, services, or facilities between the plan and a party in interest
- transfer to, or use by or for the benefit of, a party in interest of any plan assets, or
- acquisition, on behalf of the plan, of any employer security or employer real property in violation of ERISA Sec. 407(a)

Another category of prohibited transactions involves the investment in the sponsoring employer's stock or real property. First, a plan can only hold qualifying employer securities, (defined as stock or marketable obligations), and qualifying employer real property (property leased from the plan to the employer). Second, a plan may not acquire any qualifying employer security or qualifying employer real property if, immediately after such acquisition, the aggregate fair market value of employer securities and employer real property held by the plan exceeds 10 percent of the fair market value of the plan's assets. However, the 10 percent limitation does not apply to profit-sharing-type plans (including profit-sharing, stock bonus,

401(k), and employee stock ownership plans) as long as the plan provides that more than 10 percent of its assets can be invested in qualifying employer real property or qualifying employer securities.

A third category of prohibited transactions involves self-dealing. Here, the fiduciary is required to avoid using plan assets for his or her own interest or account. This prohibition includes receiving compensation from any party in connection with a transaction that involves the plan's assets.

Prohibited-Transaction Exemptions

prohibited-transaction exemptions

As you can see, the prohibited-transaction rules are extremely broad. Without **prohibited-transaction exemptions**, even common, everyday events—such as service providers receiving payment from the plan—would be prohibited. Because of the breadth of the prohibited-transaction rules, many exemptions are provided. Exemptions come in several different forms: statutory, administrative, and individual.

Statutory Exemptions

The most commonly used statutory exemptions under ERISA include

- payment of reasonable compensation to parties in interest for services rendered necessary for the plan's operation
- loans to parties in interest who are participants or beneficiaries of the plan if certain conditions are met. (This exception was described in chapter 9.)
- loans to employee stock ownership plans if specific conditions are met
- relief for plans for bank employees and insurance companies that want to invest in the sponsor's investment vehicles, as provided by several statutory exemptions
- certain pooled fund transactions involving banks, trust companies, and insurance companies
- distribution of assets in accordance with the terms of the plan

In addition to these exemptions, ERISA Sec. 408(c) clarifies that the prohibited-transaction rules do not prohibit any fiduciary from receiving benefits as a participant from a plan, receiving reasonable compensation for services rendered to the plan (full-time employees of the plan sponsor may not be paid), receiving reimbursement for expenses incurred, or serving as fiduciary in addition to being an officer, employee, agent, or other representative of a party in interest.

Also, a plan may acquire or sell qualifying securities from any party without violating the prohibited-transaction rules, as long as adequate security is paid, no commission is charged for the transaction, and the plan does not violate the 10 percent limitation.

Administrative Exemptions

ERISA Sec. 408(a) allows the Secretary of Labor to grant certain administrative exemptions from the prohibited-transaction rules. These exemptions can be individual in nature, or they may be class exemptions, which can be relied on by the general public. Class exemptions have almost the same effect as statutory exemptions. The DOL has granted a large number of class exemptions that can be relied upon by the employer.

Individual Exemptions

If neither a statutory nor a class exemption applies, then an employer can request an individual exemption from the DOL. To grant such an individual exemption, the DOL must find that the transaction is

- administratively feasible
- in the interest of the plan and its participants and beneficiaries
- protective of the rights of the plan's participants and beneficiaries

> **YOUR FINANCIAL SERVICES PRACTICE: FILING FOR A PROHIBITED TRANSACTION EXEMPTION**
>
> In their publication, "Exemption Procedures Under Federal Pension Law," the Department of Labor provides concrete advice for those considering an application for an individual prohibited transaction exemption. The publication discusses when the DOL might consider giving an exemption for transactions like a loan from the plan to the corporation, or a sale of property from the company to the plan with corresponding lease back to the corporation. With a loan to the corporation, for example, the DOL requires that the amount of the loan represents less than 25 percent of the plan's assets, that the terms of the loan are as favorable as with an arm's length transaction, that the loan is adequately secured and that the loan is reviewed and monitored by an independent fiduciary.

Common Problems

Examples of common types of transactions that would be forbidden by the prohibited-transaction rules include

- loans to the company, company owners, and relatives
- contributions other than cash, in most cases
- property that is owned by the plan (such as real estate) that is used by the company or other prohibited party

Especially in the small-plan market, the prohibited-transaction rules pose real problems. It may not be evident to the small-business owner what is wrong with the transactions described above. There are two principal reasons for this. First, the small-business owner with an entrepreneurial spirit may incorrectly look at the money in the plan as capital that should be used to build the business. As the owner often sees it, what is good for the business is good for the plan participants. Second, when a significant portion of the plan assets are for the benefit of the business owner, he or she may have a hard time distinguishing plan assets from personal assets.

Eligible Investment Advice

ERISA prohibits fiduciaries from self-dealing. This bars a plan's financial vendor from providing investment advice to plan participants for an additional fee. To ensure that participants in 401(k) plans and other plans that have individual investment direction get adequate investment advice, Congress enacted a prohibited-transaction exemption allowing for the provision of investment advice through an "eligible investment advice arrangement." If the requirements under the provision are met, then the provision of investment advice, any transactions pursuant to the advice, and the receipt of compensation by the advisor are exempt from prohibited-transaction treatment.

An eligible investment-advice arrangement has to provide that fees will not vary depending on the investment option selected, or that a computer model under an investment-advice program will be used. With defined-contribution plans the arrangement must be expressly authorized by a plan fiduciary. Also, the exemption does not preclude the use of plan assets to pay for investment advice.

If a computer model is used as the basis of any investment advice, it must apply generally accepted investment theories and use relevant information about the participant or beneficiary. An eligible investment expert must certify that the model meets these requirements. In addition, if a computer model is used, the only investment advice that may be provided under the arrangement is the advice generated by the computer model.

Defined-contribution plans must be audited annually by an independent auditor. The auditor must issue a report of the audit results to the fiduciary that authorized the arrangement. Also, before the program begins the fiduciary advisor must provide participants with written notice containing information about the terms of the arrangement, past investment performance, and any fees that will be charged. Participants also have to be notified of the advisor's status as a fiduciary of the plan.

The fiduciary advisor is defined as a provider of investment advice to a plan participant or beneficiary. To qualify, the fiduciary has to be registered as an investment advisor, registered as a broker or dealer, or an employee of a bank trust department or insurance company. Fiduciaries avoid ERISA violation by complying with the terms of the investment agreement. ERISA assigns to employers responsibility for the prudent selection and periodic review of a fiduciary advisor.

Fee Disclosure

The prohibited transaction rules generally prohibit the furnishing of goods, services, or facilities between a plan and a party in interest (ERISA 406(a)(1)(C)). As plan service providers are considered parties in interest, arrangements with service providers must generally satisfy the statutory exemption provided under ERISA Sec. 408(b)(2). This exemption provides relief as long as

- the services are necessary for the establishment or operation of the plan
- service contracts between a plan and a party in interest are reasonable, and
- no more than reasonable compensation is paid for the services

Under the second requirement, in order for certain contracts or arrangements for services to be reasonable, the covered service provider must disclose specified information to a responsible plan fiduciary. The Department of Labor issued final regulations describing the service provider fee disclosure requirements, which are effective for all services provided after January 1, 2012.[23]

Scope of the Fee Disclosure Rules

The fee disclosure rules apply to pension plans subject to ERISA, except for SEPs, SIMPLEs and IRAs. (ERISA generally applies to pension and welfare plans; these rules do not apply to welfare

---

23. See 29 CFR Sec. 2550.408b-2.

plans.) The rules focus on the disclosure of direct and indirect compensation certain service providers receive. The rules apply to service providers that expect to receive at least $1,000 in compensation in connection with their services and that provide

- certain fiduciary or registered investment advisory services
- record-keeping or brokerage services to a participant-directed individual account plan (for example, 401(k) or 403(b) plan) in connection with the investment options made available under the plan, or
- certain other services for which indirect compensation is received including accounting, auditing, actuarial, appraisal, banking, consulting, custodial, insurance, investment advisory (for plan or participants), legal, record-keeping, securities or other investment brokerage, third party administration or valuation services

Disclosure Requirements

The rules require that service providers provide in writing to the responsible plan fiduciary a description of services provided and direct and indirect compensation received by the service provider, its affiliates or subcontractors. Direct compensation is compensation received directly from the plan. Indirect compensation generally is compensation received from any source other than the plan sponsor, the covered service provider, an affiliate, or subcontractor. For indirect compensation, the service provider must disclose the services to which the compensation applies and the payer of the indirect compensation

The rules specifically require disclosure of individual services and costs without regard to whether services are furnished as part of a bundle or package. For example, service providers must disclose whether they are providing record-keeping services and the compensation attributable to such services, even when there is no explicit charge for record-keeping in the service contract. In addition, service providers must disclose whether they are providing any services as a fiduciary to the plan.

Timing Requirements

Generally, covered service providers must provide written disclosure to the responsible plan fiduciary at a reasonable time before the beginning of the arrangement. If there are any subsequent changes to fees or services provided, that information must be disclosed as soon as reasonable but not more than 60 days after service provider learns of the change. In addition, if the responsible plan fiduciary asks for any additional information, the service provider generally must provide it within 30 days.

Consequences for Failing to Satisfy Requirements

If a covered service provider fails to meet the disclose requirements, it means that the arrangement is not "reasonable" and the responsible fiduciary has engaged in a prohibited transaction. The failure to disclose also triggers the penalties under Code Sec. 4975 which can make the covered service provider subject to a 15 percent excise tax on the amount of fees involved for each year until the problem is corrected.

However, there is relief to the responsible fiduciary even if service providers fail to disclose, as long as

- fiduciary did not know that service provider would fail or did fail to disclose
- after becoming aware, fiduciary requests disclosure in writing
- failure to comply within 90 days, fiduciary must file a notice with the DOL

There is also limited relief for the service provider who makes an error in a disclosure statement. Errors do not fail to conform as long as they are disclosed when discovered and the service provider acted "in good faith and with reasonable diligence".

FIDUCIARY LIABILITY

LO 12.5   Describe the impact of failing to satisfy the fiduciary rules and ways to protect the plan and fiduciaries.

Being a plan fiduciary is a serious matter. Remember that fiduciaries are required both to satisfy the affirmative duties and to ensure that no prohibited transactions occur. Under the fiduciary liability rules, plan fiduciaries are personally liable to the plan to make good any losses that result from the fiduciary's breach of duty. In addition, a fiduciary is required to restore to the plan any profits realized by the fiduciary through the use of plan assets. A court can subject the fiduciary to other equitable or remedial relief as the court deems appropriate. In some egregious cases, the fiduciary can even be criminally liable.

As well as being personally liable for his or her own breaches, a fiduciary is generally liable for the acts of cofiduciaries. A fiduciary will be liable for the breach of a cofiduciary if

- the fiduciary participates knowingly in, or knowingly undertakes to conceal, an act or omission of such other fiduciary, knowing such act or omission is a breach
- by the fiduciary's failure to comply with ERISA, he or she enables the other fiduciary to commit a breach

- the fiduciary has knowledge of a breach by the cofiduciary, unless the fiduciary makes reasonable efforts under the circumstances to remedy the breach

Essentially, this means that if one fiduciary knows of a breach of duty by another fiduciary, he or she must take steps to correct that situation. In many cases, this can mean suing the other fiduciary.

EXAMPLE

Jill Juniper is the company's CFO and the plan administrator of the company's defined-benefit plan. She is aware that the plan's trustee has invested in real estate in violation of the plan's trust agreement. Since Jill has knowledge of the breach, to avoid liability she has to take action to remedy the breach. This could require that she notify the Department of Labor or even sue the cofiduciary.

It is important to recognize that with the role of trustee, each trustee will be considered responsible for the investment decisions of the entire portfolio unless the trust document specifically divides the responsibility.

EXAMPLE

Bob and Barry Borrows are brothers and cotrustees of their company's profit-sharing plan. Bob doesn't know much about investing and lets Barry make all the decisions. Barry borrows money from the plan violating his fiduciary duty. As Bob has failed to meet his own obligations under ERISA, he has enabled Barry to make the improper investment, which could result in cofiduciary liability.

If a plan engages in a prohibited transaction , the fiduciary that has allowed the transaction has violated ERISA and can be liable for any losses that occur. In addition, the party in interest that benefits from the transaction can also be assessed a 15 percent tax under Code Sec. 4975. The tax applies to the amount involved in the transaction and it applies for each and every year that the prohibited transaction remains.

Limiting Liability

Probably the most important step in limiting a fiduciary's liability is to carefully document the processes allowed by fiduciaries and how decisions were made. A fiduciary can also hire a service provider or providers to handle fiduciary functions and set up the agreement so that the person or entity then assumes liability for those functions selected. For example, if an employer appoints an investment manager that is a bank, insurance company, or registered investment advisor, the employer is responsible for the selection of the manager, but is not liable for the individual investment decisions of that manager. However, an employer is required to monitor the manager periodically to assure that it is handling the plan's investments prudently.

Even if the fiduciary does not delegate duties to others, it is critical to obtain appropriate advice for those matters that the fiduciary is not qualified to handle. Remember that under the prudence standard the fiduciary is going to be compared to professionals familiar with such matters. Financial advisors can be critical in fulfilling this advisory role, helping the fiduciaries better understand how to meet their obligations.

Another sometimes overlooked area is clearly allocating responsibilities among fiduciaries. This can be done by directly identifying roles and duties in the plan and/or trust documents. Also, the plan document can provide a process for fiduciaries to allocate responsibilities to others.

Fiduciary liability can also be limited when individual account plans, such as in 401(k) or profit-sharing plans, are set up so that participants have control over the investments in their accounts. As long as the plan satisfies ERISA Sec. 404(c), the fiduciaries are not responsible for the participants' investment decisions. However, the fiduciary remains responsible for selecting and monitoring the providers of the investment options and the options themselves.

ERISA does not allow agreements which relieve a fiduciary from responsibility or liability. However, ERISA Sec. 410(b) provides that a fiduciary or the employer can purchase fiduciary insurance to cover losses to the fiduciaries. Such insurance will protect the fiduciary for acts of negligence, but will not cover intentional breaches such as thefts. Similarly, the DOL has permitted indemnification agreements which leave the fiduciary fully responsible and liable, but provide that another party satisfies any liability incurred by the fiduciary in the same manner as insurance purchased under ERISA Sec. 410(b). For example, this allows an employer (but not the plan) to indemnify it's employees who perform fiduciary services.

Bonding

The fidelity bond required under ERISA Sec. 412 insures a plan against losses due to fraud or dishonesty (for example, theft) on the part of persons (including, but not limited to, plan fiduciaries) who handle plan funds or other property. The fidelity bond rules generally require that every fiduciary of an employee benefit plan and every person who handles funds or other property of such a plan (referred to as plan officials) shall be bonded. A plan official must be bonded for at least 10 percent of the amount of funds he or she handles, subject to a minimum bond amount of $1,000 per plan with respect to which the plan official has handling functions. In most instances, the maximum bond amount that can be required under ERISA with respect to any one plan official is $500,000 per plan. However, the maximum required bond amount is $1 million for plan officials of plans that hold employer securities.

In a typical bond, the plan is the named insured and a surety company is the party that provides the bond. The persons "covered" by the bond are the persons who "handle" funds or other property of the plan, that is, plan officials. As the insured party, the plan can make a claim on the bond if a plan official causes a loss to the plan due to fraud or dishonesty. The bonds must be purchased from a corporate surety that holds a Certificate of Authority issued by the Secretary of the Treasury.

Another way a plan can protect participants is to purchase liability insurance. A plan may purchase insurance for its fiduciaries or for itself to cover liability or losses occurring by reason of the act or omission of a fiduciary, as long as such insurance permits recourse by the insurer against the fiduciary.

Expanded Fiduciary Role

In 2010, the Department of Labor proposed regulations that would have expanded the ERISA fiduciary status to those individuals that work in a retirement brokerage role by accepting qualified plan asset roll-overs. In 2015, the White House and the Department of Labor made it known they were moving forward with the rules. The rules were originally designed to expand the definition of fiduciary to include those accepting roll-overs. While acting in the best interest of one's clients is universally agreed upon, the manner in which one gets to that outcome has become hotly debated with the potential expansion of the fiduciary role. This rule would have major implications for financial and retirement planning. It is important to keep a look out for any changes to the fiduciary requirements under ERISA.

Since the mid-1970s a "fiduciary" standard of care has been required for some individuals that render investment advice to retirement plans. The purpose of the rule is to protect consumers by requiring that the investment advisor acts in the best interest of their client and avoids conflicts of interest. In part because the retirement and investment worlds have changed since the 1970s, the Department of Labor (DOL) began working on an expanded fiduciary rule roughly eight years ago. On April 8, 2016, the DOL published a final rule expanding the definition of investment advice to include far more financial advisors under the fiduciary rule. The applicability date of the rule was set for April 10, 2017. However, under the direction of a February 3rd memorandum by President Trump, the DOL has published a final rule delaying the applicability date of the expanded fiduciary rule until June 9, 2017.

However, on June 9, 2017, the financial services world changed forever (maybe), as more financial advisors than ever are now acting under a fiduciary standard of care as the first roll-out of the rule occurred. This news should have been bigger, but it was not. Part of the reason is that Americans do not fully understand what it means for a financial advisor to act as a fiduciary as defined by the Employee Retirement Income Security Act (ERISA) of 1974. In a recent 2017 survey by The American College of Financial Services, only 52 percent of respondents currently working with a financial advisor were sure whether their advisor was a fiduciary or not. This leaves the remaining 48 percent totally in the dark about the fiduciary status of their advisor. Furthermore, only 31 percent stated they were extremely knowledgeable about what it means for a financial advisor to act as a fiduciary. With this in mind, it is no surprise that June 9 came and went without either the blowback or the fanfare of a rule that many are calling the most influential rule affecting financial services in two decades.

So what does it mean that a financial advisor must now act as a fiduciary under the new Department of Labor rule? From a very basic standpoint, it means that the advisor needs to act in the best interest of the client. The advisor can charge no more than a reasonable fee for his or her services, and must act with the skill, due diligence and knowledge expected of someone familiar with the responsibilities of being an advisor. Conflicts of interest must also be avoided. However, as you can imagine, the details and compliance requirements are far more complicated and nuanced. For example, this rule does not require the financial advisor to provide fiduciary level advice on all investments and advice, but only those pertaining to retirement accounts like 401(k)s and IRAs.

As a new administration gears up to take control of the implementation of the DOL rule, uncertainty reigns in the financial services industry regarding the future of the Department of Labor's new fiduciary rule, which was finalized in April 2016.

The rule was passed into law and had its initial roll-out. However, many investors, financial advisors and financial firms await the future of the rule under Donald Trump's administration as changes are expected. The rule was designed to protect retirement savers and their investments by requiring any financial firm or advisor that provides advice to an individual retirement account (IRA), 401(k) or other retirement account to act as a fiduciary, which means always in the best interest of the consumer.

The rule also takes aim at unreasonable fees, unsuitable financial products and other potential conflicts of interest. However, some in the financial services industry have pushed back against the rule, stating that compliance and costs would be overly burdensome and that the rule could ultimately harm those very consumers it is designed to protect by raising the price of doing business in financial planning.

The new definition of investment advice has been expanded to include "recommendations with respect to rollovers, transfers, or distributions from a plan or IRA, including whether, in what amount, in what form, and to what destination such a rollover, transfer, or distribution should be made[.]"9 The importance of this additional language can't be understated. Recommendations to engage in rollovers, transfers or distributions weren't considered investment advice until now. This new definition marks the first time under ERISA that a recommendation not related to a specific investment can be considered investment advice. This means that merely recommending where the investment be held or how it be distributed could trigger fiduciary responsibility. Additionally, the requirement that the advice be on "a regular basis" was removed.

Currently, the full implementation date is set for Jan. 1, 2018, however, that is expected to be delayed for an additional year and a half for further changes.

CHAPTER REVIEW

Key Terms and Concepts

- fiduciaries
- exclusive-benefit rule
- prudent-fiduciary rule
- diversification requirement
- ERISA Sec. 404(c) (individual account plan exception)
- qualified default investment alternative
- prohibited transactions
- parties in interest
- prohibited-transaction exemptions

Chapter 12: Review Questions

Review questions are based on the learning objectives in this chapter. Thus, a [12.3] at the end of a question means that the question is based on learning objective 3. If there are multiple objectives, they are all listed.

1. What types of tax-advantaged retirement plans are exempt from the fiduciary provisions of ERISA? [12.1]

2. What roles result in an individual becoming a fiduciary to a retirement plan? [12.1]

3. Who are typically the fiduciaries of a corporate-sponsored retirement plan? [12.1]

4. Name the affirmative duties that fiduciaries are required to satisfy. [12.2]

5. What are the primary requirements for fiduciaries to be eligible for ERISA 404(c) relief? [12.3]

6. If ERISA 404(c) relief is given, what decisions are still the responsibility of the fiduciaries? [12.3]

7. Under what circumstances can a fiduciary obtain relief under ERISA 404(c) even if a participant has not made an affirmative investment election? [12.3]

8. Explain whether each of the following is a prohibited transaction: [12.4]

    a. the sale of real estate owned by the ABC plan to the wife of the treasurer of the ABC Company

    b. loaning money from the plan to an officer of the corporation (the plan contains a loan provision that permits loans on a nondiscriminatory basis)

    c. the acquisition of 25 percent of employer stock by a defined-benefit plan

    d. the acquisition of real estate from the plan for less than its market value by the plan's trustee for her personal use

9. Your client is a business owner who acts as the trustee of her company's pension plan. The plan owns real estate that the expanding company would like to buy at market value. What, if anything, can your client do to avoid the consequences of the prohibited-transaction rules? [12.4]

10. When can a fiduciary be held liable for a breach of duty by a cofiduciary? [12.5]

11. How can an employer protect employees who act as plan fiduciaries? [12.5]

Chapter 12: Review Answers

1. Governmental and church plans, 403(b) plans that only contain employee salary deferrals, and plans that only cover business owners and their spouses.

2. An individual who exercises discretionary authority over the management of the plan or disposition of the plan's assets, provides investment advice for a fee, or exercises discretionary control over the plan's administration will all be considered plan fiduciaries. Note that this is functional definition, and does not require that the individual be specifically named as a fiduciary.

3. Typically, the fiduciaries will include the sponsoring company, plan trustees, investment managers, and officers of the company who participate in the selection of trustees and/or investment managers.

4. The affirmative fiduciary obligations that apply to all types of plans are (1) to maintain the plan for the exclusive benefit of the participants, (2) to discharge fiduciary duties with the prudence of a knowledgeable investment professional, (3) to diversify plan assets, and (4) to invest plan assets in accordance with the plan's documents. In addition, individual account plans that allow participant investment direction must satisfy the participant fee disclosure requirements.

5. To satisfy the individual account plan exception, participants must be given at least three core investment options and have the opportunity to make changes at least quarterly. Participants must be given information about each investment option and must have the right to request more detailed information. Employer stock can be an option, but it must be in addition to the three core options. Also, participants must be told that the plan is seeking the fiduciary relief of ERISA 404(c). Once a participant has made investment elections, he or she must be given a prospectus for each option chosen.

6. Even if the plan conforms with the ERISA 404(c) regulations, the fiduciaries are still responsible for ensuring that participants do not engage in prohibited transactions. Also, fiduciaries are never given relief from the responsibility of prudently selecting the investment alternatives.

7. ERISA 404(c) protection is available as long as assets are directed into a qualified default investment alternative. This can be a target or life-style fund, a balanced fund, or an investment management service. Participants must also be notified of the option to make an alternative election.

8. a. The sale of real estate owned by the ABC plan to the wife of the treasurer of the ABC Company is a prohibited transaction. It is considered excluded dealing to sell, exchange, or lease property between the plan and a party-in-interest. Because the treasurer's wife is a relative of an employee, she is considered to be a party-in-interest.

   b. Loaning money from the plan to an officer of the company is not a prohibited transaction. Loaning money or extending credit to a party-in-interest is generally a prohibited transaction. However, if the plan has a loan provision and loans are made available on a nondiscriminatory basis (as in this case), then there is no prohibited transaction.

   c. The acquisition of 25 percent of employer stock by a defined-benefit plan is a prohibited transaction. A defined-benefit plan cannot acquire employer securities in excess of the 10 percent allowable limit. Profit-sharing plans, stock bonus plans, and employee stock ownership plans, however, are exempt from the 10-percent limitation.

   d. The acquisition of real estate from the plan for less than its market value is a prohibited-transaction because it constitutes self-dealing with plan assets by a fiduciary.

9. Your client should obtain a prohibited-transaction exemption (PTE) from the Department of Labor. A PTE exempts the sale of the land from the plan to the company from the prohibited-transaction rules. The willingness to pay a market price for the land will weigh in favor of granting the PTE. However, the DOL will be skeptical of the transaction because of the possibility that employees will be cheated through self-dealing. The DOL will expect assurances that the participants' interests are being protected.

10. A fiduciary can also be liable for the breach of a cofiduciary if the fiduciary actively participates in the behavior, attempts to conceal the cofiduciaries breach, or even just has knowledge of the breach and fails to take steps to remedy the situation.

11. An employer can either purchase liability insurance for the employees or indemnify them from losses in their role of fiduciary.

Chapter 13
Plan Installation and Administration

Learning Objectives

An understanding of the material in this chapter should enable the student to

    LO 13.1   **Describe the steps that must be taken to install a corporate plan.**

    LO 13.2   **Identify the key ongoing responsibilities of plan administration.**

    LO 13.3   **Describe how divorce and compliance problems can complicate plan administration.**

Once the plan has been selected and designed according to employer specifications and the funding approach has been decided upon, the tasks of plan installation and plan administration begin. The role of the financial services professional in these processes varies from case to case. Some clients want you to provide ongoing consulting, while others allow you to take a more passive posture. Most financial services professionals will want to choose the latter role and delegate the responsibilities associated with plan installation and administration to a third-party administrator. This will enable you to use your time more efficiently, freeing you up for sales and design consulting. There are, however, occasions that call for client hand-holding and troubleshooting. For these times, you need a general understanding of the installation, administration processes, and the documents that are integral to these processes. The objective of this chapter is to provide you with this understanding through an overview of plan installation and plan administration. If a more detailed review of the plan-installation and plan-administration process is needed, the loose-leaf services should be consulted. These services provide a wealth of information about filing requirements, as well as supplying copies of current forms and instructions.

Also, a variety of software packages are available that aid in the process of plan installation and administration. Software packages are widely available in the following areas:

- actual deferral percentage test calculation (monitors whether 401(k) plans meet the ADP test)
- actuarial valuations (a must for firms with defined-benefit plans)
- claims processing (typically used in conjunction with welfare benefit plans)
- document preparation (both plan and summary plan description)
- employee benefit statement preparation (typically used in conjunction with welfare benefit plans)
- nondiscrimination testing (monitors whether plans meet 410(b) and 401(a)(26) tests)
- top-heavy analysis (monitors top-heavy status of plan)

- 5500 forms preparation (very popular method for simplifying government filings)
- pension check processing (processes benefit payments)
- loan processing (useful for processing loans and tracking plan loan repayments)

SETTING UP A CORPORATE PLAN

LO 13.1   Describe the steps that must be taken to install a corporate plan.

The first step in the plan-installation process is for the employer to legally adopt the plan. This can be done through a resolution by the corporate board of directors, which can either adopt a particular plan document or simply adopt the major provisions of the plan. The corporate resolution should be adopted before the end of the tax year, if the employer wants the plan to be effective in that year. If the company's securities are offered in the open market, the plan is also generally submitted for stockholder approval (although it is not legally necessary). Notice of the establishment of the plan and details about the plan should be presented to stockholders in a proxy statement.

At the same time that the plan is approved, the corporate board of directors should also approve the trust instrument (if any) that will be used. Recall that a trust provides for the irrevocable deposit of plan assets. In other words, once assets, such as individual life insurance policies or cash, are transferred to the trust, the employer or the employer's creditors cannot recapture these assets. (The employer may, however, recapture assets that exceed promised benefits at the termination of the plan.) Under some state laws, a nominal contribution to the trust may be necessary in order to establish its existence.

If a group pension contract is used instead of a trust, the board will review a specimen contract. If the board wishes to adopt the contract, it will authorize the submission of a letter of application with premium. Note that the group pension contract must be submitted for approval to the state insurance department in the state where the corporation is domiciled. The state insurance department reviews the contract to see if the insurer has sufficient reserves to pay benefits and if the contract meets other state specifications. Another step that must be completed before the end of the first tax year is notifying the participants of the new plan. This can be an oral explanation at an employee meeting or a written letter that is either mailed or posted at work—for example:

> "It is our pleasure to announce the ABC Company is adopting a qualified 401(k) plan. The details of the plan are as follows. . . ."

Alternatively, the summary plan description (see below) can be used to satisfy this requirement.

For a plan funded with employer contributions, the employer typically adopts the plan at the end of the tax year in which it wants to receive a tax-deductible contribution. The reason is that the employer may not know until the end of the year whether it has funds available to contribute to a plan. In this case, the plan is made effective retroactive to the first day of the year, and a tax-deductible contribution can be made for the whole year. For example, if the employer is on a calendar tax year, the plan may be adopted on December 31, effective as of the previous January 1. However, if the plan is a contributory plan (a 401(k) or 403(b) plan), it should be adopted prior to the beginning of the first year of the plan's operation. This is necessary to allow time to enroll participants in the program. For such a plan, application is best accomplished through one or more enrollment meetings.

enrollment meeting

If the plan is contributory or if salary reductions are required under a 403(b) plan or a 401(k) plan, an additional step must be taken. When this is the case, the employees are asked to attend an **enrollment meeting**. The enrollment of an adequate number of employees in the plan is crucial for purposes of meeting the nondiscrimination rules and passing the actual deferral percentage test (401(k) plans only). Employers usually request the financial services professional to attend the enrollment meeting and use his or her selling skills to persuade the rank-and-file employees to make the necessary contributions or salary reductions.

YOUR FINANCIAL SERVICES PRACTICE: 401(k) PLANS AND AUTOMATIC ENROLLMENT

The IRS has approved a strategy that can increase enrollment in 401(k) plans. A plan can require that all participants start off with a default contribution of a specified amount (typically 3 percent) into a default investment account. Participants have to make an affirmative election to choose not to participate. This "automatic enrollment" approach can help to include those individuals who fail to participate because they never get around to filling in the form.

The enrollment meeting begins with the financial services professional describing the plan and spelling out the benefits and trade-offs of plan participation for the employees. The meeting typically contains a question-and-answer period during which the employees can voice their concerns and receive clarification on important issues. The meeting typically concludes with the completion and signing of enrollment forms and salary reduction agreements or authorization to withhold mandatory contributions from an employee's pay. Completing investment election forms and beneficiary designations are also part of the enrollment process.

The enrollment meeting (or if an enrollment meeting is not required, a separate meeting) can be used to secure the information to apply for individual life insurance contracts if they are being used wholly or in part to fund the plan. In addition, medical examinations can also be conducted at this time, if required by underwriting.

Regardless of whether a trust or group pension contract is used, the entire first year's contribution should be made prior to filing the employer's tax return for the year in which the plan is adopted. (For a corporate employer using a calendar year, the date for filing the tax return for a given year is generally March 15 of the following year, but this can be extended to September 15.) As long as this requirement is met and the plan is in final form, the employer will be able to deduct contributions if the plan qualifies. (*Planning Note:* The plan should be adopted subject to the right to be rescinded if it does not qualify, and the trust or group pension contract should allow contributions to be returned if the plan does not qualify.)

advance-determination letter

In order to determine whether the plan qualifies, the employer should file an application for an **advance-determination letter** with the IRS. The employer is not required to receive IRS approval, but instead can wait for an IRS audit to determine whether the plan is qualified. However, this is not recommended because of the risk of disqualification (which means a retroactive loss of the tax deduction). The forms and documents used to file for an advance-determination letter include the following:

- IRS Form 5300 (Application for Determination for Employee Benefit Plan) or IRS Form 5307 (Short Form Application for Determination for Employee Benefit Plan—this form is used for master or prototype plans and volume submitter plans)
- IRS Form 8717 (User Fee for Employee Plan Determination Request)
- Schedule Q (Nondiscrimination Requirements)
- IRS Form 2848 (Power of Attorney and Declaration of Representative)
- copies of the plan and the trust or group pension contract

Make sure the determination letter is applied for before the tax return filing date (plus extensions). If the request for an advance-determination letter is submitted before the tax return is due, the IRS will extend the time limit for amending the plan. A retroactive amendment will then be possible, enabling the employer to receive a deduction for the current year. If the filing deadline is missed, it is highly unlikely that the IRS will allow the plan to be amended retroactively or that a deduction will be allowed for the initial contribution. Retroactive amendment of a plan is common if the IRS objects to some provisions of the proposed plan. (*Planning Note:* A determination letter is typically issued within 6 months after the application is filed. Although the IRS has a maximum of 270 days to make a ruling, no determination letter will be received before 60 days to give interested parties a chance to comment.)

notice to interested parties

Immediately preceding the filing of the request for an advance-determination letter, the employer should issue the notice to interested parties of the intent to install a qualified plan. The IRS will not issue an advance-determination letter unless interested parties have been notified that an application for one has been filed. The **notice to interested parties** goes to all employees eligible to be in the plan and to ineligible employees if they work at the same location as the eligible employees. The notice should indicate that qualification is being sought and that the employees have the right to submit comments on the plan to the IRS and the Department of Labor.

summary plan description (SPD)

The final and most important step in the employee communications process is the issuing of the **summary plan description (SPD)** free of cost to plan participants.[1] A summary plan description is an easy-to-read booklet that explains the plan to the participants. The SPD may be prepared by the financial services professional, the insurer, or the employer. In any case, employers are required to give SPDs to participants within 120 days after the plan is adopted by the board of directors and within 90 days of when a person becomes a plan participant. (*Planning Note:* In addition to being used with retirement plans, SPDs are also required for most welfare benefit plans. For this reason, it may be wise to suggest that your client combine all the SPDs (and other information) in an employee handbook.)

An SPD bridges the gap between the legalese of the pension plan and the understanding of the average participant by effectively communicating how a plan works, what benefits are available, how benefits vest, how benefits are calculated, how to participate in the plan, and how to obtain these benefits. The SPD must strike a balance between clarity and depth. To this end, the Department of Labor suggests the frequent use of examples, the elimination of technical jargon and long complex sentences, the inclusion of a table of contents, and the use of clear cross-references.[2] Other good ideas include the following:

- cross-referencing only to materials already discussed, not to materials that have yet to be discussed
- using short paragraphs (three or four sentences)

---

1. See 29 U.S.C. Sec. 1022 and 104(b) (setting forth the SPD requirements); See also 29 C.F.R. 2520.104b-2 (Summary Plan Description Regulation).
2. See 29 C.F.R. 2520.201–2 (Style and Format of SPD).

- using short sentences (20 words or less) and familiar words with few syllables

An SPD must be fair and evenhanded. It cannot be used to persuade employees to join the plan, but must merely explain the plan. The regulations specifically state that an SPD cannot downplay the negative consequences of involvement—for example, it cannot gloss over plan terms that may cause a participant to lose benefits or fail to qualify for them.

At the same time, the SPD must be accurate. Employees have sued and won cases where the SPD promised something that was not contained in the document.[3] The best way for the employer to protect itself is to include a disclaimer stating that if there is a conflict between the plan and the SPD, the plan provisions will be determinative.

The SPD regulations dictate what kind of language to use, what kind of information to have, and what group of people must get the information. The regulations also require that every 5 years, participants whose plans have been modified must receive an updated SPD, called a revised SPD, or in a separate document called a summary of material modification, and every 10 years—regardless of whether the plan has been modified—a new SPD must be issued. The following is a list of items that the SPD must contain:

- a provision identifying the plan—for example: "This is the ABC Company profit-sharing plan"
- the names and addresses of people responsible for the plan
- the employer identification number
- the plan administrator's name, address, and telephone number
- the name and address of the person designated for service of legal process
- the name, title, and business address of each trustee
- a statement to the effect if the plan is collectively bargained
- an explanation of the plan's eligibility requirements for participation and benefits and normal retirement age
- an explanation of any joint-and-survivor benefits
- an explanation of any terms that could result in a participant's losing benefits
- a PBGC insurance provision, if applicable
- a description and explanation of the plan provisions for determining years of service for eligibility to participate, vesting, breaks of service, and benefit accrual

---

3. *Cinga Corp. v. Amara* 131 S.Ct. 1866 (2011) (discussing SPD and ERISA violations).

- a list of the sources of plan contributions
- the name of the funding agency
- the plan year's ending date
- the procedures for presenting claims for benefits under the plan and remedies for benefits denied under the plan
- a statement of ERISA rights (this statement is standard text promulgated by the Department of Labor)

The following table summarizes the steps required to establish a qualified retirement plan.

Table 13-1
Summary of Steps in Setting Up a Corporate Plan

Steps	Timetable
1. Secure a corporate resolution adopting the plan.	Before the end of the tax year
2. Secure a corporate resolution approving the trust document or group pension contract.	Before the end of the tax year
3. Notify participants of the plan's adoption and its major terms.	Before the end of the tax year
4. Conduct an enrollment meeting if necessary.	For 401(k) and 403(b) plans, shortly after plan adoption
5. Give notice of the filing for advance determination to interested parties.	Before the date for filing the employer's tax return
6. File for an advance-determination letter.	Before the date for filing the employer's tax return
7. Make the first year's contribution.	Before the date for filing the employer's tax return
8. Supply a summary plan description to employees.	Within 120 days after the plan is adopted

ANNUAL ADMINISTRATION OF A CORPORATE PLAN

LO 13.2   Identify the key ongoing responsibilities of plan administration.

Every qualified plan has a plan administrator who is responsible for the administration of the plan. Typically, the plan administrator is the employer (in larger plans, the employer's director of human resources) or an individual or committee designated by the employer. The plan administrator receives help from a variety of sources. If the plan has a trust, the trustee may assist the plan administrator with administrative matters, but more frequently the trustee restricts his or her activities to investing the plan's assets. With insured plans, the insurer will generally provide a great number of administrative services, from computer support to producing manuals, which guide the plan administrator through the administrative process. In addition to the trustee or insurance company, the plan administrator can also look to a variety of third-party administrators (TPAs) who perform everything from turnkey services to only one specific service, such as administering the actual deferral percentage test. As a financial services professional, you will sometimes be asked to suggest or secure a TPA.

Annual Report

One of the plan administrator's principal duties is to comply with ERISA's reporting and disclosure requirements. All qualified plans are subject to these reporting and disclosure requirements (except some church and state plans). The most important reporting and disclosure requirement is filing the annual return/report with the IRS. (*Planning Note:* Financial services professionals are sometimes asked to advise plan administrators on how to comply with the reporting and disclosure requirements and may be called on to help in the filing of forms.)

Form 5500

Today, a qualified plan sponsor must file Form 5500 unless the plan qualifies as a small plan (Form 5500-SF) or is a one participant plan (Form 5500-EZ) as described below. Form 5500 is a short main form with basic identifying information. There are a number of schedule attachments focused on particular subjects and/or filing requirements. Filers will have to complete only those schedules applicable to the specific type of plan. The schedules most commonly filed by pension plans include:

- Schedule A of Form 5500 (Insurance Information). This form is filed if any benefits are provided by an insurance company.
- Schedule B of Form 5500 (Actuarial Information). This form is required for most defined-benefit plans. This report must be signed by an actuary and it addresses whether the plan has satisfied the minimum funding requirements.
- Schedule C of Form 5500 (Service Provider Information). This form is required for large plans in which a service provider earned fees of $5,000 or more or when the plan has terminated either an actuary or accountant during the year.
- Schedules H and I (Financial Information). These forms (H for large plans and I for small plans) report financial information about the plan.

- Schedule R (Retirement Plan Information). This form includes information on pension plan distributions and funding requirements, as well as information on the coverage requirements for tax-qualified plans.

When Form 5500, 5500-EZ or 5500-SF is required, it must be filed annually by the last day of the seventh month after the plan year ends. An extension of up to 2½ months may be granted if Form 5558 is filed.

In addition to Form 5500, administrators of defined–benefit plans are also required to file a report along with annual required premiums, to the Pension Benefit Guaranty Corporation. The timing requirements for this filing and the payment of premiums depends upon the size of the plan, and whether the plan is required to simply pay the flat rate—in 2017 the per-participant flat-rate premium is $69.00 for single-employer plans and $28.00 for multiemployer plans—or is required to pay an additional variable rate premium.[4]

Common 550 Filing Errors

In 2015, the IRS posted some information in its February edition of the Employee Plans News on how to help your company retirement plan avoid IRS audits. The IRS set forth a few common errors that can lead to audits. First, make sure you list the number of participants. The IRS stated that this is often left blank but must be filled out. Second, make sure that you do not check the terminated plan box until the plan has a zero balance. For IRS and form 5500 purposes, the plan is not terminated if there are still assets in the plan. Be careful when filling out the 5500. Do not copy last years form without making sure that everything was properly entered. If the plan relies upon a third party provider to fill out the form, make sure you check it for accuracy. Failing to properly fill out form 5500 can lead to IRS and DOL audits.

Audit Requirement

Federal law generally requires employee benefit plans with 100 or more participants to have an accounting audit as part of their obligation to file an annual return/report (Form 5500). The auditor must be licensed or certified as a public accountant and individual auditors should not have any financial interests in the plan or the plan sponsor that would affect their ability to render an objective, unbiased opinion about the financial condition of the plan. The scope of the audit is more limited when plan assets are held by banks or insurance companies and written certifications are provided by the institutions holding those assets.

---

4. See the PBGC website (https://www.pbgc.gov/prac/prem/premium-rates.html) for additional information.

A quality audit will help protect the assets and the financial integrity of the plan, as well as ensure that the fiduciaries carry out their responsibility to file a complete and accurate annual return/report. The IRS has indicated that the most common reason for deficient accountants' reports is the failure of the auditor to have experience with employee benefit plan audits. So it is important for the administrator to choose an auditor with the appropriate level of experience.

One-Participant Plans

Qualified plans referred to as one-participant plans are allowed to file Form 5500-EZ instead of Form 5500. A plan is considered to be a one-participant plan if it only covers (a) the business owner and his or her spouse (if the business is wholly owned by the owner and spouse) or (b) partners in a business partnership, or the partners and their spouses. In addition, to qualify as a one-participant plan, the plan must meet the minimum-coverage requirements on its own, and the plan cannot cover a business that is a member of an affiliated service group, a controlled group of corporations, or a group of businesses under common control.

A plan that satisfies all of the above one-participant requirements does not have to file any annual report if its assets total $250,000 or less at the end of the current year and every previous plan year. The same exception applies for an employer that has two or more one-participant plans that together had total plan assets of $250,000 or less at the end of every plan year. However, note that all one-participant plans must file Form 5500-EZ for their final plan year even if the total plan assets have always been less than $250,000. The final plan year is the year in which distribution of all plan assets is completed.

Small Plans

Form 5500-SF is a relatively new simplified annual reporting form for small plans. A plan sponsor can use Form 5500–SF (instead of Form 5500) if the plan meets all the following conditions.

- The plan has fewer than 100 participants at the beginning of the plan year.
- The plan is exempt from the audit requirement.
- The plan has 100 percent of its assets invested in certain secure investments with a readily determinable fair value.
- The plan holds no employer securities.
- The plan is not a multiemployer plan.

Participant Communications

summary of material modification (SMM)

Plan administrators are required not only to file forms with appropriate federal agencies, but also to keep plan participants informed. New participants must be furnished with a summary plan description within 90 days. If the plan is amended in any significant way participants must be notified of the changes. The summary plan description could be modified or the sponsor can explain the changes in a written **summary of material modification (SMM)**. Material modifications do not include every plan change, but only the major changes shown in the table below.

summary annual report (SAR)

To notify participants of the funding status of the plan, the plan administrator must automatically provide participants with a **summary of the annual report (SAR)** within 2 months after the due date of the annual report (by the end of the 9th month after the end of the plan year unless an extension applies). The summary annual report must state whether contributions were made to keep the plan funded in accordance with minimum funding requirements, or whether contributions were not made, and the amount of the deficit. The current value of plan assets is also required to be disclosed. In addition, a participant must be provided with a copy of the full annual report on written request. The Pension Protection Act replaced the SAR for defined-benefit plans with a detailed funding notice. The SAR still must be distributed for defined-contribution plans.

Furnishing plan participants with a personal benefit statement is another important aspect of plan administration. The Pension Protection Act of 2006 substantially revised these rules. Previously, benefit statements were only required upon the request of a participant or beneficiary. The rules now require regular distribution of statements and provide more guidance as to what has to be included in a benefit statement. A benefit statement must be written to be understood by the average plan participant, and must indicate the current value of accrued benefits and the extent to which benefits are vested. If the benefit structure is integrated with Social Security, the statement must explain how this works.

Table 13-2
Material Modifications
- Name and address of sponsor/employer
- Name and address of plan administrator
- Structure of plan
- Name of plan
- Type of plan
- Agent for service of process
- Persons performing functions for the plan
- Sources and method of determining contributions
- Method of asset accumulation
- Procedure for presenting claims
- Eligibility requirements
- Vesting provisions
- Features of portability or reciprocity
- Length of service to determine participation, vesting, and benefit accrual
- Break-in-service rules
- Requirements for pension benefits
- Basis for computing retirement benefits
- Circumstances causing loss of pension benefits
- Joint-and-survivor annuity rules
- Disposition of employee's contributions
- Requirements for welfare benefits
- Circumstances causing loss of welfare benefits
- Fiduciaries' names and addresses

The rules contain significant differences between the requirements for defined-contribution and defined-benefit plans. With defined-contribution plans, the sponsor must provide benefit statements at least:

- quarterly for participants who self-direct investments
- annually for all other participants
- upon written request (limited to one request per year)

The benefit statements for defined-contribution plans must also include a statement about any restrictions that apply to investment direction, the value of the participant's investments, an explanation of the importance of diversification, and direction to the DOL's website for investment and diversification information.

The administrator of a defined-benefit plan generally has to furnish a pension benefit statement at least once every 3 years to participants currently employed. As an alternative the administrator can annually distribute statements notifying participants of the availability of the pension benefit statement.

Failure to provide the required benefit statement may result in penalties of up to $100 per-day-per-participant. Regardless of the legal requirements, benefit statements are an important communication tool. Regular statements help ensure employee awareness of benefits and enable the employer to meet the organizational objectives of retaining and motivating employees.

YOUR FINANCIAL SERVICES PRACTICE: BENEFIT STATEMENTS

Defined-contribution plans that provide for participant investment direction must provide quarterly benefit statements. The law was changed effective in 2007 in response to the Enron and WorldCom bankruptcies, and may provide a valuable protection for participants. As there is no exemption for small plans (except for plans that only cover business owners) this provision can also be burdensome on small retirement plans. Compliance adds additional administrative expense, and noncompliance can result in a $100-per-day-per-participant penalty. The cost for the statements could be passed on to the plan participants, but this is not a very satisfactory result. One mitigating factor is that the law allows distribution of statements by e-mail.

Another aspect of plan administration is counseling participants about plan choices—especially about participant contributions and investment alternatives (assuming that the participants have them). Periodic notices of the plan's terms, enrollment meetings, investment alternative education, and even more general retirement planning education has become commonplace in the American workforce today. The distribution of benefits from qualified plans has become an extremely complicated and time-consuming process. The distribution process typically includes the following:

- distribution information—the process typically begins when the participant requests a distribution from the plan
- election forms—participants will be given forms identifying the
- optional forms of distribution. These forms will be supported with written materials (and sometimes personal meetings) explaining the value of each option and the impact of electing one option over another.
- qualified joint-and-survivor annuity—if the distribution is to a married participant and the qualified joint-and-survivor annuity rules apply, the participant and spouse will have to sign off on any optional form of distribution

- direct rollover—virtually all participants receiving a distribution from a qualified plan must be given an election form that allows them to elect to roll the benefit directly to an IRA
- income tax treatment—in most cases, participants must be given general information about tax implications of a pension distribution
- 1099-R forms—tax forms distributed to participants (and filed with the IRS) identifying the amount of the distribution and whether any portion is considered basis (not subject to income tax)

Calculating benefits, especially in a defined benefit is not always that easy. To get a sense of the types of errors that occur in the calculation of benefits, here is a list from the Employee Benefits Security Administration of 10 common calculation errors.

10 Common Errors in Pension Benefit Calculations

1. All relevant compensation, such as commissions, overtime, and bonuses, (if these were to be included in the plan) was not included in calculating benefits.
2. The calculation was not based on all years of service with the company, or all work within different divisions.
3. The plan administrator used an incorrect benefit formula, such as wrong interest rate.
4. Plan uses wrong social security data in calculating benefits.
5. Basic information such as birth date, and, or social security number was incorrect.
6. The company merged with another company, or went out of business, and there is confusion over which pension benefits apply.
7. Assets in your account were improperly valued.
8. Your employer failed to make required contributions on your behalf.
9. Basic mistakes were made in the mathematical calculations.
10. You failed to update your personnel office with changes (marriage, divorce, death of spouse) that may affect your benefits.

Another facet of plan administration involves amending plan documents. This may be required because the sponsor wants to make a design change or plan enhancement, or because the law has changed requiring plan amendments for the plan to remain "qualified." When a plan is amended, in general, the sponsor needs to consider whether or not to resubmit the plan for an IRS determination letter. As with the initial qualification letter, submitting the plan is generally the safer approach. In some cases, the submission process is simpler because the IRS only reviews the amendment, not the entire plan.

Summary of Plan-Administration Responsibilities
- Filing annual return or report (5500 or 5500-EZ)
- Filing annual premiums with PBGC (Form PBGC-1)
- Holding employee meetings
- Distributing SPDs to new participants
- Distributing summary annual report (SAR)
- Distributing SMM (if plan is amended)
- Furnishing personal benefit statements
- Counseling participants on participant options
- Handling benefit distributions
- Amending the plan when necessary

Special Issues Applicable to Keogh Plans

The rules for setting up and administering a qualified plan for a sole proprietor or partnership (still referred to as Keogh plans) are essentially the same as for a corporation. There are a few differences, however.

- A Keogh plan that satisfies the one-participant rule either files Form 5500-EZ or has no filing requirements if assets total $250,000 or less (see former discussion).

- A plan that covers only owners (and their spouses) may not be subject to ERISA, meaning that no summary plan description is required.

- The deductible contribution is calculated differently due to the "net income" calculation.

- A letter or some other document should be used by a sole proprietorship or partnership to formally adopt the plan. This is the corollary to the corporate resolution that adopts the plan.

The following are some other considerations that are important when installing a Keogh plan:

- The role of the financial services professional takes on greater significance when the client establishes a Keogh plan because such clients typically do not have an administrative arm to carry out the multiple functions associated with plan installation and administration.

- Like corporate plans, a qualified plan must be established by December 31 (with a calendar year tax year) in order for a deduction to be taken for the year. Plan contributions, however, can be made up until the tax return deadline plus extensions. If the year has ended, it may still be possible to adopt a SEP (simplified employee pension), which can be established up to April 15 (or later if the taxpayer files an income tax extension).

- A business owner can shift documents from one master plan to a different one without incurring penalties. (*Planning Note:* If your client is currently under another organization's master Keogh plan, the possibility for a painless switch exists.)

ADDITIONAL ADMINISTRATIVE ISSUES

LO 13.3   Describe how divorce and compliance problems can complicate plan administration.

In the life of a tax-advantaged retirement plan, there are a number of other administrative issues that periodically need to be addressed. Here are several key items that come up on a regular basis.

Divorce

qualified domestic relations orders (QDROs)

Retirement plans subject to ERISA must satisfy an anti-alienation rule, which generally prohibits a participant from assigning a pension plan asset to another individual. However, an exception to the anti-alienation rule exists in cases of divorce or legal separation. In this case, a plan is allowed to pay out benefits to an alternate payee (spouse, former spouse, child, or other dependent), but only subject to a court order, and only if the court order meets certain qualification requirements. These orders are referred to as **qualified domestic relations orders (QDROs)**.

It is the plan administrator's duty to review court orders and determine whether they qualify as a QDRO. The plan administrator is required to establish procedures for reviewing a court order, and must notify all affected parties of the procedures when the plan receives a court order. If the order fails, as long as the parties made a good-faith effort to draft the order, the administrator should explain the deficiencies and work toward an order that satisfies the rules.

YOUR FINANCIAL SERVICES PRACTICE: QUALIFIED DOMESTIC RELATIONS ORDERS

There are two ways in which a settlement of pension rights can be made under a qualified domestic relations order (QDRO):

- an immediate cash settlement (which is often made from nonpension sources)

- a settlement under which payments to the nonparticipant spouse are deferred until payments are due to the participant spouse

In both cases, valuation is fundamental. Before the parties can agree on how to divide the pension, its value must be determined. If the plan is a defined-contribution plan, valuation is relatively easy—the participant has an individual account and the plan sponsor must provide its value to the participant at least annually. However, if participation in the plan has extended over a period longer than the marriage, this amount must be reduced by a "coverture fraction" that is based on the relation between the length of the marriage and the duration of the plan coverage. This can be a simple mathematical ratio, or it can reflect rates of contribution and interest over time.

If the plan is a defined-benefit plan, the parties will probably need an actuary's assistance in determining the present dollar value of pension benefits. For a participant in a defined-benefit plan, the benefit at any time before retirement is expressed as an amount of expected pension at retirement age that the participant has accrued up to that point. For example, if the participant is aged 45, the plan might express his accrued benefit as "$10,000 per month beginning at age 65." In order to determine current worth, at age 45, an actuarial calculation must be made. In this calculation, the interest rate and mortality assumptions are critical. The assumptions do not necessarily have to be the same as those used by the plan for funding purposes. There is no federal standard for actuarial assumptions in this area, although PBGC interest rates for valuing plans on termination are sometimes used as guidelines. The total amount determined must also be multiplied by a coverture fraction, as for the defined-contribution plan where the participant was not married to the current (imminently departing) spouse during the entire time of his or her plan coverage.

Many open and controversial issues exist in these determinations. For example, should the valuation take taxes into account? What about inflation? Or possible future increases in the participant's salary? These are issues of state law that may vary and may not have been considered or decided by the state's courts. The use of an expert actuary is advisable, particularly in disputed cases, so that the actuarial assumptions and other valuation assumptions can be supported in court proceedings if necessary.

For a domestic relations order to be a QDRO, it must contain certain information, including:

- the name and address of the participant and each alternate payee
- the name of each plan affected by the order
- the amount of the benefit to be paid, which can be stated as a specific dollar amount or as a percentage of the total benefit, or use of some other methodology which allows the administrator to determine the amount to be paid out
- the number of payments to be made or the time period involved Practically speaking, it is in everyone's best interest to ensure that court orders satisfy the QDRO

requirements. The plan administrator's procedures should help the process and plans can (but are not required to) provide model language to the parties involved. The Department of Labor has drafted model QDRO documents that may be used. The DOL has very useful explanatory information at its Employee Benefit Security Administration website at www.dol.gov/ebsa.

Compliance Problems

No matter how well-intentioned the sponsor and plan administrator, it is easy to fail to satisfy one of the many requirements that apply to qualified plans and other tax-sheltered vehicles. The types of compliance problems that commonly occur include the following:

- The plan fails to include an employee who is an eligible participant under the terms of the plan.
- The plan fails to cover the number of employees required by the minimum coverage requirements.
- The plan fails to satisfy established loan procedures.
- The contribution or allocation formula does not satisfy the nondiscrimination requirements of Code Sec. 401(a)(4).
- The plan is not amended in a timely fashion when the law changes.
- The plan administrator does not follow the plan's terms.
- Plan assets are not contributed efficiently.
- The plan fails to file Form 5500 punctually.
- The plan engages in a prohibited transaction.

Over the last several years, both the IRS and the DOL have established voluntary compliance programs that reward plans for voluntarily correcting compliance problems. Today this means that when a compliance problem arises, the administrator should in most cases take the following steps:

- Determine which rules have been violated and the penalties involved.
- Determine which IRS or DOL voluntary correction program prescribes how to successfully bring the plan back into compliance with the rules.
- Determine the voluntary compliance procedure, correct the problem, make any required government submissions, and pay any required fines.

As described below, the IRS and DOL compliance programs have now become extremely comprehensive and address almost every compliance problem that could arise. In this environment, the plan administrator should always consider entering into these programs, instead of waiting until the problem is discovered by an IRS or DOL plan audit.

Plan sponsors should also consider periodic audits of their plans by an objective third party. An independent review of the plan and its operation may turn up not only hidden problems in everyday operation but opportunities to improve benefits for participants or reduce plan administration costs.

Employee Plans Compliance Resolution System (EPCRS)

The IRS has a comprehensive system of correction programs for sponsors of retirement plans that have failed to meet the qualification requirements for a period of time. This system, the Employee Plans Compliance Resolution System (EPCRS), permits plan sponsors to correct these failures and thereby continue to provide their employees with retirement benefits on a tax-favored basis. In other words, the correction and sanctions are an alternative to disqualifying the plan. A plan sponsor that has compliance problems needs to review the program carefully to see the appropriate steps involved.

Because this program continues to evolve, it is best here to talk about the program more generally than specifically. First, it's helpful to understand that the IRS established EPCRS based on the following general principles:

- Sponsors and administrators should be encouraged to establish administrative practices and procedures that ensure that these plans are operated properly.

- Sponsors and administrators should satisfy the applicable plan document requirements of the Code.

- Plan sponsors and administrators should make voluntary and timely correction of any plan failures, whether involving discrimination in favor of highly compensated employees, plan operations, the terms of the plan document, or adoption of a plan by an ineligible employer. Timely and efficient correction protects participating employees by providing them with their expected retirement benefits, including favorable tax treatment.

- Voluntary compliance is promoted by providing for limited fees for voluntary corrections approved by the Service, thereby reducing employers' uncertainty regarding their potential tax liability and participants' potential tax liability.

- Fees and sanctions should be graduated in a series of steps so that there is always an incentive to correct promptly.

- Sanctions for plan failures identified on audit should be reasonable in light of the nature, extent, and severity of the violation.
- Administration of EPCRS should be consistent and uniform.
- Plan sponsors should be able to rely on the availability of EPCRS in taking corrective actions to maintain the tax-favored status of their plans.

EPCRS includes three different programs: the Self-Correction Program (SCP), the Voluntary Correction Program (VCP), and the Audit Closing Agreement Program (Audit CAP).

- *Self-correction (SCP).* A plan sponsor that has established compliance practices and procedures may, at any time, correct insignificant operational failures without paying any fee or sanction. In addition, in the case of a qualified plan that is the subject of a favorable determination letter or in the case of a 403(b) plan, the plan sponsor generally may correct even significant operational failures without payment of any fee or sanction. In most cases to qualify for self-correction the plan must have adopted practices and procedures to ensure compliance.
- *Voluntary correction with service approval (VCP).* With more serious types of compliance problems, a plan sponsor, at any time before audit, may pay a limited fee and receive the Service's approval for correction of the problem.
- *Correction on audit (Audit CAP).* If a failure is identified on audit, the plan sponsor may correct the failure and pay a sanction. The sanction imposed will bear a reasonable relationship to the nature, extent, and severity of the failure, taking into account the extent to which correction occurred before audit.

In 2013, the IRS updated its EPCRS through Revenue Procedure 2013–12, expanding the existing system and clarifying certain areas of coverage. The most significant change was that the EPCRS's coverage of 403(b) plan errors and Sec. 436 benefit restriction errors was significantly expanded. Additionally, the ruling cleared up the treatment of some nondiscrimination testing errors, recovery of overpayment errors, and actuarial adjustment rules.

Voluntary Fiduciary Correction Program (VFCP)

The DOL also sponsors a voluntary compliance program called the voluntary fiduciary correction program (VFCP). The VFCP is a voluntary enforcement program that encourages the correction of possible violations of Title I of ERISA. The program allows plan officials to identify and fully correct certain transactions, such as prohibited purchases, sales and exchanges, improper loans, delinquent participant contributions, and improper plan expenses. The program includes 19 specific transactions and their acceptable means of correction, eligibility requirements, and application procedures. The 19 provided categories of transactions are as follows:

1. Delinquent Participant Contributions and Participant Loan Repayments to Pension Plans
2. Delinquent Participant Contributions to Insured Welfare Plans
3. Delinquent Participant Contributions to Welfare Plan Trusts
4. Fair Market Interest Rate Loans to Parties in Interest
5. Below Market Interest Rate Loans to Parties in Interest
6. Below Market Interest Rate Loans to Non-Parties in Interest
7. Below Market Interest Rate Loans Due to Delay in Perfecting Security Interest
8. Participant Loans Failing to Comply with Plan Provisions for Amount, Duration, or Level Amortization
9. Defaulted Participant Loans
10. Purchase of Assets by Plans from Parties in Interest
11. Sale of Assets by Plans to Parties in Interest
12. Sale and Leaseback of Property to Sponsoring Employers
13. Sale of Assets from Non-Parties in Interest at More Than Fair Market Value
14. Holding of an Illiquid Asset Previously Purchased by Plan
15. Benefit Payment Based on Improper Valuation of Plan Assets
16. Payment of Duplicate, Excessive, or Unnecessary Compensation
17. Improper Payment of Expenses by Plan
18. Payment of Dual Compensation to Plan Fiduciaries[5]

If an eligible party documents the acceptable correction of a specified transaction, the U.S. Department of Labor will issue a no-action letter.

Delinquent Filers Voluntary Compliance Program (DVCP)

The VFCP does not address, however, penalties resulting from the late filing of Form 5500. For these type of violations, the DOL has established the Delinquent Filers Voluntary Compliance Program (DVCP). The program provides plan administrators with the opportunity to pay

---

5. See Department of Labor website for more details at http://www.dol.gov/ebsa/newsroom/fs2006vfcp.html.

reduced civil penalties for voluntarily complying with the annual reporting requirements. For plans eligible for the program, compliance with the DVCP also results in the elimination of any penalties that the IRS is also allowed to impose for late filing of Form 5500. The program only applies to plans subject to Title I of ERISA, which means that most plans that only cover the owner and are required to file Form 5500-EZ are not eligible for the program.

CHAPTER REVIEW

Key Terms and Concepts

enrollment meeting
advance-determination letter
notice to interested parties
summary plan description (SPD)
summary of material modification (SMM)
summary annual report (SAR)
qualified domestic relations orders (QDROs)

Chapter 13: Review Questions

Review questions are based on the learning objectives in this chapter. Thus, a [13.3] at the end of a question means that the question is based on learning objective 3. If there are multiple objectives, they are all listed.

1. What role does the financial services professional play in the plan-installation and plan-administration processes? [13.1]

2. What are the steps involved in adopting a corporate plan? [13.1]

3. Why is the summary plan description (SPD) frequently used as a means of fulfilling the employer's obligation to explain the plan to participants? [13.1]

4. Discuss the makeup of an SPD with regard to [13.1]

    a. the limitations on using the SPD as a marketing piece

    b. the plan provisions that it must explain

5. a. Who is typically appointed to be the plan administrator? [13.2]

    b. What individuals and organizations help the plan administrator manage the plan?

6. Identify each of the following: [13.2]

    a. Form 5500

    b. Schedule A of Form 5500

    c. Form 5500-EZ

7. Describe the responsibility of the plan administrator with regard to [13.2]

    a. distributing the summary annual report

    b. issuing personal benefit statements

    c. counseling participants concerning plan options

    d. amending the plan document

8. How does the process of installation and administration of a Keogh plan differ from the installation and administration of a corporate plan? [13.2]

9. Describe the administrator's role when he or she is presented with a domestic relations order from a court ordering the division of a pension benefit. [13.3]

Chapter 13: Review Answers

1. Typically, the financial services advisor involves other professionals to set up and administer the plan. The advisor stays involved in plan design and troubleshooting when problems arise.

2. The steps include adopting the plan with a board resolution and plan document, obtaining an advance-determination letter from the IRS, giving notice to interested parties, explaining the plan to the employees, and, in some cases (if employees have the option to contribute or are given investment options), conducting an enrollment meeting.

3. The summary plan description (SPD) is uniquely suited for this task because it bridges the gap between the legalese of the pension plan and the understanding of the layperson. In any case, the employer is required to provide an SPD, so the use of such a description proves cost effective because a second document need not be created.

    The easy-to-read SPD also serves as a method for an employer to tout the fact that a significant employee benefit is being provided to employees and that the retirement benefit should be considered as an important part of the employee's overall compensation package.

4. a. The SPD is a legal document required by ERISA that explains but does not sell the plan.

    b. Essentially, the SPD must clearly explain eligibility for the plan's benefits and describe how to apply for benefits. It must also describe the plan's appeal procedures if the participant is denied benefits.

5. a. The plan administrator is typically the company.

    b. Specified employees carry out the administrative duties with the help of outside service providers, such as consultants, insurance companies, or accountants.

6. a. Form 5500 is the annual report required for all pension plans except one-participant plans.

    b. Schedule A is attached to the appropriate annual report when benefits are provided (in whole or in part) by an insurance company.

    c. Form 5500-EZ is the annual report filed for one-participant plans

7. a. Summary annual reports containing a summary of the information in the annual report must be distributed to participants within 2 months of the due date of the

annual report. The SAR requirement has been replaced with a detailed funding notice for defined-benefit plans.

b. In defined-contribution plans, personal benefit statements are required annually (quarterly in plans that allow participant investment direction). In defined-benefit plans, statements are required every 3 years.

c. Whenever the plan allows for employee contributions or investments, there is quite a bit of ongoing interaction between the administrator and the participants. New election forms, educational materials, investment seminars and retirement planning seminars, and software are part of the retirement planning landscape today.

d. Plan documents are amended when the sponsor wants to change the plan design or when a law change requires an amendment. In either case, the plan is typically filed for another IRS determination letter whenever a significant amendment has been adopted.

8. Plans sponsored by sole proprietors or partnerships (so-called Keogh plans) may be exempt from filing Form 5500 (or may be required to file Form 5500-EZ instead of Form 5500). They may also be exempt from the ERISA reporting requirements. As mentioned in chapter 3, a special rule applies to calculating the maximum allowable contribution.

9. It is the plan administrator's duty to review court orders and determine whether they qualify as a QDRO. The plan administrator is required to establish procedures for reviewing a court order, and must notify all affected parties of the procedures when the plan receives a court order. If the order fails, as long as the parties made a good-faith effort to draft the order, the administrator should explain the deficiencies and work toward an order that satisfies the rules.

Chapter 14

Retirement Plan Termination

Learning Objectives

An understanding of the material in this chapter should enable the student to

- **LO 14.1** Identify reasons for, alternatives to, and limitations on terminating a qualified retirement plan.
- **LO 14.2** Describe the steps for terminating a defined-contribution plan.
- **LO 14.3** Describe the steps for terminating a defined-benefit plan.
- **LO 14.4** Identify the impact of reverting assets to the employer in a defined-benefit plan.
- **LO 14.5** Explain what is unique about the distribution of plan assets at the time of plan termination.
- **LO 14.6** Review the circumstances in which a plan may be terminated by operation of law.

Business owners contemplating the establishment of a retirement plan need to know that qualified plans must be permanent, rather than temporary, programs. The IRS seeks assurance that the plan is intended to meet the retirement needs of present and future employees, rather than function as a temporary tax shelter for key employees. This does not mean, however, that the business owner must be saddled with a plan indefinitely. If business conditions change, the plan can still be terminated, as long as the plan has been drafted to reserve the employer's right to terminate it.

The term *plan termination* used herein means the complete dissolution of the plan: participants receive no additional plan benefits, contributions cease (after meeting remaining obligations), plan assets are liquidated, and benefits are distributed. Often, employers are not fully aware of the consequences and administrative burdens of plan termination. This chapter explores the procedures and ramifications of plan termination and reviews less drastic alternatives.

TO TERMINATE OR NOT TO TERMINATE

Why Plan Termination?

LO 14.1   **Identify reasons for, alternatives to, and limitations on terminating a qualified retirement plan.**

The employer may wish to terminate a plan for any number of business reasons, such as the following common ones:

- The employer is no longer in a financial position to make further plan contributions.
- The employer may want to switch plan designs (for example, switching from a defined-benefit to a defined-contribution approach) to lower plan costs and ease administrative complexity.
- The company may want to switch to an employee stock ownership plan (ESOP) to purchase the stock of a retiring owner.
- The employer may want to accommodate a substantial change in business operations, such as the sale or merger of the business.

Alternatives to Plan Termination

Plan termination is much more than simply ceasing additional employer contributions. It also means notifying proper governmental agencies, liquidating assets, and distributing funds to participants—all of which generate a great deal of paperwork and administrative expense. Before deciding to terminate a plan, the employer should consider other alternatives. Additionally, it is important to understand plan termination options before developing a company's retirement plan.

Ceasing Further Benefit Accruals

A defined-benefit or defined-contribution plan can be amended to cease further benefit accruals—as long as benefits already earned are not reduced. With defined-contribution plans, this strategy can be used to cease employer contributions. This approach may make sense for an employer expecting to resume making contributions later or who is concerned about participants squandering retirement benefits if they receive them now. Ceasing accruals in a defined-benefit plan does not always result in a complete cessation of contributions, depending upon the plan's funding status. Ceasing accruals will, however, limit the plan sponsor's future funding obligations.

Regardless of the type of plan involved, one issue that must always be considered is whether additional benefit accruals must be awarded for the current year. Under ERISA, benefit accruals cannot cease until 15 days after plan participants have been notified of the amendment.[1] Therefore, the effective date of the amendment that ceases accruals must be a minimum of 15 days after notice is given. Once the effective date is established, participants will be entitled to another year of benefit accrual if they meet all service eligibility requirements prior to the effective date of the amendment.

Effect on Defined-Benefit Plans. Ceasing further benefit accruals in a defined-benefit plan does not change the plan's essential nature—the plan is still required to pay promised benefits as they become due, employees continue to vest under the same vesting schedule,[2] and the employer is still required to meet the minimum funding obligations. If assets are not sufficient to meet the projected payouts, the actuary may determine that additional contributions are still necessary. Plans subject to the PBGC insurance program must continue paying insurance premiums. The rising costs of these premiums over the last few years could weigh in favor of terminating the plan versus discontinuing further benefit accruals.

Effect on Defined-Contribution Plans. In a money-purchase plan, or any other plan with required contributions, the only additional contributions necessary when accruals cease are those to fund the prior or current year's obligation.

Whether the same vesting provisions can continue to apply or whether full vesting occurs depends upon the type of plan involved. Any defined-contribution plan that is a pension plan (money-purchase and target-benefit plans) should be able to continue using the same vesting schedule. On the other hand, in profit-sharing plans, participants become fully vested when employer contributions are completely discontinued.

Amending the Plan into Another Type

In some circumstances, the employer has the choice to amend the plan into another type of plan, rather than terminate the plan and start up a new one. This is a tricky area and legal consultation should be sought. However, some general guidelines can be provided. A defined-contribution plan of one type usually can be amended into another type of defined-contribution plan. For example, a money-purchase plan can be amended into a profit-sharing

---

1. See 29 U.S.C. Sec. 1054 (h) and ERISA 204(h) (stating notice must be given not less than 15 days before any amendment that provides for a significant reduction in plan benefits takes effect).
2. Participants may have to become fully vested in accordance with the rule discussed in the section on partial plan terminations. Under this rule, full and immediate vesting is only an issue if the plan excess assets at the time the amendment is adopted.

plan. The plan amendment must be carefully drafted to ensure that subtle differences between the types of plans are addressed.

Likewise, a defined-benefit plan of one type can be amended into another type of defined-benefit plan. In the large plan market, this sometimes happens when a traditional defined-benefit plan is amended into a cash-balance-type plan. However, two types of amendments are clearly prohibited: defined-benefit plans cannot be amended into defined-contribution plans, and defined-contribution plans cannot be amended into defined-benefit plans.

Limitations on Plan Termination

Several issues may discourage or prohibit the plan sponsor from terminating the plan. These issues are addressed below.

Temporary Tax Shelters

As a general rule, retirement plans may not be set up as a temporary tax-shelter for the benefit of key employees. If they have been, plan termination can result in retroactive disqualification. For plans terminated within a few years after establishment, the IRS presumes the employer did not intend for the plan to be permanent. To rebut this assumption, the employer must provide a reason of "business necessity beyond the employer's control." Acceptable reasons for an early termination appear to be change in ownership by merger, substitution to another type of plan, employee dissatisfaction with the plan, financial inability to continue plan, liquidation or dissolution of the business, a change in ownership by sale or transfer, adverse business conditions, a significant change in the pension law, or a change in the company's retirement plan strategy, resulting in the adoption of a replacement plan.[3] Practically speaking, the permanency issue is not a concern when the plan has been maintained for at least 10 years.[4]

Insufficient Plan Assets

In defined-contribution plans, plan benefits are based upon the individual accounts, which represent all the assets held by the plan. This means that additional employer contributions are generally not required when a plan is terminated. However, for any plan that requires specified employer contributions, promised contributions that have not been made at the time of termination must still be made.

---

3. See Reg. 1.401–1(b)(2) and Rev. Ruling 69–25, 1969–1 C.B. 113..
4. See Reg. 1.401–1(b)(2) and Rev. Ruling 72–239, 1972–1 C.B. 107.

Defined-benefit plans, on the other hand, are a totally different story. In defined-benefit plans, assets never equal the present value of promised benefits. The plan will either have more than enough or not enough assets to pay promised benefits. When assets are insufficient to pay benefits, plans subject to the Pension Benefit Guaranty Corporation (PBGC) insurance program may not be able to be terminated at all. The PBGC has a financial interest at this point, and strict rules apply. If the plan cannot be terminated, the employer generally will want to amend the plan to cease all further benefit accruals to limit its future liability. If a plan with insufficient assets is not subject to the PBGC program, the plan may be terminated and strict rules on how plan assets are allocated to the participants apply.

Plan Problems

Plan termination is a time when the IRS scrutinizes the operation of the plan. The plan sponsor should correct any compliance problems prior to considering plan termination. The IRS currently maintains a voluntary compliance program, which allows sponsors who are willing to correct compliance problems to do so with a minimum of penalties.

TERMINATING A DEFINED-CONTRIBUTION PLAN

LO 14.2   **Describe the steps for terminating a defined-contribution plan.**

Compared with the termination of a defined-benefit plan covered by the PBGC insurance program, termination of a defined-contribution plan is relatively easy. However, each of the following steps must be taken:

- A corporate resolution terminating the plan must be adopted, and the plan and trust must be amended to terminate further accruals. As discussed above, the issue of whether participants have accrued a benefit for the current year has to be carefully considered. The plan must also be amended to fully vest all participants.

- The plan termination date must be scheduled at least 15 days after participants are notified. Because the termination effectively ceases benefit accruals, the ERISA rule requiring that participants be notified 15 days before the amendment becomes effective applies.

- The employer must make any remaining required contributions for the previous year or for this year's benefit accruals.

- Sometimes when the laws regarding qualified plans change, plan sponsors are allowed an extended period in which to incorporate amendments that reflect the new law. If this is the case at the time of a plan termination, conforming amendments should be added to the plan.

- Plan assets must be liquidated in preparation for distribution. Note that assets can be distributed in kind as long as the highly compensated employees are not given special treatment.
- Benefit distribution paperwork must be prepared.
- In the year that benefits are distributed, when the annual IRS Form 5500 is filed, it is marked as the "final form."

Submitting the Plan to the IRS

At the time of plan termination, the sponsor of a qualified plan can voluntarily request an IRS approval letter. If granted, the IRS letter states that the plan termination does not adversely affect the qualified status of the plan. Although the submission is voluntary, in recent history, the IRS has audited plans that terminate without the request of such a determination letter.

The determination letter gives the sponsor and plan participants the assurance that distributed benefits will be eligible for the special tax treatment afforded to qualified plans. Unfortunately, the IRS determination letter is not a guarantee that the plan will not be audited later. However, the auditing process should go more smoothly if the determination letter had been requested. For these reasons, it is generally a good idea for the plan sponsor to request the IRS determination letter.

To request a determination letter, the plan sponsor must complete and submit Form 5310.[5] Also, all plan participants and beneficiaries must be given notice of the submission. In addition to announcing the submission, the notice should inform participants that they are allowed to send comments to the IRS or Department of Labor (DOL). Strict rules apply to who must receive the notice as well as how and when it is to be distributed.

TERMINATING A DEFINED-BENEFIT PLAN

LO 14.3   Describe the steps for terminating a defined-benefit plan.

An extremely complex procedure applies to the termination of defined-benefit plans covered under the PBGC insurance program. For plans that are not covered, the procedures are similar to those described above. PBGC covered plans can be terminated in three possible ways, each

---

5.   Applications for a determination letter for a partial termination are filed on Form 5300.

with their own unique set of rules and procedures: 1) standard/voluntary plan termination; 2) PBGC initiated termination; and 3) distress termination.

Plans Covered under the PBGC Insurance Program

Overview of Plans Covered under PBGC

The Pension Benefit Guaranty Corporation (PBGC) is a federal agency that insures participants against the loss of benefits that arise from complete or partial termination of a defined-benefit plan. As mentioned earlier in the text, the PBGC

- covers all privately sponsored qualified defined-benefit plans (except for plans of professional-service employers with 25 or fewer active participants)
- collects compulsory premiums
- guarantees benefits vested prior to the termination up to a maximum of $5,369.32 for a 65-year-old per month (2017 indexed limit)
- oversees plan terminations initiated by the employer
- initiates terminations if a plan is financially strained
- taps up to 30 percent of the net worth of employers whose plans have terminated and left the PBGC liable for payments

Here, we will explore the PBGC's practices and requirements for plan terminations initiated voluntarily by the employer. However, note that the PBGC also has the right to terminate a plan in financial difficulty (as discussed further at the end of the chapter).

Voluntary Plan Termination

standard termination

distress termination

A plan covered by the PBGC program can only be terminated by the sponsor if the plan qualifies as a **standard termination** or **distress termination**. A standard termination is only allowed if the plan has sufficient assets to pay promised benefits (including those benefits that become fully vested because of the plan termination). To qualify for a distress termination, the employer must prove to a bankruptcy court or to the PBGC that the employer cannot remain in business unless the plan is terminated. If the application is granted, the PBGC will take over the plan as trustee and pay plan benefits, up to the guaranteed limit, using plan assets and PBGC guarantee funds.

A sponsor wishing to terminate a plan under the standard termination process must complete the following steps:

- Issue a Notice of Intent to Terminate to participants at least 60 days, and no more than 90 days, before the proposed termination date.
- Inform plan participants that PBGC's guarantee of their benefits will cease upon distribution of plan assets.
- If payouts are in the form of an annuity, inform plan participants of the identity of the private insurer from whom an annuity is being purchased.
- Send participants a notice of the benefits earned and the data used to calculate the value of the benefit.
- Submit a termination notice to PBGC, which includes certified data on the plan's assets and liabilities as of the proposed date of distribution.
- Distribute plan assets to cover all benefit liabilities under the plan.

Plans Not Covered under the PBGC Insurance Program

When a plan is not subject to PBGC regulation, it need not conform to the PBGC's rigid termination procedures. Because of this, a non-PBGC plan can be terminated even if it does not have sufficient assets to pay all of the plan benefits. When this is the case, the law prescribes a specific method for dividing the plan assets among the participants. In many cases, to avoid bad feelings (and potential lawsuits), the owners will use their own plan benefits to pay any remaining plan deficiencies.

The administrative burden is not as great with the non-PBGC plan because the PBGC filing requirements do not have to be satisfied. However, the sponsor does have to take all of the steps required for terminating a defined-contribution plan, as described above.

Reversion of Excess Plan Assets

LO 14.4 **Identify the impact of reverting assets to the employer in a defined-benefit plan.**

A defined-benefit plan may, at any point in time, have more assets than necessary to pay benefits promised under the plan. As long as the plan document specifically allows it, excess assets can revert to the employer when the plan terminates after all benefits are paid out. Reversions of excess assets are treated as taxable income to the employer. Out of concern that employers may terminate plans to access the excess assets, 26 U.S.C. Sec. 4980 provides for an additional 50 percent excise tax on the amount reverted from a qualified plan except when the employer shares the reversion with employees, in which case the excise tax is only 20 percent. To qualify for the 20 percent tax rate, the employer must either (1) establish a qualified replacement plan to which it transfers assets equal to 25 percent of the reversion, or (2) provide pro rata increases in benefits of qualified participants in connection with the plan termination equal to at least 20 percent of the reversion.

When a plan has excess assets, the employer is not under any obligation to revert the excess. The assets may be, and often are, allocated among plan participants. The law provides some discretion in the allocation method, and the actuary should provide several alternatives. In the small-plan setting, the actuary generally looks for a method that allocates the lion's share of the excess to the business owner. This can work quite well, unless the owner's benefit is already approaching the maximum benefit limitations. If the owner can get a significant piece of the excess, the reallocation method has clear tax advantages—benefits can be rolled into an IRA and tax deferral can continue. On the other hand, if the owner's share of the excess is limited, he or she may prefer the reversion approach.

DISTRIBUTIONS FROM A TERMINATING PLAN

LO 14.5 Explain what is unique about the distribution of plan assets at the time of plan termination.

The form of benefit payout at plan termination depends solely upon the terms of the plan. If the plan offers a lump-sum option, participants must be given a choice to receive a single sum or a deferred annuity. At the employer's election, a single-sum option can be added at the time of termination; however, such an option may not be removed. In most cases, when a plan has a lump-sum option, participants elect this option. With a lump-sum option, participants must be provided with the following:

- benefit election form
- notice and election forms for applicable qualified joint-and-survivor annuity rules
- notice and election forms for the right to have benefits transferred directly to an IRA or other qualified plan
- IRS Form 1099-R for lump-sum distributions

single-premium annuity contract (SPAC)

If the plan does not offer a lump-sum option, the employer purchases a **single-premium group annuity contract (SPAC)** from an insurance company. In return for the single premium, the insurance company assumes the transferred plan's liabilities and issues annuity certificates that ensure participants receive their benefits. At the time that participants retire, they choose a distribution option from among the various ones available, and the insurer handles the paperwork.

SPACs are customized products as the law generally requires that the SPAC distribution options match the options offered in the plan. This makes SPACs difficult for an insurer to price. The insurer must assess the liabilities under the plan and identify the present value of future obligations.

Out of concern that the insurance company is solely responsible for paying out plan benefits, the DOL is quite concerned about the choice of carriers when a SPAC is purchased. The employer and other plan fiduciaries may be held personally liable if the insurer cannot pay up if it is determined that the fiduciaries did not use reasonable care when choosing the carrier. On a practical level, this means the fiduciaries should

- obtain several SPAC quotes
- document how and why the particular choice was made
- review the company's insurance ratings by using a number of rating services
- be especially careful when they choose a lower quote, if that insurer is also rated lower than the competition
- consider hiring independent consultants to further analyze the company's financial condition

TERMINATIONS BY OPERATION OF LAW

LO 14.6 **Review the circumstances in which a plan may be terminated by operation of law.**

In the preceding part of this chapter, we discussed plan terminations initiated by the employer. Here, we discuss a quite different topic: plan terminations by operation of law. This may occur in three separate situations:

- a partial termination of any qualified plan, resulting from a sudden reduction in the number of plan participants or a reduction in plan benefits
- the termination of a profit-sharing plan as a result of a complete discontinuance of contributions
- the involuntary termination of a defined-benefit plan by the PBGC

Finally, we will discuss one other situation that arises periodically, abandoned plans. These typically are defined-contribution plans of employers that go out of business or otherwise terminate, so that there is essentially no employer entity to terminate the plan. The Department of Labor has established a procedure to liquidate plans for such financial services firms.

Partial Plan Termination

partial plan termination

Companies are sometimes forced to downsize through layoffs, plant closings or closing a line of business. These layoffs can have an impact on a qualified plan. If enough employees are terminated, under Code Sec. 411(d)(3) a **partial termination** has occurred and the affected workers must be fully vested in their benefits.

Under Rev. Rul. 2007-43 the IRS created a rebuttable assumption that a partial termination has occurred if a plan's turnover rate is at least 20 percent. The turnover rate is determined by dividing the number of participating employees who had an employer-initiated severance during the "applicable period" by the number of participating employees at the start of the period plus employees who became participants during the applicable period. The applicable period is generally a plan year, but could be longer period if there are a series of related severances from employment.

> **EXAMPLE**
>
> Plan X has 120 participants at the beginning of the plan year. Due to economic conditions, the company lays off 20 employees.[6] In addition, 8 employees terminate on a voluntary basis (which can be documented). No new employees become eligible during the plan year. The turnover rate is 16.67 percent (20/120).

Rev. Rul. 2007-43 notes that whether or not a partial termination occurs is ultimately dependent on all of the facts and circumstances in a particular case. If the facts and circumstances indicate the turnover rate for an applicable period is routine for the employer, that will favor a finding that there is no partial termination for that applicable period. In making the comparison, information as to the turnover rate in other periods and the extent to which terminated employees were actually replaced, whether the new employees performed the same functions, had the same job classification or title, and received comparable compensation are relevant to determining whether the turnover is routine for the employer.

---

6. See *Matz v. Household International Tax Reduction Investment Plan*, 388 F.3d 570 (7th Cir. 2004).

The IRS's 20 percent presumption test may be problematic for small employers that lay off even one or two employees.

> **EXAMPLE**
>
> **Plan Y has 6 participants at the beginning of the plan year. Due to economic conditions, the company lays off 2 employees and no new employees become eligible to participate during the plan year. The turnover rate is 33.34 percent (2/6) and the presumption is that a partial termination has occurred.**

However, the employer can rebut the presumption with facts that show that this is a normal turnover rate—which may very well be the case with a small employer. Also, the potential for problems demonstrates the necessity to keep records demonstrating that the circumstances of each employees termination.

Another way for the employer to address the uncertainty of the partial termination rules, is to simply fully vest terminated employees when a questionable situation arises. With the relatively short vesting schedules allowed today, this may not be a very costly option.

Profit-Sharing Plans

If profit-sharing-type plans (which include 401(k) plans and ESOPs), have a "complete discontinuance of contributions," participants will become fully vested in their benefits.[7] The determination is based on a facts-and-circumstances test. In making the determination, the IRS considers whether contributions have been recurring and substantial, and whether there is any reasonable probability that the lack of contributions will continue indefinitely. This vague standard makes it difficult for the sponsor to determine whether the rule applies in a particular case. As a practical matter, the issue should be reviewed if no substantial contributions are made to a plan for 2 years or more.

The IRS—especially at the time a plan terminates—will definitely review the complete discontinuance issue. In many situations, plans are terminated well after the date that contributions have ceased. In this scenario, the IRS is likely to determine that benefits became fully vested in the same taxable year when substantial contributions stopped, not when the plan was actually terminated. Such a determination can cause major headaches when forfeited benefits have already been reallocated to other participants.

---

7. See IRC Sec. 411(d)(3) & IT Reg. Sec. 1.411(d)-2(a)(1)(ii).

Involuntary Terminations of Defined-Benefit Plans

involuntary terminations

In the case of a defined-benefit plan covered by the PBGC insurance program, the PBGC has the right to initiate an **involuntary termination** in limited circumstances. The reason it does so is to protect itself from mounting liabilities under a plan that shows no promise of meeting its obligations. The PBGC can institute termination proceedings if it determines that the interests of the plan participants would be better served by the termination, and if any one of the following occurs:

- Minimum funding standards have not been satisfied.
- Benefits cannot be paid when they are due.
- A lump-sum payment has been made to a substantial owner who is a plan participant.
- The loss to PBGC is expected to increase unreasonably if the plan is not terminated.

The PBGC must terminate a plan if assets are unavailable to pay benefits currently due.

Abandoned Plan Program

Significant business events such as bankruptcies, mergers, acquisitions, and other similar transactions affecting the status of an employer can result in employers, particularly small employers, abandoning their individual-account retirement plans such as 401(k) plans. The DOL has issued guidance for custodians such as banks, insurers, and mutual fund companies are left holding the assets of the abandoned plans without the authority to terminate and distribute benefits.

Under these rules, a plan generally will be considered abandoned if no contributions or distributions from the plan have been made for a period of at least 12 consecutive months and it is determined that the sponsor no longer exists, cannot be located, or is unable to maintain the plan.[8] Only a qualified termination administrator (QTA) may determine whether a plan is abandoned under the regulations. To be a QTA, an entity must hold the plan's assets and be eligible as a trustee or issuer of an individual retirement plan under the Internal Revenue Code. The QTA can pay itself reasonable fees for services provided in connection with winding up and terminating the abandoned plan. This can result in plan participants receiving slightly less benefits.

---

8. See 29 CFR Sec. 2578.1.

The regulations establish specific procedures that QTAs must follow which include DOL and participant notification requirements, as well as instructions for calculating and distributing benefits. A QTA is not required to amend a plan to accommodate the termination and does not have to file Form 5500 Annual Report on behalf of an abandoned plan. However, the QTA must complete and file a summary terminal report at the end of the winding-up process. In addition, the regulations establish a fiduciary safe harbor provision that allows the QTA to transfer a missing participant's benefits into an IRA.

In 2012, the DOL proposed amendments to the Abandoned Plan Program to facilitate plan termination and disbursement of benefits when the plan was part of a Chapter 7 bankruptcy liquidation procedure. The proposed rules would enable to bankruptcy trustee to terminate and wind up the abandoned plan himself or appoint an eligible designee, streamlining the process for abandoned plans in Chapter 7 bankruptcy liquidation procedures.

There is now a searchable online database created by the Employee Benefits Security Administration to help beneficiaries and participants find out if a plan has been abandoned, terminated, or is the process of termination.

Additional information about the program is available under the Abandoned Plan Program section of EBSA's web site, www.dol.gov/ebsa.

CHAPTER REVIEW

Key Terms and Concepts

standard termination
distress termination
single-premium annuity contract (SPAC)

partial plan termination
involuntary terminations

Chapter 14: Review Questions

Review questions are based on the learning objectives in this chapter. Thus, a [14.3] at the end of a question means that the question is based on learning objective 3. If there are multiple objectives, they are all listed.

1. Explain the reasons employers typically terminate a qualified plan. [14.1]

2. Identify alternatives to plan termination. [14.1]

3. What problems can get in the way of a plan termination? [14.1]

4. Describe the steps required for terminating a defined-contribution plan. [14.2]

5. Explain why the employer should consider submitting the plan for IRS approval upon plan termination. [14.2]

6. What is the major difference between terminating defined-benefit plans covered by the PBGC and terminating those that are not covered? [14.3]

7. What does the employer have to do to qualify for the lower 20 percent reversion excise tax? [14.4]

8. Describe a single-premium annuity contract (SPAC). [14.5]

9. Identify the situations in which a termination by operation of law can occur. [14.6]

Chapter 14: Review Answers

1. Employers terminate qualified plans for a number of reasons. The sponsor may no longer be in a financial position to make further plan contributions. Or the sponsor may want to change plan design to another type of plan. Changes may also occur if the business is sold or merged, or if there are other substantial changes in business operations.

2. If an employer wants to cease additional benefits but does not want to distribute benefits, the plan can be "frozen." If a defined-benefit plan does not have sufficient assets to pay promised benefits, freezing benefit accruals is quite common. Also, if the employer wants to change the nature of the plan, in some cases the plan can be amended instead of terminated. For example, a traditional defined-benefit plan can be amended into a cash-balance plan.

3. If an employer is considering the termination of a qualified plan, the following issues should be considered: First, if the plan is less than 10 years old, the IRS may require a valid business reason for the plan's termination. Second, if the plan is a defined-benefit plan covered by the PBGC, it can be terminated only under certain circumstances. Third, if the plan has had any compliance problems, they should be addressed before completing the plan termination.

4. Termination of a defined-contribution plan requires a corporate resolution and plan amendments terminating further accruals. In some cases, plans also need amendments for retroactive law changes. Participants must be notified 15 days prior to the termination date. The employer must make any remaining required contributions and liquidate plan assets in preparation for distribution. Benefit distribution paperwork must be prepared and in the year that benefits are distributed, when the annual IRS Form 5500 is filed, it is marked as the "final form."

5. A plan that is not submitted to the IRS upon termination raises a "red flag" and may be audited.

6. Unlike plans covered by the PBGC program, a non-PBGC plan can be terminated even if it does not have sufficient assets to pay all plan benefits. Also, the administrative burden is not as great with the non-PBGC plan, although the plan does have to take all of the steps required for terminating a defined-contribution plan.

7. To be eligible for the lower 20 percent excise tax, the employer must share a portion of the excess with the plan participants. Either 20 percent of the excess must be

allocated to the participants in the terminating plan or 25 percent of the excess must be transferred to a replacement plan.

8. With SPACs (single-premium annuity contracts), the insurance company issues annuity certificates in the amount promised to participants under the plan. The law requires that the SPAC distribution options match the original plan distribution options and, at the time of distribution, the insurer provides election forms, qualified joint-and-survivor notices, and so on.

9. A termination by operation of law can occur without action by the employer if (1) there has been a partial termination, (2) the plan is a profit-sharing plan and there is a complete discontinuance of contributions, (3) the plan is a defined-benefit plan and the PBGC initiates a termination because one of a number of events threatening the plan's financial status has occurred or (4) the plan is abandoned (usually the sponsor no longer exists) and the financial institution holding the assets is allowed to take steps to payout benefits to participants.

Chapter 15

Nonqualified Retirement Plans: An Overview

Learning Objectives

An understanding of the material in this chapter should enable you to

- **LO 15.1** Compare nonqualified plans with qualified plans.
- **LO 15.2** Discuss the tax implications of a nonqualified plan.
- **LO 15.3** Choose the appropriate nonqualified plan for the employer.
- **LO 15.4** Identify the key design considerations when establishing a nonqualified plan.
- **LO 15.5** Review the funding requirements and the advantages of funding with life insurance.
- **LO 15.6** Describe how a plan can be designed to better protect the interests of the participants.
- **LO 15.7** Discuss the installation and administration concerns for nonqualified plans.
- **LO 15.8** Explain which deferred-compensation arrangements are subject to Code Sec. 457(b) and which are subject to Code Sec. 457(f).
- **LO 15.9** Describe an executive-bonus life insurance plan.

Up to this point, the emphasis has been on the use of a tax-sheltered retirement plan to meet the needs of the small business and the small-business owner. However, a second lucrative market is open to financial services professionals who are servicing the retirement needs of the business and the business owner. This market is the nonqualified plan market, which includes nonqualified deferred-compensation plans and executive-bonus plans. These plans help the business owner and selected employees save for retirement without being subject to the requirements that apply to qualified plans. As a trade-off for allowing the employer complete discretion in plan design and in choosing the employees who will be covered by the plan, the employer loses the central advantage of a qualified plan—that is, the ability to make a before-tax contribution on the employee's behalf that is simultaneously deductible to the business. Instead, the employer is entitled to an immediate deduction only if the employee is currently taxed, or conversely, the employee may defer tax only if the employer's deduction is deferred.

In reviewing many of the issues involved in the implementation of nonqualified plans, questions that must be addressed include the following:

- Is it more advantageous for a cost-conscious client to use a qualified or a nonqualified plan?
- What tax considerations underlie the use, design, and funding of a nonqualified plan?
- Should a nonqualified plan be funded, unfunded, or informally funded?
- Should a rabbi trust be used, and if so, how can it be designed in a state-of-the-art manner?
- Should a secular trust or a surety bond be used to secure payments under a nonqualified plan?
- What are the ERISA implications of using nonqualified plans?
- How are nonqualified plans installed and administered?
- Should life insurance products be used to fund nonqualified plan benefits?

It is only after understanding these issues that we can accurately serve our clients needs.

YOUR FINANCIAL SERVICES PRACTICE: THE ALLURE OF THE Nonqualified MARKET

Several factors prompt financial services professionals to become involved in the nonqualified market. Some get involved because nonqualified deferred-compensation and executive-bonus plans help them to provide comprehensive services to their clients. A combination of life insurance, individual annuities, qualified plans, and nonqualified plans allows the financial services professional to provide a comprehensive umbrella of retirement coverage. Others prefer the nonqualified market because it means contact with an upscale clientele, and this, in turn, provides networking opportunities. A third reason to be involved is that life insurance is often the most appropriate funding vehicle.

Nonqualified deferred-compensation plans are sometimes referred to as salary continuation plans, deferred-compensation plans, or nonqualified plans. These aliases, however, can be misleading because they all have other meanings. For example, the term salary continuation plan is sometimes used to refer to sick days and disability benefits. Likewise, deferred compensation sometimes refers to qualified pension and profit-sharing plans. The term nonqualified plans can refer to a myriad of plans that fail to meet various qualification standards. Because we will discuss only nonqualified deferred-compensation plans, we will call them nonqualified plans for short. In the marketplace, however, it is wise to make sure everybody is on the same wavelength and is not tripped up by the confusing nomenclature.

NONQUALIFIED VERSUS QUALIFIED PLANS

LO 15.1   Compare nonqualified plans with qualified plans.

As we have seen, qualified pension and profit-sharing plans are retirement plans that meet standards set out in the Employee Retirement Income Security Act (ERISA) and the Internal Revenue Code (Code). As a payback for adhering to burdensome qualification rules, plan contributions are immediately deductible by the employer, earnings on plan funds are tax deferred, and, when qualified plan funds are distributed to employees, tax-deferring strategies such as rollovers may be available.

Table 15-1
Qualified and Nonqualified Plans Compared

Characteristic	Qualified Plan	Nonqualified Plan
Tax deferred to employee	Yes—always	Yes (as long as designed properly)
Tax consequences to employer	Immediate deduction	Deduction deferred (until employees have taxable income)
Earnings accumulate on a tax-deferred basis	Yes—always	No (unless investment allows tax deferral)
Ability to rollover benefit to other tax-deferred vehicle	Yes	No
Ability to lower costs by only covering selected employees	No (must meet nondiscrimination rules)	Yes—always
Plan administration requirements	Burdensome and expensive	Minimal and inexpensive
Reporting and disclosure requirements	Burdensome and expensive	Minimal and inexpensive
Ability to attract, retain, and motivate employees	Effective	More effective (ability to target individual needs)

In contrast, a nonqualified plan cannot simultaneously give the employer the benefit of an immediate tax deduction and give the employee the benefit of a tax deferral. Most nonqualified plans are structured to defer the taxation of retirement benefits for executives. Unlike qualified plans, however, nonqualified deferred-compensation plans postpone the employer's deduction until the benefit has been paid to the executive and has been included in his or her income. In addition, earnings on money put aside to fund the plan will be taxed in the year it is earned unless a tax shelter, such as life insurance, is used. Finally, distributions from nonqualified plans cannot be rolled over to delay taxation.

Despite the dismal tax comparison, nonqualified plans are favored over qualified plans in many cases for a variety of reasons, including

- design flexibility (see below)
- lower administrative costs
- cost-saving through limiting coverage to executives

This last reason is perhaps the chief motivation for an employer to install a nonqualified plan. Business owners claim they can save significant sums of money by excluding rank-and-file employees from the plan. In the minds of many employers, the tax savings garnered under a qualified plan are overshadowed by the ability to avoid paying benefit costs for the majority of their employees. A short case study helps to illustrate this point.

Case Study: The Smallco Company

Smallco is a company of 10 people and is owned by two sisters not employed at the company. The two managers of the firm earn a salary of $100,000 each; the payroll for the additional employees is $240,000 (average salary, $30,000). If Smallco were to install a profit-sharing plan that provides a benefit of 25 percent of salary to all employees, the qualified plan would cost $110,000 plus administrative expenses ($110,000 equals 25 percent of the total payroll of $440,000). If Smallco were to provide an additional benefit of 25 percent of compensation deferred until termination of employment for the two managers and no benefits for the other employees, however, then the cost of the plan would be reduced to $50,000 plus the cost of deferring the income tax deduction until the managers received their benefits. What also changes in this scenario is that the company can simply make the promise to pay the deferred salary for the managers later; the money does not actually have to be set aside. Even if funds are earmarked for payment, they are owned by the company and can be used to pay other expenses as well.

TAX CONSIDERATIONS

With nonqualified plans, the employer receives a deduction at the time that the participant has taxable income. In almost all cases, the plan is designed to defer income tax to the participants until distributions are made. Tax can generally be deferred as long as the deferred compensation is subject to a substantial risk of forfeiture.

A substantial risk of forfeiture is a significant limitation or duty that requires the fulfillment of a meaningful effort by the executive, and there must be a definite possibility that the event that will cause the forfeiture could occur. A traditional vesting provision is clearly a substantial risk of forfeiture. Requiring that an executive continue to provide consulting services to a company after retirement may or may not be a substantial risk of forfeiture, depending upon the specific facts and circumstances.

Economic Benefit Doctrine

If the benefit is not subject to a risk of forfeiture, taxes can still be deferred as long as the distribution does not run afoul of the economic benefit doctrine generally codified in Code Sec. 83 or the constructive receipt doctrine now codified in Code Sec. 409A. Under the economic-benefit doctrine, an economic benefit conferred on an executive as compensation should be included in the person's income to the extent that the benefit has an ascertainable fair market value. In other words, if a compensation arrangement provides a current economic benefit to an executive, that person must report the value of the benefit even if he or she has no current right to receive the benefit.

The economic benefit doctrine means that if a contribution is made to an irrevocable trust for a participant and the benefit is nonforfeitable, the amount will be subject to income tax. This is one reason that nonqualified plan benefits are not as secure as those under a qualified plan. To avoid current income tax, any assets held to pay benefits must remain the property of the sponsor, or be placed in a trust that can be accessed to satisfy the claims of the sponsor's creditors (typically called a rabbi trust).

Code Sec. 409A

Another doctrine that may affect the deferral of the taxable event is the constructive receipt doctrine. Code Sec. 409A has codified many aspects of the constructive receipt rules. However, the tax rules or other legal requirements applicable to nonqualified plans under prior law are not adversely affected by Sec. 409A as long as they remain consistent with its provisions. Technically, Sec. 409A states that deferred amounts that are not subject to a substantial risk of forfeiture are currently includible in gross income and are subject to an additional 20 percent penalty tax unless they meet certain distribution, acceleration of distribution, and deferral election rules. These requirements must be contained in the plan document governing the nonqualified plan.

By way of summary, the principal requirements of Sec. 409A include the following:
- There is a broad definition of nonqualified plan that includes any plan, agreement, or arrangement that provides for the deferral of compensation, other than a tax-qualified employer plan or any bona fide vacation leave, sick leave, compensatory time, disability pay, or death benefit plan.

- An initial election to defer compensation must be made prior to the beginning of the taxable year in which the services are to be performed. There are two exceptions to this requirement which apply to (i) deferral elections by newly eligible participants who are given a 30-day grace period and (ii) performance-based compensation where the performance period is 12 months or more. In the latter case the deferral election can be made up to 6 months prior to the end of the performance period.

- Nonqualified deferred compensation may only be distributed upon the occurrence of any of the following six specified events: a separation from service, the participant's death or disability, a specified time (or fixed schedule) provided under the plan or elected by the participant at the date of deferral, a change in ownership or effective control of the corporation or in the ownership of a substantial portion of the assets of the corporation, or the occurrence of an unforeseen emergency (generally a severe financial hardship as defined in Sec. 457). Distributions of nonqualified deferred compensation may no longer be made based on a haircut provision under which a small penalty (such as 6 percent) was imposed on the amount withdrawn. Unfortunately, under prior law, a haircut provision was an important safeguard. If the employee felt that financial or other conditions within the company might threaten the employee's deferral compensation benefit, the employee could withdraw his or her money under the plan's haircut provision. It was a form of safety valve that no longer exists.

- Specified employees (as determined under Sec. 416) of a publicly traded corporation may not receive a distribution of nonqualified deferred compensation for at least 6 months following a separation from service.

- A taxable event will occur if the corporation transfers assets to an offshore trust (even if the trust is otherwise subject to the claims of the corporation's creditors) used for the purpose of paying nonqualified deferred compensation.

A nonqualified deferred-compensation plan is not limited to an arrangement between an employer and an employee, but includes arrangements between any person who is the recipient of services and the person providing the services. Thus, arrangements covering corporate directors, independent contractors, agents, consultants, and partners can be a nonqualified deferred-compensation plan subject to Sec. 409A. Likewise, the service providers who may be subject to Sec. 409A can include individuals, personal service corporations, or similar noncorporate entities. (Similar to the nomenclature used in the Sec. 409A regulations, the individual who is providing the services covered by the nonqualified deferred-compensation plan will be hereafter referred to as a "service provider" and the individual receiving those services will hereafter be referred to as a "service recipient".)

Timing of Deferral Elections

For a deferral election to be considered properly made under Sec. 409A, it must be irrevocable and must specify (i) the amount of compensation being deferred, (ii) the timing of when the deferred compensation will ultimately be paid out, and (iii) the form in which the deferred compensation will ultimately be paid out. For bonuses that relate to services provided over one or more years, the deferral election with respect to such bonuses must be made before any services are performed during the bonus period. Accordingly, an election must be made in 2016 with respect to a 2017 bonus period. "Evergreen" elections are also permitted; that is, a deferral election for one year remains in effect for the following year unless terminated or changed before the last day of the year preceding the year in which the election is to be effective. For example, an evergreen election for 2016 remains in effect for 2017 if it is not terminated or changed by December 31, 2016.

There is a special deferral election rule applicable to newly eligible participants. Under this rule, if an employee becomes newly eligible, he or she can make a deferral election within 30 days after he or she becomes eligible, but only with respect to compensation payable for services performed after the election. In addition, a special deferral election rule applies to performance-based compensation. A deferral election with respect to performance-based compensation may be made no later than 6 months before the end of the period over which the performance is measured and prior to when the compensation amount is readily ascertainable.

One quite useful provision of Sec. 409A relating to deferral elections is that as long as certain timing requirements are satisfied, an election can be made to delay the timing, or change the form, of a previously elected distribution. The Sec. 409A regulations elaborate on this provision by authorizing a subsequent election to delay a payment or to change the form of a payment if

- The plan requires that any such subsequent election postponing a payment must be made at least 12 months before any payment is scheduled to be made.
- The plan requires that the redeferred payment must be deferred for a period of not less than 5 years from the date such payment would have otherwise been made. During that 5-year period distributions may be made on account of death, disability, or unforeseeable emergency, but not on account of separation from service or change of control.

For purposes of applying these subsequent election rules, the term "payment" refers to each separately and objectively identified amount to which a service provider is entitled under a plan at a particular date. Under this definition a life annuity is treated as a single payment with the first date that a payment could be made being considered the payment date. However, changing from one type of life annuity to another type of life annuity before any annuity payment has been made is not considered a change in the time or form of payment, as long as the two annuities are actuarially equivalent using reasonable actuarial assumptions. Similarly, a series of installment payments is treated as a single payment, however, if a specific election is made each can be treated separately, giving the participant more flexibility in the timing of payments.

Distribution of Benefits

Sec. 409A(a)(2)(A) significantly limits the circumstances under which nonqualified deferred compensation can be paid. A nonqualified deferred-compensation plan will fail to satisfy the distribution restrictions of Sec. 409A(a)(2)(A) unless distributions cannot be made earlier than (i) a separation from service, (ii) the date a service provider becomes disabled, (iii) the date of a service provider's death, (iv) a specified time or pursuant to a fixed schedule specified in the plan, or (v) the occurrence of an unforeseeable emergency (hereafter together referred to as the "enumerated events"). A distribution may also be made on account of a change in control event involving any of the following: (i) the service provider's employer, (ii) the service recipient or other corporation liable for the nonqualified deferred-compensation payment, or (iii) the parent corporation of the employer or service recipient. For a public company's "specified employees," as defined for purposes of the "top-heavy plan" rules found in Code Sec. 416(i), there is an additional 6-month waiting period, commencing with the date of separation, before any distribution of deferred compensation can be made on account of a separation from service. Finally, the acceleration of distributions is prohibited, except as provided in the Sec. 409A regulations.

The Sec. 409A regulations elaborate on these distribution requirements in several respects. It is permissible for a plan to provide for a distribution of nonqualified deferred compensation on the "earliest of" or "latest of" more than one of the enumerated events. Furthermore, a different form of distribution can be used for payments occurring before or after a particular date. For example, a plan can provide a lump-sum payment if separation from service occurs before age 65, and installment payments if the separation occurs on or after age 65. This rule also allows for different forms of distribution to be associated with different payment events. Thus, the nonqualified deferred-compensation payments triggered by a change in control can always be made in the form of a lump sum, while all other nonqualified deferred-compensation payments are made in five installments.

The occurrence of an "unforeseeable emergency" is determined in a similar manner to a hardship withdrawal under a Sec. 401(k) plan, but without the safe harbors. In other words, payments to satisfy an unforeseeable emergency are allowable only upon severe financial hardship of the service provider or a beneficiary resulting from illness or accident or other similar extraordinary and unforeseeable circumstances from events beyond the control of the service provider or beneficiary. Only the amount necessary to satisfy the need can be withdrawn. Moreover, an emergency will not qualify to the extent that the emergency can be relieved by insurance, liquidation of other assets, or cessation of any deferrals under the plan. Clearly, plan administrators must take care in making the determination of the need and the service provider's other available assets and may want to borrow procedures and representations from the hardship withdrawal regulations for Sec. 401(k) plans.

Tax Consequences

LO 15.2   Discuss the tax implications of a nonqualified plan.

A nonqualified deferred-compensation plan that satisfies the rules of Sec. 409A will be taxed under the same rules as applied under prior law. Assuming the requirements of prior law have been satisfied, the executive includes the nonqualified deferred compensation in gross income when the executive receives it; the employer deducts the nonqualified deferred compensation from gross income when the executive includes it in income; and the investment income, if any, attributable to the nonqualified deferred compensation between the time of the initial deferral and the time of distribution is taxed to the employer.

On the other hand, a nonqualified deferred-compensation plan that fails to satisfy Sec. 409A will result in accrual-based taxation for the affected executive. This means that in each year the executive will include in gross income the total amount of vested nonqualified deferred compensation, including actual or notional investment returns, if any, less any amounts included in income in all prior years. Sec. 409A also imposes a flat 20-percent surtax on the nonqualified deferred compensation taxable to the executive. If a nonqualified deferred-compensation plan initially meets the requirements of Sec. 409A, but subsequently fails them, the executive must pay an interest charge, that is, the IRS underpayment rate plus one percentage point, from the time of the initial vesting of the nonqualified deferred compensation.

Code Sec. 83

In the typical nonqualified plan where the employee simply has a contractual right to receive money in the future and even if the plan uses informal funding, as discussed below, Code Sec. 83 is not a consideration. However, if a nonqualified plan becomes funded, Sec. 83 will control the tax consequences of the plan.

Sec. 83 of the Code taxes the transfer of property in connection with the performance of services. If, in connection with the performance of services, property is transferred to a person other than the person for whom the services are performed, the excess of (i) the property's fair market value at the first time the ownership rights of the person having the beneficial interest in the property are transferable or are not subject to a substantial risk of forfeiture, whichever occurs first, over (ii) the amount, if any, paid for the property becomes taxable income to the person providing the services. For this purpose, property is defined to include real and personal property, other than money or an unfunded and unsecured promise to pay money in the future. Property also includes a beneficial interest in assets (including money) which are transferred or set aside from the claims of the transferor's creditors—for example, in a trust or escrow account.

Code Sec. 3121(v)(2)

Code Sec. 3121(v)(2) provides a special timing rule for determining when amounts deferred under a nonqualified plan must be designated as wages for purposes of the employment taxes imposed by the Federal Insurance Contributions Act (FICA) (unlike the regular income tax provisions, which generally require income recognition when deferred amounts are actually or constructively received). The special timing rule states that an amount deferred under a nonqualified plan must be considered wages for employment tax purposes as of the later of the date the services are performed, or when there is no substantial risk of forfeiture of the rights to such amount—even if the deferred amount is not subject to income taxes at that time. There is also a nonduplication rule which generally provides that once a deferred amount is taken into account for employment tax purposes, neither that amount nor income attributable to it will be treated as FICA wages in the future.

Once it is determined that benefits are being provided under a nonqualified plan, the determination of the deferred amount that will be subject to employment taxes depends on whether the amounts are held in an account balance plan or a nonaccount balance plan. An account balance plan is one in which

- principal amounts are credited to an individual account for an employee.
- the income attributable to the principal amounts is credited (or debited) to the individual account.
- the benefits payable to the employee are based solely on the balance credited to the individual account.

Under an account-balance plan, the amount taken into account as wages is the principal amount that is credited to the executive's account, increased (or decreased) by income (or loss) attributable to that amount through the date the amount is required to be taken into account as FICA wages.

> **EXAMPLE**
>
> Under Woodsworth Company's nonqualified plan for employee Frank Myers, 10 percent of his annual compensation is credited on his behalf on December 31 of each year. In addition, a reasonable rate of interest is credited quarterly on the balance credited to Frank as of the last day of the preceding quarter. All amounts credited under the plan are 100 percent vested after Frank completes 5 years of service. The benefits payable to Frank are based solely on the balance credited to his account under the plan. Frank was hired on March 1, 2012, and began participation in the plan on January 1, 2013. When Frank became vested on January 1, 2017, his account under the plan had a balance of $88,456. The company must treat the $88,456 account balance as wages for employment tax purposes for 2017.

A nonaccount balance plan, such as a defined-benefit plan, does not meet the requirements for an account-balance plan. In a nonaccount balance plan, the amount taken into account is the present value of the future payments to which the executive has obtained a legally binding right (that is, he or she has met the vesting requirement). The income attributable to the amount taken into account is defined as the increase, due to the passage of time, in the present value of any future payments to which the executive has a legally binding right. Employers may use any reasonable actuarial assumptions and methods in determining present value. Moreover, an employer can elect not to take into account any amount, even if vested, unless the value is "reasonably ascertainable." An amount is "reasonably ascertainable" when there are no actuarial or other assumptions needed to determine the amount deferred other than interest, mortality, or cost-of-living assumptions.

> **EXAMPLE**
>
> Software Development, Inc., has a fully vested nonqualified plan that gives Bill Vista, now aged 45, the right to a $500,000 lump sum benefit at age 65. The amount deferred is reasonably ascertainable because only interest and mortality assumptions are needed to determine it. If the $500,000 is instead payable to Bill at the later of age 55 or his termination of employment, the amount deferred will no longer be reasonably ascertainable because the present value of the benefit is contingent on when Bill terminates his employment.

Due to the potential mismatch of income and employment taxes, employment taxes should not be an afterthought in planning for deferred compensation. Tax planning that considers income tax consequences but neglects employment taxes is inadequate. The combined employment tax rate for employers and employees is 15.3 percent on wages up to the taxable wage base, but it falls to 2.9 percent on wages over the taxable wage base. Thus, timing is an important factor in planning for the avoidance of employment taxes. To the extent possible, deferred amounts should be treated as wages under Sec. 3121(v)(2) after an executive has earned more than the taxable wage base for the year.

Finally, nonprofit organizations and governments have different tax considerations than do their taxable counterparts. These considerations are discussed below as part of the material on Sec. 457 plans.

CHOOSING A NONQUALIFIED PLAN

LO 15.3   **Choose the appropriate nonqualified plan for the employer.**

Choosing the right nonqualified plan requires that the advisor consider the employer's objectives and understands the various options available.

Determining the Company's Needs

The nonqualified plan market is a very important part of a financial services practice in the retirement field because it allows financial services professionals to deal successfully with client situations that are otherwise unsolvable, such as the following:

- The client wants to provide a second tier of executive retirement benefits in addition to the qualified plan in order to attract and retain strong executives.
- The client wants to limit coverage to certain executives.
- The client wants a plan that is less of an administrative burden than a qualified plan.
- The client wants to give executives the opportunity to save more of their current income. Sometimes the program dovetails with a 401(k) plan, and only salary deferrals above the applicable 401(k) plan limit go into the nonqualified program.
- The client is an owner of a closely held business who is looking to temporarily save taxes and may want to have income retained in the company. This makes sense when the corporate tax rate is lower than the individual tax rate. Note, however, that the IRS may challenge a plan that allows a controlling (50 percent) shareholder to defer compensation.1
- The client is the controlling owner of a closely held business that is just starting up and the company lacks the cash to pay other owner-employees their full salaries. Making the promise to pay such owner-employees' compensation later establishes

the obligation to pay additional income and helps avoid problems with the IRS about "reasonable compensation" in later years when the owner-employees are receiving large payouts.

- The client wants to meet the organization's objectives of attracting executives, retaining executives, and providing for a graceful transition in company leadership. Although qualified plans can achieve similar objectives, nonqualified plans can be more effective because they are subject to fewer design restrictions.

NONQUALIFIED PLAN FACT FINDER

Client Name: _____

Step 1: Identify concerns

Listed below are some typical concerns that organizations have when instituting a nonqualified plan. Grade each of these concerns by scoring 1 for very valuable, 2 for valuable, 3 for moderately valuable, and 4 for least valuable.

1. Avoid the nondiscrimination requirements of a qualified plan. [1][2][3][4]
2. Allow executives to defer current income for their own tax-shelter purposes. [1][2][3][4]
3. Exceed the Sec. 415 maximum benefit and contribution limits of a qualified plan. [1][2][3][4]
4. Supplement qualified-plan benefits that are not stretched to the maximum limits. [1][2][3][4]
5. Recruit talented executives from outside the company. [1][2][3][4]
6. Retain executives by inducing them to stay with the company. [1][2][3][4]
7. Induce executives to take early retirement. [1][2][3][4]
8. Induce executives to provide consulting services after retirement. [1][2][3][4]
9. Keep executives from competing with the company. [1][2][3][4]
10. Adjust executive retirement benefits to include not only the compensation considered under the qualified plan but all compensation. [1][2][3][4]

Step 2: List in order the primary reasons for establishing a nonqualified plan.

1.
2.
3.

Once your client has indicated that one or more of the above situations is applicable, your next step is to focus the client on the important issues involved in selecting and designing a nonqualified plan. In addition, you need to discern the organization's needs and objectives. A nonqualified plan fact finder can accomplish these steps.

The fact finder the previous table will:

- provide a working framework for soliciting the client's goals

- serve as a due-diligence checklist, which will ensure that important discussions have not been omitted
- operate as a training tool for those who have little or no experience with nonqualified plans
- educate the client about the various needs, objectives, and considerations that are relevant to plan selection and design

Choosing the Right Type of Plan

LO 15.4 **Identify the key design considerations when establishing a nonqualified plan.**

When you have a full understanding of the client's objectives, you can choose the proper nonqualified plan. There are many varieties of nonqualified plans, but our focus will be primarily on deferred-compensation plans. Several terms commonly used in this field that are helpful to understand include:

golden handshakes

- **golden handshakes**—additional benefits that are intended to induce early retirement

golden handcuffs

- **golden handcuffs**—additional benefits that are intended to induce an executive to remain employed, rather than leaving prematurely

golden parachutes

- **golden parachutes**—substantial payments made to executives who are terminated upon change of ownership or corporate control

incentive pay

- **incentive pay**—bonuses given for accomplishing short-term goals that can be used by the executive for retirement purposes

There are two major types of nonqualified plan designs: the salary reduction plan and the supplemental executive-retirement plan. Each approach is discussed below.

Salary Reduction Plans

salary reduction plan

If the employer wants to permit executives to defer current income (in essence, to allow a nonqualified 401(k) look-alike arrangement), a so-called **salary reduction plan** can be used. Salary reduction plans typically give participants the option to defer regular compensation, bonuses, or commissions. These plans are appropriate when executives in the highest marginal income tax bracket anticipate being in a lower tax bracket after retirement. It can also be appropriate simply as a means of income leveling for highly compensated employees whose income would otherwise drop sharply after retirement. What makes the nonqualified salary reduction plan more flexible than the 401(k) plan is that it has no maximum deferral limits. It should also be designed to exclude rank-and-file employees.

A salary reduction plan either can be initiated at the executive's individual option during contract negotiations or offered as a package of perks to selected managers or highly compensated employees. In either circumstance (consistent with the requirements of Sec. 409A), the agreement of deferral should be entered into prior to the beginning of the year on which the services are actually performed to avoid unwanted tax consequences.

Candidates for a salary reduction plan include:

- employers who want to provide a low-cost benefit for highly compensated and management employees (the only employer cost is the cost of the deferral of the tax deduction and the tax imposed on the earnings from the deferred amounts)
- small closely held businesses whose owners' individual marginal tax rate is higher than the applicable corporate tax rate
- organizations that wish to set conditions on a certain amount of executives' salaries or bonuses to induce desired results

EXAMPLE

Before the beginning of each year, the Baltimore Company offers its top executives the opportunity to defer up to $50,000 of their following year's compensation. Deferred amounts grow at some specified interest rate and the accumulated amount will be paid out over a 15-year period, beginning at the later to occur of age 55 or termination of employment.

Supplemental Executive Retirement Plans

supplemental executive retirement plan (SERP)

A **supplemental executive retirement plan (SERP)** satisfies the employer's objective of complementing an existing qualified plan that is not already stretched to the maximum limits by bringing executive retirement benefits (or contributions) up to desired levels. Unlike salary reduction plans, SERPs make available additional employer-provided benefits.

SERPs can complement the underlying qualified plan in one of two ways. They can be designed to provide the "missing piece" of retirement benefit (or contribution) that the employer wants the executive to have. For example, if the employer wants to provide a replacement of 60 percent of an executive's final-average salary and the underlying qualified plan only provides for a 40-percent replacement, the SERP can be designed to provide a benefit equal to 20 percent of the final-average salary. However, in cases where the exact benefit (or contribution) is unknown, such as when an integrated unit-benefit formula is used, SERPs can be designed a second way: to provide for the desired total benefit or contribution (for example, 60 percent of final average compensation), taking into account or offsetting the benefit provided by the qualified plan. This type of SERP is called an offset SERP.

Candidates for SERPs include employers who want to

- cut back benefits under their qualified plans due to increased costs
- provide a higher income replacement ratio for executives than the employer can afford (or may want) to provide for rank-and-file employees
- defeat the $270,000 cap (as indexed for 2017) on compensation that can be considered in determining benefits
- provide a benefit based on total compensation for executives while continuing to provide a benefit based on base pay for rank-and-file employees
- provide a COLA benefit for executives without having to provide a similar benefit to rank-and-file employees

Nonqualified Plan Objectives
- Alternative to qualified plan
- Second tier of benefits
- Cover a select group of highly paid employees
- Salary deferral for executives
- Instant benefit program for executives of a new company
- Meet a wide range of compensation goals
- Satisfy special needs of specific highly compensated employees

DESIGN CONSIDERATIONS

LO 15.6 Describe how a plan can be designed to better protect the interests of the participants.

Even though they are designed to avoid the rules of ERISA (which, as discussed later, most plans are), salary reduction plans and SERPs still have tremendous design flexibility. Without legislative and regulatory constraints, plan design is an interesting and challenging assignment. Let's look at the most common design features used in these plans.

Forfeiture Provisions

A forfeiture provision in a nonqualified plan sets forth certain conditions under which an employee forfeits the benefits he or she would normally get under the plan. Salary reduction plans do not typically contain forfeiture provisions because they represent an employee election to reduce the employee's own salary, which he or she had an absolute right to receive. However, forfeiture provisions are very common in SERPs because they help to achieve a multitude of employer objectives. Let's look at some client problems and see how forfeiture provisions can help solve them.

Successful Transition of Company Leadership

Some businesses are dependent on the special contributions of a few key executives. The retirement of these executives may prove devastating to the organization's profit-making ability. To prevent a drop in revenue and to ensure a smooth transition, a nonqualified plan can contain a provision that requires the executive to provide consulting services after retirement or else forfeit any benefit under the plan.

Retention of Executives

If your client is concerned about inducing an executive to stay on board instead of leaving prematurely, a so-called golden-handcuffs provision should be incorporated into the plan. Many plans accomplish this with a traditional vesting schedule. Since most nonqualified plans are exempt from ERISA, there are no vesting limitations—so a long vesting provision such as 10 year cliff vesting is allowed. A plan could also choose a graded vesting schedule. Longer vesting schedules may help retain executives, but the trade-off is that it may make it more difficult to recruit new executives.

Another approach is to provide that benefits will be forfeited if certain performance goals are not met. These are becoming more common in deferred compensation plans, to ensure that the executives have the same priorities as the board of directors.

It is much more likely that a forfeiture provision will be included in a SERP, that is funded by the employer and provides a supplemental benefit, than in a salary deferral plan that allows employees to make salary deferrals. A forfeiture provision in a salary deferral plan would have the effect of discouraging salary deferral elections.

Competition from Former Employees

A major problem for employers in service industries is an employee who goes to work for a competitor or sets up a competing business. A covenant-not-to-compete provision can deter this behavior. A covenant-not-to-compete provision calls for the forfeiture of nonqualified benefits that have not yet been paid if the employee enters into competition with the employer by opening a competing business. To avoid legal problems, the covenant-not-to-compete provision must be carefully drafted and must be supported by adequate consideration. Towards that end, the covenant-not-to-compete provision should ideally be entered into at the commencement of employment where the new job serves as the adequate consideration. Alternatively, if the need for a covenant-not-to-compete provision arises following the employee's initial date of employment, the nonqualified plan benefits may be able to serve as the adequate consideration. However, if a covenant-not-to-compete is added to a preexisting nonqualified plan, then some other form of consideration must be provided by the employer. Furthermore, the noncompete provision must be reasonable in terms of the geographical area and the time period it covers. For example, a covenant that says a former employee cannot compete in the Northeast for 10 years after the employee leaves employment is probably a violation of public policy and not valid. If the employee is restricted from working for 2 years in the same county, however, the provision is probably valid. The particular facts and circumstances of each case will be determinative. Because the rules for noncompetition clauses vary from state to state, your client should consult an attorney before designing such a provision.

Protecting the Executive

Up to this point, the assumption has been that your client is a taxable business entity. However, your financial services practice may also include solving problems for executives who are negotiating a nonqualified arrangement with their employer. If this is the case, keep the following points in mind:

- Nonqualified plans can protect the executive against involuntary termination because of a change in the control of the business by including a takeover trigger. Also, called a golden parachute, the plan can provide for additional benefits, immediate vesting, and/or immediate payouts at the time of the change in control. The challenge is to design the golden parachute provision to satisfy the Code Sec. 409A change in control provision, and to ensure that the payout is not so large as to deter potential buyers. Under Sec. 409A, a payment upon a change of control is not treated as an accelerated distribution only if the new owners control enough additional stock to own more than 50 percent of the corporation's total fair market value or of the total voting power of the corporation's stock.

- Nonqualified plans can be designed to allow withdrawals prior to termination of employment in cases of an unforeseeable emergency. As required by Section 409A, the plan should spell out the circumstances that constitute an allowable distribution, or it should provide for an independent third party to make the determination.

- Your client should ask for a binding-arbitration clause in case of a dispute. This will save on litigation costs.

Other Features in Plan Design

In addition to forfeiture provisions, there are several other important design features to be considered in nonqualified plans. In fact, in the circumstance where a plan is not required to meet ERISA standards, the only real constraints on plan design are the competitive forces applicable to the employer and the designer's imagination. In general, however, the design features of a nonqualified plan are similar to those of a qualified plan except that they are not inhibited by the Code's restrictions. The following is an overview of some of those standard design features.

Benefit or Contribution Structure

Nonqualified plans can be designed as either defined-benefit or defined-contribution plans. Salary reduction plans are usually designed as defined-contribution plans because they allow executives to defer a specified portion of their salaries each year. SERPs can also be set up as defined-contribution plans, but are more frequently set up as defined-benefit plans. When SERPs are set up as defined-benefit plans, the benefit formula should be consistent with the employer's objectives. This may mean supplementing the employer's qualified plan or avoiding duplication in benefits by the coordination of all benefits received under the employer's qualified and other benefit plans, retirement benefits earned with other employers, and Social Security benefits.

Eligibility

Participation in nonqualified plans is typically restricted to company executives. In fact, it is almost always necessary to restrict participation to management and highly compensated employees in order for the plan to be exempt from ERISA requirements. Under what is referred to as the "top-hat exemption" of ERISA, the plan must be unfunded and maintained "primarily" for a select group of management or highly compensated employees.

In a salary reduction plan or a SERP, the executive's title or position typically dictates inclusion in, or exclusion from, the plan. (For example, all executives above the level of first vice president might be included.) A second way to determine eligibility is by salary. When salary determines eligibility, the chosen dollar amount should be indexed. By taking this precaution, the employer does not risk substantial cost increases caused by the inclusion of executives who are not at the top level but whose salaries have inflated over time. A third common way to determine eligibility is to appoint a compensation committee. When this is done, the members of the committee are given the authority to determine who should be eligible for plan membership.

Disability Provisions

Nonqualified plans frequently contain disability provisions. The employer can stipulate whether disability will be treated like any other termination of employment or whether special provisions will apply. However, care should be taken to coordinate any plan disability benefit with any insured disability benefit that may also cover the employee Most disability insurance policies reduce the insured benefit by any other disability benefits paid by the employer. In addition, the employer must choose whether service will continue to accrue if a disability occurs—in which case the plan should contain a clear definition of disability.

Retirement Age

Another key plan design issue is retirement age. In general, the normal retirement age of the nonqualified plan is the age at which benefits become payable without forfeiture. The employer's personnel objectives determine whether a "young" retirement age (50–62) or an "old" retirement age (65–70) is chosen. If the employer wants to control salary costs by keeping a young work force, then a young retirement age should be chosen (typically, this is coordinated with a young normal retirement age in the qualified plan). If the executives involved have knowledge or experience that is crucial to the employer, however, a later retirement age should be selected.

Key Plan Design Considerations
- Salary deferral or supplemental benefit
- Benefit structure
- Eligibility
- Disability and death benefits
- Forfeiture provisions
- Withdrawals for emergencies
- Change in control and trigger

Death Benefits

Nonqualified plans can provide death benefits, which can cover the preretirement period, the postretirement period, or both. The death benefit chosen depends in part on what type of life insurance is used to fund the plan (if any) and what type of annuity is used for the distribution of benefits from the plan. The choice of a death benefit should, therefore, be closely coordinated with the life insurance product used to fund the plan.

PLAN FUNDING

Nonqualified plans can be funded, unfunded, or informally funded. As you have probably concluded by now, plan funding for tax purposes and "storing" assets to pay future nonqualified promises are two different things from a tax standpoint. Let's take a closer look.

Funded Plans

A nonqualified plan is considered funded for tax purposes when, in order to meet its promise of providing benefits under the nonqualified plan, the company contributes specific assets to an escrow or trust account in which the executive has a current beneficial interest. In other words, to pay benefits, the company sets aside funds that are beyond the reach of the company's general creditors. In addition, a nonqualified plan is funded if the obligation to the executive is backed by a letter of credit from the employer or by a surety bond obtained by the employer. If a nonqualified plan is considered funded, the executive is subject to taxation upon the later to occur of either when contributions are made to the plan or when the employee becomes vested in the benefit (under the economic-benefit doctrine codified in Sec. 83). As discussed later, ERISA rules concerning participation, funding, vesting, fiduciary enforcement, and reporting and disclosure also apply to a funded plan. Because these adverse tax consequences generally defeat the purpose of the plan, most nonqualified plans are designed to be unfunded for both tax and ERISA purposes. One exception, discussed later, is the secular trust, which is typically utilized when benefit security is determined to outweigh the need for income tax deferral.

Unfunded Plans

A nonqualified plan is considered unfunded for tax purposes if there is no reserve set aside to pay the promised benefit under the plan. The Sec. 83 regulations state that a mere promise to pay that is not represented by notes or secured in any way is not regarded as a receipt of property. Therefore, as long as the requirements of Sec. 409A are satisfied, an unfunded and unsecured promise by an employer to pay compensation at some future date does not constitute current taxable income to an executive.

Informally Funded Plans

Unfunded nonqualified plans that do not involve a mechanism for storing funds to pay the nonqualified promised benefits pose a major problem for the executive because his or her benefit payments hinge on the employer's fiscal health at the time benefits become payable. In addition, many executives wonder if their own status will be different by the time they become entitled to collect. Management changes, business buyouts (through a hostile takeover or otherwise), or a demotion due to performance problems or "office politics" may put the executive in an untenable position when he or she approaches the time to collect benefits. The executive is relying mainly on the employer's unsecured (albeit contractual) promise to pay. Thus, executives are caught on the horns of a dilemma. On the one hand, if the plan is funded, executives will be taxed immediately. On the other hand, executives do not want to risk their retirement on an unsecured promise to pay. Because executives want the best of both worlds—as much security as possible without triggering immediate taxation—many plans are informally funded. A plan is informally funded when a reserve is set up to pay the nonqualified benefit, but the assets of the reserve are retained as assets of the company, subject to the claims of the company's creditors. In other words, as long as the executive does not have a current beneficial interest, the plan is considered unfunded for tax purposes. When a plan is informally funded, it is important to consider the other side of the equation—the company's deduction.

Income Tax Effects on the Employer

Under the cash method of accounting, a taxpayer is not entitled to a deduction until benefits have been paid to executives. Some employers are subject to the accrual method of accounting. However, under this method, a taxpayer is entitled to a deduction in the year during which all events have occurred that give rise to the liability, if the amount of such liability can be determined with reasonable accuracy. However, the timing of deductions for the payment of nonqualified deferred compensation comes under special IRS regulations. Unlike the usual tax accounting rules applicable to other deductions, Reg. Sec. 1.404(b)-1T allows a deduction for nonqualified deferred compensation only in the year in which the payment is includible in the executive's gross income. Although unfunded deferred-compensation arrangements often qualify as deductible expenses under the usual accrual requirements, Reg. Sec. 1.404(b)-1T takes precedence and delays the employer's deduction until the income is taxable to the executive.

"Funding" Nonqualified Plans with Life Insurance

LO 15.5 Review the funding requirements and the advantages of funding with life insurance.

Corporate-owned life insurance (COLI) is a popular way for most publicly held and almost all closely held businesses to set up a reserve against future obligations under a nonqualified plan. No single type of contract is best. Most employers, however, prefer policies with premium and investment flexibility and low mortality and expense costs. Because the policy values are generally used to finance retirement benefits, permanent rather than term coverage is indicated.

Advantages of COLI

The use of COLI is attractive for many reasons:

- The tax-free inside buildup that occurs in a life insurance policy is important to a nonqualified plan because, unlike those of a qualified plan, earnings on nonqualified plan assets are not tax deferred.

- Life insurance proceeds received by the employer can protect the employer against an executive's premature death. This works two ways. If the executive is not fully vested in his or her promised benefit at death, or if no death benefit is provided, the excess death benefit received by the employer can be used to cushion the employer against anticipated losses owing to the executive's death. If the executive is fully vested in a substantial death benefit and dies shortly after entering the plan, the life insurance policy will be able to pay the promised benefit in full, whereas the other reserves would have been inadequate.

- Life insurance proceeds received by the employer upon the death of the executive are generally tax free.

- Policies can be borrowed against to help pay the cost of future premiums. If cash flow is a problem, knowing that the funding of his or her benefit will not suffer should give the executive an added sense of security.

- Life insurance funding provides the employer with flexibility. The employer can either use the policy's cash values to pay nonqualified benefits, or use other assets and keep the policy in force until death. If the latter course is taken, the employer can often receive more from the insurance company as death proceeds than it pays out under the nonqualified plan.

- Life insurance policies can be used to provide a supplemental disability benefit. The waiver-of-premium clause in a life policy will enable the executive to get the full nonqualified benefit even if he or she becomes disabled.

- If the life insurance policy purchased on the executive's life is owned by the employer, if the premiums are paid by the employer, and if the employer is the sole beneficiary, then constructive-receipt, economic-benefit, and Sec. 83 problems are avoided.

- If the nonqualified plan requires the company to pay a life income to the executive, by electing a life-income option, the company can transfer to the insurance company the risk that the executive will live beyond his or her normal life expectancy.

Disadvantages of COLI

As with any life insurance product, the financial strength of the company and the insurance company's ability to meet it's promises is of primary concern when using COLI as a funding vehicle for nonqualified deferred-compensation plans. There are several important tax issues to consider as well. First, if policy loans are used to pay retirement benefits, there is a limitation on the corporate deduction for interest paid on policy loans. For policies purchased after June 20, 1986, no deduction is allowed for interest on loans totaling more than $50,000 per insured individual under policies covering officers and employees. Second, the alternative minimum tax (AMT) offers some impediment to the use of life insurance to fund a nonqualified plan because the life insurance that is payable to the employer, although not subject to regular taxes, may be subject to the AMT. If so, employer costs are increased. Employers should be advised that they may need to purchase additional insurance so they can pay any AMT as well as their obligations under the plan. Although the AMT is usually about 15 percent of the death benefit (and in many cases far less), some experts suggest that the employer obtain slightly over 15 percent more life insurance than the amount needed to fund the plan. In any case, the employer's tax advisor should be consulted to determine whether the AMT will apply.

In addition, the Pension Protection Act of 2006 (PPA) added Sec. 101(j) to the Code, which was aimed primarily at curbing the use of COLI covering a broad-based employee group which were in effect an investment vehicle for the employer. The rules codified what many refer to as the insurance industries' "best practices" relating to the use of employer-owned life insurance. The rules allow for the death benefits of the typical COLI policies on key employees issued after August 17, 2006, to remain nontaxable to the employer as long as certain requirements are satisfied. First, policies must be limited to one of the following categories:

- the insured is a director or a highly-compensated employee (among the highest paid 35 percent of all employees) when the COLI is purchased;
- the insured was an employee within 12 months before death; or
- the death benefits are paid to the insured's heirs or used to purchase an equity interest in the employer from the insured's heirs.

Second, the insured must be notified of, and consent to, the life insurance coverage. Third, the employer must file an annual information return which reports certain information regarding the COLI and must keep whatever records are necessary to establish that the requirements for income exclusion have been met.

BENEFIT SECURITY

Because of the income tax and ERISA issues involved in nonqualified plans, it is quite difficult to make benefits as secure for the participants as they are with qualified plans. To solve the security issue, there are three possible solutions: the rabbi trust, the secular trust, and the surety bond. (Unfortunately, no solution is totally satisfactory.)

Rabbi Trust

rabbi trust

With the **rabbi trust** (first conceived in 1981 to provide benefit security for a rabbi), contributions are made to a separate trust. Under the terms of the trust, assets generally cannot revert to the company—meaning that plan assets will be available to pay plan benefits, even if new hostile management takes over the company. However, to avoid current taxation to the participants, the trust's assets remain subject to the claims of the employer's creditors.

For many years, an employer wanting the IRS to rule on the validity of the rabbi trust agreement had to request a private letter ruling. In Rev. Proc. 92-64, the IRS made the use of the rabbi trust more secure by providing a model trust agreement. In order to have IRS approval of a deferred compensation agreement today, the employer in almost all cases must use the IRS's model rabbi trust form.

The model trust generally conforms to IRS guidelines already well known from prior IRS private letter rulings. Optional paragraphs are provided to allow some degree of customization. The model contains some relatively favorable provisions. For example, it allows the use of "springing" irrevocability. Springing irrevocability is a provision under which, if there is a change in employer ownership, the trust becomes irrevocable. Similarly, at the change in control, the employer can be required to make an irrevocable contribution of all remaining deferred compensation. Also, the model permits the rabbi trust to own employer stock. However, the model does not allow "insolvency triggers" that hasten payments to executives when the employer's net worth falls below a certain point. (The IRS fears that accelerating benefit payments when the employer's financial position deteriorates may result in all benefits being paid before any creditors have a chance to attach the trust's assets.) Other requirements, either contained in the model trust or in prior rulings, include the following:

- The assets in a rabbi trust must be available to all general creditors of the company if the company files for bankruptcy or becomes insolvent.
- The participants must not have greater rights than unsecured creditors.
- The plan must provide clear rules describing when benefits will be paid.
- The company must notify the trustee of any bankruptcy or financial hardship that the company is undergoing. When a bankruptcy or financial hardship occurs, the trustee should suspend payment to the trust beneficiary and hold assets for the employer's general creditors.

Another way to protect the participants in the event of a hostile takeover is to give the trustee control over the investment of plan assets upon the change in control. This prevents the "bad guys" from making investments in illiquid employer-leased real estate or an employer-related venture.

Consistent with the requirements of Sec. 409A, participants can elect the form of distribution from the rabbi trust when contributions to the trust are made without triggering constructive receipt. In addition, a change in the form of business organization by the employee's company (from a partnership to an S corporation, for example) will not adversely affect the rabbi trust.

Finally, consistent with the requirements of Sec. 409A (discussed above), executives can take a hardship withdrawal from a rabbi trust without triggering constructive receipt. The withdrawal is limited to an amount reasonably needed to meet the emergency. In addition, the emergency must be unforeseeable—that is, it must pose a severe financial hardship to the participant or result from a loss of property due to casualty or other similar extraordinary and unforeseeable circumstances beyond the participant's control.

Although rabbi trusts accomplish the dual objectives of deferring taxation and providing a measure of retirement security to executives, they have one important disadvantage: they provide no benefit security for executives should the employer go bankrupt. In other words, the executive must stand in line with other general creditors if the employer files for bankruptcy. Rabbi trusts, therefore, are very effective in providing retirement security if the employer is unwilling to pay promised benefits, but they do not provide security if the employer becomes insolvent.

Secular Trusts

secular trust

In situations where the employer's ability to pay promised benefits comes into question, some professionals recommend a secular trust in lieu of a rabbi trust. Like a rabbi trust, a **secular trust** calls for an irrevocable contribution on the employer's part to finance promises under a nonqualified plan. Unlike a rabbi trust, however, funds held in a secular trust cannot be reached by the employer's creditors. This means that executives can expect to receive promised benefits even if the employer goes bankrupt (giving the participants a similar level of security that qualified plans have). However, there is a significant price for this security. Contributions to the trust are taxable at the later of the date when contributions are made or benefits become nonforfeitable. (See the earlier discussion of Sec. 83.)

Unfortunately, several IRS private letter rulings have also indicated that in some circumstances, trust earnings would be subject to double taxation: once when earned at the trust level and again when actually paid out to the employee. Because of the unsettled tax issues and because individual tax rates (for executives) are generally higher than the corporate rate, secular trusts are not commonly used today.

Table 15-2
Comparison of Funding Approaches

Type of Plan	Funds Set Aside Prior to Retirement	Secured against Unwillingness to Pay	Secured against Employer Insolvency	Delayed Taxation for Executives
Unfunded pay-as-you-go plan	No	No	No	Yes
Rabbi trust	Yes	Yes	No	Yes
Secular trust	Yes	Yes	Yes	No

Surety Bonds

For the executive who feels uncomfortable with the possibility of benefits going unpaid from a rabbi trust because of an employer bankruptcy but who wants to avoid the use of a secular trust because of the tax consequences, an alternative may be available. A surety bond provides for a bonding company to pay promised benefits if the employer defaults on the promise to pay nonqualified benefits—thus providing the executive with an indirect means of securing the employer's unsecured promise.

surety bonds

In order to prevent the purchase of a surety bond from triggering a constructive-receipt, economic-benefit, or Sec. 83 problem, certain precautions must be taken. The executive must bear the cost of the **surety bond**, and the employer should not have an involvement with the bonding company. If these precautions are taken, the executive can have the security of continued protection for nonqualified retirement payments.

The downside is that surety bonds for nonqualified plans can be expensive and difficult to obtain. Premiums are typically one to 3 percent of the annual amount deferred, plus earnings. The employer must also have a strong balance sheet to qualify for the coverage. In addition, very few insurance companies provide this type of coverage. Finally, renewal of the bond can be difficult if the employer experiences an economic downturn. Surety bonds are issued for a range of from 3 to 5 years and may not be renewed if bankruptcy is on the horizon. Ironically, this is when they are most needed!

THE INSTALLATION OF NONQUALIFIED PLANS

ERISA Considerations

LO 15.7 Discuss the installation and administration concerns for nonqualified plans.

top-hat exemption

When designing a nonqualified plan, in almost all cases, the employer will want to avoid coverage under ERISA by satisfying the **top-hat exemption** of ERISA. This requires that the plan be unfunded and maintained by an employer, primarily for the purpose of providing deferred compensation for a select group of management and/or highly compensated employees. The "unfunded" requirement is generally not problematic, as the employer can still utilize one of the informal funding approaches discussed above. The more difficult task is determining which employees can be covered as highly compensated employees. Unfortunately, the DOL has not provided any clear guidance on this issue. It is clear, however, that the Code's definition of highly compensated is not determinative here. From a practical perspective, a plan that covers only a few highly paid executives will probably comply. As the group gets bigger, however, there is less certainty. To safeguard the plan, the plan documents should specify that the employer has the right to amend the plan to limit the group of covered employees, conforming to any future DOL guidance on this issue.

An unfunded top-hat plan is exempt from ERISA's participation, vesting, benefit accrual, funding, and fiduciary provisions. It is still subject to ERISA's reporting, disclosure, administration, and enforcement provisions. However, the reporting provisions can be satisfied simply by filing a statement with the DOL (at the time the plan is established) that includes the following information: the employer's name and address, the employer's identification number, a declaration that the employer maintains the plan primarily to provide deferred compensation to a select group of management or highly paid employees, the number of such plans maintained by the employer, and the number of employees in each plan.

A second type of nonqualified plan that is exempt from ERISA coverage is an excess-benefit plan. This type of plan is not as prevalent as the top-hat plan, but it nevertheless can be useful in the appropriate circumstances. An excess-benefit plan is a plan maintained by an employer solely for the purpose of providing benefits for certain employees in excess of the limitations on contributions and benefits imposed by Sec. 415 on plans to which that section applies, without regard to whether the plan is funded. Unfunded excess-benefit plans are totally exempt from ERISA; those which are funded are partially exempt.

EXAMPLE

An employer's profit-sharing plan provides for a contribution of 25 percent of compensation. For an employee who is earning compensation equal to the Sec. 401(a)(17) cap ($270,000 in 2017), Section 415 limits the contribution on the employee's behalf to $54,000 (2017). Without Section 415, the employee would be entitled to a contribution of $67,500 ($270,000 x .25) if he or she was earning the compensation cap. The employer can adopt an excess-benefit plan to enable the employee to receive an additional annual contribution of $113,500 ($67,500 - $54,000) (based off of 2017 numbers but this could be higher if the person earned more than the compensation cap, a number that the employer is also not bound by in the nonqualified world).

The advantage of using an excess-benefit plan as compared to a top-hat plan is that an excess-benefit plan can cover any employee, not just a member of a select group of management and highly-compensated employees. The disadvantage of an excess-benefit plan is that only a small number of employers provide a qualified retirement plan that by design provides the maximum contributions or benefits allowable under Sec. 415. In addition, the Sec. 415 limitations are not the only provisions which can operate to reduce a participant's benefits or contributions. The following are rules that also impose restrictions which could have a similar impact: Sec. 401(a)(17) (imposing a cap on COLA-adjusted compensation), Section 401(a)(30) (limitation on elective deferrals), and the Sec. 401(k) ADP and ACP nondiscrimination tests. However, for those plans that can qualify, an excess-benefit plan is relatively easy to design and implement.

Installation Process

The final issue we will consider in connection with your client's nonqualified plans is their installation and administration. In order to install a nonqualified plan, the employer should adopt a corporate resolution authorizing the purchase of life insurance to indemnify the business for the expenses it is likely to incur. A second resolution should authorize the production of either a contract or plan document that will spell out both the employer's and the executives' benefits and obligations. In addition, a rabbi trust document or a secular trust document should be created. Finally, the ERISA statement referred to above should be completed and sent to the Department of Labor.

SEC. 457 PLANS

LO 15.8   **Explain which deferred-compensation arrangements are subject to Code Sec. 457(b) and which are subject to Code Sec. 457(f).**

Up to this point, nonqualified plans have been examined in the context of the for-profit business where the business owner and selected employees want to save for retirement without being subject to the requirements that apply to qualified plans. In that context, the employer is entitled to an immediate deduction only if the employee is currently taxed, or conversely, the employee may defer tax only if the employer's deduction is deferred.

The tax tension that exists between employers and employees of for-profit companies is absent for employers that are tax-exempt entities. Because a tax deduction is meaningless for a tax-exempt employer, the tax-exempt employer is more inclined to allow an employee to defer compensation than is its for-profit counterpart. Recognizing this difference between for-profit and tax-exempt employers, Congress established a separate tax regime applicable to deferred compensation for employees and independent contractors employed by state and local governments and tax-exempt organizations. These tax rules are found in Sec. 457.

Sec. 457 deferred compensation plan

There are two types of **Sec. 457 deferred compensation plans**: 457(b) eligible plans and 457(f) ineligible plans. The former are similar to qualified retirement plans and are intended to ensure that tax-favored savings are used primarily for retirement purposes. The deferred compensation in an eligible plan is taxed when it is paid or made available to the employee. A participant in a 457(f) ineligible plan will be taxed on deferred compensation if his right to receive those amounts is not subject to a substantial risk of forfeiture.

457(b) Eligible Plans

The five principal requirements applicable to a 457(b) eligible plan are the following:

- Participation limited to service providers—Only employees and independent contractors who perform services for the employer may participate.

- Maximum annual deferral amount—The plan must provide that the maximum amount of compensation which may be deferred under the plan for the taxable year may not exceed the lesser of $18,000 (the applicable dollar amount for 2017) or 100 percent of the participant's includible compensation. (457(b) contributions can be made in addition to 403(b) or 401(k) salary deferrals, as these limits are not aggregated.) The term includible compensation means compensation for services performed for the employer which is currently includible in gross income (after taking into account the deductions allowed under Sec. 457 and other similar income tax provisions.) Prior to 2002, amounts excluded from income under Section 403(b) and Sec. 401(k) plans were required to reduce the maximum allowable Sec. 457(b) deferral. This was a major deterrent to the use of 457(b) eligible plans. However, since 2002 this is no longer the case, and it has provided a significant impetus to the adoption of 457(b) eligible plans as supplemental plans in recent years.

- Timing of deferral election—The plan must provide that compensation will be deferred for a calendar month only if an agreement providing for such deferral has been entered into before the beginning of the month. However, with respect to a new employee, a plan may provide that compensation is to be deferred for the calendar month during which the participant first becomes an employee if an agreement providing for such deferral is entered into on or before the first day on which the participant becomes an employee.

- Timing of distributions—Amounts cannot be made available under the plan to participants or beneficiaries earlier than (i) the calendar year in which the participant attains age 70½, (ii) when the participant has a severance from employment with the employer, or (iii) when the participant is faced with an unforeseeable emergency. In addition, the plan must comply with the minimum-distribution requirements of Sec. 409(a)(9). Finally, a plan may permit a distribution of benefits pursuant to a qualified domestic relations order. If an amount becomes available pursuant to one of the distribution events described in (i), (ii) or (iii), above, a participant can elect, but only once, to defer commencement of distributions, provided that payments have not yet begun. Participants in a nongovernmental 457(b) eligible plan cannot avoid taxation by rolling over a distribution into an IRA or another plan.

- Property rights—All amounts of compensation deferred under the plan, all property and rights purchased with such amounts, and all income attributable to such amounts must remain solely the property of the employer, subject to the claims of the employer's general creditors, until the deferred compensation is made available to the participants and beneficiaries.

EXAMPLE

Smithtown Health System (SHS), a Sec. 501(c)(3) organization, maintains a Sec. 403(b) plan for its employees. Under this plan, employees can contribute the maximum allowable deferrals. SHS matches 50 percent of these deferrals up to 6 percent of compensation. SHS also makes a nonelective contribution equal to 5 percent of compensation. SHS can adopt a 457(b) eligible plan, which will allow its highly compensated employees to supplement their 403(b) elective deferrals by making additional elective deferrals up to the $18,000 limit (for 2017).

From a planning perspective it's important to note that 457(b) contributions can be made in addition to salary deferrals under a 401(k) or 403(b) plan, meaning that a nonprofit organization can have both a 403(b) and a 457(b) plan. Also, 457(b) plans can allow a special catch-up contribution in the last three years prior to normal retirement age of up to twice the annual contribution limit. This amount is reduced if an individual has always contributed close to or the maximum allowable amount.

Another interesting difference between 457 plans and other types of retirement plans is that the 10 percent early withdrawal penalty tax does not apply to withdrawals made prior to age 59½.

Government-Sponsored Plans

Code Section 457 was at first a provision that primarily limited the nonqualified deferred compensation for employees of nonprofit organizations and government entities. With regard to nonprofits this is still the case, and for the most part these plans operate like nonqualified plans sponsored by for-profit entities. For example, benefits cannot be rolled over into an IRA, and plans must remain "unfunded" and be limited to key executives to avoid ERISA coverage.

Several changes to the rules over the years have made plans sponsored by government entities quite different. In reaction to several municipalities filing bankruptcy and participants losing benefits, government 457(b) plans must now be held in an irrevocable trust.

Also, because government entities (other than public school systems) cannot sponsor 403(b) or 401(k) plans, government 457(b) plans have become the 401(k) for state and local governments. The law allows benefits from these plans to be rolled to an IRA or other tax-advantaged plan, and participants have the right to elect a direct rollover as they do in qualified plans and 403(b) arrangements. Government 457(b) plans can also give participants the option to make the catch-up contribution after age 50 that is allowed in 401(k) and 403(b) plans (as long as the special catch-up election is not made in the same year). Also, government plans can give participants the option to make a Roth election on salary deferrals.

Coordination with ERISA

A 457(b) eligible plan is technically allowed to cover any group of employees or independent contractors. However, as a practical matter, a plan sponsored by a nonprofit organization must limit coverage to a select group of management and highly compensated employees to satisfy what is called the ERISA top-hat exemption. Otherwise, the plan would be subject to the ERISA funding requirements which would violate the 457(b) requirement that the plan be unfunded. A 457(b) eligible plan established by a state or local government is exempt from ERISA and consequently, does not have to satisfy the top-hat plan exemption.

457(f) Ineligible Plans

If a plan does not meet the requirements of Sec. 457(b), then the deferred compensation is included in the compensation of the participant when there is no longer a substantial risk of forfeiture. These noncomplying plans are referred to as 457(f) ineligible plans. Because employees do not want to pay tax on compensation they have not yet received, almost all 457(f) ineligible plans provide for distributions when the deferred compensation vests. A 457(f) ineligible plan is broadly defined to include any agreement or arrangement.

> **EXAMPLE**
>
> John Donovan is an executive of a nonprofit corporation. John has earned a bonus of $100,000, payable in 3 years together with interest, provided that John remains employed for the entire 3-year period. Since the $100,000 amount exceeds the limit

under Sec. 457(b), this deferred arrangement is a 457(f) ineligible plan. Because John must work for 3 years in order to receive the bonus, it is subject to a substantial risk of forfeiture and will not be taxable until the end of the 3-year period. At that time the bonus will be paid.

Although 457(b) eligible plans are exempt from Sec. 409A, 457(f) ineligible plans are not. Accordingly, 457(f) ineligible plans must satisfy the Sec. 409A restrictions on the timing of distributions, acceleration of deferrals, and deferral elections. However, unlike taxable employers, the penalty for failing to meet the Sec. 409A requirements is not so much the acceleration of taxation, since employees of tax exempts are already subject to tax when the substantial risk of forfeiture lapses. Rather, the real penalty is the 20-percent additional tax imposed on a service provider who has violated the requirements of Sec. 409A.

EXECUTIVE-BONUS LIFE INSURANCE PLANS

LO 15.9   Describe an executive-bonus life insurance plan.

Sec. 162 plan

An alternative that can be used in combination with, or in lieu of, the previously discussed nonqualified plans is an executive-bonus life insurance plan (also known as a **Sec. 162 plan**). Like a nonqualified plan, an executive-bonus life insurance plan can be provided on a discriminatory basis to help business owners and select executives save for retirement. The executive-bonus life insurance plan, however, does not provide for the deferral of income. Under an executive-bonus life insurance plan, the corporation pays a bonus to the executive for the purpose of purchasing cash-value life insurance. The executive is the policy owner, the insured, and the person who designates the beneficiary. The corporation's only connection (albeit a major one) is to fund premium payments and, in a few cases, to secure the application for insurance. Bonuses can be paid out by the corporation in either of two ways. The corporation can pay the premiums directly to the insurer or pay the bonus to the executive, who in turn pays the policy premiums. In either case, the corporation deducts the contribution at the time it is made (this is in direct contrast to most deferred-compensation plans) and includes the amount of the payment in the executive's W-2 (taxable) income.

> **YOUR FINANCIAL SERVICES PRACTICE: NONRETIREMENT APPLICATIONS FOR EXECUTIVE-BONUS PLANS**
>
> In addition to being a retirement planning tool, executive-bonus life insurance plans can be used in several other ways to serve your clients. Some planners use them in lieu of superimposed group term life insurance (life insurance over the tax-sheltered $50,000

limit). Another use of Sec. 162 plans is to help the executive to purchase an insurance policy to fund a cross-purchase buy-sell agreement. Without these agreements, partners may not have the assets to continue the business when one of them retires or dies. A third use of executive-bonus life insurance plans is to provide the executive's estate with a source of liquid funds to pay estate taxes. Restrictions on the amount of insurance that may be used under group term life plans and qualified retirement plans make the liquidity issue an important executive concern.

Because payments made under executive-bonus life insurance plans are W-2 income, bonuses are subject to federal, state, and local tax withholding requirements, to Social Security taxes (unless the wage base has already been exceeded) and to Medicare taxes.

Implementation of Sec. 162 Plans

Executive-bonus plans are fairly easily implemented. First, as with all forms of nonqualified compensation, a corporate resolution that authorizes the business expenditure should be obtained. Second, those in charge should select the executives to be included in the plan and the amount of benefits they will receive. Third, either the executive or the corporation should secure the application for insurance. And finally, the executive should apply for the policy as the owner and designate the policy's beneficiary.

Double-Bonus Plans

double-bonus plan

Concern over the receipt of additional taxable income from executive-bonus life insurance plans has caused many employers to provide a second bonus to alleviate any tax that the business owner or executive may pay. (These plans are typically called **double-bonus plans**.) There will be a tax on the second bonus, so the work sheet below helps to calculate the total amount needed for both bonuses.

Table 15-3 Double-Bonus Worksheet	
Step 1: State the target premium (the amount of the first bonus).	_____
Step 2: Specify the applicable tax rate (including federal state, local, and all other applicable taxes).	_____
Step 3: Subtract the step 2 amount from 1.00	_____
Step 4: Divide the step 1 amount by the step 3 amount to find the amount of both bonuses.	_____

EXAMPLE

JANCO wants to provide executive Kathy Beamer with a $10,000 nontaxable bonus to pay the premium under her cash-value life insurance policy. JANCO will have to provide Kathy with $16,666.67, determined as follows:	
Step 1: State the target premium.	$10,000.00
Step 2: State the individual's tax rate	.40
Step 3: Subtract the step 2 amount from 1.00	.60
Step 4: Divide the step 1 amount by the step 3 amount to find the amount of both bonuses.	$16,666.67
Note that the 40 percent aggregate tax rate used in the example includes a 31 percent federal income tax rate, a 4 percent state income tax rate, a city income tax rate of 3.55 percent and Medicare taxes of 1.45 percent. In lieu of the work sheet, the following formula can be used: Amount of first bonus ÷ (1 – tax rate) = Amount of both bonuses	

CHAPTER REVIEW

Key Terms and Concepts

- golden handshakes
- golden handcuffs
- golden parachutes
- incentive pay
- salary reduction plan
- supplemental executive retirement plan (SERP)
- rabbi trust
- secular trust
- surety bonds
- top-hat exemption
- Sec. 457 deferred compensation plan
- Sec. 162 plan
- double-bonus plan

Chapter 15: Review Questions

Review questions are based on the learning objectives in this chapter. Thus, a [3] at the end of a question means that the question is based on learning objective 3. If there are multiple objectives, they are all listed.

1. What are the advantages for a financial services professional of becoming involved in the nonqualified deferred-compensation market? [15.1]

2. Discuss the differences between a qualified plan and a nonqualified plan. [15.1]

3. Will a postretirement consulting agreement always be considered a substantial risk of forfeiture? [15.2]

4. An executive has just become fully vested in a $20,000 account balance held in an irrevocable trust. The benefit cannot be paid out for 5 more years. Under what theory is this deferred vested amount subject to current income tax? [15.2]

5. Sec. 409A would allow distributions from a nonqualified plan in which of the following circumstances? [15.2]
   a. Upon the death of the participant
   b. Payable to the participant 10 years from now
   c. As a financial hardship to pay for a family member's college tuition
   d. As a financial hardship for a spouse's funeral expenses

6. What is the general rule that determines when deferred compensation is considered wages for employment tax purposes? [15.2]

7. Identify the planning situations in which a nonqualified plan should be used. [15.3]

8. Rhonda Rolodex is the owner of The Mainline Office Supply Company. In order to "keep her top people happy," Rhonda would like to set up a nonqualified plan for the top 20 executives in her 200-employee company. Rhonda has asked her financial services professional how she can best accomplish this objective. How should the planner advise Rhonda? [15.3]

9. Briefly describe the following: [15.3]
   a. golden handshakes
   b. golden handcuffs
   c. golden parachutes
   d. incentive pay

10. Describe a salary reduction plan. [15.3]

11. Describe a supplemental executive retirement plan (SERP). [15.3]

12. Jersey Technical Electronics (JTE) has been a very successful business, thanks to the personal contacts Sue Edison has throughout the electronics industry. The owners of JTE fear that Sue, now 60, will retire shortly and the business will suffer. How can a nonqualified plan with a consulting clause help? [15.4]

13. Explain how a nonqualified plan can be designed to help in the following situations: [15.4]

a. Rayco, Inc. is concerned about its key executives leaving prior to retirement age.

b. Lawyer Prudence Juris is concerned that one of her junior partners will leave, taking some of the firm's clients with her.

14. Howard Hayes, an executive at a local manufacturing firm, has asked his insurance agent what provisions he should ask the firm's owners to put into his nonqualified plan. What provisions should the agent suggest? [15.4]

15. Briefly describe how nonqualified plans can be designed with regard to their [15.4]
    a. benefit structure
    b. eligibility provisions
    c. disability provisions
    d. retirement age provisions
    e. death benefit provisions

16. List the reasons why life insurance is frequently used to fund nonqualified plans. [15.5]

17. How does a rabbi trust work? [15.5]

18. How does a secular trust work? [15.6]

19. What is the top-hat exemption from ERISA? [15.7]

20. Discuss the procedures for installing and administering a nonqualified plan. [15.7]

21. Describe the two forms of 457 plans. [15.8]

22. Describe an executive-bonus life insurance plan. Also, calculate the correct bonus amount if the insurance premium is $5,000 and the executive's tax rate is 40 percent. [15.9]

Chapter 15: Review Answers

1. Financial services professionals working in the pension area may want to offer nonqualified plans for a number of reasons: (1) to provide comprehensive services, (2) to gain access to an upscale market, and (3) to find a good market for significant life insurance sales (for funding the nonqualified plans).

2. In a qualified plan, the sponsor is given tax advantages in exchange for covering a wide group of employees and meeting a large number of "qualification requirements." In a nonqualified plan, the employer is subject to the normal rules that apply to the taxation of compensation, but in exchange has much more design freedom.

3. It will depend upon the facts and circumstances of the case. The parties must demonstrate that the consulting agreement requires the fulfillment of a meaningful effort by the executive, and there must be a definite possibility that the failure to consult could occur.

4. Under the concept of economic benefit, deferred compensation may be taxed currently if the amount is set aside irrevocably for an executive, even if the benefit is not available currently.

5.
   a. Yes.
   b. Yes.
   c. No. College tuition for a child is not considered an unforeseeable emergency in the regulations.
   d. Yes.

6. An amount deferred under a nonqualified plan must be considered wages for employment tax purposes as of the later of the date the services are performed, or when there is no substantial risk of forfeiture of the rights to such amount.

7. The course materials identify many objectives that a nonqualified plan can meet. These objectives fall into three general categories. Nonqualified plans can be used as an alternative to qualified plans, as supplemental benefits for executives, or as a tax-sheltering device for a business owner.

8. One of the first concerns the advisor should have is whether Rhonda would be better served by a nonqualified plan or some other form of executive compensation, such as an incentive stock option plan, incentive pay, salary increases, executive bonuses, or some form of noncash reward (a company car or a country club membership). Rhonda

should be made aware of the various executive-compensation techniques available, and the advisor should discuss the advantages and disadvantages that each technique holds in Rhonda's situation.

If Rhonda feels a nonqualified deferred-compensation plan is appropriate, the advisor should help her fill out a nonqualified plan fact finder. The fact finder will help Rhonda to prioritize her objectives and it will enable the agent to gather the information necessary for making insightful suggestions and rendering accurate advice.

9. a. The term golden handshakes implies any type of plan that encourages retirement through the use of a financial reward.

   b. The term golden handcuffs implies a plan that provides additional benefits that are intended to induce an executive to remain employed.

   c. The term golden parachutes denotes benefit plans provided to soften financial hardship if an executive is terminated upon a change in the company's ownership.

   d. The term incentive pay refers to bonuses given for accomplishing short-term goals that can be used by the executive for retirement purposes.

10. A salary reduction plan gives participants the option to defer compensation as a way for them to lower their current income taxes and build retirement income.

11. A SERP provides additional employer-provided retirement benefits to executives. The objective is typically to complement an existing qualified plan.

12. Because JTE is dependent on Sue to bring in business through her personal contacts, JTE should strive to secure her unique talents beyond her retirement. The firm can protect against a drop in revenue when Sue retires by setting up a nonqualified plan that provides retirement benefits and requires her to continue working on a part-time consulting basis.

13. a. The Rayco nonqualified plan can be designed to include a golden-handcuffs provision, which discourages executives from leaving the employment of your client by providing for the forfeiture of substantial benefits if service is voluntarily terminated prior to normal retirement age.

   b. The law firm's nonqualified plan can be designed to include a covenant-not-to-compete provision, which calls for the forfeiture of nonqualified benefits if the employee enters into competition with the employer, either by opening a competing business herself or by working for a competitor. In order to be considered valid, the covenant-not-to-compete provision must be carefully drafted. The provision should be reasonable in terms of the geographical area and the time period over which it applies.

14. An executive may want benefits to accelerate in case of a change in control in the event that the financial condition of the company deteriorates. He or she may also want the ability to access benefits prior to retirement in case of a financial hardship.

15. a. Salary reduction plans are usually designed as defined-contribution plans, while supplemental executive retirement plans (SERPs) can be either defined-contribution or defined-benefit plans.

    b. Participation generally needs to be restricted to a select group of management or highly compensated employees in order to avoid ERISA coverage.

    c. The plan can provide for full vesting, distribution, and/or additional retirement accruals when a participant goes out on disability. Of course, it is crucial to coordinate benefits between the nonqualified plan and other employer plans.

    d. With no legal limitations, choosing the plan's retirement age is strictly a matter of meeting the plan's benefit objectives at a cost that is affordable to the employer.

    e. Nonqualified plans can provide preretirement and/or postretirement death benefits. The choice of a death benefit should, therefore, be closely coordinated with the life insurance product used in the plan.

16. Life insurance as a funding vehicle for nonqualified plans has the following strengths: (1) it has tax-free inside buildup; (2) in most circumstances, the company receives tax-free death benefits; (3) preretirement death benefits can protect the employer from financial losses or can be used to fund the participant's benefit; (4) it has funding flexibility; and (5) there are supplemental disability benefits.

17. In a rabbi trust, assets contributed to the trust are typically irrevocable to the extent that they cannot be returned to the employer, which protects the participants in case of a change in management. However, to avoid current taxation to the participants (at the time contributions are made to the trust), assets must continue to be available for the claims of unsecured creditors.

18. In contrast, a secular trust can protect against both change in control and insolvency, but with the adverse consequence that assets are taxable at the time they are contributed (or when the participant's benefits become nonforfeitable).

19. Almost all executive nonqualified deferred-compensation plans are drafted to satisfy the top-hat exemption of ERISA. Without an exemption, the plan would have

to satisfy certain vesting, participation, and funding requirements. To satisfy the top-hat exemption, the plan must be unfunded and be maintained by an employer primarily for the purpose of providing deferred compensation for a select group of management and/or highly compensated employees. A final requirement of the exemption is that the plan sponsor send a one-page notice of the plan to the Department of Labor.

20. In order to install a nonqualified plan, the employer should accept a corporate resolution adopting the plan and authorizing the funding mechanism (typically the purchase of life insurance). The sponsor must also create a plan document. If a rabbi trust is used, a trustee must be appointed and a trust document drafted. Finally, a one-page ERISA notice should be completed and sent to the Department of Labor.

21. Think of Code Sec. 457 as a provision that limits and controls the taxation of any nonqualified plan sponsored by a nonprofit organization or government entity. There are two types of Sec. 457 plans, an eligible plan and an ineligible plan. The former limits the amount of salary deferral contributions that a participant can contribute, but the participant's accounts are not taxed until distributed. The latter does not limit the amounts that can be contributed by either the participant or the employer, but the participant's accounts are taxed as soon as they become nonforfeitable.

22. An executive-bonus life insurance program, sometimes known as a double-bonus plan, is a plan in which the employer pays the premium for a life insurance policy for the executive. With this type of plan, the executive is the owner and selects the beneficiary. The premium payments are taxed as compensation to the executive. The employer may also pay an additional amount to cover the taxes due on the premium payments (the double-bonus part). To determine the double-bonus amount, divide the premium by 1 minus the individual's marginal tax rate. For a $5,000 insurance premium, the bonus is $8,333, calculated as follows: $5.000/(1 − .40).

Chapter 16

Equity-Based Compensation Plans: And Overview

Learning Objectives

An understanding of the material in this chapter should enable the student to

- **LO 16.1** Identify the reasons for using equity-based compensation.
- **LO 16.2** Identify the factors in assessing whether one or more forms of equity-based compensation are appropriate for a particular closely held corporation.
- **LO 16.3** Describe common features of a nonqualified stock option program and the tax consequences of such a program.
- **LO 16.4** Compare incentive stock options with nonqualified stock options.
- **LO 16.5** Identify uses of employee stock purchase plans and the advantages of such programs.
- **LO 16.6** Explain the tax treatment of restricted stock, phantom stock and stock appreciation rights programs.

Up to this point, the emphasis has been on the use of a tax-sheltered retirement plan or a nonqualified deferred-compensation plan to meet the needs of the small business and the small-business owner. However, another lucrative market is open to financial services professionals who are servicing the retirement and capital accumulation needs of businesses and their owners. This market involves the various methods and arrangements by which employees are compensated through the transfer of stock or equity of the employer to its executives and managers. These compensation techniques utilizing the employer's stock are generally referred to as equity-based compensation.

REASONS FOR EQUITY-BASED COMPENSATION

LO 16.1 Identify the reasons for using equity-based compensation.

Equity-based compensation is a popular component of a company's total compensation package for at least three reasons. First, because stock is a capital asset under current tax law, it has the potential to offer the employee who receives it capital gain treatment for any increase in its value. Second, it serves as an incentive for employees who receive it. Once an employee owns stock in the employer, he or she can share directly in the consequences of his or her efforts through increases in the stock's value. Third, in the appropriate circumstances it may be a less costly form of compensation than cash or other forms of property to the employer and its controlling shareholders. However, as will be discussed later in this chapter, in the private company context this potential advantage has to be examined very closely.

Whether an employer is a public company or a closely held corporation, there is a positive cachet associated with receiving an award of stock in the employer. The receipt of stock is generally perceived as an acknowledgment that the recipient is such a valued employee that he or she is worthy of receiving a "piece of the action." Moreover, in large public companies stock compensation also aligns the interests of the executives with those of the shareholders. In this context, incentives are structured so that the executives will perform in a manner that will cause the value of the stock to increase.

In "start-up" companies, stock compensation is often used because cash is in short supply and stock is the best way to attract and retain qualified executives. The executive expects that a substantial gain will be realized if the employer is successful and is subsequently sold or eventually goes public. Conversely, stock compensation is not as popular with closely held corporations where there is little possibility of the company going public and where the stock has less value to the executive because there is no public market for it. Nevertheless, there are ways to overcome these disadvantages and to utilize stock compensation to reward and motivate the executives of smaller companies.

Equity-based compensation plans help the business owner and selected employees accumulate wealth for retirement and for other financial needs without being subject to the requirements that apply to qualified retirement and savings plans. Moreover, they have the potential of turning what otherwise might have been ordinary income into the more favorable capital gains. However, similar to nonqualified deferred-compensation arrangements, there is a trade-off for allowing the employer complete discretion in plan design and in choosing the employees who will be covered by an equity-based compensation plan—that is, the employer loses the ability to make a before-tax contribution on the employee's behalf that is simultaneously deductible to the business. Instead, the employer is entitled to an immediate deduction only if the employee is currently taxed, or conversely, the employee may defer tax only if the employer's deduction is deferred.

Current tax law generally provides favorable tax treatment to equity-based compensation for both the employer and the employee. As will be seen when each form of equity-based compensation is analyzed individually, the thrust of the applicable tax provisions is to ensure that, from the employee's perspective, the transfer of a stock award is properly analyzed so that it can be divided into the proper amounts of compensation income and capital gain and that the timing of the income realization is properly determined. Similarly, from the employer's perspective, the tax law seeks to limit the employer's deduction to the amount of the employee's ordinary income and to correlate the timing of the deduction with the occurrence of the employee's taxable event.

ASSESSING THE CLOSELY HELD BUSINESS

LO 16.2   Identify the factors in assessing whether one or more forms of equity-based compensation are appropriate for a particular closely held corporation.

As a financial services professional, the primary market for the design of and the planning for equity-based compensation is the closely held corporation and its owner-employees. In assessing whether one or more forms of equity-based compensation are appropriate for a particular closely held corporation, the following seven considerations should be evaluated and discussed with the client.

Valuation

By definition, equity-based compensation arrangements relate in one way or another to the value of the employer's stock. Such valuation can be important in at least four points in time: when the program is established, when a stock award is received by an employee, when the stock award becomes vested, and when the employee decides to sell or otherwise dispose of the stock award. These valuation issues are particularly acute when there is no public market for the employer's stock. Under these circumstances, the employer must decide on an appropriate valuation formula for the stock awarded under its program. As will be discussed in greater detail later in this chapter, a proper valuation formula is also important for tax purposes. If the valuation formula produces a value that the IRS determines to be less than fair market value, a stock award may be treated as deferred compensation and may become subject to the requirements of Code Sec. 409A.

There is no single approach to determining the best valuation formula. Any number of factors, such as book value, earnings per share, or net revenue, can be taken into account under the valuation formula. However, no matter how the stock's value is measured or determined, the valuation should be sensitive to those aspects of the corporation's financial performance that the corporation wants the recipients of the stock awards to be motivated to improve. In addition, the same valuation formula should be used for all purposes under the program. In other words, it should be applied evenhandedly so that stock awarded under the program is valued no differently than the stock that is being repurchased by the corporation.

Mechanism for Repurchasing Stock

If an equity-based compensation program is to be successful in retaining and motivating employees, the award recipients must have a market within which the employee can sell or otherwise realize an economic benefit from his or her equity interest. This is fairly simple when the employer's stock is publicly traded and there is an institutional market for the shares. However, in the case of a closely held corporation, the "market" typically takes the form of a contractual obligation of either the corporation or the other shareholders to repurchase the employee's equity interest at a formula price, whenever the employee decides to sell or when the employee's relationship with the employer is terminated. Consequently, in this context, both employer and employee have a strong interest in entering into some form of shareholders' agreement, which will prevent shares from being sold to third parties or from being retained by a person who is no longer an employee.

When an employer provides the market for the stock awarded to employees under an equity-based compensation program, the program becomes hard to differentiate from a typical deferred-compensation arrangement. For example, if an employee exercises an option in order to obtain stock having a value of $1,000 and the stock's value increases at the rate of 10 percent per year, this is no different than the employee deferring $1,000 from his or her income and receiving a 10 percent return on that deferral. In either event, at the end of 15 years, the employee is entitled to a payment of almost $4,200. A significant difference between these two arrangements arises in connection with how the $4,200 is treated for tax purposes. Under the stock program, the employer makes the $4,200 payment with after-tax dollars—that is, the payment represents a capital transaction, and the employee recognizes a capital gain of $3,200 ($4,200 less the $1,000 purchase price). Under the deferred-compensation arrangement, the employer is entitled to a tax deduction for its $4,200 payment, as additional compensation, and the employee is taxed on $4,200 of ordinary income. The after-tax result of the stock award favors the employee while the after-tax result of the deferred-compensation arrangement favors the employer. Consequently, in determining whether to adopt an equity-based compensation plan, the employer must factor into its decision the additional tax cost associated with having to repurchase the shares awarded under the program.

Performance Criteria

Equity-based compensation plans can differ in the degree to which they reward both the overall success of the employer and the performance of particular employees. Some equity-based compensation plans allow employees to benefit from the change in the employer's overall worth. For employees whose responsibilities can directly affect such net worth, this may be an appropriate measure of their performance. On the other hand, for employees whose responsibilities don't directly affect the "bottom line," it may be more appropriate to have their equity compensation determined by matters which are within their control. Thus, their equity compensation might relate to growth in the sales of one or more product lines or to improvements in the efficiency with which various products are produced. The choice of whether to use explicit performance criteria and, if such criteria are appropriate, which ones should be utilized, should be left to the employer to determine, based on the purpose for the equity-based compensation plan.

Extent of Employee's Economic Risk

Another factor that provides a basis for distinguishing among various forms of equity-based compensation is the extent to which the employee is economically put at risk as a consequence of entering into the equity compensation arrangement. For example, a direct purchase of stock by an employee generally results in economic risk to the employee to the extent of the purchase price. In other words, if the stock falls in value, the employee will suffer an economic loss. On the other hand, in the case of some equity-based compensation programs, the employee suffers no out-of-pocket cost and in turn will not suffer a loss if the stock does not appreciate in value. For example, an employer may sell shares of stock to an employee for $100 a share. In conjunction with the sale, the employee agrees that upon termination of his or her employment, he or she will sell the stock back to the employer for the greater of its fair market value or the amount paid for the shares. In this case, the employee, as a practical matter, has not incurred any economic risk. In designing an equity-based compensation program, the employer must determine the extent to which its employees will incur an economic risk as a consequence of receiving a stock award.

Federal Tax Consequences

The federal tax consequences of a particular equity-based compensation program are an important consideration from both the employee's and employer's perspectives. The employee's objective is to maximize the after-tax benefit of any stock award. Under current tax law, the maximum tax rate applicable to compensation income is 35 percent, while the maximum federal tax rate on long-term capital gains is 15 percent. Thus, there is a significant tax advantage to the employee arising from the adoption of an equity-based compensation program that results in the recognition of long-term capital gains income.

Moreover, almost without exception, the most frequently used forms of equity-based compensation involve a trade-off between the employer and employee as to the timing of the taxable event. In general, the employer cannot claim a tax deduction with respect to an equity-based compensation award until the employee is taxed on the income realized in connection with the receipt of the award. As a result, the employer generally prefers forms of equity-based compensation that permit it to claim a tax deduction as soon, and in as large an amount, as possible. The employee, on the other hand, can be expected to favor a stock award that defers the imposition of tax or that enables the employee to realize capital gain, rather than compensation income.

In the context of private companies, one of the major planning issues faced by the financial services professional is how to maximize the tax benefits of a stock award program for both the employer and its employees. In many circumstances, the interests of the employer and its employees may very well be contradictory. For example, under Sec. 83, if an employee can reduce the ordinary income consequence of a property transfer and increase its capital gain potential, he or she is better off. But the employer, on the other hand, has given up a deduction to the extent that ordinary income has been changed to capital gain.

Given the structure of the tax law, in many cases the employer nevertheless utilizes compensation techniques that tend to favor the employees' interests. There is nothing wrong with this approach, as long as it is undertaken with a clear understanding of what the costs, including lost tax benefits, are to the employer. Consequently, good planning should not focus solely upon the tax results to the employee, but should consider the total effect of any proposed program on both employer and employee. This concept will be looked at more closely in the context of choosing between the issuance of nonqualified stock options and incentive stock options.

Corporate Structure

Up to this point, it has been assumed that a closely held corporation that is considering the adoption of an equity-based compensation arrangement is treated as a C corporation for federal tax purposes. However, given the increased use of pass-through entities by business owners, the employer may have elected to be taxed under Subchapter S of the Code (an "S corporation") or that the employer is a limited liability company (LLC) that has elected to be taxed as a partnership. In both of these circumstances, there are additional considerations to be evaluated before adopting an equity-based compensation arrangement.

S Corporation

With respect to an S corporation, an individual who owns more than 2 percent of the corporation's outstanding stock is treated as a partner in a partnership for purposes of the provisions of the Code which relate to employee fringe benefits. For this purpose, employee fringe benefits include, among other things, group term life insurance and medical plans. Thus, an employee who receives more than a 2 percent interest in an S corporation's stock may find that his life insurance coverage and medical benefits are no longer excludible from income. This reduction in the employee's tax benefits should be understood and accepted by the employee before any stock awards are made.

LLC

Even though a business owner who operates his or her business in the form of an LLC may perceive the business as being no different than a regular corporation, the award of equity-based compensation to an employee of the LLC has tax consequences that differ in several material respects from those of a grant of equity compensation by a corporation to an employee.

First, an LLC can provide an unrestricted equity award in one of two forms, a profits interest or a capital interest. A profits interest is an unrestricted interest in the LLC's future profits. However, a profits interest does not entitle the holder to receive a share of the proceeds from the sale of the LLC's assets in connection with its liquidation. On the other hand, a capital interest typically includes a profits interest as well as the right to receive a share of the sales proceeds if the LLC's assets are sold in connection with its liquidation.

If an employee of an LLC is awarded a profits interest in exchange for providing services, he or she is generally not subject to taxation at the time of receipt. However, future allocations or distributions to the recipient with respect to the profits interest will be taxable. If an employee receives a capital interest in exchange for services, the recipient of the capital interest is immediately subject to taxation on ordinary income equal to the fair market value of the capital interest (reduced by any amount paid for the interest), and the LLC becomes entitled to a deduction equal to the amount of income recognized (the deduction is allocated to the member or members of the LLC whose capital has been transferred to the recipient). There also may be other tax consequences to the LLC and its members associated with the transfer of the capital interest.

Following the transfer of either a profits interest or a capital interest, the recipient must be treated as a member of the LLC. This means that in most circumstances the recipient no longer can be treated as an employee for tax purposes. Similar to what happens to a 2 percent S corporation shareholder, the new LLC member will lose the tax benefits associated with those welfare and fringe benefits that are only available to employees, such as group term life insurance and medical plans. Given the complexity of the possible tax consequences to the LLC and its members, an LLC should not undertake the adoption of an equity-based compensation program without the advice of a tax attorney, an accountant, or another qualified tax advisor.

OTHER LEGAL AND ACCOUNTING CONSIDERATIONS

Apart from the design and operational considerations addressed above, there are a number of legal and accounting factors that must be considered in assessing whether an employer is a candidate for implementing an equity-based compensation program.

- The employer must evaluate whether the accounting treatment of a particular form of equity-based compensation is acceptable from a financial reporting standpoint.
- State or federal law may require that certain forms of equity-based compensation receive stockholder approval before they become effective.
- To avoid the requirements of Title I of ERISA, certain equity-based compensation arrangements that operate like deferred compensation should be designed to satisfy the requirements for being a "top hat" plan—that is, an unfunded plan that is maintained primarily for the purpose of providing deferred compensation for a select group of management or highly compensated employees.

Another consideration for a closely held corporation that is related to the ERISA "top-hat" issue is whether stock awards made under a particular equity-based compensation arrangement will be considered a public offering, which requires filing a registration statement with respect to those awards under the Securities Act of 1933 (1933 Act) or comparable state securities laws. Generally, a stock plan that issues stock or options to a limited number of key executives who are familiar with the employer's overall operations and affairs can be considered a private offering that will not require registration under the 1933 Act. Conversely, if the plan covers a broad group of employees, some or all of whom are not familiar with the employer's operations, then the awards may constitute a public offering that requires a registration statement to be filed under the 1933 Act or under state securities laws. Because all closely held corporations want to avoid this result, it is important to include the employer's corporate attorney and accountant in the planning process.

OTHER PRELIMINARY CONCERNS

Creating a Plan or Program

Two common approaches are used to grant equity-based compensation awards. Under the more favored approach, the awards are granted pursuant to a plan maintained by the employer issuing the stock. The plan establishes the general terms of any awards to be granted, and permits the employer's compensation committee or other designated group to exercise discretion in granting individual awards to employees or other recipients and in establishing the individual terms and conditions applicable to the awards, consistent with the plan's general limitations or restrictions. Under the second approach, each award is granted on an ad hoc basis by the board of directors or other granting authority without any governing document. Under this approach, the only limitations on the terms of the award are found in applicable law, stock exchange requirements, and the employer's own bylaws or other governing corporate documents. This chapter will generally address equity-based compensation awards that are granted pursuant to some form of plan or other governing document or agreement.

One of the more practical reasons that plans are the preferred approach to awarding equity-based compensation is that several forms of equity-based compensation require shareholder approval; the use of a plan document greatly simplifies the process of obtaining the required approval. For example, as will be discussed later in this chapter, shareholder approval is required for the issuance of incentive stock options and for the adoption of an employee stock purchase plan. In addition, shareholder approval is required to exempt certain stock awards from the $1 million cap on deductible compensation paid to top officers of public companies and (under some stock exchange rules) to use authorized and unissued shares to satisfy awards made to officers and directors.

For public companies, use of a plan is also important to maintain favorable shareholder relations. Due to the potential dilution associated with equity-based compensation, institutional shareholders often have a negative view of such awards unless they are made pursuant to a plan that identifies the type of awards that can be made as well as the total value of the equity-based compensation to be delivered and that has been submitted to shareholders for approval. Similarly, stock plans may have a positive effect on employee relations. Stock awards will be more effective in motivating executives if the executives are satisfied that the stock awards will not be made on an arbitrary basis.

Accounting Considerations

For public companies, at one time the use of equity-based compensation received favorable treatment for financial accounting purposes on the books of the company. This is no longer the case. Under generally accepted accounting principles (as articulated in FAS 123(R), Share-Based Payment), all stock awards now have some accounting expense associated with them. FAS 123(R) generally requires companies to measure compensation costs based on the award's grant date fair value. For example, the grant date value of stock options must be estimated using option pricing models that take into account the option's exercise price, the expected option term, the current price of the underlying stock and that price's expected volatility, expected dividends, and the risk-free interest rates for the option's expected term. Acceptable pricing models include the binomial option-pricing model (a lattice model) and the Black-Scholes-Merton option-pricing formula.

The resulting compensation cost must be recognized over the period during which the employee is required to provide service in exchange for the award—that is, the vesting period. However, the total amount of the compensation cost recognized for an award of stock options is based solely on the number of options that eventually vest. The compensation cost attributable to nonvested options (the options for which the requisite service is not rendered) is never recorded. FAS 123(R) also requires that if a stock award is modified, an incremental compensation cost must be recognized in an amount equal to the excess of the fair value of the modified award over the fair value of the original award before its modification.

Finally, FAS 123(R) requires expense recognition of employee stock purchase plan (ESSP) options if certain criteria are not met. Under such criteria, any purchase discount may not exceed the per share amount of share issuance costs that would have been incurred to raise a significant amount of capital by a public offering. The safe harbor discount for this purpose is 5 percent or less. Accordingly, if the purchase discount under the ESSP is more than 5 percent (a discount of up to 15 percent is allowed under Code Sec. 423), an expense recognition will be required with respect to options issued under the ESSP.

Public Corporations

If a financial services professional counsels a public company or represents employees of one or more public companies, there are special limitations that affect stock awards granted to employees of public companies. Financial services professionals must be familiar with these limitations when working with such clients.

$1 Million Cap on Compensation

Sec. 162(m) of the Code limits to $1 million per covered individual the amount that a public company may deduct as "employee remuneration." This limitation applies to any publicly held company whose chief executive officer and certain other officers are required to have their compensation reported in the employer's proxy statement. Not all compensation is taken into account for purposes of the Sec. 162(m) deduction cap. Sec. 162(m) defines "applicable employee remuneration" by what it is not, providing that the limit takes into consideration all remuneration, other than commissions, qualified plan and fringe benefit contributions, and performance-based compensation. The latter form of compensation is the primary exception to the Sec. 162(m) limitation.

Generally, performance-based compensation is paid only if certain preestablished objective performance formulas or goals are met. Moreover, the performance goals must be established by a compensation committee consisting of two or more outside directors of the corporation. However, because stock rises and falls in value based on the employer's stock price which in turn reflects corporate performance, stock options and stock appreciation rights (SARs) are automatically considered to have satisfied the requirements for performance-based compensation as long as certain other conditions are satisfied. These conditions include that the option exercise price equal fair market value on the date of grant and that the shareholders approve the terms of the option plan. Once a stock option or SAR qualifies as performance-based compensation, the amounts realized in connection with the exercise of those forms of compensation are no longer subject to the $1 million cap on compensation. Thus, for executives whose compensation can be limited by Sec. 162(m), the goal is to maximize the amount of performance-based compensation that they receive. In general, restricted stock falls into the $1 million limit and stock options as performance-based awards are not counted. Additionally, a review of company profits and the impact of Sec. 162(m) has yielded disappointing results, as it has had a minimal impact. The lost deduction has not really impacted company decisions in part because it was significantly watered down from the original proposal. Additionally, many executives and companies have found ways around the rule or just do not care that much about the financial impact of the rule.

Insider Trading Restrictions

Rule 16b-3, referred to as the short swing profit recovery rule, is issued by the SEC under the authority of Sec. 16 of the Securities Exchange Act of 1934. Under this section, insiders (a corporation's officers, directors, and greater than 10 percent shareholders), must disgorge profits from purchases and sales within 6 months of each other. A purchase for purposes of this restriction includes the grant of an option. However, Rule 16b-3 does provide an exemption for securities issued under a employee benefit plan if certain requirements are satisfied. Chief among these requirements is that the shareholders approve the plan. Thus, if the requirements of Rule 16b-3 are met, the grant of an option will not be characterized as a purchase under the short swing profit recovery rule. In 2016 and 2017, a number of cases have been working their way through the court system in an attempt to clarify and, in some areas, challenge the applicability of 16b-3.

Proxy Disclosure Requirements

The SEC requires that a public company disclose in its annual proxy statement the compensation paid to its senior executives and directors. However, for proxy statements issued after December 15, 2006, the SEC substantially revised and enlarged the scope and form of disclosure of a public company's reportable compensation practices and arrangements. The SEC attempted to update and changes this controversial rule in 2010, however, it was struck down by the United States Court of Appeals for the District of Columbia Circuit in 2011 and the SEC has not revived any further attempts at changes. In addition to salary, bonuses, and other forms of compensation, the new disclosure rules require that options and any other forms of equity awards granted to senior executives and directors during the applicable year must be disclosed in a table, using the award's compensation cost as recognized by the corporation for financial accounting purposes under FAS 123(R). Thus, for a corporation's senior executives and directors, there is more transparency as to the value of the compensatory equity awards that they receive.

STOCK OPTION PLANS

Up until the recent changes in accounting rules that affect how stock options are treated for financial statement reporting purposes, stock option programs had been one of the most popular forms of equity-based compensation, both from the employer's and the participants' perspectives. Yet, despite the accounting treatment changes, stock options are still a popular form of equity-based compensation, particularly from the employee's perspective. In this section, we will review the three types of stock option plans, design considerations, and planning for the participant. Even if a financial services professional does not work with employers to design stock option programs, he or she must nevertheless be familiar with the tax considerations when working with employees who have been awarded one or more of the various forms of stock options.

What Is an Option?

An option affords its holder the right to acquire the property subject to the option privilege by paying the exercise price within the period set forth in the option agreement. Typically, an option is only exercised when it is "in the money;" that is, the value of the underlying property exceeds the exercise price. At the time of grant, a stock option's value includes the following three components:

- **the intrinsic value of the option.** This element refers to the excess, if any, of the stock's value over the exercise price. In most cases involving compensatory stock options, this element does not have any value because when granted those options typically have an exercise price equal to the fair market value of the stock on the date of grant.
- **the leverage value of the option.** This element refers to the fact that an option allows an employee to hold onto it without risking capital or having to pay taxes until the

option is exercised. This value is equivalent to the return that the holder could earn on funds that do not otherwise have to be committed to paying the exercise price. This leverage value is similar to an interest-free loan. However, the leverage value decreases as the period to the expiration of the option draws nearer.

- **the option's price protection.** This element refers to the fact that an option holder suffers no economic loss if the value of the underlying stock falls below the exercise price. This price protection value is particularly relevant for more volatile stocks where the probability of an option finishing out of the money is higher.

Nonqualified Stock Options (NQSOs)

LO 16.3 Describe common features of a nonqualified stock option program and the tax consequences of such a program.

nonqualified stock options (NQSOs)

Nonqualified stock options (NQSOs) are options to purchase shares of company stock at a stated price over a given period of time (frequently 10 years). The option price normally equals 100 percent of the stock's fair market value on the date the option is granted, but if adverse tax consequences are to be avoided, it is no longer possible, as a practical matter, to set the option price below this level. Typically, the employee may exercise the option by paying cash equal to the exercise price or by tendering previously owned shares of stock.

At the time the NQSO is exercised, the excess of the fair market value of the stock over the option price is taxed as ordinary income and is also subject to FICA tax and income tax withholding. The company receives a tax deduction in the amount of the executive's income recognized from the exercise of the option in the year of such recognition, as long as the withholding requirements are met. The executive's tax basis in the shares received upon exercise of the option is equal to the sum of the exercise price and the amount that the executive recognizes as income.

> **EXAMPLE**
>
> The employer grants to Ellie Executive the right to purchase 500 shares of common stock at the market price ($20/share at the time of issuance) at any time over the next 10 years. After 3 years, the market price has risen to $60/share. Ellie purchases all 500 shares at $20/share ($10,000). She now has $20,000 ($40 × 500) of ordinary income, which is the difference between the purchase price ($10,000) and the current market value ($30,000). Ellie's basis in her 500 shares is $30,000, the sum of the $10,000 exercise price and her $20,000 of ordinary income.

Clearly NQSOs will be valuable to the employee only if the price of the underlying stock has risen since the date the option was issued. However, there is a possibility of a large gain if the price increases substantially. The employee generally may choose to exercise the options at any time during a specified period (typically 10 years) without limitation.

Many NQSOs are not exercisable for a period of time after the options are granted. Sometimes all options granted at a specific time become vested at once (referred to as cliff vesting) after a specified number of years. For example, the company grants 500 options that become exercisable 3 years from the date of the grant as long as the participant is still employed on that date. Another approach is to vest a portion of the options each year (referred to as graded vesting). For example, one third of the options is vested after one year and two thirds after 2 years, with full vesting after 3 years. It is also possible to have accelerated vesting upon the occurrence of a change in control of the company or upon the participant's death or disability. Also, be aware that the vesting provisions within a single company can be different for options granted at different times or to different individuals. Unless the terms of the stock option plan provide otherwise, there are no nondiscrimination or uniformity requirements applicable to stock option grants.

Several newer vesting approaches are being used today. In some cases, vesting is subject to the company (or employee) satisfying certain performance goals. Another approach offered in some pre-IPO (prior to the initial public offering) companies is referred to as early exercise. Under this arrangement, the participant is allowed to immediately exercise options when they are granted, but the stock remains restricted (forfeitable if the employee does not complete a specified period of service or does not remain employed until the IPO is completed). Because the employee could forfeit the stock, there is generally no income tax consequences until the vesting restrictions lapse. As an alternative, the employee can make a Sec. 83(b) election and pay tax at the time of the early exercise. Once exercised, the program is really a form of restricted stock plan.

noncompete clause

The duration of the exercise period for an NQSO is most often 10 years, but termination of employment prior to the end of that period can shorten the duration. It is common for a terminating employee to have the options lapse between 60 and 180 days after termination of employment, but it is also possible for the options to lapse at termination of employment if the participant is terminated for cause or violates a **noncompete clause**.

To exercise the options, the employee needs cash to pay the option price for the stock. Although this often requires borrowing, once the options are exercised, the employee may sell a sufficient number of the shares to repay the loan. If the employer is the source of the employee's loan, care must be taken in how the loan is structured. If the employer provides a nonrecourse loan (that is, the employee does not have any personal liability) that is only secured by the stock obtained through the exercise of an option, this form of loan will cause the exercise of the stock option to be ignored for tax purposes pursuant to Code Sec. 83. This is the case because the employee has not taken any personal risk that the stock's value will decline. Accordingly, even though the option has been exercised, there has been no transfer of stock for tax purposes. The employee does not recognize any income as a consequence of the exercise of the option and will not have a taxable event until the loan has been repaid and the stock no longer secures the loan. At that time, the employee will recognize income equal to the excess of the then value of the stock over the exercise price.

For example, an employee has an option to purchase 1,000 shares of Company X stock with an exercise price of $50. When the value of Company X stock has reached $100 a share, the employee decides to exercise the option by obtaining a nonrecourse loan from Company X in the amount of $50,000, which must be repaid one year from the date of the loan. The employee will not have a taxable event when the option is exercised. Rather, the taxable event will occur one year later when the employee repays the loan. For tax purposes, a transfer of property is considered to have occurred at that time. When the loan repayment is made, if Company X stock has a value of $125 a share, the employee will be required to report $75,000 of compensation income, the difference between the exercise price and the fair market value of the stock on the date the stock is transferred for tax purposes. The $25 of additional stock value that accrued between the time that the option was exercised and the time that the loan was repaid must be treated as ordinary income and not capital gain. This tax result is the same whether the loan proceeds are used to exercise an option or to purchase the stock directly from the employer. In either event, no transfer of property occurs until the loan is repaid and the employee's income recognition is deferred until a transfer of property has taken place. However, if the loan is obtained from an unrelated third party, the usual taxation rules apply. The special rule described above only applies where the loan is from the employer. Accordingly, if loans are to be used to exercise options or to purchase stock, then, if possible, the employer should negotiate with its bank to provide the loans to the employees so that they do not have to come from the employer.

Many stock option programs adopted by public companies today offer cashless exercise transactions pursuant to Regulation T issued by the Federal Reserve Board. Under Regulation T a stockbroker is permitted to extend credit to an employer on behalf of an employee for the purpose of exercising an option. In other words, the options are exercised with broker financing and the broker simultaneously sells some or all of the stock received in connection with the option exercise in order to repay the broker's loan. What the employee receives are shares, cash, or both having a value equal to the gain realized upon the exercise of the option (the spread), net of any brokerage commissions and any required tax withholding. Although this transaction is substantially similar to a stock appreciation right that is payable in cash, the employer avoids having to make any cash payment.

If the employee prefers to hold option shares for their potential future appreciation, devising a method to raise the cash necessary to purchase those shares becomes an important part of the employee's retirement planning. In addition, if employer stock constitutes a disproportionate share of a retiring employee's investment portfolio, planning for the systematic repositioning of the portfolio is another consideration for the financial services professional.

Impact of Sec. 409A

Prior to the addition of Code Sec. 409A, the grant of an NQSO with an exercise price of less than fair market value was generally a nonevent for tax purposes. There may have been adverse accounting treatment at the time of grant, but the taxable event continued to arise only when the option was exercised. Sec. 409A has added a new consideration to this scenario.

As discussed in the last chapter, Sec. 409A was added to the Code for the purpose of regulating deferred compensation. Although stock options had never previously been characterized as deferred compensation for tax purposes, under Sec. 409A discounted stock options are nevertheless treated as deferred compensation and must satisfy the Sec. 409A requirements. The most relevant of these requirements to stock options is that deferred compensation may not be distributed earlier than separation from service, disability, death, a specified time, or pursuant to a fixed schedule. For an option, this means that the exercise of the option can only take place upon the occurrence of one of those events, which is not how the typical stock option is written.

If a discounted stock option runs afoul of Sec. 409A, the holder of the option will be subject to income tax at the time that the option becomes exercisable, that is, vested, rather than the date on which the option is exercised. The amount subject to tax is the spread between the exercise price and the fair market value of the underlying stock on the vesting date. In addition, the option holder will incur a 20 percent penalty on the amount of income that is treated as additional compensation under Sec. 409A. Moreover, the employer has an employment tax and withholding obligation with respect to the amount required to be included in the employee's income.

EXAMPLE

The employer grants to Paula President an option to purchase 500 shares of common stock. At the time of this grant, the stock has a fair market value of $20 per share.

However, the exercise price of the option is $10 per share. The option can be exercised at any time after the third anniversary of the date of grant. After 3 years, the value of the stock has increased to $60 per share. On the third anniversary of the grant date, Paula must recognize income equal to $25,000 (500 × $50). In addition, Paula is also subject to a penalty of $5,000 ($25,000 × .2).

The application of Sec. 409A to discounted stock options is of particular importance to closely held corporations that grant stock options. This is because closely held corporations may inadvertently grant discounted stock options due to a faulty evaluation. Although there has yet to be any meaningful experience with how Sec. 409A will be applied, it is very possible that the IRS may apply a strict interpretation of Sec. 409A with respect to the valuation of a closely held corporation's stock in determining whether options presumed to be granted "at the money" should instead be treated as discounted stock options. The same issue can arise in connection with the issuance of incentive stock options (discussed below), which are required to be granted at fair market value, but on closer examination it may be determined that the exercise price was not fair market value. Accordingly, closely held corporations should give serious consideration to having an independent appraisal of their stock prepared prior to the grant of any stock options in order to confirm that the exercise price of each stock option is not less than the stock's fair market value.

The regulations under Sec. 409A provide guidance on three safe harbor methods of determining fair market value, one of which is an independent appraisal. Pursuant to these regulations, it will be advantageous to use one of the safe harbor methods. It will shift the burden to the IRS to establish that both (i) the option's exercise price is below fair market value and (ii) the company's method of valuation was unreasonable.

Finally, the option grants that are now subject to Sec. 409A are grants made after October 3, 2004 and options issued before October 3, 2004 that are either (i) amended after October 3, 2004, or (ii) not fully vested as of December 31, 2004. On the other hand, it is not impossible to structure an option so that it complies with Sec. 409A. It primarily requires that stricter rules regarding the timing of exercise have to be built into the option grant. For example, a closely-held corporation that expects to be acquired for its current fair market value may determine that a discounted option that is exercisable solely upon a change in control is a better compensation device than is a regular option that is exercisable at any time.

Incentive Stock Options (ISOs)

LO 16.4   Compare incentive stock options with nonqualified stock options.

incentive stock option (ISO)

An **incentive stock option (ISO)** is an option to purchase shares of company stock at 100 percent or more of the stock's fair market value on the date the option is granted, for a period of up to 10 years. The option plan itself may not have a duration of more than 10 years and must be approved by shareholders within one year before or after the date of the plan's adoption. ISOs are taxed more favorably to the employee than NQSOs, but are less flexible. The stock's aggregate fair market value (determined at the date of grant) subject to ISOs which become exercisable for the first time by an employee in any calendar year cannot exceed $100,000. This means that if an employer grants 20,000 ISOs to an employee and the value of the underlying stock is $10 per share, then no more than 50 percent of the ISOs (10,000 × $10 = $100,000) may become vested in any calendar year. An ISO is exercisable only by an employee and cannot be transferred to anyone, except in the event of death. The favorable tax treatment is also conditioned on satisfying certain holding period requirements before any sale of the option shares. In addition, any option granted to a shareholder of 10 percent or more of a company's voting stock must be priced at 110 percent or more of the stock's fair market value, with an option term of no more than 5 years. As in the case of NQSOs, the options may be exercised by paying cash or by tendering previously owned shares of stock.

When the employee exercises the ISO, there is no regular income tax owed. However, the excess of the stock's fair market value at the time of exercise over the option exercise price—that is, the spread—is a tax-preference item that may trigger an alternative minimum tax obligation (discussed below). If the shares are held for at least 2 years from the date the option was granted and at least one year from the date of exercise, the tax on the gain realized upon the sale of the option stock is payable at a long-term capital-gains rate. This gain is equal to the increase in the stock's value from the date the ISO is granted to the date the stock is sold.

> **EXAMPLE**
>
> Alex, an executive of Private Company, receives an ISO for 1,000 shares of company stock. The exercise price of the options and the stock's fair market value on the date of grant is $10. One year later, Alex exercises his ISOs and receives 1,000 shares of stock. Alex holds these shares for another 2 years and then sells them for $15 per share. At that time Alex has a long-term capital gain of $5,000 (1,000 × $5).

If the holding period requirements are not met, the gain to the extent of the spread at the time of exercise is taxed as ordinary income; the remainder of the gain is taxed as capital gain.

Such an early sale is referred to as a disqualifying disposition. In the event of a disqualifying disposition, the employer becomes entitled to a deduction in the taxable year of such disposition equal in amount to the ordinary income recognized by the employee.

> **EXAMPLE**
>
> Same facts as the preceding example except that Alex exercises his ISOs 6 months after the date of grant when the value of the stock is $12 per share. Alex then sells his shares a year later for $15 a share. This is a disqualifying disposition since Alex did not hold his shares for at least 2 years from the date of grant. As a result, Alex recognizes ordinary income in the year of the disqualifying disposition in the amount of $2,000 (1,000 × $2). In addition, because Alex held his shares for a year, he will also report a long-term capital gain of $3,000 (1,000 × $3).

Because the capital-gains tax rate can be significantly lower than ordinary income tax rates, satisfying the holding period requirements for capital-gains treatment is quite important. In addition to the lower rate, capital gains on the sale of stocks acquired through incentive stock options can be used to offset capital losses from the sale of other securities. Still, the employee needs to consider the alternative minimum tax implications of holding stock after exercise.

As with NQSOs, ISOs provide the employee with the possibility of large gains. Within limits, the employee can choose the timing of exercise of the ISOs to maximize gains. Also, as with NQSOs, the employee needs to have a full appreciation of the terms of the program, including the vesting and option duration provisions, before any liquidation strategy can be conceived.

Finally, one of the tax consequences associated with the exercise of ISOs is that the spread upon exercise of an ISO is treated as a preference item for purposes of the alternative minimum tax (AMT). This means that an employee may be surprised to learn that he or she has an income tax liability as a result of exercising an ISO even though the general rule is that the exercise of an ISO is not a taxable event. Looking back at the first example above, if at the time of exercise the stock has a value of $12 a share, Alex will have a tax preference amount equal to $2,000 when the ISOs are exercised (1,000 × $2). This AMT preference item may or may not affect Alex's actual income tax liability, depending on his overall tax situation. However, if an employee does pay AMT in connection with the exercise of an ISO, that AMT amount is available to offset any capital gains tax due on the sale of the option shares. Thus, in the original example, if the AMT attributable to the ISO exercise is $500 and the capital gain tax on the subsequent sale of the shares following the 1-year holding period will be $4,500 ($5,000 − $500).

It is important that the financial services professional pay attention to the danger of the AMT. If an employee exercises a large number of ISOs at a time when the value of the underlying stock has increased substantially, the employee may incur an AMT liability. However, with proper planning the employee can minimize the effect of an ISO exercise on AMT liability. Some strategies that can be used to minimize the AMT include the following:

- Limit the number of ISOs exercised in any year. Calculate the number of ISOs to exercise in a year so that the regular tax will equal the AMT.

- Plan ahead by estimating how many ISOs can be exercised in each future year without triggering AMT.

- Exercise ISOs as early in the year as possible and then monitor the stock price throughout the year. If the stock price decreases and the employee believes that the decline will continue, then he or she should consider selling the stock. This technique eliminates the tax preference item and avoids the risk of paying AMT on phantom income. If the stock price increases and the employee believes that the appreciation will continue, then he or she should hold the stock. In that event the increasing value of the stock will hopefully result in any AMT payment being recouped when the stock is eventually sold.

Tax Withholding and Employment Taxes

In order to engage in cash flow planning, it is important for an employee to understand the income tax withholding and employment tax obligations that apply to stock options. With respect to ISOs, there is no federal income tax withholding requirement, even when the employee has a disqualifying disposition. Similarly, no employment taxes are payable in connection with the exercise of an ISO. This is another advantage that ISOs have over NQSOs.

With respect to NQSOs, income tax withholding is required, as is the payment of FICA, FUTA, and Medicare taxes. These withholding and employment tax obligations arise at the time that the NQSO is exercised, assuming that the option stock is nonforfeitable.

Choosing and Designing a Plan

Similar to deferred-compensation plans, stock option programs can be used to attract, motivate, and retain the services of an employee. Unlike compensation programs, stock programs can transform the executive's interest in the company from that of an employee to a partowner. Apart from the possible payment of employment taxes, a stock option program also does not involve the outlay of any cash by the employer, either at the time of issuance or at the time the participant exercises the option.

However, this does not mean there is no cost associated with the establishment of a stock option program. If the value of the company's stock increases a great deal, there is the lost opportunity of selling the stock to a third party at the market price. A company should not consider a stock option program unless it has first carefully evaluated the potential costs and has a clear understanding of the objectives it is trying to accomplish.

When choosing between the two types of stock option programs, remember that the tax impact on the employer is quite different. With an ISO, the employer gets no tax deduction, while under a nonqualified program, the employer receives a deduction in the amount the participant recognizes as income at the time of exercise. This makes the cost of providing benefits with an ISO more expensive than with a nonqualified program. In addition, the nonqualified program is more flexible.

In the review of NQSOs and ISOs, we discussed the major plan design alternatives that the employer has with each type of option plan. As you can see, as with nonqualified deferred compensation, there is a great deal of flexibility in choosing the proper plan design.

What may be a little different about designing an option program is that the employer and employees do not have the same interest in which type of option program is adopted. Due to the favorable capital gains treatment, employees generally favor ISOs. Because employers do not obtain any deduction from the exercise of an ISO, they tend to favor NQSOs. However, this tension is not irreconcilable. Due to the flexibility of NQSOs, a program can be designed where the employer obtains a full tax deduction for the options granted and the employee is effectively taxed at a capital gains rate on the income recognized when the options are exercised.

EXAMPLE

Widget Corporation adopts an NQSO program for its employees. The program provides for the grant of NQSOs and for the company to pay a bonus to employees who exercise their options equal to the sum of (i) the additional federal taxes payable by the employees by reason of using an NQSO and (ii) an amount equal to the federal taxes payable on the amount determined in (i). If Frank has a marginal tax rate of 30 percent and has annual earnings in excess of the taxable wage base, it would take a payment of $16.45 by the company to make up for the excess income and Medicare taxes that Frank would have to pay on each $100 of gain. The tax gross-up amount determined under (ii) is $7.55. This makes the total amount payable to Frank for each $100 of gain equal to $24. Consequently, after Frank pays his federal income and Medicare taxes on each $100 of gain and the bonus amount attributable to that gain, he is left with $85 ($124 × (100% − 31.45%)), which is equivalent to being taxed at a 15 percent capital gains rate.

In the example above, from Widget Corporation's perspective, if its marginal tax rate is 35 percent, it receives a tax benefit of $35 from each $100 of Frank's gain. Because each $100 of Frank's gain is a noncash expense for the company, the $35 tax benefit represents a true economic gain. The company also realizes a tax benefit from the bonus paid to Frank as well as the additional Medicare taxes paid on the sum of the $100 gain and the bonus amount. This additional tax benefit is $9 (($1.45 + $24.35) × 35%). This results in a net tax savings to the company of $18.20 ($44 - $25.80) per $100 of gain. If Frank's state and local taxes are factored in (assuming that they impose a more favorable tax rate on capital gains, which is not always the case), the net tax savings will be reduced somewhat, but the company will still be better off than if it had issued ISOs.

Exercising NQSOs and ISOs

Employees who participate in an NQSO or ISO program have a difficult time choosing the optimal timing strategy for exercising their stock options. There are no rules of thumb that apply to every situation. Because there is a risk to every alternative, in some ways making the right choice is more of an art than a science. Also, remember that the most serious mistakes employees make are often the simplest ones—for example, letting valuable options lapse because of a misunderstanding or a failure to monitor the options.

An employee's decision making can be facilitated by having a clear structure to the process. The following provides a logical process to follow. The first step is to identify clear financial goals. Knowing for what the proceeds will be used, such as buying a home in 2 years or retiring in 10 years, will go a long way to bringing the right decision into focus.

The next step is to get a complete understanding of the option program. The types of questions to ask include:

- Are the options nonqualified or ISOs?
- When do options become vested and does vesting occur at once (cliff vesting) or over time (graded vesting)?
- Will the options become vested earlier if the participant dies, becomes disabled, or if there is a change in ownership?
- Are the options exercisable before they become vested?
- What is the duration of the option period?
- For how long are options exercisable after termination of employment due to (a) death, (b) disability, (c) retirement, (d) voluntary termination, or (e) an involuntary termination?
- Do options lapse if the participant goes to work for a competitor?
- Does the employer intend to grant additional options in the future?

- Where the employer is a closely held corporation, what are the terms that control the repurchase of option shares by the employer?

Knowing the rules also means understanding the tax implications. Once the type (nonqualified or ISO) is determined, the client needs to have a full appreciation of the tax timing issues. An employee does not really know the value of the options until he or she knows the value after the exercise price and after all taxes have been paid. As discussed above, the alternative minimum tax is a real issue for those holders of ISOs who choose to retain the stock to take advantage of the lower capital-gains rate.

The development of an option exercise and a stock liquidation strategy is generally best suited to employees who hold stock in, or options issued by, a public company. Once the employee of a public company understands the plan and has a general idea of what the funds will be used for, the next step is to develop a long-term liquidation plan. This can be facilitated by asking questions such as

- How many additional options are likely to be granted?
- How much wealth should be tied up in the employer's stock?
- How long will employment with the employer continue?

Because many employees of public companies acquire sizable blocks of stock in their company through various incentive plans, one important planning consideration is often the systematic liquidation of this stock and the purchase of other securities to better diversify the employee's investment portfolio at his or her retirement. The plan should include a strategy for which shares of stock to sell first.

The plan should also have an action strategy. For example, who is going to notify heirs if the participant dies and still has stock options? What steps are in place to ensure that valuable options do not lapse? How often will the plan be reevaluated and adjusted for changing conditions?

The financial advisor can be a very important part of this process because the advisor is typically better suited than the employee to help model asset allocations, long-term projections, and tax planning alternatives.

When devising a long-term plan, in addition to taking the above steps, the employee may want to consider some of the following strategies:

- Because stock prices historically rise over time, holding the options until the end of the exercise period is a good place to start when formulating a strategy.

- Countervailing considerations, such as diversifying the portfolio, exercising the options to meet a specific financial goal, or a realistic assessment that the stock price is unlikely to continue to increase, can be good reasons to sell sooner.

- Arguably, because options are a bonus, liquidating the position (selling the stock) at the time the options are exercised ensures a positive cash position—and does not tie up the employee's assets.

- Alternatively, if stock appreciation is relatively certain, an employee in a high tax bracket (who can afford to take some risk) should exercise early and hold the stock to change the tax treatment from ordinary income (up to a 35 percent tax rate) to long-term capital gains (15 percent tax rate). However, this strategy requires cash to purchase the stock and the risk that some or all of the gain will be lost.

- When choosing which options to exercise, first consider exercising the oldest options, even if they are not the lowest priced.

- Pay attention to the price behavior of the company's stock.

- Consider exercising the options and selling the stock (cashless transactions) over a period of time instead of all at once. This allows the price to be averaged and reduces the risk of receiving a low price for all the options, and it allows the employee to invest the proceeds into new investments over time, also reducing risk.

Gifting Opportunities

NQSOs are assets with a strong potential for growth. Accordingly, they are attractive candidates for gifts so that the anticipated appreciation can be removed from the donor's estate. The most important feature of a stock option for gift tax purposes is that it can be transferred. As discussed above, ISOs are required to be nontransferable in order to obtain favorable tax treatment. Thus, ISOs are not available for making gifts.

On the other hand, NQSOs are a more favorable vehicle for estate planning. NQSOs do not have to be nontransferable to obtain favorable tax consequences and there is no other non-tax reason why NQSOs have to be nontransferable. Moreover, in 1998 the IRS approved the transfer of NQSOs as an acceptable estate planning technique and confirmed the income and gift tax consequences of such transfers.

The favorable estate planning results that can be obtained from the transfer of NQSOs are dependent upon the making of a completed gift. A gift is complete when the donor has parted with all dominion and control over the property so that the donor no longer has the power to change its disposition. If a donor makes an incomplete gift, the gift tax consequences are deferred until the gift is completed, at which time the property may have appreciated in value.

The income and gift tax consequences of the transfer of an NQSO are determined by the regulations under Sec. 83 that address the disposition of a stock option. If the disposition of nonvested property is made in an arm's length transaction, compensation is realized by the employee to the extent that the amount realized from the disposition exceeds the amount, if any, paid for the property. In that event, the property is no longer subject to Sec. 83. If the disposition of nonvested property occurs in a non-arm's length transaction, like a gift, the employee realizes compensation income equal to the amount of money or the value of property, if any, received by the employee in connection with the disposition. In addition, Sec. 83 continues to apply to the transferred property, except that the amount previously included in income when the property was transferred is treated as an amount paid for the property.

Applying these principles to gifts of NQSOs, the IRS has determined that when an NQSO is transferred to a family member as a gift, there is no income tax consequence at that time. However, when the option is subsequently exercised by the donee, the donee receives the option shares, but the income tax consequences of the exercise are imposed on the donor as if the transfer had not occurred. In other words, the donor reports the difference between the exercise price and the fair market value of the stock on the date of exercise as income. This income continues to be wages for purposes of federal income tax withholding and employment taxes. The good news for the donor is that the shares and the income tax paid in connection with the exercise of the option have been removed from the donor's estate. The latter payment can also be characterized as a further gift to the donee without any gift tax liability. The donee, on the other hand, has obtained the shares for a bargain price and has a basis in those shares equal to their fair market value.

EXAMPLE

The employer grants to Dan Donor a vested option to purchase 500 shares of common stock at the market price ($20/share at the time of issuance) at any time over the next 10 years. After 3 years, the market price has risen to $60/share. Dan then gives the option to his son, Peter. After 5 more years, the stock price has increased to $120/share. At that time, Peter purchases all 500 shares at $20/share ($10,000). Dan now must report $50,000 ($100 × 500) of ordinary income, which is the difference between the purchase price ($10,000) and the current market value ($60,000). Peter's basis in his 500 shares is $60,000, the sum of the $10,000 exercise price and the $50,000 of ordinary income recognized by Dan.

Looking at the gift tax side of the transfer, the IRS takes the position that the transfer of nonvested NQSOs is not a completed gift. The rationale for this position is that, until the employee has completed all of the services required in order for the options to become vested, he or she does not possess an enforceable property right, which can be transferred for federal gift tax purposes. Thus, only vested NQSOs can be the subject of a completed gift. When a gift of vested NQSOs is made, the NQSOs must be valued for gift tax purposes. The IRS provides Rev. Proc. 98-34 for the purpose of establishing a safe harbor method of valuing nonpublicly traded stock options on publicly traded stock for gift and estate tax purposes. Under this revenue procedure, the taxpayer can use a generally recognized option pricing model, such as the Black- Scholes model or an accepted version of the binomial model, as long as certain conditions are met. The trade-off for using this safe harbor valuation method is that the options may be overvalued. The safe harbor approach does not allow any discount to be applied to the valuation produced by the option pricing model. For example, no discount can be taken for lack of transferability or due to the termination of the option following a termination of employment.

NQSOs are very attractive for gift-giving to family members and can also be used to make charitable gifts. In addition, NQSOs can play an important role in facilitating estate planning in any number of ways. As an example, consider this hypothetical plan of a husband and wife who own an incorporated family business. As part of his estate planning, the husband sells to each of his four children for fair market value (FMV) an option to purchase the shares of the business on a pro rata basis. The options are exercisable on the death of the last survivor of the husband and the wife and the exercise price is the FMV of the shares at the time the options become exercisable. By their terms, the options may be exercised by tendering cash or an installment note payable in no more than 15 years, or a combination of both.

At the same time, the family established a private foundation. The husband, wife, and the four children are members of the foundation's board and participate in its gift-giving program. The husband's will bequeaths the stock of the business to a marital trust for the wife's benefit. On the wife's death, or on the husband's death if the wife predeceases him, the shares pass to the foundation. This avoids estate tax due to the estate tax charitable deduction.

Under this plan, the children are required to pay the foundation the FMV of the shares of the business that it holds. The purchase price can be paid over a 15-year period, thus allowing payment to be made from the cash flow of the business.

EMPLOYEE STOCK PURCHASE PLANS

LO 16.5   **Identify uses of employee stock purchase plans and the advantages of such programs.**

A third form of stock option program which can be an addition to, or a substitute for, an ISO or NQSO program is the employee stock purchase plan (ESPP). These plans are designed to satisfy and take advantage of the special tax rules contained in Sec. 423. Since participation in a Sec. 423 stock purchase plan must be broad based, resulting in widespread employee ownership of the employer's stock, such plans are usually only adopted by employers who want to promote that goal. Moreover, due to the valuation, accounting, securities law, and record-keeping requirements that apply to a program covering large groups of employees, ESPPs are typically adopted by large, publicly held companies.

ESPP

Under an **ESPP**, the employer provides its employees with the opportunity to use after-tax income to purchase the employer's common stock at a discount from its fair market value. In a typical ESPP, employee contributions are accumulated by payroll deduction over a 6-month (or longer) offering period. At the end of the offering period the accumulated employee contributions are used to purchase shares of the employer's common stock at a 15-percent discount off the market price generally at the beginning of the offering period. Since no purchase of stock is made until the end of the offering period, in operation the ESPP is generally administered as if it were a stock purchase plan. But for purposes of Sec. 423, it is nevertheless treated as a stock option plan.

As a practical matter, the discount available under an ESPP will be greater than 15 percent. This will occur if the stock appreciates in value from the first day of the offering period or if the ESPP utilizes what is referred to as the look-back rule. Under the look-back rule, an ESPP is allowed to offer the employees the option to purchase the stock using an option price that is the lesser of 85 percent of the fair market value of the stock at the beginning of the offering period, or 85 percent of the fair market value of the stock at the end of the offering period. When the ESPP utilizes the look-back rule, two other requirements must be satisfied: First, the offering period must be no more than 27 months. Second, the ESPP must designate a maximum number of shares that an employee may purchase during any offering period or must include a formula by which such maximum number may be calculated for each employee.

EXAMPLE

Breen, Inc. maintains an ESPP that gives eligible employees the right to purchase stock over a 12-month offering period at 85 percent of the market price at the beginning or the end of the offering period, whichever is less. If the stock price is $10 at the beginning of the offering period and goes up to $20 at the end of the period, the purchase price is just $8.50 per share. If the stock price goes down to $5 at the end of the period, the purchase price is $4.25 per share.

Tax Consequences

At the time stock is purchased under an ESPP, there are no tax consequences. Taxes are paid only at the time of the sale of the stock, and the tax consequences depend upon whether a holding period requirement has been satisfied. The requirement is that the stock is not sold within 2 years after the date that the option is granted, i.e., typically the first day of the offering period, nor within one year after the shares are purchased, typically the last day of the offering period. When the holding period is satisfied and there is a gain from the sale, the gain is ordinary income up to the amount by which the stock's fair market value, when the option was granted, exceeded the option price. Any excess gain is capital gain. If there is a loss from the sale, it is a capital loss, and there is no ordinary income or loss. The employer gets no deduction when the holding period requirements have been satisfied.

EXAMPLE

Under an ESPP Yodell Corporation grants an option to buy 100 shares of common stock of Yodell Corporation for an exercise price that is 15-percent less than the stock's fair market value at the beginning of the offering period. On the first day of the offering period the stock had a market value of $24 per share. Thus, the option price under the ESPP was $20.40. The ESPP's offering period is 18 months and at the end of that period the value of the stock is $25 per share. Rachel Rhinehart has made contributions to the ESPP sufficient to purchase 100 shares, and 14 months after the end of the offering period she sells her stock for $30 per share. In the year of sale, Rachel must report as wages the difference between the option price ($20.40) and the value at the time the option was granted ($24). The rest of the gain ($6) is capital gain, figured as follows:

Selling price ($30 × 100 shares)	$3,000
Purchase price (option price) ($20.40 × 100 shares)	-2,040
Gain	$960
Amount reported as wages [($24 × 100 shares) - $2,040]	-360
Amount reported as capital gain	$ 600

If the employee does not meet the holding period requirement, the ordinary income is the amount by which the stock's fair market value exceeded the option price at the time of exercise, the date the stock was purchased. This ordinary income is not limited to the gain from the sale of the stock. The basis in the stock then becomes the market value for determining future capital gains or losses. The employer receives a deduction in this case equal to the amount of ordinary income recognized by the employee.

EXAMPLE

The facts are the same as in the previous example, except that Rachel sold the stock only 6 months after she purchased her shares. Because she did not hold the stock long enough, she must report $460 as wages and $500 as capital gain, calculated as follows:

Selling price ($30 × 100 shares)	$3,000
Purchase price (option price) ($20.40 × 100 shares)	-2,040
Gain	$960
Amount reported as wages [($25 × 100 shares) - $2,040]	-460
Amount reported as capital gain	$ 500

Qualification Requirements

The employer that is considering the adoption of an ESPP must be aware that to qualify for favorable tax treatment, the plan must meet the following requirements:

- The plan must provide that options to purchase stock can only be granted to employees of the adopting employer and its parent or subsidiaries.

- The plan is approved by the employer's stockholders within 12 months before or after the date such plan is adopted.

- No employee can be granted an option if such employee, immediately after the option is granted, owns stock possessing 5 percent or more of the total combined voting power or of the total value of all classes of the employer's stock.

- The plan must cover all employees except those with less than 2 years of employment, employees whose customary employment is 20 hours or less per week, employees whose customary employment is for not more than 5 months in any calendar year, and those who are highly compensated employees, as defined under Sec. 415(q).

- All employees granted options must have the same rights and privileges, except that the limit on the amount of stock which may be purchased by any employee under such option may bear a uniform relationship to the employee's total compensation, or his or her basic or regular rate of compensation. Alternatively, the plan may provide that no employee may purchase more than a maximum amount of stock fixed under the plan.

- The employer cannot permit an employee to buy more than $25,000 of stock in any one year. This limit is applied with respect to each calendar year, beginning with the calendar year in which the grant date occurs and ending with the calendar year in which the option is exercised. This limit is based upon the stock's fair market value when the option is granted. This limit, however, is cumulative. For example, if the stock's fair market value on the date of grant in 2017 is $200 per share and no shares are purchased in 2017, 250 shares may be purchased in 2018.

Planning

If the employer sponsors an ESSP, employees can earn a significant return on their investment. If the plan does not use the look-back rule, but simply provides a 15 percent discount off the current market price, the employees immediately earn a return of 17.6 percent when they purchase stock. For example, if the stock is selling at $10 and the employee purchases the stock at $8.50 (a 15 percent discount), the participant has earned $1.50. On an investment of $8.50, the return is 17.6 percent ($1.50/$8.50). Of course, if the participant holds the stock to satisfy the holding period requirements, the stock's value could possibly decline.

When the ESPP has a look-back purchase price, the potential gain is much higher. If, for example, the stock can be purchased at a 15 percent discount off the price at the time the offering period begins and the stock price rises from $10 at the beginning of the period to $20 at the end of the offering period, the participant has a return of 135 percent ($11.50/$8.50).

From the employer's perspective, establishing an ESSP is a much bigger commitment than that made under the other forms of stock option programs. Regular stock option programs are generally limited to officers and certain key executives while ESSPs must cover substantially all full-time employees. The employer must be committed to the concept (and the cost) of encouraging employee stock ownership through a discount program.

OTHER FORMS OF EQUITY-BASED COMPENSATION

LO 16.6 **Explain the tax treatment of restricted stock, phantom stock and stock appreciation rights programs.**

phantom stock

Phantom stock is the name given to what is essentially a bookkeeping entry on behalf of the executive as if he or she had been given stock in the company. Units analogous to company shares are granted to executives pursuant to a contractual undertaking, and the value of the units generally equals the market value of the stock underlying the units at the time of grant. Phantom units mature at a fixed date, typically at retirement, death or a fixed period, such as 5 to 15 years after the grant of the phantom stock. On the maturation date, the company generally pays the executive (in cash or stock) the difference between the initial value of the units and the current value of the units based on the stock's current market price. In some plans, dividend equivalents may be credited to the units just as dividends would be paid on the underlying stock.

> **EXAMPLE**
>
> Employer grants Executive A 100 shares of phantom stock valued at $5,000 ($50 per share). The phantom stock matures after 5 years and at maturity its value has increased to $7,500 ($75 per share). At that time, the employer pays the employee $2,500, the difference between the value at the time of the grant and the value at the time of maturity.

On the payment date, the appreciation in the value of the units is taxed to the executive as ordinary income and is subject to withholding and employment taxes. The company takes a tax deduction in the amount of the executive's taxable income from the units.

As with other incentive plans, the executive has the possibility of large gains. Although one advantage of phantom stock over stock options is that the executive avoids the financing cost associated with the exercise of the options, in some cases gains may be capped by company-imposed maximums designed to limit the company's potential payment. Because payment is typically triggered by retirement, the executive generally has no flexibility in choosing when to value the award. In cases where the issuer is a public company and the executive can control the form or timing of the unit's valuation or settlement, trading restrictions similar to those applicable to stock options also apply to insiders holding phantom stock.

Restricted Stock

restricted stock plan

In a **restricted stock plan**, the executive is given (usually at no cost) shares of his or her employer's stock. The shares are actually stamped with specific restrictions, which require that the executive give the shares back to the employer upon a specified event. Most commonly, the restriction is that if the executive stops working prior to some specified date, he or she will have to forfeit some or all of the shares. Another common restriction is a clause that requires forfeiture if the executive terminates employment and goes to work with a competitor (commonly called a noncompete clause). Dividends on the stock are usually paid to the executive during the entire period in which he or she holds the restricted stock.

From a tax perspective, the shares of restricted stock are generally not taxed until the substantial limitations on the stock lapse. At that time, the value of the stock will be treated as ordinary income to the executive and will be deductible as compensation expense by the employer. Any dividends paid to the executive will also be treated as compensation income—both includible as income to the executive and deductible as compensation by the employer.

EXAMPLE

Company grants to Billy Bigshot, age 55, 200 shares of stock worth $20,000. The stock is restricted and will be forfeited unless Billy works until age 65, at which time the stock becomes nonforfeitable and freely transferable by Billy. At age 65, Billy retires and decides to hold the stock, which is now valued at $80,000. For the year in which Billy attains age 65, he must report $80,000 of ordinary income and the company is entitled to an $80,000 deduction.

In the preceding example, Billy could have chosen to report income in the year that the restricted stock was transferred to him. This decision to accelerate the reporting of income is referred to as a "Sec. 83(b) election," taking its name from the section of the Code that authorizes the election. When a Sec. 83(b) election is made, the amount of ordinary income that is recognized is based on the stock's fair market value on the date of transfer. The employer is also entitled to a corresponding deduction. Subsequently, when the stock vests and is sold, there is a capital gain, assuming that the stock has appreciated in value. The capital gain is long-term or short-term, depending on the holding period which is measured from the date of transfer, rather than the date on which ownership of the stock vests in the employee.

EXAMPLE

If in the preceding example Billy had decided to make a Sec. 83(b) election, in the year of transfer he would have recognized $20,000 of ordinary income. Then at his retirement he would not have had to report any additional income. Later, if Billy sold the stock for $100,000, he would have had a long-term capital gain of $80,000.

While a Sec. 83(b) election can often result in considerable tax savings, it is not a decision that should be taken lightly. A Sec. 83(b) election involves no small amount of risk. For example, if Billy had left the company before becoming vested in his stock, he would have reported $20,000 of income that he never received. The tax law does not permit Billy to take a tax deduction of any kind for the taxes paid in connection with his Sec. 83(b) election. Moreover, if the stock goes down in value after the Sec. 83(b) election is made and the stock is eventually sold at a loss, the loss must be taken as a capital loss on the employee's tax return even though the income from the Sec. 83(b) election was previously taxed at ordinary income rates. Nevertheless, an executive who (1) does not expect to lose the stock, (2) has the money to pay taxes at the time of the grant, and (3) expects the stock to greatly appreciate in value may want to consider the election.

In order to make a Sec. 83(b) election, certain procedures must be followed. These procedures include the following:

- The election must be made within 30 days of the stock transfer date.
- The election must be sent to the IRS within that 30-day period.
- A copy of the election must be attached to the executive's tax return for the year in which the election is made.
- A copy of the election must be provided to the executive's employer.

For all intents and purposes, a Sec. 83(b) election should be considered irrevocable. It is only under the most highly unusual circumstances that the IRS will consider allowing a taxpayer to revoke a Sec. 83(b) election.

For the employer, restricted stock plans are another way to tie the employee to the company (through the vesting provision) and to tie the benefit to the performance of the company stock. From the employee's perspective, this type of deferred compensation is relatively secure because the stock is titled in the executive's name, meaning that the company's creditors cannot get to this asset if the company performs badly. (However, if the company performs badly, the stock may not be worth very much in any event.) Another advantage is that the employee does not have to pay anything in order to get stock ownership, unlike stock option plans. The biggest limitation, from the employee's perspective, is the possibility of forfeiture.

Stock Appreciation Right

stock appreciation right (SAR)

A **stock appreciation right (SAR)** is an arrangement under which an executive has the right to receive the amount of the increase in the value of employer stock during a specified period. The executive receives the increase in value by cashing out or exercising the SAR, similar to a stock option.

> **EXAMPLE**
>
> Wanda Wunderkind receives SARs with respect to 1,000 shares of employer stock when the stock is valued at $100 a share and the SARs may be exercisable for 3 years. For a period of 3 years, Wanda has the right at any time to receive cash in the amount of the increase in value of up to 1,000 shares of stock since the time that the SARs were granted. If after year 1 the stock value has increased to $110 a share, Wanda can exercise 100 of her SARs and receive a cash payment of $1,000. Similarly, if after year 2 the stock

value has increased to $200 per share, Wanda can exercise her remaining 900 SARs and receive a cash payment of $90,000.

The grant of an SAR does not result in taxation because the executive only has the right to receive income in the future. However, due to the fact that an employee has the unfettered right to receive the current increase in the value of the underlying stock upon request, an SAR does raise an issue of constructive receipt. However, based on a consistent line of revenue rulings (issued before the enactment of Sec. 409A), the IRS has taken the position that a substantial limitation on the executive's ability to receive the current increase in stock value results from the fact that the executive loses the right to future appreciation in the stock once she exercises the SAR. In other words, the executive must surrender a valuable right in order to exercise the SAR. However, care must be taken at the end of the SAR term. Since there will be no more future appreciation to be lost, any value in the SAR at that time may be constructively received by the holder if the SAR has not been exercised.

Once an SAR has been exercised, the amount received by the executive is taxable as ordinary income. The employer generally receives a deduction for the same amount. The ordinary income recognized by the executive is subject to income tax withholding and is considered wages subject to employment taxes.

CHAPTER REVIEW

Key Terms and Concepts

nonqualified stock options (NQSOs)
noncompete clause
incentive stock option (ISO)
ESPP

phantom stock
restricted stock plan
stock appreciation right (SAR)

Chapter 16: Review Questions

Review questions are based on the learning objectives in this chapter. Thus, a [16.3] at the end of a question means that the question is based on learning objective 3. If there are multiple objectives, they are all listed.

1. What are three key reasons that equity-based compensation is a popular compensation component? [16.1]

2. What are the points in time that valuation of the stock is important in the life span of an equity-based compensation program? [16.2]

3. Describe what is meant by the concept of the employee's "economic risk." [16.2]

4. What legal considerations must be used in evaluating an equity-based compensation program? [16.2]

5. What are the advantages of granting awards under a clearly defined plan or program? [16.2]

6. What is the intrinsic value of a stock option? [16.3]

7. What are the tax consequences of nonqualified stock options? [16.3]

8. What are the tax consequences of incentive stock options? [16.4]

9. What requirements must an ESPP satisfy? [16.5]

10. What are the tax consequences of the sale of 100 shares of stock, assuming the stock was purchased under a Sec. 423 stock purchase plan and the participant satisfied both the 2-year and one-year holding requirements? [16.5]

Stock price at beginning of option period ($5 × 100)	$500
Purchase price ($4.25 × 100)	$425
Stock price at the time of purchase ($10 × 100)	$1,000
Stock price at the time of sale ($15 × 100)	$1,500

11. What is the objective of a phantom stock plan? [16.6]

12. Explain the tax-timing strategies available to an executive covered by a restricted stock plan. [16.6]

13. Explain how an SAR rewards the executive. [16.6]

14. Explain why the grant of an SAR does not result in the constructive receipt of income. [16.6]

Chapter 16: Answers

1. The first reason is that it has the potential to offer the employee who receives it capital gain treatment for any increase in its value. Second, it serves as an effective incentive for employees who receive it. Third, in the appropriate circumstances it may be a less costly form of compensation than cash or other forms of property to the employer and its controlling shareholders.

2. Such valuation can be important (1) when the program is established, (2) when a stock award is received by an employee, (3) when the stock award becomes vested, and (4) when the employee decides to sell or otherwise dispose of the stock award.

3. There is the possibility of loss to the employees. For example, a direct purchase of stock by an employee generally results in economic risk to the employee to the extent of the purchase price.

4. First, it is important to recognize that many plans require stockholder approval. To ensure that the plan is not subject to most of the provisions of ERISA, the plan should be designed to satisfy the top-hat exemption. Also, care should be taken to ensure that the plan does not result in a public offering of stock, requiring SEC filing.

5. Advantages include: a plan facilitates the process of obtaining shareholder approval, a plan helps maintain shareholder relations in a public company, and can help employee relations as well.

6. This element refers to the excess, if any, of the stock's value over the exercise price.

7. At the time the options are granted, there are no income tax consequences. At the time of exercise, the participant has ordinary income in the amount of the difference between the option price and the current market price. The employer receives a deduction of this same amount. When the stock is later sold, the gain is taxed as short-term or long-term capital gain, depending upon the holding period.

8. There are no income tax consequences to the participant either at the time the options are granted or at the time the options are exercised. However, at the time of exercise, there could be an alternative minimum tax. The employer gets no deduction. At the time the stock is sold, the whole taxable amount (the difference between the sale price and the option price) is taxed as long-term gains if certain holding period requirements are satisfied.

9. An ESPP 1) may only cover employees, 2) must be approved by the shareholders, 3) must exclude 5 percent owners, 4) must cover full-time employees (with a few exceptions), 5) all employees granted options must have the same rights and privileges, 6) employees can not buy more than $25,000 of stock in any one year.

10. Because the purchase price was $425 and the value of the stock at the beginning of the period was $500, the participant will pay $75 of ordinary income. Because the sale price was $1,500, the participant pays capital gains tax on $1,000.

11. The objective is to reward the executive for increasing the value of the company stock.

12. The participant can pay taxes at the time the restrictions are removed or within 30 days from the time the stock is transferred to the participant.

13. The executive is entitled to the increase in the value of a stock over a stated period.

14. Even though the executive has the right to exercise the SAR at any time, cashing in on the current gain means giving up the right to any future potential gain.

Chapter 17

Individual Retirement Plans—Part I

Learning Objectives

An understanding of the material in this chapter should enable the student to

- **LO 17.1** Identify the different types of individual retirement arrangements.
- **LO 17.2** Describe the contribution limits that apply to IRAs and Roth IRAs.
- **LO 17.3** Determine who is eligible to make deductible and nondeductible IRA contributions.
- **LO 17.4** Determine who is eligible to make a Roth IRA contribution.
- **LO 17.5** Describe a Roth IRA conversion and when this transaction is allowed.

OVERVIEW OF INDIVIDUAL RETIREMENT PLANS

LO 17.1 Identify the different types of individual retirement arrangements.

Individual retirement plans are a vital part of the financial planning business. They are important both to the financial security of clients and to the business efforts of financial services professionals. Even though the best opportunities are for lower- and middle-class workers, wealthy individuals often have plans with large sums that have been rolled over from employer-sponsored tax-advantaged retirement plans.

Over the years, Congress has changed the IRA rules numerous times. The changes in the last few years have all been favorable. The Taxpayer Relief Act of 1997 added the Roth IRA and made the deductible IRA available to more taxpayers. The Economic Growth and Tax Relief Reconciliation Act of 2001 increased the maximum allowable contribution limits and added a catch-up contribution for older participants. The Pension Protection Act of 2006 made the increased contribution limits permanent and added a cost-of-living adjustment to the various IRA and Roth IRA income phaseout limits. As a result, proper use of traditional IRAs, Roth IRAs, and rollover IRAs can go a long way toward providing retirement security. The financial services professional can help clients achieve their goals by explaining the IRA rules, encouraging saving for retirement, and marketing IRA investments.

Roth IRA

IRA

With the introduction of the **Roth IRA**, there are now two types of savings vehicles that are called IRAs (individual retirement accounts). The traditional plan is still referred to as an **IRA**; the newer plan is referred to as a Roth IRA. Traditional IRAs are similar to employer-sponsored tax-sheltered retirement plans in many ways. Both are tax-favored savings plans that encourage the accumulation of savings for retirement because they allow contributions to be made with pretax dollars and earnings to be tax deferred until retirement. With Roth IRAs, contributions are made on an after-tax basis, but earnings are not taxed and qualifying distributions are tax free. Because the tax benefits of both types of plans result in a significant loss of revenue to the federal government, the stringent rules encourage retirement savings but at the same time try and minimize revenue loss.

The funding vehicles and types of allowable investments are the same for both traditional IRAs and the Roth IRA. Both types of IRAs can have as funding instruments a trust or custodial account (individual retirement account) or an annuity contract (individual retirement annuity). With either type of funding vehicle, a wide array of traditional investment strategies can be used.

CONTRIBUTION LIMITS

LO 17.2 Describe the contribution limits that apply to IRAs and Roth IRAs.

The maximum allowable contribution to an IRA or Roth IRA for 2017 is the lesser of $5,500 or 100 percent of compensation. The $5,500 limit applies to all traditional IRAs and Roth IRAs to which a taxpayer contributes for the year. For example, if the taxpayer makes a $5,500 contribution to a traditional IRA, no contributions can be made to a Roth IRA for the year.

> **EXAMPLE**
>
> Dana is a college student and earns $2,500 for the year from a part-time job. The maximum contribution she can make to an IRA or Roth IRA is $2,500 because her earnings are less than the maximum contribution.

Compensation is earnings from wages, salaries, tips, professional fees, bonuses, and any other amount a taxpayer receives for providing personal services. In addition, alimony and separate-maintenance payments are also considered compensation for IRA purposes. Compensation does not include earnings and profits from property, such as rental and dividend income, or amounts received as a pension or annuity. As a general rule, if it is income the taxpayer worked for in a given year, the contribution can be made; if it is derived from investments or retirement income, it is not eligible.

For self-employed persons, compensation includes earned income from personal services, reduced by any contributions to a qualified plan on behalf of the individual. Self-employeds with a net loss from self-employment cannot make IRA contributions unless they also have salary or wage income. In this case, they do not have to reduce the amount of salary income by the net loss from self-employment. If there are both salary or wage income and net income from self-employment, the two amounts are combined to determine the amount that can be contributed.

> **EXAMPLE**
>
> In his first year in business, Don, a self-employed creator of computer software, had a net loss of $17,000, largely due to start-up costs. However, he received $8,000 from part-time teaching. Don may contribute up to $5,500 to an IRA (2017) because his salary will not be reduced by his self-employment loss.

Spousal IRAs

spousal IRAs

If a married person does not work or has limited compensation, his or her spouse can contribute up to $5,500 to a spousal IRA (2017) (which can be either a traditional or a Roth IRA) as long as the following conditions are satisfied:

- The taxpayer is married at the end of the year and files a joint tax return.
- The spouse earns less than the taxpayer.
- The couple has compensation that equals or exceeds contributions to the IRAs of both persons ($11,000 if $5,500 is contributed for each in 2017).

Spousal IRAs can be set up even if the taxpayer does not contribute to his or her own account, or contributions can be made for both spouses, or the taxpayer can make contributions just to the taxpayer's IRA even though a spousal IRA already exists. However, no more than $5,500 (2017) can be placed in either IRA for the year (unless the individual is eligible for the catch-up contribution discussed below).

Catch-up Election

An individual who has attained age 50 before the end of the taxable year can make an IRA catch-up contribution of up to $1,000 (the limit for 2017). For example, in 2017, a 55-year-old individual could contribution up to $6,500 to an IRA or Roth IRA (assuming he or she was otherwise eligible under the phaseout limits discussed below).

> **EXAMPLE**
>
> In 2017, John and Sarah are married, file jointly, and have an AGI of $120,000. They are each eligible to make Roth IRA contributions. Because they are both over 50 years old, the maximum contribution for each is $6,500, or $13,000 in total.

Timing of Contributions

Contributions to an IRA or Roth IRA can be made at any time during the tax year for which the contribution relates or up to April 15 of the following year. Contributions for the year can be made at once or over time.

Excess Contributions

excess contribution

An **excess contribution** is any amount contributed to an IRA or Roth IRA that exceeds the maximum contribution limit. Excess contributions will result in an excise tax of 6 percent on the excess. The penalty tax can be avoided by withdrawing the excess amount (plus earnings) by the federal income tax filing deadline for the year. The taxpayer does have to include the excess amount in his or her gross income and may be subject to the 10-percent Sec. 72(t) premature distribution tax on the earnings withdrawn. With traditional IRAs, excess contributions are relatively rare because most taxpayers can contribute $5,500, even though only a portion of that may be deductible. However, excess contributions may be more common in the Roth IRA because the maximum allowable contribution is reduced when the taxpayer's adjusted gross income (AGI) exceeds a specified amount.

Recharacterization

recharacterization

A taxpayer may be able to treat a contribution made to one type of IRA as made to another type of IRA. This transaction is called a **recharacterization** and it requires that the contribution be transferred from the trustee of the first IRA (the one to which the contribution was made) to the trustee of the second IRA by the due date, plus extensions, of the individual's federal income tax return for the year that the contribution was made. Taxpayers may make this change simply because they change their minds or to solve a tax problem. Take the person who contributes $5,500 to a Roth IRA during the year, and then discovers after the year's end that he or she earned too much and was not eligible to make the contribution. If that person was eligible for either a nondeductible or deductible contribution to a traditional IRA, the Roth IRA contribution could be recharacterized as a traditional IRA contribution to resolve the problem of the excess contribution to the Roth IRA. A recharacterization also requires the following steps:

- Include in the transfer any net income attributable to the contribution. If there was a net loss, the contribution transferred is reduced by the amount of the loss.
- Report the recharacterization on your tax return for the year during which the contribution was made.
- Treat the contribution as having been made to the second IRA on the date that it was actually made to the first IRA.

TRADITIONAL IRAs

Any person under age 70½ who earns compensation can make a contribution to an IRA. For some, the contribution will not be deductible, but earnings will be tax deferred until benefits are distributed. However, most individuals making traditional IRA contributions do so in order to receive an income tax deduction. Not all taxpayers are eligible.

Eligibility for Deductible Contributions

LO 17.3 Determine who is eligible to make deductible and nondeductible IRA contributions.

IRA contributions will always be deductible if neither the taxpayer nor the taxpayer's spouse is an active participant in an employer-maintained retirement plan. If the taxpayer is an active participant, then the contribution is deductible only if his or her adjusted gross income falls below prescribed limits (designed to approximate a middle-class income). If an individual is not an active participant, but his or her spouse is, then the contribution is deductible (for the nonparticipant) if the couple's income is less than a different higher income threshold.

EXAMPLE

Brendan, who is single and has an AGI of $265,000 for 2017, is self-employed and is not an active participant in a retirement plan. Because he has more than $5,500 of income from employment and is not an active participant in an employer-sponsored plan, he can make a deductible contribution of $5,500 to an IRA. This example illustrates that when a single person is not an active participant, he or she can always make a deductible IRA contribution, regardless of the income level.

Active Participant Status

active participant

An individual is an **active participant** if he or she is a participant in an employer-maintained retirement plan. Employer plans include every type of qualified plan—defined-benefit pension plans, money-purchase plans, target-benefit plans, profit-sharing plans, and stock plans. They also include 403(b) tax-sheltered annuity plans, SEPs, and SIMPLEs. Federal, state, or local government plans are also taken into account. An employee who is covered only by a nonqualified plan is not considered an active participant and can, therefore, make deductible IRA contributions.

The term active participant has a special meaning that depends on the type of plan involved.

Defined-Benefit Plans. An individual who is eligible to participate in a defined-benefit plan is considered an active participant in the plan. This is true even if he or she declines to participate or does not earn a benefit accrual for the year. One exception is that if the defined-benefit plan is frozen—meaning that no additional benefits are accruing for any participant—then participants will not be considered active participants in the plan.

Defined-Contribution Plans. A person is an active participant in a defined contribution plan if the plan specifies that employer contributions must be allocated to the individual' account (as in a money-purchase pension plan). For defined-contribution plans with discretionary contributions, such as profit-sharing plans and 401(k) plans, the participant must actually receive a contribution to be considered an active participant. Any type of contribution will count, including elective salary deferral contributions and even reallocated forfeitures from a terminated participant's account. SEPs, SIMPLEs, and 403(b) plans are treated as defined-contribution plans under these rules.

A special rule applies when contributions are completely discretionary under the plan and are not made until after the end of the plan year (ending with or within the employee's tax year in question). In this case, to recognize that a plan participant may not know whether he or she is an active participant by the time the IRA contribution deadline arrives, the employer's contribution is attributable to the following year.

> **EXAMPLE**
>
> Sally first becomes eligible for XYZ Corporation's profit-sharing plan for the plan year ending December 31, 2016. The company is on a calendar fiscal year and does not decide to make a contribution for the 2016 plan year until June 1, 2017. Sally is not considered an active participant in the plan for the 2016 plan year. However, due to the 2017 contribution, she is an active participant for the 2017 plan year.

When the plan year of the employer's plan (regardless of whether the plan is a defined-benefit or defined-contribution plan) is not the calendar year, an individual's active-participant status is dependent upon whether he or she is an active participant for the plan year ending with or within the particular calendar year in question.

> **EXAMPLE**
>
> Susan first becomes eligible for the ABC Corporation's money-purchase pension plan for the plan year June 1, 2016 to May 30, 2017. Susan is an active participant for 2017 (but not 2016) because the plan year ended "with or within" calendar year 2017.

Finally, note that in determining active-participant status, participation for any part of the plan year counts as participation for the whole plan year, and that whether or not the participant is vested in his or her benefit has no bearing on the determination.

> **EXAMPLE**
>
> Jeffrey makes salary deferral contributions to the GHI Corporation's 401(k) plan in January. The plan has a calendar plan year. On February 1, he terminates employment and does not participate in another retirement plan for the rest of the year. Jeffrey was not entitled to the employer-matching contribution or any other employer contribution for the year. However, Jeffrey is still an active participant because salary deferral contributions count as an allocation to his account, and he was in the plan for a portion of the plan year.

Income Level

If an individual is an active participant, fully deductible contributions are allowed only if the taxpayer has adjusted gross income (AGI) below a specified level. The deduction is then phased out over a range, with no deduction allowed if a specified AGI threshold is exceeded. The phaseout ranges as shown in the table below depend upon the participant's income tax filing status.

When applying the phaseout limits, calculation of the AGI is somewhat modified. AGI is determined without regard to the exclusion for foreign earned income, but Social Security benefits includible in gross income and losses or gains on passive investments are taken into account. Also, contributions to an IRA or Roth IRA are not deducted.

Table 17-1
2017 Limits for Deductible IRA Contributions

Filing Status	Full IRA Deduction	Reduced IRA Deduction	No IRA Deduction
Individual (or head of household)	$62,000 or less	$62,000.01 – $71,999.99	$72,000 or more
Married filing jointly	$99,000 or less	$99,000.01 – $118,999.99	$119,000 or more
Married filing jointly (spouse is active participant and individual is not)	$186,000	$186,000.01 – $195,999.99	$196,000 or more
Married filing separately	$0	$.01 – $9,999.99	$10,000 or more

For taxpayers whose AGI falls between the no-deduction level and the full-deduction level, the deduction is reduced pro rata. To compute the reduction, use the following formula:

$$\text{Deductible amount} = \text{max. contribution} - \{\text{max. contribution} \times [(\text{AGI} - \text{filing status floor}) \div \text{phaseout range}]\}$$

Two operational rules apply to taxpayers who fall into the reduced IRA category. First, the IRS allows the adjusted limitation to be rounded up to the next $10 increment. For example, if the formula for Kay shows her eligible to make a deductible contribution of $758.43, her deductible contribution is rounded up to $760. The second rule that applies to the reduction formula mandates a $200 floor. In other words, even if Ed's deductible IRA contribution works out to $57, Ed is still entitled to make a $200 deductible contribution.

EXAMPLE

Bob and Rita Dufus (a married couple under age 50 filing jointly) are both working, are both active participants, and have a combined adjusted gross income of $109,000 for 2017. Bob and Rita can each make the full IRA contribution of $5,500 (total $11,000). However, only a portion of each contribution is deductible. Because their AGI is $10,000 more than the lower limit for married couples ($99,000), they each lose one half (totally phased out over $20,000 ($119,000-$99,000 = $20,000)) of the deductible contribution. Each can deduct $2,750 (total $5,500). Using the formula,

$$\$5{,}500 - \{\$5{,}500 \times [(\$109{,}000-\$99{,}000) \div \$20{,}000]\}$$

Married Taxpayers with Spouses Who Are Active Participants

If a married taxpayer and his or her spouse are both active participants, then the deduction rules just described apply to both IRAs. However, the rules are different when only one spouse is an active participant. In this case, a $5,500 deductible IRA contribution is allowed for the nonactive participant spouse as long as the couple's AGI does not exceed $186,000 (2017). The deduction is phased out if the couple's joint AGI exceeds $186,000 (2017) and will be gone entirely if their AGI is $196,000 or more (as indexed for 2017). These phaseout rules apply in the same way as the other deductible IRA phaseout rules. A deductible contribution is not available for the nonactive participant spouse if the couple files separate tax returns.

> **EXAMPLE**
>
> Joe and Jane Morgan, each aged 43, ask you whether they are allowed to make deductible contributions for 2017. They file a joint tax return. Only Joe works outside of the home, and their expected modified AGI for 2017 is $130,000. Only Joe is an active participant in an employer-sponsored retirement plan. Joe cannot make a deductible IRA contribution on his own behalf because their modified AGI will exceed $119,000 (the phaseout amount in 2017). However, the couple can make a $5,500 deductible IRA contribution to Jane's spousal IRA because their AGI is less than $186,000.

Rollover Contributions

In addition to annual contributions, an IRA is allowed to accept certain rollover contributions. The IRA rollover permits the financial services professional to manage and service large asset accumulations. This opportunity continues to grow as more company pension plans today give participants a lump-sum option and workers continue to accumulate large sums in their company's 401(k) plan.

rollover

There are several types of rollovers that involve individual retirement arrangements:

- *Rollover* from one individual retirement arrangement to another individual retirement arrangement. Taxpayers can withdraw all or part of the balance in an IRA and reinvest it within 60 days in another IRA. The reasons for doing this include changing trusts or custodial accounts (because of dissatisfaction with investment performance or service) or even the temporary use of the IRA asset. This type of **rollover** can only occur once each year. Only one IRA-to-IRA rollover is allowed in a 1-year period. See *Bobrow v. Commissioner*, 2014. Direct trustee to trustee IRA transfers are not considered a rollover and are not subject to the one rollover-per-year limitation of Sec. 408(d)(3)(B). Remember, this allows you to either rollover into the same IRA or to a different IRA or account, but limits the total number of rollovers to 1 per year, not one per IRA.

trustee-to-trustee transfer

- *Trustee-to-trustee transfer.* An IRA owner who wants to change service providers can transfer the account directly from one trustee (or custodian) to another. **Trustee-to-trustee transfers** ensure that the participant does not violate the 60-day rule.

- *Rollover from a qualified plan or 403(b) plan to an IRA.* Under the rules applicable today, most distributions made from a qualified plan, 403(b) plan, or 457 plan sponsored by the government can be rolled over (in full or in part) into a new or existing IRA. The rollover is not allowed when the distribution is part of a series of periodic payments over the participant's life expectancy or over a period of 10 years or more, or if the distribution is a hardship withdrawal from 401(k) plan. The problem with this type of rollover is that distributions from the qualified plan, 403(b) annuity, or 457 plan will be subject to a 20 percent income tax withholding.

direct rollover

- *Direct rollover.* To avoid the 20 percent withholding, a participant in a qualified plan, 403(b) annuity, or 457 plan should elect instead what is referred to as a **direct rollover** from the plan to the IRA. These plans are required to give participants a form in which they elect the direct payment to the IRA trustee. When the direct rollover is elected, the normal 20 percent income tax withholding requirements on the distribution do not apply.

Tax Treatment of Distributions

Taxpayers can generally withdraw all or part of their IRAs at any time. Unless the participant has made nondeductible contributions, distributions from IRAs are treated as ordinary income and are subject to federal income tax. Nondeductible contributions are withdrawn tax free on a pro rata basis. If the participant dies, payments to beneficiaries are still subject to income tax. However, the income is treated as "income in respect to a decedent," which means that income taxes are reduced by the amount of estate taxes paid as a result of the IRA.

If distributions are made prior to age 59½, the Sec. 72(t) excise tax imposes an additional 10 percent tax unless an exception applies. Exceptions are made for payments on account of death, disability, or for the payment of certain medical expenses. Another exception allows substantially equal periodic payments over the remaining life of the participant and a chosen beneficiary. Another allows payments for qualified higher education expenses for education furnished to the taxpayer, the taxpayer's spouse, or any child or grandchild of the taxpayer or taxpayer's spouse at an eligible educational institution. A final exception is for distributions to pay for acquisition costs of a first home for the participant, spouse, or any child, grandchild, or ancestor of the participant or spouse. However, this exception has a $10,000 lifetime limit per IRA participant.

IRAs are also subject to rules that control the maximum length of the tax-deferral period. These are minimum-distribution rules that generally require distributions to begin when the participant attains age 70½ and also require specified payments at the participant's death.

ROTH IRAS

LO 17.4   Determine who is eligible to make a Roth IRA contribution.

Determining whether an individual is eligible to make a contribution to a Roth IRA is simpler than with a traditional IRA. Eligibility is entirely dependent upon an individual's modified AGI and tax filing status. An individual's active participant status is not relevant. Also, unlike traditional IRAs, contributions can even be made after attainment of age 70½.

A single taxpayer with AGI of $118,000 or less (as indexed for 2017) can make the maximum allowable Roth IRA contribution (as long as he or she has compensation from employment and has not made contributions to other IRAs or Roth IRAs). The ability to contribute to a Roth IRA is phased out for single taxpayers with an modified AGI between $118,000 and $133,000 (2017) (pro rata reduction over $15,000 income spread). For married couples filing jointly, each spouse can make the maximum contribution as long as the couple's modified AGI is $186,000 or less (as indexed for 2017). The ability to contribute to a Roth IRA is phased out for joint filers with an AGI between $186,000 and $196,000 (pro rata reduction over $10,000 income spread). For married taxpayers filing separately, the phaseout range is $0 to $10,000. For purposes of this calculation, the AGI is adjusted in the same way as for traditional IRAs.

> **EXAMPLE**
>
> Joe and Jane Morgan, the same couple who asked about deductible IRA contributions, also want to know about their Roth options for 2017. Remember that they are each aged 43, they file a joint tax return, and their expected modified AGI for 2017 is $140,000. Only Joe is an active participant in an employer-sponsored retirement plan. Assuming that they don't make any contributions to other traditional IRAs or Roth

IRAs, a $5,500 contribution to a Roth IRA could be made for both Joe and Jane Morgan because their income does not exceed $186,000. Now that they know their options, the couple decides to make a $5,500 deductible IRA contribution for Jane and a Roth IRA contribution for Joe.

Rollovers and Conversions

LO 17.5   Describe a Roth IRA conversion and when this transaction is allowed.

Distributions from one Roth IRA can be rolled over tax free to another Roth IRA. As with traditional IRAs, the rollover has to occur within 60 days and can only occur once a year. The transaction can also be made as a trustee-to-trustee transfer.

Also, amounts in a traditional IRA can be rolled over to a Roth IRA. Such transactions are referred to as Roth IRA conversions, and today all taxpayers are allowed to convert. The conversion can be accomplished with a distribution from a traditional IRA, which is contributed (rolled over) to a Roth IRA within 60 days. Or the conversion can be accomplished with a direct transfer of assets to a Roth IRA, either with a new trustee or with the same trustee. A conversion can also occur if the IRA is a SEP-IRA or a SIMPLE-IRA, except that SIMPLEs cannot be converted in the first 2 years. A conversion to a Roth IRA can also be made through a rollover or transfer from a qualified plan, 403(b) plan, or even a government-sponsored 457(b) plan.

When an amount is rolled over from a traditional IRA, the distribution (valued at the time of the distribution from the IRA) is subject to income tax (taxed as ordinary income), but is not subject to the 10 percent early distribution excise tax. However, because this could result in the avoidance of the 10 percent early distribution tax, individuals who withdraw converted amounts from a Roth IRA within 5 tax years of the conversion are subject to the 10 percent Code Sec. 72(t) penalty tax on early withdrawals (unless one of the exceptions to that tax applies).

EXAMPLE

Candy Street converted a $100,000 IRA last year when she was age 44. The following year Candy decides to start a business and withdraws $60,000. Since she paid income tax on the $100,000 at the time of the conversion, she can withdraw the $60,000 without paying ordinary income tax. However, since the withdrawal is within 5 years of the conversion Candy will have to pay a $6,000 Code Sec. 72(t) early withdrawal penalty tax. The tax can still be avoided if one of the exceptions to the penalty tax applies, for example if Candy was taking the withdrawal to pay for qualified higher-education expenses.

The rules require that the conversion occur before the end of the year for which the conversion is being made. Technically, this means that if an individual wants to convert an IRA in 2017, the amount must be distributed from the traditional IRA by December 31, 2017. However, it can still be rolled over within 60 days of the end of the year.

> **EXAMPLE**
>
> Brendan Bartels is single and wants to convert his $80,000 IRA to a Roth IRA in 2017. He withdraws the $80,000 from the traditional IRA on December 31, 2017. On February 15, 2018, he rolls the benefit into a Roth IRA. This transaction is treated as a 2017 transaction, and Brendan is taxed on the value at the time the amount was distributed from the IRA.

One useful planning tool is that the law allows an undoing of the Roth IRA conversion without penalty as long as the amount is transferred back to a traditional IRA by the due date of the income tax return (plus extensions) for the year, and that any earnings on the account are also returned. In IRS Publication 590, the IRS indicates that even if the taxpayer has filed his or her tax return, the recharacterization can occur up until October 15, as long as an amended return is filed. Recharacterizations can only occur once for each tax year.

> **YOUR FINANCIAL SERVICES PRACTICE: RECHARACTERIZING ROTH IRA CONVERSIONS**
>
> When an IRA is converted into a Roth IRA, the participant pays taxes on the value of the converted amount on the date of conversion. This means that when the market is down and IRA values are low, it is a good time to convert an IRA into a Roth. However, it is possible that the value of the converted Roth IRA will decline after the conversion, in which case the participant would prefer to undo this transaction and convert again later at the lower value. With a recharacterization, the transaction can be reversed generally up until the October 15 of the following year.

Tax Treatment of Roth IRA Distributions

Any "qualified distribution" from a Roth IRA is free from federal income taxes. Qualified Roth IRA distributions must satisfy two requirements. First, the distribution must be made after the 5-tax-year period beginning with the first tax year for which a contribution was made to any Roth IRA established for the individual. Second, the distribution has to be (1) made on or after the date on which the owner attains age 59½, (2) made to a beneficiary or the owner's estate on or after the date of the owner's death, (3) attributable to the owner's disability, or (4) made to pay for up to $10,000 of qualified first-time homebuyer expenses.

If these requirements are not satisfied, the distribution is referred to as a nonqualifying distribution. Generally, an individual can withdraw his or her Roth IRA contributions (or converted contributions) without income tax consequences. Once all contributions have been withdrawn, amounts representing earnings are subject to both income tax and the 10 percent Sec. 72(t) excise tax.

CHAPTER REVIEW

Key Terms and Concepts

Roth IRA
IRA
spousal IRAs
excess contribution
recharacterization

active participant
rollover
trustee-to-trustee transfer
direct rollover

Chapter 17: Review Questions

Review questions are based on the learning objectives in this chapter. Thus, a [17.3] at the end of a question means that the question is based on learning objective 3. If there are multiple objectives, they are all listed.

1. How are traditional IRAs similar to qualified plans? [17.1]

2. How is a Roth IRA different from a traditional IRA? [17.1]

3. Answer these common client questions about contributions to IRAs and Roth IRAs for 2017. [17.2]

    a. If I make the maximum contribution to a traditional IRA, can I make additional contributions to a Roth IRA?

    b. I'm a college student and I'm not planning to work in 2017. Can my parents make a Roth IRA contribution for me?

    c. When is the last date I can make a contribution for 2017?

    d. I made a Roth IRA contribution of $5,500, expecting that my income would be under the allowable threshold. I ended up earning too much and now am ineligible to make the contribution. What do I do now?

4. What do you think are the governmental policies that are fostered with the IRA deduction rules that consider active participant status and income phaseouts? [17.3]

5. Which of the following employees is considered an active participant? [17.3]

   a. John has a target-benefit Keogh plan to which he contributes annually.

   b. Barb works for an employer who maintains a defined-benefit plan, but Barb is not eligible to participate in the plan.

   c. Patty is a member of a 401(k) plan and makes a 5 percent salary reduction that is not matched.

   d. Bob is a member of his employer's profit-sharing plan; the employer has announced that no contribution will be made for the year.

   e. Tim's employer does not have any form of retirement plan. Tim's wife works for an employer who contributes an amount equal to 10 percent of her salary each year to a money-purchase plan.

6. For taxpayers who are active participants in an employer-sponsored retirement plan, what are the modified AGI phaseout ranges for deductible IRA contributions in 2017 for [17.3]

   a. a single taxpayer?

   b. a married taxpayer who is filing jointly?

7. George and Mary Barke (marrieds filing jointly) have a combined modified AGI of $104,657 in 2017. Each is aged 45. George is an active participant in an employer-maintained plan but Mary is not. What is the amount of the deductible IRA contribution that George and Mary can make for 2017, assuming that both earn more than $5,500? [17.3]

8. John is changing jobs at age 35. He is entitled to a distribution of $47,000 from his former company's 401(k) plan. This amount is about the same amount that a terrific car that John wants to buy costs. He's asked you for your advice. What would you say to John? [17.3]

9. Answer the following common Roth IRA client questions. [17.4]

   a. How do I know if I'm eligible to make a Roth IRA contribution?

   b. I'm 72 years old. Can I make a contribution to a Roth IRA?

   c. I'd like to start a Roth IRA, but I'm concerned about needing some of the money in the case of emergencies. Could you explain the tax consequences?

10. In 2017, Joe, age 52, converts a $100,000 IRA to a Roth IRA. [17.5]

    a. What are tax consequences of this transaction?

    b. Assuming that the conversion was Joe's first Roth IRA, what are the tax consequences of a withdrawal of $15,000 2 years later to pay for a new car?

11. Given the following facts, what are Edward and Alice's IRA and Roth IRA options for 2017? [17.5]

    - Names: Edward and Alice Sillyman
    - Ages: Edward 53, Alice 48
    - Modified AGI: $ 140,000
    - Employment status: Alice is employed and earns $109,000 and Edward is not employed
    - Marital status: Married
    - Tax filing status: Joint tax return
    - Active participant status: Alice is an active participant, Edward is not

Chapter 17: Review Answers

1. Both qualified plans and traditional IRAs are tax-favored savings plans that encourage the accumulation of savings for retirement because they allow contributions to be made with pretax dollars (if the taxpayer is eligible) and earnings to be tax deferred until retirement.

2. Contributions are not deductible in a Roth IRA, but qualifying distributions are tax free.

3. a. No; the contribution limits apply to contributions to all IRAs and Roth IRAs in aggregate.

   b. No; you must have employment income in order for them to make a Roth IRA contribution. Because that Roth IRA contribution will grow tax free for many years, this is a great idea. I would hope that you could fit in some work so that your parents could make this contribution to your future.

   c. You must make the contribution on or before April 15, 2018.

   d. You have made an excess contribution and will be subject to a 6 percent penalty tax for the tax year that you made the contribution unless you can withdraw the contribution and any earnings on the contribution before the due date of your tax return for the year (including extensions). If you've missed the deadline, you will have to pay the tax and resolve the problem for that tax year. This would mean using the contribution as next year's contribution if you were eligible. There is one more alternative: You can recharacterize the Roth IRA contribution as a nondeductible IRA contribution.

4. The rules encourage those who do not participate in employer-sponsored pension plans to establish their own IRAs by giving them the opportunity to make tax deductible contributions. Allowing tax-deductible contributions for lower-income individuals who participate in employer plans makes sense in that it targets a group that is likely to be financially unprepared for retirement. However, many in this group are not able to afford to make the IRA contributions. The most likely reason for the income caps is to limit the tax expenditure on deductible contributions.

5. a. John is considered an active participant. In general, anyone covered by a qualified plan is considered an active participant, and a Keogh plan is considered a qualified plan.

   b. Barb is not considered an active participant, even though her employer has a qualified plan, because she is not eligible to participate.

c. Patty is an active participant because salary reductions to a 401(k) plan are treated as employer contributions.

d. Unless there are contributions as a result of a forfeiture, Bob is not an active participant because no contributions will be allocated to his account for the year.

e. Tim is not an active participant because his spouse is an active participant in a qualified plan.

6. a. For 2017, the deduction for a single taxpayer is phased out for adjusted gross income between $62,000 and $72,000.

   b. For 2017, the deduction for a married taxpayer who files jointly is phased out for adjusted gross income between $99,000 and $119,000.

7. Using the formula in the text, George Barke can deduct $5,500 − {$5,500 × [($104,657 − $99,000) ÷ $20,000]}. The actual amount is $3,944.33 which is rounded up to $3,950. The AGI is $104,657, the threshold is $99,000, the phaseout range is $20,000 and the maximum contribution is $5,500. Mary can deduct $5,500, because she is not an active participant and the couple's AGI is less than $186,000.

8. John, if you take a withdrawal from the 401(k) plan, 20 percent of the distribution will be withheld for taxes. However, this is not the total tax picture. At the end of the year, you must include the $47,000 in taxable income and pay taxes at your marginal tax rate. In addition, because you are younger than age 59½, you will have to pay an additional 10 percent penalty tax. After all the taxes, you may have only 60 percent or less of the benefit remaining. Even worse, you just spent a retirement asset that would be worth over $134,000 at age 65 (assuming a conservative 6 percent rate of return each year). John, I would strongly encourage you to elect a direct rollover of the $47,000 to an IRA.

9. a. Eligibility depends solely on your adjusted AGI and your tax filing status.

   b. Yes, there are no age limits on a Roth IRA.

   c. You can always withdraw up to the amount of your total contributions without paying any income tax. If you have the Roth IRA for at least 5 years and you wait until age 59½, all distributions will be tax free. If you take out more than your total contributions before age 59½, you will have to pay income taxes, and possibly a 10 percent penalty tax for a premature withdrawal.

10. a. Joe will have to pay income tax on the $100,000 conversion. Because this amount is added to his ordinary income, it might put him into a higher tax bracket. Even

though Joe is age 52, conversions are not subject to the 10 percent Sec. 72(t) penalty tax on early withdrawals.

b. The $15,000 withdrawal is a nonqualifying distribution since Joe has not maintained the Roth IRA for 5 years and he has not met one of the qualifying trigger events. However, Joe's contribution basis is $100,000, the amount included in income at the time of the conversion. Because basis can be withdrawn first, there are no income tax consequences. However, Joe is subject to the Sec. 72(t) 10 percent penalty tax because of the special rule that applies to withdrawals within 5 years of the conversion.

11. Given that Alice is an active participant and their adjusted AGI exceeds $119,000, Alice cannot make a deductible IRA contribution. However, she could make a $5,500 nondeductible contribution to a traditional IRA. Even though Edward has no earnings from employment, he is eligible for a deductible spousal IRA since their AGI is less than $186,000. The Sillymans can make a $6,500 ($5,500 plus the $1,000 catch-up contribution, since Edward has attained age 50) deductible contribution to Edward's traditional IRA.

Alternatively, they could make contributions to Roth IRAs. The maximum contributions are $5,500 for Alice and $6,500 for Edward. They could also use a combination of plans, as long as contributions do not exceed the maximum contribution. For example, they could make a $3,500 deductible contribution for Edward and also make a $3,000 Roth IRA contribution on his behalf.

Chapter 18

Individual Retirement Plans—Part II

Learning Objectives

An understanding of the material in this chapter should enable the student to

- **LO 18.1** Describe the two types of funding vehicles that can be used with IRAs.
- **LO 18.2** Identify appropriate as well as prohibited investments in an IRA.
- **LO 18.3** Discuss appropriate uses of IRAs and Roth IRAs.

In addition to the legal and tax implications concerning IRAs, there are also several financial implications. Note that both traditional IRAs and Roth IRAs are subject to the same investment rules. Let's take a closer look.

FUNDING VEHICLES

LO 18.1 Describe the two types of funding vehicles that can be used with IRAs.

Individual retirement plans can be established with one of two IRA funding vehicles:

- individual retirement accounts
- individual retirement annuities

Individual Retirement Accounts (IRAs)

Individual retirement accounts (IRAs) are the most popular type of individual retirement arrangement. The IRA document itself is a written trust or a custodial account whose trustee or custodian must be a bank, a federally insured credit union, a savings and loan association, or a person or organization that receives IRS permission to act as the trustee or custodian (for example, an insurance company). No one receives IRS permission to be the trustee of his or her own IRA because the IRS mandates arm's-length dealing between the beneficiary of the IRA trust and those in charge of enforcing IRA rules.

The IRA trust or custodial account must be established for the exclusive benefit of the participant and his or her beneficiaries, and benefits must be nonforfeitable. The document must limit contributions to the maximum allowable deductible or nondeductible contribution allowed each year. The document must also state that distributions will satisfy the required minimum-distribution provisions. IRA funds may not be commingled with other assets except in a common trust fund or common investment fund.

Individual Retirement Annuities (IRA Annuities)

An individual retirement annuity (IRA annuity) is an annuity contract typically issued by insurance companies. IRA annuities are similar to IRAs except that the following additional rules apply because of their annuity investment feature:

- The IRA annuity is nontransferable. In other words, unlike the proceeds from other annuities, the IRA annuity proceeds must be received by either the taxpayer or a beneficiary. Individuals cannot set up an IRA annuity and then pledge the annuity to another party or put the annuity up as a security for a loan. For example, if loans were made under an automatic premium-loan provision, the plan would be disqualified.

- The premium cannot exceed the current year's maximum contribution amount. Any refund of premiums must be applied before the close of the calendar year following the year of the refund toward payment of future premiums or the purchase of additional benefits.

The primary reason for choosing one IRA funding vehicle over another is the investor's desired return balanced against the amount of risk he or she is willing to accept. There are, however, secondary reasons that make IRA annuities worth considering when the return/risk factors are comparable with other investments. If a deferred annuity is chosen, features like a guaranteed death benefit, waiver-of-premium coverage in case of disability, and a guaranteed rate of return can have value to certain individuals. Immediate annuities provide guaranteed payments for a specified period.

TYPES OF INVESTMENTS

self-directed IRAs

IRAs can be invested in a multitude of vehicles, running the gamut from mutual funds to limited partnerships, from investments with minimal risk and modest returns to speculative investments with promises of greater return. IRAs are typically invested in certificates of deposit, money market funds, mutual funds, limited partnerships, income bond funds, corporate bond funds, and common stocks and other equities. **Self-directed IRAs** (IRAs in which the taxpayer is able to shift investments between general investment vehicles offered by the trustee) are also popular because they give the investor investment flexibility and the ability to anticipate or react to interest-rate directions and market trends.

Clearly, investment decisions need to follow from the client's retirement goals. The job of a financial services professional is to induce the client to generate a retirement strategy first and an investment strategy second. The financial strategy needs to consider the client's lifestyle, other financial resources, and the client's degree of risk aversion.

When forming an investment strategy, another consideration is the tax-advantaged nature of IRAs. Investment earnings are not subject to income tax while held in the plan. This means that it is generally not appropriate to invest in tax-sheltered vehicles, such as municipal bonds—which generally offer a lower rate of return than taxable investments.

Investment Restrictions

LO 18.2 Identify appropriate as well as prohibited investments in an IRA.

Investment of IRAs is generally open to all of the investment vehicles available outside IRAs. There are, however, a few prohibited IRA investments:

- investment in life insurance
- investment in collectibles
- prohibited transactions

Life Insurance

Investment in life insurance is not allowed for an IRA even though defined-benefit and defined-contribution retirement plans allow an "incidental" amount of life insurance. IRAs, however, are not subject to the same rules (or underlying logic) and are considered to be strictly for retirement purposes. Therefore, no incidental insurance is available.

Collectibles

If IRA funds are invested in collectibles, the amount invested is considered a distribution, subject to income tax and possibly the 10 percent excise tax on distributions made prior to age 59½. Collectibles include works of art, Oriental rugs, antiques, rare coins, stamps, rare wines, and certain other tangible property.

There is an exception for certain coins and precious metals. IRA funds can be invested in one, one-half, one-quarter, or one-tenth ounce U.S. gold coins, or one-ounce silver coins minted by the Treasury Department. Funds can also be invested in certain platinum coins and certain gold, silver, palladium, and platinum bullion. However, investments in bullion are allowed only when the IRA trustee has physical possession of the bullion.

Prohibited Transactions

Generally, a prohibited transaction is the improper use of an IRA by the participant, a beneficiary, or any disqualified person. Disqualified persons include fiduciaries and members of the IRA participant's family (spouse, ancestor, lineal descendant, and any spouse of a lineal descendant). These are the same prohibited transaction rules that apply to qualified plans.

The following are examples of prohibited transactions with a traditional IRA:

- borrowing money from it
- selling property to it
- receiving unreasonable compensation for managing it
- using it as security for a loan
- buying property for personal use (present or future) with IRA funds

In many cases, an IRA will not have an outside fiduciary, but it may in some cases. Just as with employer-sponsored retirement plans, a fiduciary includes anyone who does any of the following:

- exercises any discretionary authority or discretionary control in managing an IRA or exercises any authority or control in managing or disposing of its assets
- provides investment advice for an IRA for a fee, or has any authority or responsibility to do so
- has any discretionary authority or discretionary responsibility in administering an IRA

Penalties

Failure to satisfy the investment restrictions can be severe. If the participant borrows any money from an annuity the entire value of the annuity contract (not just the amount borrowed) is included in the owner's income. Similarly, if a loan is taken from an IRA account, the account is disqualified. If the participant pledges the account as collateral for a loan, then the amount pledged is treated as a distribution.

If the participant or a beneficiary engages in a prohibited transaction in connection with an IRA at any time during the year, the account stops being an IRA as of the first day of that year, and all its assets are treated as a distribution, subject to income tax. If someone other than the owner or beneficiary of a traditional IRA engages in a prohibited transaction, that person may be liable for certain taxes. In general, there is a 15-percent tax on the amount of the prohibited transaction and a 100-percent additional tax if the transaction is not corrected.

Investment in a prohibited collectible has a somewhat less severe penalty. Here the result is that the value of the collectible purchased is deemed to be distributed and will be subject to tax. Since investments in life insurance are prohibited by the terms of the investment vehicle, a life insurance investment would disqualify the IRA.

In addition to these penalties, deemed distributions to a participant under age 59½ will also be subject to the 10-percent Sec. 72(t) early withdrawal penalty tax.

Clearly, clients and their advisors need to be very careful not to violate the investment restrictions in order to avoid penalties.

IRAs Used with SEPs and SIMPLEs

IRAs are also used as the funding vehicle for two types of employer-sponsored retirement plans, SEPs and SIMPLEs. Obviously, the contribution limits are different, but in most other ways the IRAs operate under the same rules that apply to IRAs established by individuals. This means that the investment restrictions are the same, benefits must be fully vested at all times, distributions are taxed the same, and in most instances benefits can be rolled from one IRA to another. (Note that the IRA rules prohibit loans to participants. This prohibition means that SEPs and SIMPLEs cannot include participant loan programs.)

When an employer establishes a SEP, SEP IRA accounts are established for each participant. When an employer establishes a SIMPLE, a SIMPLE IRA is adopted for each participant. SIMPLE IRAs are subject to several special rules. If a distribution is made from a SIMPLE IRA in the first 2 years of participation and the participant is under age 59½, the penalty tax under Code Sec. 72(t) becomes a 25 percent excise tax (the tax is usually 10 percent). Because of this tax, there is a prohibition on transfers from a SIMPLE IRA to a regular IRA in the first 2 years of participation. Otherwise, participants could circumvent the 25 percent tax. SIMPLE IRAs may not accept rollovers from any vehicle other than another SIMPLE IRA account.

IRAS AND THE FINANCIAL SERVICES PROFESSIONAL

For the financial services professional, understanding IRAs requires more than just knowing the various rules, restraints, and tax implications associated with them. The financial services professional must also analyze whether a current client's interests are best served by making IRA contributions and must identify potential clients who need IRA assistance. Many financial services professionals must even ask themselves whether selling IRAs is appropriate for them. Here we will discuss proper planning with IRAs.

Should Your Client Make an IRA or Roth IRA Contribution?

LO 18.3   Discuss appropriate uses of IRAs and Roth IRAs.

The first step in determining whether a client should use IRAs is to determine his or her eligibility for the various options. The tables below summarize the available options for both single and married (filing jointly) taxpayers in 2017. The last several decades have seen important favorable changes for IRAs. Even though IRA planning has become considerably more complicated, it has also opened up opportunities for your clients. Looking at IRAs under the current playing field, here are some general observations for your clients.

- The maximum contribution to IRAs has risen over the years. For 2017, the limit is $5,500. Those aged 50 or older can make an additional contribution of $1,000.

- The special spousal rule provides that for married couples filing jointly with AGI less than $183,000 and only one spouse covered in an employer-sponsored retirement plan, the other spouse can contribute the maximum amount on a deductible basis to a traditional IRA.

- The Roth IRA offers a significant tax benefit that is available to many taxpayers who cannot make deductible IRA contributions. For example, a single individual earning $100,000 and who is a 401(k) plan participant cannot make a deductible IRA contribution, but can make a $5,500 contribution to a Roth IRA.

- Choosing between a Roth IRA and a deductible IRA (or other pretax savings vehicle like a 401(k) plan) can be difficult (see below). However, both are great ways to save for retirement.

- Now that all taxpayers have the opportunity to convert tax-deferred accounts to Roth IRAs, clients and their advisors should think carefully about taking advantage of this opportunity.

- Because of the income phaseout rules, high-income taxpayers may only be able to make nondeductible contributions—which have limited tax benefits. This opportunity has become more valuable as nondeductible accounts for taxpayers of any income level can be converted to a Roth IRA.

- Older, more affluent individuals can also provide encouragement—and funds—to their children and grandchildren to take advantage of these opportunities.

- The IRA rules offer little to those at the lower end of the earnings scale. These individuals are least likely to have sufficient income to afford a contribution, and will be most likely to need emergency withdrawals that will not qualify for special tax treatment.

Let's look at several of these points in greater depth.

Table 18-1
IRA Options for Singles in 2017

Type of Contribution	Tax Benefit	Availability
Nondeductible	• After-tax contributions with tax deferral on earnings • Distributions of earnings taxed as ordinary income	• Individuals who have not yet attained age 70½ with compensation from personal services (does not include investment income)
Deductible	• Tax deduction on contributions with tax deferral on earnings • All distributions taxed as ordinary income	• Individuals who have not yet attained age 70½ with compensation who are not active participants in an employer sponsored retirement plan • Deduction phased out for individuals who are active participants with AGI between $61,000 and $71,000
Roth	• After-tax contributions • No tax on qualifying distributions	• Individuals of any age with compensation • Ability to make contribution phased out with AGI between $116,000 and $131,000
Converting an IRA to a Roth IRA	• Income tax paid at the time the IRA is converted to the Roth IRA	• Conversions are allowed regardless of income

Table 18-2
IRA Options for Marrieds Filing Jointly in 2017

Type of Contribution	Tax Benefit	Availability
Nondeductible	• After-tax contributions with tax deferral on earnings • Distributions of earnings taxed as ordinary income	• Individuals* who have not yet attained age 70½, with compensation from personal services (does not include investment income)
Deductible	• Tax deduction on contributions with tax deferral on earnings • All distributions taxed as ordinary income	• Individuals* who have not yet attained age 70½ with compensation who are not active participants in an employer-sponsored retirement plan • If one spouse is an active participant, then the deduction is phased out (for the spouse who is not an active participant) for AGI between $183,000 and $193,000 • Deduction phased out for individuals who are active participants with AGI between $98,000 and $118,000

Table 18-2
IRA Options for Marrieds Filing Jointly in 2017

Type of Contribution	Tax Benefit	Availability
Roth IRA	• After-tax contributions • No tax on qualifying distributions	• Individuals* of any age with compensation • Ability to make contribution phased out with AGI between $186,000 and $196,000
Converting an IRA to a Roth IRA	• Income tax paid at the time the IRA is converted to the Roth IRA	• Conversions are allowed regardless of income

* For a married couple, a spousal IRA can be established if one spouse does not have compensation from employment.

Easier Access to IRA funds

Sometimes it is difficult to convince your clients of the importance of saving for retirement. With younger clients, it can be helpful to point out that by making just 10 $5,000 contributions from age 25 through age 34—and no contributions thereafter—an IRA at age 65 will be larger than an IRA funded with a $5,500 contribution each year from age 35 through age 64 (see table below). Individual savings is also necessary to supplement company-sponsored retirement plans. One reason is that most company-sponsored pension benefits do not provide inflation protection, and if postretirement inflation is 4 percent per year, a $1 loaf of bread at age 65 will cost $2.19 at age 85.

Another concern of clients is that they may need access to the account at some point prior to retirement. If money is withdrawn before age 59½, income tax and the 10 percent early withdrawal penalty may apply. One answer to your client's concerns, is that withdrawals can be made to pay for educational expenses and up to $10,000 of first-time home buying expenses. These exceptions mean that young persons who are also concerned about saving for home ownership and for their children's college education can withdraw funds for these purposes without penalty. It is also true that there is a point at which it pays a taxpayer to make IRA contributions, even when a premature withdrawal is the taxpayer's intention. The break-even or get-ahead date depends on the tax bracket of the employee when contributions are made, the interest earned under the IRA, the tax bracket of the person when distributions are withdrawn, and the ratio of nondeductible contributions to the total IRA balance at the time of withdrawal. If the taxpayer's tax bracket is lower at the time of withdrawal, the break-even point will be shorter. (The converse is also true: a higher tax bracket at distribution time will mean a longer break-even point.)

Table 18-3
IRA Funding Plans[1]

Plan One			Plan Two		
Age start		25	Age start		35
Age end		34	Age end		64
Amount per year		$5,500	Amount per year		$5,500
Rate of return		6.5%	Rate of return		6.5%
Value at age 65		$556,807	Value at age 65		$538,827
Total amount contributed		$55,000	Total amount contributed		$165,000
Age	Amount	Value	Age	Amount	Value
25	$5,500	$ 5,858	25	0	0
26	5,500	12,096	26	0	0
27	5,500	18,739	27	0	0
28	5,500	25,815	28	0	0
29	5,500	33,351	29	0	0
30	5,500	41,376	30	0	0
31	5,500	49,923	31	0	0
32	5,500	59,025	32	0	0
33	5,500	68,719	33	0	0
34	5,500	79,044	34	0	0
35	0	84,181	35	5,500	$5,858
36	0	89,653	36	5,500	12,096
37	0	95,481	37	5,500	18,739
...	...	...	...	...	...
60	0	406,403	60	5,500	373,213
61	0	432,819	61	5,500	403,329
62	0	460,952	62	5,500	435,403
63	0		63		469,562
64	0	522,823	64	5,500	505,941
65	0	556,807	65	0	538,827

[1] This comparison is hypothetical; no guarantees are implied for specific investments. The interest rate is assumed to remain unchanged for the entire period.

Choosing the Roth IRA over the Nondeductible IRA

Many taxpayers who do not have the option to make deductible IRA contributions will, however, have the opportunity to make Roth IRA contributions. The ability to contribute to Roth IRAs is phased out for single taxpayers with AGI between $118,000 and $132,000 (2017) and married couples filing jointly with AGI between $186,000 and $196,000 (as indexed for 2017). Individuals who have the choice between nondeductible IRA contributions and Roth IRA contributions should almost always choose the Roth IRA. Tax-free distributions are clearly better than tax deferral.

In fact, it's difficult to argue for nondeductible contributions at all today because the price of tax deferral is turning investment gain into ordinary income. Arguably, investing directly in securities (outside of the IRA context) may be more attractive, since capital gains can be deferred until the sale and qualifying sales will be taxed at the capital gains rate (currently the maximum rate is 15 percent). Also, securities left to heirs avoid income taxes on the growth over the participant's life.

In contrast, the tax advantages of the Roth IRA are clear. As long as distributions satisfy the eligibility requirements, the entire distribution avoids income tax—even distributions to death beneficiaries. Even the Roth IRA participant who needs early withdrawals can withdraw up to the amount of total contributions without any income tax consequences.

A good candidate for the Roth IRA would be a 401(k) participant who has maximized his or her contribution to the 401(k) plan, is not eligible for a deductible IRA contribution, and still wants to save more for retirement. In this case, the next place to save is definitely the Roth IRA. The harder question to answer would be, "Should the 401(k) participant who has been putting away 6 percent of compensation each year and who wants to save more contribute additional amounts to the 401(k) plan or contribute to a Roth IRA?" This individual is now choosing between deductible savings and tax-free saving alternatives. The issues involved in this decision are discussed below.

The best candidate for a nondeductible IRA is the high-income individual who earns too much to contribute to a Roth IRA. Since the Roth IRA conversion rules no longer have an income limit, the nondeductible contributions can periodically be converted to a Roth IRA.

> **EXAMPLE**
>
> John and Jill are both age 58, married and have AGI of $250,000. Both are employed and maximize contributions to their companies' 401(k) plans. They do not currently have

any IRA accounts. They want to know if they can contribute more to tax-advantaged retirement plans?

They are good candidates to establish nondeductible IRA accounts, contribute the maximum amount and then immediately convert those amounts into a Roth IRA. Since they do not have other IRAs, the conversion will be tax-free (assuming no earnings accrue before the conversion occurs). If they have other IRAs, the situation is more complicated as IRA accounts are aggregated when determining the tax treatment of the conversion—and the conversion will generally result in taxable income.

Choosing the Roth IRA over the Deductible IRA

Some taxpayers will be in the position to choose between a deductible IRA contribution or the Roth IRA. Similarly, many employees may be choosing between making additional tax-deferred contributions to a 401(k) plan or the Roth IRA. In the 401(k) setting, if the employer does not offer a Roth election and is going to match the contribution, the advantage usually goes to the 401(k) tax-deferred contributions, because the employer match is like an instant return on the participant's contribution. However, if the contribution is not matched (or the employer allows a Roth election), then the 401(k)-to-Roth IRA comparison (as well as a 401(k) tax-deferred versus Roth election) is essentially the same as the deductible IRA-to-Roth IRA comparison.

Comparing the financial effect of the two options is difficult, mainly because it involves assumptions about rates of return in the future, tax rates in the future, and the timing of withdrawals. Numerous computer software programs are available to help with this comparison, and they can be quite valuable in helping to make choices.

Even though individual analysis is best, here are some general considerations. It is clearest that when the individual expects to be in a higher tax bracket in retirement than at the time of the contribution, the Roth IRA is the more appropriate vehicle. For example, take the young person in the 17 percent (15 percent federal and 2 percent state) bracket today who expects to be in a 42 percent bracket at the time of distribution. The table below gives an example of such an individual, who has $2,000 to contribute at age 25 and withdraws this amount at age 70. If $2,000 is contributed at age 25 to the traditional IRA, after taxes are paid at age 70, she will have $37,027.

However, if $1,660 is contributed to a Roth IRA ($2,000 less taxes), at age 70 she will have $52,967. This is a significant difference.

Table 18-4
Comparing Deductible IRAs to Roth IRA Accumulations

Age	30%/17%		30%/30%*		17%/42%*		30%/42%*	
	Roth	Deductible	Roth	Deductible	Roth	Deductible	Roth	Deductible
25	$1,400	$2,000	$1,400	$2,000	$1,660	$2,000	$1,400	$2,000
70	$44,688	$52,987	$44,688	$44,688**	$52,967	$37,027**	$44,688	$37,027**

* The first number represents the combined federal and state income tax rate at the time of contribution and the second number represents the tax rate at the time of distribution.

** Assumes that the entire accumulation is distributed and taxed at age 70. Assumes growth at 8 percent.

If an individual expects his or her tax rate to go down in retirement, the opposite is true—the deductible IRA shows a greater accumulation ($52,987 for the deductible IRA versus $44,688 for the Roth IRA). However, for many taxpayers this is a relatively unlikely scenario.

If the tax rates are the same at the time of contribution and at the time of withdrawal, the accumulations shown in the table above for the Roth IRA and the deductible contribution are the same (each $44,688). However, if the tax rates remain the same, there are still advantages to the Roth IRA. In our example, the participant withdraws all of the Roth IRA at age 70, but one of the Roth IRA's powerful features is that distributions are not required during the participant's lifetime. If the beneficiary is the spouse, distributions can be delayed even further to the death of the spouse. After that, distributions can be made over the expected lifetime of the beneficiary or beneficiaries. This tax deferral can be quite powerful, and makes the Roth IRA a good way to pass on wealth to the next generation.

Also, there is another strength to the Roth IRA. The tax-free source of income gives the participant more flexibility in how and when to liquidate other taxable assets in retirement. The tax-free funds in a Roth IRA can be used in retirement to

- minimize taxable withdrawals from traditional IRAs or qualified plans
- minimize taxable income to stay in a lower tax bracket
- provide for a source of income that will not increase the portion of Social Security benefits that are taxed
- fund life insurance premiums for estate planning purposes
- provide liquidity for estate taxes
- minimize liquidation of other taxable investments such as stocks and mutual funds—which receive a step-up if left intact to heirs

Because of the Roth IRA's many strengths, the following types of clients should consider the Roth IRA over the deductible IRA:

- individuals in the 15 percent federal income tax bracket (or lower) who expect higher earnings in the future
- individuals in the 25 and 28 percent federal income tax brackets who expect to be in a higher bracket at retirement
- individuals expecting tax rates to increase
- individuals who have already accumulated significant assets for retirement on a tax-deferred basis and who may want to use the Roth IRA as a way to create a more balanced (from a tax perspective) portfolio
- individuals who are more concerned about estate planning than retirement planning

IRA-to-Roth IRA Conversions

The Roth IRA conversion is an important strategy now that it is available to all taxpayers. It is important to understand that the question of whether or not to convert has many of the same considerations as whether to choose new Roth contributions. This means that clients can now access the tax advantages of the Roth in a number of ways: conversion, new contributions to a Roth IRA, or new Roth contributions to a 401(k), 403(b) or 457 plan. Accessing the Roth through a conversion has the psychological implication that most clients have difficulty paying taxes earlier than required. In making a conversion decision, here are some important considerations:

- Just as when comparing deductible IRA and Roth IRA contributions, if tax rates go up from the time of conversion to the time of withdrawal, conversion results in a larger accumulation than leaving the funds in a tax-deferred plan. If tax rates are lower at the time of withdrawal than at the time of conversion the opposite is true. If tax rates remain the same the after-tax accumulation is the same in both scenarios. Since future tax rates are uncertain, it is important to look at other factors as well.

- It is better to pay taxes on the conversion from a source of funds other than the converted account. If IRA funds are used, the individual has taken a withdrawal subject to income taxes and possibly the 10 percent penalty tax if the taxpayer is under age 59½. Using outside funds leaves the maximum amount earning a tax-free return in the Roth IRA.

- Tax diversification can protect against uncertainty and change. Many middle- and upper-income taxpayers have a great deal of retirement savings in tax-deferred accounts. Converting a portion of the account allows better planning options if future tax rates were to increase.

- Many clients do not like to take required distributions that they will not need. A conversion accelerates income tax—but another way of looking at it is that you are eliminating future tax uncertainty. Once converted, amounts can be saved until needed. If the participant does not need them, the account makes an excellent vehicle to leave to heirs.

- As a conversion increases AGI, the decision can have other income tax consequences. For example, increased AGI can increase the portion of Social Security benefits that are taxed or result in an increase in the Medicare Part B premium.

- A conversion can have unexpected tax benefits. Withdrawals from a Roth IRA, under current law, are not counted toward determining the taxable portion of Social Security or the calculation of the Medicare Part B premium.

- Taxes paid at the time of the conversion are based on the value of the account on the date of the conversion and conversions relate to the year in which the amount is converted. For example, a conversion on January 15, 2017 can only be treated as a 2017 conversion and the tax will be calculated based on the value of the account on January 15, 2017. Converting when the value of the account is low is optimal but this is like giving the advice buy low and sell high. However, the IRS actually offers a valuable safety valve. If the account value drops after the conversion but before the due date of the tax return for the year of conversion (generally the October 15th of the following year) the transaction can be essentially undone through a recharacterization and reconverted in a later year.

- Even though it may appear at first glance that older persons should not convert, conversion can also have significant estate-planning implications. Even if the older participant were to die shortly after the conversion, the income taxes paid at the conversion reduce the value of the estate, reducing estate and inheritance taxes. This effect reduces the effective tax rate on the conversion. Also, under the minimum-distribution rules, a spousal beneficiary can continue to defer withdrawals and, with other beneficiaries distributions, can be spread over the beneficiary's entire lifetime.

Based on these considerations, here are some ideas about the types of clients who should or should not consider conversion:

- Many expect that future tax rates for those in the highest income tax bracket will rise. Those in the top bracket should give serious consideration to converting.

- For a number of reasons, an individual can have lower income for a year. This can offer the opportunity to convert at a low (or even zero) tax bracket. Remember, partial conversions are allowed. A common strategy is to convert enough to take advantage of a 15 percent or even 25 percent tax rate, assuming that tax rates will be higher later. This may be especially effective for those early in retirement who have reduced their taxable income.

- Those who do not need withdrawals from the account to meet living expenses will benefit from converting as a way to avoid required minimum distributions.

- Taxpayers likely to face a significant estate or inheritance tax should seriously consider converting to maximize benefits received by heirs.

- Taxpayers who have accumulated most of their retirement savings on a tax deferred basis need to be considering a Roth conversion as a way to diversify.

- On the other hand, many middle-class taxpayers will have lower income in retirement and may still be in a lower tax bracket. This weighs against conversion, although for diversification purposes or the ability to convert some at a low tax rate may suggest that converting a small amount is appropriate.

- For those struggling to meet retirement needs, converting reduces available resources and may not be the best approach—unless conversion can be accomplished at a zero or extremely low tax rate.

EXAMPLE

Alex and Alicia are married, each age 63, and retired. They are taking $80,000 of withdrawals from their taxable investment account to pay for living expenses. They have made some good choices, deferring Social Security and holding onto their substantial 401(k) accounts until later. They do not have any Roth IRAs at this point. Because of their current strategy, they have a very low taxable income for the year. Is there any other option to improve their situation?

They are great candidates for converting a portion of either of their 401(k) plan benefits, since their taxable income will be much higher once they start Social Security benefits and begin withdrawals from their 401(k) plans. Together with their accountant, they should determine how much they should convert—the objective is converting as much as possible at a lower-than-normal tax rate (for example 15 percent when the normal rate is 25 percent). The conversion provides more tax diversification, reduces their future required minimum distributions from qualified plans and provides a source of income that can be held in the Roth IRA until it is needed.

Deemed IRAs

For financial services professionals who work primarily with employers, note that qualified plans, 403(b) annuities, and even government 457 plans may be written to allow participants to make voluntary IRA or Roth IRA contributions directly to the plan. These accounts are referred to as deemed IRAs. If a plan so provides, the document must require separate accounting for the IRA or Roth IRA contributions, and the contributions would have to meet the requirements applicable to either traditional IRAs or Roth IRAs.

deemed IRAs

Having a deemed IRA account does not affect the qualification and contribution limits that otherwise apply to the qualified plan or 403(b) plan. For example, in a 401(k) plan, a participant could make both the maximum salary deferral and the IRA or Roth IRA contribution to the plan (as long as he or she is eligible under the IRA rules to make the contribution). The **deemed IRA** is also not subject to the ERISA reporting and disclosure, participation, vesting, funding, and enforcement requirements that are otherwise applicable to the plan.

If you are considering whether to advise your employer-client to institute a deemed IRA, your client must consider the following factors:

- Because these accounts are treated as IRAs and Roth IRAs, the normal rules concerning eligibility to make a contribution or deduct it still apply.
- There may be an advantage to the individual to have an IRA account within a company plan because the IRA contributions are subject to ERISA's exclusive benefit and fiduciary rules. This may mean that the accounts will be eligible for more protection from attachment by a taxpayer's creditors than traditional or Roth IRAs.
- The downside for the employer is that there will be increased administrative effort and expense to maintain the additional accounts. The plan also becomes more complicated and difficult to explain to participants.

CHAPTER REVIEW

Key Terms and Concepts

self-directed IRAs
deemed IRAs

Chapter 18: Review Questions

Review questions are based on the learning objectives in this chapter. Thus, an [18.3] at the end of a question means that the question is based on learning objective 3. If there are multiple objectives, they are all listed.

1. a. What is an individual retirement account (IRA)? [18.1]

b. What is an individual retirement annuity, and what special rules apply to the annuity contract?

2. What are some of the advantages of investing in an individual retirement annuity? [18.2]

3. Which of the following items is/are permissible IRA investments? [18.2]

   a. investment in life insurance
   b. investment in antiques
   c. investment in gold bullion
   d. investment in real estate that is owned by the client

4. How are SIMPLE IRAs different from traditional IRAs? [18.3]

5. Explain the IRA and Roth IRA options for the following individuals in 2017: [18.3]

   a. Carlos, a single 35-year-old taxpayer, has an adjusted gross income (AGI) of $85,000 and is not an active participant in an employer-sponsored retirement plan in 2017.

   b. Anthony, a single 45-year-old taxpayer, has an AGI of $150,000 and is an active participant in a qualified retirement plan.

   c. Sam and Sally, each under age 50, are married and file a joint tax return. The couple has AGI of $150,000 and is an active participant in an employer-sponsored retirement plan. Sally does not work outside of the home.

   d. Della and George, aged 40, are married and file a joint tax return. Their AGI is $220,000). They are both active participants in employer-sponsored retirement plans.

6. Why may the nondeductible IRA be an inappropriate retirement investment vehicle in today's tax environment? [18.3]

7. What type of clients may find Roth IRA contributions potentially more advantageous than deductible IRA contribution? [18.3]

8. What type of clients may be good candidates for a Roth IRA conversion. [18.3]

Chapter 18: Review Answers

1. a. An individual retirement account (IRA) is a trust or a custodial account whose trustee or custodian must be a bank, a federally insured credit union, a savings and loan association, or a person or organization that receives IRS permission to act as the trustee or custodian.

   b. An individual retirement annuity is an annuity contract issued by an insurance company. It is not transferable and the premium cannot exceed the current year's maximum contribution amount.

2. An individual retirement annuity can be used to reduce exposure to the risk of "living too long." The annuity will also typically have a waiver-of-premium feature if the individual becomes disabled.

3. Life insurance and collectibles (antiques) are prohibited investments. Gold bullion is allowed if it meets the exception to the collectible prohibition. Real estate owned by the participant would most likely be prohibited under the prohibited transaction rules.

4. A SIMPLE IRA is different from a traditional IRA in one regard: Distributions from SIMPLE IRAs in the first 2 years of participation are subject to a 25 percent early withdrawal penalty tax. Because of this tax, there is a prohibition on the transfer out of a SIMPLE IRA and into a regular IRA during the first 2 years of participation.

5. a. Carlos can make either a $5,500 deductible IRA contribution or a $5,500 Roth contribution for 2017 (or he could divide the $5,500 contribution up into both).

   b. Anthony cannot make a deductible IRA contribution or a Roth IRA contribution because he earns too much. He could make a nondeductible IRA contribution.

   c. Sam cannot make a deductible IRA contribution (AGI over $119,000), but Sally can (AGI less than $186,000). Both can make Roth IRA contributions (AGI less than $186,000).

   d. Neither can make a deductible IRA contribution or a Roth IRA contribution. Of course, both can make a nondeductible IRA contribution.

6. Investing directly in stock or mutual funds may be a better alternative to nondeductible IRA contributions because of the disparity in the tax rate. Long-term capital gains are taxed at a maximum 15-percent rate while IRA withdrawals will always be ordinary income.

7. Determining when the Roth makes economic sense is a complicated analysis that involves a review of the individual's entire retirement and estate planning picture. The Roth can be quite valuable to young persons, those with estate planning problems, and individuals with a large percentage of their assets already in tax-sheltered retirement plans.

8. The clients that may want to consider a conversion include: those in the top tax bracket that expect taxes to rise in the future; those with lower income for a particular year that can take advantage of converting at a low tax rate; those who do not need required minimum distributions; those who face estate or inheritance taxes; and those who need tax diversification.

Chapter 19
Social Security

Learning Objectives

An understanding of the material in this chapter should enable the student to

- **LO 19.1** Identify workers who are and those who are not covered by the Social Security system.
- **LO 19.2** Understand the breadth of coverage that Social Security provides concerning the retirement security of Americans.
- **LO 19.3** Describe how Social Security is funded.
- **LO 19.4** Explain the eligibility requirements for retirement benefits, survivors benefits, and disability benefits.
- **LO 19.5** List and explain the types of benefits clients receive from the Social Security system.
- **LO 19.6** Describe how to calculate benefits.
- **LO 19.7** Identify the impact of taking benefits early or late and what happens if an individual works after benefits begin.
- **LO 19.8** Explain how to request information about and apply for benefits.
- **LO 19.9** Calculate the portion of Social Security benefits that is subject to tax.
- **LO 19.10** Determine when it is appropriate to begin benefits prior to full retirement age.

BACKGROUND/HISTORY

Social Security

Social Security is arguably the most important retirement plan in the United States. Social Security is much more than retirement, however. Technically, Social Security is the Old-Age, Survivors, Disability, and Health Insurance (OASDHI) program of the federal government. In addition to retirement benefits, the Social Security system also provides benefits to disabled workers and to families of workers who have died, retired, or become disabled. Currently, approximately 52 million Americans—one out of every six—receive retirement, survivors, and disability benefits from Social Security. In addition, the hospital insurance (HI) program provides health care coverage through Medicare to retirees, the disabled, and their families.

Historically, Social Security has been a work in progress. The system has been changed a number of times to meet the ever-changing needs of the people it serves. Currently further changes are being debated in Washington. When these changes are sorted out, they will represent another chapter in a long and storied history for the Social Security system. For an overview of the history of Social Security, see the time line in Table 19-1.

Planners need to be familiar with the entire Social Security system. This chapter focuses on OASDI benefits, which include old-age retirement benefits, disability benefits, and survivor benefits. Medicare, along with other retiree health care issues, will be discussed in a later chapter.

EXTENT OF COVERAGE

LO 19.1 **Identify workers who are and those who are not covered by the Social Security system.**

Close to 90 percent of the workers in the United States are in covered employment under the Social Security program. This means that these workers have wages (if they are employees) or self-employment income (if they are self-employed) on which Social Security taxes must be paid. For this reason, it is important for the planner to understand potential clients who are not covered under the Social Security program. The following are the major categories of workers who may not receive benefits under the program:

- people with less than 40 quarters of coverage (discussed later)
- civilian employees of the federal government who were employed by the government prior to 1984 and who are covered primarily under the Civil Service Retirement System. Coverage for new civilian federal employees under the entire program was one of the most significant changes resulting from the 1983 amendments to the Social Security Act. It should be noted, however, that all federal employees have been covered under Social Security for purposes of Medicare since 1983.
- railroad workers. Under the Railroad Retirement Act (RRA), employees of railroads have their own benefit system that is similar to OASDI. However, they are covered under Social Security for purposes of Medicare.
- employees of state and local governments unless the state has entered into a voluntary agreement with the Social Security Administration. However, this exemption applies only to those employees who are covered under their employer's retirement plan. Under an agreement with the Social Security Administration, the state may

either require that employees of local governments also be covered or allow local governments to decide whether to include their employees.

- American citizens working abroad for foreign affiliates of U.S. employers, unless the employer owns at least a 10 percent interest in the foreign affiliate and has made arrangements with the Secretary of the Treasury for the payment of Social Security taxes. However, Americans working abroad are covered under Social Security if they are working directly for U.S. employers rather than for their foreign subsidiaries.
- ministers who elect out of coverage because of conscience or religious principles
- workers in certain jobs, such as student nurses, newspaper carriers under age 18, and students working for the school at which they are regularly enrolled or doing domestic work for a local college club, fraternity, or sorority
- certain family employment. This includes the employment of a child under age 18 by a parent. This exclusion, however, does not apply if the employment is for a corporation owned by a family member.
- certain workers who must satisfy special earnings requirements. For example, self-employed persons are not covered unless they have net annual earnings of $400 or more.

One last point concerning the extent of coverage—many of the groups not covered (for example, federal workers in the civil service retirement system and railroad workers covered by the RRA) have significant pensions that account for the lack of Social Security coverage.

Table 19-1
History of Social Security

Year	Event
1935	FDR signs the Social Security Act providing for old-age insurance
1939	Survivors benefits are added
1940	First benefits are paid out
1950	Truman extends coverage to many farm and domestic workers, state and municipal employees, and some professionals
1956	Disability coverage added by Eisenhower; women become eligible for some benefits at 62 rather than 65
1965	Johnson adds Medicare
1972	Benefit increases pegged to the cost of living
1983	Social Security Reform Act
2006	Medicare Part D drug benefits added

BREADTH OF COVERAGE

LO 19.2 **Understand the breadth of coverage that Social Security provides concerning the retirement security of Americans.**

According to the Social Security Administration, Social Security replaces about 40 percent of the wage-indexed average of lifetime earnings. For more affluent clients, this percentage will be lower, however, because of the way benefits are structured to favor lower-paid workers over higher-paid workers. America's reliance on Social Security, particularly for middle- and lower-income Americans, is staggering. Consider this:

- Social Security benefits represent about 34 percent of the income of elderly.
- For more than one in three (34 percent), Social Security is more than 90 percent of income.[1]
- For seniors (24 percent), Social Security is more than one-half of what they have to live on in retirement.
- Roughly 66 million people received benefits from Social Security programs in 2017.

One can conclude from these statistics that the breadth and importance of the Social Security system is divided along (for lack of a better term) "class" lines. For people in the upper-middle- and upper-income groups, Social Security, while important, is not as vital. For people below those levels, however, Social Security is crucial to financial well being.

Social Security Trust Funds
- Disability
- Old-age and survivors
- Medicare Part A
- Medicare Part B

Out of every dollar paid in Social Security taxes, 70 cents goes to the old-age and survivors trust fund, 19 cents goes to the Medicare trust fund, and 11 cents goes to the disability trust fund.[2]

---

1. Fact Sheet, Social Security, available at https://www.ssa.gov/news/press/factsheets/basicfact-alt.pdf (2017).
2. InCharge Debt Solutions, https://www.incharge.org/financial-literacy/where-do-my-social-security-tax-dollars-go/ (2017).

FUNDING

LO 19.3   Describe how Social Security is funded.

All benefits of the OASDI program are financed through a system of payroll and self-employment taxes paid by all persons covered under the program. Employers of covered persons are also taxed.

FICA tax

SECA tax

taxable wage base

Over the years, both the tax rate and the wage base have been dramatically increased to finance increased benefit levels under Social Security as well as new benefits that have been added to the program. Social Security benefits are financed through a system of payroll (**FICA tax**—Federal Insurance Contributions Act) and self-employment (**SECA tax**—Self-Employment Contributions Act) taxes paid by all persons covered under the program as well as their employers. For employees, both the employee and the employer pay 6.2 percent on wages up to the **taxable wage base** (which is $127,000 in 2017) to pay for retirement, death, and disability benefits (OASDI), and 1.45 percent on all wages to pay for Medicare and Medicaid (HI). The tax rate for the self-employed is double, that is 12.4 percent on self-employment income up to the taxable wage base and 2.9 percent on all self-employment income. An individual must continue paying FICA (or SECA) taxes as along as he or she continues employment, even if Social Security benefits have already begun. As of January 2013, individuals earning more than $200,000 and married couples filing jointly earning more than $250,000 pay an additional 0.9 percent in Medicare taxes as part of the Affordable Care Act (ACA).

The Social Security program is essentially based on a system of pay-as-you-go financing with limited trust funds. This means that current payroll taxes and other contributions the program receives are used to pay the current benefits of persons who are no longer paying Social Security taxes because of death, old age, or disability. This is in direct contrast to private insurance or retirement plans, which are based on advance funding, whereby assets are accumulated from current contributions to pay the future benefits of those making the contributions.

All payroll taxes and other sources of funds for Social Security (such as income tax on Social Security benefits and interest earned by the current surplus) are deposited into four trust funds: an old-age and survivors fund, a disability fund, and two Medicare funds. Benefits and administrative expenses are paid out of the appropriate trust fund from contributions to that fund and any interest earnings on excess contributions.

In the early 1980s, considerable concern arose over the potential inability of payroll taxes to pay promised benefits in the future. Through a series of changes, the most significant being the 1983 amendments to the Social Security Act, these problems were addressed for the OASDI portion of the program—at least in the short run. The changes approached the problem from two directions. On the one hand, payroll tax rates were increased; on the other hand, some benefits were eliminated and future increases in other benefits were scaled back.

The trust fund for old-age and survivors benefits will continue to grow and will be very large by the time the current baby boomers retire. At that time, the fund will begin to decrease as the percentage of retirees grows rapidly. Projections indicate that the combined OASI and DI trust funds will be adequate only to the year 2034, after which time the fund will only be able to pay approximately 75 percent of the benefits owed.[3] This shortfall, for the next 75 years, equates to roughly 2.66 percent of taxable payroll or roughly 1 percent of the GDP. Social Security's total income is projected to exceed its total cost through 2019, as it has since 1982. However, after 2019, interest income and redemption of trust fund asset reserves from the General Fund of the Treasury will provide the resources needed to offset Social Security's annual deficits until 2034, when the reserves will be depleted. (See Social Security Trustee Report 2016).

ELIGIBILITY FOR BENEFITS

LO 19.4 **Explain the eligibility requirements for retirement benefits, survivors benefits, and disability benefits.**

To be eligible for benefits under OASDI, an individual must have credit for a minimum amount of work under Social Security. This credit is based on "quarters of coverage, or sometimes referred to as a 'Social Security credit' or just 'credit.'" For 2017, a worker receives credit for one quarter of coverage for each $1,300 in annual earnings on which Social Security taxes are paid. However, credit for no more than 4 quarters of coverage may be earned in any one calendar year. Consequently a worker paying Social Security taxes on as little as $5,200 (that is, $1,300 × 4) during the year will receive credit for the maximum 4 quarters. As in the case of the wage base, the amount of earnings necessary for a quarter of coverage is adjusted annually for changes in the national level of wages.

---

3. 2016 Social Security Trustee's Report.

quarters of coverage

fully insured status

Quarters of coverage are the basis for establishing an insured status under OASDI. The three types of insured status are fully insured, currently insured, and disability insured. A person is fully insured if he or she has 40 quarters of coverage. Once a client acquires 40 quarters of credit, he or she is fully insured for life even if covered employment under Social Security ceases. **Fully insured status** requires fewer than 40 quarters of coverage for an individual who dies or becomes disabled before age 62. The number of quarters required in either of these situations is based on the number of years from age 21 until the year before the individual dies or becomes disabled.

Currently Insured

currently insured

If a worker is fully insured under OASDI, there is no additional significance to being **currently insured**. However, if a worker is not fully insured, certain survivors' benefits are still available if a currently insured status exists. To be currently insured, it is only necessary that a worker have credit for at least 6 quarters of coverage out of the 13-quarter period ending with the quarter in which death occurs.

Disability Insured

disability insured

In order to receive disability benefits under OASDI, it is necessary to be **disability insured**. At the minimum, a disability-insured status requires that a worker (1) be fully insured and (2) have a minimum amount of work under Social Security within a recent time period. In connection with the latter requirement, workers aged 31 or older must have credit for at least 20 of the last 40 quarters ending with the quarter in which disability occurs; workers between the ages of 24 and 30, inclusively, must have credit for at least half the quarters of coverage from the time they turned 21 and the quarter in which disability begins; and workers under age 24 must have credit for 6 out of the last 12 quarters, ending with the quarter in which disability begins.

A special rule for the blind states that they are exempt from the recent-work rules and are considered disability insured as long as they are fully insured.

TYPES OF BENEFITS CLIENTS RECEIVE

LO 19.5   List and explain the types of benefits clients receive from the Social Security system.

As its name implies, the OASDI portion of Social Security provides three principal types of benefits:

- retirement (old-age) benefits
- survivors benefits
- disability benefits

Retirement Benefits

full retirement age

A worker who is fully insured under OASDI is eligible to receive monthly retirement benefits as early as age 62. However, the election to receive benefits prior to attainment of full retirement age results in a permanently reduced benefit. In 2017, the **full retirement age** is age 66. The table below indicates a client's full retirement age, depending on their year of birth. In addition, the following dependents of persons receiving retirement benefits are eligible for monthly benefits once the worker claims retirement benefits:

Table 19-2
Social Security Normal Retirement Age

Year of Birth	Retirement Age
1937 and earlier	65 years
1938	65 and 2 months
1939	65 and 4 months
1940	65 and 6 months
1941	65 and 8 months
1942	65 and 10 months
1943–54	66 years
1955	66 and 2 months
1956	66 and 4 months
1957	66 and 6 months
1958	66 and 8 months
1959	66 and 10 months
1960 and after	67 years

- a spouse aged 62 or older. However, benefits are permanently reduced if this benefit is elected prior to the spouse's reaching full retirement age.
- Planners should be aware that this benefit is also available to an unmarried divorced spouse if the marriage lasted at least 10 years. However, the benefit is not payable to a divorced spouse who has remarried unless the marriage is to a person receiving Social Security benefits as a widow, widower, parent, or disabled child.
- a spouse of any age if the spouse is caring for at least one child of the retired worker, and the child is (1) under age 16 or (2) disabled and entitled to a child's benefit as described below. This benefit is commonly referred to as a mother's or father's benefit.
- dependent, unmarried children under 18. This child's benefit will continue until age 19 as long as a child is a full-time student in elementary or secondary school. In addition, disabled children of any age are eligible for benefits as long as they were disabled before reaching age 22.

It is important to note that retirement benefits, as well as all other benefits under Social Security, are not automatically paid upon eligibility but must be applied for.

Survivors Benefits

All categories of Social Security survivors benefits are payable if a worker is fully insured at the time of death. However, three types of benefits are also payable if a worker is only currently insured. The first is a lump-sum death benefit of $255, payable to a surviving spouse living with a deceased worker at the time of death or, if there is no such spouse, to children eligible for monthly benefits. If neither category exists, the benefit is not paid.

There are two categories of persons who are eligible for income benefits as survivors if a deceased worker was either fully or currently insured at the time of death:

- dependent, unmarried children under the same conditions as previously described for retirement benefits
- a spouse (including a divorced spouse) caring for a child or children under the same conditions as previously described for retirement benefits

The following categories of persons are also eligible for benefits, but only if the deceased worker was fully insured:

- a widow or widower at age 60. However, benefits are reduced if taken prior to full retirement age. This benefit is also payable to a divorced spouse if the marriage lasted at least 10 years. In addition, the widow's or widower's benefit is payable to a disabled spouse at age 50 as long as the disability commenced no more than 7 years after (1) the worker's death or (2) the end of the year in which entitlement to a mother's or father's benefit ceased.

- a parent aged 62 or over who was dependent on the deceased worker at the time of death

Disability Benefits

A disabled worker under the full retirement age is eligible to receive benefits under OASDI as long as he or she is disability insured and meets the definition of disability under the law. The definition of disability is very rigid and requires a mental or physical impairment that prevents the worker from engaging in any substantial gainful employment. The disability must also have lasted (or be expected to last) at least 12 months or be expected to result in death. A more liberal definition of disability applies to blind workers who are aged 55 or older. They are considered disabled if they are unable to perform work that requires skills or abilities comparable to those required by the work they regularly performed before reaching age 55 or becoming blind, if later.

Social Security disability benefits are subject to a waiting period and are payable beginning with the sixth full calendar month of disability. Besides the benefit paid to the worker, other categories of benefits—the same as those described under retirement benefits—are available to the spouse and dependents of the worker.

As previously mentioned, certain family members not otherwise eligible for OASDI benefits may be eligible if they are disabled. Disabled children are subject to the same definition of disability as workers. However, disabled widows or widowers must be unable to engage in any gainful (rather than substantial gainful) employment.

Eligibility for Dual OASDI Benefits

In many cases, a person is eligible for more than one type of OASDI benefit. Probably the most common situation occurs when a person is eligible for both a spouse's benefit and a worker's retirement benefit based on his or her own Social Security record. In this case and in any other case when a person is eligible for dual benefits, only an amount equal to the highest benefit is paid.

Termination of Benefits

Monthly benefits to any Social Security recipient cease upon death. When a retired or disabled worker dies, the family members' benefits that are based on the worker's retirement or disability benefits also cease, but the family members are then eligible for survivors benefits. When a married worker dies, if his or her spouse was receiving a spousal benefit of 50 percent, the surviving spouse will be bumped up to the full amount that the deceased worker was receiving.

Disability benefits for a worker technically terminate at the full retirement age for that worker, but are then replaced by comparable retirement benefits. In addition, any benefits payable because of disability cease if the definition of disability is no longer satisfied. However, the disability benefits continue during a readjustment period that consists of the month of recovery and 2 additional months.

As long as children are not disabled, benefits will usually terminate at age 18, but may continue until age 19 if the child is a full-time student in elementary or secondary school.

The benefit of a surviving spouse terminates upon remarriage unless remarriage takes place at age 60 or later.

AMOUNT OF BENEFITS CLIENTS CAN EXPECT

primary insurance amount (PIA)

average indexed monthly earnings (AIME)

With the exception of the $255 lump-sum death benefit, the amount of all OASDI benefits is based on a worker's **primary insurance amount (PIA)**. The PIA, in turn, is a function of the worker's **average indexed monthly earnings (AIME)**, on which Social Security taxes have been paid.

Calculation of AIME

LO 19.6   Describe how to calculate benefits.

Even though calculation of the AIME is rather complex and somewhat unnecessary (the Social Security Administration will do it for the client or the client can use the Social Security Web site (www.ssa.gov) to do it for himself or herself), planners should still be aware how the system works. A rough understanding of how to calculate the AIME will enable an advisor to maximize planning opportunities. The list below sketches how the process works, as well as pointing out planning issues.

- First, list the earnings on which Social Security taxes were paid for each year up to and including the year of death or the year prior to disability or retirement. This list

- includes all applicable years even if there were no wages subject to Social Security tax, in which case zero is used for covered wages. Also note that in any given year someone earning in excess of the taxable wage base for the year will be credited only up to the taxable wage base that year and not his or her actual salary. *Planning Note:* "Zero years" can really hurt a client's benefit. This is one reason that women who took time off to have children often have lower benefits than their male counterparts.

- Second, index these earnings by multiplying them by an indexing factor that reflects changing wage levels. The only years that are indexed are those prior to the indexing year, which is the year a worker turned 60 for retirement purposes or 2 years preceding the year of death or disability for purposes of survivors or disability benefits. Therefore, the indexing factor for the indexing year and subsequent years is one. For years prior to the indexing year, the indexing factor for each year is equal to the average annual covered wages in the indexing year divided by the average annual covered wages in the year in which earnings are to be indexed. Average annual covered wages are the average wages on which Social Security taxes were paid. Each year the government makes the figure for the previous year available. *Planning Note:* Earnings after age 61 (which are not indexed) can be substituted for earnings in earlier years if they result in a higher benefit.

- Third, determine the number of years to be included in the calculation. For retirement and survivors benefits, the number of years is typically 35 (5 less than the minimum number of quarters necessary to be fully insured). Disability benefits, too, may be calculated by subtracting a certain number from the minimum number of quarters necessary for fully insured status. This number is five for workers aged 47 or over, four for workers aged 42 through 46, three for workers aged 37 through 41, two for workers aged 32 through 36, one for workers aged 27 through 31, and zero for workers under age 27. However, for survivors or disability benefits, at least 2 years must remain for purposes of calculating benefits. (Note: Up to 3 additional years may be dropped from the calculation if the worker had no income during the year and had a child under the age of 3 living in his or her household during the entire year.) *Planning Note:* Because only 35 years are used, a client who has earned the taxable wage figure or more for 35 years will typically get the maximum benefit. Consequently, working longer will typically not help the client to optimize his or her benefit because it is already at the maximum.

- Fourth, determine the years to be excluded from the calculation. These will be the years with the lowest indexed earnings. Of course, the number of years determined in the previous step must remain. *Planning Note:* Typically the lowest 5 years are dropped, including years with zeros.

- Fifth, add the indexed earnings for the years to be included in the AIME calculation and divide the result by the number of months in these years.

As mentioned earlier, the calculation of the AIME for retirement or disability benefits excludes the year in which retirement or disability takes place. However, the indexed earning for that year can be substituted for the lowest year in the calculation if the result will be a larger AIME.

Determination of PIA and Monthly Benefits

Once a worker's AIME has been calculated, his or her PIA is determined by applying a formula to the AIME. The 2017 formula is as follows:

- 90 percent of the first $885 of AIME
- plus 32 percent of the AIME in excess of $885 and less than $5,336
- plus 15 percent of the AIME in excess of $5,336

The dollar figures in this formula are adjusted annually for changes in the national level of wages.

The formula used to determine a worker's retirement benefit is the formula for the year in which the worker turned age 62. Therefore, a worker retiring at age 66 in 2017 would use the 2013 formula rather than the 2017 formula. The formula used to determine survivors and disability benefits is the formula in existence for the year in which death or disability occurs, even if application for benefits is made in a later year.

The PIA is the amount a worker will receive if he or she retires at normal retirement age or becomes disabled, and it is the amount on which benefits for family members are based.

In 2017, the average monthly retirement benefit for workers was of $1,360 ($16,320 per year). A worker who has continually earned the maximum income subject to Social Security taxes and retires at age 66 in 2017 can expect a benefit of $2,687 a month ($32,224 annually) for retirement purposes and a lower benefit for purposes of disability and survivors benefits. If a worker is retired or disabled, the following benefits are paid to family members:

Category	Percentage of Worker's PIA
Spouse at full retirement age	50%
Spouse caring for disabled child or child under 16	50%
Child under 18 or disabled	50% each

If the worker dies, survivors benefits are as follows:

Category	Percentage of Worker's PIA
Spouse at full retirement age	100%
Spouse caring for disabled child or child under 16	75%
Child under 18 or disabled	75% each
Dependent parent	82.5% for one, 75% each for two

family maximum

However, the full benefits described above may not be payable because of a limitation imposed on the total benefits that may be paid to a family. This **family maximum** will usually be reached if three or more family members (including a retired or disabled worker) are eligible for benefits. The family maximum for purposes of retirement and survivors benefits can be determined for 2017 from the following formula, which, like the PIA formula, is adjusted annually based on changing wage levels:

- 150 percent of the first $1,131 of PIA
- plus 272 percent of the PIA in excess of $1,31 through $1,633
- plus 134 percent of the PIA in excess of $1,633 through $2,130
- plus 175 percent of the PIA in excess of $2,130

The family maximum for purposes of disability benefits is limited to 85 percent of the worker's AIME or 150 percent of the worker's PIA, whichever is lower. However, in no case can the maximum be reduced below the worker's PIA. If the total amount of benefits payable to family members exceeds the family maximum, the worker's benefit (in the case of retirement and disability) is not affected, but the benefits of other family members are reduced proportionately.

When the first child loses benefits at age 18, the other family members will each have benefits increased. When a second family member loses eligibility, the remaining two family members will each receive the full benefit because the total benefits received by the family will now be less than the family maximum.

Other Factors Affecting Benefits

Benefits Taken Early

LO 19.7   Identify the impact of taking benefits early or late and what happens if an individual works after benefits begin.

Persons can retire as early as age 62, but the monthly benefit is subject to an early retirement reduction. The reduction is 5/9 of 1 percent for each of the first 36 months of entitlement immediately preceding the age at which 100 percent of PIA is payable (scheduled to increase to age 67 by the year 2022), plus 5/12 of 1 percent for each of up to 24 earlier months.

> **EXAMPLE**
>
> Georgia is aged 62 in 2017. Since she was born in 1955 she has a full retirement age of 66 and 2 months. If she retires at age 62 in 2017 and is 50 months prior to her full retirement age, the reduction in her benefit would be 25.83 percent, 36 months multiplied by 5/9 of 1 percent (a 20-percent reduction) plus 14 months multiplied by 5/12 of 1 percent (a 5.83 percent reduction).

A spousal benefit is reduced 25/36 of one percent for each month before normal retirement age, up to 36 months. If the number of months exceeds 36, then the benefit is further reduced 5/12 of one percent per month.

Delayed Retirement

Workers who delay applying for retirement benefits until after attainment of normal retirement age are eligible for an increased benefit. The increase for those born in 1943 or later is 8 percent for each full year of deferral up to age 70.

Earnings Test

earnings test

Benefits are reduced for Social Security beneficiaries under the full retirement age if their work wages exceed a specified level. The rationale behind having a reduction tied to wages, referred to as an **earnings test,** is that Social Security benefits are intended to replace lost wages but not other income such as dividends or interest. In 2017, Social Security beneficiaries under full retirement age are allowed earnings of $16,920 ($1,410/month). This figure is adjusted annually on the basis of national wage levels. If a beneficiary earns in excess of the allowable amount, his or her Social Security benefit is reduced. For persons under full retirement age the reduction is $1 for every $2 of excess earnings. A different formula applies for the calendar year in which an individual attains the full retirement age. For that year, the reduction is only $1 for every $3 of excess earnings and counts only earnings before the month the individual reaches full retirement age. Also, for that year the threshold is higher: $44,880 ($3,740/month) in 2017. Once an individual attains the full retirement age, he or she can earn any amount of wages without a reduction of benefits.

The reduction in a retired worker's benefits resulting from excess earnings is applied to all benefits paid to the family. If large enough, this reduction may totally eliminate all benefits otherwise payable to the worker and family members. In contrast, excess earnings of family members are charged against their individual benefits only. For example, a widowed mother who holds a job outside the home may lose her mother's benefit, but any benefits received by her children will be unaffected.

Cost-of-Living Adjustments

COLA

OASDI benefits are increased automatically each January as long as there has been an increase in the CPI for the one-year period ending in the third quarter of the prior year. This is known as a cost-of-living adjustment (**COLA**). The increase is typically the same as the increase in the CPI since the last COLA, rounded to the nearest 0.1 percent. There have been proposals over the year to reduce the COLA adjustments to S.S. and to tie S.S. benefits to the CPI-E, which tracks the spending habits of the elderly, instead of tying the adjustments to the CPI-W, which does not track the spending habits of the elderly.

Table 19-3
Social Security COLAs

Year	COLA	Year	COLA
2000	2.4%	2009	5.8%
2001	3.5%	2010	0%
2002	2.6%	2011	0%
2003	1.4%	2012	3.6%
2004	2.1%	2013	1.7%
2005	2.7%	2014	1.5%
2006	4.1%	2015	1.7%
2007	3.3%	2016	0%
2008	2.3%	2017	0.3%

Offset for Other Benefits

Disabled workers under full retirement age who are also receiving workers' compensation benefits or disability benefits from certain other federal, state, or local disability programs will have their OASDI benefits reduced to the extent that the total benefits received (including family benefits) exceed 80 percent of their average current earnings at the time of disability. In addition, the monthly benefit of a spouse or surviving spouse is reduced by two-thirds of any federal, state, or local government pension that is based on earnings not covered under OASDI.

REQUESTING INFORMATION AND FILING FOR BENEFITS

LO 19.8 Explain how to request information about and apply for benefits.

Earnings and Benefit Estimate Statement

Beginning in 1999, the Social Security Administration began to send an annual **Earnings and Benefit Estimate Statement** to each worker who is not currently receiving benefits and who is over age 25. In March of 2011 statements were suspended due to budgetary constraints. The cut was projected to save about $70 million a year. However, in 2014, due to low online enrollments of just 14 million people, paper statements are now mailed. Statements are now mailed every five years, age 25, 30, 35, etc., and annually after age 60.

If the Social Security Administration has underestimated your clients' yearly earnings, they will get less Social Security than they are entitled to. Have clients' W-2s or tax returns available for the affected years.

The statements also contain important information for both planner and client, including:

- The estimated Social Security retirement benefit the client will receive—the Social Security Administration calculates its estimated benefits by assuming that the client will make about the same as his or her latest earnings. If your client's earnings are likely to increase or decrease from present levels, then the benefit will change accordingly.
  Planning Note: You can estimate benefits with different wage assumptions using one of several available calculators at the Social Security website.

- The Social Security benefit estimates given are in current dollars. Let the client know that each subsequent year's calculation will be adjusted for cost of living increases. What's more, depending on the accumulation model (calculation of client needs) that you use, you may have to estimate adjustments to the projected benefit in "retirement time" dollars.

- The estimated disability and survivors benefits that your client will get from Social Security

- The full retirement age of the client—according to the Retirement Confidence Survey, 59 percent of workers in the nation expect to reach full eligibility sooner than they actually are scheduled to reach it.

Obtaining additional information about the Social Security system generally or getting specific information about benefits is easy—simply a telephone call away. The Social Security Administration can be reached at (800) 772-1213. Forms, brochures, and even applications for benefits can be obtained by calling this number; in fact, applications can even be made by phone or online at socialsecurity.gov.

OASDI benefits will not begin until an application for benefits is made. Most applications can be taken by phone at the number mentioned above or on the Internet. To ensure timely commencement, clients should be encouraged to apply for benefits 3 months in advance. However, benefit claims can technically be filed up to 6 months after benefits are due to commence because benefits can be paid retroactively for 6 months (longer in the case of a disability). If a client believes that he or she is entitled to a benefit, encourage him or her to file an application. A simple information request will not be given the same attention as a benefit application. Another important reason for filing an application is that if benefits are erroneously denied, they will be paid retroactively as of the application date once the snafu is straightened out. Also if, after benefits begin, an individual becomes aware that he or she is eligible for a second, larger benefit (for example, a spousal benefit), he or she must file an application in order to ensure receipt of the correct benefit.

YOUR FINANCIAL SERVICES PRACTICE WWW.SSA.GOV

There are few websites as helpful as the one sponsored by the Social Security Administration (ssa.gov). At this site, you and your client can

- obtain a benefit estimate
- apply for Social Security retirement benefits on-line
- use retirement, disability, or survivors planners and calculators to help with financial decisions
- replace, correct, or change the name on the Social Security card
- download publications about benefits
- look up technical details in the Social Security handbook

TAXATION OF SOCIAL SECURITY BENEFITS

LO 19.9   Calculate the portion of Social Security benefits that is subject to tax.

Until 1984, all Social Security benefits were received free of federal income taxation. Since that time, however, the rules have required individuals with substantial additional income to pay tax on a portion of their benefits. Until 1994, the maximum amount of Social Security benefits subject to tax was 50 percent. However, in 1994 the maximum percentage increased to 85 percent for certain taxpayers.

provisional income

The portion of the OASDI benefit that is subject to tax is based on what is referred to as the individual's provisional income. **Provisional income** is the sum of the following:

- the taxpayer's adjusted gross income
- the taxpayer's tax-exempt interest for the year
- half of the taxpayer's Social Security benefits for the year

If the provisional income is less than what is referred to as the base amount—$25,000 for a single taxpayer and $32,000 or less for a married taxpayer filing jointly—Social Security benefits are not taxable. If the provisional income is between the base amount and $34,000 ($44,000 for a married taxpayer filing jointly), up to 50 percent of the Social Security benefit will be includible in taxable income. If the provisional amount exceeds $34,000 ($44,000 for a married taxpayer filing jointly), up to 85 percent of the Social Security benefit will be includible in taxable income. To summarize, the table below identifies the various cutoff points.

Table 19-4
Portion of OASDI Benefits Subject to Federal Income Tax

Taxpayer Filing Status	Provisional Income Threshold	Amount of Benefits Subject to Federal Income Tax
Single	under $25,000	0 percent
Single	$25,000–$33,999	up to 50 percent
Single	$34,000 or more	up to 85 percent
Married filing jointly	under $32,000	0 percent
Married filing jointly	$32,000–$43,999	up to 50 percent
Married filing jointly	$44,000 or more	up to 85 percent
Married filing separately (and living in the same household)	$0	up to 85 percent

The general description of how much is included and the various cutoffs is often sufficient for planning purposes. However, the planner may have occasion to actually calculate the specific amount of benefits that are includible as taxable income. The following explanation and example can be used to make this determination.

Step 1: Calculate provisional income.

Step 2: Determine appropriate thresholds based on the individual's tax filing status.

Step 3: The amount of Social Security benefits included as taxable income is the smallest number obtained from performing the following three calculations:

(a) 50 percent of any provisional income that exceeds the base threshold plus 35 percent of any amount in excess of the second threshold

(b) 85 percent of the benefits

(c) 50 percent of the benefits, plus 85 percent of any amount in excess of the second threshold

EXAMPLE

Peggy and Larry Novenstern are married and file jointly. They have an adjusted gross income of $40,000 (not considering Social Security benefits) plus $5,000 of tax-free bond interest, and are entitled to a $15,000 Social Security benefit.

Step 1: Provisional income equals:

preliminary adjusted gross income	$40,000
tax-free bond interest	$5,000
50 percent of Social Security benefits	$7,500
provisional income	$52,500

Step 2: Determine income in excess of the applicable thresholds.

Excess over base threshold: ($52,500 − $32,000) $20,500

Excess over second threshold: ($52,500 − $44,000) $8,500

Step 3: Amount includible in taxable income is the lowest of the following three amounts:

(a) 50 percent of excess over base threshold plus 35 percent of excess over second threshold (.5 × $20,500 + 35 × $8,500) = $13,225

(b) 85 percent of $15,000 = $12,750

(c) 50 percent of $15,000 + 85 percent of $8,500 = $14,725

In this case, the $12,750 (85 percent of the benefit) is included as adjusted gross income.

WHEN TO TAKE EARLY RETIREMENT BENEFITS

LO 19.10 Determine when it is appropriate to begin benefits prior to full retirement age.

One of the questions most frequently asked by clients considering early retirement is whether they should begin taking Social Security retirement benefits early, that is prior to the date that full benefits are payable. A worker covered by Social Security can retire at full retirement age and receive full benefits or begin receiving reduced benefits as early as age 62. A large number of Americans currently choose to take benefits early. According to Social Security's 2007 Annual Statistical Supplement, in 2006, 52 percent of men and 56 percent of women who claimed retired-worker benefits were age 62. However, there has been a slow increase in the average claiming age since 2004. In 2014, only 34.5 percent of men claimed at age 62. Similarly, the number of women claiming at age 62 also dropped to 39.7 percent in 2014. (See Social Security Annual Statistical Supplement for 2015). Whether or not this is the right decision depends on a number of issues. First we will address some rules and other threshold issues that impact on this decision, and then look at the economic impact of the timing of the benefit election.

Threshold Issues

The decision of whether an individual should elect to receive benefits early comes up in different contexts. For the retiring worker, it generally arises in three situations: as part of the decision regarding at what age to retire, as an issue of need for the individual who has been involuntarily terminated, and as an economic issue for the individual who has other potential sources of income in the early years of retirement. For this third category, the primary issue is an economic one, which is discussed in depth below. However, even for this group, one threshold issue must be addressed: Is the individual considering returning to work at any time prior to full retirement age? If so, then he or she will have a reduction in benefits if earnings exceed the earnings threshold.

For the group considering what age to retire, the Social Security early retirement reduction factor is only part of the impact of retiring at an earlier age. More central to this decision is whether the individual will have sufficient pension benefits and/or personal savings to meet retirement needs. When advising these clients, be aware that they (1) generally are not fully aware of the financial effects of having a longer retirement period, (2) do not fully understand the impact on their pension benefits when they choose to retire early, and (3) do not understand that there are other factors other than the early reduction factor that can result in a reduction in Social Security benefits.

Early commencement will have the most negative impact on Social Security benefits when the individual has a short working history (especially for those who have worked fewer than 35 years) or when the individual has recently seen a drastic upswing in wages. However, in most cases continuing to work will increase benefits at least modestly, as the more recent years of higher wages are typically replacing lower wages in the benefit formula. In order to determine the impact of retiring at different ages, the Social Security Administration website offers several different benefit calculators that allow benefit modeling at different ages.

For the group that is involuntarily terminated and is forced to begin benefits, there are two rules that can mitigate against losses that may occur from taking benefits early. First, an individual beginning benefits early is allowed to pay back the benefits within one year (without interest) and have benefits recalculated based on the later retirement age. Second, under the earnings limit, there is an automatic recalculation of benefits at full retirement age when benefits have been reduced. For example, if under the earnings test an individual loses 6 months of payments, at full retirement age benefits are recalculated based on a retirement age that is 6 months later then under the initial calculation. If the worker returns after full retirement age, he or she can elect voluntary suspension, which again allows an increase in benefits when benefits are started later.

When to Elect Early Benefits: The Economic Issue

First, let's focus on the group of individuals who are struggling to make ends meet in retirement. Approximately two-thirds of Americans rely as Social Security for more than half of their retirement income, and that statistic is not expected to change any time soon. A surprising percentage of these individuals still choose to retire and begin benefits early. For this group deferring could result in a significantly higher replacement ratio. Considering that Social Security has a built in cost of living increase and provides benefits for a surviving spouse, deferring retirement benefits is an important option to consider.

> **EXAMPLE**
>
> Dick and Pat are married and currently age 62. Dick earns $80,000 and Pat does not work outside the home. Pat is entitled to a Social Security spousal retirement benefit. Using the Social Security "Retirement Estimator" calculator, if this couple retires and both begin benefits at 62, Social Security replaces only 31 percent of income. If instead Dick continues to work until age 66 and both defer benefits until age 66 the replacement ratio increases to 42 percent. If Dick defers retirement and Dick begins benefits at age 70 the replacement rate jumps to 57 percent, a much more secure situation for this couple!

For wealthier clients that can choose alternative sources of retirement income, a good place to start in the decision making process is to compare the expected present value of lifetime benefits assuming different benefit start dates. Not surprisingly, the Social Security system is designed so that individuals living the average life expectancy will receive the same expected present value for retirement ages between age 62 and full retirement age. According to research from the Center of Retirement Research at Boston College, there is a major exception to this rule. Because of the spousal benefit, married men who retire and begin benefits early (those that live the average life expectancy) will receive a smaller present value than if they defer. The reason for this is that post-death spousal benefit is based on the amount of benefit that the participant was receiving. This is a significant finding, since it surmises that, on average, married participants will receive a greater expected present value by deferring, and that lots of participants are leaving money on the table by beginning benefits early. There are a number of articles at the Center for Retirement Research at Boston College discussing this research.

When considering whether to take early or defer, assuming that an individual will live much shorter or longer than the average life expectancy will have an impact on the analysis. The most obvious case may be the individual who is ill and has a high probability of a short life expectancy. In this case clearly benefits are maximized by beginning early. On the other hand, a long life expectancy weighs in favor of deferring. Historically, this break-even analysis based on life expectancy has been a common approach for determining the optimal retirement age. The analysis is fairly complex, however, and requires assumptions about rates of return on investments. The major flaw with this type of analysis is that we do not know when people are going to die, and break-even analysis becomes a dangerous gamble. The person who starts early and dies early wins the gamble. The one who lives too long loses the gamble and runs out of money, a frightening proposition. With married men, in many cases the spouse lives longer and the spouse suffers from the participant's bad choice.

A newer way of looking at this issue is to look at deferring benefits as the purchase of an inflation adjusted joint-and-survivor (for married participants) annuity. The annuity amount "purchased" is the additional benefit earned from deferral and the "price" is the loss of benefits by electing deferral. The price of deferral can be compared with the actual price of buying an inflation adjusted fixed annuity in the amount of the additional monthly benefit. It is likely that the cost of purchasing the annuity will be more, partially because of the high cost of purchasing the inflation adjustment. Looking at it this way, an individual looking for additional guaranteed lifetime income may want to look first at ways to maximize Social Security benefits before seeking additional annuity income.

YOUR FINANCIAL SERVICES PRACTICE FUNDING SOCIAL SECURITY DEFERRAL

There are a number of ways to finance retirement needs while maximizing Social Security benefits by deferring benefits. There's continued work or using other assets to fund the first retirement years. What can also be helpful is that beneficiaries eligible to receive more than one benefit may in some cases be able to benefit from deferring the more valuable benefit, but still taking a different benefit at a younger age. Here are several examples:

- Spousal benefits taken first. At or after full retirement age, a married (or divorced) spouse may have the option to claim the spousal benefit and claim the worker's benefit later—at age 70 to maximize the worker's benefit. An eligible divorced spouse can take advantage of the same rule. This option is not available if benefits are claimed before full retirement age, because under the deemed-filing rule an individual filing before full retirement age is treated as claiming both benefits, if eligible. Note that a currently married spouse can begin a spousal benefit only if the worker has claimed benefits. However, the worker can claim and suspend benefits (at

or after full retirement age) to trigger eligibility for the spouse.
- Worker's benefits taken first. The spouse with a small worker's benefit may consider claiming benefits from his or her own earnings history at 62, and, once the higher-earning spouse retires, receive the higher spouse's benefit. The deemed-filing rule is not an impediment here since the spouse is not entitled to the spousal benefit until the worker claims retirement benefits.
- Widow(er)'s benefit options. A widow(er) eligible for both widow's benefits and worker's benefits can choose one benefit and later choose the other. For example, a widow could take a reduced widow's benefit at age 60 or 62 and then switch to her maximum retirement benefit when she reaches age 70.

CHAPTER REVIEW

Key Terms and Concepts

Social Security
FICA tax
SECA tax
taxable wage base
quarters of coverage
fully insured status
currently insured
disability insured
full retirement age

primary insurance amount (PIA)
average indexed monthly earnings (AIME)
family maximum
earnings test
COLA
Earnings and Benefit Estimate Statement
provisional income

Chapter 19: Review Questions

Review questions are based on the learning objectives in this chapter. Thus, a [19.3] at the end of a question means that the question is based on learning objective 3. If there are multiple objectives, they are all listed

1. Which workers are not covered under Social Security? [19.1]

2. What percentage of seniors have Social Security as their only source of income? [19.2]

3. What is the Social Security tax rate for employees, employers, and self-employed individuals? [19.3]

4. In 2017, Sally earns $5,500 for employment subject to Social Security taxes between January 1 and April 1. She does not work for the remainder of the year. How many quarters of coverage does she earn? [19.4]

5. What is the earliest age at which a retired worker and his or her spouse are entitled to receive Social Security benefits? [19.5]

6. How long must a couple be married before a divorced spouse is eligible for a spousal retirement benefit? [19.5]

7. Describe the survivor and disability benefits available under the Social Security system. [19.5]

8. Discuss the general rule that applies when a client is eligible for dual benefits under the Social Security system. [19.5]

9. How many years of income are generally used to calculate the average indexed monthly earnings (AIME) for an individual eligible for retirement benefits? [19.6]

10. Calculate the primary insurance amount (PIA) for an individual retiring at age 62 in 2017 with an AIME of $5,500. [19.6]

11. Patty, born in 1964, is planning on taking Social Security benefits at age 62. Her PIA will be decreased by what percentage? [19.7]

12. George, currently age 62 (assume full retirement age of 67), is planning to retire and begin receiving Social Security benefits at age 68. His PIA will be increased by what percentage in order to reflect his late retirement? [19.7]

13. How does the earnings test work? [19.7]

14. Describe the information contained in the benefit estimate available to Social Security participants at the Social Security website. [19.8]

15. What steps must be followed to ensure timely payment of all Social Security benefits to which a client is entitled? [19.9]

16. From an economic perspective, when will clients be better off electing Social Security benefits? [19.10]

Chapter 19: Review Answers

1. The workers who are not covered under Social Security include:
   - people with less than 40 quarters of coverage
   - civilian employees of the federal government who were employed by the government prior to 1984 and who are covered primarily under the Civil Service Retirement System
   - railroad workers covered under the Railroad Retirement Act
   - some employees of state and local governments, unless the state has entered into a voluntary agreement with the Social Security Administration.
   - some American citizens working abroad for foreign affiliates of U.S. employers
   - ministers who elect out of coverage because of conscience or religious principles
   - student nurses, newspaper carriers under age 18, and students working for the school at which they are regularly enrolled or doing domestic work for a local college club, fraternity, or sorority
   - certain family employees

2. Social Security is the only source of income for nearly one-third of seniors.

3. The Social Security tax rate for employees is 6.2 percent on income up to the taxable wage base and 1.45 percent on all income. This is the same amount paid by the employer. Self-employed individuals pay both the employee and employer amount (total of 15.3 percent).

4. For 2017, a worker receives credit for one quarter of coverage for each $1,300 in annual earnings on which Social Security taxes are earned, up to a maximum of four quarters of coverage. Sally earns four quarters of coverage because she has earned more than $5,200. It does not matter that she works for only part of the year.

5. Age 62 is the earliest age at which benefits can be received.

6. Ten years is the length of time a couple must have been married before a divorced spouse would be entitled to a spousal benefit.

7. All categories of survivors benefits are payable if a worker is fully insured at the time of death (see below). However, three types of benefits are also payable if a worker is only currently insured. The first is a lump-sum death benefit of $255. The second

are dependent, unmarried children, and the third is a spouse (including a divorced spouse) caring for a child or children.

The following categories of persons are also eligible for benefits, but only if the deceased worker was fully insured:

- a widow or widower at age 60. However, benefits are reduced if taken prior to full retirement age. This benefit is also payable to a divorced spouse if the marriage lasted at least 10 years. In addition, the widow's or widower's benefit is payable to a disabled spouse at age 50 as long as the disability commenced no more than 7 years after (1) the worker's death or (2) the end of the year in which entitlement to a mother's or father's benefit ceased.

- a parent aged 62 or over who was dependent on the deceased worker at the time of death

A disabled worker under the full retirement age is eligible to receive benefits under OASDI as long as he or she is disability insured and meets the definition of disability under the law. The definition of disability is very rigid and requires a mental or physical impairment that prevents the worker from engaging in any substantial gainful employment. The disability must also have lasted (or be expected to last) at least 12 months or be expected to result in death.

8. In many cases, a person is eligible for more than one type of OASDI benefit. Probably the most common situation occurs when a person is eligible for both a spouse's benefit and a worker's retirement benefit based on his or her own Social Security record. In this case and in any other case when a person is eligible for dual benefits, only an amount equal to the highest benefit is paid. However, there are situations in which a person can file for one benefit and later change to another.

9. For retirement benefits, the number of years is 35 (5 less than the minimum number of quarters necessary to be fully insured).

10. Because the PIA is based on the formula used for the year in which an individual attains age 62, use the current (2017) PIA formula.

.9 x $885	=	$796.50
.32 x ($5,336– $885)	=	$1,424.32
.15 x ($5,500 – $5,336)	=	$24.60
Total		$2,245.42

11. Persons born in 1964 can retire as early as age 62, but the monthly benefit is permanently reduced. Patty's full retirement age is 67. The reduction used is 5/9 of 1 percent for each of the first 36 months of entitlement immediately preceding the age at which 100 percent of PIA is payable (20 percent), plus 5/12 of 1 percent for each of up to 24 earlier months (10 percent). Patty's reduction is therefore 30 percent of her PIA.

12. The actuarial increase is 8 percent per year after full retirement age. George is age 62, with a given full retirement age of 67 and 2 months. Deferring benefits until age 68 means he will increase his benefit by 8 percent (8 percent for the year he waited).

13. Under the earnings test, benefits are reduced for Social Security beneficiaries under the full retirement age if their work wages exceed a specified level. The rationale behind having a reduction tied to wages is that Social Security benefits are intended to replace lost wages, but not other income such as dividends or interest. In 2017, Social Security beneficiaries under full retirement age are allowed earnings of $16,920. This figure is adjusted annually on the basis of national wage levels. If a beneficiary earns in excess of the allowable amount, his or her Social Security benefit is reduced. The reduction is generally $1 for every $2 of excess earnings. There is a special rule for the year that the individual attains full retirement age. For that year, the earnings limit is higher and the reduction is only $1 of benefits for $3 earned in excess of the limit.

14. In addition to earnings history, the benefit estimate includes:
    - the estimated Social Security retirement benefit the client will receive (the Social Security benefit estimates given are in current dollars)
    - the estimated disability and survivors benefits that your client will get from Social Security
    - the client's full retirement age

15. OASDI benefits will not begin until an application for benefits is made. Most applications can be made by phone or on the Internet. To ensure timely commencement, clients should be encouraged to apply for benefits 3 months in advance. However, benefit claims can technically be filed up to 6 months after benefits are due to commence because benefits can be paid retroactively for 6 months (longer in the case of a disability).

16. Those clients who expect to live a shorter than average life are the most obvious candidates for beginning benefits early. However, for married couples, the joint life expectancy must be considered. Since anticipating life expectancy is difficult

to do, clients should consider deferring benefits as a way to increase this source of guaranteed, inflation-adjusted lifetime income.

Chapter 20

Introduction to Individual Retirement Planning

Learning Objectives

An understanding of the material in this chapter should enable the student to

LO 20.1 List the skills that a pension student has learned regarding individual retirement planning.

LO 20.2 Identify the role of the retirement planner and the steps in the retirement planning process.

LO 20.3 Describe the following critical issues that affect retirement planning:

- availability of private pensions
- women and retirement
- need for education and planners
- changing face of retirement
- baby boomers and retirement
- roadblocks to retirement savings
- retirement objectives

LO 20.4 Discuss the potential sources of retirement income.

In addition to servicing the pension needs of a business and a business owner, identifying the Roth and regular IRA opportunities for individual clients, and understanding how the Social Security system applies to a client's situation, practitioners must also attend to the individual financial goals that clients have for their retirement.

In essence, you have come to the logical conclusion concerning your study of planning for retirement needs. You started with an analysis of the pension system as codified in ERISA and the Internal Revenue Code. At that time, your client was the small business owner. You focused on the qualified plan needs of the business and then turned to the nonqualified plan needs for executives and business owners. Once again you served two masters—both the business and the business owner. You then turned your attention to the needs of the individual client and the individual retirement plan system (Roth and regular IRAs). Finally, you explored the workings of the Social Security system. Now, in this last part of the text, you continue to focus on the individual as your client and take a comprehensive look at planning for his or her successful retirement.

LO 20.1 List the skills that a pension student has learned regarding individual retirement planning.

YOUR FINANCIAL SERVICES PRACTICE: PENSION KNOWLEDGE HELPS WITH RETIREMENT PLANNING EXPERTISE

When you were studying ERISA, IRAs, and Social Security, you were also learning a great deal about individual retirement planning. For example, you are now proficient in the following skills that an individual retirement planner must have. These include:

- understanding the type(s) of retirement plan(s) being provided to your clients including the plans' benefit or contribution formula
- analyzing the key provisions of your clients' retirement plan including their vesting schedules, hardship withdrawal and loan rules, and matching contribution and elective deferral options
- identifying and using documents like the summary plan description and the personal benefit statement
- appreciating the importance of before-tax and/or tax-free savings vehicles as a method to maximize retirement savings
- diagnosing the ramifications of starting Social Security benefits prior to full retirement age
- choosing an appropriate Keogh plan for a self-employed person with Schedule C income
- recognizing the specifications for and importance of the ESOP diversification rules
- determining the IRA options that best fit your clients' needs
- interpreting the tax rules applicable to Social Security benefits and nonqualified stock plans
- explaining how Social Security and pension benefits are calculated and how your client can optimize his or her benefits under each system
- cataloging the fiduciary protection, QDRO assurance, and PBGC refuge and bankruptcy shield afforded your clients under law

As you can see a significant foundation has already been laid for our study of individual retirement planning.

THE ROLE OF THE RETIREMENT PLANNER

LO 20.2 Identify the role of the retirement planner and the steps in the retirement planning process.

It may surprise you to know that retirement planning is a relatively young discipline. Consider this: In 1930, only one in 10 workers was covered by a pension program and Social Security did not exist! For Americans who lived early in the 20th century, "retirement" meant moving from fieldwork to household chores. In the middle of the century, retirement was thought of as a short and sedentary experience. Consequently the need for a retirement planner did not exist until recently.

Today, however, retirement is no longer synonymous with rocking chairs. Instead retirement is thought of as a vibrant and significant time of life, which may last 30 years or longer. If Norman Rockwell, the renowned American illustrator, were alive today, he might put a face on today's retirement by portraying active seniors engaged in a variety of recreational activities. Gone are the days of the frail seniors sitting in rocking chairs. They have been replaced with active and involved people who need help in planning for a dynamic time of life.

Does the Retirement Planner Have an Impossible Task?

Retirement planning is a multidimensional field that requires the planner to be schooled in the nuances of many financial planning specialties as well as other nonfinancial areas. Unfortunately, some so-called planners approach retirement planning from only one point of view (for example, investments). The perspective offered by limited specialization, however, is inadequate for dealing with the diversified needs of the would-be retiree. A client is better served by a team of planners who have complementary specialized backgrounds or by a single planner who is experienced in a variety of important retirement topics.

Whether the retirement team or the multi-area individual is the vehicle, the holistic approach to retirement planning is the most professional method by which a client's needs can be fully and adequately met. Holistic retirement planning requires the planner to communicate with clients concerning the following topics:

- the effect of financial well-being on the quality of life
- employer-provided retirement plan options
- Social Security considerations
- personal savings and investments
- IRAs and Roth IRAs
- income tax issues
- tax planning for distributions and other distribution issues
- Medicare choices
- health insurance planning including medigap insurance and long-term care insurance
- wealth accumulation for retirement

- asset allocation and risk
- long-term care options (living options)
- retirement communities
- relocation possibilities and reverse mortgages
- wellness, nutrition, lifestyle choices, and other gerontological issues
- assessment of current savings needed to achieve retirement goals
- financial gerontology
- estate planning

A word of caution is in order at this point. Understanding how to plan for a client's retirement is much more art than science. There is no one-size-fits-all approach to retirement planning. For example, an attempt to describe the average retiree is like trying to describe the average book—even if it could be done, the information would not be very useful. Retirees are wealthy and poor, male and female, old and not-so-old. They are single, married, and widowed; they have children and they do not have children. They are healthy and unhealthy, happy and unhappy, active and sedentary, sophisticated and naive.

A further complication is that planning does not always begin early enough in the financial life cycle. While the axiom "it's never too early or too late to plan for retirement" is true, it requires a completely different approach to plan for a client's retirement when it is too late to influence the client's ability to retire with financial security. Conversely, planning at a relatively young age opens up a multitude of opportunities for clients and presents different planning challenges.

Because client circumstances and objectives are like snowflakes—there are no two alike—planners must be able to meet a variety of situations creatively and cannot rely on a "formula approach" to solve their clients' problems.

YOUR FINANCIAL SERVICES PRACTICE: ADDITIONAL RESPONSIBILITIES

In addition to being a "Jack of all trades," retirement planners now must undertake several responsibilities that may not have been a part of their traditional financial practice. These aspects of a retirement planning practice include

- incorporating retirement planning as a segment of comprehensive financial planning
- dealing with other professionals who advise the client
- dealing with clients from every age group (Retirement planning is for young clients as well as clients who are near or at retirement or who have retired already.)
- conducting retirement planning seminars

Retirement Resources

In order to measure up to the Herculean task of retirement planning, retirement planners must familiarize themselves with the various resources available in this field. Organizations such as the Society of Financial Service Professionals, the Financial Planning Association, the National Council on Aging, and the American Society on Aging offer a forum that provides newsletters, conferences, and a chance for interaction with other planners. In addition, planners should make their clients aware of the American Association of Retired Persons, an organization that provides information on services for the elderly including a valuable resource for retirement information. Planners may also want to check the numerous retirement planning websites.

1. www.ssa.gov —This site allows individuals to project the benefits they will receive from Social Security; it also provides a great deal of information regarding Social Security.

2. www.EBRI.org —The home page of the Employee Benefit Research Institute presents updates, databases, and surveys that have been recently issued.

3. www.ASEC.org —The American Savings Education Council provides the ballpark estimate calculator that enables people to calculate their savings need for retirement. It also contains links to different financial calculators.

4. www.irs.gov —The IRS website provides useful publications on many retirement issues.

5. www.benefitscheckup.org —This is a service that allows seniors, their families, and caregivers to quickly and easily identify what programs and services they may qualify for and how to access them.

6. http://crr.bc.edu —The Center for Retirement Research at Boston College promotes research and publishes it for the public and policy community. This valuable resource offers information on a wide range of subjects including Social Security, private pensions, work and retirement, and savings and consumption.

7. www.mrrc.isr.umich.edu —The Michigan Retirement Research Center also promotes quality research on retirement and Social Security policy and communicates findings to the policy community and the public.

8. http://retirement.theamericancollege.edu/ —The New York Life Center for Retirement Income provides planning videos for financial advisors on retirement income topics and conducts a variety of advisor and consumer focused research products.

Steps in the Retirement Planning Process

The retirement planning process is similar to the process for financial planning.

Step 1: Establish Client-Planner Relationships

It is essential to establish a working relationship with the client. This involves the identification and explanation of issues, concepts, and products related to the retirement process. The planner should describe the services he or she provides, the steps involved in the process, and the documentation (such as the summary plan description) required.

Step 2: Determine Goals and Expectations and Gather Client Data

This step begins by listening to the client's goals and hopes for retirement. Listening skills are important because it is easy for a planner to impose his or her concept of retirement on the client or to assume that he or she believes is important is also important to the client. However, clients have a variety of objectives that range from never working again to working full time during retirement. Clearly, planners have their work cut out for them as they deal with a plethora of client expectations and, in some cases, help frame those expectations through the education process.

In addition to sorting through the various lifestyle options for retirement, planners must also focus at this stage on conducting a financial inventory of retirement assets and an assessment of the strategies available to a client. For example, planners must account for all resources allocated to retirement and all opportunities a client has, such as the ability to contribute to a Roth IRA or the availability of a 401(k) plan at work.

> **YOUR FINANCIAL SERVICES PRACTICE: IMPORTANT FACT-FINDING TOOLS**
>
> In addition to the typical information concerning assets and liabilities, securities holdings, and annual income, retirement planners need to look at the following:
> - wills and trusts
> - long-term care policies
> - Social Security statements
> - employer health benefit policies
> - employer summary plan descriptions
> - employer benefit statements

Step 3: Analyze and Evaluate the Client's Financial Status

In this step, the planner looks at the client's current situation as well as his or her future goals in order to determine the appropriate strategies for that particular client. This includes conducting a retirement needs analysis as well as an analysis of the client's risk tolerance, risk management strategies, and risk exposures. For example, do clients have adequate disability insurance and long-term care insurance? Do their current investment allocations adequately achieve their financial goals? Are they currently saving enough for retirement? What tax planning and distribution strategies are available and do they make sense for the client's situation? Planners need to evaluate and analyze current retirement plan exposures (for example, premature distribution tax), current retirement plans, current retirement strategies, and Social Security benefits.

Step 4: Develop and Present the Retirement Plan

The planner should develop and prepare a retirement plan tailored to meet the client's goals and objectives and commensurate with the client's values, objectives, temperament, and risk tolerance. In addition to the client's current financial position, the plan should include the client's projected retirement status under the status quo as well as projected statements if the planner's recommendations are followed. The planner should also provide a current asset allocation statement along with strategy recommendations and a statement that assumes that recommendations will be followed. Investments should be summarized, and the planner should propose an investment policy statement and additional policy recommendations. The plan should also include an assessment of distribution options and tax strategies for retirement. Finally, the plan should include a list of prioritized action items and engage issues such as housing and health care.

After developing and preparing the plan, the planner should present it to the client for review. The planner should collaborate with the client to ensure that the plan meets the stated goals and objectives; then the planner should revise it as appropriate.

Step 5: Implement the Retirement Plan

The planner should assist the client in implementing the recommendations. Often this requires coordinating with other professionals, such as human resource professionals, accountants, attorneys, real estate agents, investment advisors, stock brokers, and insurance agents.

Step 6: Monitor the Retirement Plan

After the plan is implemented, the planner should periodically monitor the plan, evaluate the soundness of recommendations, and review its progress with the client. The planner should discuss and evaluate changes in the client's personal circumstances such as family births or deaths, illness, divorce, or change in job status. Any relevant changes in tax laws, benefit and pension options, and the economic environment should be reviewed and evaluated before the planner makes recommendations to accommodate new or changing circumstances.

CRITICAL ISSUES THAT AFFECT RETIREMENT PLANNING

LO 20.3   Describe the following critical issues that affect retirement planning:

- **availability of private pensions**
- **women and retirement**
- **need for education and planners**
- **changing face of retirement**
- **baby boomers and retirement**
- **roadblocks to retirement savings**
- **retirement objectives**

To better understand the retirement planning discipline, let's look at the different issues affecting the world of retirement today. By laying this foundation, the planner should be able to understand the rules and strategies discussed later in the book in the context of the retirement planning environment as it currently exists.

> **YOUR FINANCIAL SERVICES PRACTICE: HELPING YOUR CLIENTS SAFEGUARD THEIR PENSIONS**
>
> Help your clients get all the pension benefits that they are entitled to. Pass along to your clients these Department of Labor consumer tips for safeguarding pension benefits.
> - Know your pension plan. Obtain and review your Summary Plan Description (SPD).
> - Review your individual benefit statement and individual account information. Know what your accrued and vested benefits are.
> - Maintain a pension file. Keep records of where you've worked, dates you've worked there, your salary and any plan documents or benefit statements you've received.
> - Notify your plan administrator of any changes that may affect your benefit payments (i.e., marriage, divorce, death of a spouse).
> - Know the person in your company who has information about your pension plan and can give you plan documents.

- Know how the merger or acquisition of your company will affect your pension benefit.
- Know your pension rights. Request information on your pension rights and how to protect your pension.
- Contact the Department of Labor's Employee Benefits Security Administration if you have any additional questions about your rights under the law.

Issue One: Employer Sponsored Retirement Plan Availability

Clients who work for medium- and large-sized employers typically have an advantage over their counterparts in small firms when it comes to retirement planning. One fact of life in retirement planning is that as the size of the organization increases, the chance of having a employer sponsored retirement program increases. According to the Bureau of Labor Statistics, roughly 66 percent of the private industry employees in the United States had access to an employer sponsored retirement plan and about 49 percent of the private industry workforce was participating in a plan, which equated to a take-up rate of roughly 75 percent, meaning about 25 percent of those with access to a retirement plan were not participating. However, in the state and local government sector, access was much higher at roughly 90 percent and participation was higher with roughly 81 percent participating in the plan, giving state and local government plans a higher take-up rate of roughly 90 percent. The BLS noted that participation rates are largely driven by the plan type, as more state and local governments still offer defined benefit plans which have a higher take-up rate. The BLS also noted a few important characteristics about plan access. First, access to retirement benefits ranged depending on the type of job. For instance, only 47 percent of service workers had access to an employer sponsored plan while 84 percent of management and professional service workers had access to a plan. Companies with more than 100 employees were also far more likely to offer a retirement plan as nearly 86 percent offered a plan, while roughly 50 percent of smaller firms offered a plan. Additionally, income also appeared to play a role. Unfortunately, those individuals that earned the least amount of money a year, were also the least likely to have access to a retirement plan at work. For instance, only 22 percent of civilian workers in the bottom 25 percent of wages had access to a retirement plan. This is a huge difference when compared to state and local government employees as nearly 76 percent of the lower 25 percent wage earners still had access to a retirement plan.[1]

Issue Two: Women and Retirement

While the elderly in the U.S. struggle with retirement—millions of elderly live in poverty—gender also plays an important role.[2] That women struggle more financially in retirement than

---

1. https://www.bls.gov/news.release/pdf/ebs2.pdf.
2. Census Bureau, *Income and Poverty in The United States*: 2015, https://www.census.gov/library/publications/2016/

men is not just hyperbole. Approximately 70 percent of the elderly living in poverty are women according to analysis of the U.S. Census on poverty for 2014. One interesting fact is that nearly 1.5 percent of the population lived below the federal poverty line in 2015 but only 8.8 percent of those aged 65 and older fell below the line. According to the Census Bureau, the poverty rate for all women age 65 and older was 10.3 percent in 2015, just over one in 10. In contrast, the overall poverty rate for men was just 7.0 percent, or about two-thirds the poverty rate of women. According to a 2016 report, retired women receive, on average, about 33 percent less in pension payments and have about 34 percent less saved on average in 401(k) accounts. (See *National Institute on Retirement Security, 2016 Report, Shortchanged in Retirement, The Continuing Challenges to Women's Financial Future*).[3] In 2014, the Federal Government in its annual Income and Poverty in the United States census release stated that women earn roughly 78 percent of what men earn on average. However, the good news is that this number is up from roughly 60 percent in 1980. Additionally, a women reaching age 65 today can expect to live, on average, until age 86.6, while a man only can expect to live until age 84.3. As such, women are expected to live almost two years longer than men in the United States.

Women have unique problems that make it difficult to achieve a financially successful retirement. For one thing, women are less likely than men to have a pension at work. According to the Department of Labor, of the 62 million wage-earning and salaried women (age 21 to 64) working in the United States, just 45 percent participated in a retirement plan. Second, they have lower earnings, which obviously makes it harder to save for retirement. In 2014, women who were full-time wage and salary workers had median usual weekly earnings of $719, about 82.5 percent of median earnings for male full-time wage and salary workers ($879). In 1979, the first year for which comparable earnings data are available, women earned 62 percent of what men earned. Third, they experience higher turnover than men, so they are more adversely affected by plan vesting schedules. Fourth, they outlive men so, all else being equal, women need to save more than men. Fifth, they are more likely to be caregivers than men, and thus often forgo income to care for a loved one. According to Workforce Management, women give up on average 12 years of work for caregiving responsibilities. The care-giving responsibility also impacts women in the workforce as women are more likely to be part-time employees than are men. Sixth, they are more likely to be single or widowed, and the responsibility of retirement in these instances is not shared. And finally, according to studies, they invest pension assets too conservatively and thus self-inflict an additional savings burden.

---

demo/p60-256.html.

3. Society of Actuaries. Key Findings and Issues: The Impact of Retirement Risk on Women. *2005 Risks and Process of Retirement Survey Report*, (Schaumburg, IL. August 2006.).

A real strength for women and retirement planning is that, as a rule, women are receptive to coaching. They appreciate assistance in understanding their financial situation and they look for guidance in taking action to improve their position. They tend to value ongoing relationships, and planning for retirement involves a long-term process that requires regular interaction with the financial advisor. A recent Ameriprise study identified that more than three quarters of those with a comprehensive financial plan feel well prepared for retirement, as compared to less than half (46 percent) of those with no professional support. Additionally, a 2012 HSBC study showed that planners accumulate roughly 2.5 times the amount of wealth for retirement as compared to nonplanners. According to a 2016 research report by the Transamerica Center for Retirement Studies, women are significantly less confident about their retirement preparedness than men. Women also reported a higher reliance on Social Security and working in retirement than men. As a result, women were more concerned about the future financial security of Social Security.

Issue Three: The Need for Education and Planners

Many studies have shown the lack of financial literacy in the United States. Many lack knowledge of financial concepts, such as diversification, the interest compounding, and the difference between nominal and real values. The problem is widespread, but is particularly problematic with women, African-Americans, Hispanics and those with low education.[4] Half of older workers know little about their pensions and the rules governing Social Security benefits.

It is logical to think that improving financial education is one way to improve financial decisions—including financial preparedness for retirement. One recent pilot program[5], demonstrated this effect. A program was creating offering financial education and individualized financial planning in the workforce. The study found that increased financial literacy did help people make better decisions about their money. The researchers observing the program was successful in part because of the planning component. They also found that the program had a net positive effect on the employer as well. In another workplace seminar program[6], workers who participated reported changing their investment strategy by appropriately diversifying or being more aggressive in their investment choices.

Consider the following factors that indicate the importance of a planner:

---

4. *Household Saving Behavior: The Role of Literacy, Information and Financial Education Programs,* Luscardi, 2008.
5. *Weighing the Effects of Financial Education in the Workplace,* Edmiston, Gillett-Fisher, and McGrath, 2009.
6. *Financial Education in the Workplace: Results of a Research Study,* Kratzer, Brunson, Garman, Kim, and So-hyun Joo.

- A 2010 study (during the recession) showed that people getting "help" outperformed those that did not by about 2 percent.[7]
- A similar 2007 study (prerecession) showed a 3 percent improvement in performance for those that used a computerized advice tool.[8]
- According to the 2010 EBRI Retirement Confidence Survey, less than half of workers have calculated how much they need to save each year to reach their retirement goal.
- According to a research project by David Blanchett, "Alpha, Beta, and Now Gamma," showed that good planning and better decisions can improve retirement income by 38 percent.

Based on the above insights, it is apparent that clients will need education and active involvement from financial service professionals.

Issue Four: The Changing Face of Retirement

It is very important for planners to realize that retirement planning is a dynamic environment. Not only do products, services, and tax laws seem to change on a regular basis, but the very nature of retirement also is in flux. Some interesting studies show differences for those planning to retire in the future. For example, surveys show that current workers expect to work longer than current retirees actually worked before retiring. Surveys also show that many baby boomers say they plan to work after they retire because they enjoy working and want to stay involved. According to EBRI's 2017 Retirement Confidence Survey, only about 29 percent of retirees keep working in retirement, but 79 percent of workers state they plan to work for pay in retirement.

---

7. *Help in Defined Contribution Plans, is it Working and for Whom?* Hewitt Associates and Financial Engines, 2010.
8. Charles Schwab Data, News Release Nov. 28, 2007.

Table 20-1
Reasons for Working in Retirement

	Reason
• Wanting to stay active and involved	90%
• Enjoying working	82
• Wanting money to buy extras	67
• A job opportunity	47
• A decrease in the value of savings or investments	23
• Needing money to make ends meet	42
• Keeping health insurance or other benefits	13

Source: Employee Benefit Research Institute 2017 Retirement Confidence Survey.

Another responsibility changing the nature of retirement is that of a caregiver. The retirees of today and tomorrow are increasingly responsible for caring for parents, children, and grandchildren. Caregiving by retirees of aging parents is well-documented. Apparently, however, a parent's job never ends! According to the U.S. Census Bureau, in 2012, about 7 million grandparents lived in a house with their grandchildren, and for about 4.9 million of the 7 million, the grandparent was the householder. About ten percent of children in the U.S. lived with a grandparent, totaling 7.5 million.

Issue Five: Baby Boomers and Retirement

baby-boom generation

Retirement planning is important for every generation—a person is never too old or too young to plan for retirement. Special attention must be paid, however, to the needs of those born from 1946 to 1964, the so-called **baby-boom generation**. This generation represents roughly one-third of the population and, as it has progressed through the life cycles, it has greatly impacted everything from crowding in grammar schools to the housing market. The question remains: What will the implications of this demographic tidal wave have on retirement?

YOUR FINANCIAL SERVICES PRACTICE:
THE GRAYING OF AMERICA

Considering that the number of people over age 60 will triple by 2030 to 1.4 billion (16 percent of the world's population), the need for retirement planners and practitioners familiar with eldercare issues is certain to intensify as the baby-boom generation matures. In fact, the closer a person gets to retirement, the more he or she realizes the great need for products and services provided by the financial services industry.

> Ironically, retirement planning is not just about older people. Planners are well-aware that the process should begin at the early stages of a client's life cycle. However, over the next 10 years, the fledgling field of retirement planning should mature along with the baby-boom generation. For this reason, the timing of practitioners currently entering this field is perfect because the opportunities to serve both clients and themselves in a rewarding career are great.

Issue Six: Roadblocks to Retirement Saving

No matter what the generation, the question remains: Why don't more Americans plan for retirement? The answer lies in the many distractions that hinder retirement savings.

Perhaps the biggest roadblock to retirement planning is the tendency of many working people to use their full after-tax income to support their current standard of living. Whatever the reason for their lack of retirement savings, clients must follow a budget that allows them to live within their means and that also provides for retirement savings. Make your clients aware that a 90/10 spending ratio is generally desired. Under a 90/10 spending ratio, 90 percent of your clients' earnings is directed toward their current standard of living, and at least 10 percent is directed toward other long-term financial objectives, such as their own retirement.

A second impediment to retirement saving is unexpected expenses including uninsured medical bills; repairs to a home, auto, or major appliance; and periods of unemployment. The client should set up an emergency fund to handle these inevitable problems. Approximately 3 to 6 months' income is usually set aside for this objective.

Inadequate insurance coverage is a third impediment to retirement saving. Regardless of whether it is life, disability, health, home, or auto, many individuals continue to remain uninsured or underinsured. Because the client cannot always recover economically from such losses, one important element of retirement planning is protection against catastrophic financial loss that would make future saving impossible. Agents should conduct a thorough review of their clients' insurance needs to make sure they are adequately covered. Two areas that are often overlooked are disability insurance and liability insurance for the professional. Make sure your client is adequately protected in both of them.

Whatever distractions face your clients, it is important to educate them about the need to plan for retirement. Clients must realize that saving is possible only for a limited time during their lives, but consumption occurs throughout their lives and can increase at any time because of illness or inflation. This imbalance makes it essential for clients to save sufficient assets during their working years to ensure attainment of retirement goals.

Issue Seven: Retirement Objectives

A client's retirement objectives vary significantly depending on many factors including health, age, marital status, number and ages of children, differences in the ages of husband and wife, and personal preferences. Also, a client's objectives vary depending on his or her personal definition of retirement. For some, retirement is the last day they have to work; for others it is the last day they want to work; and for still others it is the last day they can work. The table below contains a ranking of some typical retirement objectives. (The ranking identifies how a surveyed group of CLUs, ChFCs, and members of the Registry of Financial Planning Practitioners feel their clients would generally rate their retirement objectives.)

Table 20-2
Ranking of Retirement Objectives in Order of Priority

1. maintaining preretirement standard of living
2. maintaining economic self-sufficiency
3. minimizing taxes
4. retiring early
5. adapting to noneconomic aspects of retirement
6. passing on wealth to others
7. improving lifestyle in retirement
8. caring for dependents

THE RETIREMENT LADDER: SOURCES OF RETIREMENT INCOME

LO 20.4   Discuss the retirement ladder.

For years, traditional thinking indicated that financial needs during retirement are met from three primary sources often referred to as the legs of the three-legged stool. The sources include Social Security benefits, employer-sponsored pension plan benefits, and personal savings. There is no doubt that these sources remain an integral part of retirement security. However, the three-legged stool analogy does not do justice to the myriad sources of income needed for financial independence in retirement. For this reason, let us now think of the stool being replaced by the retirement ladder.

The federal Social Security system provides retirement benefits to a large portion of retired workers. Two statistics clearly demonstrate the importance of Social Security benefits: (1) around 90 percent of all individuals aged 65 and older report Social Security benefits as a source of income, and (2) Social Security represents more than 40 percent of total income for this group. Company-sponsored retirement plans also remain an important foundation for a secure retirement. Nearly 95 million Americans are covered by a company-sponsored retirement plan. However, only slightly more than 30 percent of the population aged 65 and older have pension income and, to the surprise of many, pension income for current retirees represents only about 20 percent of total retirement income. Personal savings also remain important. However, just from watching the news most of us are aware of the low savings rate for Americans today. It should be noted, however, that over 50 percent of people aged 65 and older have interest income, and approximately 25 percent have dividend income.

In addition to the big three sources, one of the key rungs on the ladder of retirement success is proper planning. As we discussed a few pages ago, this represents a huge opportunity and challenge for financial services professionals.

Another key resource for retirement security is sufficient insurance protection in all forms of insurance. In all phases of life, an insurance checkup is needed to ensure financial security. From renter's insurance to long-term care, seniors often find themselves lacking the protection they need. Clients who have medigap coverage, long-term care insurance, and other protections will not only be more financially secure but they will feel more secure than clients who do not have these protections.

fiscal welfare

social assistance

Supplemental Security Income (SSI)

For individuals of limited means, one of the keys to financial security in retirement concerns **fiscal welfare** and **social assistance**. Fiscal welfare is an indirect payment made to individuals through the tax system. An example is the retirement savings contribution credit. The retirement savings contributions credit is a tax credit of up to $2,000 ($4,000 if married filing jointly in 2017) that is given as an incentive for lower income clients to save for their future. It is available to the client if he or she makes an "eligible contribution" that includes a contribution to a traditional or Roth IRA; a 401(k), 403(b), or 457 plan; a SIMPLE; or a salary reduction SEP (SARSEP). Social assistance is a type of social benefit that contains eligibility criteria designed in part to encourage the able-bodied poor to work by providing minimal benefits. An example of social assistance would be supplemental security income. **Supplemental Security Income (SSI)** is a benefit program administered by the Social Security Administration that pays monthly income to low income individuals who are 65 or older, blind, or disabled. In 2017, an individual client who qualifies for the full benefit can receive up to $735 per month and a couple can receive approximately $1,103 per month. In addition, state supplements may increase these amounts depending on the client's state of residence. Planners need to assist clients in understanding these important social programs. In 2017, there are roughly 8 million Americans receiving some SSI benefits. So, while it might not be your clients, it might be your client's family or friends.

Part-time wages are another important rung on the retirement ladder. Over 2 million people or 23 percent of the 65–69 cohort remain in the labor force. Also, according to a recent AARP survey, 66 percent of older workers plan to work well into their retirement years. For all people aged 65 and older, 16.3 percent have earned income and the median income is $15,000.

For some clients, inheritances will add to their financial security in retirement. According to AARP, only 15 percent of baby boomers expect to receive any future inheritances. The median value of inheritances already received by baby boomers was $47,900, and less than 2 percent received over $100,000. It is important to know that the bulk of wealth is concentrated in the hands of the wealthiest 10 percent. It is also important to know that parents are living longer and spending down accumulated assets or have annuitized their wealth so that second generation inheritances are unlikely. This does not mean that clients will not get an inheritance from their parents. It does mean, however, they should count on inheritances as a financial planning tool only in limited circumstances.

Figure 20-1
The Ladder of Retirement Security

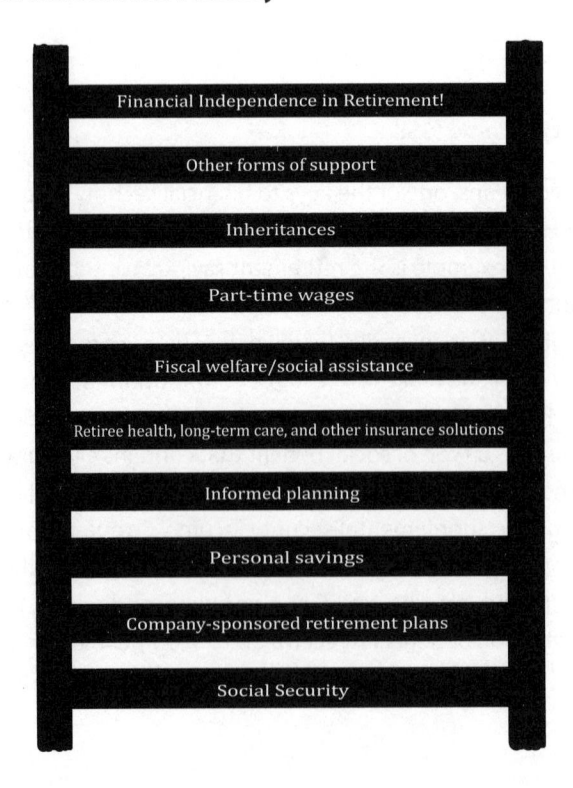

- Financial Independence in Retirement!
- Other forms of support
- Inheritances
- Part-time wages
- Fiscal welfare/social assistance
- Retiree health, long-term care, and other insurance solutions
- Informed planning
- Personal savings
- Company-sponsored retirement plans
- Social Security

There are a variety of other sources of retirement income including:

- *Home equity.* For many, this represents the largest asset they will have in the later retirement years. Strategies such as downsizing to free up cash or using a reverse mortgage may be considered.
- *Life insurance.* Receiving life insurance from a deceased spouse or cashing out a whole life policy may provide retirement protection for some.
- *Family business assets.* Clients who owned their own business may be able to capitalize on the business by selling it at retirement.
- *Rental property.* Some clients may receive rental income from property they own.

Tomorrow's retirement will be funded from sources beyond the traditional three-legged stool. The time has come for planners and clients to adjust projections for how much they will need in retirement to account for additional streams of income. Planning based on a stool can get clients only so high. Planning based on a ladder will bring them to greater heights.

CHAPTER REVIEW

Key Terms and Concepts

baby-boom generation
fiscal welfare
social assistance
Supplemental Security Income (SSI)

Chapter 20: Review Questions

Review questions are based on the learning objectives in this chapter. Thus, a [20.3] at the end of a question means that the question is based on learning objective 3. If there are multiple objectives, they are all listed.

1. Gina Neuman is an insurance agent who would like to conduct individual retirement planning for her clients. What topics does she already have expertise from her ERISA training that will allow her to serve her clients? [20.2]

2. List the topics that comprise the field of holistic retirement planning. [20.2]

3. List some organizations that can supply retirement planners with information and strategies for their clients. [20.3]

4. Identify and discuss the six steps in the retirement planning process. [20.3]

5. What are the problems specific to the retirement security needs of women? [20.3]

6. What are some characteristics of the changing face of retirement? [20.3]

7. List some of the roadblocks to successful retirement. [20.3]

8. List and explain the rungs of the retirement ladder. [20.4]

Chapter 20: Review Answers

1. Gina has learned the following from her ERISA training:

    - Understanding the type(s) of retirement plan(s) being provided to your client, including the plan's benefit or contribution formula.

    - Analyzing the key provisions of your clients' retirement plan, including their vesting schedules, hardship withdrawal and loan rules, and matching contribution and elective deferral options.

    - Identifying and using documents like the summary plan description and the personal benefit statement.

    - Appreciating the importance of before tax and/or tax-free savings vehicles as a method to maximize retirement savings.

    - Diagnosing the ramifications of starting Social Security benefits prior to full retirement age.

    - Choosing an appropriate Keogh plan for a self-employed person with Schedule C income.

    - Recognizing the specifications for and importance of the ESOP diversification rules.

    - Determining the IRA options that best fit your clients' needs.

    - Interpreting the tax rules applicable to Social Security benefits and nonqualified stock plans.

    - Explaining how Social Security and pension benefits are calculated and how your clients can optimize their benefits under each system.

    - Cataloging the fiduciary protection, QDRO assurance, PBGC refuge, and bankruptcy shield afforded your clients under law.

2. The topics that comprise holistic retirement planning include:

    - the effect of financial well-being on the quality of life
    - employer-provided retirement plan options
    - Social Security considerations
    - personal savings and investments
    - IRAs and Roth IRAs
    - income tax issues

- tax planning for distributions and other distribution issues
- Medicare choices
- health insurance planning, including medigap insurance and long-term care insurance
- wealth accumulation for retirement
- asset allocation and risk
- long-term care options (living options)
- retirement communities
- relocation possibilities and reverse mortgages
- wellness, nutrition, lifestyle choices, and other gerontological issues
- assessment of current savings needed to achieve retirement goals
- financial gerontology
- estate planning

3. Organizations include:
    - The Society of Financial Service Professionals
    - The Financial Planning Association
    - The National Council on Aging
    - The American Society on Aging
    - The American Association of Retired Persons (AARP) Planners may also want to check the numerous retirement planning websites.

4. The six steps in the retirement planning process include:
    - Establish Client-Planner Relationships (Step 1). This involves the identification and explanation of issues, concepts, and products related to the retirement process.
    - Determine Goals and Expectations and Gather Client Data (Step 2). This step begins by listening to the client's goals and hopes for retirement. Clients have a variety of objectives that range from never having to work again to working full time during retirement. Clearly, planners have their work cut out for them as they deal with a plethora of expectations and, in some cases, help frame the expectations of their clients through the education process. In addition to sorting through the various lifestyle options for retirement, planners must also focus at this stage on conducting a financial inventory.

- Analyze and Evaluate the Client's Financial Status (Step 3). In this step, the planner looks at the client's current situation as well as his or her future goals in order to evaluate the appropriate strategies for that particular client. This includes the performance of a retirement needs analysis as well as the analysis of the client's risk tolerance, risk management strategies, and risk exposures.

- Develop and Present the Retirement Plan (Step 4). In addition to the client's current financial position, the plan should include the client's projected retirement status under the status quo as well as projected statements if the planner's recommendations are followed. The planner should also provide a current asset allocation statement along with strategy recommendations and a statement that assumes that recommendations will be followed. Investments should be summarized, and the planner should propose an investment policy statement and additional policy recommendations. The plan should also include an assessment of distribution options and tax strategies for retirement. Finally, the plan should include a list of prioritized action items and address issues such as housing and health care.

- Implement the Retirement Plan (Step 5). The planner should assist the client in implementing the recommendations. Often this requires coordinating with other professionals.

- Monitor the Retirement Plan (Step 6). After the plan is implemented, the planner should periodically monitor and evaluate the soundness of recommendations and review the progress of the plan with the client.

5. Women have unique problems that make it difficult to achieve a financially successful retirement.

- Women are less likely to have a pension at work than men.
- Women have lower earnings, which obviously make it harder to save for retirement.
- Women outlive men, so all else being equal, women need to save more than men.
- Women are more likely to be caregivers than men.
- Women are more likely to be single or widowed and the burden of retirement in these instances is not shared.
- Women invest pension assets too conservatively and, thus, self-inflict an additional savings burden.

6. It is very important for planners to realize that retirement planning is a dynamic environment. Not only do products, services, and tax laws seem to change on a regular basis, but the very nature of retirement also is in flux. For example, surveys show that current workers expect to work longer than current retirees actually worked before retiring. Surveys also show that many baby boomers say they plan to work after they retire because they enjoy working and want to stay involved. Another responsibility changing the nature of retirement is that of caregiver. The retirees of today and tomorrow are increasingly responsible for caring for parents, children, and grandchildren.

7. Roadblocks to a successful retirement include:
   a. the tendency of many working people to use their full after-tax income to support their current standard of living
   b. unexpected expenses, including uninsured medical bills; repairs to a home, auto, or major appliance; and periods of unemployment
   c. inadequate insurance coverage (an insurance review should be conducted)

8. The retirement ladder includes the following:
   - Social Security: The bottom rung (the most important rung of the retirement ladder) is Social Security. Social Security provides retirement benefits to around 90 percent of all individuals aged 65 and older, and it represents more than 40 percent of total income for this group.
   - Company-sponsored retirement plans: Company-sponsored retirement plans cover nearly 95 million Americans employees. However, only slightly more than 30 percent of the population aged 65 and older have pension income, and pension income for current retirees represents only about 20 percent of total retirement income.
   - Personal savings: Just from watching the news, most of us are aware of the low savings rate for Americans today. However, note that 50 percent of people aged 65 and older have interest income, and approximately 25 percent have dividend income.
   - Informed planning: One of the key rungs on the ladder of retirement success is proper planning. As we discussed a few pages ago, this represents a huge opportunity and challenge for financial services professionals.
   - Insurance solutions: Another key resource for retirement security is sufficient insurance protection in all forms of insurance. In all phases of life, an insurance checkup is needed to ensure financial security. From renter's insurance to

long-term care, seniors often find themselves lacking the protection they need. Clients who have medigap coverage, long-term care insurance, and other protections will not only be more financially secure but they will feel more secure than clients who do not have these protections.

- Fiscal welfare/social assistance: For clients of limited means, one of the keys to financial security in retirement concerns fiscal welfare and social assistance. Fiscal welfare is an indirect payment made to individuals through the tax system. An example is the retirement savings contribution credit, which is a tax credit of up to $1,000 ($2,000 if married filing jointly) that is given as an incentive for lower-income clients to save for their future. It is available to the client if he or she makes an "eligible contribution" that includes a contribution to a traditional or Roth IRA; a 401(k), 403(b), or 457 plan; a SIMPLE; or a salary reduction SEP (SARSEP). Social assistance is a type of social benefit that contains eligibility criteria designed in part to encourage the able-bodied poor to work by providing minimal benefits. An example of social assistance would be Supplemental Security Income. Supplemental Security Income (SSI) is a benefit program administered by the Social Security Administration that pays monthly income to clients who are 65 or older, blind, or disabled. An individual client who qualifies for the full benefit can receive close to $735 per month in 2017, and a couple can receive approximately $1,103 (in 2017) per month. In addition, state supplements may increase these amounts depending on the client's state of residence. Planners need to assist clients in understanding these important social programs.

- Part-time wages: Part-time wages are another important rung on the retirement ladder. Over 2 million people or 23 percent of the 65–69 cohort remain in the labor force.

- Inheritances: This is an important supplemental source of retirement income for some—probably fewer than we would expect. Only 15 percent of baby boomers expect to receive any future inheritances.

- Other forms of support: Living off home equity, life insurance proceeds, proceeds from sale of a family business, and rental income are other common sources of retirement income.

Chapter 21

Retirement Needs Analysis: The Assumptions

Learning Objectives

An understanding of the material in this chapter should enable the student to

- **LO 21.1** Discuss the factors that should be considered when choosing a retirement age and a life expectancy assumption.

- **LO 21.2** Describe the replacement-ratio approach for determining the income needed in the first year of retirement, considering the
  a. estimated replacement ratio
  b. decrease in taxation for retirees
  c. factors that reduce living expenses for retirees
  d. factors that increase living expenses for retirees

- **LO 21.3** Describe the expense-method approach for determining the income needed in the first year of retirement.

- **LO 21.4** Describe the impact inflation has on funds needed for retirement.

- **LO 21.5** Discuss the total return on investment assumption and some of the common retirement investing strategies that help to shape it.

One major question that is encountered when planning for retirement is whether sufficient savings exist to provide enough income for the retirement years. More specifically, clients want to know how much they have to squirrel away each year so that they can maintain their current standard of living after they retire. There is no precise method that specifies exactly how much is enough. However, the planner can take several steps to create a workable retirement plan and calculate a funding target for the client.

ASSUMPTION ONE: RETIREMENT AGE

The existence of the Social Security and Medicare programs has created an expectation that Americans would retire when both Social Security and Medicare benefits were available. Until recently, most retirement planning tended to support this perception by anticipating retirement to occur at age 65. Thus, workers and advisors almost invariably planned, economically and psychologically, for retirement at this age. However, for a variety of reasons that will be discussed later, age 65 is no longer a magic number for retirement.

What, then, is retirement age? As a practical matter, the average retirement age (which is slightly over age 62) is irrelevant to the retirement planner. What is important is the unique retirement-age goal for each individual client.

Major factors that help to frame that goal include government and employer programs and policies. For example, not only the key Social Security and Medicare ages (age 62 for early (albeit reduced) Social Security benefits, age 65 for Medicare coverage, and depending on the year of birth, anywhere between age 65 and 67 for full (unreduced) Social Security benefits) but also the early, normal and deferred retirement ages in the client's qualified plan. Also important are the client's lifestyle goals, family responsibilities, and individual financial circumstances, as well as his or her willingness to incur the risks of portfolio performance, inflation, and adverse changes in government and employer policies. Let's take a closer look at some other things that should be considered when your client selects a retirement age.

LO 21.1   Discuss the factors that should be considered when choosing a retirement age and a life expectancy assumption.

Factors Affecting the Choice of a Retirement Age
1. Early Social Security benefits available at age 62. (These benefits are reduced).
2. Medicare eligibility at age 65.
3. Full retirement age for Social Security. (Anywhere from 65 to 67 depending on the year of birth)
4. Early retirement age as defined in the employer plan.
5. Normal retirement age as defined in the employer plan.
6. Lifestyle goals.
7. Family responsibilities.
8. Specific financial conditions applicable when the decision is being made.
9. Perspective on investment performance, inflation and changes in government programs that may impact financial resources.

Reasons Clients Choose Early Retirement (Or Have It Thrust Upon Them)

Several factors encourage younger retirement ages. Some workers have succeeded in saving and investing and are able to retire before 65 in comfort, even with reduced Social Security and retirement benefits. Other people simply want to retire earlier and will accept a lower standard of living if necessary.

A trend in recent years is for corporations to trim expenses by offering incentives for older, higher-paid employees to retire early. These so-called golden handshakes are dangled in front of employees in the forms of extra lump-sum payouts (typically based on years of service—for example, two weeks pay for each year of service), extra retiree medical coverage (for example, the employer promising to pick up COBRA payments) and increases in accrual rates (for defined-benefit plans). Golden handshakes provide tempting offers even in cases where they are not a wise financial decision. What's more, in some cases corporations cut back by eliminating the older employees without offering any incentives. Because older people can have trouble finding new positions, an employer cutback often amounts to the end of a worker's career—a forced retirement that is early and permanent.

Another reason people choose to retire early centers on health. Some clients' personal heath situation makes continuation of work difficult or impossible. For others, the need to care for a spouse or parent with health problems (even though they are in good health themselves) forces an early retirement. Fear of bad health in the future becomes an impetus for some workers to retire now while they have the health to enjoy it.

Summary of Reasons for Early Retirement

1. Financial goals have been met. The client can continue his or her standard of living throughout retirement.
2. Financial goals have been compromised. The client has a personal desire to trade a lower standard of living for freedom from employment.
3. Corporate downsizing with incentives (golden handshakes). These incentives often encourage an early retirement.
4. Corporate downsizing without incentives. When a business contracts in size, some people who are near retirement age are forced into early retirement.
5. Actual health issues. Clients may retire early because they have health concerns and work compounds their problems.
6. Caregiving health issues. Some clients retire early because they have caregiving responsibilities for a parent or spouse.
7. Perceived health issues. Clients in good health may want to retire early while they can enjoy life. They fear poor health later will limit their activity and do not want to ruin the opportunity of an active retirement.
8. Health and pension incentives. The structure of the employer's health and pension plan may encourage early retirement. For example, a client with retiree health coverage at age 62 and a pension that provides 60 percent of salary may perceive that he or she is working for 40 cents on a dollar.
9. Nonfinancial factors. In some instances, the death of a spouse can encourage early retirement. In others, such as in the two-wage-earner family, there may be a desire to retire together even though one spouse is younger than the other (the younger spouse would take early retirement).
10. Problems in the workplace. Some people retire because their jobs have grown

> intolerable. For example, a recent change makes the job environment a difficult one. These changes range from, "I cannot work in this changed environment" to "I feel they just do not care about quality any more and I cannot work that way."

Yet another reason people choose early retirement is the availability of company-paid health benefits and a good pension system at their place of employment. Many corporations offer medical insurance at reduced rates to early retirees to bridge the gap until eligibility for Medicare. Others continue to pay for retirement benefits throughout the retirement period. Some clients with defined-benefit plans feel they are working for only part of their salary. In other words, some argue that if their pension will be $50,000 and their salary is $100,000, then it makes no sense to keep working.

Other reasons early retirement occurs include:

- spouse's death
- spouse's retirement
- problems and/or changes in the workplace

A recent Retirement Confidence Survey, sponsored by the Employee Benefit Research Institute and the Principal Financial Group, revealed that 45 percent of current retirees retired earlier than they had planned! Reasons most frequently cited for earlier-than-planned retirement include health problems or disability (40 percent), downsizing or closure (14 percent), family reasons (14 percent), other work-related reasons (12 percent), and miscellaneous (20 percent). Because these reasons typically arise unexpectedly, few of these retirees had enough time to prepare adequately. They simply did not know when they would retire.

Reasons Clients Should View Early Retirement Skeptically

From the planner's perspective, there are many reasons to advise a client against early retirement. First, the Social Security full retirement age is being increased from 65 to 67. Clients affected by this change should be aware that the early retirement benefit paid at age 62 will also be reduced. For an individual born in 1937 or earlier, it is 80 percent of the individual's primary insurance amount. For those with a full retirement age of 67, the benefit will drop to 70 percent of the client's primary insurance amount.

Early retirement also affects the client's pension benefits. In a defined-benefit plan, the final-average salary and years-of-service components of the client's benefit formula will be lower than they otherwise would be if the client remained employed. In addition, there is typically an actuarial reduction in the pension annuity to account for a larger payout period. In a defined-contribution plan, a client's account balance will be smaller than it otherwise would be if the client remained employed. The client loses the opportunity to make (or have his or her employer make) contributions based on a percentage of peak (end-of-career) salary and, where applicable, may lose the matching contributions attributable to those contributions.

Other ways in which early retirement can affect financial security include the following:

- increased exposure to inflation (because of the longer retirement period)
- lack of health insurance prior to Medicare. Some employers either do not offer retiree coverage or reserve the right to cancel it. An accounting rule known as FASB 106 discourages health plans for retirees by requiring firms to lower current reported earnings in anticipation of future health care costs. Since its implementation, some corporations have reneged on what retirees thought was a pledge of future coverage.
- an adverse effect on the calculation of Social Security benefits (the 35 years used in the PIA calculation may have to include years with reduced or no earnings)

Planning Note: If you err on the conservative side and plan for a retirement date that occurs prior to your client's actual retirement date, you will overestimate the retirement need and, consequently, the client will have more funds than necessary. Conversely, a planned retirement date that occurs after the actual retirement starting date will underestimate the retirement income need and leave the client with less funds than necessary.

For Your Financial Services Practice: Deferring the Company Pension

Recently, there have been significant discussions regarding the advantages of deferring Social Security benefits. However, the benefits associated with deferring a defined-benefit plan benefit can also have tremendous value. For example, take the client enrolled in a defined-benefit plan with a benefit formula that is a life annuity payable at age 65 in the amount of one percent of final average monthly compensation times years of service. If the client at age 65 has 30 years of service and $10,000 of final average monthly compensation, the benefit is $3,000 a month. If the client defers retirement for a year, to age 66, (and assuming an increase in final average compensation to $10,500), the benefit becomes $3,255 a month (a 7.5 percent increase). The benefit may actually be larger as most plans provide an actuarial increase for deferring benefits for a year.

Since benefits are typically tied both to years of service and the highest 3–5 years of earnings, a client's retirement age decision can have a significant impact on the amount of benefits that he or she receives. Other additional key considerations include:

- Late career job change—changing from a company with a defined-benefit plan to one that only has a 401(k) late in one's career can have a significant negative impact on benefits.

- Service cap in benefit formula—if a plan caps service and the individual has earned the maximum number of years of service allowed, deferring retirement has less of an impact.
- Impact of increasing or decreasing compensation—the definition of final average compensation is a significant factor. For example, if the plan only uses the highest three years of compensation, it is easier to increase compensation than if the plan counts the highest 5 years.
- Actuarial adjustments—another important factor is the actuarial increase (for deferring benefits) or decrease (for those that retire early) that is determined in the plan.

Other Considerations

Be aware that some clients are planning to work past age 65. At one time, turning 65 meant mandatory retirement. Now federal law (the Age Discrimination in Employment Act) specifies that many mandatory retirement policies represent age discrimination and are illegal except for certain people.[1] What's more, pension benefits that continue to increase after age 65, lack of success in personal investing, and longer life expectancies are among the factors that encourage older retirement ages. Also, many people choose to retire long after 65 because they enjoy their work and/or they derive a large part of their personal identity from work.

Another consideration when determining a "later" target retirement date is the client's fixed long-term liabilities, such as educational expenses incurred for children. In some cases, the client has very little discretion over the retirement date until these liabilities have been paid.

For most clients, specification of a retirement age is based on nonfinancial criteria. If the client indicates the desire to retire at age 64, the planner's responsibility is to help determine whether that is a financially viable goal. At the same time, the planner must advise the client of negative aspects of the chosen age. Often the planner provides the client with a variety of scenarios (for example, if x age is targeted, y level of savings is needed per year); in some circumstances, this information may cause the client to postpone retirement so that a proper amount of income can be saved.

---

1. While the Age Discrimination in Employment Act ended broad mandatory retirement policies, certain military, government, and professionals (pilots, air traffic controllers, judges, etc.) can still be subject to mandatory retirement.

ASSUMPTION TWO: LIFE EXPECTANCY

Clients are living longer than prior generations and, in many cases, living longer than expected. According to the U.S. Census Bureau, there were 71,991 estimated centenarians in the United States as of Dec. 1, 2010. The projected number of centenarians in the United States in 2050 is 601,000.

Many clients mistakenly rely on life expectancy at birth to set their expectations. However, life expectancy at age 65 is much different (89.5 versus 85.1 for females) and a more accurate measure for retirement. Even if clients were to use accurate life expectancy tables, remember that many clients will outlive the tables. Earlier-than-expected retirement (issue one) in combination, with increased longevity (issue two) can be a disastrous one-two punch for knocking out retirement security and sending clients into financial trouble.

To establish the proper life expectancy, planners must take a close look at clients' personal and family health history. For example, an obese, alcoholic smoker with diabetes, a heart condition, a family history of cancer, and multiple reckless driving citations is unlikely to reach the life expectancy. A cautious, healthy, and health-conscious individual with a good family medical history and an enthusiasm for life is likely to live beyond the expected span.

How long will retirement last? To estimate the expected retirement period, take the following steps:

- Look up statistical life expectancy data by using the retirement ages of the client and his or her spouse.
- Adjust the estimate up or down for factors such as health, lifestyle, and family history.
- Use consumer Web sites or proprietary software that projects longevity based on family and personal health history.

Even after this analysis, remember it is only an estimate. Financial conservatism dictates that planner and client should assume a longer-than-expected retirement period and add a few years to the estimate. Alternatively, the planner can set aside a separate class of assets that will only be consumed if the client outlives his or her planned life expectancy (otherwise these assets can be used for estate planning). Consider that it is the anxiety of possibly outliving one's money that causes clients to select life annuities or interest-only payout provisions at retirement. Such clients implicitly assume a longer-than-average life span. For any reasonable life span estimate, there is some probability that the typical client will outlive his or her assets. Although this statement is mathematically obvious, it often serves as a wake-up call, further emphasizing the importance of accumulating a substantial retirement fund that the client will not outlive.

ASSUMPTION THREE: EXPECTED STANDARD OF LIVING DURING RETIREMENT

The standard of living enjoyed during the years just prior to retirement largely influences the client's expectations for his or her postretirement standard of living. For this reason, the planner encounters different situations depending on how close the client is to his or her retirement date. With this in mind, let's examine the differences that exist between clients of various age groups.

Late-Career Clients

For almost all clients, the years immediately prior to retirement represent their peak earning years and their highest standard of living. Clients who are near the end of their careers are concerned about maintaining their current standard of living. As a group, these clients are the most interested in retirement planning and are the most willing to make adjustments to their preretirement lifestyle to compensate for inadequate retirement savings.

Mid-Career Clients

The client who is in the middle of his or her career has a different perspective on his or her postretirement standard of living. Employment has permitted this client to establish a comfortable standard of living, but he or she envisions still further increases in income and in lifestyle. For these clients, the desired standard of living during retirement will be based on their expectations of success in their career and the attendant increases in their standard of living. In other words, these clients will prefer to enjoy an unknown and yet-to-be-realized standard of living during their retirement years. Planners must first make the best estimate possible based on the client's educational background, job experiences, personal ambitions, and career plan. The estimated retirement standard of living can be computed by applying a growth factor to the client's current salary and approximating the client's final-average salary.

Early-Career Clients

These clients typically have too little experience to estimate what their retirement needs will be and probably have not thought about the standard of living they will expect at that time. For this reason, estimating a retirement standard of living at this stage is too tentative. The planner should instead concentrate efforts on encouraging these clients to use regular IRAs or Roth IRAs, or to make contributions to the employer 401(k) plan. Note also that early-career clients as well as mid-career clients are less likely than late-career clients to adjust their current lifestyle for retirement planning purposes. Younger clients are more likely to be distracted by other priorities and will tend to ignore the future because current problems take precedence. In this situation, the retirement planner must try to make saving for retirement a priority in spite of these distractions. One way to accomplish this is to talk about retirement planning in terms of financial independence planning. The change in terminology focuses clients on the goal of being able to control their own financial future, which is desirable even to younger clients.

In addition to understanding the standard of living the client expects during retirement, planners must also be prepared to estimate the income stream a client will need during retirement. One of the essential parts of this process is estimating the income a client will need in the first year of retirement. Let's examine the two generally accepted methods for determining this, the replacement-ratio method and the expense method.

The Replacement-Ratio Method

LO 21. 2 Describe the replacement-ratio approach for determining the income needed in the first year of retirement, considering the

      a. estimated replacement ratio
      b. decrease in taxation for retirees
      c. factors that reduce living expenses for retirees
      d. factors that increase living expenses for retirees

replacement-ratio method

One way to estimate how much a client will need in the first year of retirement is to apply the **replacement-ratio method**. The replacement-ratio method assumes that the standard of living enjoyed during the years just prior to retirement will be the determinant of the standard of living needed in the first year of retirement. Under the replacement-ratio method, the planner can estimate the amount needed in the first year of retirement, regardless of the client's age, by using a replacement ratio that is geared to continue the same standard of living (for late-career clients) or the estimated standard of living (for mid-career clients). In general, a 60 to 80 percent replacement ratio is used. In other words, the amount of income needed to be financially independent in the first year of retirement without drastically altering the client's standard of living varies between 60 and 80 percent of the average gross annual income of the average of the last 3 years of employment. For example, if a client with an income in the years prior to retirement of $95,000, $100,000, and $105,000, respectively, has an 80 percent target rate, then the client should target a replacement ratio of about $80,000 (80 percent of the $100,000 average). Support for this range rests upon the elimination of some employment-related taxes and some expected changes in spending patterns that reduce the retiree's need for income (such as expenditures that will either decrease or disappear in the retirement years).

Reductions in Taxation

In many circumstances, retirees can count on a lower percentage of their income going to pay taxes in the retirement years. Some taxes are reduced or eliminated, and in other cases retirees may enjoy special favorable tax treatment. Let's take a closer look at the potential reductions in taxation that are granted to retirees.

Social Security Taxes. FICA contributions (old-age, survivors, disability, and hospital insurance) are levied solely on income from employment. Distributions from pensions, IRAs, retirement annuities, and other similar devices are not considered income subject to FICA or SECA (self-employment FICA) taxes. Hence, for the retiree who stops working entirely, Social Security taxes are no longer an expenditure.

Increased Standard Deduction. For a single taxpayer aged 65 or over, $1,500 (indexed for 2017) is added to the standard deduction. If the taxpayer is married and his or her spouse is also 65 or older, both spouses receive an additional $1,250 (indexed for 2017).

Social Security Benefits Exclusion. Some or all of a client's Social Security benefits will be received tax free. To reiterate, the table below identifies the various cutoff points. The provisional income thresholds have not been indexed or modified in a long time. However, there have been multiple proposals to increase the provisional income thresholds but at this time there have been no changes. It is an area worth keeping an eye on for future modifications.

Table 21-1
Portion of OASDI Benefits Subject to Federal Income Tax

Taxpayer Filing Status	Provisional Income Threshold	Amount of Benefits Subject to Federal Income Tax
Single	under $25,000	0 percent
Single	$25,000–$33,999	up to 50 percent
Single	$34,000 or more	up to 85 percent
Married filing jointly	under $32,000	0 percent
Married filing jointly	$32,000–$43,999	up to 50 percent
Married filing jointly	$44,000 or more	up to 85 percent
Married filing separately (and living in the same household)	$0	up to 85 percent

State and Local Income Taxation. In some states, Social Security benefits are fully exempt from state income taxation; in others, some taxation of these benefits might occur if the state's income tax is assessed on the taxpayer's taxable income as reported for federal income tax purposes. In addition, some states grant extra income tax relief for seniors by providing increased personal exemptions, credits, sliding scale rebates of property or other taxes (the amount or percent of which might be dependent on income), or additional tax breaks. For instance, in Pennsylvania, distributions from IRAs, 401(k)s, and pensions are not subject to state income taxes. As such, it can be beneficial for some people to relocate to a state that does not tax distributions. However, some states do not allow for state income tax deductions for contributions to those accounts. The worst case tax scenario would be if you live in a state that does not allow a deduction for contributions and then later move to a state that also taxes distributions.

Deductible Medical Expenses. As taxpayers' age it becomes more likely that they will be eligible for deductible medical expenses. Under the rules, taxpayers who itemize deductions can deduct medical expenses that exceed 10 percent of adjusted gross income. Qualifying medical expenses include costs for long-term care insurance.

Work-Related Expenses

The costs of proper clothing for work, commuting, parking, and meals purchased during work hours are eliminated when a person retires. In addition, other expenses, such as membership dues in some professional or social clubs, may be reduced because of retired status or may be eliminated if no longer necessary.

Home Ownership Expenses

By the time of retirement, many homeowners have "burned the mortgage" and no longer have this debt-reduction expenditure. However, this is changing as more and more retirees are now entering retirement with a mortgage. The addition of mortgage payments in retirement can create a serious cash flow issue for retirees.

Absence of Dependent Children

The expense of supporting dependent children is usually completed by the time a client enters retirement. Be cautious, however, because retirees, especially those who married later in life, occasionally have children who are not self-supporting and will require continued financial support during some of the clients' retirement years.

Senior Discounts

Senior discounts can reduce prices from 5 to 15 percent of an item's cost. Some reductions, such as certain AARP discounts, are available at age 50. Many businesses, however, require proof of age 65 (usually by having a Medicare card) to qualify for discounts on prescriptions, clothing, and restaurant meals.

No Longer Saving for Retirement

For many retirees, retirement is not a time to continue to save for retirement. Payments to contributory pension plans, lack of eligibility for IRA or Keogh plan contributions, or just the psychological fact of being retired help to weaken retirees' motivation to save for the future. Note that a retired worker's income can fall by the amount being saved with no concurrent reduction in standard of living. Therefore, a retired worker who has been saving 10 percent of income needs only to maintain an inflation-protected 90 percent (before tax) of income to enjoy the same purchasing power.

Fewer Automobiles

Retirees often consciously decide to reduce their automobile expenditures, either by owning fewer automobiles or by purchasing a replacement less frequently. In either case, the dollar cost for automobile insurance and the cash flow for financing automobiles tend to decline during the retirement years.

Age-Related Reductions

As a client grows older in retirement, he or she often cuts back on expenses and adopts a more sedentary lifestyle. For example, at some age driving becomes impossible or restricted and, at that point, car and other expenses decline. Some practitioners argue that these declines are mitigated by increased costs for medical care. Data from the Bureau of Labor Statistics, however, indicates that even though health care expenses increase over retirement, the increase does not significantly mitigate the decrease in other expenses.

Living Expenses in the Early Years of Retirement

Some retirement planners are uncomfortable with recommending a planned reduction in income in the first year of retirement. These planners believe that certain factors suggest that during the first year of retirement, at least as much, if not more, income will be required to maintain the preretirement standard of living. Let's take a closer look at these factors.

Medical Expenses. Without question, medical expenses will increase over time for virtually all clients. The mere act of aging and the associated health problems generate additional demands for medical services. Even if advancing age does not create an increase in an individual's demands for medical services, inflation in these costs will. Furthermore, increases in inflation are not evenly distributed in the various medical care disciplines, and those services that will potentially affect retirees have been hit hardest. Although retirees are often covered by Medicare and other health insurance, the trend in these coverages has been toward cost containment—defined by the government and the insurance companies as shifting more of the medical cost to the insured via larger deductibles and coinsurance payments. These higher medical expenses would be in addition to the increased premiums for the insurance. While some elderly people have seen increased out of pocket costs due to the Affordable Care Acts changes, most researchers predict decreased total out of pocket costs for retiree health care due to improvements in Medicare.

Table 21-2
Justification of a 60 to 80 Percent Replacement Ratio

Joe Jones, aged 64, has a fixed salary of $100,000 and would like to maintain his current purchasing power when he retires next year. If Joe has no increased retirement-related expenses, he can do this by having a retirement income of 70 percent of his final salary (as illustrated below). If Joe has increased retirement-related expenses, a somewhat higher figure should be used. (Note that postretirement inflation will be accounted for later.)

Working salary		$100,000
less retirement savings		15,000
less FICA taxes		7,030
less reduction in federal taxes	(extra $1,250 deduction for being 65)	350
	(no tax on portion of Social Security received)	1,138
less annual commuting expenses to work		500
less mortgage expenses	(mortgage expires on retirement date)	6,032
Reductions subtotal		30,000
Total purchasing power needed at 65		$70,000
Percentage of final salary needed		70%

YOUR FINANCIAL SERVICES PRACTICE:
WARNING YOUR CLIENTS ABOUT THE RISKS

Whether or not your clients accept a 60 to 80 percent replacement ratio or feel that something more is necessary, there is no definitive answer to absolutely determine if the postretirement income should be less than, equal to, or greater than that of the preretirement years.

Estimating financial needs during the first year of retirement is like trying to hit a moving target when you are blindfolded: Your aim is obscured by many unknown variables and it is hard to draw a bead on the target. For example, the planner and client must establish what standard of living is desired during retirement, when retirement will begin, what inflation assumptions should be made before and after retirement, and what interest can be earned on invested funds. In addition, for clients who are forced by economic necessity to liquidate their retirement nest egg, the client and planner must estimate the life expectancy over which liquidations will occur. Many of these variables can dramatically change overnight and without warning—for example:

- The client may be planning to retire at age 65 when health considerations, or perhaps a plant shutdown, force retirement at age 62.
- A younger client may be planning on a relatively moderate retirement lifestyle, but business success mandates that a more lucrative retirement lifestyle be planned.

Travel, Vacations, and Other Lifestyle Changes. Many clients expect to devote considerably more time to travel and vacations upon retirement than they did during their working years. Increased leisure time, once a scarce commodity, now provides the opportunity to travel. Unfortunately, vacationing can be an expensive activity. Indeed, an increase in vacation activities represents a rise in the standard of living and will require additional income.

Dependents. As previously stated, parents usually need less income during the first year of retirement because they no longer financially support their children, who typically become self-supporting prior to parental retirement. However, many retirees still have dependents to support. Many parents have children with mental or physical problems who will require long-term custodial and financial care throughout the retirement years. Other retirees, because medical care, surgical techniques, and drugs are helping to prolong life, may have to provide for their aged parents who no longer possess the wherewithal to do so themselves.

The Expense Method

LO 21.3 Describe the expense-method approach for determining the income needed in the first year of retirement.

A second way planners can estimate their client's retirement needs is by using the expense-method approach. The expense method of retirement planning focuses on the projected expenses that the retiree will have in the first year of retirement. As with the replacement-ratio method, it is much easier to define the potential expenses for those clients who are at or near retirement. For example, if the 64-year-old near-retiree expects to have $3,000 in monthly bills ($36,000 annually), then the retirement income for that retiree should maintain $36,000 worth of purchasing power in today's dollars. If, however, a younger client is involved, more speculative estimates of retirement expenses must be made (and periodically revised).

A list of expenses that should be considered includes expenses that may be unique to the particular client, as well as other, more general expenses.

Some expenses that tend to increase for retirees include the following:

- utilities and telephone
- medical/dental/drugs/health insurance
- house upkeep/repairs/maintenance/property insurance (until a move occurs)
- recreation/entertainment/travel/dining (during the early years of retirement)

Conversely, some expenses tend to decrease for the retiree. These include the following:

- mortgage payments
- food
- clothing
- income taxes
- property taxes
- transportation costs (car maintenance/insurance/other)
- debt repayment (charge accounts, personal loans)
- child support/alimony
- household furnishings

To illustrate the expense method, assume that your clients, Bob and Betty Smith, both aged 64, would like to maintain their current purchasing power when they retire next year. Estimating their actual expenses, they can do this by having an annual income of $40,860 (as illustrated in the following table). Estimates expenses are in current dollars; postretirement inflation will be accounted for later.

Table 21-3
Understanding the Expense Method

Living Expenses		Per Month × 12 =	Per Year
1. Food		$ 500	$ 6000
2. Housing			
	a. Rent/mortgage payment.	400	4,800
	b. Insurance (if separate payment)	25	300
	c. Property taxes (if separate payment)	150	1,800
	d. Utilities	180	2,160
	e. Maintenance (if owned)	100	1,200
3. Clothing and Personal Care			
	a. Wife	75	900
	b. Husband	75	900
4. Medical Expenses			
	a. Doctor (HMO)	75	900
	b. Dentist	20	240
	c. Medicines	75	900
5. Transportation			
	a. Car payments	130	1,560
	b. Gas	50	600
	c. Insurance	50	600
	d. Car maintenance (tires and repairs)	30	360
6. Miscellaneous Expenses			
	a. Entertainment	150	1,800
	b. Travel	200	2,400
	c. Hobbies	50	600
	d. Other	100	1,200
	e. Club fees and dues	20	240
7. Insurance		100	1,200
8. Gifts and contributions		50	600
9. State, local, and federal taxes (if any)		800	9,600
10. Total expenses (current dollars)		$3,405	$40,860*

*Note: An adjustment should be made for future years to reflect a more sedentary lifestyle and reduced spending on the part of the client.

ASSUMPTION FOUR: EXPECTED INFLATION BEFORE AND DURING RETIREMENT

LO 21.4   **Describe the impact inflation has on funds needed for retirement.**

Another assumption that greatly affects the postretirement monetary need is the amount of expected inflation before and after retirement. The importance of inflation's effect on retirement cannot be overstated. Inflation erodes the client's purchasing power over time, making it difficult to maintain economic self sufficiency. Consider that if a client needed $2,000 in 1987, he or she will need around $4,288.79 in 2017 (a thirty year retirement period) to maintain the same purchasing power. According to LPI inflation calculator provided by Bureau of Labor Statistics, planners can use the inflation calculators at www.bls.gov to demonstrate the long-term deleterious effects of inflation to their clients. Also, inflation's importance can be illustrated by showing the changes in retirement savings needed when the assumption in a computer model or worksheet is changed. For example, changing from 3 percent inflation to 4 percent inflation in one retirement needs calculator increased the amount of savings needed by 15 percent!

Forecasting inflation is not an easy task. Lacking a crystal ball, a proxy for the expected inflation rate is needed. Because retirement income planning can encompass a long time span, one school of thought is to recommend taking historical averages of inflation over 40 years or more. The average inflation rate from 1913 to 2017 is 3.22 percent. However, the cumulative inflation rate over this time was 2360.6 percent. This means an item that cost $10 in 1913 would cost roughly $246.06 in 2017.

A second school of thought suggests that the structure of the economy and prices have changed too drastically to use 40 years or more. This group would argue that the figures from the last 20 years are a more appropriate measure of inflation. Note that in both cases long-term inflation is used instead of focusing on the yearly consumer price index reports. The average inflation rate from 1995 through 2014 was 2.28 percent, significantly lower than for the longer period. However, some decades like the 1970s saw an average inflation rate of 7.25 percent and the 1980s experienced an average rate of 5.82 percent.

In addition to considering long-term historical rates (no matter what the period), the planner must be aware of the forces that are likely to operate in the future and the following factors:

- Personal buying habits affect a clients actual inflation experience (keep in mind that services, which tend to be used more often by retirees, inflate at a higher rate than goods).
- There are significant regional variations in inflation.

- Retirees buy more services than goods, which historically have inflated at a higher rate than goods.
- The CPI may not be an accurate gauge of inflation for seniors because it relies heavily on housing.
- Planning for a younger worker can be troublesome because inflation over 60 years needs to be considered.

Because there is no exact method of predicting the inflation rate, you must use your best judgment as to future economic prospects and your clients' risk-aversion tendencies. A risk-averse client will probably want a more conservative figure projected, whereas a risk taker may feel comfortable with an optimistically low-inflation assumption. Many planners choose a long-term inflation rate between 3 and 4 percent. This is also an assumption that needs to be revisited over time if the actual inflation rate does not match the expected rate.

Illustrating the Effect of Increases in Inflation and Standards of Living

In general, the higher the inflation rate and standard-of-living increases that a client experiences, the greater the amount of retirement income that will be needed. The compound interest formula can be used to make the necessary projection for the purpose of illustrating this. This formula is

$$FV = PV (1 + r)^n$$

where FV = the target dollar expenditure at retirement

PV = the dollar expenditures for the current standard of living

r = a rate of growth in the dollar expenditures for the standard of living

n = the number of years from time of planning until target retirement date

The rate of growth, or r, can stand for (1) the rate of increase in the level of the standard of living, (2) the rate of inflation that requires more dollars being spent to maintain the current standard of living, or (3) a combination of both. For example, if no inflation is expected, but the client anticipates a 20 percent increase in his or her standard of living between now and retirement 10 years hence, the result is an average annual 1.84 percent compound increase in the standard of living and r equals .0184 in the formula. If no growth in the standard of living is anticipated before retirement, but inflation is expected to average 4 percent annually over the 10 years to retirement, then r equals .04 in the above formula.

When the standard of living is expected to rise during the planning period and inflation is expected to continue, then r, the growth rate, can be approximated by adding the rates of growth in both the standard of living and inflation to estimate the needed income at or during retirement. For example, if the standard of living is expected to rise at 1.84 percent annually and inflation at 4 percent annually, then the combined result is a needed 5.84 percent increase in income. In this case, r equals 5.84. (For technical accuracy, these rates should be multiplied together [1.0184 × 1.04 = 1.059] rather than added, but because of the many necessary assumptions about the future, the inaccuracy from approximating is acceptable.)

ASSUMPTION FIVE: TOTAL RETURN ON INVESTMENTS

LO 21.5 Discuss the total return on investment assumption and some of the common retirement investing strategies that help to shape it.

The traditional way to estimate a client's total return on investments is to determine his or her risk tolerance, select an appropriate portfolio based on it, and then use historical averages to predict future returns. In other words, if a client currently has an asset allocation model in place, the historical averages of that portfolio should be used as a proxy for future returns. Planners should be mindful of the after-tax rate of return, which will depend in part on the ability to invest in qualified plans and other tax shelter vehicles. Planners should also be aware of a client's ability to increase savings based on future salary increases (called a step-up rate). In other words a step-up rate represents the amounts savings will be increased each year.

A thorough discussion about total return on investments would require another textbook to do it justice. In the remaining part of this chapter, however, we would like to propose some commonly accepted strategies about retirement investing that will help to frame the total return on investment assumption.

Retirement Investment Strategies

There are a variety of investment strategies and planning opportunities available to clients who are in the process of accumulating a nest egg for retirement. It is appropriate at this point to sketch out some of the thinking on which the financial planning community generally agrees in order to better understand the assumptions used for total return on investments. Below you will find a brief overview of these commonly accepted retirement investment strategies.

risk tolerance

A good place to start might be to discuss the relationship between risk tolerance and retirement investing. One of the first obligations of a financial planner is to assess a client's risk tolerance. Risk tolerance identifies the point at which a client falls on a spectrum that ranges from risk averse (that is, risk intolerant or conservative) to aggressive. Once a **risk tolerance level** has been identified, the planner can make suitable investment recommendations. The first strategy deals with the fact that whatever the clients' risk tolerances, they should be encouraged to be aggressive—particularly in the earlier years—when it comes to building their retirement portfolio. This so-called concept of "time diversification" recommends that investors with long-term investment objectives should be willing to invest in what are considered higher risk, higher return investments than they would tolerate for short-term objectives. Although there is academic debate over the validity of this concept, experts agree that when clients have many years of employment before they retire, they can alter their savings habits should substantial investment losses occur in the early years of saving for retirement. Hence, they are in a position to accept additional risk. In order to facilitate long-term aggressive investing (relatively speaking), it may be a good idea to educate clients about financial risks (because unknown risks naturally loom larger than known risks) and to suggest they reduce the frequency with which they review their portfolios (because constant scrutiny leads to second-guessing and excessive concern about risk). (*Planning Note:* The retirement planner must exercise caution when recommending investment vehicles. The portfolio must fall within the client's "zone of acceptance." Otherwise the client may reject the full set of recommendations and either do nothing, which would be detrimental to the client, or, worse yet from the planner's standpoint, look to someone else to do his or her retirement planning.)

dollar cost averaging

A second retirement investment strategy centers on the integration of buy-and-hold philosophy, **dollar cost averaging**, and asset allocation modeling. Most planners agree that retirement investing should not be influenced by attempts at market timing. Long-term goals are likely to be achieved by a buy-and-hold strategy that includes periodic monitoring and selective repositioning. For this reason, the second strategy is to use dollar cost averaging with individual stocks (diversifying by adding new stocks over time) and to hold those stocks for a long period of time. Individual stocks should be utilized instead of mutual funds in portfolios that should grow to be sizable and where regular cash additions are expected. This is because, over time, individual holdings allow more opportunities for tax-efficient investing and they avoid the fees associated with funds. In portfolios that are not expected to be large or where the menu is restricted to mutual funds, mutual funds are fine. However, care should be exercised to acquire funds with negligible or no loads, no 12b(1) charges, low expense ratios, and low portfolio turnover ratios. (*Planning Note:* Dollar cost averaging (DCA), an approach in which a fixed dollar amount is invested in a security in each period, is consistent with a buy-and-hold strategy. Clients who use this approach will purchase more units of a security when its price is low and fewer units of a security when its price is high. Over a long period of time, the investor ends up with a lower average cost for the security than was the average acquisition price for each transaction. For example, dollar cost averaging occurs when an individual makes monthly contributions to a specific mutual fund in a 401(k) plan.)

Another idea concerns the risk of investing for retirement using the stock of one's employer. Investments in company stock may be desirable in some instances (for example, when a discounted stock purchase plan is offered or when a 401(k) match in employer stock is offered), but such investments must be limited. The third strategy therefore is to limit an employee's investment in company stock. The primary problem of over-investment in employer stock is the double whammy of the company's performance declining and the employee simultaneously being laid off. At this point, not only have the securities of the company declined in value, but also the employee/investor takes on the extra burden of being unemployed. Hence, there could be concurrent substantial declines in both his or her current standard of living and his or her financial position. A second troublesome reason for over-investment in employer stock centers on diversification requirements. Even investing in other companies in the same industry presents a similar problem.

The next idea involves tax efficiency in retirement investing. Because there is no taxation of earnings of investments in tax-qualified plans as the assets accumulate prior to distribution, a commonly suggested rule of thumb (and a fourth strategy) is to hold fixed income investments in tax-deferred accounts and equity investments in taxable private savings accounts. The reasoning for this rule of thumb is simple. Fixed-income investments pay interest, which is taxed as ordinary income anyway. Holding these investments in a tax-deferred account, therefore, does not change the fact that this income will still be taxed as ordinary income and still has the benefit of delaying taxation. With Roth IRA or Roth 401(k) accounts, an investor can even avoid taxation on what is otherwise taxable as ordinary income.

Equity investments pay dividends and provide capital gains (assuming the investor is fortunate enough to own stocks that go up in value). Under current tax laws, most dividend income and all capital gains are taxed at lower marginal rates. Furthermore, capital gains are not taxed until the investments are sold. By placing equities in tax-deferred accounts (except for Roth IRAs and Roth 401(k)s), the dividend income and capital gains are eventually taxed as ordinary income (that is, a withdrawal from a tax-deferred account) and do not retain their special tax status. The exception to this rule is that the current allocation of investment dollars between tax-deferred accounts and taxable private savings accounts should not determine the equity-bond allocation decision. In some cases, a client must compromise between the most tax-efficient form of investing and the desired asset allocation mix.

Another strategy focuses more on savings than investing. It is important that clients make the most of their IRA and 401(k) opportunities. In 2017, the amount a client can save each year in an IRA and 401(k) is $5,500 and $18,000, respectively. The contribution limit is $1,000 more for an IRA and $6,000 more for a 401(k) if the client is 50 or older because of catch-up provisions written into the law. One way to accumulate the additional savings is to encourage the client to bank either a percentage or the whole amount of any raise he or she expects. What they never receive, they won't miss! As they grow closer to retirement, banking the raises tends to set a more manageable standard of living for which they can plan. In other words, they will be better able to reach their retirement expectations because they chose to bank their raises in the final years of employment.

Finally, it is important to involve both spouses in retirement investing decisions. All too frequently only one spouse manages the family's finances. If this spouse is the first to die or has any type of dementia, the surviving spouse faces a significant financial crisis because of his or her lack of financial awareness. Many financial advisors insist that the financially unaware spouse be involved with all retirement financial decisions and also become involved in the day-to-day finances.

Table 21-4
Summary of Accumulation Strategies

1. Clients should be encouraged to invest at the aggressive limit of their risk tolerance.
2. Use dollar cost averaging to invest in individual stocks over time and use a buy-and-hold approach to these stocks.
3. Investment in employer stock should be limited because of diversification concerns (both stock diversification and human capital diversification).
4. Hold fixed income investments in tax-deferred accounts (such as 401(k) plans) and equity investments in taxable private savings accounts.
5. Make the most of tax deferral opportunities by using future raises as fodder for future savings.
6. Include both spouses in the decision making and planning process.

CHAPTER REVIEW

Key Terms and Concepts

replacement-ratio method
risk tolerance

dollar cost averaging

Chapter 21: Review Questions

Review questions are based on the learning objectives in this chapter. Thus, a [21.3] at the end of a question means that the question is based on learning objective 3. If there are multiple objectives, they are all listed.

1. List the factors that affect the choice of a retirement age. [21.1]

2. What factors may encourage a client to retire early? [21.1]

3. Why should early retirement be viewed skeptically from a financial planning perspective? [21.1]

4. What factors should be considered when estimating life expectancy. [21.1]

5. What ranges of replacement ratios are generally chosen by retirement planners in order to maintain a client's preretirement standard of living during the first year of retirement? [21.2]

6. Why can retirees, in some cases, count on less of their income going to pay taxes during their retirement years? [21.2]

7. Explain the expense-method approach to retirement planning. [21.3]

8. What factors tend to
   a. increase a client's living expenses after retirement? [21.2]
   b. reduce a client's living expenses after retirement?

9. What inflation assumption is considered appropriate for a client who is willing to accept a moderate risk? [21.4]

10. List and briefly define some investing strategies for accumulating retirement assets. [21.5]

Chapter 21: Review Answers

1. The factors that affect the choice of a retirement age include:
   - early Social Security benefits available at age 62
   - Medicare eligibility at age 65
   - full retirement age for Social Security
   - early retirement age as defined in the employer plan
   - normal retirement age as defined in the employer plan
   - lifestyle goals
   - family responsibilities
   - specific financial conditions applicable when the decision is being made
   - perspective on investment performance, inflation, and changes in government programs that may affect financial resources

2. Factors that encourage clients to choose early retirement include:
   - financial goals that have been met
   - financial goals that have been compromised
   - corporate downsizing with incentives (golden handshakes)
   - corporate downsizing without incentives
   - actual health issues
   - caregiving health issues
   - perceived health issues
   - health and pension incentives
   - nonfinancial factors
   - problems in the workplace

3. Planners may want to advise clients against early retirement for several reasons. The Social Security full retirement age is increasing to 67. Another reason early retirement causes a concern for your client is the impact on the client's pension benefits. In a defined-benefit plan, the final-average salary and years-of-service component of the client's benefit formula will be lower than they otherwise would be if the client remained employed. In addition, there is typically an actuarial reduction in the pension annuity to account for a larger payout period. In a defined-contribution

plan, the account balance a client has will be smaller than it otherwise would be if the client remained employed. The client loses the opportunity to make (or have his or her employer make) contributions based on a percentage of peak (end-of-career) salary and, where applicable, may lose the matching contributions attributable to those contributions. Other ways in which early retirement can affect financial security include the following:

- increased exposure to inflation
- lack of health insurance prior to Medicare (the Affordable Care Act health care exchanges now make pre-age 65 retirement easier as access to health care has been increased. However, the premiums for certain individuals can still be incredibly expensive.)
- adverse effect on the calculation of Social Security benefits

4. Planners should consider the following factors when estimating life expectancy:

- clients' personal and family health history
- the statistical life expectancy data by using the retirement ages of the client and his or her spouse
- consumer websites or proprietary software that project longevity based on family and personal health history
- financial conservatism (which dictates that the planner and client should assume a longer-than-expected retirement period)

5. In general, a 60 to 80 percent replacement ratio is used. In other words, the amount of income needed to be financially independent in the first year of retirement without drastically altering the client's standard of living varies between 60 and 80 percent of the average gross annual income of the average of the last 3 years of employment.

6. In many circumstances, retirees can count on a lower percentage of their income going to pay taxes in the retirement years. Some taxes are reduced or eliminated, and in other cases retirees may enjoy special favorable tax treatment.

- FICA contributions (old-age, survivors, disability, and hospital insurance) are levied solely on income from employment.
- For a taxpayer aged 65 or over, an additional amount is added to the standard deduction. If the taxpayer is married and his or her spouse is also 65 or older, both spouses receive the additional standard deduction.
- Some or all of a client's Social Security benefits will be received tax free.

- In some states, Social Security benefits are fully exempt from state income taxation; in others, some taxation of these benefits might occur if the state's income tax is assessed on the taxpayer's taxable income as reported for federal income tax purposes.
- Some states grant extra income tax relief for seniors by providing increased personal exemptions, credits, sliding scale rebates of property or other taxes (the amount or percent of which might be dependent on income), or additional tax breaks.
- Taxpayers may be able to exceed the 10 percent threshold for deductibility of qualifying medical expenses

7. The expense method of retirement planning focuses on the projected expenses that the retiree will have in the first year of retirement. As with the replacement-ratio method, it is much easier to define the potential expenses for those clients who are at or near retirement.

    A list of expenses that should be considered includes expenses that may be unique to the particular client, as well as other, more general expenses.

8. a. Some expenses that tend to increase for retirees include the following:
    - utilities and telephone
    - medical/dental/prescription drugs/health insurance
    - house upkeep/repairs/maintenance/property insurance (until a move occurs)
    - recreation/entertainment/travel/dining (during the early years of retirement)

    b. Some expenses tend to decrease for the retiree. These include the following:
    - mortgage payments
    - food
    - clothing
    - income taxes
    - property taxes
    - transportation costs (car maintenance/insurance/other)
    - debt repayment (charge accounts, personal loans)
    - child support/alimony
    - household furnishings

9. A 4 percent assumption could prove to be a viable rate to use during both the accumulation period and the retirement period. However, both you and your client must recognize that if long-term inflation does not match the expected rate, revisions in planning must be made.

10. Investing strategies for the accumulation period include the following six ideas.
    a. Clients should be encouraged to invest at the aggressive limit of their risk tolerance.
    b. Use dollar cost averaging to invest in individual stocks over time and use a buy-and-hold approach to these stocks.
    c. Investment in employer stock should be limited because of diversification concerns (both stock diversification and human capital diversification).
    d. Hold fixed income investments in tax-deferred accounts (such as 401(k) plans) and equity investments in taxable private savings accounts.
    e. Make the most of tax deferral opportunities by using future raises as fodder for future savings.
    f. Include both spouses in the decision making and planning process.

Chapter 22

Developing Retirement Savings and the Building Blocks of a Retirement Income Plan

Learning Objectives

An understanding of the material in this chapter should enable the student to

- **LO 22.1** Communicate the importance of having a well-funded retirement plan.
- **LO 22.2** Explain phased retirement plans and the financial benefits of delayed retirement.
- **LO 22.3** Understand the role of safe savings rates in a retirement savings plan.
- **LO 22.4** Understand the unique challenges and risks of turning retirement savings into retirement income.
- **LO 22.5** Explain the systematic withdrawal approach to retirement income planning.
- **LO 22.6** Review the bucketing approach to retirement income planning.
- **LO 22.7** Describe the flooring approach to retirement income planning.

LO 22.1 Communicate the importance of having a well-funded retirement plan.

Retirement is a broad term that means a lot of different things to different people. For some, retirement represents a complete end of employment. For others, it means transitioning into a secondary career or part-time work. However, for most people, retirement also represents opportunity. It is an opportunity to do "bucket-list" items, spend time with family, travel, golf, or just relax. This active view of retirement is the enjoyable part, but retirement is often a continuum of phases. This first active period, is often called the go-go period, followed by the slow-go period as the retiree becomes less active, and ultimately the no-go period towards the end of retirement when travel and physical activities become even more restricted. Regardless of your specific retirement goals and vision, you will need sufficient funding in order to retire with independence, dignity, and security. As such, it's important for everyone to have a well-funded retirement plan.

In the United States, we often refer to the retirement funding sources as the three-legged stool. The stool is made up of government programs, self-funding, and employer-sponsored retirement plans. However, the reality is that saving for retirement is much more complicated and detailed. While an employer might provide a vehicle to save for retirement, a lot of the work and responsibility of saving now falls on the individual employee. As employers move away from pensions and towards 401(k) plans funded mostly by employee salary deferrals, the retirement savings landscape will shift. The three-legged stool in a sense becomes unbalanced as more burden is placed on the individual.

Furthermore, while the government plays a huge role in retirement preparation in the United States, the social and government-provided programs are often not sufficient to fully fund everyone's retirement. Social Security, Medicare, Medicaid, tax breaks, and Supplemental Security Income can provide a baseline of security and benefits to retirees; however, they are often not sufficient to cover all retirement needs. As such, Americans need to save additional resources to fill in the funding and coverage gaps of these government programs.

There are a few funding gaps that almost all Americans need to consider for retirement. First, there is longevity risk. Since it is uncertain how long someone will live in retirement, you need to have sufficient funds set aside to cover longevity risk. While projecting longevity starts with the life expectancy of an individual, it's always an estimate. If we plan for averages, we will be wrong 50% of the time. As such, the safe way to plan is to take an individual's situation, look at the mortality tables for someone their age, and modify based off of their unique health history and family situation. Furthermore, it's often a good idea to add a few buffer years onto any plan. But to deal with longevity requires the individual to save enough money to fund an uncertain time period. This is one of the greatest challenges for saving for retirement, as you do not know if you need money for 20 years or 40 years.

Another big risk for having a well-funded retirement plan is inflation. Inflation impacts a retiree's purchasing power over time. What this really means is that a dollar today is not worth a dollar tomorrow as it cannot buy the same amount of goods and services. This means you need income sources and investments that can keep pace with inflation over time. It also means your retirement savings need to keep pace with inflation while preparing to fund retirement during your working years. To determine a good inflation rate for retirement, it is suggested that you look at long-term rates (over the past 30-40 years). You can think about inflation as a "raise" you will need to build in for retirement each year to cover increasing retirement costs. Furthermore, it usually means you need to save a percentage of your income each year while working and a set dollar amount will not properly address inflation. Hopefully your salary will adjust to keep pace with inflation and perhaps even outpace it while you work.

A third risk for a well-funded retirement plan is health care. Health care can be a very expensive budget item before retirement and in retirement. Health care out of pocket costs for retirees can be hundreds of thousands of dollars through the course of retirement, requiring the retiree to have set aside additional funds to cover medical costs where Medicare coverage gaps, premiums, and co-payments exist. Furthermore, the lack of proper health care insurance before retirement can drain an individual's assets leaving them unprepared financially for retirement if a big medical emergency and bill becomes due. Tied to medical expenses, but often dealt with separately, are long-term care expenses. While long-term care needs can arise before retirement, most people need long-term care towards the end of retirement, which can run well over $100,000 a year in a nursing home in 2017. This can quickly deplete a couple's savings leaving the couple in an uncomfortable financial situation.

A well-funded retirement plan will address these risks and a number of other pre- and post-retirement risks. A quality retirement savings plan starts by setting aside a proper amount of money each year, investing it properly, having proper insurance coverage, and then understanding how to generate sustainable lifetime income from the assets once the retiree reaches retirement. However, as we will see later in this chapter, there is no magic retirement savings number that guarantees a successful retirement. Instead, it requires a number of moving pieces and varies depending on each unique individual situation.

LO 22.2   Explain phased retirement plans and benefits of delaying retirement on savings.

Many Americans state that they plan to work in retirement. However, this perception is not always reality as far less actually end up working in retirement. Declining health, cutbacks at work, and caregiving responsibilities can force a person out of the workforce earlier than planned. At that point, the individual might just accept early retirement as the prospect of finding a new job appears daunting. This is really reemployment risk, the inability to supplement retirement income through additional work due to a number of economic and personal factors. However, for some, phased retirement might be possible. This can allow the individual to continue to work longer, test drive retirement, and not have to retire 'cold turkey.'

Research from the EBRI Retirement Confidence Survey asks retirees about work and retirement. Every year, the report has shown the percentage that actually work in retirement is much lower than the percentage of pre-retirees reporting that they expect to work in retirement. One big challenge is that many employers do not offer any formal type of phased retirement. In fact, there is no legal or industry standard definition. Many retirees engage in an informal type of phased retirement by taking consulting positions, part-time jobs, or even turning their hobbies into profit-making activities. Employment prospects among retirees vary depending on health, family circumstances, and demands for the retiree's skills.

While most employers do not offer phased retirement, other phased retirement options can include getting a bridge job with another employer or getting rehired as a consultant or part-time worker with the same company. Working part-time may result in a reduction in pay, but many report increased job satisfaction. In some cases, if an employee has a defined-benefit plan at work it can be preferential to leave the employer and be rehired in order to lock in the previous benefit at higher salaries. While in defined-contribution plan situations it is almost always preferable to have continuous employment and not be rehired, with defined-benefit plans it's not always clear as it will depend, in part, on the plan's definition of final average monthly compensation.

Based on the statistics, planning on earning significant employment income in retirement may be unrealistic. Jobs may be unavailable or the client may be unable to work. If the client really needs income to meet retirement objectives, it may be best to postpone retirement from a career that pays better and offers health insurance and other benefits. For those looking to work in retirement, be sure to use available resources to find employment opportunities that are meaningful and meet income requirements. Books like *What Color is Your Parachute for Retirement?* and websites like "AARP" can be quite helpful. It is also important to be open to learning new skills to be successful in the job market. Recognize that work in retirement can have important rewards other than money. The retiree may use a job to add some purpose, fill time, or build a social network.

When available, phased retirement can play a very important role in a successful retirement plan. Phased retirement can be thought of as a broad range of employment arrangements that allows a retiree to continue working at a reduced workload while he or she gradually shifts from full-time employment to full-time retirement. Because of the lack of an industry standard, phased retirement can include jobs that require the same amount of work, less work, or even just more flexible work hours. For people working in retirement, there is a mix of people working at their same employer, a new employer, or becoming self-employed.

A formal workplace phased retirement policy or program can allow an employee to continue working with their current employer at a reduced schedule. However, retirement benefits will need to be coordinated with the program. In some instances, employees are given the opportunity to receive retirement benefits while still working and in others cases may not be given the opportunity. If a formal policy does exist, they are often contained in the personnel or employee handbooks of the employer. It is more common to have a formal phased retirement program with a larger employer than it is with a smaller employer.

More likely, the employee will have access to an informal phased retirement plan. These are informal workplace arrangements and practices that might allow an employee to continue working with their current employer at a reduced or modified schedule. Informal phased retirement is more common than formal plans. However, it cannot be as easily relied upon and fit into a plan because it is not a guarantee. Instead, companies often decide on a case-by-case basis if they want to accommodate the wishes of an employee who wants to phase into retirement.

For some individuals, phased retirement could represent a huge shift. They could switch jobs and careers entirely, basically creating an encore career. In this situation, the individual will likely need to have a strong desire to try out something new or work in an area where they find personal meaning. However, a person could also just phase a little, perhaps just going to part-time or working more remotely. Regardless of how much the person changes their work, continued employment income can significantly increase the client's cash flow and retirement security. Phased retirement also enables the individual to test drive retirement in order to figure out what they want and how they will find meaning in their life after work. For others, work will remain a part of their retirement because it is what they enjoy doing, they get meaning out of their job, and they want the income.

While phased retirement offers many benefits, it can also have some negative impacts or impediments to continuing phased retirement. First, an employee that goes part-time as part of a phased retirement program might lose their health insurance. This could be an issue for a retiree that is not ready to go on Medicare. However, someone participating in phased retirement who is age 65 or older will likely need to enroll in Medicare. Continued work in retirement can also impact Social Security through the earnings test if the individual is younger than their full retirement age and collecting benefits. There are also times when part-time work could negatively impact a defined-benefit plan by having higher years of income replaced by lower earning years.

There are impediments for an employer that can get in the way of offering a phased retirement plan. Many employers want a graceful transition in the workplace in which their older, more expensive employees retire so they can bring in younger, less expensive employees. Additionally, phased retirement plans can still cost money as the employer might need to provide health insurance, retirement benefits, and other workplace benefits to a part-time phased employee. Another challenge for phased retirement jobs is that the employer must be able to have the work and structures in place to offer such flexibility in the workplace. Many employers will not be able to cover the benefits, pay, support, and other requirements for a phased retirement plan. In some cases, they might be able to offer it for a short period of time, but might end up needing to change the plan over time, which might not work out for the employee. There are also situations in which ERISA rules might make it hard for an employer to offer a phased retirement plan and still stay compliant with their qualified retirement plan.

Ultimately, the decision of when to retire has a big impact on retirement security. The longer you can keep working, the better off you will be in retirement. By pushing off retirement, the individual shortens his or her retirement period and increases their income. It's really a double win for retirement security. A shorter retirement period means you need to have less saved up and also means that you can spend a higher percentage of your wealth each year and still not run out of money. So, if there is a phased retirement program available to the employee it could be very beneficial to at least look into the plan or discuss the possibility of an informal arrangement with his or her employer. However, if that is not available, the employee might need to look at other employers or even consider being self-employed for a while in retirement.

LO 22.3   Understand safe savings rates on a retirement savings plan.

As someone begins saving for retirement, it can be incredibly difficult to determine how much needs to be saved. One issue is that there is no magic retirement savings number. You might have heard that retirees need $1 to $2 million saved for retirement. Realistically, that is much more money than most people need in investable assets for retirement. Nonetheless, for some it's not nearly enough. Perhaps you have heard that people need a multiple of 10 to 20 times their current income? Again, that could be enough for some and not enough for others. What you need saved for retirement depends on so many factors and your individual situation. While these rules of thumb can be helpful in bringing attention to retirement savings, the focus cannot be on accumulating a set amount of money on a specific date, as that is not realistic or doable due to market volatility and fluctuations.

The focus instead should be on the individual's unique goals, needs, risks, and income sources. In order to figure out how much you need for retirement, you need to first be able to visualize retirement and come up with realistic retirement expenses. Once you can estimate your expenses, you can then start figuring out how much income you need in retirement. Meeting your income needs and generating a steady paycheck is really the goal for retirement income planning, not just wealth accumulation. Furthermore, you need to consider all of the assets at your disposal to meet your income needs, not just your investable assets. This means considering how you will use Social Security, your home equity, your pension, your 401(k), your life insurance, and whether you will keep working part-time in retirement. Someone who works part-time in retirement and has Social Security and a pension will often need far fewer investable assets to meet their retirement income needs than someone with the same income needs who only has Social Security and a 401(k).

human capital

Remember, when saving for retirement you should focus on all of the income sources you have available to meet your retirement needs and not just your accumulated investable assets. This also includes human capital. **Human capital** is an individual's earning potential, which is the single most valuable asset that most people have before retirement. Human capital can be expressed as the present value of wages that someone can earn over the course of their lifetime.

So how does human capital fit into a retirement savings plan? First, at a young age an individual should invest in themselves. The best thing you can do to improve your retirement security it to increase your earning potential. This could be investing in an education, which could increase your human capital. Over time, as you age, human capital will likely start to decline as you have less working years left in life to earn money. As such, the present value of your human capital will go down. However, the goal is to convert human capital into financial capital over time because at retirement, human capital will be very low or nearly fully extinguished. At this time, you will no longer be able to rely on your wages but instead on your savings.

Human capital can also be expressed as an asset class. For some people, like a professor with tenure, human capital is very much like a bond as future earnings are stable, predictable, and not impacted by stock market conditions. So one theory of investing says that as your human capital decreases over time you should replace it with more bond-like assets in your investment portfolio. However, for others, it could be more analogous to a stock. For example, if you are in a pure commission-based job, income could be uncertain, unpredictable, and impacted by poor market conditions. In both situations, you can see that if you consider human capital to be an asset class it is very risky to hold too much of your investable assets in employer stock. So you could encourage the person to invest in other markets that are not as correlated to the individual's own employer and work.

So how much of your human capital do you need to convert into savings each year to have a secure retirement? Again, the answer is not so simple. One strategy is to look at a concept called the "safe savings rate." This strategy was first tested by Dr. Wade Pfau, a Professor at The American College of Financial Services, who has since published this research in a number of academic journals. In order for someone to achieve a wealth accumulation target for retirement, they need to set money aside in their 401(k) and perhaps in a brokerage account as well. But to figure out how much you will have in the future you need to make a number of assumptions. First, you need to assume some growth in your salary, investment returns, and the sequencing of those investment returns.

safe savings rate

The **safe savings rate** is the maximum of all the minimum necessary savings rates from overlapping historical periods needed to accumulate an individual's desired wealth in order to meet a certain level of spending in retirement. The safe savings rate will tell you how much you need to save over a 20, 30, or 40-year working career, as a percent of your salary, to replace either 50% or 70% of your final salary in retirement based on your investment asset allocation. The investment returns are based off of historical returns. For example, if you want to work for 40 years and have a 30-year retirement of 70% replacement rate of your final salary in retirement you will need to save roughly 10.35% of your salary in an 80% stock and 20% bond investment portfolio to ensure enough money at retirement.

The safe savings rate is essentially saying how much do you need to save, for what period of time, in what investment mix to ensure that you can replace a certain amount of money in retirement. It is also looking at worst case scenarios based on historical data. Many people could still reach their spending goals without saving as much if they get lucky and just happen to live through a good market cycle of returns and retire at the right time. However, most people probably do not want to leave their retirement to chance.

Another important takeaway from the safe savings rate research is that the more conservatively you invest, the less likely you are to meet your retirement goals. So, when you are young and just starting to save, you want to consider taking a lot of investment risk and having a high allocation of stocks to bonds in your portfolio. Again, this ties back to your human capital – take risk at an early age. Additionally, the longer you expect your retirement to last, the more money you will need to save. Lastly, the earlier you start saving, the better. The percent of salary someone needs to save each year to replace 50% of their income in retirement is often three or four times higher if you are only saving for a 20-year time period as compared to someone who can save for a 40-year time period. Time is on your side as an investor. Start saving early, take market risks, and realize you will likely have to save more than 10% of your annual salary to have a secure retirement.

Table 22-1 Safe Minimum Savings Rates

Replacement Rate = 50% of Final Salary		Retirement Phase							
		40/60 Fixed Asset Allocation			60/40 Fixed Asset Allocation			80/20 Asset Allocation		
		20 Years	30 Years	40 Years	20 Years	30 Years	40 Years	20 Years	30 Years	40 Years
Accumulation Phase	20 Years	31.98	39.5	47.02	30.94	35.91	38.92	30.52	34.45	35.94
	30 Years	15.64	19.33	22.19	13.88	16.62	18.63	12.85	15.14	16.54
	40 Years	10.26	12.42	13.84	7.57	8.77	9.22	6.26	7.39	8.06

Replacement Rate = 70% of Final Salary		Retirement Phase							
		40/60 Fixed Asset Allocation			60/40 Fixed Asset Allocation			80/20 Asset Allocation		
		20 Years	30 Years	40 Years	20 Years	30 Years	40 Years	20 Years	30 Years	40 Years
Accumulation Phase	20 Years	44.78	55.30	65.82	43.31	50.28	54.49	42.73	48.24	50.31
	30 Years	21.90	27.07	31.06	19.43	23.77	26.08	17.99	21.20	23.16
	40 Years	14.36	17.38	19.38	10.60	12.27	12.91	8.76	10.35	11.28

Wade Pfau, "Safe Savings Rates: A New Approach to Retirement Planning over The Life Cycle," *Journal of Financial Planning*, May 2011.

LO 22.4   Understand the unique challenges and risks of turning retirement savings into retirement income.

As retirement approaches, concerns shift from the accumulation phase to the decumulation phase. The focus is no longer just on accumulating wealth, although that might remain important throughout life, but instead, the individual's concerns now focus on generating income from their savings to last throughout retirement. Retirement income planning really is goal-based planning. A successful retirement income plan would be tailored to the individual's situation, assets, needs, goals, and desires. The plan would also address a number of retirement income related risks such as inflation, longevity risk, investment risk, health care expenses, loss of a spouse, and long-term care. However, retirement income planning is a complex task that this chapter just briefly touches upon. The task is complex because retirement income planning needs to address a number of unknown risks while coordinating with other financial objectives such as estate and legacy planning.

longevity risk

As we have discussed a few times now, longevity risk has a huge impact on retirement income planning. Because no one can predict how long he or she will live, a retiree needs to secure an income stream to cover expenses in retirement for an unpredictable length of time. As such, **longevity risk** is really the risk of outliving your savings because you live longer than expected. For example, if you plan to retire for 25 years, age 65 until 90, but you live until 95 and end up retiring two years earlier at 62, can your savings and income sources cover your expenses for an additional 7 years? The answer for a lot of people is going to be no.

Dealing with longevity really starts with picking a realistic retirement date and a well-developed life expectancy number. While the average life expectancy age for someone alive today at 65 is roughly 84 for males and 86 for females, averages do not tell the whole story. In fact, if you plan for an average life expectancy in retirement there is a 50% chance you are wrong! That just will not do. Instead, planning needs to be tied to the individual's personal health history and family history. Furthermore, many plans just add on additional years to help plan for some longevity risk. Dealing with longevity also means coming up with a realistic withdrawal rate from your retirement portfolio that will last throughout retirement and secure guaranteed sources of lifetime income. While longevity risk is hard to completely eliminate from a retirement income plan, you can transfer a lot of the risk onto someone else. You can greatly increase the likelihood that your money lasts throughout retirement by purchasing guaranteed lifetime sources of income like a deferred annuity or qualified longevity annuity contract (QLAC), by selecting the annuity distribution from your pension plan, or by deferring Social Security.

contingency fund

Other strategies can help with longevity such as using a sustainable withdrawal rate from your retirement portfolio or by building a contingency fund that can be used for longevity as well as other risks. A **contingency fund** is a reserve of money or other assets that is set aside to cover possible unforeseen or unknown future expenses. A contingency fund could be a well-diversified investment portfolio that focuses on long-term growth. A Roth IRA could function as a tax-efficient and useful account for a contingency fund because of the tax-free growth, tax efficiency for estate planning if the money is not used, and because the Roth IRA is not subject to required minimum distributions at age 70½ so it can continue to grow throughout retirement. Other assets like a cash value life insurance policy or home equity can also be used as a contingency fund for longevity risk.

inflation risk

While having a contingency fund and guaranteed sources of lifetime income can go a long way to building a secure retirement income plan, you also need to deal with a decline in purchasing power (DIPP) over time due to inflation. **Inflation risk** is the general increase in prices and the decline in purchasing power of money over time. Inflation, while not always a huge factor in purchasing decisions from one year to the next, compounds over time. Additionally, while still employed and working, inflation is often offset to some degree by an increasing salary. However, in retirement, inflation makes retirement more expensive over time which can impede the client's ability to maintain his or her desired standard of living. This is especially true of anyone living off of a fixed income in retirement. As such, something that cost $1,000 today could double in price over the course of retirement and become unaffordable if your income did not also adjust for inflation.

Even modest inflation can significantly erode purchasing power over time. For example, a 3% annual inflation will mean that costs double for a client who retired at 62 and is now 86. The first part of the plan to address inflation is building in realistic estimates of long-term inflation when calculating how much to save for retirement. In this modeling, sophisticated retirement software can apply different inflation rates to different expense categories. Next, to protect a retiree from this decline in purchasing power, the retirement income plan needs to include inflation-adjusted or protected assets and income sources. To a certain extent, Social Security is inflation protected because it is geared toward increases in the consumer price index (CPI-W). This assumes, however, that the law will remain unchanged and that the CPI accurately reflects inflation as it affects seniors. There have been some unsuccessful attempts over the years to adjust Social Security's inflation protections by tying it more directly to the spending habits of seniors. Additionally, stocks and dividends tend to have some inflation protections. Dividend income from a stock portfolio is generally considered to be inflation protected if the principal is left intact. However, focusing too much of your investments in dividend paying stocks can cause an individual to become too concentrated in their investments and actually increase some other investment risks. Furthermore, some annuities offer inflation protection riders; however, they can be very expensive.

excess withdrawal risk

When taking withdrawals from a portfolio during retirement to fund income needs, there is a risk that the rate of withdrawals will deplete the portfolio before the end of retirement, resulting in an **excess withdrawal risk**. The client can also create a huge risk here by just spending outside of their means. However, just because you have investments that have averaged 8% returns, it does not mean you can spend 8% of the initial portfolio value (plus a little more for inflation each year) and be okay. In reality, to protect against the uncertainty of the market you may have to limit withdrawals to 4% or less. What this really comes down to is making sure the income sources and portfolio investments can provide for a retiree's expenditures throughout retirement without having a shortfall. A longer time horizon, bad investment returns, increased expenses, or higher inflation could all cause the income to fall short of needs.

There is a lot of research on how much can be withdrawn from a portfolio without risking portfolio failure. Unfortunately the answer is complicated, and depends upon the length of retirement, the asset allocation, and whether rates of return will match historical returns. Choosing an appropriate withdrawal rate should be done with the help of a qualified advisor with expertise in this area and with the assistance of computer software. While there is no one software program that everyone uses, retirement income planning needs software today. Another factor that affects how much can be withdrawn is whether the client is willing to make adjustments over time. If the income need is determined—let's say its $50,000 and increased for inflation each year and the client cannot tolerate a reduction—the possibility of portfolio failure increases. Furthermore, the ability to stay within the discipline of a withdrawal plan is very important when discussing excess withdrawal risk. Taking withdrawals from a portfolio allows for flexibility, but that can be a disadvantage as well. When the adult children are buying houses, the grandchildren are going to college, or other compelling reasons to spend appear, it's hard to stay within the discipline of a spending plan. All of a sudden, the retiree could have overspent and now faces a retirement income shortfall. However, to ensure that a portfolio lasts a lifetime, the withdrawal rate needs to be conservative. This has the downside that retirees may not fully enjoy retirement out of a concern of running out of money. So taking withdrawals from a portfolio presents both a risk of spending too much and a risk of spending less than can be afforded.

Building a plan to address excess withdrawal risk requires an understanding of the research about rates of withdrawals that can be sustained over a retirement period. Choosing a withdrawal rate also means weighing a client's desire for increased spending in relation to willingness to reduce spending. That is in part the client's attitude, but it's also a function of his risk capacity as well. If a retiree has Social Security and a substantial pension that is payable for life, then the client has more capacity for risk in taking withdrawals from the portfolio. A real and serious consideration is sticking with the withdrawal plan. It should be helpful to have regular client meetings reviewing the plan and making sure that the client has a clear understanding of the consequences of failing to follow the plan. Whether the plan is realistic is also a function of whether other contingencies have been planned for, or whether the portfolio is being relied upon to meet long-term care needs, unexpected health care expenses, and other risks faced in retirement. Sometimes clients simply determine their income needs without considering those big periodic expenditures like replacing a roof or buying a new car.

In general, a lot of sustainable withdrawal rates are built around Monte Carlo analysis and the 4% rule. The 4% rule is a rule of thumb used to determine the amount of funds that can be withdrawn from a retirement account each year without depleting the portfolio before 30 years. For example, the rule would state that you could safely withdraw $40,000 (4%) of a $1,000,000 portfolio for 30 years, adjusting the withdrawal for inflation if you were investing in 50% stocks and 50% bonds without running out of money based on historical U.S. data. Essentially, the rule says that even in the worst case scenario this is what works. However, it is entirely based on past data, and previous success does not guarantee future success. But, the 4% rule can be used to show a reasonable withdrawal rate for a portfolio even if it is not guaranteed to work in all situations moving forward.

sequence of returns risk

Many seniors rely on investments to provide them returns and protect against inflation in retirement. However, investment returns are variable and very unpredictable. Not only do average returns matter for the senior, but the order of returns has an impact on how long a portfolio will last if the portfolio is in the distribution stage and if a fixed amount is being withdrawn from the portfolio. Negative returns in the first few years of retirement can significantly add to the possibility of portfolio ruin. This risk is called sequence of returns risk. **Sequence of returns risk** is the risk of receiving low or negative investment returns early in retirement when withdrawals are being made from those investments.

> **EXAMPLE**
>
> Peggy's portfolio is worth $10,000. She draws $1,100 at the end of each period. Peggy earns returns in years 1 through 5: 40%, 20%, 0%, –20%, –40%. Peggy has a 0% average rate of return.
>
> Gregg starts with the same amount, makes the same withdrawals, and earns the same returns, except in reverse order. However, Peggy ends up with $4,614 left over at the end while Greg only has $249, despite having the same average returns and same withdrawal amount. The only difference was the order of the market returns. Gregg was unlucky and retired at a bad time!

Table A: Peggy

Period	BOP	ROR	Value	Withdrawal	EOP
1	$10,000	40%	$14,000	$1,100	$12,900
2	$12,900	20%	$15,480	$1,100	$14,380
3	$14,380	0%	$14,380	$1,100	$13,280
4	$13,280	-20%	$10,624	$1,100	$9,524
5	$9,524	-40%	$5,714	$1,100	$4,614

Table B: Greg

Period	BOP	ROR	Value	Withdrawal	EOP
1	$10,000	-40%	$6,000	$1,100	$4,900
2	$4,900	-20%	$3,920	$1,100	$2,820
3	$2,820	0%	$2,820	$1,100	$1,720
4	$1,720	20%	$1,720	$1,100	$964
5	$964	40%	$1,349	$1,100	$249

Sequence of returns risk cannot be fully avoided if the retiree is invested in the market. However, it is important to remember that the risk is most impactful for retirement during the first few years in retirement and the last few years right before retirement. As such, there are a number of strategies used to help reduce the impact of sequence of returns risk. One strategy is to reduce the investment portfolio's volatility early in retirement. By reducing volatility in the retirement portfolio during the withdrawal stage, the sequence of returns risk is reduced. This can be done by (1) purchasing life annuities, (2) using bonds to build a specified income stream over a specified number of years, or (3) by investing in a better diversified portfolio of stocks.

Another successful strategy to reduce sequence of returns risk is to be flexible in your spending. If a client is able to adjust withdrawals for market volatility and actually lower his or her withdrawal rate in bad market years, the portfolio can limit the impact of sequence of returns risk to some degree. The problem with adjusting spending in bad markets is that the amount withdrawn each year may vary significantly and it may not meet the client's income needs. A compromise is to start with the standard withdrawal definition and then make some minor adjustments based on market conditions. Other strategies for dealing with sequence of returns risk could be to rely on non-market correlated assets like a reverse mortgage line of credit or cash value life insurance during bad market years. Additionally, derivatives and puts can be useful during the first few years of retirement to provide some downside protection in a portfolio in order to mitigate sequence of returns risk.

health care and long-term care risks

One of the top expenses for retirees is health care. While Medicare is available for most retirees, for those that had employer health care coverage, retirement may mean paying more for medical insurance (Medicare Parts B and D and Medicare Supplement policies). Even with insurance, some expenses will be paid out of pocket. Also, chronic or acute illnesses and long-term care costs may mean more significant and unexpected out-of-pocket expenses. Normally, **health care and long-term care risks** are separated when discussed because different government programs cover health care and long-term care. However, for an individual retiree, the two are very related. The amount needed to cover health insurance premiums for Medicare and other out-of-pocket expenses in retirement is significant. Furthermore, long-term care is not covered by Medicare. Instead, an individual would need long-term care insurance, self-funding, or would have had to spend down most of their assets to qualify for Medicaid.

When planning for health care and long-term care it's important that people understand how both Medicare and Medicaid work. Make sure you have the right type of Medicare insurance coverage and that you sign up at the right time. Individuals become eligible for Medicare at age 65. Almost everyone is eligible for Medicare Part A, which covers hospital expenses at no cost, and for Part B upon paying a monthly premium. Individuals aged 65 can purchase prescription drug coverage under Medicare Part D. Individuals choose from among available private plans. Choosing a plan is an important decision, and changes can be made each year in an open enrollment period. Plans with higher premiums may offer more comprehensive benefits and may result in lower total out-of-pocket costs for a retiree with significant drug expenses. Medicare Parts A and B are quite comprehensive, but they do have deductibles and copays, and some health care needs of older adults are not covered. Some of the gaps can be addressed through Medicare Supplement insurance. Insurance companies must sell plans that provide standard benefits; however, premiums can vary from company to company. There are a number of available plans; the more comprehensive have higher premiums but can have the important function of making costs more predictable and putting a cap on out-of-pocket expenses.

Controlling health care costs can also be part of the solution. This can be by getting the right preventative care and living a healthy lifestyle. It can also be accomplished by relocating to an area that has lower medical care costs and by using generic brand drugs. Furthermore, you can also set aside money specifically for long-term care and health care in special tax-advantaged accounts like Health Savings Accounts (HSAs). HSAs can be funded while working and provide income to cover both Medicare premiums and long-term care insurance premiums. However, there are a number of restrictions on funding HSAs. First, you cannot fund one if you are enrolled in Medicare and need a high deductible health plan (HDHP). However, setting aside money to help cover the costs of insurance and out-of-pocket costs can be an effective strategy for dealing with health care and long-term care risks, and HSAs are the most tax-efficient way to do that.

frailty risk

Aging brings on a number of wonderful opportunities, but it also has its challenges. As many individuals age, some tasks like managing financial affairs, mowing the lawn, cleaning the gutters, painting, and cleaning the house can become more difficult. The inability or difficulty associated with completing some of these household tasks can require the senior to reach out and hire help. The increased assistance also brings with it increased risks and costs. **Frailty risk** is the risk that as a result of deteriorating mental or physical health, a retiree may not be able to execute sound judgment in managing his or her financial affairs and/or may become unable to care for his or her home. The majority of retirees will suffer from frailty during retirement and it's important to plan for the event. Frailty can have a significant impact on retirement as it can increase costs, increase the risk of financial elder abuse, and decrease one's ability to work in retirement.

So how can you plan for and deal with frailty? Frailty, along with declining mental decision making due to disease, needs to be planned for ahead of time. Once it has kicked in, it might be too late. For many retirees, family members will have to play a role here. This means a client might have others step in to make decisions which may mean involving a family member, hiring a daily money manager, or even selecting a corporate trustee to make investment decisions. Giving someone control is generally done with a power of attorney, which is either currently in force (durable power) or becomes effective only when you are no longer able to make decisions (springing power). Having assets in a living trust is another option, and you can remain the trustee until such time that you name a successor. However, preplanning with the documents described here is critical to avoid having to go through a court incompetency hearing in which a court-appointed guardian is chosen. Simplifying finances can also be helpful by using direct deposit for income payments and automatic withdrawals for regular bills. Some retirement products are simpler to manage as well, such as an immediate life annuity. Remember that there is no one simple solution for frailty risk as it depends on every situation. However, it can be managed in a number of different ways.

LO 22.5   Explain the systematic withdrawal approach to retirement income planning.

Once a client reaches retirement, his or her assets need to be turned into income. This is really the heart and soul of retirement income planning. However, there is no one agreed upon solution for most effectively turning assets into income in retirement. One reason is because every client is different. They have different assets, risks, desires, goals, and risk tolerance levels. However, the retirement income field has broken down into a mix of three different mindsets around retirement income. The three most prevalent approaches to retirement income are 1) the systematic withdrawal approach, 2) the bucket approach, and 3) the flooring approach. However, as you will see, these strategies are not completely exclusive of each other and can be used together in a combination type strategy. However, it is crucial to have a baseline understanding of the three different strategies, the products utilized in each, and the theory and research behind each strategy.

systematic withdrawal approach

The most commonly utilized of the three strategies is the systematic withdrawal approach. A **systematic withdrawal approach** to retirement income attempts to generate sustainable income for a retiree by withdrawing investments, both growth and principal, on an annual basis from a well-diversified portfolio based on guidelines in order to make the portfolio last for a desired amount of time. To implement this approach, guidelines must be established for safe withdrawals from year to year, including which investments should be converted into income, giving consideration to tax implications.

Financial planners use several schools of thought around creating guidelines for safe withdrawals from year to year. However, most systematic withdrawal strategies base the withdrawal guidelines at least in some part on the 4% safe withdrawal rate research.

- **Fixed Amount Adjusted for Inflation.** Take an initial withdrawal from the portfolio at retirement (for example, assuming a portfolio of $1,000,000, 4% or $40,000 in the first year), and then adjust the $40,000 each subsequent year for inflation regardless of the current value of the portfolio. In other words, the initial value is adjusted without "consulting" the current value of the portfolio on a year-by-year basis. This is the method suggested in the initial and ground-breaking research on the topic that using historical data would prove to be a fail-safe method for 30 years even if the market repeats its worst case 30-year pattern. Under this approach, the payments are fixed year to year on an inflation-adjusted basis. Planning can proceed accordingly for 30 years (or whatever the chosen time horizon) in a worst case scenario.

- **Fixed Amount Not Adjusted for Inflation.** Take an initial withdrawal from the portfolio at retirement (for example, 4% of $1,000,000, or $40,000 in the first year), and make that the "salary" each year for the client. There is no adjustment for inflation, nor is the year to year value of the portfolio "consulted" with regard to future distributions. This is a variation from the traditional approach. Under this approach, the payments are fixed year-to-year on a nominal (noninflationary adjusted) basis. Planning must account for loss of purchasing power separately. However, planning can proceed accordingly for 30 years (or whatever the chosen time horizon) in a worst case scenario.

- **Variable Amount Based Upon Prior Year-End Value.** Take an initial withdrawal of the portfolio at retirement (for example, 4% of $1,000,000, or $40,000 in the first year) and make that the "salary" for the first year of retirement. In each subsequent year, continue using the 4% guideline, but apply it to the ending year's account balance. For example, if the portfolio value at the start of year 2 is $1,200,000, the client would take a $48,000 distribution. If it is $800,000, the client will take a $32,000 distribution. This is a variation from the traditional approach. Under this approach, the payments are variable. They are not fixed from year to year but instead are linked to investment performance. Planning must account for dramatic shifts in annual income separately.

- **Fixed Amount Adjusted for Inflation and Based on Change in Portfolio Value.** Follow the methodologies in Step 1. For example, take an initial withdrawal of the portfolio at retirement such as 5% of $1,000,000, or $50,000 in the first year and then adjust the $50,000 each subsequent year for inflation regardless of the current value of the portfolio. However, if the portfolio value is more or less than a specified value, make adjustments to the percentage withdrawn accordingly. In other words, the initial value is adjusted without "consulting" the current value of the portfolio on a year-by-year basis unless that value triggers an adjustment.

This is the method suggested by building on the groundbreaking research on the topic. It allows for a larger initial withdrawal rate that would prove to be a fail-safe method for 30 years because future withdrawals may need to be adjusted (up or down) based on future market conditions. Under this approach, the payments are fixed year to year on an inflation-adjusted basis. Planning can proceed accordingly for 30 years (or whatever the chosen time horizon) in a worst case scenario. However, adjustments to annual income must be made when trigger events occur.

PRODUCTS FOR THE SYSTEMATIC WITHDRAWAL APPROACH

Systematic withdrawal strategies rely heavily on stock market investment return to generate the income needed for sustainable withdrawals. As such, any investment portfolio needs to be adequately diversified and properly allocated between investment classes in order to meet the client's goals. A financial services professional and client must develop an asset allocation model that covers:

- decisions about risk and returns (trade-offs the client faces)
- accounting for the types of returns needed to make the retirement income plan work

- accounting for the types of risks that the client can tolerate

When the asset allocation model is set, the products often fall naturally in place to fill the necessary allocations needed. Products should limit the client's risk exposures (not just investment risk, but all types of risk). A variety of products can be used to invest client assets when the systematic withdrawal approach is used. What follows is a list of some of the strengths, weaknesses, and applications of some of the more common products. While systematic withdrawal strategies tend to favor market investments due to their high returns, the strategy is in some way agnostic when it comes to products. Systematic withdrawal strategies just want to generate the highest level of risk for the lowest level of return. So if one product, like an annuity, can provide a higher rate of return for lower amount of risk than a bond, then the annuity would likely win out for the increased income.

- Bond mutual funds, which are actively managed, may be appropriate for the income producing portion of the portfolio.
- Deferred fund annuities may be appropriate for the income producing portion of the portfolio. Surrender charges should be avoided.
- Deferred variable annuities may be appropriate for the equity side of the portfolio held for the later years. They can help to protect the withdrawal rate.
- Growth and value equity funds might be appropriate for the side of the portfolio held for later years.
- Mutual funds are excellent vehicles for tax-deferred products such as IRAs and 401(k) funds.
- Managed funds or ETFs where the growth can be taxed as capital gains can be beneficial products for the systematic withdrawal method.
- Individual bonds work for the current income producing side of the systematic withdrawal portfolio.
- Bond UITs (unit investment trusts) have target maturity dates for the bond portfolio and can give the client the best of diversification as well as maturity dates (with low cost).
- Individual stocks can be used in the growth portion but can present a risk if the entire portfolio is not properly diversified.
- Treasuries and high quality bonds may be able to provide income when equity markets are down.
- The role of bonds is different when the client is taking distributions and has an additional responsibility to manage volatility. The principal of the bond becomes the

source of the withdrawal. The changing value of bonds is meaningful to the retirement income portfolio.

Planning Point: Avoid purchasing bonds that are likely to decline in price the most when equities also suffer big losses. They will not be helpful to provide sustainable withdrawals. Additionally, try to hold bonds inside of tax-advantaged vehicles like a Roth or IRA whenever possible due to the tax-deferred nature on growth of both vehicles. However, stocks already have preferential tax treatment and can be held in brokerage accounts to receive long-term capital gains treatment.

Target date mutual funds may also be used in a retirement portfolio. These funds are really designed to get you to retirement, not get you through retirement. Target date funds can be too conservative for the entirety of retirement. For example, a target date fund for any given year might have a wide range of how much is invested in equities. A financial planner must be aware of the underlying allocation of a target date fund. Balanced, diversified target funds can be good, but (1) the wide range of equity funds for the same year can be misleading; (2) the granularity of owning pieces individually may be important for systematic withdrawals; (3) planners need to be aware of how the asset allocation will change over time (and it's hard to map this); (4) if a planner is familiar with the details of the target date fund, it may work for the client. Furthermore, the target date fund is probably not well suited to be the only investment for the client even if the asset allocation within the fund appears appropriate.

LO 22.6 Review the bucketing approach to retirement income planning.

bucket approach

time-based segmentation approach

age-banded approach

The **bucket approach**, also referred to as the **time-based segmentation approach** or the **age-banded approach**, sets aside different investments for different time periods in order to match up investment risk to income needs. For instance, the near-term bucket or time horizon is usually filled with low-risk investments such as cash and bonds while the far-term buckets are filled with the riskiest growth portfolio assets. Income for each year comes out of the current bucket of assets. The biggest challenge of a bucket approach tends to be answering the question of when and how to refill the near-term buckets with safe income sources over the course of retirement. Generally speaking, once the first bucket is depleted, assets from the second segment are used for income. However, this requires reallocating a portion of each bucket in order to ensure the client does not get too heavily invested in high risk assets as they age.

Instead of looking at the portfolio as a whole, this method will break the portfolio into a series of groups. Most bucket strategies use three to five buckets or time periods. For instance, bucket one could include the spending goals from ages 60 to 70. This bucket accounts for travel, Medicare premiums, and other costs. As such, the financial planner will design a portfolio that meets that time horizon and goal, putting the most secure assets in the near-term bucket because these are the most likely to occur and are needed the soonest so their time horizon is the shortest. As such, risky assets should not be used to fund these near-term goals.

A second bucket, with spending goals from ages 70 to 80, will be filled with a better mix of assets. The financial planner will invest this time frame differently because there is a longer time horizon. This could be a 50% stock and 50% bond portfolio, but it will depend in part on the retiree's goals and overall funding status. The third bucket, spending goals from age 80+, will again see a different mix of investments. This bucket will most likely be made up of primarily growth assets like stocks, mutual funds, and perhaps a variable annuity.

As described, several different age bands are used. Each band has its own specific goals. Each band has its own time horizon. However, the buckets are also determined based on the individual's time horizon, market trends, assets, and risk tolerance.

By way of illustration, Chuck and Sarah divide their retirement portfolio into three "buckets." The first bucket will be used to provide their income from ages 65–75. This bucket will be invested more conservatively than the other two parts of their retirement assets. The second bucket will be used to provide income from ages 75–85 and can be invested with a moderate amount of aggressiveness (moderate risk/moderate return). The third bucket can be used to provide the needed income from ages 85–95 and can be invested with the highest tolerable degree of aggressiveness (higher risk/higher return).

The bucket approach to retirement income planning calls for special attention to be paid to investment products used for the "near-term" bucket. Buckets beyond the near-term bucket can use many of the products used with systematic withdrawals. The bucket approach uses more investment accounts than the systematic withdrawal approach. A financial services professional and his or her client will want to identify and work with the short-term money bucket, so these assets must be specifically identified and segregated. The short-term bucket is less likely to be able to use institutional shares because of the lower amount of resources devoted to it. The short-term bucket will rely on a more retail approach. The short-term bucket needs to remove volatility for the client. The short-term bucket is usually more cash heavy. In the aggregate, the systematic withdrawal approach and bucket approach may have a similar asset allocation model.

The long-term buckets are typically subject to more volatility because the "safe" assets are clustered in the near-term bucket, and the long-term bucket includes more of the "risky" assets. The short-term bucket identifies where the cash flows come from for the next set of years in the client's life. Short-term buckets invest in cash, individual bonds, bond UITs with clear maturity dates, and fixed annuities with fixed maturity time horizons.

Short-term buckets not only identify that the portfolio will liquidate what it needs, but also identify where the money will come from for the next few years, and they specifically identify the assets which are to be liquidated. A client using a short-term bucket knows exactly where the cash is coming from. The products that are used need to reflect the client's knowledge of where the money is coming from. Products in the short-term bucket should minimize liquidation fees and transaction costs. Any "distant" buckets will be more identified with the equity investment portion of the need for asset allocation.

Bucketing can be very beneficial as a strategy from a behavioral finance perspective. Bucketing allows clients to easily do mental accounting of their assets and visualize why they have safe assets and why they have growth assets. Presenting growth assets as in a bucket for future needs can also lessen concerns about holding volatile assets because they are not needed for the short term. However, as mentioned before, the biggest challenge of a bucket approach is figuring out how to rebalance the buckets over time. As the short-term bucket is used up and exhausted, riskier assets will need to be liquidated to refill the safe investments and short-term bucket. As such, this can be a challenge if the market drops. Do you refill the short-term bucket that year or can you wait a few years to replenish the assets? Financial planners use different tests and measurements in order to determine the best way to rebalance. Some look at funding status, and if the client is overfunded for retirement that is a good time to "lock" in gains and rebalance. For others, a look at PE ratios or some other market measurement is used to figure out if it's a good time to sell assets. Even more just rebalance on a calendar year model, which is the simplest and cheapest, but perhaps not always the most efficient.

LO 22.7   **Describe the flooring approach to retirement income planning.**

essential-versus-discretionary approach

flooring approach

Another strategy commonly utilized for generating retirement income is the **essential-versus-discretionary approach**, also known as flooring. The **flooring approach** starts by having the client categorize his or her retirement expenses as essential or discretionary and then builds a portfolio of investment and income sources to guarantee the essential expenses throughout retirement. Essentially, the flooring strategy creates a "floor" or baseline amount of guaranteed income each year to ensure that the client's basic needs are met. This strategy is often best for a more risk averse client who wants to remove the fear of not meeting basic expenses in retirement. Then, discretionary expenses are funded with more volatile assets either through a bucketing approach or a systematic withdrawal approach.

The flooring approach takes a much different view of retirement income planning than does the systematic or bucketing approach. While the systematic withdrawal and bucket approaches rely heavily on long-term returns and market assets to provide income later in retirement, the flooring strategy relies more heavily on guaranteed income sources. Regardless of which approach is used, Social Security (when available) creates at least a partial floor. Systematic withdrawal approach usually relies on the 4% rule being the floor, while bucketing only worries about a near-term floor. If someone is thinking about building a floor in retirement, the first thing they should do is defer Social Security to age 70. Deferring Social Security to 70 is more efficient than buying an annuity to provide that future income. However, annuities are a core piece of the flooring strategy as they are a way to provide guaranteed lifetime income.

A flooring approach does bring with it a number of challenges. First, it can be very difficult for a client to actually split out his or her income into essential and discretionary expenses. People do not like to change their current standard of living, so cutting out any normal expense could feel like a cut to essential expenses. Secondly, flooring can become very expensive. It is not always easy to generate risk-free returns. As you know, higher risk investments tend to provide higher returns over time, meaning you do not need as much money to make it through retirement if you are willing to take on some risk. If you want to floor most of your retirement income, it could take a lot of money.

Generally, with the flooring approach low-risk investments or annuity guarantees are selected to fund the essential expenses, and a mix of medium- and higher-risk investments is selected to fund the discretionary expenses. Income is drawn from the respective pools to cover essential and discretionary expenses.

By way of illustration, Cliff and Claire have essential expenses such as food, rent, and utilities that amount to $5,000 per month. Social Security will provide them with an inflation-protected $3,000 a month. Cliff and Claire buy an annuity with a cost of living rider that provides an inflation-protected $2,000 a month to augment Social Security to cover mandatory expenses. They then draw down income from the remainder of their assets to pay for their discretionary expenses.

The flooring approach to retirement planning calls for special products that reduce risk and provide guaranteed income to be used to set the floor. In other words, products used for essential spending are much different than products used for discretionary spending. Items included in the floor are basic needs such as food, shelter, clothing, and transportation.

Immediate annuities can serve as an excellent base for the floor (if the environment is right to purchase them). TIPs can also be used to set up a floor. Laddering annuities may help to set the floor. Immediate annuities become very viable at interest rates over 5%.

Discretionary expenses raise the following considerations:

- The products used depend on the importance of the expenditure to the client.
- There is a continuum of expenses in retirement ranging from critical for survival, to critical for enjoyment of life, to not critical at all but nice to have.
- Once a client has effectively set a floor, then he or she can choose products that fit his or her other goals and wishes.

Options for flooring include

- Social Security and inflation-adjusted fixed annuity
- I-bonds: These are attractive in today's interest rate environment and they also provide inflation protection
- TIPs

Options for discretionary expenses include

- equities and mutual funds
- deferred annuity with a death benefit
- stock mutual funds that invest in less liquid stocks

Regardless of what retirement income approach is utilized, the client will need a well-funded retirement. This starts with saving the right amount while working, investing in the right asset mix, and utilizing tax-advantaged savings vehicles like 401(k)s, IRAs, and Roth accounts. Furthermore, any retirement income approach also needs to consider human capital, employer-sponsored pension plans, and Social Security. Social Security is the largest retirement income source for most retirees and needs to be coordinated with any other assets. Decisions about asset allocation and income generation cannot be made in a vacuum but need to be coordinated with other assets and income sources. The best way to maximize retirement income is through a comprehensive retirement income plan. This plan could utilize any of the three retirement income approaches as each approach can align better for any individual retiree depending on his or her situation and risk tolerance levels. Retirement income planning is challenging, but a well-educated and prepared advisor can help craft the right plan for any client.

CHAPTER REVIEW

Key Terms and Concepts

human capital
safe savings rate
longevity risk
contingency fund
inflation risk
excess withdrawal risk
sequence of returns risk
health care and long-term care risks

frailty risk
systematic withdrawal approach
bucket approach
time-based segmentation approach
age-banded approach
essential-versus-discretionary approach
flooring approach

Chapter 22: Review Questions

Review questions are based on the learning objectives in this chapter. Thus, a [22.3] at the end of a question means that the question is based on learning objective 3. If there are multiple objectives, they are all listed.

1. What is the amount of money that Americans need saved in order to have a successful retirement? [22.1]

2. Is a client more likely to have access to a formal or informal phased retirement program at work? What is the difference between the two programs? [22.2]

3. What are the main benefits of phased retirement? [22.2]

4. Explain the "safe savings rate." [22.3]

5. Is the safe savings rate different for a more conservative investor or an investor willing to take on more risk? [22.3]

6. How can longevity risk impact a retirement income plan? [22.4]

7. What are some solutions to dealing with longevity risk? [22.4]

8. Is inflation usually more impactful for retirees in the short term or long term? [22.4]

9. What are some strategies for dealing with inflation in retirement? [22.4]

10. What is sequence of returns risk? [22.4]

11. How can a retiree mitigate sequence of returns risk in generating retirement income? [22.4]

12. What is the role of investment products in the systematical withdrawal strategy for generating retirement income? [22.5]

13. What is the 4% safe withdrawal rate rule's role in a systematic withdrawal strategy? [22.5]

14. Explain why the bucket strategy can be an effective retirement income plan from a behavioral finance perspective. [22.6]

15. How does the flooring strategy differ from the bucket and systematic withdrawal strategies? [22.7]

Chapter 22: Review Answers

1. There is no magic retirement savings number that guarantees a successful retirement. Instead, saving and planning for retirement requires a number of moving pieces and varies depending on each unique individual situation. Those with higher costs of living will need to save more money than those with lower costs of living. Additionally, retirement is all about income generation and not just about savings. Obviously, you need savings to produce the income, but savings alone will not create a successful retirement.

2. Clients are way more likely to see an informal phased retirement program than a formal program at work. Formal phased retirement programs are not very common in the United States, despite a high desire from Americans to continue working in retirement. A formal workplace phased retirement policy or program, if one exists, is usually contained in the personnel or employee handbook of the employer and explains how the employee can continue working with their current employer at a reduced schedule. An informal retirement program might allow an employee to reduce or modify his or her schedule, but occurs on a case-by-case basis from the employer and cannot be as easily relied upon or planned for by an employee.

3. Phased retirement has a lot of benefits. For example, continued employment income can significantly increase the client's cash flow and retirement security. Phased retirement also enables the individual to test drive retirement in order to figure out what they want and how they will find meaning in their life after work. Additionally, continued work can help retirees to find meaning in retirement.

4. In short, the safe savings rate tells a client what percentage of their salary they need to save in order to be financially prepared for retirement. The safe savings rate is the maximum of all the minimum necessary savings rates from overlapping historical periods needed to accumulate an individual's desired wealth in order to meet a certain level of spending in retirement. The safe savings rate will tell you how much you need to save over a 20, 30, or 40-year working career, as a percent of your salary, to replace either 50% or 70% of your final salary in retirement based on your investment asset allocation.

5. The safe savings rate is determined based on what the client invests in. A client with a more conservative portfolio of 40% in stocks and 60% in bonds will have to save more during his or her working years than someone with 80% in stocks and only 20% in bonds. As such, a more conservative investor will have to save more (a higher safe savings rate) than a more risk tolerant investor.

6. Longevity risk has a huge impact on retirement income planning. Living just a few years longer than expected could mean you need hundreds of thousands of dollars more for retirement. Because no one can predict how long he or she will live, a retiree needs to secure an income stream to cover expenses in retirement for an unpredictable length of time. As such, longevity risk is really the risk of outliving your savings because you live longer than expected. For example, if you plan to retire for 25 years, age 65 until 90, but you live until 95 and end up retiring two years earlier at 62, can your savings and income sources cover your expenses for an additional seven years? The answer for a lot of people is going to be no.

7. While longevity risk is hard to completely eliminate from a retirement income plan, you can transfer a lot of the risk onto someone else. You can greatly increase the likelihood that your money lasts throughout retirement by purchasing guaranteed lifetime sources of income like a deferred annuity or qualified longevity annuity contract (QLAC), by selecting the annuity distribution from your pension plan, or by deferring Social Security.

8. Inflation has a bigger impact over time because it compounds. Even a small inflation rate of 3% per year can double the cost of goods over the course of retirement due to compounding rates.

9. To protect a retiree from this decline in purchasing power, the retirement income plan needs to include inflation-adjusted or protected assets and income sources. To a certain extent, Social Security is inflation protected because it is geared toward increases in the consumer price index (CPI-W). This assumes, however, that the law will remain unchanged and that the CPI accurately reflects inflation as it affects seniors. There have been some unsuccessful attempts over the years to adjust Social Security's inflation protections by tying it more directly to the spending habits of seniors. Additionally, stocks and dividends tend to have some inflation protections. Dividend income from a stock portfolio is generally considered to be inflation protected if the principal is left intact. Treasury Inflation-Protected Securities (TIPS) can also be used as an effective inflation protection measure. TIPs are unique in that they are considered by most to be free of credit risk and also have an inflation protection. TIPs can help take the guesswork out of estimating inflation because they automatically adjust for changes in consumer prices.

10. Sequence of returns risk is the risk of receiving low or negative investment returns early in retirement when withdrawals are being made from those investments. Bad early years of returns in a portfolio subject to withdrawals can dramatically reduce the longevity and sustainability of that portfolio. This means a few bad years of returns

early in retirement can make a retiree run out of money later in retirement much earlier than someone who has good investments in the first few years of retirement.

11. Sequence of returns risk cannot be fully avoided if the retiree is invested in the market. However, it is important to remember that the risk is most impactful for retirement during the first few years in retirement and the last few years right before retirement. As such, there are a number of strategies used to help reduce the impact of sequence of returns risk. One strategy is to reduce the investment portfolio's volatility early in retirement. By reducing volatility in the retirement portfolio during the withdrawal stage, the sequence of returns risk is reduced. This can be done by (1) purchasing life annuities, (2) using bonds to build a specified income stream over a specified number of years, or (3) by investing in a better diversified portfolio of stocks.

12. While systematic withdrawal strategies tend to favor market investments due to their high returns, the strategy is in some ways agnostic when it comes to products. Systematic withdrawal strategies just want to generate the highest level of risk for the lowest level of return. So if one product, like an annuity, can provide a higher rate of return for a lower amount of risk than a bond, then the annuity would likely win out for the increased income. Investment products are sold each year in order to generate the income needed for the retiree.

13. Most systematic withdrawal strategies base the withdrawal guidelines at least in some part on the 4% safe withdrawal rate research. The reason is that the 4% safe withdrawal rate is viewed as a floor or baseline for most systematic withdrawal strategies. However, in practice, many strategies will assume a higher withdrawal rate and accept a 5-10% likelihood that the client runs out of money in the worst-case scenarios.

14. Bucketing can be very beneficial as a strategy from a behavioral finance perspective. Bucketing allows clients to easily do mental accounting of their assets and visualize why they have safe assets and why they have growth assets. Presenting growth assets as in a bucket for future needs can also lessen concerns about holding volatile assets because they are not needed for the short term.

15. The flooring approach takes a much different view of retirement income planning than the systematic or bucket approaches. While the systematic withdrawal and bucket approaches rely heavily on long-term returns and market assets to provide income later in retirement, the flooring strategy relies more heavily on guaranteed income sources. Investment products can be used solely for the purpose of removing risk, meaning that insurance plays a much bigger role for risk mitigation in the flooring

approach, whereas insurance products are only used to produce income in the other strategies.

Chapter 23

Additional Retirement Planning Issues

Learning Objectives

An understanding of the material in this chapter should enable the student to

- **LO 23.1** Identify what a client needs to know about the home as a financial asset.
- **LO 23.2** Describe housing alternatives, including age-restricted housing and life-care communities.
- **LO 23.3** List the factors to consider when a client decides to retire out of state.
- **LO 23.4** Review ways to use the home as a financial asset.
- **LO 23.5** Identify benefits that are included and excluded under Medicare.
- **LO 23.6** Identify the solutions to the pre-Medicare/postretirement health care gap.
- **LO 23.7** List and explain the characteristics of long-term care insurance policies.
- **LO 23.8** Identify the types of documents individuals can use to control their own medical care after they become unable to make decisions for themselves.

CHOOSING TO MOVE

LO 23.1 Identify what a client needs to know about the home as a financial asset.

Housing issues that face the retiree vary from client to client. Planners need to understand that the disposition of the family homestead and the decision of where to reside during the retirement years are, first and foremost, personal choices with a different meaning for every client. In other words, the psychological attachment to the home in many cases far outweighs the financial and tax wisdom involved with thinking of the home as an asset. It is in this context that financial services professionals must deal with planning for the disposition of a retired client's home. Factors to take into consideration include:

- Although one's house remains the same, the character of the neighborhood can change during retirement with the deaths and/or departures of friends.
- The house that was suitable for raising a family may not be suitable for retirement.

- The costs of heating, cooling, cleaning, and maintaining a house with empty rooms and a child-sized yard can be prohibitive.
- Even a mortgage-free house can be a financial drain that robs the retiree of income. Besides the additional costs involved in maintaining a home, the equity that can be gained from its sale can be used to provide needed retirement income.

Tax Implications of Selling a Home

When considering whether or not to move into another living arrangement, clients need to understand the tax implications of selling their home. Today the rules are quite liberal, and in most cases the gain will not be subject to federal income tax (note that some states do not follow the federal scheme). This means that if the client would prefer condo living or a smaller home, replacing the old home with a less expensive one will free up assets.

IRC Sec. 121

Specifically, **IRC Sec. 121** provides that taxpayers of any age who sell their homes can exclude up to $250,000 of their gain ($500,000 for married taxpayers filing jointly). To qualify for the exclusion, the property must have been owned and used by the taxpayer as a principal residence for an aggregate of at least 2 years out of the 5 years ending on the date of sale.

For married taxpayers, both spouses have to meet the 2-year use requirement—otherwise the available exclusion is $250,000 rather than $500,000. However, the couple can qualify for the higher $500,000 amount even if just one spouse owns the home.

The exclusion may generally be used only once every 2 years. If a single taxpayer marries someone who has used the exclusion within the past 2 years, that taxpayer is allowed a maximum exclusion of $250,000 (rather than $500,000) until 2 years have passed since the exclusion was used by either spouse. If the taxpayer fails to meet the ownership and use rules and the sale of the home is due to a change of employment, change of health, or other "unforeseen" circumstance, a reduced exclusion may still be available.

Planning for a Move

downsize

A common reason for changing residences at retirement is to **downsize**—that is, to purchase a retirement residence that costs less than the one being sold in order to transfer a portion of the gain (enhanced by tax breaks) into cash for retirement. Retirees may also change residences to relocate to an area where their dollars can be stretched further because the living costs are lower. Others move to avail themselves of living circumstances uniquely geared to the retired population. These residences include life-care communities and other senior living arrangements. Still others move because they need current care, such as nursing homes and assisted living arrangements. Let us take a look at these issues, starting with life-care communities.

YOUR FINANCIAL SERVICES PRACTICE: RESIDENCE CHOICES LITERATURE

The Internet offers easy access to a wealth of information about senior housing. Several resources are listed here. See www.seniorresource.com for housing information for seniors. The American Seniors Housing Organization (www.seniorhousing.com) is an organization for those in the senior housing industry. Senior sites (www.seniorsites.com) list housing and services offered through nonprofit organizations. New LifeStyles (www.newlifestyles.com) is a resource for senior residential care housing options. Finally, AARP (www.aarp.org) is an excellent resource for a wide range of information for seniors.

Life-Care Communities

LO 23.2 Describe housing alternatives, including age-restricted housing and life-care communities.

life-care community

There are many varieties of **life-care communities** (also called continuing-care retirement communities) throughout the United States. In fact, because of the number of options that exist, it may be best to explain what life-care communities are by explaining what they are not. Life-care communities are not simply retirement villages where people over a specified age reside; nor are they simply nursing homes where senior patients go for custodial and medical care. A life-care community is a combination of the two extremes, plus a little bit of everything in between. Although life-care communities are often thought to be only for the wealthy, the truth is that there are substantial variations in price among these communities, and the majority of them are nonprofit organizations.

While it is true that facilities, fees, and services vary widely from one life-care community to the next, several common features do exist. Most frequently your clients will pay a one-time up-front fee that is often fairly expensive as the average in 2014 was roughly $250,000. In some cases, the fee is nonrefundable; in others, the fee is fully refundable if the individual retiree, couple, or surviving spouse leaves. And in still other cases, the fee is refundable based on an agreed-upon schedule. In addition to a one-time up-front fee, residents generally pay a monthly fee that can range from less than $1,000 per month to more than $12,000 per month. In part, the monthly fee depends on the dwelling unit chosen and any services rendered.

The residential accommodation may be a single-family dwelling or an apartment. It can change with the retiree's needs to a skilled-nursing facility or a long-term care facility. Most life-care communities point with pride to the safety of the facility and its accessibility to those who are suffering from one or more diseases associated with aging.

Services may include the following:

- some level of housekeeping, including linen service
- some level of meal preparation (taking one or more meals in a common dining hall)
- facilities for crafts, tennis, golf, and other types of recreation
- transportation to and from area shopping and events
- supervision of exercise and diet
- skilled-nursing care (if needed)
- long-term care, including custodial care (if needed)

One key element to the life-care contract is the guarantee of space in a nursing home or assisted living facility if it becomes necessary. The guarantee of long-term care can be approached in several ways. One approach is to pay in advance—generally through a large up-front fee—for unlimited nursing home care at little or no increase in monthly payments. Another approach is to cover nursing home care up to a specified amount with a per diem rate paid by your client for usage over and above the specified amount. Today a wide range of contracts are available. As some potential residents have balked at large nonrefundable initial fees, some contracts even offer an equity approach—allowing the resident or the estate to recover the initial fee through selling the interest back to the facility or to a third party.

Retirees need to be careful when choosing a life-care community. With such a large financial commitment, the retiree will want to scrutinize contract details. Many of these arrangements are difficult to undo later if the resident is not satisfied. Also it's critical to review the financial health of the organization to ensure that it will be able to fulfill its long-term promises.

Other Housing Options

age-restricted housing

There is a wide range of senior housing arrangements between independent living and a life-care community. **Age-restricted housing** options include apartment buildings, retirement hotels, condominiums, subdivisions, and mobile home parks. These housing communities can provide safety, companionship, and special services. It is not uncommon for these communities to have special recreation and leisure facilities, such as golf courses, craft rooms, swimming pools, game rooms, and libraries. Many housing communities also contain amenities to make living almost self-contained—for example, food stores, banks, hairdressers, and other services.

Under the Federal Fair Housing law, a community can restrict age but only if the rules of one of two statutory exemptions are followed. Under the first, a community can restrict residents to age 62 or older. However, if this limitation is imposed, no individuals younger than that age are allowed. This could cause a problem if a retiree moved in and later found that a child or grandchild needed housing. A more flexible exemption allows a community to limit eligibility to age 55. With this exception, some individuals under age 55 can be allowed as long as 80 percent of all residents are 55 or older and at least one resident in each living unit is aged 55 or older. This alternative is often a better option for many retirees.

Of course, age-restricted housing is not for everyone; some find this type of living depressing and prefer being in a broader community with a variety of ages. A client needs to weigh this concern with the services offered by the facility.

Relocation Out of State

LO 23.3 **List the factors to consider when a client decides to retire out of state.**

The decision to relocate to another state is often motivated by such factors as climate, location of friends and relatives, and affection for the area itself. For clients considering such a move, it is important to weigh the decision carefully because it is not easily reversible. Factors to consider with respect to relocating out of state include:

domicile

- If one spouse should die, will the other want to cope with another uprooting?
- What are state income taxes, property taxes, transfer taxes, and death taxes?
- For the client with more than one home, which state would be declared the domicile? (**Domicile** is the client's intended permanent home. Such factors as where the client spends time, is registered to vote, has a driver's license, where his or her planner resides, and where his or her will is executed help to determine what residence is the client's permanent home.)
- Does the state or local government provide specific tax breaks for seniors?

Finally, before any move, the individual should consider looking for a replacement home that is equipped to meet his or her needs. Obviously, changes could later be made to a home, but it would probably be less expensive to purchase a home that already includes such characteristics.

PLANNING FOR CLIENTS REMAINING IN THEIR HOMES

A financial planner may look at a client's large, four-bedroom house and see unnecessary heating and maintenance costs. The client, on the other hand, sees the extra rooms as necessary for returning children and visiting relatives. There are other benefits to remaining in a current home. Starting life over in a new location means developing new routines, finding new merchants and service providers, and losing old friends and neighbors who can be relied on for companionship and favors. The value of the retiree's social network is often crucial to his or her sense of well-being. The reality is that most clients will want to age in place and stay in their current home for as long as possible in retirement. Homeowners as they age become attached to their home and become less and less likely to move out willingly the longer they stay in the home in retirement.

Retirees who stay in their homes will probably want to make some changes to make the home safer and to minimize ongoing maintenance. This means taking actions such as adding guard rails in the shower and slip-proofing bathroom and tub floors and other floor surfaces. The outside of the home should be examined for cracked or uneven sidewalks and inadequate lighting. Additional handrails may be appropriate both inside and outside the house. Other changes that might be helpful to reduce ongoing home maintenance are the addition of siding or replacement windows. Appliances such as dishwashers, garbage disposals and compactors, central vacuuming systems, and water filters (versus bottled water) can reduce daily labor.

Retirees who stay in their homes also need to be prepared for the possibility of needing additional services. This requires financial readiness, but also research to see what is available in their area. The types of services that may be needed include:

- outdoor home maintenance and gardening
- indoor home maintenance
- cleaning services
- driving services
- home care ranging from meal preparation to help with bathing and dressing

- emergency call/response systems

Creating Income from the Home

LO 23.4 Review ways to use the home as a financial asset.

Clients who have paid off their mortgages and want to "age in place" may still be able to tap the equity in their homes if they need finances to maintain their current standard of living. There are a number of options for this group, including a sale-leaseback, a home-sharing arrangement, and a reverse mortgage. The reality is that home equity is the largest asset for most Americans. As such, financial advisors need to consider the home and home equity when doing comprehensive financial planning. Additionally, advisors doing "comprehensive" or "retirement income" planning need to better incorporate home equity into their process. Sometimes this even requires advisors to push back against compliance in order to enact planning changes. That does not mean that an advisor should ignore compliance, but at times advisors need to challenge the status quo in order to do better planning.

sale-leaseback

Under a **sale-leaseback arrangement**, your client sells his or her house to an investor and then rents it back from the investor under a lifetime lease. Thus, your client can garner extra retirement resources, make use of the home sale exclusion, and still remain in his or her home. Often the purchaser is a family member, because the sale of the house removes it from the retiree's estate. The sale-leaseback agreement can specify future rents or stipulate how changes in the rental rate will be determined (for example, a periodic market value appraisal by a neutral third party). The agreement should also clearly spell out that it is the new owner's responsibility to pay property taxes, special assessments, insurance, and major maintenance and repairs.

Another way to use the home as an asset is a home-sharing arrangement. Home sharing helps people stay independent; it can also provide companionship and reduce housing costs. In forging a home-sharing arrangement, the client should carefully consider what he or she is looking for. Is the arrangement more about friendship and companionship or simply a means of lowering expenses? Either motivation can result in a successful relationship, as long as the parties entering into the arrangement are clear. If the arrangement is with a relative or friend, it is important either to enter into a formal agreement or at least to discuss expectations about how the arrangement will work and also to agree on how the arrangement will end.

Reverse Mortgages

reverse mortgage

A **reverse mortgage** is a loan against an individual's home that requires no repayment as long as the individual continues to live in the home. In other words, a reverse mortgage is a strategy that allows a client to live in his or her home and take substantial amounts of money for current needs with no current payments. Except for certain special needs loans offered by state or local government programs, virtually all reverse mortgages today are made under the federally sponsored Home Equity Conversion Mortgage (HECM) program. Lenders are willing to make reverse mortgage loans, since the FHA insures HECM loans to protect lenders against loss if amounts withdrawn exceed equity when the property is sold. Any lender authorized to make HUD-insured loans, such as banks, mortgage companies, and savings and loan associations, can participate in the HECM program.

Under the HECM program, loans are only available when all of the owners are aged 62 or older or if a married couple owns the residence and at least one of them is aged 62 or older and when their home is the principal residence. The homeowners must live in the home. New rules in 2014 allow for one spouse to take out a reverse mortgage in his or her name only and still protect the nonborrowing spouse. If that spouse dies, the surviving spouse can still live in the home as long as tax, insurance, and maintenance costs are paid. Also, if the home has a current mortgage, balance must be paid off at the time the reverse mortgage is made. A unique feature of these loans is that the borrower must receive consumer information from a HECM certified counselor before obtaining the loan.

The amount of loan payments made to the client under the HECM program depends on the youngest borrower's age, the lesser of the appraised value of the home or the current HECM lending limit (currently $636,150 in 2017), and the interest rate and fees that are being charged. For example, using one of the available loan estimators,[1] a 70-year-old could borrow approximately 65 percent of the value of the home while an 80-year-old could borrow approximately 70 percent. The loan estimator is a good place to identify the fees involved. In addition to loan initiation fees and other closing costs, HECM loans require insurance premiums to support the FHA insurance program. There is an initial premium based on the value of the home, and an annual premium applied to the outstanding loan balance. In 2013, the HECM program was simplified. Today, borrowers will be charged an upfront initial mortgage insurance premium (MIP) at closing of .5 percent or 2.5 percent of the home value, depending on the amount of initial loan disbursement. Additionally, the borrower will have to pay other traditional closing costs like third party charges, origination fees, and servicing fees. However,

---

1. *Reverse Mortgage, Getting Started.* Your Guide to Reverse Mortgages, 2015. http://www.reversemortgage.org.

many lenders offer credits like in the forward mortgage world to help offset some of these costs. The reverse mortgage loan still requires an ongoing 1.25 percent annual mortgage premium (which increases the loan interest rate by 1.25 percent) on the amount of outstanding debt.

In addition, the HECM program has been made more difficult to qualify for by HUD due to concerns over the number of technical defaults occurring. As such, individuals applying for a HECM will now need to undergo a financial assessment to ensure that there will be enough income to pay living expenses. Additionally, an individual could be required to set-aside funds in order to pay property taxes and other fees. This could reduce the total amount of available reverse mortgage assets for the homeowner.

Under the HECM program, borrowers may choose one of five payment options, or a mix of the options:

- *tenure*, which gives the borrower a monthly payment from the lender for as long as the borrower lives and continues to occupy the home as a principal residence
- *term*, which gives the borrower monthly payments for a fixed period selected by the borrower
- *line of credit*, which allows the borrower to make withdrawals up to a maximum amount, at times and in amounts of the borrower's choosing
- *modified tenure*, which combines the tenure option with a line of credit
- *modified term*, which combines the term option with a line of credit

YOUR FINANCIAL SERVICES PRACTICE: FINDING A REVERSE MORTGAGE PROGRAM

To find out more about the HECM program call (888-466-3487) or visit HUD at www.hud.gov for lists of approved counseling agencies that counsel individuals about the program and of approved lenders. Additional information is available from two nonprofit organizations: the American Association of Retired Persons (AARP) Home Equity Conversion Information Center (202-434-6044) and the National Center for Home Equity Conversion (NCHEC) at 7373 147th St., Room 115, Apple Valley MN 55124. To find out about other types of reverse mortgage programs, visit the National Reverse Mortgage Lenders Assn. at www.reversemortgage.org or call 202-939-1765 for an up-to-date list of lenders that clearly tells you which reverse mortgage products are offered by each listed lender.

The amount of the debt grows based on the amount paid, any fees that are financed, and accumulated interest. Typically, the loan only has to be repaid when the last surviving borrower dies, sells the home, or permanently moves away. Reverse mortgages are by definition nonrecourse, meaning the maximum amount that has to be repaid is the value of the home. If property values have eroded, the borrower has received a windfall and the lender ends up with a loss. However, the HECM program is insured by the extra mortgage insurance premium that is paid, to ensure that the lenders do not take a loss. Lenders transfer the debt obligation to the Government once the loan reaches a certain threshold. When the loan is repaid, any interest paid is deductible just like regular mortgage interest. Additionally, it is important to remember that you can make monthly payments on a reverse mortgage. Very few people do, but you can.

Because these programs are truly loans, if the retiree wants or needs to sell the home, any equity that exceeds the loan balance is the property of the retiree. If the property is sold at death, the heirs receive the additional equity. Also, because these are loans, payments received by the retiree as part of the mortgage program are not considered taxable income and interest expense is deductible but only at the time it is paid (when the loan is repaid). Reverse mortgages are no longer the reverse mortgage of the past. Financial advisors need to understand the program and recognize when it might be appropriate for a client. There are three main ways a reverse mortgage can be utilized. First, a reverse mortgage can be used to pay off a traditional mortgage, stemming the outflow of cash each month for the retiree. This is really a cash flow management situation. A second strategy is by setting up a line of credit reverse mortgage the retiree can borrow from the line of credit when the stock market drops. This is really a substitution for a cash buffer strategy. Lastly, a reverse mortgage can simply be used as a way to generate more cash flow for the retiree to meet his or her needs. Professor Wade Pfau has a reverse mortgage book on the market which can be a great resource to anyone wanting to learn more about the product and how to effectively use them. Unfortunately, very few financial advisors or financial service companies are using reverse mortgage and home equity best practices today.

YOUR FINANCIAL SERVICES PRACTICE:
USING A REVERSE MORTGAGE IN A RETIREMENT PLAN

There are a number of ways that clients (along with their advisors) are choosing to use reverse mortgages in retirement planning. Here are a few common options.

- <u>Meet emergency expenses:</u> Some take out a line of credit which is used to meet extraordinary expenses in retirement, allowing the individual to remain in the home and live more comfortably. An advantage to this approach is that the outstanding balance on the loan grows slowly, saving home equity for other purposes.
- <u>Funding long-term care needs:</u> Home equity can be an integral part of planning for long-term care expenses. Home care can be funded with a reverse mortgage and institution care can be funded in part with the sale of a home. Some make this the primary funding approach, although a better approach may be to use home equity as

a supplement to long-term care insurance or other funding source.
- **Paying off a mortgage:** More borrowers today are using reverse mortgages to reduce monthly expenses by paying off an outstanding mortgage. This approach may be effective, but it is likely to use up a large amount of the home equity.
- **Increasing monthly income:** Another common approach is to choose a tenure option and receive monthly payments as long the borrower remains in the home. This can supplement other income, while using up equity slowly as the outstanding balance of the loan grows slowly with monthly payments and accumulated interest.
- **Funding the deferral of Social Security benefits:** A newer strategy is to use a line of credit to borrow in the early years of retirement, to afford the deferral of Social Security benefits.

MEDICARE AND RETIREE HEALTH CARE

LO 23.5 Identify benefits that are included and excluded under Medicare.

Any discussion of planning for a retiree's health care should start with an analysis of the Medicare system. Today, discussing Medicare is a fairly complex proposition, because eligible persons can choose from the original system as well as a number of other options.

Medicare Part A

Medicare Part B

The original Medicare program consists of two parts. **Medicare Part A** is the hospital portion. It provides benefits for expenses incurred in hospitals, skilled-nursing facilities, hospices (in limited circumstances), and for home health care for a condition previously treated in a hospital or skilled-nursing facility. **Medicare Part B** is the supplementary medical insurance portion of Medicare. It provides benefits for physicians' and surgeons' fees, diagnostic tests, certain drugs and medical supplies, rental of certain medical equipment, and home health service when prior hospitalization has not occurred. Part C of Medicare is a series of options that beneficiaries can elect in lieu of the original program. Part D is a drug benefit that is available to all Medicare beneficiaries. Let's take a closer look at the entire Medicare system, starting with the question of eligibility.

Eligibility for Medicare

Most of your senior clients will be eligible to receive health benefits under the federal government's Medicare program. Part A is available at no cost to most persons aged 65 or older. Among those eligible are:

- everyone aged 65 and over who is receiving a monthly Social Security retirement or survivor's benefit
- people aged 65 and over who have deferred receiving Social Security retirement benefits (these people must apply for Medicare; others in "pay status" are automatically enrolled)
- 65-year-old civilian employees of the federal government who did not elect into the Social Security system under the 1983 law
- people who receive or are eligible to receive railroad retirement benefits
- any spouse aged 65 and over of a fully insured worker who is at least aged 62

Any other people (aged 65 or older) who do not meet the requirements to receive Part A at no cost may voluntarily enroll by paying a premium ($413 per month in 2017). Any person enrolled for Part A of Medicare is eligible for Part B. However, a monthly premium must be paid. This annually adjusted premium represents only about 25 percent of the cost of the benefits provided for many clients. For retirees with modest income the Part B premium in 2017 is $134 per month. Medicare Part B enrollees with higher incomes ($85,000 single, $170,000 MFJ) will pay higher premiums based on the extent their income exceeds the threshold. See the chart below.

Medicare: Part B Monthly Premium Changes

The Medicare Modernization Act require those with higher incomes to pay a greater percentage of Medicare Part B costs. Before the law change, Part B beneficiaries were responsible for premiums approximately equal to 25 percent of the total cost of the benefit. (The federal government pays the remaining 75 percent.) In order to bolster Medicare's sustainability, beneficiaries with incomes over specified thresholds now pay a higher percentage of the total cost, depending on their income level. Income earned 2 years prior is used to determine the applicable premium for the year. This means that income earned in 2015 is used to determine premiums for 2017 as listed below.

	2015 Modified Adjusted Gross Income	Part B Premium 2017
Single	$85,000 or less	$134
MFJ	$170,000 or less	
Single	Over $85,000 up to $107,000	$187.50
MFJ	Over $170,000 up to $214,000	
Single	Over $107,000 up to $160,000	$267.90
MFJ	Over $214,000 up to $320,000	
	2015 Modified Adjusted Gross Income	Part B Premium 2017
Single	Over $160,000 up to $214,000	$348.30
MFJ	Over $320,000 up to $428,000	
Single	Over $214,000	$428.60
MFJ	Over $428,000	

Enrolling in Medicare is quite simple. Those who will have started receiving Social Security at or before age 65 will receive a notice that they will be automatically enrolled at age 65. If a client does not want Part B coverage, he or she must reject it in writing within 2 months of receiving the notice. Others should contact their local Social Security office (see the phone book for the local address and phone number or go online at medicare.gov about 3 months before their 65th birthday to sign up for Medicare.

YOUR FINANCIAL SERVICES PRACTICE: MISCONCEPTIONS ABOUT MEDICARE ELIGIBILITY

Clients can have several misconceptions about eligibility for Medicare that should be corrected. It is important to point out the following:

- Those who retire early and elect to start Social Security at age 62 are not eligible for Medicare until they reach age 65.
- Spouses who are younger than 65 and are married to a retiree over age 65 are not eligible for Medicare until they turn 65.
- Despite the Part B premiums, the system offers a relatively good value. In other words, rejecting Part B coverage to avoid paying premiums is not usually the best choice.

Part A Benefits

benefit period

lifetime reserve days

Part A pays for inpatient hospital services for up to 90 days in each **benefit period** (also referred to as a *spell of illness*). Benefit period is a key concept. A benefit period begins the first time a Medicare recipient is hospitalized and ends only after the recipient has been out of a hospital or skilled-nursing facility for 60 consecutive days. A hospitalization after that 60-day period then begins a new benefit period. There is no limit on the number of benefit periods a person may have during his or her lifetime. In addition to 90 days of hospital coverage within each benefit period, Medicare covers an additional 60 **lifetime reserve days** over an individual's lifetime.

> **EXAMPLE**
>
> Barbara goes into the hospital for 45 days, goes home for 2 weeks, and returns to the hospital for 80 days. Barbara's 125 days of hospitalization will be considered to be within one benefit period because there was not a gap of 60 days between hospital visits. Barbara is covered for 90 days under the benefit period rule. In addition, Barbara chose to use 35 of her reserve days to cover the full amount of time she spent in the hospital (125 days).

Covered services for Part A hospital benefits include what you would expect, including operating expenses, semi-private room and meals, nursing services, social services, use of hospital equipment, rehabilitation services, and diagnostic testing. In each benefit period, covered hospital expenses are paid in full for 60 days, subject to an initial deductible of $1,260 per benefit period. A coinsurance charge applies to each of the next 30 days (days 61–90), and a larger coinsurance charge applies to lifetime reserve days.

In many cases, a patient may no longer require continuous hospital care but may not be well enough to go home. Consequently, Part A provides benefits for care in a skilled-nursing facility. This coverage can be triggered only if a physician certifies that skilled-nursing care or rehabilitative services are needed for a condition that was treated in a hospital within the last 30 days. Days 1-20 are fully covered for each benefit period. The Part A skilled-nursing facility per diem for days 21 through 100 is $164.50 (2017). Days 101 and beyond are not covered by original Part A Medicare.

Starting in 1998, Parts A and B of Medicare began to share the costs of providing home health care. If a patient can be treated at home for a medical condition, Part A will pay up to the full cost for up to 100 home visits by a home health agency, but only if the visits occur after a hospital or skilled-nursing facility stay. Home health agencies specialize in providing nursing services and other therapeutic services. Part B covers additional visits or visits that do not occur after a hospital stay. To receive these benefits, a person must be confined at home and treated under a home health plan set up by a physician. The care needed must include skilled-nursing services, physical therapy, or speech therapy.

Hospice benefits are available under Part A of Medicare for terminally ill persons who have a life expectancy of 6 months or less. The election of hospice benefits has an effect on the participant's other eligible benefits under Medicare.

There are some circumstances under which Part A of Medicare will not pay benefits. Luxury services and elective surgeries are not covered and most services provided outside of the United States are not covered. Procedures performed in a federal facility, such as a veterans' hospital, and services covered under workers' compensation are also excluded. In other cases, Medicare is the secondary payer of benefits. This is the case:

- when primary coverage under an employer-provided medical expense plan is elected by (1) an employee or spouse aged 65 or older or (2) a disabled beneficiary
- when medical care can be paid under any liability policy, including policies providing automobile no-fault benefits

- in the first 18 months for end-stage renal disease when an employer-provided medical expense plan provides coverage. By law, employer plans cannot specifically exclude this coverage during the 18-month period.

Medicare pays only if complete coverage is not available from these sources, and then only to the extent that benefits are less than would otherwise be payable under Medicare.

Part B Benefits

Part B (medical insurance) helps cover medically-necessary doctors' services, outpatient care, home health services, durable medical equipment, and other medical services. Part B also covers many preventive services. Medicare's annual publication "Medicare and You" is the best place to look to identify specific services that are covered. Remember that you will pay a monthly premium while enrolled in Part B. The part B premium is determined in part by your modified adjusted gross income as reported on your IRA tax return from 2 years ago.

With some exceptions, Part B pays 80 percent of the approved charges for covered medical expenses after the satisfaction of an annual deductible ($183 in 2017). Out-of-hospital psychiatric services are generally limited to 50 percent reimbursement. Annual maximums may also apply to some services, such as psychiatric services and physical therapy.

What may be more important than what is covered is what is not covered by Part B, some of which represents significant expenses for senior clients. They include the following:

- long-term custodial care
- routine dental and eye care
- dentures
- routine foot care
- cosmetic surgery
- hearing aids and exams for fitting hearing aids
- acupuncture

Part D Drug Benefits

Medicare Part D is a voluntary prescription drug benefit available to all

Medicare beneficiaries entitled to Part A and enrolled in Part B. There is an incentive to join when an individual first becomes eligible, as those who choose to defer coverage (and who do not have other creditable prescription drug coverage), will pay a late enrollment penalty if they join later. Obtaining Medicare prescription drug coverage requires joining a plan run by an insurance company or other private company approved by Medicare. Each plan can vary in cost and specific drugs covered, although there are required minimum benefits and every plan must cover at least two prescription drugs in each therapeutic category and class.

There are two ways to get prescription drug coverage, stand alone Medicare Prescription Drug Plans, and Medicare Advantage Plans (like an HMO or PPO) or other Medicare health plans that offer Medicare prescription drug coverage.

Most drug plans charge a monthly fee that varies by plan that is paid in addition to the Part B premium. For those in a Medicare Advantage Plan that includes Medicare prescription drug coverage, the monthly premium may include an amount for prescription drug coverage. Also note that like the Part B premium, those with high earnings are required to pay both the plan's premium and an additional amount, based on income. The income thresholds are the same as for Part B.

Plans may also have a yearly deductible, and copayments or coinsurance amounts. Most Medicare drug plans have a coverage gap (also called the "donut hole"). This means that there's a temporary limit on what the drug plan will cover for drugs. The coverage gap begins after the participant and the plan have spent a certain amount for covered drugs. In 2017, once entering the coverage gap, the participant pays 40 percent of the plan's cost for covered brand-name prescription drugs. In 2017, once a participant has spent $3,700 on covered drugs they are in the coverage gap. In 2017, participants pay roughly 51 percent of the price of generic drugs in the coverage gap. However, the "donut hole" is being phased out each year until 2020 when the coverage cap will go away, providing retirees with much more complete prescription drug coverage under Part D.

Some plans offer additional coverage during the gap, like for generic drugs, but they may charge a higher monthly premium. In addition to the discount on covered brand name prescription drugs, there will be increasing coverage for drugs in the coverage gap each year until the gap closes in 2020, at which time you will just pay 25 percent. Once out of the coverage gap, catastrophic coverage requires only a small coinsurance amount or copayment for covered drugs for the rest of the year.

ADDITIONAL COVERAGE FOR THOSE ELIGIBLE FOR MEDICARE

Medigap insurance

For many years, individuals who wanted more coverage than the original Medicare plan could purchase a supplemental plan, generally called **Medigap insurance**, through an insurance company. This is still true, but today those eligible for traditional Medicare can now opt out of it in favor of a managed care plan. These alternatives typically limit the participant's choice of medical service providers in exchange for additional services. Also, some Medicare recipients may be eligible for retiree medical coverage at work. Each of these three options is discussed below.

No matter what the medical program, few if any cover long-term custodial care. For this contingency, many individuals should consider a long-term care policy. This is discussed in a later section of the chapter.

Medicare Supplement (Medigap) Insurance

For retired clients who do not have employer-provided insurance or who have inadequate amounts, there is Medicare supplement (Medigap) insurance. Medigap is a tool that can be used by private insurance planners to supplement the inadequacies of the Medicare program and to relieve seniors of part or all of their cost-sharing burden. In other words, as one expert puts it, Medigap "eliminates the risk of unpredictable and uncontrollable bills by converting them into a predictable and affordable series of insurance payments."

Medigap policies are regulated by both the state and the federal governments. Laws protect consumers and provide for the following:

- notice that no individual needs more than one Medigap policy
- notice that Medicaid-eligible individuals do not need a Medigap policy
- easy comparison among rival policies
- guaranteed renewability
- automatic policy changes whenever Medicare deductibles and coinsurance change

Most important is that the law guarantees that, for 6 months immediately following enrollment in Medicare medical insurance (Part B), a person aged 65 or older cannot be denied Medigap insurance because of health problems. To protect insurance companies, there is the possibility that a preexisting conditions clause will apply during the first 6 months of the policy's life. This clause, however, is the maximum insurer protection against adverse selection allowed under the law.

Every Medigap policy must be clearly identified as "Medicare Supplement Insurance." Insurance companies can only sell a "standardized" policy identified in most states by letters A–N. All policies offer the same basic benefits, but some offer additional benefits so you can choose which one meets your needs. In Massachusetts, Minnesota, and Wisconsin, medigap policies are standardized in a different way. Plans E, H, I, and J are no longer available to purchase, but policies in force are grandfathered.

In some states, a type of Medigap policy is available called Medicare SELECT. These are policies that require the use of specific hospitals and, in some cases, specific doctors or other health care providers to get full coverage.

Choosing a Medigap policy requires comparing benefits from the standardized policies and choosing the plan that results in the lowest possible out-of-pocket costs. For those with significant medical expenses, this may be accomplished by choosing a more comprehensive policy that has higher premiums but covers more. Medicare's publication, "Choosing a Medigap Policy: A Guide to Health Insurance for People with Medicare," can help a client choose a policy.

Managed Care Option under Medicare

Under Part C of Medicare, participants may now elect to have their Medicare benefits provided by a managed care plan such as a health maintenance organization (HMO), a preferred-provider organization (PPO), or an insurance company. The participant must still pay the Part B premium for Medicare and may—in some plans, in some regions of the country—have to pay an additional premium to the managed care plan.

Each managed care plan subcontracts for the Department of Health and Human Services to provide benefits at least equal to, and sometimes better than, those available under Medicare. Medicare then reimburses the managed care plan for services it provides to participants electing the managed care coverage. The managed care plans usually provide additional benefits, such as prescription drugs, eyeglasses, hearing aids, and routine physical exams; also, they usually eliminate deductibles and lower copay amounts to very nominal levels. These additional benefits are often similar to what is provided by Medigap policies. Because of this redundancy, those who choose Part C cannot be sold a Medicare supplement program.

The important factor in managed care plan operations is that services must be provided to participants by qualified providers who are affiliated with, or have contracted with, the plan.

The participant is not able to seek covered services from health care providers outside the plan except in emergencies.

By electing the managed care option, the participant gives up the right to covered benefits from any licensed provider of his or her choice. The choices are narrowed to those approved by the specific managed care plan. For these reasons, it may not be advisable for people who travel frequently or live part of the year outside the geographic region of the plan to select managed care.

Persons who elect the managed care option may drop the plan coverage and return to the regular Medicare program by notifying both the local Social Security office and the managed care plan. Medicare coverage will usually be restored within a month of the request.

There are some limits for those returning to Medicare on obtaining Part D and medigap supplements. The rules are complex, but it is an issue that someone choosing Part C needs to understand. This issue is covered in great detail in the annual "Medicare and You" Medicare publication.

YOUR FINANCIAL SERVICES PRACTICE: THE MEDICARE WEBSITE

The Medicare website can be an invaluable tool for you and your clients (medicare.gov). It contains search tools that can help you choose the best Medicare plan option and more. Below are search tools offered as links on the site.

Medicare Plan Finder	**Nursing Home Compare**
Helps you to compare health plans in your area	Compares nursing homes in your area
Pharmaceutical Assistance Programs	**Publications**
Shows programs that offer discounted or free medications	Views, orders, or downloads Medicare publications
Physician Compare	**Supplier Directory**
Locates Medicare participating physicians in your area	Locates participating Medicare suppliers in your area
Medicare Helpful Contacts	**Dialysis Facility Compare**
Finds phone numbers and websites	Compares dialysis facilities in your area
Your Medicare Coverage	**How to Compare Medigap Policies**
Shows your health care coverage in the original Medicare plan	Locates supplemental insurance policies to cover expenses not paid by Medicare
Your Plan Comparison	**Home Health Compare**
Compares health plans in your area	Compares home health care in your area

Employer-Provided Health Benefits

In addition to Medicare, some individuals (generally employees of large private and public employers) receive employer-provided health care coverage that continues after retirement. Although coverage has been shrinking in recent years, this type of benefit is still available to a significant number of employees in larger companies.

The types of plans provided by employers vary a great deal—some are quite generous and others pay only a small proportion of the retiree's medical expenses. Also, in most cases, the employer retains the right to amend or terminate benefits into the future.

If the retiring employee has to pay some or all of the premium for the plan, then he or she must decide whether to buy into the program or to pursue an individual Medigap policy. Even if the coverage is provided without cost, both the adviser and the retiree must fully understand the extent of the coverage in order to determine whether additional Medigap coverage is still necessary. Also note that some employers will actually offer retirees regular Medicare-supplement policies similar to those that individuals can buy on their own.

MEDICAL COVERAGE BEFORE ELIGIBILITY FOR MEDICARE

One problem that is not solved by a Medigap policy is the health gap that occurs after early retirement and before age 65 when Medicare (and Medigap) starts. Statistics show that slightly over 50 percent of those who retire early do not have employer-provided health insurance. For those in that group, the effect can be devastating. A financial planning challenge awaits clients and planners alike, especially because poor health may have been the reason for early retirement in the first place. Let's take a closer look at what can be done.

COBRA Coverage

The Consolidated Omnibus Budget Reconciliation Act of 1985 (COBRA) established the option for a retiring employee to buy into the employer's group health plan. COBRA continuation coverage allows an employee to continue health benefits under the employer's plan for 18 months after retirement. The period is extended to 29 months in the case of retirement due to disability and 36 months if the insurance is through a spouse's plan and the spouse dies, the couple divorces, or the spouse becomes eligible for Medicare.

The COBRA requirements apply to all health care plans of employers (except for churches) with 20 or more employees. If the employer has a medical plan but COBRA does not apply, state law may provide for a similar continuation requirement. The continuation period varies; it may be as short as 3 months and as long as 18 months.

Under COBRA, your client will take over the entire premium for coverage. This can equal the full cost of group coverage, and the employer can add an additional 2 percent for administrative charges. In many cases, the group coverage is a relative bargain, especially in cases of poor health or a preexisting condition, where comparable coverage is not available at any price. If the individual is healthy, he or she may want to compare the price of an individual policy to the COBRA benefits to get the best possible deal. COBRA coverage can be very expensive and might not be financially suitable for every client. Additionally, COBRA will not qualify as group health coverage from an active employer, even if the coverage is identical to the employer plan. This means, even if an individual has COBRA coverage, he or she will need to enroll in Medicare when they turn 65 as Medicare will be the primary payer and COBRA the secondary. However, in some cases COBRA coverage might qualify for creditable prescription drug coverage, allowing the individual to delay signing up for Part D without facing a late-enrollment penalty.

Other Options

LO 23.6 Identify the solutions to the pre-Medicare/postretirement health care gap.

One solution to the pre-Medicare health care gap can be coverage under a spouse's plan. For couples who can keep one spouse in the workforce, this coverage offers the best solution possible. A problem, however, is that one reason for early retirement may be to perform caregiving services for a spouse. In such cases—and in other cases—spousal coverage may not be a viable solution.

A second option is to purchase an individual policy. Surprisingly, this can be a viable solution in some instances. Individual policies may be available through a conversion from an employer provided group plan. If this is not the case, most states have a program to ensure that insurance is available. The problem with individual policies generally will not be their availability; it will be their prohibitive cost.

LONG-TERM CARE INSURANCE

The Need for Long-Term Care

LO 23.7   **List and explain the characteristics of long-term care insurance policies.**

As the nearly 78 million baby boomers move into retirement, the need for long-term care will soar. In addition to the growing need for long-term care services, the costs associated with long-term care are also expected to increase substantially over the next generation as traditional long-term care providers, such as family members, are becoming less available to provide care. As such, government funding, personal savings, and financial products, primarily long-term care insurance (LTCI), will be required to help fund these costs. Currently, the population aged 65 and over represents about 15 percent of the population, a figure that is expected to increase to between 20 and 25 percent over the next 50 years. The segment of the population aged 85 and over is growing at an even faster rate. While roughly 10 percent of the over-65 group is over 85 today, this percentage is expected to double over the next two generations.

Planners should keep in mind that the likelihood of a person needing long term care services increases dramatically with age. One percent of persons between the ages of 65 and 74 reside in nursing homes, and the percentage increases to 6 percent between the ages of 75 and 84. At ages 85 and over, the figure rises to approximately 25 percent. Additionally, 60 percent of all people will need some long-term care during their life and 40 percent of people will need long-term care in a facility at some point.

While government programs such as Medicaid, and to a lesser extent Medicare, provide the majority of long-term care funding in the U.S., out-of-pocket expenditures and long-term care insurance coverage is a crucial part of paying for long-term care needs. Nearly $50 billion is spent each year on nursing home care. In 2016, a year of long-term care in a semi-private nursing home room costs on average $82,125 according to Genworth's Annual Cost of Care study. However, certain states are well over $250,000. For example, Alaska, New York, Hawaii, DC, DE, NJ, CT, MA, NH, VT, and Maine all cost on average over $100,000 a year. This cost is increasing faster than inflation because of the growing demand for nursing home beds and the shortage of skilled medical personnel. The cost of complete long-term care for a client can be astronomical, with annual costs reaching over $100,000 for some people.

Characteristics of Individual Policies

For many types of insurance, policies are relatively standardized. For long-term care insurance, the opposite is true. Significant variations (and, therefore, differences in cost) exist from one insurance company to another. State laws also vary, although many have adopted some or all of the provisions in the model NAIC legislation. The model legislation limits provisions somewhat and also limits the way policies can be marketed. Additionally, state partnership programs put significant restrictions on policy provisions in order to have a policy qualify for the program.

Regardless of the state, a policyowner will typically have options with respect to various policy provisions. The following are a few of the key issues that need to be reviewed for each policy.

Issue Age

Substantial differences exist among insurance companies with respect to the age at which they will issue policies. There is considerably more variation with respect to the youngest age at which coverage will be written. Some companies have no minimum age. Other companies sell policies to persons as young as age 20. Still other companies have minimum ages in the 40-to-50 age range. Most companies also have an upper age of 80 or 85, beyond which coverage will not be issued. In addition to age limitations, these policies have medical underwriting requirements and many elderly people might not qualify for long-term care insurance coverage. As such, it can be a good planning idea to purchase a base long-term care insurance policy with a future purchase option for additional benefits to protect insurability both based on health and on age.

Benefits

Benefits under LTCI policies can be categorized by type of coverage, amount of benefit, duration of coverage, the ability to restore benefits, spousal benefits, return of premium riders, and a variety of inflation protections.

Types. There are several levels of care that are frequently provided by long-term care policies:

skilled-nursing care

- **skilled-nursing care**, which consists of daily nursing and rehabilitative care that can be performed only by, or under the supervision of, skilled medical personnel and must be based on a doctor's orders

intermediate care

- **intermediate care,** which involves occasional nursing and rehabilitative care that must be based on a doctor's orders and can be performed only by, or under the supervision of, skilled medical personnel

custodial care

- **custodial care,** which is primarily to handle personal needs, such as walking, bathing, dressing, eating, or taking medicine, and can usually be provided by someone who does not have professional medical skills or training

home health care

- **home health care,** which is received at home and includes part-time skilled-nursing care, speech therapy, physical or occupational therapy, part-time services from home health aides, and help from homemakers

adult day care

- **adult day care,** which is received at centers specifically designed for seniors who live at home but whose spouses or families are not available to stay home during the day. The level of care received is similar to that provided for home health care. Most adult day-care centers also provide transportation to and from the center.
- care coordination, which is usually a standard benefit under the policy, but can be optional, that provides the services of a care coordinator who works with the insured and family to assess the person's long-term care needs to help develop an individualized care plan.
- respite care, which is usually a benefit that is provided for someone other than the insured. Respite care is designed to provide temporary relief to a primary caregiver, such as the wife or husband of the insured.
- specialized facilities, some policies might cover or exclude care in specialized facilities, such as Alzheimer's facilities, that provide care for a very specific type of long-term care need.

YOUR FINANCIAL SERVICES PRACTICE:
THE BEST TIME TO SELL LTC INSURANCE

Many planners feel the best time to sell long-term care insurance is when clients are in their early 50s. One reason for this is that these clients have often recently undergone the experience of dealing with the long-term care needs of their parents. More important, however, the "numbers" seem to work well for this age group as compared to those who are in their mid- to late 60s, because costs are more reasonable.

Most policies cover at least the first three levels of care, and many "comprehensive" LTCI policies cover all of the above. While some policies also provide benefits for respite care, which allows occasional full-time care at home for a person who is receiving home health care, this is almost always an additional benefit that must be added to the basic policy. Respite-care benefits enable family members who are providing much of the home care to take a needed break. This can be beneficial for both the health of the caregiver and care recipient. It is also an important consideration because the majority of long-term care services are provided at home by family members.

It is becoming increasingly common for policies to contain a bed reservation benefit. This benefit continues payments to a long-term care facility for a limited time (such as 20 days) if a patient must temporarily leave to be hospitalized. Without a continuation of payments, the bed may be rented to someone else and unavailable upon the patient's release from the hospital.

Most newer policies provide assisted-living facility (ALF) benefits. These benefits are for facilities that provide care for frail seniors who are no longer able to care for themselves but who do not need the level of care that is provided in a nursing home.

Benefit Amounts. Benefits are usually limited to a specified amount per day that is independent of the actual charge for long-term care. The insured purchases the level of benefit he or she desires up to the maximum level the insurance company will provide. For example, an insured can purchase a policy that offers a $150 daily benefit with coverage up to 2 years. Benefits are often sold in increments of $10 per day up to frequently found limits of $100 or $150 or, in a few cases, as much as $300. Most insurance companies will not offer a daily benefit below $50.

Another important consideration is how the benefit is paid as the type of policy can result in staggeringly different results based on how and when care is received. Indemnity policies (also called per diem policies) pay the purchased daily benefit regardless of the actual cost of the services as long as the insured is receiving some type of long-term care. Another per diem policy is the disability or cash-based policy which pays benefits as long as the insured satisfies the policy's benefit triggers, regardless of if long-term care is being received. Reimbursement policies pay the actual cost of the services up to the daily benefit. Most policies today are reimbursement policies, because they pose less risk to the insurance company. Additionally, reimbursement policies typically will result in lower premiums for the insured.

Duration. LTCI policies contain both an elimination (waiting) period and a maximum benefit period. Under an elimination period, benefit payments do not begin until a specified time period after long-term care has begun. The elimination period is analogous to an insurance deductible. While a few insurance companies have a set period (such as 90 days), most allow the policyowner to select from three or four optional elimination periods. Choices may occasionally be as low as 30 days or as high as 365 days. The policyowner is also usually given a choice regarding the maximum period for which benefits will be paid. For example, one insurer offers durations of 2, 3, or 4 years; another makes 3-, 6-, and 12-year coverage available. At the extremes, options of one year or lifetime (that is, unlimited) may be available. Currently, there are very few unlimited benefit policies still available because of the potential costs to the insurance companies. However, because most people only need long-term care insurance for roughly 90 days, it might be wise to consider a policy that offers a lower elimination period. Additionally, elimination periods are also measured by service days and calendar days. Service day elimination periods only run on a day when the insured receives long-term care services. Therefore, if an insured is only receiving long-term care services once a week and he or she has a 90-service-day elimination period, it will take 90 weeks before the policy starts paying any benefits. Typically, shorter elimination periods increase the policy's premiums and service day elimination periods are also less expensive.

Inflation Protection. Most LTCI policies offer some type of inflation protection that the policyowner can purchase, either as part of the policy or as a policy rider. In some cases, the inflation protection is elected (for a higher premium) at the time of purchase; future increases in benefits are automatic. In other cases, the policyowner is allowed to purchase additional benefits each year without evidence of insurability.

Inflation protection is generally in the form of a specified annual increase, often 5 percent. Some policies limit aggregate increases to a specified multiple of the original policy, such as two times. Other policies allow increases only to a maximum age, such as 85. Inflation protection maybe less than adequate to offset actual inflation. The maximum annual increase in benefits is usually 5 percent. This is significantly below recent annual increases in the cost of long-term care, which have been over 5 percent in the last decade. Inflation protections can be both compounding and straight.

Eligibility for Benefits

activities of daily living

Almost all insurance companies now use a criterion for benefit eligibility that is related to several so-called **activities of daily living (ADLs)** or instrumental activities of daily living (IADLs). While variations exist, ADLs include eating, bathing, dressing, transferring from bed to chair, using the toilet, and maintaining continence. In order to receive benefits, there must be independent certification that a person is totally dependent on others to perform a certain number of these activities. For example, one insurer lists seven activities and requires total dependence for any three of them; another insurer requires dependence for two out of a list of six (the most common eligibility requirement).

Newer policies contain a second criterion that, if satisfied, will result in the payment of benefits even if the activities of daily living can be performed. This criterion is based on cognitive impairment or IADLs, which can be caused by Alzheimer's disease, stroke, or other brain damage.

Exclusions

Most LTCI policies contain the exclusions permitted under the NAIC model act. One source of controversy is the exclusion for mental and nervous disorders. Similarly, many policies also use the model act preexisting conditions limit, excluding benefits within the first 6 months of a policy for a condition for which treatment was recommended or received within 6 months prior to policy purchase.

Underwriting

The underwriting of LTCI policies, like the underwriting of medical expense policies, is based on the health of the insured. However, underwriting for the long-term care risk focuses on situations that will cause claims far into the future. Most underwriting is done on the basis of questionnaires rather than on the use of actual physical examinations. Underwriting tends to become more restrictive as the age of an applicant increases. As stated earlier, purchasing a base policy with future purchase options is a way to protect a client's insurability. Additionally, employer-provided group plans often have less strict underwriting requirements that can also be used to provide coverage to an otherwise uninsurable client.

Renewability

guaranteed renewable

LTCI policies currently being sold are **guaranteed renewable**, which means that an individual's coverage cannot be canceled except for nonpayment of premiums. While premiums cannot be raised on the basis of a particular applicant's claim, they can (and often are) raised by class. Since 2000, there have been significant long-term care insurance premium increases due to rising long-term care costs and higher than expected persistency rates with those buying long-term care insurance policies. This means more people are keeping their long-term care insurance policies than originally anticipated by insurance companies. Additionally, gender based premium increases are likely to occur in the near future because women often need long-term care for a significantly longer period of time.

Deductibility of Premiums and Taxation of Benefits

LTCI policies are treated like health insurance policies under the federal income tax laws. Employer expenditures on LTCI are a deductible business expense, and the employee does not recognize income when the employer pays the premiums. Additionally, an individual paying his or her own LTCI premiums can deduct them as an itemized medical expense if it exceeds 10 percent of their adjusted gross income in 2017. However, the amount of premiums excludable as an itemized medical expense is capped by federal limits and depend on the insured's age at the end of the taxable year. However, the law currently prohibits individuals from paying LTCI premiums through a flexible spending account. This limitation makes it clear that individuals are not allowed to pay the premiums with pretax dollars. However, LTCI premiums can be reimbursed from a health savings account up to specific age-based federal limits.

Another limitation in the law prohibits employers from offering LTCI policies as a choice under a cafeteria plan for benefits. Employers can provide LTCI coverage outside a cafeteria plan. Most existing plans are merely a payroll deduction for premium payments where the employee is paying all of the premium.

Individuals may deduct their LTCI premium payments as a medical expense provided they have enough medical expenses to satisfy the adjusted gross income threshold. If the threshold is not satisfied, the deduction will be lost.

In addition to traditional LTCI, hybrid policies have grown in popularity in the past decade. In fact, in 2016, about twice as many hybrid LTCI policies were sold as traditional or stand-alone LTCI. Hybrid policies consist of life insurance or annuity contracts with long-term care riders or benefits. The annuity-long-term care products can often have simpler underwriting requirements than a traditional LTCI policy. As such, advisors should check out hybrid policies for clients that want some long-term care protection but were denied coverage under a traditional product. Hybrid products also qualify for tax-free 1035 exchange treatment from life insurance products. This can allow someone with a traditional life insurance product to 1035 exchange the outstanding product into a hybrid product to obtain some long-term care coverage. However, it is important to price these hybrid policies as compared to two separate stand alone policies.

ADVANCE DIRECTIVES

LO 23.8 Identify the types of documents individuals can use to control their own medical care after they become unable to make decisions for themselves.

Individuals by law have the right to make their own medical choices based on their own values, beliefs, and wishes. But what happens if a person has an accident or suffers a stroke and can no longer make decisions? Would the person want to have his or her life prolonged by any means necessary, or would he or she want to have some treatments withheld to allow a natural death? Usually, directives will go into effect only in the event that the person cannot make and communicate his or her own health-care decisions. Preparing an advance directive lets the physician and other health-care providers know the kind of medical care the individual wants (or does not want) if he or she becomes incapacitated. It also relieves family and friends of the responsibility of making decisions regarding life-prolonging actions.

advance directive

living will

do-not-resuscitate order

The term **advance directive** can describe a variety of documents. A **living will** is a document in which an individual states whether he or she wants his or her life prolonged through medical intervention if he or she has a terminal illness or if her or she is permanently unconscious. **Do-not-resuscitate orders** are more specific and are typically signed by terminally ill patients to address the withholding of CPR (cardiopulmonary resuscitation) or other forms of resuscitation if they would only temporarily prolong life and perhaps increase pain.

health-care power of attorney (HCPOA)

A **health-care power of attorney (HCPOA)** allows an individual to name an agent to make health-care decisions for the person if he or she is unable to do so. The HCPOA is more flexible than a living will and can cover any health-care decision, even if the person is not terminally ill or permanently unconscious. Some states also have a document specifically called an advance health-care directive that addresses all of the issues contained in both a living will and in a health-care power of attorney. The term advance directive may be used to refer to any of these specific documents or to all of them in general.

States differ widely on what types of advance directives they officially recognize. Some states require a specific style for the format and content of the advance directive. Moreover, the laws regarding honoring advance directives from one state to another are not clear. If a person lives in one state but travels to other states frequently, he or she may want to consider having the advance directive meet the laws of other states. A good source of information is the Office of the State Attorney General for each state.

Under the federal Patient Self-Determination Act, hospitals and other health-care providers across the country are required to give patients information about their rights to make their own health-care decisions. This includes the right to accept or refuse medical treatment. If an individual has an advance directive, it is appropriate to provide a copy to relevant health-care providers. These directives are more likely to be followed if a friend or family member becomes an active advocate for the patient.

Individuals should keep a number of issues in mind when considering advance directives. First, no one has to have an advance directive if he or she does not want one. Second, if an advance directive is adopted, it is crucial to do the following:

- Tell family members and make sure they know where it is located.
- Inform the person's lawyer.
- Discuss the advance directive with the family doctor before signing it. It is important that both the patient and the doctor are comfortable with the contents. The doctor may have some additional suggestions that the patient had not thought to include. Make sure the advance directive is part of the patient's medical records.
- If a person has a durable power of attorney, give a copy of the advance directive to the person holding the power of attorney.
- Be sure to comply with the state's signature and witness requirements. States have various requirements about who can be a witness, how many witnesses are needed, and if the directive must be notarized.
- The person should keep a small card in his or her wallet to notify emergency medical services (EMS) providers of his or her wishes. (EMS generally refers to ambulance companies and paramedics.) In an emergency situation, however, EMS staff members do not have much time to look for or to evaluate different types of documentation. They may only acknowledge cards issued by a state's EMS program and only when the cards are signed by a personal physician.

An individual may change or cancel an advance directive at any time. Any change or cancellation should be written, signed, and dated. Copies should be given to the doctor and to anyone else who had a copy of the original. Some states allow a person to change an advance directive by oral statement. Even if the advance directive is not officially withdrawn, a patient with a clear mind who is communicating his or her wishes directly to the doctor carries more weight than a living will or durable power of attorney.

CHAPTER REVIEW

Key Terms and Concepts

IRC Sec. 121	skilled-nursing care
downsize	intermediate care
life-care community	custodial care
age-restricted housing	home health care
domicile	adult day care
sale-leaseback	activities of daily living
reverse mortgage	guaranteed renewable
Medicare Part A	advance directive
Medicare Part B	living will
benefit period	do-not-resuscitate order
lifetime reserve days	health-care power of attorney
Medigap insurance	(HCPOA)

Chapter 23: Review Questions

Review questions are based on the learning objectives in this chapter. Thus, a [23.3] at the end of a question means that the question is based on learning objective 3. If there are multiple objectives, they are all listed.

1. Answer the following questions about the exclusion of gain provisions upon the sale of a personal residence. [23.1]

    a. What are the ownership and use requirements?

    b. What is the maximum amount that can be excluded for the sale of a personal residence by a single taxpayer?

    c. What is the maximum amount that can be excluded for the sale of a personal residence by a married taxpayer filing jointly?

2. If a couple is planning to marry, and each owns a home that he or she is planning to sell, what should they do about the two properties? [23.1]

3. Describe the typical fee structure of a life-care community and what the promise of lifetime care can mean for the client. [23.2]

4. Explain the differences between the age-62 restriction and the age-55 restriction to your client, who is interested in an age-restricted housing community. [23.2]

5. What factors should be considered by clients planning to relocate out of state? [23.3]

6. What type of home improvements should a retiree staying in the home typically consider? [23.4]

7. Describe a sale-leaseback arrangement. [23.4]

8. What are the requirements for a reverse mortgage ? [23.4]

9. How are lenders protected under the HECM program? [23.4]

10. How much will the lender be able to borrow under a reverse mortgage? [23.4]

11. What happens under a reverse mortgage if the retiree dies and the amount of the outstanding loan exceeds the value of the home? What if the value of the home exceeds the amount of the outstanding loan? [23.4]

12. Identify who is eligible to receive Medicare benefits. [23.5]

13. Joan (aged 66) is hospitalized for 80 days (January–March), goes home for 6 months, and is hospitalized again in October for an additional 30 days. How will Medicare treat each stay for payment purposes? [23.5]

14. Identify the key benefits that are not covered by Parts A or B of Medicare. [23.5]

15. Describe how a managed care plan works under Medicare. [23.5]

16. Discuss how COBRA coverage can help solve the pre-Medicare/postretirement gap. [23.6]

17. In addition to COBRA, what other options are available to people who face pre-Medicare/postretirement problems? [23.6]

18. Briefly discuss the need for long-term care insurance. [23.7]

19. Discuss the following characteristics of long-term care policies: [23.7]
    a. issue age
    b. benefits
    c. costs
    d. duration

20. Describe each of the following: [23.8]

a. living will
b. health care power of attorney
c. advance care directive
d. do-not-resuscitate order

Chapter 23: Review Answers

1. a. To qualify for the exclusion, the property must have been owned and used by the taxpayer as a principal residence for an aggregate of at least 2 years out of the 5 years ending on the date of sale.

    b. The maximum exclusion is $250,000.

    c. The maximum exclusion is $500,000.

2. Even though the current home sale exclusion rule is quite flexible, it could cause problems for a couple planning to marry if each owns a home that he or she plans to sell. If the sales occur after the marriage, the 2-year rule could prohibit the use of the exclusion for both homes. In this case, the couple should consider selling one or both homes prior to the marriage.

3. Most frequently, the resident pays a one-time fee (which may or may not be refundable) and a monthly fee that can range widely depending on the facility. The key element to the life-care contract is typically the guarantee of space in a nursing home if it becomes necessary.

4. Under the age-62 restriction, all residents must be aged 62 or older. The more flexible exemption allows a community to limit eligibility to age 55. With this exception, some individuals under age 55 can be accepted as long as 80 percent of all residents are 55 or older and at least one resident in each living unit is aged 55 or older.

5. Retirees planning a relocation should be concerned about financial considerations, such as the tax situation in the new state. They should also consider personal issues like whether both spouses would be comfortable living in the new state. Also, individuals should look for replacement homes that are equipped to meet their needs.

6. Improvements can include installing guard rails in the shower and making sure that bathroom, tub, and other floor surfaces are slip proof. The outside of the home should also be examined for cracked or uneven sidewalks and inadequate lighting. Additional handrails may be appropriate both inside and outside of the house. Adding siding or replacement windows may help reduce ongoing home maintenance. Appliances such as dishwashers, garbage disposals and compactors, central vacuuming systems, and water filters (versus bottled water) can reduce daily labor.

7. Under a sale-leaseback arrangement, your client sells his or her house to an investor and then rents it back from the investor under a lifetime lease.

8. A reverse mortgage is typically available only when all of the owners are aged 62 or older or if a married couple only one needs to be aged 62 or older and the home is the principal residence. Also, the home must either have no debt or only a small debt that can be paid off with part of the reverse mortgage loan.

9. FHA insures HECM program loans to protect lenders against loss if amounts withdrawn exceed equity when the property is sold.

10. The amount of loan payments made to the client depends on the client's age (or client's joint ages), the amount of equity the home currently has or is expected to have, and the interest rate and fees that are being charged.

11. Because most loans are "nonrecourse," the only security for the loan is the home. This means that if the outstanding loan amount exceeds the value of the home, neither the retiree nor his or her heirs will be responsible for any shortfall. On the other hand, the transaction is a loan and, if the value of the home exceeds the outstanding balance, any remainder is the property of the retiree or his or her heirs.

12. Those individuals who are aged 65 and are eligible for Social Security retirement benefits are covered, as are their spouses as long as they are aged 65. A 65-year-old spouse can be covered as long as the worker is aged 62 or older. In addition, certain federal employees and railway workers are also eligible at age 65.

13. Part A of Medicare pays for inpatient hospital services for up to 90 days in each benefit period. Because Joan was out of the hospital for more than 60 days, each illness will be treated as a new benefit period.

14. Part A has a deductible and excludes elective surgeries and luxury items such as private rooms. Part B has a 20 percent copay for most expenses and excludes custodial care, dentures, eyeglasses, and hearing aids, as well as other things.

15. All Medigap policies cover the Part A hospital daily copay amounts as well as an additional 365 lifetime reserve days. The Part B copay amounts are also covered after the deductible.

16. A Medicare SELECT policy must meet all of the requirements that apply to a Medigap policy, and it must be one of the prescribed benefit packages. The only difference is that a Medicare SELECT policy may require that the recipient use doctors or hospitals within its network in order to receive full benefits.

17. Medicare participants may elect to have their Medicare benefits provided by a managed care plan such as a health maintenance organization (HMO) or a preferred

provider organization (PPO). The participant must still pay the Part B premium for Medicare and may be required to pay an additional premium. Each managed care plan subcontracts for the Department of Health and Human Services to provide benefits at least equal to, and often better than, those available under Medicare. The important factor in managed care plan operations is that services must be provided to participants by qualified providers who are affiliated with, or have contracted with, the plan (except in emergencies).

18. When an individual retires from a company under COBRA, he or she has the right to purchase coverage under the plan for the next 18 months. This guarantees coverage under a health insurance plan for this period of time. The problem is that some small employers are not required to offer COBRA coverage and the 18-month period may not take the retiree up to eligibility for Medicare at 65.

19. a. Issue age—There is little uniformity here, with some companies having a minimum and/or a maximum age.

    b. Benefits—Policies usually include skilled nursing, intermediate care, and custodial care. Some policies cover home care and/or adult day care.

    c. Cost—Benefits are usually paid regardless of the actual cost of the services provided.

    d. Duration—Policies will have both a waiting period and maximum benefit period.

20. a. Living will—gives people the opportunity to state whether they want their lives prolonged through medical intervention if they will soon die from a terminal illness or if they are permanently unconscious.

    b. Heath care power of attorney—allows an individual to name someone (an agent) to make health care decisions for the person if he or she is unable to do so. The HCPOA is more flexible than a living will and can cover any health care decision, even if the person is not terminally ill or permanently unconscious.

    c. Advance care directive—addresses all of the issues contained in a living will and in a health care power of attorney.

    d. Do-not-resuscitate order—often signed by terminally ill patients to address the specific issue of withholding CPR (cardiopulmonary resuscitation) or other forms of resuscitation if they would only prolong dying and perhaps increase pain.

Chapter 24

Distributions from Retirement Plans—Part I

Learning Objectives

An understanding of the material in this chapter should enable the student to

LO 24.1 Identify the exceptions to the general rule that distributions from qualified plans, 403(b) annuities, and IRAs are included as ordinary income.

LO 24.2 Clarify the legal limitations and planning strategies for avoiding the Sec. 72(t) early withdrawal penalty tax.

LO 24.3 Identify the various methods for recovering cost basis from qualified and other tax advantaged retirement plans.

LO 24.4 Explain the tax treatment of qualified and nonqualified distributions from a Roth IRA or a Roth account in a 401(k) or 403(b) plan.

LO 24.5 Distinguish between distributions that can be rolled over into other tax-advantaged retirement plans and those that cannot.

LO 24.6 Discuss the special tax rules that may apply to lump-sum distributions from qualified plans.

LO 24.7 Describe when required minimum distributions must begin, and how to calculate the required minimum distributions during the participant's lifetime and after the participant's death.

LO 24.8 Describe the postmortem planning opportunities under the required minimum-distribution rules.

Planning for the distribution of funds from employer-sponsored retirement plans and IRAs can be one of the most challenging aspects of retirement planning. Any strategy selected must account for the following factors:

- the client's needs and goals
- the variety of distribution options that are available in your client's particular situation
- the implications of choosing one option over another from a tax perspective
- the implications of choosing one option over another from a cash-flow perspective
- the implications of choosing one option over another from a death benefit and estate tax perspective
- the ability to delay the receipt and taxation of a distribution by rolling the distribution over into an IRA or another qualified plan

This chapter examines the tax implications of the withdrawal.

TAX TREATMENT

Tax Treatment in General

LO 24.1 **Identify the exceptions to the general rule that distributions from qualified plans, 403(b) annuities, and IRAs are included as ordinary income.**

From the employee's perspective, the advantage of tax-sheltered retirement plans (qualified plans, 403(b) plans, IRAs, SEPs, and SIMPLEs) is that taxes are deferred until benefits are distributed—the day of reckoning. Generally, the entire value of a distribution is included as ordinary income in the year of the distribution. If the individual has made after-tax contributions or receives an insurance policy and has paid Table 2001 costs, he or she will have a cost basis that can generally be recovered. Taxable distributions from tax-sheltered retirement plans made prior to age 59½ are also subject to the 10 percent Sec. 72(t) penalty tax, unless the distribution satisfies one of several exceptions.

If the benefit is distributed in a single sum, the taxable portion may be eligible for one of several special tax benefits, but only if the distribution is from a qualified plan and satisfies certain lump-sum distribution requirements. Persons born before 1936 may be eligible for 10-year forward averaging or special capital-gains treatment. Any participant who receives employer securities as part of a lump-sum distribution can defer tax on the unrealized appreciation until the stock is later sold.

In many cases, all taxes, including the Sec. 72(t) penalty tax, can be avoided by rolling—or directly transferring—the benefit into an IRA or other qualified plan. Today, most distributions are eligible for rollover treatment. Taxes cannot be deferred indefinitely, however. Under the minimum-distribution rules, distributions generally have to begin shortly after attaining age 70½.

Estate Taxation of Pension Accumulations

Qualified plan and other tax-sheltered benefits payable to a beneficiary at the death of the participant are included in the participant's taxable estate. Benefits payable to beneficiaries are still subject to income tax, although the benefit amount is treated as income in respect of a decedent, meaning the income taxes are reduced by the estate taxes paid as a result of the pension benefit.

Sec. 72(t) Penalty Tax

LO 24.2   Clarify the legal limitations and planning strategies for avoiding the Sec. 72(t) early withdrawal penalty tax.

Sec. 72(t) penalty tax

Distributions prior to age 59½ from all types of tax-advantaged retirement plans are subject to the 10 percent **Sec. 72(t) penalty tax** (unless an exception applies). The 10 percent penalty applies to distributions that are made from a qualified plan, a Sec. 403(b) plan, an IRA, or a SEP. The rule also applies to SIMPLEs with a modification. During the first 2 years of plan participation, the early withdrawal penalty is 25 percent instead of 10 percent.

The 10 percent tax applies only to the portion of the distribution subject to income tax. This means the tax does not apply when a benefit is rolled over from one tax-deferred plan into another. It also does not apply to the nontaxable portion of a distribution (which may occur with a distribution of after-tax contributions).

substantially equal periodic payments

However, a distribution made prior to age 59½ can escape the 10 percent penalty if it qualifies under one of several exceptions. To avoid the 10 percent penalty, the distributions must be

- to a beneficiary or an employee's estate on or after the employee's death
- attributable to a disability that generally prevents the employee from engaging in any substantial gainful activity
- part of a series of **substantially equal periodic payments** made at least annually over the life or life expectancy of the employee or the joint lives or life expectancies of the employee and a beneficiary. (If the distribution is from a qualified plan, the employee must separate from service.)
- after a separation from service for early retirement after age 55 (not applicable to IRAs, SEPs, or SIMPLEs)
- made to cover medical expenses deductible for the year under Sec. 213 (medical expenses that exceed 7.5 percent of adjusted gross income)

YOUR FINANCIAL SERVICES PRACTICE: ASKING THE RIGHT QUESTIONS

In most cases, taxation of a distribution from a pension plan or IRA is simple. The distribution is fully taxable as ordinary income. However, there are a number of critical exceptions. (This whole chapter is about the exceptions.) Here is a series of questions to ask your client to determine if any of the special rules apply.

1. What type of plan is the distribution from?

    There are some rule differences among the different types of plans. For example, the grandfathered lump-sum distribution rules only apply to qualified plans.

2. Is a portion of the distribution attributable to amounts that have already been taxed?

    After-tax employee contributions or Table 2001 costs in a qualified plan or nondeductible contributions to an IRA are treated as cost basis and will not be taxed twice. The methodology for recovering the basis is complicated and depends on the type of plan involved. Form 1099-R, which is provided to the recipient, will reveal such amounts. However, if a Form 1099-R has not yet been issued, the recipient's latest plan account statement may be a source of information.

3. Is the benefit payable to an individual who has not attained age 59½?

    If the answer is yes, then in addition to income taxes, a 10 percent penalty tax may apply if the recipient is not eligible for one of the exceptions.

4. Is the distribution to a plan participant or to a beneficiary receiving a death benefit?

    If it is a distribution to the death beneficiary, the beneficiary still pays income taxes, but he or she might be entitled to a deduction if the participant had paid federal estate taxes on the value of the pension.

5. Is some or all of the distribution attributable to stock of the sponsoring entity?

    If the distribution is from a qualified plan and it qualifies as a lump-sum distribution, the taxpayer may be entitled to deferral of gain on the unrealized appreciation on the employer stock.

6. Is the distribution from a qualified plan payable as a lump sum to an individual born before 1936?

    If the distribution is from a qualified plan, the recipient may be entitled to a special tax rate using grandfathered 10-year averaging or the grandfathered capital-gains rule.

7. Is the distribution from a Roth IRA or a Roth account in a 401(k) or 403(b) plan?

    The tax treatment of distributions from Roth IRAs and Roth accounts is different than distributions from other types of tax-advantaged plans. Qualifying distributions are tax free. The tax treatment of nonqualifying distributions depends upon the type of plan involved.

Several additional exceptions apply to IRAs (which include SEPs and SIMPLEs). Distributions from IRAs escape the penalty if the distribution is for the

- purpose of paying health insurance premiums by an individual who is collecting unemployment insurance

- payment of qualified home acquisition expenses (paid within 120 days of the distribution) of a first home for the taxpayer, spouse, or any child, grandchild, or ancestor of the taxpayer or spouse (with a lifetime limit of $10,000 per IRA participant)
- payment of qualified higher education expenses for education furnished to the taxpayer, the taxpayer's spouse, or any child or grandchild of the taxpayer or taxpayer's spouse at an eligible postsecondary educational institution

Qualified home acquisition expenses are those used to buy, build, or rebuild a first home. To be a first-time homebuyer, the individual (and spouse, if married) must not have had an ownership interest in a principal residence during a 2-year period ending on the date the new home is acquired. Qualified higher education expenses include tuition, fees, books, supplies, and equipment required for enrollment in an eligible postsecondary education institution. For at least half-time students, room and board are also qualified education expenses.

The following examples should help to illustrate when the Sec. 72(t) 10 percent penalty applies and when it does not.

EXAMPLE 1

Greg Murphy, aged 57, takes a $50,000 distribution from his profit-sharing plan account. If Greg terminated employment after age 55 and before receiving the benefit, the penalty does not apply. If Greg is still employed at the time of the distribution, then the $50,000 distribution will be subject to a $5,000 (10 percent) penalty.

EXAMPLE 2

Jane Goodall, aged 45, takes a life annuity from Biological Researchers, Inc., when she quits and goes to work for The Primate Institute. Jane's distribution is not subject to a penalty because of the substantially equal periodic payments exception.

EXAMPLE 3

Ed Miller, aged 35, takes a $10,000 distribution from his 401(k) plan account as a downpayment on his first home. Ed's distribution is subject to the 10 percent penalty.

EXAMPLE 4

Sandra Smalley, aged 45, takes a distribution from her IRA to pay her child's college tuition. Sandra's distribution is not subject to the 10 percent penalty.

EXAMPLE 5

Catherine Thegrate, aged 45, withdraws $10,000 from her IRA to make the down payment on her first home. The distribution is exempt from the 10 percent penalty. However, no additional withdrawals from any of Catherine's IRAs (or Roth IRAs) can qualify for this exception.

Avoiding the Sec. 72(t) Penalty Tax

Clients may need to make withdrawals prior to age 59½ to pay personal or business expenses. Voluntary early retirement, involuntary termination of employment followed by a period of not working, or leaving a job to start a business are common scenarios. Within the exceptions to the Sec. 72(t) penalty tax, some helpful planning opportunities do exist.

Age 55 Exception. Distributions taken directly from a qualified plan or 403(b) plan to a participant who separates from employment during or after the calendar year of attainment of age 55 are exempt from the penalty tax. If the participant rolls the benefit into an IRA, the exception is no longer available. This exception allows the participant to take a portion of the distribution into income now to meet current income needs, and still roll over the rest to an IRA. It also will eliminate the 10 percent penalty when the participant elects a stream of installment distributions or an annuity payment from the plan. The primary limit of this exception is the extent that the plan provides the distribution flexibility that the participant needs. For example, it is not uncommon for defined-contribution plans to only allow a lump-sum distribution option.

YOUR FINANCIAL SERVICES PRACTICE: TAX FORMS REQUIRED WITH EARLY WITHDRAWALS

When a participant receives a distribution from a pension plan or IRA the payor must provide Form 1099-R, which reports the amount and nature of the distribution to the IRS. If the recipient has not yet attained age 59½, the payor will identify in box 7 of the form whether an exception to the Sec. 72(t) tax applies (in this case, the payor identifies "2", "3", or "4" in the box.) If the payor writes "1" in the box, "no known exception," then the recipient is required to file Form 5329 with his or her tax return. On Form 5329, the taxpayer identifies the taxable amount, but also has the opportunity to identify the applicable exception to the penalty tax.

Education Expenses. For IRA participants (this includes SEPs and SIMPLEs), the exception for educational expenses can also be useful. The education expense exception requires that the taxpayer pay qualified education expenses for the family member, but the expenses do not have to be paid directly from the IRA. The actual education payments can be paid from employment income, loans, gifts, or inheritances. However, education expenses paid with a tax-free distribution from a Coverdell education account, tax-free scholarships, Pell grants, employer-provided educational assistance or veterans' educational assistance do not qualify.

Qualified education expenses include tuition, fees, books, supplies, and equipment required for enrollment in a postsecondary education institution. Room and board is also included for students attending school at least half time. An eligible educational institution is any college, university, or vocational school eligible to participate in the student aid programs administered by the Department of Education. It includes virtually all accredited, public, nonprofit, and proprietary postsecondary institutions.

> **EXAMPLE**
>
> Randolph, aged 56, withdraws $50,000 during the year from his IRA to pay for a new boat (before calling his financial advisor). It is determined that during the same year he also took out a second mortgage to pay $25,000 of tuition, $1,000 for books, and $12,000 for room and board for his daughter, a full-time student at Private University. Since Randolph incurred $38,000 of qualified education expenses for his daughter, he only has to pay the 10 percent penalty on $12,000 of the $50,000 withdrawal.

Substantially Equal Periodic Payments. The most helpful Sec. 72(t) penalty tax exception is the substantially equal periodic payment exception. This exception applies to all types of plans. However, with qualified plans, the participant must separate from service before distributions begin in order to be eligible. Moreover, the qualified plan has to provide for a form of lifetime payments. Payments can begin at any age, as long as the stream of distributions is set up to last for the life of the participant or the joint lives of the participant and his or her beneficiary. For the individual who needs the withdrawals for ongoing financial needs, periodic distributions may be just right. If, on the other hand, a large single-sum amount is needed, this strategy could still work. Assuming the individual qualifies for a loan from a third party, the individual can borrow the sum needed and repay the loan from the periodic distributions. The borrower, however, is not allowed to use the pension or IRA account as collateral for the loan.

Under this exception, if the payments are to be made from an IRA, there is usually some flexibility in calculating the annual withdrawal amount. Withdrawals must be made at least annually (or more often) and the stream of withdrawals can be calculated under one of three IRS-approved methods. The first is the required minimum-distribution method. Under this approach, the annual payment for each year is determined by dividing the account balance for that year by the number from the applicable life expectancy table for that year. Under this method, the account balance, the number from the applicable life expectancy table, and the resulting annual payments are redetermined for each year.

The second method is the fixed-amortization method. The annual payment for each year is determined by amortizing, in level amounts, the account balance over a specified number of years determined using the applicable life expectancy table and an assumed interest rate. The calculation involves three factors: the account balance (IRS guidance allows choosing the account balance from the end of the previous year or any time between that time and the time of the distribution), the applicable interest rate and the participant's life expectancy. With these three factors and a financial calculator, it is not difficult to determine the required annual payment.

The third method is the fixed-annuitization method. The annual payment for each year is determined by dividing the account balance by an annuity factor that is the present value of an annuity of one dollar per year beginning at the taxpayer's age and continuing for the life of the taxpayer (or the joint lives of the taxpayer and a beneficiary). The annuity factor is derived by using the mortality table in appendix B of Rev. Rul. 2002-62 and by using an assumed interest rate. Under this method, the account balance, the annuity factor, the assumed interest rate, and the resulting annual payment are determined once for the first distribution year and then the annual payment is the same amount in each succeeding year.

The life expectancy tables that can be used to determine distribution periods are the uniform lifetime table (found in Rev. Rul. 2002-62), the single-life table or the joint and survivor table (found in appendix A). These are the same tables used for determining the required minimum distribution. The number that is used for a distribution year is the number shown from the table for the participant's age on his or her birthday in that year. If the joint and survivor table is being used, the age of the beneficiary on the beneficiary's birthday in the year is also used. In the case of the required minimum-distribution method, the same life expectancy table that is used for the first distribution year must be used in each following year. Thus, if the taxpayer uses the single-life expectancy table for the required minimum-distribution method in the first distribution year, the same table must be used in subsequent distribution years.

The interest rate that may be used is any interest rate that is not more than 120 percent of the federal mid-term rate for either of the 2 months immediately preceding the month in which the distribution begins. For example, 120 percent of the annual mid-term rate was 2.36 percent percent for January, 2017.

EXAMPLE

George, aged 50, has an IRA with an account balance of $500,000. In February, 2017 he decides that he wants to take the maximum withdrawals allowed under the substantially equal periodic payment rule. The annuitization and amortization methods give similar results, and the calculation using the amortization method is quite easy to calculate. To get the maximum withdrawal, use the highest allowable interest rate (2.36 percent in January, 2017) and the single life expectancy table. The life expectancy factor is 34.2 for an individual aged 50. Using a financial calculator with the present value of $500,000, 2.36 (i), and 34.2 (n), and beginning payments, the required annual stream of payments is $21,468.

There are several other important considerations. First, even though the distribution amount is calculated based on lifetime payments, the rules do not actually require that payments continue for life. Payments can be stopped without penalty after the later of 5 years after the first payment or age 59½. For example, an individual who began distributions in substantially equal payments at age 56 in January 2017 must continue taking the distributions until January 2022. Or, in the case of an individual beginning withdrawals at age 47, the payments must continue until he or she attains age 59½, which is a period of 12½ years.

Second, once the amount is determined under one of the three methods, that exact amount must be distributed throughout the prescribed period. Distributing too little or too much violates the rules. There is one exception; an individual can make a one-time switch from either the amortization approach or the annuitization approach to the minimum distribution method. This is generally a way to reduce the required withdrawal.

Third, if a client fails to follow the rules exactly, the 10 percent penalty will be due on all distributions made before age 59½, as well as interest on the penalty tax that was avoided during the years in which distributions were made. A client who uses the substantially equal payment exception needs to understand the rigidity built into the rules and the penalty for failing to follow them.

YOUR FINANCIAL SERVICES PRACTICE: THE SUBSTANTIALLY EQUAL PAYMENT EXCEPTION IN A DOWN MARKET

The biggest limitation of the substantially equal periodic payment exception is the inability to change the calculation methodology after the first year. With the amortization and annuitization approaches, the amount withdrawn in each and every year must remain the same for the prescribed period. This can cause problems in a down market when the value of the account can drop suddenly. A participant who is concerned about this issue should consider using the required minimum-distribution approach. Under this approach, the required distribution each year is based on the prior year's account balance. Interestingly, in Rev. Rul. 2002-62, the IRS has indicated that anyone who chooses either the amortization or annuitization method can, after the first year, make a one-time election to change the method to the required minimum-distribution approach. This gives taxpayers a safety net if the value of the account suddenly drops.

Nontaxable Distributions

Most distributions made from qualified plans, IRA accounts, and 403(b) annuities or custodial accounts are fully taxable as ordinary income. However, if some of the participant's benefit under the plan is attributable to dollars in the plan that have already been subject to taxation—for example, employee after-tax contributions and amounts attributable to term insurance premiums—then a portion of a distribution may be exempt from tax until the total nontaxable amount has been distributed.

The calculation of the appropriate tax treatment for periodic payments can become quite complex. The rules are different, depending upon the type of plan and type of distribution involved. At the same time, fewer and fewer participant benefits contain nontaxable basis. This is true in part because of law changes that almost eliminated all new after-tax contributions to qualified plans beginning in 1987 (with the exception of a few large 401(k) plans that still allow after-tax contributions). Also, life insurance benefits in qualified plans have become more and more uncommon, thus, reducing the amount of recoverable Table 2001 costs. One more complicating factor is that under current rules, participants are allowed to roll nontaxable contributions into an IRA. The tax treatment of withdrawals from the IRA are different than those from a qualified plan. Even though these situations are not that common, they still come up and the financial services professional needs to have a basic understanding of the rules. A summary of the rules follows.

IRA Distributions

Let's begin with the simplest case, the traditional IRA. A participant can accumulate nontaxable amounts (referred to as cost basis) from either nondeductible contributions to the IRA or nontaxable amounts that have been rolled over from qualified plans. The rule is simply that if an individual has unrecovered cost basis, then a portion of each IRA distribution is tax free. The amount excluded from income is:

$$\text{Unrecovered cost basis} \div (\text{Total IRA account} + \text{Current year's distribution})$$

$$\times \text{Distribution amount} = \text{Tax-free portion}$$

This calculation is made by looking at all of the IRAs an individual owns—which can have quite a negative impact on the recovery of cost basis if the participant has both nondeductible and deductible IRA contributions. This method applies until the individual has recovered all of his or her nondeductible contributions. After that, any distribution is fully taxable. If the IRA owner dies prior to recovering all nondeductible contributions, the remaining amount can be deducted on the decedent's final income tax return.

EXAMPLE

Julia decides to withdraw $50,000 from her IRA account. After the withdrawal, her account is valued at $750,000 and $50,000 represented after-tax contributions that were rolled over into the IRA. Julia will only recover $3,125 tax free out of the $50,000 withdrawal. The calculation is $50,000 ÷ ($750,000 + $50,000) × $50,000.

Recovering Cost Basis with a Life Insurance Policy

LO 24.3 **Identify the various methods for recovering cost basis from qualified and other tax advantaged retirement plans.**

When a participant has had a life insurance policy as part of his or her benefit in a qualified plan or 403(b) annuity, there is generally an accumulation of cost basis over the years, as the cost of the term insurance portion of the policy is included in income each year (often referred to as Table 2001 costs). Note, however, that self-employed persons (sole proprietors and partners) do not technically accumulate Table 2001 costs and are, therefore, not allowed to recover them upon distribution.

Table 2001 costs can only be recovered if the policy is actually distributed to the participant. However, if a participant does not want to continue the policy, there is a way around this problem. The trustee can strip the policy's cash value (by borrowing) to reduce it to the accumulated Table 2001 costs and then distribute the contract and the cash. The participant then cancels the policy and recovers the tax free cost basis. The cash can be rolled to an IRA to avoid all taxation.

If the participant dies and the policy proceeds are paid out to a beneficiary, then the Table 2001 costs can again reduce the taxable portion of the distribution to the death beneficiary. When paid out as a death benefit, the death beneficiary pays income tax only on the cash value of the policy less Table 2001 costs. The remaining value is income tax free.

EXAMPLE

Serena dies while still employed. She had a life insurance policy with a face value of $100,000, a cash value of $20,000, and $4,000 of accumulated cost basis. Serena's daughter Tina is the beneficiary and she elects a lump-sum withdrawal of the $100,000 benefit. Tina will pay income tax on $16,000, the difference between the cash value and the unrecovered cost basis; $84,000 is recovered tax free.

Rollovers from Qualified Plans

When a participant receives a distribution from a qualified plan that is eligible to be rolled into an IRA, the whole distribution (including after-tax contributions) may be rolled into an IRA. However, if the after-tax amount is rolled over, it is subject to the IRA recovery rules. As described above, these rules are not very favorable, especially with large rollover accounts. A participant may want to choose instead to roll over all but the nontaxable amount. In IRS Publication 575, Pension and Annuity Income, the IRS clarifies that the participant is not required to pay any income taxes if he or she rolls over all of the distribution except for the amount of after-tax contributions.

> **EXAMPLE**
>
> Assume in the Julia example above that the $800,000 IRA was recently rolled over from a qualified plan. Remember that in the example Julia had $50,000 in after-tax contributions. If at the time of the IRA rollover she would have rolled only $750,000 into the IRA, she would have avoided income taxes on the entire $50,000 amount.

As mentioned above, when a participant receives a life insurance policy from a qualified plan, the Table 2001 costs may be recovered tax free if the policy is distributed. Special consideration must be made when the participant wants to receive the policy but minimize the tax consequences by rolling over as much of the benefit into an IRA as possible. Because a life insurance policy may not be rolled into an IRA, the tax consequences of this transaction can be minimized by having the trustee strip the cash value of the policy (by borrowing) to reduce the cash value to the accumulated Table 2001 costs. Then the extra cash is distributed as part of the benefit and may be rolled over.

Single-Sum Distributions

If a participant receives the entire benefit and does not roll it into an IRA or other tax-sheltered retirement plan, recovery of basis occurs at the time of the distribution.

Distribution of After-Tax Contributions Prior to the Annuity Starting Date

Prior to 1987, an amount up to the participant's cost basis could be withdrawn prior to the annuity starting date (the time periodic retirement benefits begin) without income tax consequences. The Tax Reform Act of 1986 changed this rule significantly. A grandfather provision still allows a participant to withdraw an amount equal to the pre-1987 cost basis as long as the plan provided for in-service distributions on May 5, 1986. Post-1986 amounts attributable to the cost basis, however, are now subject to a pro rata rule. The general rule is that the amount of the distribution that is excluded from tax is based on a ratio, with the numerator being the cost basis and the denominator being the total account balance at the time of the distribution. However, when determining the ratio, an individual may treat employee after-tax contributions and the investment experience thereon separately from the rest of the participant's benefit. This rule still allows a participant to withdraw after-tax contributions with limited tax liability. This principle can be best illustrated with an example.

EXAMPLE

Joe has an account balance of $1,000, $200 of which is attributable to post-1986 employee contributions and an additional $50 is attributable to investment earnings on the $200. Joe takes an in-service distribution of $100. The exclusion ratio is $200/$250 or 80 percent. Therefore, Joe will receive $80 income tax free and will owe tax on $20.

YOUR FINANCIAL SERVICES PRACTICE: AFTER-TAX CONTRIBUTIONS

It is not uncommon for a business owner to have made after-tax contributions prior to 1987. These amounts can be withdrawn tax free, making them an excellent source of funds if the owner has a life insurance need or some other reason to need cash. After 1986, large company 401(k) plans are typically the only plans that still have an after-tax contribution feature.

Periodic Distributions from Qualified Plans and 403(b) Annuities

When the participant has a cost basis and begins to receive periodic annuity payments from a qualified plan or 403(b) annuity, the amount of each distribution that is not subject to income tax is determined by dividing the cost basis by the number of expected monthly annuity payments. When the annuity is on the participant's life only, the number of months are as cited in Table 24-1. For a joint and survivor annuity, use the number of months in Table 24-2.

Table 24-1
Number of Months—Single Life Annuity

Age of Distributee	Number of Payments
55 and under	360
56–60	310
61–65	260
66–70	210
71 and over	160

Table 24-2
Number of Months—Joint Annuity

Combined Age of Annuitants	Number of Payments
Not more than 110	410
More than 110 but not more than 120	360
More than 120 but not more than 130	310
More than 130 but not more than 140	260
More than 140	210

The cost basis is the aggregate amount of after-tax contributions to the plan (plus other after-tax amounts such as Table 2001 costs and repayments of loans previously taxed as distributions) minus the aggregate amount received before the annuity starting date that was excluded from income.

The distributee recovers his or her cost basis in level amounts over the number of monthly payments determined in the tables above. The amount excluded from each payment is calculated by dividing the investment by the set number of monthly payments determined as follows:

$$\text{Investment} \div \text{Number of monthly payments} = \text{Tax-free portion of monthly annuity}$$

This amount is excluded from each payment until the entire investment is recovered. After that, each monthly payment is fully taxable.

EXAMPLE

John Thomas is about to begin receiving a retirement benefit in the form of a single life annuity. His investment in the contract is $40,000. John is aged 65 at the time benefit payments begin. The set number of months used to compute the exclusion amount is 260 (for age 65). Because his cost basis is $40,000, the amount excluded from each monthly payment is $154 ($40,000 ÷ 260).

Roth IRAs and Roth Accounts

With the maturation of the Roth IRA and the availability of Roth 401(k) and Roth 403(b) accounts beginning in 2006, tax questions involving these accounts became more prevalent. Conceptually, with all Roth accounts the participant is forgoing a deduction at the time of the contribution in exchange for tax-free withdrawals. It is true that qualifying distributions are entirely free of federal income tax; however, nonqualifying distributions may or may not be subject to tax. Unfortunately, there also is a difference between the tax treatment of nonqualifying distributions from Roth IRA and Roth 401(k) (or 403(b)) accounts. We will first discuss Roth IRAs and then identify the differences that apply to Roth 401(k) and Roth 403(b) accounts.

Tax Treatment of Roth IRA Distributions

LO 24.4 **Explain the tax treatment of qualified and nonqualified distributions from a Roth IRA or a Roth account in a 401(k) or 403(b) plan.**

The tax treatment of Roth IRA distributions are not quite as simple as they first seem. Any qualified distribution from a Roth IRA is free from federal income taxes. Qualified distributions must satisfy two requirements. First, the distribution must be made after the 5-tax-year period beginning with the first tax year for which a contribution was made to an individual's Roth IRA (or converted Roth IRA). For an individual with multiple Roth IRAs, the 5-year period begins for all Roth IRAs the first time a contribution is made to any Roth IRA. The 5-tax-year period ends on the last day of the individual's fifth consecutive taxable year beginning with the taxable year described in the preceding sentence (even if the participant dies prior to this date).

> **EXAMPLE**
>
> Karen Crumbcake made her first Roth IRA contribution on April 15, 2013, for the year 2012. The 5-year period ended on December 31, 2017, and distributions in 2018 or later have satisfied the 5-tax-year requirement. Because of the aggregation rule, if Karen opened another Roth IRA in 2015, the 5-year period ends at the end of 2017 for that IRA as well.

The second requirement for a qualified distribution is that the distribution may only be made after any one of the four following events has occurred:

- The participant has attained age 59½.
- The distribution is paid to a beneficiary due to the participant's death.
- The participant has become disabled so that he or she can no longer engage in any gainful activity.
- The withdrawal is made to pay qualified first-time homebuyer expenses.

Qualified first-time homebuyer expenses include acquisition costs of a first home (paid within 120 days of the distribution) for the participant, spouse, or any child, grandchild, or ancestor of the participant or spouse. This exception, however, has a $10,000 lifetime limit per IRA (or Roth IRA) participant.

Distributions that do not satisfy both the 5-year waiting period and the triggering event requirements are referred to as nonqualified distributions. Tax treatment of nonqualified distributions from a Roth IRA is still quite favorable. The law allows the withdrawal of the participant's Roth IRA contributions (or converted contributions) first without any income tax consequences. Once all contributions have been withdrawn, any additional amounts withdrawn are subject to both income tax and the 10 percent Sec. 72(t) excise tax. However, all of the exceptions to the premature distributions penalty that apply to traditional IRAs apply to distributions from the Roth IRA as well.

> **EXAMPLE**
>
> Sheila made her first Roth IRA contribution on April 15, 2007. As of the end of 2016, her total contributions equaled $14,000 and her total account was valued at $26,000. In 2015, at age 53, she withdraws $18,000 to pay for her son's college education expenses. Although she has met the 5-year requirement, the withdrawal does not match up with any of the specified trigger events. As a nonqualified distribution, $14,000 (her total contribution) can be withdrawn tax-free. She will have to include $4,000 as ordinary income on her tax return. The $4,000 technically is subject to the Sec. 72(t) 10 percent early withdrawal tax. However, the education expense exception to that tax applies and no penalty tax is due.

There is a special tax rule that applies to Roth IRAs created with a conversion. Under this rule, the Sec. 72(t) early withdrawal penalty tax applies to any distributions from a converted IRA made within the 5-year period starting with the first day of the tax year in which the conversion occurred. This tax rule is necessary to ensure that individuals cannot use the conversion as a way to avoid the Sec. 72(t) early withdrawal penalty tax.

> **EXAMPLE**
>
> Rhonda, converted an IRA on December 31, 2014, to a Roth IRA in the amount of $50,000 (she paid tax in 2014 on the $50,000 converted). In 2017, at age 45 she takes her first withdrawal from the converted IRA in the amount of $10,000 to purchase a new car. This withdrawal is not treated as ordinary income subject to income tax because it does not exceed the value of the converted amount. However, the $10,000 distribution is subject to the Sec. 72(t) early withdrawal penalty because it is within the 5-taxable-year period subsequent to the conversion. Since none of the exceptions applies, Rhonda is subject to a $1,000 penalty tax.

Tax Treatment of Roth Accounts

As with Roth IRAs, qualifying distributions from Roth 401(k) and Roth 403(b) accounts will not be subject to federal income tax. Because the tax treatment of these two programs is identical, we will refer to them both as Roth 401(k) accounts.

The qualification requirements for tax-free treatment are the same as with a Roth IRA—there is the same 5-tax-year rule and a triggering event requirement. The major difference is in the application of the 5-tax-year requirement. With Roth 401(k) plans, each Roth 401(k) has to satisfy the 5-tax-year rule separately; plans cannot be aggregated. The only exception is if an individual elects a direct rollover from one Roth 401(k) to another Roth 401(k) plan. In this situation, the time earned under the first plan is aggregated with the years of participation in the second plan.

The second major difference is the tax treatment of nonqualifying distributions. In a Roth IRA, contributions can be withdrawn without income tax consequences. With a Roth 401(k), nonqualifying distributions are subject to the same pro rata requirement that applies to distributions of after-tax contributions made after 1986 (see discussion above). That is, the distribution is taxed using a pro rata rule, looking solely at the value of the Roth account.

Even though Roth accounts are subject to required minimum distributions and a less favorable method of taxing nonqualified distributions, these issues are not likely to cause difficulties for most plan participants. Because the law allows rollovers from a Roth account to a Roth IRA, many participants will roll over their benefits at termination of employment. Once in a Roth IRA, these amounts are subject to the more liberal Roth IRA rules.

Exclusion of Income for Charitable Contributions

If a participant takes a withdrawal from an IRA or other tax-advantaged retirement plan during his or her lifetime and then contributes the amount to a charity, the distribution is treated as a taxable distribution and the participant may also be eligible for a deduction for part or all of the contribution to the charity. There are numerous rules that limit the charitable deduction, one being that an individual must itemize deductions in order to benefit from the contribution. Other complex rules limit the deduction to a specified percentage of income. For these reasons, it is quite possible that the deduction will not equal the amount taken into income.

As an attempt to encourage lifetime gifts to charities, the Pension Protection Act of 2006 allows distributions from IRAs and Roth IRAs (excluding SEPs and SIMPLEs) to simply be excluded from the participant's income. The exclusion may not exceed $100,000 per taxpayer per taxable year. The limit is based on the aggregate amount of a taxpayer's qualified charitable distributions in a year, meaning that an individual's tax-free IRA donations may consist of one or more distributions from one or more IRAs. Also to be eligible for the exclusion, the distribution must be made from the trustee directly to the charitable organization; the participant cannot receive the funds and later make the donation. Only contributions to public charities are allowed; contributions to donor-advised funds or private foundations are prohibited. Also, the donation must qualify as a deductible contribution under the current rules that apply to charitable deductions.

However, the exclusion only applies to distributions made on or after the date that the participant attains age 70½. The qualified charitable distribution (QCD) was made permanent in 2016 as part of the Consolidated Appropriations Act of 2016. Using the QCD can be very beneficial for any retiree that is subject to RMDs and gives money to a charity each year. The QCDs help satisfy the RMDs, can qualify as an income tax deduction as a charitable gift and the amount is not included in the taxpayer's income.

For the charitably inclined individual, there are several reasons to take advantage of the income exclusion. But one major reason to use the QCD is that the charitable contribution is fully excluded from income. By avoiding an increase in AGI, other tax problems can be avoided. For example, individuals with AGIs that exceed specified thresholds begin to lose the personal exemption and itemized deductions. This can help keep Medicare premiums, tax rates, and Social Security taxes lower. Another advantage of this strategy is that the distributions count toward satisfying the required minimum-distribution rules. Also, the amount contributed to the charity reduces the value of the individual's taxable estate.

ROLLOVERS

When a plan participant retires, changes jobs, or wants to change service providers (in the case of an IRA), in most cases a plan benefit can be rolled out of one plan and into another tax-deferred vehicle without any income tax consequences. Even though the rollover rules are relatively straightforward today, that doesn't mean that things don't go wrong, and a mistake could result in one of the biggest tax problems that an individual will ever encounter.

Distributions from Qualified, Governmental 457, and 403(b) Plans

LO 24.5 Distinguish between distributions that can be rolled over into other tax-advantaged retirement plans and those that cannot.

eligible rollover distribution

The regulatory scheme is virtually the same for distributions from qualified plans, 403(b) annuities, and 457 plans sponsored by a governmental agency. A participant receiving an **eligible rollover distribution** can defer tax on the distribution by rolling it over in total or in part to a qualified plan, 403(b) annuity, 457 governmental plan, or a traditional IRA. Most distributions qualify as eligible rollover distributions with a few limited exceptions. The most common distributions that do not qualify are as follows:

- minimum required distributions
- hardship withdrawals from a 401(k) plan
- distributions of substantially equal periodic payments made
    - over the participant's remaining life (or life expectancy)
    - over the joint lives (or life expectancies) of the participant and a beneficiary
    - over a period of more than 10 years

In addition, certain corrective distributions, loans treated as distributions, dividends on employer securities, and the cost of life insurance coverage are not eligible rollover distributions.

> **EXAMPLE**
>
> Your client, Jean Jones, calls you to say she is receiving a life annuity from her former employer's defined-benefit plan. This month Jean does not need the money. She wants to know whether she can roll the benefit into an IRA account. The answer is no. Because it is part of a stream of life annuity payments, it is not an eligible rollover amount.

Rollover

rollover

The term **rollover** is used to describe the situation in which the participant physically receives the distribution and subsequently deposits the amount into an eligible plan. A distribution must be rolled over by the 60th day after the day it is received, or the entire distribution is subject to income tax and, if applicable, the 10 percent Sec. 72(t) penalty tax. The IRS can waive the 60-day requirement when the failure to satisfy that requirement is beyond the individual's reasonable control (discussed further below). Remember that only one rollover is now allowed each year. However, that does not impact the amount of direct transfers allowable each year.

Direct Rollover

Rollovers are problematic because eligible rollover distributions from qualified plans, 403(b) annuities, or 457 governmental plans are subject to 20 percent mandatory income tax withholding. This means that a participant wanting to roll over the benefit only receives 80 percent of the total benefit. The entire benefit could be rolled over, but the other 20 percent would have to be contributed from other funds.

direct rollover

Mandatory withholding is not required if the participant elects a **direct rollover**. Qualified plans, 403(b) plans, and 457 governmental plans are required to give participants the option to elect a direct rollover for eligible distributions to an IRA or other employer-sponsored retirement plans. When a participant elects the direct rollover, instead of receiving the distribution, the funds are paid directly to the trustee of the new plan.

Planning Considerations

For many retiring plan participants, the best strategic decision is to elect a direct rollover of the entire benefit into an IRA. The direct rollover bypasses the 20 percent withholding rules, and once in the IRA the participant has maximum investment and withdrawal flexibility. In some cases (especially defined-benefit plans) it might be economically beneficial to take the distribution directly from the employer's retirement plan. There is also the occasional situation in which a participant receiving a lump-sum distribution from a qualified plan will want to consider electing one of the special tax rules that applies to lump-sum distributions.

There may also be several good reasons not to elect to roll over the entire distribution. As discussed earlier, the portion of the benefit that represents after-tax contributions should not be rolled over in most cases. Second, if the distribution includes the sponsoring company's stock, then the participant needs to carefully evaluate whether the net unrealized appreciation rules make it advantageous to take the stock portion of the distribution in income.

A participant over age 55 (but not yet age 59½) who needs funds might consider withdrawing the amount of the current need and rolling over the rest to avoid the 10 percent early withdrawal tax.

If the participant is changing jobs, the new employer's qualified plan, 403(b) annuity, or 457 governmental plan may (but is not required to) permit rollovers. Most individuals prefer the investment and withdrawal flexibility of an IRA. Also, if a participant dies while the money is held in the qualified plan (or 403(b) annuity or 457 governmental plan), the death beneficiary will be limited by the distribution options offered by the plan. The plan may require a single sum distribution or limited installment payments. If the benefit was in an IRA, the beneficiary typically can withdraw the funds over his or her entire life expectancy as allowed under the minimum-distribution rules. Stretching out the payments defers income taxes, resulting in additional tax deferred growth and a larger after-tax benefit for the heirs.

On the other hand, the ability to borrow, or to take advantage of specialized investment options, like a guaranteed investment contract, may create an incentive to choose the new employer's plan instead of an IRA. If the participant is approaching or has attained age 70½ and is continuing to work, the rollover to the new employer's plan can potentially delay the timing of required minimum distributions.

Distributions from IRAs

Rollovers from SEPs and SIMPLEs (as well as traditional IRAs) are somewhat easier to accomplish because the 20 percent mandatory withholding rules do not apply. SIMPLE distributions have the most limitations. They can be rolled into another SIMPLE or, 2 years after the SIMPLE was established, into a traditional IRA. Once in a traditional IRA, in most cases the entire IRA amount can be rolled into another IRA or, for that matter, a qualified plan, 403(b) annuity, or 457 governmental plan. One exception is that required minimum distributions for the year cannot be rolled over.

Even though the mandatory withholding rules do not apply, a participant wishing to roll over a distribution from a SEP, SIMPLE, or IRA should have the assets transferred directly from one trustee to the other. This transaction, referred to as a trustee-to-trustee transfer, ensures that the participant does not violate the 60-day rollover rule. This is an important consideration because failure to meet the 60-day requirement means the entire distribution is subject to income tax and, if applicable, the 10 percent Sec. 72(t) penalty on the entire taxable portion of the distribution.

Even considering the potential for a tax problem, there will be some occasions in which the participant will want short-term access to an IRA account. It is possible to withdraw some or all of the assets from a plan for 60 days. If a withdrawal is made and then returned within the 60 days, this is considered a rollover; no additional rollover can occur in that plan for one year from the time of the withdrawal. However, this requirement applies to each IRA separately; consequently, a participant with multiple IRAs could have one rollover in each plan annually.

For purposes of the one-year rule, trustee-to-trustee transfers and direct transfers from a qualified plan to an IRA are not counted as a rollover.

YOUR FINANCIAL SERVICES PRACTICE: CLIENT QUERY

Question: Your client Rudolph, aged 50, has found out that he is eligible to receive a hardship withdrawal from his profit-sharing plan account in the amount of $5,000. The withdrawal is to pay college education expenses for his daughter. He wants to know the withholding rules and income tax consequences of this distribution.

Solution: Because a hardship withdrawal is not an eligible rollover amount, he can receive the entire $5,000—the plan administrator is not required to withhold 20 percent for payment of income taxes. However, at the end of the year, Rudolph will have significant tax consequences. He will have to pay ordinary income taxes and the 10 percent Sec. 72(t) penalty tax. If the withdrawal were from an IRA account instead, the 10 percent penalty would not apply because the withdrawal is to pay for a family member's college education expenses.

Rollovers by Beneficiaries

Until this point, we have been discussing rollovers by participants. There are several situations in which rollovers by beneficiaries are allowed. A beneficiary who is the surviving spouse receiving an eligible rollover distribution may roll it over in total or in part to a qualified plan, 403(b) annuity, 457 governmental plan, or traditional IRA. Similarly, a spouse or former spouse entitled to a payout of benefits under a qualified domestic relations order (QDRO) is also entitled to a rollover.

Distributions in these cases are also subject to the direct rollover requirement and the 20 percent mandatory withholding requirements. When a spouse or former spouse rolls the benefit into an IRA or other plan, the spouse is treated as if he or she were the participant. This characterization is significant. Under the minimum-distribution rules, required distributions are calculated treating the spouse as the participant and not a beneficiary.

A spousal death beneficiary inheriting an IRA can leave the IRA account in the name of the decedent or roll the benefit into an IRA in his or her own name. Technically, the account can be retitled without even changing the IRA vehicle. The decision whether or not to retitle the account in the spouse's name has an impact on several related tax rules. If the spouse has not yet attained age 59½, changing the title could result in penalty taxes if withdrawals are made prior to age 59½. If the account is left in the participant's name, any payments to the spouse are death benefits exempt from the 10 percent penalty tax. On the other hand, retitling typically has advantages under the minimum-distribution rules. Fortunately there is no time limit on the ability to retitle the IRA, so the spousal beneficiary could leave the benefit in the name of the participant until the spouse attains age 59½ and then retitle it in his or her own name.

If a nonspouse is the death beneficiary of an IRA, then the IRA is treated as an inherited IRA. The IRA is generally a flexible vehicle that allows the death beneficiary to take withdrawals as slowly as required under the minimum-distribution rules. As discussed in the minimum-distribution rules, when there are multiple beneficiaries, it may even be possible to separate the inherited IRA into separate accounts to facilitate separate investing and withdrawal plans by the beneficiaries.

Under the Pension Protection Act of 2006, nonspouse death beneficiaries, including trusts, are allowed to roll distributions from a qualified plan, 403(b) plan, or government-sponsored 457 plan into a newly established inherited IRA—as long as the transfer of funds is made by a direct trustee to trustee payment. If the distribution is received directly by the non-spouse beneficiary, the beneficiary loses the ability to roll over the funds to an IRA. As with any inherited IRA, the newly established IRA is identified with respect to both the decedent and the beneficiary. For example, an acceptable designation is " Mary Jones as beneficiary of Peter Smith." The primary reason for requiring the rollover into an inherited IRA instead of an individual's own IRA has to do with the required minimum-distribution rules. Under those rules nonspouse beneficiaries have to take withdrawals over a specified period of time, described later in the chapter.

Waivers for the 60-Day Rollover Requirement

Code Sec. 402(c)(3) provides that the IRS may waive the 60-day rollover requirement when the failure to waive such requirement "would be against equity or good conscience, including casualty, disaster, or other events beyond the reasonable control of the individual subject to such requirement."

When the 60-day rule has been violated, Rev. Proc. 2003-16 clarifies the conditions in which a waiver can be granted. The waiver is automatic (no application to the IRS is required) if a financial institution receives funds prior to the expiration of the 60-day rollover period, the taxpayer follows all procedures for depositing the funds into an eligible retirement plan within the 60-day period, and, solely due to an error on the part of the financial institution, the funds are not deposited into an eligible retirement plan within the 60-day rollover period. Automatic approval is granted only: (1) if the funds are deposited into an eligible retirement plan within one year from the beginning of the 60-day rollover period; and (2) if the financial institution had deposited the funds as instructed.

If an automatic waiver is not available, the taxpayer can file for a waiver using the same procedures for a private letter ruling. Rev. Proc. 2003-16 provides that in determining whether to grant a waiver of the 60-day rollover requirement the IRS will consider all relevant facts and circumstances, including: (1) errors committed by a financial institution; (2) inability to complete a rollover due to death, disability, hospitalization, incarceration, or restrictions imposed by a foreign country or postal error; (3) the use of the amount distributed (for example, in the case of payment by check, whether the check was cashed); and (4) the time elapsed since the distribution occurred.

A review of the private letter rulings that have been granted show that the IRS has been quite generous in granting the waiver of the 60-day requirement. Typically, the waiver has been granted when:

- the facts and circumstances consisted of an error by the financial institution
- erroneous investment advice was given
- plan administrator errors were made
- the taxpayer's medical condition made it difficult to comply with the rules
- taxpayer errors occurred that ran contrary to the taxpayer's intention to make a rollover
- there was an existence of intervening causes such as the death of a spouse, weather conditions, or fraud by the taxpayer's child

Typically the waiver has been denied in situations where the taxpayer intended to use the amount for personal purposes and could not return it to the IRA before the 60-day time limit.

LUMP-SUM DISTRIBUTIONS

LO 24.6 **Discuss the special tax rules that may apply to lump-sum distributions from qualified plans.**

Instead of taking periodic payments from a qualified plan, employees are frequently permitted to receive their retirement benefit in a lump-sum distribution. In the past, participants who received a lump sum from a qualified plan had the opportunity to take advantage of several special tax rules. Most of these rules have been repealed, but individuals born before 1936 who receive a lump sum distribution from a qualified plan may still be eligible for grandfathered 10-year averaging. To be eligible, however, the participant must receive the entire benefit in one year, which disqualifies anyone who has already begun taking required minimum distributions. Because the group eligible for this grandfathered tax treatment is so small, we will not discuss it here.

There is one remaining special tax rule that applies to lump-sum distributions that include stock of the sponsoring employer. This rule, which allows the deferral of the net unrealized appreciation of distributed employer securities, is quite important for stock bonus plans and ESOPs as well as profit-sharing and 401(k) plans that invest in employer securities.

Net Unrealized Appreciation

net unrealized appreciation (NUA)

Whenever a recipient receives a lump-sum distribution from a qualified plan, he or she may elect to defer paying tax on the **net unrealized appreciation (NUA)** in qualifying employer securities. If the distribution is not a lump-sum distribution, NUA is excludible only to the extent that the appreciation is attributable to nondeductible employee contributions.

lump-sum distribution

To qualify as a **lump-sum distribution**, the participant's entire benefit (referred to as the balance to the credit) must be distributed in one tax year (typically a calendar year) on account of death, disability, termination of employment, or attainment of age 59½. Under the balance-to-the-credit rules, all pension plans of a single sponsor (defined-benefit, money-purchase, target-benefit or cash-balance plan) are treated as a single plan; all profit-sharing plans (including those with 401(k) features) are treated as a single plan; and all stock-bonus plans are treated as a single plan. This means, for example, that a participant in both a defined-benefit plan and a money-purchase plan would have to receive both benefits in the same year to receive the balance to the credit.

The NUA in the employer's stock that is included in a lump-sum distribution is excluded when computing the income tax on the distribution. NUA is the difference between the stock's value when credited to the participant's account and its fair market value on the date of distribution. The plan provides the participant with the value of the stock when it was credited to the account (referred to as the stock's cost basis). The plan can choose one of several methods for valuing the cost basis as found in Treas. Reg. Sec. 1.402(a)-1(b)(2)(i).

This NUA is taxable as long-term capital gain to the recipient when the shares are sold, even if they are sold immediately. If the recipient holds the shares for a period of time after distribution, any additional gain (above the NUA) is taxed as long- or short-term capital gain, depending on the holding period (long term if held for one year or more).

To ensure that the participant's unrealized appreciation is taxed at some point, if the stock is left to an heir, the unrealized appreciation is not entitled to a step up in basis, but is treated as income in respect of a decedent (IRD). As with other IRD, the amount retains its character as long-term capital gain, and the beneficiary is entitled to a deduction for the amount of estate taxes paid on the IRD amount.

Taking Advantage of the NUA Rule

Many mid-size and large companies provide employer securities as an investment alternative or even make employer-matching contributions in employer stock. Because the current long-term capital-gains rate is much lower than the top marginal tax bracket, participants receiving a lump sum that includes employer stock should seriously consider the impact of this tax opportunity, before electing to roll the entire lump sum into an IRA. Once the lump sum is rolled over, the NUA tax advantages are lost and the future distributions will be subject to ordinary income tax. The opportunity can also be lost if the individual sells the stock prior to retirement, or chooses to receive the distribution in cash instead of in stock.

Another reason the NUA rule can be quite useful is that a participant may elect to take advantage of the deferral of income recognition on NUA and roll over the remainder of the lump-sum distribution (see private letter ruling 9721036). This means a participant in a 401(k) plan with an employer securities account can elect NUA treatment on the employer stock account and roll over any other investments tax free into an IRA.

> **EXAMPLE**
>
> Joe retires at age 62 and receives a lump-sum distribution with a current market value of $700,000. The market value of employer securities is $200,000, but the cost basis is $50,000. Joe should consider rolling the cash (worth $500,000) into an IRA but not rolling over the $200,000. At the time of the distribution, Joe will have to pay tax on the $50,000 cost basis. When he sells the stock, he will pay long-term capital gains on the $150,000 NUA, and he will pay long-term gain on any subsequent appreciation (as long as he holds the stock for at least one year). If Joe is in the 35 percent federal income tax bracket, he pays 35 percent on the $50,000 distribution, but he pays only 15 percent on the rest of the gain. If he rolls the employer securities into an IRA, all subsequent distributions will be taxed at 35 percent.

This example illustrates the importance of considering NUA tax treatment. It is the type of situation in which the election may well be the right choice. However, in each individual case, determining whether or not to roll the benefit into an IRA or to take the employer stock in income will not be an easy decision. Factors in the decision-making process include the following:

- The rule only has a positive impact when the cost basis of the securities is significantly lower than the current market value.
- If the participant needs cash in the near future, then taking the stock in income is probably a good idea since it results in a conversion of a portion of the taxable income from ordinary income to capital gains. Also, if the individual is under age 59½, the Section 72(t) tax will only apply to that portion of the income subject to ordinary income tax.
- Electing NUA tax treatment may offer an opportunity to take withdrawals at a lower than normal tax rate and provide tax diversification.
- A younger person receiving a distribution that includes company stock will generally want to sell the stock to diversify his or her retirement portfolio. Because the sale will result in current taxation, the individual is giving up what could be significant income tax deferral if he or she decides not to roll the stock into an IRA. Deferral is very valuable, even if the tax rate in the future is somewhat higher than the rate today.

In addition to the above considerations, the participant's attitude about paying taxes and projections about future tax rates are important considerations. The planner's main objective should be to present all of the alternatives clearly so the participant can make the right election.

MINIMUM-DISTRIBUTION RULES

The minimum-distribution rules contained in IRC Sec. 401(a)(9) are designed to limit the deferral of taxation on plan benefits. The primary reason for allowing the deferral of taxes is to encourage savings for retirement. This tax-preferred item comes at a great cost to the government; therefore, the minimum-distribution rules have been designed both to ensure that a significant portion of a participant's benefit is paid out during retirement and to limit the period for benefits paid after death.

General

The rules of Sec. 401(a)(9) apply in essentially the same way (with a few exceptions) to all tax-deferred retirement plans, including qualified plans, IRAs (including SEPs and SIMPLEs), 403(b) plans, and even IRC Sec. 457 plans. This means that any Roth accounts in a 401(k) plan or 403(b) plan would be subject to the minimum-distribution rules. Roth IRAs are not subject to the rules governing lifetime distributions to the participant, but are required to make minimum distributions to the beneficiary after the death of the participant.

It is important to understand that there are actually two separate minimum-distribution rules. One rule applies to those individuals who live until the required beginning date (generally April 1st following the year the participant attains age 70½) and a separate rule that applies when the participant dies before the required beginning date.

Another complicating factor is that Sec. 402 allows a spouse the option to roll over a benefit received at the death of the participant into an IRA in his or her own name. The rollover is treated as a complete distribution from the participant's plan, meaning that the minimum-distribution rules will have to be satisfied, treating the spouse as the participant. This rule provides planning opportunities, but can also be confusing.

Failing to satisfy the minimum-distribution rules results in an extremely harsh penalty. Under Sec. 4974, if the minimum distributions are not made in a timely manner, the plan participant is required to pay a 50 percent excise tax on the amount of the shortfall between the amount actually distributed and the amount required to be distributed under the minimum-distribution rules. In addition, if the plan is a qualified plan, it may lose its tax-favored status if the minimum-distribution rules are not satisfied.

To help enforce the minimum-distribution rules, IRA trustees are required to report on Form 5498 participants who have a required minimum distribution. At the same time, IRA trustees are also required to notify participants by January 31 that a required distribution is due for that year. Trustees can either provide a calculation of the required minimum distribution or offer to make the calculation at the participant's request. At the present time, there are no similar reporting requirements for qualified plans. The requirement also currently ends at the participant's death; no reporting is required concerning required distributions for death beneficiaries.

Required Minimum Distributions at the Required Beginning Date

LO 24.7 **Describe when required minimum distributions must begin, and how to calculate the required minimum distributions during the participant's lifetime and after the participant's death.**

The next several pages describe the required minimum-distribution rules that apply when the individual has lived until the required beginning date (generally April 1 of the year following attainment of age 70½). The rules for determining the minimum distribution differ depending on whether the distribution is from an individual account plan or is payable as an annuity—either from a defined-benefit plan or from a commercial annuity. The account plan rules apply to all IRAs, 403(b) plans, SEPs, SIMPLEs, Sec. 457 plans, and qualified plans of the defined-contribution type, unless a commercial annuity is purchased prior to the required beginning date. The account plan rules are reviewed below, followed by a discussion of the annuity distribution rules.

Required Beginning Date

required beginning date

The date benefit payments must begin is called the **required beginning date**. This date is generally April 1st of the year following the calendar year in which the participant attains age 70½. However, there are two important exceptions:

- Any participant in a government or church plan who remains an employee after reaching age 70½ does not have to begin distributions until April 1st following the later of either the calendar year in which the participant reaches age 70½ or the calendar year in which he or she retires.

- Any qualified plan participant who reaches age 70½ and who is not considered a 5 percent owner of the entity sponsoring the plan does not have to begin distributions until April 1st following the later of either the year of attainment of age 70½ or the year in which the participant retires. This exception also applies to 403(b) plans without regard to the 5-percent-owner rule.

Note that there are no exceptions to the required beginning date for IRAs—which also includes SEPs and SIMPLEs. For these plans, the required beginning date is always the April 1st of the year following the calendar year in which the covered participant attains age 70½.

first distribution year

The required beginning date is somewhat of a misnomer because a minimum distribution is required for the year in which the participant attains age 70½ or, if one of the exceptions applies, the year in which the participant retires. Because a distribution must be made for this year, it is referred to as the first distribution year. The distribution for the **first distribution year** can be delayed until the following April 1st, but required distributions for all subsequent distribution years must be made by December 31 of the applicable year.

> **EXAMPLE**
>
> Shelley, who has an IRA, turned 70 on March 15, 2017. On September 15, 2017, she turned 70½. The first required distribution from Shelley's IRA is for the year ending

December 31, 2017, but she has the option to take the distribution any time in 2017 or delay it up to the required beginning date of April 1, 2018. However, if she delays the distribution into 2018, she will still have to take a minimum distribution for the second distribution year by December 31, 2018.

As you can see, delaying the first distribution into the second year doubles up the required distribution for that year and increases taxes for that year—not a desirable result in some cases.

Table 24-3
Uniform Lifetime Table

Age of Participant	Distribution Period	Age of Participant	Distribution Period
70	27.4	93	9.6
71	26.5	94	9.1
72	25.6	95	8.6
73	24.7	96	8.1
74	23.8	97	7.6
75	22.9	98	7.1
76	22.0	99	6.7
77	21.2	100	6.3
78	20.3	101	5.9
79	19.5	102	5.5
80	18.7	103	5.2
81	17.9	104	4.9
82	17.1	105	4.5
83	16.9	106	4.2
84	15.5	107	3.9
85	14.8	108	3.7
86	14.1	109	3.4
87	13.4	110	3.1
88	12.7	111	2.9
89	12.0	112	2.6
90	11.4	113	2.4
91	10.8	114	2.1
92	10.2	115 and older	1.9

Account Plan Distributions During the Participant's Life

Once the participant attains the required beginning date, a minimum distribution is required for each and every distribution year (and no credit is given for larger distributions in prior years) through the year of the participant's death. The required distribution is calculated by dividing the participant's benefit by the applicable distribution period. The participant's benefit in a defined-contribution plan, 403(b) plan, or IRA is based on the participant's account balance. In an IRA account, the participant's benefit for a distribution year is the IRA account balance at the end of the previous calendar year. For qualified plans and 403(b) plans, the employee's benefit is his or her individual account balance as of the last valuation date in the calendar year immediately preceding the distribution year.

The distribution period comes from Table 24-3 Uniform Lifetime Table and is determined based on the age of the participant at the end of the distribution year. The same methodology is used for every year the participant is alive. Each year the applicable distribution period is determined by simply looking at the uniform table based on the oldest age of the participant during that year.

EXAMPLE

Sally, an IRA participant, is aged 71 at the last day of the first distribution year (the year she attains age 70½). Her IRA balance at the end of the preceding year is $200,000. The first year's required distribution is $200,000/26.5 = $7,547. This is the required minimum regardless of the beneficiary unless Sally's sole beneficiary is her spouse and he is more than 10 years younger than she. For the second distribution year the applicable distribution period is 25.6 (table amount for a 72-year-old participant).

Table 24-4
Joint and Last Survivor Table

Ages	45	46	47	48	49	50	51	52	53	54
68	39.6	38.7	37.9	37.0	36.2	35.3	34.5	33.7	32.9	32.1
69	39.5	38.6	37.8	36.9	36.0	35.2	34.4	33.6	32.8	32.0
70	39.4	38.6	37.7	36.8	35.9	35.1	34.3	33.4	32.6	31.8
71	39.4	38.5	37.6	36.7	35.9	35.0	34.2	33.3	32.5	31.7
72	39.3	38.4	37.5	36.6	35.8	34.9	34.1	33.2	32.4	31.6
73	39.3	38.4	37.5	36.6	35.7	34.8	34.0	33.1	32.3	31.5
74	39.2	38.3	37.4	36.5	35.6	34.8	33.9	33.0	32.2	31.4
75	39.2	38.3	37.4	36.5	35.6	34.7	33.8	33.0	32.1	31.3
76	39.1	38.2	37.3	36.4	35.5	34.6	33.8	32.9	32.0	31.2
77	39.1	38.2	37.3	36.4	35.5	34.6	33.7	32.8	32.0	31.1
78	39.1	38.2	37.2	36.3	35.4	34.5	33.6	32.8	31.9	31.0

*Source: Treas. Reg. Sec. 1.401(a)(9)-9

An exception applies if the participant's sole beneficiary is the participant's spouse and the spouse is more than 10 years younger than the participant. In that case, the participant is permitted to use the longer distribution period measured by the joint life and last survivor life expectancy of the participant and spouse (calculated looking at the IRS Joint and Last Survivor Table, a portion of which is reproduced below. The complete table appears in the appendix.) This exception will apply for any distribution year in which the spouse (who is more than 10 years younger than the participant) is the sole beneficiary as of January 1 of the distribution year. This means that if the spouse dies or the couple gets divorced after January 1, the joint life table can still be used for that year.

Table 24-5
Single Life Table*

Age	Multiple	Age	Multiple
40	43.6	66	20.2
41	42.7	67	19.4
42	41.7	68	18.6
43	40.7	69	17.8
44	39.8	70	17.0
45	38.8	71	16.3
46	37.9	72	15.5
47	37.0	73	14.8
48	36.0	74	14.1
49	35.1	75	13.4
50	34.2	76	12.7
51	33.3	77	12.1
52	32.3	78	11.4
53	31.4	79	10.8
54	30.5	80	10.2
55	29.6	81	9.7
56	28.7	82	9.1
57	27.9	83	8.6
58	27.0	84	8.1
59	26.1	85	7.6
60	25.2	86	7.1
61	24.4	87	6.7
62	23.5	88	6.3
63	22.7	89	5.9
64	21.8	90	5.5
65	21.0		

*Source: Treas. Reg. Sec. 1.401(a)(9)-9.

EXAMPLE

If Sally's beneficiary in the previous example was her 51-year-old spouse, the minimum distribution would be $200,000/34.2 = $5,848. In this case, for the second distribution year the applicable distribution period is 33.2—their joint life expectancy calculated at the end of that distribution year.

Death of the Participant after the Required Beginning Date

For the participant who dies after the required beginning date, distributions must continue to satisfy the required minimum-distribution rules. In the year of death, the heirs must take the decedent's required distribution (if this distribution was not taken before death) based on the method under which the decedent had been taking distributions.

In subsequent years, the required distributions will depend upon who is the chosen beneficiary. When the beneficiary is an individual who is not the spouse, the applicable distribution period is that individual's life expectancy (using the IRS Single Life Table) as of the end of the calendar year following death. If the beneficiary is older than the decedent participant, then the participant's life expectancy is used instead. In subsequent years, the applicable distribution period is the life expectancy from the previous year less one. This means that remaining distributions are now made over a fixed period. This is true even if the beneficiary at the time of the participant's death subsequently dies and leaves the benefit to another payee.

EXAMPLE

John dies at age 82 with an $800,000 IRA account (at the end of the previous year). For the year of death, the required minimum distribution is $800,000 ÷ 17.1 = $46,783. Assuming that, at the end of the year of death, the value of the account is $840,000 and on September 30 of the following year the sole beneficiary is John's daughter, Sarah, who is aged 54 at the end of that year, the minimum distribution is $840,000 ÷ 30.5 = $27,540. The remaining distribution period is now fixed. In the next year, the applicable distribution period is 29.5 (30.5 – 1), and so on in future years. In total, distributions can continue for 31 years after the death of the participant. This would be true even if Sarah dies before the end of the period and leaves the benefit to another individual.

If there is no designated beneficiary as of September 30th of the year after the participant's death (which would be the case if a nonperson such as a charity or the estate is the designated beneficiary), the distribution period is the participant's life expectancy calculated in the year of death, reduced by one for each subsequent year. However, if the plan so provides, the beneficiary can nevertheless elect to receive a single-sum distribution of the death benefit.

EXAMPLE

Sandra dies at age 80 with her estate as the beneficiary. Her account balance at the end of the year of her death is $240,000, and her life expectancy is 9.2 years (10.2 – 1) in the year following death. The required minimum distribution in the year following death is $26,087 ($240,000 ÷ 9.2). In each following year, the applicable distribution period is reduced by one, until all amounts are distributed after 10 years.

If the participant's spouse is the chosen beneficiary, there are a number of options. In most cases, the spouse will elect to roll the benefit into his or her own IRA (or, in some cases, treat the account as his or her own). In this case, subsequent distributions (in the year following death) are calculated by using the same methodology as when the participant was alive—with the spouse now treated as the participant.

EXAMPLE

Rollo dies at age 80; his spouse Cassandra, aged 75, is the beneficiary. Cassandra rolls the benefit into her own IRA and names their only child, Alexis, as beneficiary. During Cassandra's life, the uniform table is still used to calculate the minimum required distribution. For example, in the year following Rollo's death, the applicable distribution period is 22.0 (see table for individual aged 76). Assume that Cassandra dies at age 86 and, on the September 30th following the year of her death, her daughter Alexis is the beneficiary. At the end of that year, Alexis is aged 53. The applicable distribution period is 31.4 for that year (see table). This is now the fixed remaining distribution period, even if Alexis dies prior to the end of that time period. Her beneficiaries can continue distributions over the remaining period. In this example, the minimum required distributions are spread over a 50-year period!

If the participant's spouse is his or her sole beneficiary as of September 30th in the year following the year of death, and the distribution is not rolled over, the distribution period during the spouse's life is the spouse's single life expectancy, recalculated each year. For years after the year of the spouse's death, the distribution period is the spouse's life expectancy calculated in the year of death, reduced by one for each subsequent year.

Annuity Payments

When a defined-benefit pension plan pays out a benefit in the form of an annuity, or if a commercial annuity is purchased to satisfy benefit payments in a defined-contribution plan, the regulations provide a method for determining whether the annuity satisfies the minimum-distribution rules. Under these rules, the determination only has to be made one time—when the annuity payments begin.

If the annuity is meant to satisfy the required minimum-distribution rules, it must begin on or before the participant's required beginning date. Most life annuity and joint and survivor annuities will satisfy the rules as long as the payment interval is uniform, does not exceed one year, and the stream of payments satisfies a nonincreasing requirement. The term nonincreasing is defined broadly in the regulations, and variable annuities and annuities that increase due to cost-of-living increases fit within the definition. An annuity with a cash-refund feature also qualifies.

Joint and survivor annuities with a survivor benefit of up to 100 percent are generally allowed. The only exception is for nonspousal beneficiaries who are more than 10 years younger than the participant. In this case, the maximum survivor benefit will be something less than 100 percent. To determine the applicable survivor percentage, see the IRS Table reproduced below. The example below explains how this works.

Table 24-6
Table for Determining the Maximum Applicable Survivor Annuity Percentage

Excess of Age of Employee over Age of Beneficiary	Applicable Percentage	Excess of Age of Employee over Age of Beneficiary	Applicable Percentage
10 years or less	100%	28	62%
11	96	29	61
12	93	30	60
13	90	31	59
14	87	32	59
15	84	33	58
15	84	33	58
16	82	34	57
17	79	35	56
18	77	36	56
18	77	36	56
19	75	37	55
20	73	38	55
21	72	39	54
22	70	40	54
23	68	41	53
24	67	42	53
25	66	43	53
26	64	44 years and more	52
27	63		

Source: Treas. Reg. Sec. 1.401(a)(9)-2

EXAMPLE

Sandra wants to elect a 100 percent joint and survivor benefit from her company's defined-benefit plan beginning at age 70. She is considering her son, Albert, aged 45, as the contingent beneficiary. In the table, notice that the maximum survivor benefit for a beneficiary who is 25 years younger than the participant (70 – 45 = 25) is 66 percent.

The life annuity can have a period certain (or the annuity can be a period certain annuity without a lifetime contingency) as long as the period certain does not exceed the joint life expectancy of the participant and beneficiary using the uniform table (or joint and survivor table in the case of a spouse more than 10 years younger than the participant).

EXAMPLE

Suppose Herb, aged 70 (at the end of the first distribution year), chooses a joint and survivor annuity with Sally, aged 80, as the contingent beneficiary. Herb wants to have a period-certain feature and wants to know if there are limitations on the length of the period certain. Because the joint life expectancy under the uniform table for Herb (age 70) is 27.4, this is the maximum length for period-certain payments for an annuity beginning at age 70.

YOUR FINANCIAL SERVICES PRACTICE: ANNUITIZING AFTER THE REQUIRED BEGINNING DATE

It's quite possible that an IRA participant past the required beginning date would want to purchase an immediate annuity. This transaction is allowed as long as the amount of the distribution satisfies the account plan rules in the year the annuity is purchased, and the annuity purchased satisfies the annuity limitations. Another implication of the annuity purchase is that payments from the annuity cannot be used to satisfy the minimum-distribution requirements from other IRAs. If, for example, a client has two IRAs and purchases an annuity with one, the total required withdrawals after the annuity purchase may be substantially higher than with two IRA account plans.

Preretirement Death Benefits

When the participant dies prior to the required beginning date, and does not designate a beneficiary or chooses a nonperson, such as a charity, an institution or an estate, as the beneficiary the participant's entire interest must be distributed by December 31st of the calendar year that contains the fifth anniversary of the date the participant dies. Under this rule, the entire interest could be distributed at the end of the 5-year period.

When the chosen beneficiary is a person distributions can generally be paid out over the beneficiary's lifetime. However, it is important to review the plan document, since the plan may give the beneficiary the option to choose the "five-year" rule as an alternative. The rules are somewhat different for spousal and nonspousal beneficiaries. For nonspousal beneficiaries, the minimum-distribution rule is satisfied if distributions are made over the expected lifetime of the beneficiary, as long as the benefit begins by December 31st of the year following the year of death. The calculation of each required distribution is determined using the same methodology as with a nonspousal beneficiary when the participant dies after the required beginning date.

> **EXAMPLE**
>
> Suppose that Gilligan dies at age 65 and his daughter Ginger is the beneficiary of his IRA. In the year following death, Ginger is aged 40 and her life expectancy is 43.6 years. If the lifetime exception is used and the account balance is $300,000 at the end of the year in which Gilligan dies, the required distribution in the following year is $300,000 ÷ 43.6 = $6,880. Note that as long as distributions begin by the end of the year following the year Gilligan died, distributions can continue for 44 years. If this deadline is not met, the entire distribution must be made within 5 years!

When the beneficiary is the participant's spouse, the distribution may be made over the life of the spouse, as long as payments begin on or before the later of (1) December 31st of the calendar year immediately after the calendar year in which the participant dies or (2) December 31st of the calendar year immediately after the year in which the participant would have reached age 70½. However, if the spouse dies prior to the commencement of benefit payments, then benefits may be distributed to his or her beneficiary under the same rules that would apply to the participant. Note that the spousal exception is generally not utilized since the spouse will typically elect to roll the benefit into his or her own account.

Beneficiary Issues

All of the required minimum-distribution rules involve the identification of the participant's beneficiary. Under the current regulations, the beneficiary used to determine the required distribution is the beneficiary that actually inherits the benefit. Technically, it is the beneficiary identified as of September 30th of the year following death. (See the discussion of postdeath planning below.)

If there are multiple designated beneficiaries on September 30th of the year following death (and separate accounts for each participant have not been established), the life expectancy of the oldest beneficiary (with the shortest life expectancy) is used to determine the required distributions. If one of those beneficiaries is a nonperson, then the participant is deemed to have no designated beneficiary. If there are multiple designated beneficiaries and separate accounts are provided for, the required minimum distributions of his or her separate share are taken by each beneficiary over the fixed-term life expectancy of each respective beneficiary.

Generally, a beneficiary must be an individual (that is, not a charity or the participant's estate) in order to take advantage of the ability to stretch out payments over a beneficiary's lifetime. A nonperson beneficiary (estate, charity, trust) is treated as having no beneficiary, unless the beneficiary is a trust and the following requirements are satisfied:

- The trust is irrevocable at death.
- The beneficiaries under the trust are identifiable.
- The trust document or a statement identifying the distribution provisions is provided to the plan's administrator following the participant's death.

In the case of a trust that conforms to these rules, the beneficiaries of the trust will be treated as the beneficiaries for purposes of the required minimum-distribution rules. If there are multiple beneficiaries then the multiple-beneficiary rule applies here, too. However, there is no opportunity to create separate accounts within the trust.

Additional Rules

Multiple Plans

With qualified retirement plans, required minimum distributions must be calculated—and distributed—separately for each plan subject to the rules. The rules are more liberal with multiple IRAs or 403(b) plans. With IRAs, the minimum distribution must be calculated separately for each IRA, but then the actual distributions can come from any of the IRAs. If, however, an individual has accounts in his or her own name as well as inherited IRAs, he or she has to treat each category separately. Similarly, an individual with multiple 403(b) plans can take the required minimum distributions from any of the 403(b) plans. IRAs and 403(b) plans may not be aggregated.

Rollovers and Transfers

As we have discussed, liberal rules allow participants the right to roll or transfer benefits from one type of tax-sheltered retirement plan to another. This transaction is relatively simple except in the case of the individual rolling over the benefit after attainment of age 70½. In order to ensure that the minimum required distributions are made, the rules clarify what to do in this special situation.

Special rules apply to amounts rolled (or transferred) from one tax-sheltered retirement plan to another. From the perspective of the distributing plan, the amount distributed (to be rolled over or transferred) is credited toward determining the minimum required distribution from that plan. However, if a portion of the distribution is necessary to satisfy the minimum-distribution requirements, that portion may not be rolled (or transferred) into another plan.

> **EXAMPLE**
>
> Shirley, aged 71½, receives a single-sum distribution from a qualified retirement plan. She intends to roll the distribution into an IRA. She may not roll the portion of the lump-sum distribution that represents the minimum required distribution for the current distribution year into the IRA, assuming such distribution has not already been taken from the retirement plan.

After the amount is rolled into the transferee plan, it will count toward determining the participant's account balance which is used for determining future required minimum distributions. However, because the required minimum distribution is based on the benefit in the previous year, the amount rolled over does not affect the minimum until the following year.

Spousal Rollovers

When the spouse is the beneficiary of the participant's retirement plan benefit, the spouse has a unique opportunity to roll the benefit into an IRA in his or her own name. Under the required minimum-distribution rules, the rollover is treated as a complete distribution of the participant's benefit, satisfying the required minimum-distribution rules from the perspective of the participant's plan. After the benefit is in the spouse's name, the required minimum-distribution rules have to be satisfied with the spouse treated as the participant. The spouse has the opportunity to name a beneficiary and calculate future required minimum distributions based upon the joint life expectancy of the spouse and the beneficiary.

Grandfather Provisions for Qualified Plans and 403(b) Plans

There are two situations in which the current distribution rules do not apply. In a qualified plan, participants with accrued benefits as of December 31, 1983, were allowed to sign an election form (prior to January 1, 1984) to indicate the time and method of distribution of their plan benefit. The benefit election form had to be specific and had to conform to pre-TEFRA rules, which allowed distributions to be deferred much later than age 70½. These grandfather provisions were contained in Sec. 242(b) of TEFRA and are generally referred to as Sec. 242(b) elections.

The Sec. 242(b) elections continue to be valid if benefits are being paid from the original plan in which the election was made, and if the plan distributions follow the Sec. 242(b) distribution election. If it is not followed exactly with regard to the form and timing of the payments, the election is considered revoked. A substitution or addition of a beneficiary generally does not result in the revocation of the election. If the benefit election is changed or revoked after the individual has reached the required beginning date under the current rules, the participant will be forced to "make up" distributions that would otherwise (absent the Sec. 242(b) election) have been required under the current rules.

Sec. 242(b) elections can delay the timing of required distributions substantially. The retirement planner should be sure to ask if the client has retained a Sec. 242(b) election form in his or her files. As noted above, the election has to be followed exactly in order to avoid having to take a potentially large distribution at some later date.

In a 403(b) plan, a separate grandfathering rule allows the participant to delay the distribution of amounts earned prior to 1987 until the participant attains age 75 as long as such pre-1987 amounts can be identified. There are no special grandfathering exceptions that apply to IRA distributions.

Planning

LO 24.8   **Describe the postmortem planning opportunities under the required minimum-distribution rules.**

Under the current rules, the designated beneficiary does not have to be determined until September 30th of the year following the year of the participant's death. This permits some flexibility for determining the postdeath minimum required distributions from the deceased participant's retirement plan or IRA. Of course, the decedent's potential beneficiaries are "carved in stone" at the time of his or her death, because the decedent can no longer make additional beneficiary designations. However, the use of a qualified disclaimer or early distribution of a beneficiary's share could be effective in changing the designated beneficiary to contingent beneficiaries by the time specified to determine such beneficiary.

> **EXAMPLE**
>
> Helen dies at age 80. At the time of her death, her son, Bud, from her first marriage, The American College, and her second husband, Saul, are each beneficiaries of one-third of her 401(k) plan death benefit. Before September 30th of the year following Helen's death, Saul rolls his benefit into a spousal IRA and benefits are paid out to The American College, leaving Bud as the sole beneficiary. This means subsequent required minimum distributions will be based on Bud's life expectancy. If Helen had also named

a contingent beneficiary for Bud's benefit (for example, Bud's child, Kelly), Bud could disclaim his benefit in favor of Kelly and the distribution could continue over Kelly's longer life expectancy.

Another way to limit problems that could arise with multiple beneficiaries is to divide benefits into separate accounts. The regulations define acceptable separate accounting to include allocating investment gains and losses, and contributions and forfeitures, on a pro rata basis in a reasonable and consistent manner among each separate portion and any other benefits. If these rules are followed, the separate beneficiary of each share determines his or her minimum required distribution based on his or her life expectancy according to his or her age on the birthday that occurs in the year following the year of the decedent's death. The regulations clearly state that the decedent's account can be divided into a separate account for each beneficiary up to the end of the year following the death of the participant.

YOUR FINANCIAL SERVICES PRACTICE: BENEFICIARY ELECTIONS

Under the regulations, taking advantage of the maximum allowable deferral is an option that remains open even after the death of the participant. But to do so, the beneficiary designation must be reviewed during the life of the participant and an appropriate list of contingent beneficiaries chosen. For example, with a married person with children, the following beneficiary designation including three layers of contingent beneficiary elections may be an appropriate choice:

- payable to the spouse and if disclaimed
- payable to a credit-shelter trust with the spouse as income beneficiary and the children as remainder beneficiaries, and if disclaimed
- payable directly to the children, and if disclaimed
- payable to a trust with the grandchildren as beneficiaries

Because of the ability to disclaim benefits, to pay them out, or to establish separate accounts after the death of the participant, postmortem planning is an important consideration. However, to effectively use these tools, the participant should give careful thought to the beneficiary election form. For many individuals, this means the establishment of multiple layers of contingent beneficiaries on the designation form in order to provide the most flexibility after the participant's death.

CHAPTER REVIEW

Key Terms and Concepts

Sec. 72(t) penalty tax
substantially equal periodic payments
eligible rollover distribution
rollover
direct rollover

net unrealized appreciation (NUA)
lump-sum distribution
required beginning date
first distribution year

Chapter 24: Review Questions

Review questions are based on the learning objectives in this chapter. Thus, a [24.3] at the end of a question means that the question is based on learning objective 3. If there are multiple objectives, they are all listed

1. Describe the federal income tax treatment of benefit distributions to a participant from a tax-advantaged retirement plan. [24.1]

2. Describe the estate tax treatment of the balance in a qualified plan account or IRA and how this affects the income tax treatment of a distribution to a death beneficiary. [24.1]

3. Which of the following plan distributions is subject to the 10 percent Sec. 72(t) penalty? [24.2]

    a. a death benefit from a defined-benefit plan payable to a beneficiary upon the death of an employee aged 52

    b. a lump-sum benefit from a money-purchase pension plan payable to a disabled employee aged 57

    c. a distribution from a 401(k) plan to an employee aged 52 who qualifies under the plan's "financial hardship" distribution provision

    d. an in-service distribution made to an employee aged 63 from a profit-sharing plan

    e. a $10,000 distribution from a SIMPLE to pay for qualifying acquisition costs of a first home for the participant

4. Ralph withdraws $100,000 from his IRA for start-up costs for his new business. In the same year, he pays $40,000 in tuition, $12,000 in room, board, and fees, and $2,000 for

books for his two daughters, who are full-time students at Haverford College. What is the applicable Sec. 72(t) penalty tax? [24.2]

5. What method for avoiding the 10 percent early-withdrawal penalty is the most useful and flexible for planning purposes? [24.2]

6. What are the risks of relying on the substantially equal periodic payments exception? [24.2]

7. Ralph has two IRAs, one created with nondeductible contributions (contributions of $12,000 and a current value of $43,000) and one created by a rollover from a qualified plan ($357,000). He has not taken any previous withdrawals. Ralph withdraws $12,000 from the nondeductible IRA, thinking this transaction will have no income tax ramifications. In reality, how much of the distribution is taxable? [24.3]

8. Your client, Cherie Reisenberg, is single and plans to retire at age 62. Payments from her employer's qualified plan will start at the end of the first month after her 62nd birthday. The monthly retirement benefit that will be paid to Cherie in the form of a single-life annuity without any guaranteed payments is $1,000. Her cost basis in the plan is $72,900. What portion of her first distribution will be nontaxable? [24.3]

9. Mick Jagner (aged 60 in 2017) made his first Roth IRA contribution on January 20, 2012, for the 2011 tax year. On February 1, 2017, he withdraws $19,000 from the Roth IRA to help purchase a new car. This is the first withdrawal from the Roth IRA that he has taken. As of February 1st the value of the account is $24,000 and $15,000 represents Roth IRA contributions. [24.4]

   a. Based on these facts, what is the tax treatment of the withdrawal?
   b. Now assume that Mick is aged 55, not aged 60. What is the tax treatment of the withdrawal?

10. Sally is receiving a life annuity from her former employer's defined-benefit pension plan. Sometimes she doesn't need the money for day-to-day expenses. Can she roll over some of the payments into an IRA? [24.5]

11. Carole Gumley, aged 54, is retiring early and has a profit-sharing plan account balance of $150,000. She receives a notice of the right to elect a direct rollover, but she hasn't yet decided where she would like to invest her retirement money so she receives the distribution from the plan directly. [24.5]

    a. How much will Carole actually receive from the plan?
    b. Can Carole roll over the entire benefit?

c. What are the tax ramifications if she doesn't get around to rolling over the benefit for 75 days?

d. Would the situation be different if the reason that she waited 75 days is that a financial advisor told her that she had 90 days to accomplish the rollover?

12. In what situations is it more prudent to take some or all of a distribution into income instead of rolling the benefit into an IRA? [24.5]

13. What conditions must a lump-sum distribution meet in order to qualify for special tax treatment? [24.6]

14. Andrew Fiddler, aged 45, receives a distribution of $400,000 in cash and $100,000 of company stock from his employer's 401(k) plan. Andrew rolls over the cash portion of the distribution and elects to take the stock portion into income. The company tells him that the cost basis for the stock is $25,000. Andrew sells the stock 3 years later for $125,000. What are the tax ramifications of these two transactions? [24.6]

15. What types of plans are subject to the required minimum-distribution rules? [24.7]

16. Sara Stewart must take a required minimum distribution of $2,000 from a qualified retirement plan at the required beginning date. The distribution does not occur. What penalties arise from this failure? [24.7]

17. James Daniel was born on July 15, 1945. State his required beginning date in the following situations: [24.7]

    a. He is a participant in an IRA.

    b. He is an employee of Alpha Corp. and he is a participant in a 401(k) plan. He is not a 5-percent owner. He plans to terminate employment on June 1, 2019.

18. Distributions for the first two distribution years have to be made by when? [24.7]

19. Joe is aged 70 at the end of the first distribution year. His IRA account balance was $250,000 at the end of the previous year. His beneficiary is his 65-year-old spouse, Jenny. What is the required minimum distribution for the first distribution year? [24.7]

20. Taking the facts from the previous question, what is the required distribution for the second distribution year if the account balance at the end of the first distribution year is $265,000? [24.7]

21. Joe is aged 70 at the end of the first distribution year. His IRA account balance was $250,000 at the end of the previous year. His beneficiary is his 52-year-old spouse, Jenny. What is the required minimum distribution for the first distribution year? [24.7]

22. Sally dies at age 75 and leaves her benefit to her 48-year-old son. How is the required minimum distribution calculated in the year of her death and for subsequent years? [24.7]

23. If a participant dies at age 55 and has named a 30-year-old child as beneficiary, what must happen to ensure distributions can be made over the child's life expectancy? [24.7]

24. Will an individual with two IRAs satisfy the required minimum-distribution rules by taking the required distribution from only one of the IRAs? [24.7]

25. Describe four important planning tools that can be used to maximize the potential deferral period after the participant's death under the required minimum-distribution rules. [24.8]

Chapter 24: Review Answers

1. Generally, the entire value of a distribution will be included as ordinary income in the year of the distribution, except if a portion of the distribution is deemed to be recoverable cost basis. Taxable distributions made prior to age 59½ will also be subject to the 10 percent Sec. 72(t) excise tax unless the distribution satisfies one of several exceptions. Taxation may be avoided if the benefit is rolled over into another tax-sheltered plan.

2. At death, any remaining benefits will be included in the participant's taxable estate. Distributions to a death beneficiary are subject to income tax, although the benefit amount is treated as income in respect of the decedent, meaning the income taxes will be reduced by the estate taxes paid as a result of the pension benefit.

3. a. A death benefit payable from a defined-benefit plan to a beneficiary upon the death of a 52-year-old employee is not subject to the 10 percent Sec. 72(t) penalty because distributions as a result of death are exempt from the penalty.

   b. A lump-sum benefit payable from a money-purchase pension plan to a 57-year-old disabled employee is not subject to the Sec. 72(t) penalty because distributions made due to disability are exempt from the penalty.

   c. A distribution from a 401(k) plan to a 52-year-old participant because of financial hardship is subject to a Sec. 72(t) penalty—there is no applicable exception to the tax.

   d. The penalty tax does not apply because the participant has attained age 59½.

   e. Because a SIMPLE plan is funded with IRAs, distributions are eligible for the educational expense and first-time home buyer exceptions to the 10 percent penalty tax.

4. Tuition and books are qualified education expenses, as are room and board for full-time students. Because Ralph pays $54,000 in total expenses, he is required to pay the 10 percent penalty on $46,000 of the $100,000 IRA withdrawal. The tax is $4,600.

5. The most useful exception to the Sec. 72(t) penalty tax is the substantially equal payment exception. The rules provide a significant amount of flexibility for calculating the amount of the distribution; distributions can stop after the later of 5 years or the attainment of age 59½, and benefits can be divided into separate accounts to meet the required income goal. If a lump sum is needed, the participant can borrow from another source (possibly a deductible home equity loan) and repay the loan with the periodic distributions.

6. If substantially equal periodic payments do not continue for the prescribed period or stray from the calculated amount, the participant could be required to pay the 10 percent penalty (including past due interest) on all nonconforming distributions prior to the participant attaining age 59½.

7. Only $360 is excluded from tax and $11,640 is taxable. The calculation of the amount excluded from tax is $12,000/$400,000 (the total value of both IRA accounts) multiplied by $12,000.

8. The answer is $280. The amount of the first distribution that is excluded from tax is calculated by dividing Cherie's investment in the plan (cost basis = $72,900) by 260, the number used for an individual who is aged 62.

9. a. This is a qualifying distribution. The 5-year period has elapsed and Mick is older than age 59½.

   b. This is a nonqualifying distribution because Mick has not satisfied one of the triggering events. The $15,000 representing return of contributions is not taxed. The additional $4,000 is subject to income tax and the 10 percent Sec. 72(t) early withdrawal excise tax.

10. No, she cannot. A payment that is part of stream-of-life annuity payments cannot be rolled over into an IRA.

11. a. Carole will receive $150,000 less 20 percent withholding or $120,000.

    b. Even though Carole only received $120,000, if she can come up with the additional cash, she can roll over the entire $150,000 benefit.

    c. If the benefit is not rolled over within 60 days, the $150,000 amount is subject to income tax and the Sec. 72(t) 10 percent penalty tax. If Carole actually rolled it into an IRA after the 60-day period, it would be considered an excess contribution and would have to be withdrawn.

    d. Carole can file for a private letter ruling to grant her an extension to the 60-day rollover requirement. The IRS has granted waivers when a financial advisor has provided a client with incorrect information.

12. The following are common situations in which the rollover option needs to be considered carefully.

    - Consider rolling over all but the portion of the distribution that is not subject to income tax.

- If the distribution is a lump-sum distribution that includes employer stock, consider the effect of the net unrealized appreciation rules.

- If the participant over age 55 (but not yet age 59½), consider withdrawing the amount of the current need and rolling over the rest to avoid the 10 percent early withdrawal tax.

13. The participant must receive the balance to the credit within one taxable year and receive the distribution upon death, disability, termination of employment, or attainment of age 59½.

14. At the time of the distribution, Andrew includes $25,000 as ordinary income on his tax return (the cost basis of the stock). He is also required to pay the Sec. 72(t) 10 percent penalty tax on $25,000. When he sells the stock, the $75,000 of net unrealized appreciation is taxed as long-term capital gains. Because the one-year holding period has been met, the $25,000 of additional gain also is taxed as long-term capital gain.

15. The minimum-distribution rules apply to IRAs (including SEPs and SIMPLEs), qualified plans, 403(b) plans, and even 457 plans. Although Roth IRAs are not subject to the rules governing lifetime distributions to the participant, they are required to make distributions to a death beneficiary.

16. Sara is subject to a 50 percent excise tax ($1,000), which she (not the plan administrator) is responsible for paying.

17. a. James Daniel reached age 70 on July 15, 2015, and age 70½ on January 15, 2016. His required beginning date is April 1, 2017 (the April 1 following the calendar year in which he became 70½).

    b. Because James was a participant in a qualified plan, was not a 5-percent owner, and is still employed when he attained age 70½, his required beginning date will be the April 1 following retirement. Based on these facts, his first distribution year will be 2019 and his required beginning date is April 1, 2020.

18. Even though the minimum distribution for the first year is not due until the following April 1, the distribution for the second (and all subsequent years) must be made by December 31.

19. The required minimum distribution is $9,124 ($250,000/27.4).

20. The required minimum distribution is $10,000 ($265,000/26.5).

21. The required minimum distribution is $7,485 ($250,000/33.4).

22. In the year of her death, the minimum distribution is calculated by using the uniform table. In the year following her death, the remaining distribution period is fixed, based on the beneficiary's age at the end of that distribution year.

23. Distributions must begin by the end of the year following the year of death. Otherwise, the beneficiary will be facing a penalty for failing to make the required distribution (if he/she wants to take distributions over life expectancy) or be forced to withdraw the entire account within 5 years.

24. Yes; however, the first step is to calculate the required minimum distribution from each plan separately. Then the distribution can be made from either or both plans.

25. The four planning tools are (1) spousal rollovers, (2) making payouts prior to the September 30 of the year following death, (3) using qualified disclaimers to direct distributions to contingent beneficiaries, and (4) setting up separate accounts when there are multiple beneficiaries.

Chapter 25

Distributions from Retirement Plans—Part II

Learning Objectives

An understanding of the material in this chapter should enable the student to

- **LO 25.1** Review the types of benefit distribution options that are available in qualified plans, IRAs, and 403(b) plans.
- **LO 25.2** Identify the key distribution issues for the middle-class client who is concerned about financing retirement needs.
- **LO 25.3** Identify the key distribution issues for the wealthier client who is concerned about both financing retirement needs and building an estate for his or her heirs.

CHOOSING A DISTRIBUTION OPTION

Choosing the best distribution option at retirement can be a complex decision that involves personal preferences, financial considerations, and the interplay between tax incentives and tax penalties. Planners must keep a myriad of factors in mind in order to render effective advice. For example, typical considerations include whether

- the periodic distribution will be used to provide income necessary for sustaining the retiree or whether the distribution will supplement already adequate sources of retirement income
- the client has properly coordinated distributions from several different qualified plans and IRAs
- the retiree will have satisfactory diversification of his or her retirement resources after the distribution occurs
- the client has complied with the rules for required minimum distributions from a qualified plan

The first step in making a choice is to fully understand the available options. Following is a discussion of the options that are available from qualified plans, SEPs, SIMPLEs and 403(b) plans. Of course, the only way to understand the options for a plan is to read the appropriate plan documents.

Distribution Options Available from the Plan

LO 25.1 Review the types of benefit distribution options that are available in qualified plans, IRAs, and 403(b) plans.

When discussing the distribution options available in tax-advantaged retirement plans, it is important to distinguish qualified plans from IRAs (SEPs and SIMPLEs) and 403(b) plans. Qualified plans are subject to a significant number of limitations, while the others are more open-ended.

Qualified Plans

Every qualified retirement plan specifies when payments may be made and what distribution options are available. Each plan also has a default option if the participant fails to make an election. The distribution options are generally quite limited in a qualified plan. This is because any option that is available must be available to all participants. Also, under the anti-cutback rules, certain annuity options cannot be taken away once they are made available in the plan. To find out when benefits are payable and what the optional forms of benefit are requires a careful review of the plan's summary plan description and, in some cases, a review of the actual plan document.

A qualified plan is allowed to defer the payment of distributions until participants attain normal retirement age, but more typically, the plan will also allow payment upon attainment of early retirement age, death, or disability. Today, most plans also make distributions available to employees who terminate employment (prior to retirement age) with vested benefits. This is almost always the case in defined-contribution plans, but is increasingly common in defined-benefit plans as well. Plans in the profit-sharing category can also allow in-service withdrawals after a stated amount of time or upon a stated event.

involuntary cash-out option

When the participant terminates employment with a vested benefit of $5,000 or less, the plan can provide that such small benefits will be cashed out in a lump sum—without giving the participant any choice in the timing or form of benefit. Most plans choose this **involuntary cash-out option** to simplify plan administration. A recipient of an involuntary cash out retains the right to elect a direct rollover to an IRA or to receive the distribution directly. If the involuntary cash out is $1,000 or more and the participant fails to make an affirmative election, the plan administrator is required to roll the involuntary cash out directly to a designated IRA. When the benefit exceeds $5,000, participants must be given all the benefit options allowed under the plan as well as the right to defer receipt of payment until normal retirement age.

Due to the fiduciary responsibility issues associated with the selection of an IRA provider, many plan sponsors have determined to avoid the automatic rollover requirement by reducing their defined contribution plans' involuntary cash-out amount to $1,000. The consequence of this reduction is to avoid having to make an involuntary cash-out of amounts subject to the automatic rollover requirement. This means that participants with accounts having balances between $1,000 and $5,000 who fail to make an affirmative distribution election will have the payment of their accounts deferred until normal retirement age. The bottom line is that there may be more smaller accounts left in the plan, but the plan sponsor avoids a potential fiduciary liability.

In some cases, a plan will also allow withdrawals prior to termination of employment. This type of provision is generally not allowed in plans in the pension category, which include defined-benefit, cash-balance, target-benefit, and money-purchase pension plans. However, distributions may be available even from these types of plans at the earlier of age 62 or the plan's normal retirement age.

In-service withdrawals are allowed in profit-sharing-type plans (including profit-sharing, 401(k), stock bonus, and ESOP plans) even though many plans do not elect to have such a provision. A special rule applies to the salary deferral account in a 401(k) plan—the in-service withdrawals cannot be made prior to age 59½, unless the participant has a financial hardship. Because in-service withdrawals result in taxable income, some plans (especially 401(k) plans) also provide for participant loan programs. All types of qualified plans may allow distributions at the attainment of normal retirement age, even if the participant is still working.

The normal form of benefit for a married individual—in qualified plans that are subject to the qualified joint-and-survivor annuity rules—must be a joint-and-survivor benefit of not less than 50 percent nor greater than 100 percent and a life annuity for a single participant. In addition to the required form for married participants, the plan must give married participants the option to elect a 75-percent survivor option (if the normal form has a survivor benefit of less than 75 percent) and a 50-percent option (if the normal form is more than 75 percent).

In qualified plans not subject to the qualified joint-and-survivor annuity rules (generally, profit-sharing, 401(k), and stock bonus plans), the normal form of payment is usually a single-sum payment. Even if the plan's normal form of benefit is a single sum payment, participants frequently choose one of the alternative forms of distribution allowed under the plan. Such alternative forms of distribution may include

- annuity payments
- installment payments

Let's take a closer look at some of the more common distribution options available.

Life Annuity. A life annuity provides monthly payments to the participant for his or her lifetime. Payments from a life annuity stop when the participant dies and no other benefit is paid to any beneficiary. A life annuity can be an appropriate option for individuals who want the guarantee of lifetime payments but who have no need to provide retirement income to a spouse or other dependent.

Joint-and-Survivor Annuity. A joint-and-survivor annuity provides monthly payments to the participant during his or her lifetime and if, at the participant's death, the beneficiary is still living, a specified percentage of the participant's benefit continues to be paid to the beneficiary for the remainder of his or her lifetime. The plan will specify the survivor portion and may allow the participant to choose from a 50-percent to a 100-percent survivor portion. Joint-and-survivor annuities can be appropriate if there is a need to provide for the continuation of retirement income to a spouse or other beneficiary who outlives the participant.

Life Annuity with Guaranteed Payments. A life annuity with guaranteed payments (sometimes referred to as a life annuity with a period-certain guarantee) provides monthly benefit payments to the participant during his or her lifetime. Payments are made for the longer of the life of the participant or some specified period of time. The plan may offer a 5-year, 10-year, or other specified guarantee period.

> **EXAMPLE**
>
> Sandy has elected a life annuity with a 10-year certain guarantee in the amount of $1,000 a month. If Sandy dies after 8 years, her designated beneficiary will continue to receive a $1,000 a month for 2 years. If, instead, Sandy dies 12 years after payments begin, there are no additional payments following her death.

Participants with no real income concern for a beneficiary may still elect guaranteed payments to ensure that, at least, minimum payments are made in case of an untimely death. *Planning Note*: If a client outlives the guarantee period, he or she has, in effect, gambled and lost, because lower monthly benefits will be paid under a life annuity with guaranteed payments than under a straight life annuity. Also, guaranteed payments can be a good option when the spouse (or some other beneficiary) is ill and has a short life expectancy. For example, if a retiring husband expects to outlive his wife who is in relatively poor health, then a life annuity with a minimum guarantee might be purchased to protect against the unlikely case of the husband predeceasing the wife. The period chosen should reflect, to some extent, the planner's best estimate of the wife's maximum life expectancy and, if applicable, the client's desire to pass on wealth.

Annuity Certain. The annuity certain provides the beneficiary with a specified amount of monthly guaranteed payments, after which time all payments stop (for example, payments for 20 years). An annuity certain continues to be paid whether the participant survives the annuity period or not. If the client dies prior to 20 years, payments will be made to the client's beneficiary. This type of annuity can be appropriate when the participant's income need has a predictable period, such as for the period prior to beginning Social Security payments.

Lump-sum Distribution. This is what it sounds like—the entire benefit is distributed at once in a single sum. A participant interested in rolling the benefit into an IRA will elect the lump-sum distribution option. Some individuals elect this option from qualified plans in order to take advantage of the special tax treatment (10-year averaging for those born before 1936) and deferral of gain for those who receive a portion of their benefit in qualifying employer securities.

Installments. The installment option is similar to, but definitely different from, a term-certain annuity. With installment payments, the participant elects a payout length and, based on earnings assumptions, a payout amount is also determined. Payments will be made from the participant's account, not an insurance carrier, and there are no guaranteed payments. If the funds run out before the period is over, payments will stop. If the assumptions are exceeded, the participant typically gets a distribution of the remaining account at the end of the period. This option would not be available in a defined-benefit plan because there is no individual account.

For Your Financial Services Practice:
More Retirement Income Solutions

Recent IRS and DOL guidance makes it easier to offer a wider array of retirement income solutions within a qualified plan. It is too early to tell whether employers will add these options, in part because most of the new rules do not become effective until they are finalized. Practitioners should stay tuned to this evolving trend. Here's a summary of the current guidance.

- Proposed regulations allow defined-benefit plans to offer participants the option to elect a lump sum for part of the benefit and an annuity for the other part.
- Proposed regulations allow participants in IRAs and defined-contribution plans to buy longevity insurance. This was added in 2014.
- Rev. Rul. 2012-3 simplifies the application of the qualified joint-and-survivor rules to defined-contribution plans that choose to offer annuities.
- Rev. Rul. 2012-4 allows 401(k) rollovers to purchase an annuity in a company's defined-benefit plan.

QLACs

In 2014, the Treasury Department passed regulations allowing for the use of deferred annuities called qualified longevity annuity contracts (QLACs) inside of qualified retirement accounts including 401(k)s and IRAs. The new rules limit the cumulative dollar amount invested across all retirement accounts that can be invested in QLACs to not exceed the lesser of $125,000 or 25 percent of an employer sponsored plan or 25 percent of all pretax aggregated IRAs. Additionally, these limitations apply to each spouse individually. The QLAC must not have a cash surrender value but can have a return-of-premium death benefit and must begin payouts by age 85 or earlier. The payouts must be fixed, except for the allowance of a cost of living adjustment. The new regulations exempt the QLAC from RMDs, which otherwise would have had to come out of the account at age 70 ½ taking into consideration the value of the QLAC. As such, the QLAC could have created liquidity issues for the owner under the old rules. QLACs make a lot of sense for those people who are concerned about longevity risk and expect to live a long time. Additionally, QLACs can also provide a nice buffer income stream later in retirement to help meet long-term care costs and the rising health care costs people often experience in the later years of retirement. QLACs cannot be purchased inside of a Roth IRA because Roth IRAs are not subject to the RMD rules while the account owner is alive, however, that is not a real limitation as an unlimited amount of longevity annuities can be purchased within a Roth IRA.

Reasons to Consider a Longevity Annuity

Over the last few years, annuities have begun to take a more prominent role in the retirement income planning process and part of the reason is longevity risk. In 2014, *annuity sales for the U.S. reached nearly $230 billion*, representing a 3.8 percent increase over 2013 and a nearly 8 percent increase over 2012 sales. Product innovations and enhanced company offerings have continued to come to market allowing for a wider range of benefits for consumers as different types of annuities are suitable for certain situations and not for others. One particular type of annuity, often referred to as a deferred-income annuity, or longevity insurance, is one product that has seen the fastest growth (*from $211 million in 2011 to about $2.7 billion in 2014*).

The deferred income annuity is a relatively simple product. It promises a specified monthly income amount beginning at a future date in exchange for a premium. Payouts can be made for a single life or over a joint lifetime (to protect income for a couple) and the promise can include death benefits and inflation protection. For example, a 65-year-old man willing to use $50,000 of retirement assets to buy a single life annuity beginning at age 85 will receive $2,109 a month beginning at 85, (using the average of the three best paying products available—pricing data from Cannex Financial Exchanges). This is over $25,000 a year, meaning that the payout rate is about 50 percent of the initial premium. A nonreducing joint annuity, assuming a same-age female spouse, drops the payout to about $1,194 a month because of the longer assumed payout period. Add a return-of-premium death benefit to the joint annuity if death occurs before payouts begin and the monthly payment drops again to $981.

One barrier to use this product within a qualified plan (401(k)) or IRA was recently lifted by IRS regulations in November 2014. Without the guidance, purchasing a deferred income annuity with a start date after age 70½ could have violated the required minimum-distribution rules. The new regulations allow for deferred income annuities with start dates as late as age 85 as long as certain other requirements are met (qualifying products are called qualified longevity annuity contracts (QLAC)). To qualify as a QLAC,

1. the total premiums paid on any given date in all IRAs owned by an individual cannot exceed the lesser of $125,000 or 25 percent,
2. the start date cannot be later than the first day of the month after the individual turns 85,
3. payouts can only be for a single or a joint life, and
4. the only allowable death benefit is a return of premium.

The new regulations are a meaningful change as many retirees have a significant portion of their retirement assets tied up in IRAs and qualified plans and now these funds can be used to purchase this product. There are only a few companies offering the QLAC in an IRA. However, another half-dozen or so companies rolled out QLACs later in 2015. Since, many more companies have developed QLAC products and sales have started to increase. While a number of companies are offering QLACs inside of IRAs, very few companies have rolled out QLACs for 401(k)s yet. Even more limited is the number of 401(k)s that have introduced QLACs as an option. QLACs will not offer all the features and options available in other types of deferred income annuities, but they represent an important shift from the Government to recognize the importance of longevity insurance as part of a retirement income plan and bring increased attention to a viable planning technique. As such, we will take a quick look at six reasons why someone would want to purchase longevity insurance as part of their retirement income plan.

1. **Protect Against Longevity Risk:**

    Retirees are living longer than ever before, which also means their assets need to last longer than ever before. One of the biggest challenges in retirement planning is dealing with longevity risk, the risk of outliving one's assets. Especially for those who only have Social Security as a guaranteed source of retirement income, building in more sources of lifetime income can help insure sufficient income at the end of life when going back to work to fix a shortfall is not an option. The annuity has an impact on how much can be withdrawn each year from the remaining IRA account, as the portfolio only has to last until the annuity income kicks in. This means that withdrawals can be somewhat larger as the time horizon for withdrawals is fixed.

2. **Maintain More Flexibility:**

    The advantage of the longevity insurance annuity approach over simply buying an income annuity at retirement is that the portion of the portfolio needed to buy the income is much smaller. This means "locking-in" with a smaller portion of the portfolio. Systematic withdrawals can be taken until annuity payments begin. This allows the flexibility to change spending as needs change and modify investments with market, tax law, or other changes. Some experts claim that the real reason to buy an annuity or longevity insurance right now is to "lock-in" the highest longevity credits that we will likely ever see. It also means committing fewer assets to longevity risk in case life is not as long as expected—allowing a larger legacy for heirs.

3. **Prepare for Long-Term Care Costs:**

    Long-term care costs can be one of the biggest impediments to living a financially secure retirement as the expenses can quickly become overwhelming. For instance, a year in a semi-private nursing home room can easily cost more than $100,000. While family members provide the majority of long-term care services without financial compensation, there is often still a negative financial impact on the family due to lost time, additional care costs, and missed work opportunities. As such, even someone planning on having family members provide long-term care services could consider a longevity annuity to help fund some of the costs. While longevity insurance will not match up as perfectly with the actual long-term care costs incurred by an individual in the manner that long-term care insurance could, the deferred annuity can still provide an increased stream of income when someone is most likely going to need long-term care. Long-term care is much more prevalent with retirees aged 80 and older than it is for those aged 65. As such, starting a stream of income later in life can help pay for long-term care costs, as nearly 70 percent of people over age 65 will need some long-term care services.

4. **Prepare for Frailty**

    The need for long-term care is just one aspect of the changing needs of aging retirees. Years before long-term care is needed there can be additional costs of maintaining a home such as lawn care, house cleaning, and other services need to be purchased.

As mental capacity changes, financial decisions become more difficult as well. Having annuity income kicking in at a later age allows for simplifying financial affairs.

5. **Replace Other Lost Income Sources:**

    Prepurchasing income that starts later in life can meet other needs as well. An income source that kicks in later in retirement can replace part-time income from wages, lost benefits from Social Security after the death of a spouse, or loss of purchasing power due to inflation. Some sources of income may not be entirely reliable as well. For example, unless the Social Security system is revised, it is only expected to be able to pay out about 77 percent of promised benefits after 2033. While there is a good chance this will not happen, someone concerned about this drop in income could use longevity insurance to address this contingency as well.

6. **Peace of Mind:**

    Besides all the other reasons to consider longevity insurance, research shows that retirees with more guaranteed income sources are happier. They are less concerned about their finances after they have secured guaranteed income sources, income they know they cannot outlive. As such, individuals with guaranteed income, such as longevity insurance, feel more confident about meeting their financial goals.

With longevity insurance finally available in an IRA and qualified retirement plans, where many people have most of their investable retirement assets, this tool should be considered when building a retirement income plan. This is a complex decision that has to be made in the context of a comprehensive retirement income plan and there are other annuity products which may be better suited for a specific situation. If longevity insurance is a possibility, there are still important decisions about how much income to buy, when to start the income, and the features of the annuity product. For these reasons, it is best to work with a qualified financial planner with retirement planning expertise when building a retirement income plan.

Value of the Benefit

To understand the value of the benefit provided by the plan, it is important to discuss defined-contribution plans and defined-benefit plans separately. In a defined-contribution plan, the benefit is always based on the value of the account balance. If the participant elects a lump-sum withdrawal, it will represent the entire value of the vested account balance. If installment options are elected, the account balance (along with continued investment return) is simply liquidated over the specified time period. If the participant elects an annuity option, the plan will purchase the annuity from an insurance company. Depending upon the service providers involved in investment of plan assets, the plan may be able to get a favorable annuity purchase rate.

actuarial equivalent

In a defined-benefit plan, the value of each benefit is almost always the **actuarial equivalent** of a specified form of payment—most typically a single life annuity. For example, if the participant chooses a lump-sum benefit, the amount of the lump sum is based on the single-sum value of a life annuity using the actuarial assumptions prescribed in the plan. Under current law, actuarial assumptions must be tied to the PBGC long-term rate, which is reassessed each month. This means that over time the value of the lump sum may go up or down as the PBGC interest rate changes.

To get a sense of the relative values of different distribution options, the table below provides an example based on a $1,565 monthly life annuity. The other annuity options pay less than the life annuity because of the longer guaranteed payout period.

Table 25-1
Comparison of Optional Benefit Forms (Defined-benefit plan with a monthly life annuity payment of $1,565; assume both participant and spouse are aged 65)

Annuity Form	Monthly Benefit
Life	$ 1,565
Life annuity/10-year guarantee	$ 1,506
Life annuity/20-year guarantee	$ 1,364
Joint-and-survivor (50 percent)	$ 1,414
Joint-and-survivor (66 2/3 percent)	$ 1,371
Joint-and-survivor (100 percent)	$ 1,284
Lump-sum payment	$ 259,000

subsidized benefits

Occasionally, in a defined-benefit plan, all forms of benefit will not be the actuarial equivalent. Forms of payment that are more valuable than the standard form of payment are referred to as **subsidized benefits**. Some plans provide an unreduced qualified joint-and-survivor benefit. For example, a single participant would be entitled to a $1,000 a month life annuity and a married participant with the same benefit accrual would be entitled to a $1,000 a month qualified joint-and-survivor annuity (a more valuable benefit). It is also not uncommon to see early retirement benefits that are subsidized. For example, the plan may allow an individual aged 60 with 30 years of service to receive the full normal retirement benefit payable at age 65 at the earlier age of 60.

IRAs

Typically, form-of-distribution options from IRAs are much more flexible than qualified plans because the individual is the owner and beneficiary. Withdrawals can be made on a discretionary basis or the participant can purchase any of the types of annuities discussed above with some or all of the balance in the IRA. However, the type of financial institution that sponsors the IRA may determine the form of distribution options that are available from a particular IRA. If a participant wants to be able to purchase an annuity form of distribution, the IRA should generally be issued by an insurance company. In addition, the participant can purchase an immediate variable annuity contract, which can guarantee lifetime payments while allowing some potential upswing in monthly payments.

Variable Annuities

A variable immediate annuity is one in which the periodic payments received from the contract vary with the investment experience of the underlying investment vehicle. The variable immediate annuity was developed to answer the problem of a fixed-payment immediate annuity's purchasing power being eroded by inflation. The variable immediate annuity can often accomplish this objective, but not without risk to the annuity owner that the payments can decrease as well as increase.

With fixed immediate annuities, the insurance company accepts the mortality risk, the expense risk, and the interest rate risk. The contract owner accepts the liquidity and the purchasing power risks. With the variable annuity, the contract owner trades guarantees and unwavering income for variable payments. The mortality and expense risks stay with the insurance company.

Currently, the market for variable immediate annuities is small, but it is expected to increase as baby boomers deal with retirement. Trying to live for several decades on money from a 401(k) plan can be stressful and difficult. It is likely that those with extreme longevity in their families will opt to have some portion of their income guaranteed for life while still being able to withstand inflation.

Operation of a Variable Annuity

In the process of implementing a variable immediate annuity, the annuity owner selects from among the various subaccounts offered in the contract to create a diversified portfolio and a suitable asset allocation. In most cases, this asset allocation can be changed among the subaccounts offered within the contract. The annuity owner may also select automatic rebalancing within most variable immediate annuity contracts. The proceeds to be immediately annuitized buy units of the selected subaccounts on the date of purchase; future changes in value of the selected subaccounts will determine the amount of the future annuity payments.

assumed interest rate (AIR)

The amount of the two initial monthly annuity checks will be determined based on the **assumed interest rate (AIR)**. The contract owner may be given a choice of AIRs, such as 4 percent, 5 percent, or 6 percent. After the two initial checks, the underlying investment accounts have to exceed the AIR to increase the amount of future checks. If the subaccount performance is below the chosen AIR, future checks will decrease. Accepting a low AIR increases the chances of receiving higher future checks, whereas accepting a high AIR increases the chances of receiving lower future checks.

403(b) Plans

Withdrawal flexibility from 403(b) plans generally falls somewhere between the limited options in a qualified plan and the more open-ended options of the IRA. 403(b) plans take two forms, one funded by mutual funds purchased through a custodial account and one funded through an annuity contract. Both forms have some restrictions on withdrawals prior to termination of employment. Also, if the 403(b) plan contains an employer contribution, it is subject to ERISA fiduciary rules and will generally be subject to the qualified joint-and-survivor annuity rules.

Still, the participant may have more distribution options than with a qualified defined contribution plan, especially if the 403(b) plan is funded with an annuity. In that case, the participant may have virtually any annuity option commercially available from the insurance carrier, including an immediate variable annuity.

PUTTING IT ALL TOGETHER

Throughout the text, we have discussed rules that affect pension distributions. Learning this information and integrating it into a cohesive package can be highly difficult. To help with these concerns, we will first review the rules as they apply to qualified plans, IRAs, and 403(b) plans. Then we will examine common issues that can arise when you are working with different types of clients.

Qualified Plans

Qualified plans must have clear and precise rules regarding the amount, timing, and form of available benefits. The following discusses the tax treatment of these distributions and summarizes the rules that affect qualified plan distributions:

- Distributions are taxed as ordinary income unless the distribution is a lump sum and one of the special tax rules applies (the deferral of gain on employer securities and for participants born before 1936 the grandfathered 10-year averaging and capital gains rules), or unless the participant has basis. Basis includes after-tax contributions and Table 2001 costs.

- The 10 percent premature distribution excise tax applies to the taxable portion of a distribution made prior to age 59½. Exceptions apply if the distribution is made because of death or disability, to pay for certain medical expenses, or if substantially equal periodic payments are withdrawn (after separation from service). Another exception (that does not apply to IRAs) is that of distributions to a terminating participant after attainment of age 55.

- If a participant has a qualified plan balance payable to a beneficiary at his or her death, the value of the benefit is included in the taxable estate. Payments to beneficiaries are treated as income in respect of a decedent—meaning that beneficiaries who receive benefit payments pay income tax, but may get a deduction for any estate taxes paid because of the value of the pension.

- In-service distributions are subject to limitations. No in-service withdrawals are allowed from plans categorized as pension plans. Profit-sharing-type plans may allow distributions upon a stated event; 401(k) plans are subject to more limiting hardship withdrawals.

- In lieu of taxable in-service withdrawals, plans may offer participant loan programs. Loans within prescribed limits are not subject to income tax.

- Distributions from most plans are subject to the qualified joint-and-survivor annuity (QJSA) requirements. A limited exception applies for certain profit-sharing plans.

- Distributions are subject to the required minimum-distribution rules. Participants (except for 5-percent owners) who continue working until they are past age 70 can defer the required beginning date until April 1 of the year following the year in which they retire.

- Distributions other than certain annuity payments, hardship withdrawals from 401(k) plans, and required minimum distributions can be rolled over into another qualified plan, 403(b) plan, 457 government plan, or IRA.

- Qualified plans are required to give participants the option to directly roll over distributions to an IRA or other qualified plan. Distributions that are not directly rolled over are subject to a 20 percent mandatory income tax withholding.

IRAs

The following is a brief review of the distribution rules that apply to IRAs. With one exception (described below), these rules apply to regular IRAs or IRAs associated with SEPs or SIMPLEs.

- Distributions are always taxed as ordinary income unless the participant has made nondeductible IRA contributions (or rolled over after-tax contributions from a qualified plan). None of the special tax rules that apply to qualified plans apply here.

- The 10 percent premature distribution excise tax applies to the taxable portion of a distribution made prior to age 59½. Exceptions apply if the distribution is made because of death or disability, to pay for certain medical expenses, or if substantially equal periodic payments are withdrawn. With IRAs, there are three additional exceptions: withdrawals to cover medical insurance premiums for certain unemployed individuals, withdrawals to cover postsecondary education expenses, and withdrawals of up to $10,000 for first-time homebuyer expenses.

- With SIMPLE IRAs, the 10 percent penalty tax becomes a 25 percent penalty if withdrawals are made in the first 2 years of participation. Since this tax cannot be avoided, as a practical matter, SIMPLE IRAs cannot be rolled over or transferred into a regular IRA during the first 2 years of participation.

- If a participant has an IRA payable to a beneficiary at his or her death, the value of the benefit is included in the taxable estate. Payments to beneficiaries are treated as income in respect of a decedent—meaning that beneficiaries who receive benefit payments pay income tax but may get a deduction for any estate taxes paid because of the value of the pension.

- Participants can make withdrawals from IRAs (as well as SEPs and SIMPLEs) at any time, without limitation. No participant loans are available, however.

- Distributions are subject to the required minimum-distribution rules under which the required beginning date is always the April 1 following the year of attainment of age 70½.

- The QJSA rules do not apply to IRAs.

- The 20 percent mandatory withholding rules do not apply to IRAs.

- Except for amounts that satisfy the required minimum-distribution rules, distributions can be rolled over or transferred to another IRA, qualified plan, 403(b) plan, or 457 government plan. 403(b) Plans

The following is a brief review of the distribution rules that apply to 403(b) plans:

- Distributions are generally taxed as ordinary income. Although there are rarely after-tax contributions, it is possible for the participant to have basis due to the Table 2001 costs that may be recovered tax free.
- The 10 percent premature distribution excise tax applies in the same way as it does to qualified retirement plans.
- If a participant has a 403(b) account payable to a beneficiary at his or her death, the value of the benefit is included in the taxable estate. Payments to beneficiaries are treated as income in respect of a decedent—meaning that beneficiaries who receive benefit payments pay income tax but may get a deduction for any estate taxes paid because of the value of the benefit.
- In-service distributions are subject to limitations. When a plan (funded with annuity contracts) contains a salary-deferral feature, contributions attributable to the deferral election may not be distributed until the employee attains age 59½, separates from service, becomes disabled, incurs a financial hardship, or dies. When the plan is funded with mutual fund shares, the special distribution requirements apply to all contribution amounts. 403(b) plans can have participant loan programs.
- Distributions are subject to the required minimum-distribution rules. Participants who continue working past age 70½ can defer the required beginning date until the April 1 following the year in which they retire.
- Distributions (other than required minimum distributions and certain annuity payments) from a 403(b) plan sponsored by a governmental entity can be rolled over into another 403(b) annuity, qualified plan, 457 government plan, or IRA. Distributions from nongovernmental 403(b) plans can be rolled to another 403(b) plan or IRA.
- A participant can generally continue to maintain his or her account in the 403(b) plan even after termination of employment. This may be a better option than rolling the benefit into an IRA because of the pre-87 exception to the required minimum-distribution rules and the ability to continue to take a loan, if the 403(b) plan is funded through an annuity contract.
- Participants must be given the option to directly rollover distributions to a new trustee or custodian. Distributions that are not directly rolled over are subject to a 20 percent mandatory income tax withholding.
- In most cases, distributions are subject to the qualified joint-and-survivor annuity (QJSA) requirements.

Working with Clients

Financial services professionals work with a wide variety of clients, and each of their needs is unique. The checklist in the table below identifies typical client issues. Generally, the specific issues that need to be addressed can be anticipated based on the client's economic status. There are two general groups: clients with limited resources who are trying to make those resources last throughout the retirement years, and wealthier individuals who will not use up all of their assets during their own lifetime. The latter group faces the dual concern of financing retirement and maximizing the after-tax estate that they leave to their heirs. We will address each of these situations.

Table 25-2
Checklist of Issues and Decisions at Retirement

- Do you want an annuity for all or part of your funds?
- What type of annuity is best for your situation?
- Can you maximize the monthly payment of your annuity by rolling it into an IRA or another qualified plan—in other words, shop your annuity?
- Should you delay taxation of a distribution by rolling it into an IRA or another tax-deferred plan?
- Is a rollover possible from a cash-flow perspective?
- Is a direct rollover to the new trustee preferable to a rollover?
- Do you want a single-sum distribution for part or all of your funds?
- Can you elect the grandfathered 10-year averaging or capital-gains treatment for pre-1974 income?
- Should you elect 10-year averaging or the capital-gains treatment?
- What is the best tax strategy for dealing with the distribution of employer stock?
- Have you complied with the rules for minimum distributions from the qualified plan?
- When do distributions have to begin?
- Have your beneficiary elections been carefully prepared?
- In what order should assets be cashed in order to maintain optimum tax-shelter and proper asset allocation ratios?
- Has there been proper coordination of distributions from qualified plans and IRAs?
- Will distributions be used to provide necessary income for sustaining your lifestyle, or will they supplement already adequate sources of retirement income?
- Did you meet the need to provide for surviving dependents?
- Have you integrated your retirement planning with proper estate planning?

Primary Concern: Funding Retirement Needs

LO 25.2 Identify the key distribution issues for the middle-class client who is concerned about financing retirement needs.

For most of us, accruing adequate retirement resources is a daunting task. In many cases, the most significant retirement asset is the benefit payable from our employer's retirement plan. For this reason, it is imperative that the distribution decisions maximize the family's available after-tax dollars. The following materials address the vital issues that apply to clients whose primary concern is affording retirement.

Preretirement Distributions. The major concern for the individual who receives a pension distribution prior to retirement is ensuring that pension accumulations are used to finance retirement and are not spent beforehand. In this regard, participants must satisfy rollover rules so inadvertent taxes do not have to be paid. Meeting the rollover requirements has become much easier now that participants in qualified plans and 403(b) plans must be given the option to transfer benefits directly to an IRA or other qualified plan. Note that these direct rollover rules do not apply to IRA-funded plans, including SEPs and SIMPLEs. However, when a participant leaves an IRA-funded plan, there is generally no reason for a rollover.

Still, some clients are tempted to spend preretirement pension distributions. If you have clients in this position, showing them the power of the compounding return sometimes convinces them otherwise.

> **EXAMPLE**
>
> Sonny Shortview, aged 40, is changing jobs. He will be receiving a much higher salary in his new job and he is feeling quite well off. Sonny has the opportunity to receive a pension distribution from his old employer's retirement plan in the amount of $35,000. Even though he does not really need the funds, the amount seems small enough to Sonny that he is considering paying taxes and using the after-tax proceeds for an auto upgrade. Hopefully, Sonny will change his mind when he learns that if he rolls the distribution into an IRA and earns a 10 percent rate of return, his $35,000 distribution would grow to $367,687 by the time he reaches age 65.

Another difficult situation arises in the case of involuntary dismissal. An employee who is terminated due to downsizing or other reasons may experience a prolonged period of unemployment. In this case, the individual may need to tap into his or her pension. If the participant is younger than age 59½, he or she must pay the 10 percent premature distribution excise tax unless one of the exceptions applies. The substantially equal periodic payment exception is one way to avoid this tax, but the problem is that distributions must be made for the longer of 5 years or until attainment of age 59½, and this period will probably be much longer than the period of unemployment. This problem can be mitigated somewhat by dividing assets into a number of IRAs. For example, part of the need can be met by using a periodic payment from one IRA and simply paying the excise tax for certain short-term needs from another IRA. If a lump sum is needed, the individual could consider borrowing from another source and repaying the loan with periodic distributions from an IRA.

Form of Retirement Distribution. For the client who will be living on his or her pension distribution, the two most important decisions are usually when to retire and the form of payment that should be received. As we discussed previously in this book, the effect of early retirement can be quite profound, especially in defined-benefit plans. Even if the plan subsidizes some part of the early retirement penalty, there is always a cost for early retirement. Other timing issues that need to be understood are the consequences of delaying payments to some time after retirement and of retiring after the plan's normal retirement age. Spend time with your clients to make sure they understand these important timing issues—it is rare that a plan participant will fully understand them without your help. Of course, the answers always depend upon the specific terms of the plan, so be sure to review the summary plan description.

Once the client has a full understanding of the timing issues, the next decision is choosing the form of retirement benefits. Almost all individual account-type plans (including qualified plans of the defined-contribution type, SEPs, SIMPLEs, and 403(b) plans) give the participant the option to receive a lump-sum distribution, which can be rolled into an IRA without tax consequences. This benefit option affords the participant the most flexibility because he or she can take money out as slowly or as quickly as it is needed.

Defined-benefit plans may or may not have a lump-sum option, depending upon the terms of the plan. Also note that a lump sum from a defined-benefit plan is based on the actuarial equivalent of a normal form of payment, usually a life annuity. If the lump sum is calculated with unfavorable assumptions, this option may not be advisable. One way to test the value of the lump sum is to compare the amount payable as a life annuity from the plan to the amount that would result from taking a lump sum, rolling it into an IRA, and then buying a life annuity at commercially available prices.

Many participants will be satisfied with the IRA rollover approach because it provides both investment and withdrawal flexibility. However, this method does not ensure that the participant will not outlive pension distributions. Even with careful distribution planning, investment performance may not meet expectations, or the individual may live too long. To protect against this contingency, retirees should consider having at least a portion of their retirement income payable as some form of life annuity. We reviewed the advantages and disadvantages of various annuity options. Participants can generally receive the type of annuity that they want, even if it is a not offered by the particular plan involved. They can accomplish this by electing a lump-sum option, rolling the benefit into an IRA, and then purchasing the annuity. Variable annuities should be considered because they can combine the promise of lifetime benefits with the possibility of increasing payments over time to offset the effects of inflation.

Qualified Joint-and-Survivor Considerations. A married participant who receives a pension distribution in a form other than a qualified joint-and-survivor annuity generally must have his or her spouse sign a waiver. Unless there is marital discord, the receipt of an alternate form of benefit generally poses no special concerns. In fact, the disclosure and paperwork involved probably ensure that the participant is carefully considering all the available distribution options. Still, this is a matter that retirees may not understand.

Explaining the effect of the joint-and-survivor form of payment is an excellent way to provide service to the client and solidify the advisory relationship.

Tax Issues. If the client receives a single-sum distribution in most situations it is appropriate to elect a direct rollover to an IRA. However, as discussed in the previous chapter, it often is appropriate not to roll over the portion of the benefit that represents after-tax contributions. If the distribution includes employer stock, the effect of the net unrealized appreciation rules should be considered before rolling over employer securities.

To maximize the benefit of tax deferral, once the rollover occurs, amounts should be distributed only when needed (unless, of course, the required minimum-distribution rules mandate a larger distribution).

Another concern is whether the client should elect to convert his or her pension distribution to a Roth IRA. Conversion results in taxable ordinary income in the amount of the conversion. Once in the Roth IRA, growth is tax free as long as the distribution meets certain eligibility requirements. The determination of whether or not to convert is a complex issue that requires a full understanding of the client's retirement and estate planning concerns. However, there are some general considerations that will affect the client's decision.

- The Roth IRA conversion is more appropriate when the income tax rate is higher at the time of distribution than at the time of conversion. For many, the postretirement income tax rate is probably lower than the rate at the time of distribution. This factor weighs against conversion.

- Any portion of an IRA can be converted to a Roth IRA. An individual who has saved primarily for retirement with tax-deferred accounts may want to convert some retirement income to a Roth IRA as a hedge against future tax rate increases.

- For retirees who are struggling to meet their retirement needs, converting and paying taxes does not seem like an appropriate choice.

Primary Objective: Maximizing the Estate

LO 25.3 **Identify the key distribution issues for the wealthier client who is concerned about both financing retirement needs and building an estate for his or her heirs.**

When examining your clients' needs, you will find there is a distinct difference between those who will probably spend most of their assets during their retirement and those who can afford to leave an estate to their heirs. However, even for wealthier clients, the first and foremost concern is retirement security, with estate planning as a secondary objective.

Tax-deferred retirement plans are excellent vehicles for accumulating wealth for retirement, but they also can pose problems on the distribution end. Lifetime distributions can be subject to income tax and the 10 percent premature distribution excise tax. If money that is still in the plan is left to heirs, the amount is included in the taxable estate, and distributions are still subject to federal income taxes. If assets are distributed at death, in order to pay Federal Estate or state inheritance taxes, a large portion of the pension asset can be confiscated by taxes.

Fortunately, there are a number of ways to minimize the tax threat at the time of the participant's death. Under the required minimum-distribution rules, it is possible to distribute assets over the remaining life expectancy of the beneficiary after the death of the participant. This strategy spreads out the payment of income taxes, meaning that the IRA balance can continue to generate significant income for the beneficiaries. However, in order to take advantage of the extra deferral period, the IRA balance cannot be used to pay estate taxes. Readers familiar with estate planning know that the IRA balance problem is similar to problems that can arise with other illiquid assets. In many cases, the solution to the illiquid asset problem is to purchase life insurance—usually using an irrevocable life insurance trust—because the insurance proceeds will not be subject to estate taxes. This approach generates capital for paying estate taxes. In fact, the IRA balance problem is often less difficult to solve than the problem of illiquid assets because distributions from the IRA can function as a source of insurance premiums. In many cases, the premiums are simply paid out of distributions that are already mandated under the required minimum-distribution rules.

When the participant is uninsurable or unwilling to purchase insurance, the problem becomes more difficult to solve. One option is to use IRA distributions to fund a family gifting program. Another solution for the charitably inclined is to leave the IRA balance to charity. When the charity receives the IRA balance, it pays no income taxes and the estate receives an estate tax deduction for the amount of the contribution.

This type of client also needs to consider whether or not to convert some or all of his or her pension assets or traditional IRAs to a Roth IRA. Today, all taxpayers are allowed to convert. The conversion can be valuable for the wealthier client for a number of reasons. First, for estates subject to estate or inheritance taxes, a conversion reduces the estate by the amount of income taxes paid due to the conversion. This reduces the effective tax-rate on the conversion.

Second, once the conversion occurs if the asset is not needed for retirement the entire account can continue to grow tax-free for heirs. The amount of tax-free growth can be staggering, as there are no required minimum distributions during the participant's (or a spousal beneficiary's) lifetime. A nonspousal beneficiary must take required distributions over his or her life expectancy, but this can still result in many years of tax-free growth in the account. For example, with a conversion at age 65, the Roth IRA will grow income tax free for possibly 25 or more years, followed by distributions that can be spread over the next 30 to 40 years (the life expectancy of the beneficiaries). Third, the Roth IRA can also be used in retirement as an emergency fund, or as a tax planning tool to minimize taxes.

Since one objective of the Roth conversion is to stretch out payments as long as possible, the Roth IRA is more valuable when the heirs do not need to take withdrawals to pay inheritance taxes. As with tax-deferred retirement plans, purchasing life insurance can be the appropriate means to prepare for this contingency.

Making sure you leave the right assets to your heirs is an important estate planning goal. In 2014, the Supreme Court in *Clark v. Rameker* determined that inherited IRAs are not "retirement funds" within the meaning of the code and are therefore not exempt from the bankruptcy estate. As such, how someone leaves an IRA to his or her children should be reviewed if there is a spendthrift or creditor concern regarding the heirs. There are strategies available to protect the IRA assets from the heir's creditors. However, these strategies usually involve the use of a see-through trust. However, trusts do bring forth additional management fees and can complicate the distribution of assets.

YOUR FINANCIAL SERVICES PRACTICE: CLIENT QUERY

Question: Your client Wanda is single, aged 73, and has an IRA worth $150,000. Because she does not need to take distributions from the plan to live on, she asks you whether she can avoid taking minimum distributions from the plan. Upon further inquiry, you find out she has three adult children who are all successful financially and six grandchildren. Her goal is to leave the IRA money to her family.

Solution: Wanda sounds like a great candidate for a conversion to a Roth IRA. Once the assets are in a Roth IRA, she can avoid minimum distributions during her lifetime. She will have to pay income taxes at the time of conversion, but the prepaid income taxes also reduce her taxable estate. If she names her six grandchildren as the beneficiaries, at Wanda's death, this account can be divided into six accounts and distributed over the lifetime of each grandchild.

Form of Distribution Option. For a client with substantial assets, the IRA rollover option is generally the appropriate choice. This type of client can afford to self-insure against the contingency of living a long life and, therefore, will generally not want to annuitize the benefit. The IRA provides both investment and distribution flexibility. The rollover option may not be the best option for after-tax contributions or for distributions of employer securities eligible for the net unrealized appreciation tax treatment.

MINI-CASES: DISTRIBUTIONS FROM RETIREMENT PLANS

Case One—Facts

Jerry Jobchanger, aged 32, terminated employment with Midsize Corporation in order to take a job with Mega Corporation as a systems analyst. He was in both a defined-benefit plan and a 401(k) plan at Midsize Corporation. The present value of his accrued benefit in the defined-benefit plan is $4,200, and the 401(k) account balance is $9,500. He has come to you to discuss what he should do with his pension distributions from Midsize. He also has told you that he will not be eligible for Mega Corporation's pension plans for one year. He is thinking about withdrawing both benefits and buying a car better suited for his position as a young executive. Discuss his options with him.

Case Two—Facts

Joseph Professional is 55 years old and has accumulated $1.3 million in his company's profit-sharing plan. That is good news, but the trouble is that this asset represents 80 percent of his net worth. He is a dentist and does not expect to be able to sell his practice for a large sum. He has a house, some other personal property, and little other savings. Joseph is married and his wife is aged 52. He has two children, ages 24 and 27. His first concern is his retirement security, but he is also concerned about passing on wealth to his children. He enjoys his work and intends to continue working until age 70. After he retires, he anticipates withdrawing his current salary, $150,000 a year, from the IRA (in today's dollars).

Case Three—Facts

Mary Middle Class is single (divorced) and works for ABCD University as an administrator. Her current income is $42,000. She is aged 62 and is thinking of retiring in the near future. The university has a defined-benefit pension plan and a 403(b) plan. The benefit formula in the defined-benefit plan is one and one-half percent of final-average compensation times years of service (limited to 30 years). Mary currently has 12 years of service. She has an account balance of $95,000 in her 403(b) plan.

Mary has come to you to help her determine whether she can afford to retire now and, if so, how she should take her distributions from her qualified plans.

After asking Mary more about her retirement planning goals, you find out that Mary was married for 15 years (to a well-paid lawyer) and several years ago she got a large house in the divorce settlement. The house has a small mortgage payment, high taxes, and a significant amount of equity buildup. Other than the house, she has no significant investments. You also find that she would like to live closer to her adult children so that she can spend more time with the grandchildren. She has little interest in travel, but would like to get additional education.

CHAPTER REVIEW

Key Terms and Concepts

involuntary cash-out option
actuarial equivalent
subsidized benefits
assumed interest rate (AIR)

Chapter 25: Answers to Mini-Cases

Case One

The first step is to clarify Jerry's distribution options. To learn about this, review the summary plan descriptions for both plans, any benefit statements that have been distributed, and any benefit paperwork that has been given to Jerry from the company regarding the distributions. If there is still any ambiguity, remember Jerry has the right to receive a copy of the entire plan document. After that, Jerry may still have to ask the plan administrator a number of questions.

In the past, defined-benefit plans typically required that terminating participants wait until retirement age to begin receiving benefits. More and more plans allow immediate lump-sum distributions to terminating employees. Also, most plans take advantage of the option to cash out those participants with benefits worth less than $5,000. Because Jerry's benefit is less than $5,000, let's assume that Jerry will be cashed out, meaning he will receive the single sum within a reasonable time after termination of employment. Even with the cash out, the plan is required to give him the option of having the benefit rolled directly to an IRA or other qualified plan or having the benefit distributed directly, in which case 20 percent of the distribution must be withheld for taxes.

Like most other 401(k) plans, Jerry's 401(k) plan allows for distributions as soon as administratively feasible after termination of employment. Jerry can choose from a lump sum or installment payments over a period not to exceed 10 years. As required by law, Jerry can also defer receipt of his benefit until age 55 (early retirement age).

Jerry's decision to cash out his benefit and buy a car is not a good one. Many people do not understand the tax implications of such a withdrawal. They think the distribution is taxed at 20 percent (the amount withheld for taxes). The reality is that the distribution is subject to tax as ordinary income, (let's assume that Jerry's marginal tax rate is 25 percent) and the 10 percent early withdrawal excise tax. If there are also state and local taxes, Jerry's tax rate could be above 40 percent. More importantly, Jerry probably cannot afford to spend the retirement benefits that he has earned with Midsize Corporation. He thinks that he is giving up $13,700 in benefits (about $8,000 after taxes), but he is wrong. He is giving up the $147,000 that this amount will be worth at age 60 (growing at 9 percent) or $347,000 if he does not begin spending the amount until age 70.

Now that you have convinced Jerry not to spend the benefits, what should he do with them? Remember that he has few choices with the defined-benefit amount because the plan calls for a cash out. He should elect to transfer (also referred to as a direct rollover) the cast out from the defined-benefit plan to an IRA or the new company's qualified plan, if it is allowed. If, instead, he were to receive the check directly, the plan administrator would have to withhold 20 percent of the distribution. Jerry should consider the new company's plan if fees are much lower than if he maintains a separate IRA or if there is an investment option (such as a guaranteed investment contract that promises an excellent return) that would not be available in the IRA. Also, the benefit amount might be more secure from the claims of his creditors in the pension plan than in the IRA, although most participants choose to establish an IRA.

Similarly, he will most likely choose to have a direct rollover of his 401(k) benefit into an IRA. He could leave benefits in the Midsize plan and, in some cases, may choose to do so because of fees or investment options. In this case, these are not an issue and Jerry chooses to have both benefits transferred to a new IRA account.

Once in the IRA, Jerry has several more choices. First, he will have the option to convert any portion of the IRA into a Roth IRA. Because he is only 32, this is an attractive option. Even though he would have to pay income taxes, he would not have to pay the 10 percent excise taxes, and any future growth would be tax free (assuming the distributions were made after age 59½). The conversion also makes sense for Jerry because he will probably be in a higher tax bracket later. If he does not want to pay taxes on the whole $14,200, it would still be beneficial for him to convert part of the benefit.

The final consideration is how to invest either the IRA (or converted Roth IRA). With a 30-year investment horizon, Jerry would probably be best served with all or most of his holdings in common stock or stock mutual funds. With only $13,700 to invest, he should probably choose mutual funds or some other pooled investment to obtain professional management and proper diversification.

Case Two

This is a common situation these days. More and more people are accumulating a large portion of their wealth in tax-sheltered retirement plans. This does not mean that these people have made a mistake; they have most likely accumulated a lot more this way than if they had saved on an after-tax basis. However, there are certain tax problems that need to be addressed when planning for liquidation of pension assets.

The first tax concern, of course, is that any withdrawals are ordinary income subject to income tax. Therefore, it is generally appropriate to defer withdrawals until they are needed or as required under the minimum-distribution rules. Deferral also allows the continued tax-deferred growth of the entire principal. The second tax issue is that any assets remaining in the retirement plans at death will be subject to estate taxes. If funds have to be withdrawn from the pension to pay estate taxes, the distributions are also subject to income tax. If there is another source from which to pay estate taxes, then the pension distributions can continue as long as permitted under the required minimum-distribution rules. This period could easily be an additional 30 years or more, and an extremely large amount can be paid out to heirs.

Because most of the couple's assets are in the profit-sharing plan in Joseph's name, several other estate planning techniques become more difficult. First, to lower estate taxes, it is generally a good idea for both the husband and wife to each have significant assets in his or her own name. This often means retitling assets from one spouse to the other. When the asset is in a profit-sharing plan (or other tax-advantaged plan), the asset cannot be retitled without a distribution that would trigger income taxes.

Another useful estate planning technique is the credit-shelter trust. This device allows the individual to minimize estate taxes and still take care of the remaining spouse. Without going into detail here, note that using a tax-sheltered plan asset to fund the trust is not as tax efficient as using an asset that will not be subject to additional income tax to the recipient.

A good way to get a feel of how these issues affect Joseph is to use a pension distribution software program to see whether Joseph's pension is sufficient to meet his needs. This example was run on Brentmark Software's Pension and Roth IRA Analyzer. The results of the illustration were eye opening. The first thing that became clear was that, because Joseph will wait until age 70 to begin withdrawals, his $1.3 million profit-sharing benefit will grow (without any additional contributions) to more than $4.5 million (assuming a 9 percent annual return). If he withdraws the equivalent of $150,000 in today's dollars, he will withdraw $270,000 the first year (assuming a 3.5 percent inflation rate). Assuming that Joseph dies at age 88 and his wife dies at age 90, they will have been able to generate an inflation-adjusted stream of income of $270,000 a year ($550,000 in the final year) and still have $4 million left in the plan for their children. Given these assumptions, distributions can continue for approximately 10 more years to the children, generating more than $5 million of distributions to them.

Joseph and his family are in great shape as long as the pension asset does not have to be liquidated to pay estate taxes. What this means from the planning perspective is that Joseph needs to create a source to pay estate taxes. Those familiar with estate planning know that the pension asset problem is similar to those that arise with other illiquid assets. In many cases, the solution to the illiquid asset problem is to purchase life insurance—often a second-to-die policy using an irrevocable life insurance trust. If the trust is designed properly, the insurance proceeds will not be subject to estate taxes. This approach generates capital for paying estate taxes. Because Joseph is continuing to work until age 70, he may be able to afford the premiums out of current income. If he is unwilling to do so, he may choose to make withdrawals from the pension plan to pay the premium. Because Joseph is under age 59½, if he chooses to make withdrawals, he needs to meet the "substantially equal periodic payment exception" from the 10 percent early withdrawal excise tax. Many clients like the idea of paying the premium from the pension asset because it feels like the estate planning problem is being solved with the asset that is causing the problem.

We also learned from running the software program that Joseph does not need to make additional contributions to his plan to be financially secure in retirement. If he can afford additional savings, this should be done outside the plan and probably in his wife's name. They might want to consider investments that pay off primarily in capital gains (such as stock or stock mutual funds) to lower their income taxes and to take advantage of the step up in basis that occurs with capital investments at death. They may also want to consider making their more aggressive, higher return investments outside the plan, where growth is taxed at a capital gains rate, instead of inside the pension plan, where distributions are all taxed as ordinary income.

One final thought is a Roth IRA conversion. The reason a conversion can be so valuable for the wealthier client is that there are no required minimum distributions during the participant's lifetime. If the spouse is the beneficiary, no distributions have to be made over the spouse's lifetime either. After the spouse's death, distributions must be made over the life expectancy of the beneficiaries at that time. This may mean that if the conversion occurs at age 55, the Roth IRA will grow income tax free for possibly 25 or more years, followed by distributions that can be spread over the next 30 to 40 years.

Case Three

This is also not an uncommon scenario. If you work with teachers or other middle-class professionals, you will have many clients like Mary.

Since you've determined Mary's retirement planning goals and objectives, you will need to ascertain what financial resources she needs to meet these goals and objectives. Because she is close to retirement, it is appropriate to inventory her specific expenses to determine an appropriate budget.

The next step is to inventory her traditional retirement assets. This includes Social Security, company pensions, and any income that can be generated from her savings. Because of what you learned, Mary's divorced spousal Social Security benefit may be higher (50 percent of her ex-spouse's PIA) than the benefit earned on her own wages. You need to let Social Security know about her divorce benefit to make sure that her benefit is calculated both ways. Because she is thinking of retiring early, be sure to identify a retirement age under her full retirement age to show the effect of the earlier payments.

To understand her company pension benefits, review her benefit statements and summary plan description. It is crucial that the advisor fully understand Mary's pension benefits. Without knowing all of the facts, it appears that Mary will have a difficult time affording retirement. With no substantial investment income, she will be extremely dependent on her pension income. In the discussion of the pension plan, especially in the defined-benefit plan, Mary's early retirement will penalize her three ways: she will have shorter service, lower salary, and the benefit will be reduced for payment beginning before age 65. Waiting until 65 or even later gives her a chance to earn a significantly larger benefit. With the 403(b) plan, retiring now means that 3 years of contributions will not be made and also earnings will be reduced as distributions are made. These timing-of-payment issues are complex and need to be reviewed and discussed carefully with Mary, who is unlikely to fully appreciate the effects of the deferral decision.

One factor in Mary's favor is a less obvious asset—the equity in her home. Because she is predisposed to moving, she may want to purchase a condominium or smaller home. Better yet, she may want to rent for a while to be assured that she likes her new location. Under the current Sec. 121 tax rules, she can exclude up to $250,000 of gain without having to purchase a replacement home. If she decides to stay in the home, she could look into a reverse annuity mortgage to free up some equity.

Now that you have gathered the facts, you can help Mary form a retirement planning strategy. At first blush, it looks like Mary will have to defer retirement. In addition to the penalties on her pension and Social Security benefits for retiring early, it also turns out that her company does not have post-retirement medical benefits and, if she retires before 65, she will have to purchase individual medical insurance. However, before sending Mary away disappointed, it is time for some serious brainstorming. Maybe Mary can meet some of her goals and still keep working. Simply by thinking through what she wants, she has decided to sit for her grandchildren more and have her grandchildren stay with her over their summer vacations on her own vacation time. It turns out that under the company's flexible benefit program, Mary can buy additional vacation time and still be a full-time employee entitled to medical benefits and additional pension accruals.

This fact pattern illustrates the importance of the advisor's expertise and skill. Mary's situation could not be adequately understood simply by taking out a retirement planning software package and running the numbers. There are many nuances here—the equity in the home, the divorced spouse Social Security benefit, the complicated pension calculations, and an understanding of her medical insurance coverage.

After successfully formulating a plan and picking a retirement date, there is one more important issue to consider—choosing the best form of distribution from her retirement plans.

Let's assume that her defined-benefit plan has a lump-sum option. The amount payable will be based on the "actuarial equivalent" of the normal form of payment—usually a life annuity. If the lump sum is calculated with unfavorable assumptions, this option may not be advisable. One way to test the value of the lump sum is to compare the amount payable as a life annuity from the plan to the amount that would result from taking a lump sum, rolling it into an IRA, and then buying a life annuity at commercially available prices.

Many participants will be satisfied with the IRA rollover approach because it provides both investment and withdrawal flexibility. However, this method does not ensure that the participant will not outlive pension distributions. Even with careful distribution planning, investment performance may not meet expectations, or the individual may live too long. To protect against this contingency, Mary should consider having at least a portion of her retirement income payable as a life annuity. Because Mary is single and does not have any dependents, a single life annuity will provide her with the largest payment and adequate protection. She can either elect the life annuity in the plan or roll over the benefit into an IRA and then purchase an annuity. In this way, she could purchase a variable annuity that ensures lifetime payments and addresses the effect of inflation. To obtain the security of a base income for life and the flexibility of an IRA, she might choose to annuitize her defined benefit and roll over the 401(k).

One final point is that Mary is exactly the kind of client who is not a good candidate for a Roth IRA conversion. Because she is near retirement, has a low tax rate, and will be living on her pension benefits, she really cannot afford to take the chance of reducing her pension benefits by paying taxes up front in exchange for tax-free growth.

Chapter 25: Review Questions

Review questions are based on the learning objectives in this chapter. Thus, a [25.3] at the end of a question means that the question is based on learning objective 3. If there are multiple objectives, they are all listed.

1. What considerations affect an individual's decision concerning the appropriate form of pension distribution? [25.1]

2. When do qualified plans typically allow for benefit payments? [25.1]

3. What options does a participant have with regard to the timing and form of payment of benefits? Is there any situation in which the participant does not have these same rights? [25.1]

4. What is the major limitation of a life annuity? [25.1]

5. Why can a life annuity with guaranteed payments be used to provide for the income needs of a beneficiary? [25.1]

6. Describe an installment payment option from a defined-contribution plan. [25.1]

7. In a defined-benefit plan, what does it mean to say that if a participant elects a life annuity with 10-year-certain payments the amount of the distribution is the actuarial equivalent to a life annuity? [25.1]

8. In a defined-benefit plan, what does it mean to say that a benefit is subsidized? [25.1]

9. What is the impact on the benefit payments in an immediate variable annuity contract when the actual rate of return exceeds the assumed interest rate? [25.1]

10. Explain the following: [25.1]

    a. Are distributions from qualified plans always taxed as ordinary income?

    b. What exception to the 10 percent Sec. 72(t) excise tax applies to qualified plans and 403(b) plans, but does not apply to IRAs?

    c. What is the exception that applies to the required minimum-distribution rules for qualified plans?

    d. Do the 20 percent mandatory income tax withholding rules apply to distributions from IRAs?

    e. In an IRA, is the required beginning date ever later than the April 1 following the year in which the participant attains age 70½?

11. Sheila, single and aged 50, is laid off from her job. She receives a $150,000 distribution from a 401(k) plan that she rolls directly into an IRA. She decides to take some well-deserved time off and plans to go back to work in about a year. She needs living expenses for the current year. How could she make withdrawals from her IRA that would avoid the 10 percent penalty tax? [25.1]

12. Why is choosing the right distribution option so important for someone with a relatively small account balance? [25.2]

13. Explain the estate tax threat that faces those with significant retirement plan balances and the strategies to minimize its effect. [25.2]

14. Can the Roth IRA conversion be used as an effective tax planning strategy for the wealthier individual? [25.2]

Chapter 25: Review Answers

1. The types of considerations include the need for retirement income, life expectancy, nonretirement income, and estate tax.

2. Qualified plans must begin to pay benefits at normal retirement age. Most plans also pay out benefits upon death, disability, termination of employment (for any reason), and, in the case of profit-sharing-type plans, in-service withdrawals.

3. A participant generally has the right to choose from all of the benefit options allowed under the plan. The participant also has the right to defer payment of benefits until attainment of normal retirement age. However, if the benefit is $5,000 or less, the plan is allowed to force the participant to take the benefit in a lump sum at the time of termination of employment.

4. Life annuity payments cease when the participant dies, so there are no benefits for beneficiaries.

5. If the beneficiary has a limited life expectancy, a life annuity with guaranteed payments can provide for continued payments to the beneficiary if the participant were to die prematurely.

6. With installment payments, an estimated payment is determined over a specified period of time, but because the benefit is tied to the actual account balance, the payout period may be shorter or longer depending upon the investment return in the account.

7. When a participant elects a life annuity with 10-year certain payments, the payments are reduced to reflect the "cost" of including the guaranteed payment period.

8. Subsidized means that the benefit is more valuable than the standard form of payment. In most plans, all forms of payouts are actuarially equivalent to the standard or normal form. Occasionally you will see a subsidized early retirement (the benefit is not reduced for payment prior to the normal retirement age) or a subsidized qualified joint-and-survivor annuity (the benefit is not reduced to be the actuarial equivalent of the standard or normal form—typically a life annuity option).

9. When the actual rate of return exceeds the expected rate of return, the annuity payments increase.

10. a. Certain amounts can be distributed tax free (after-tax contributions and Table 2001 costs), and lump-sum distributions could be eligible for one of several special tax rules.

　　b. Separating from service after attainment of age 55 exception

　　c. TEFRA 242(b) elections

　　d. No, they do not.

　　e. No, there are no exceptions to this date for IRAs.

11. There is no exemption that would cover Sheila's living expenses for one year. However, she could borrow the amount needed from another source in a lump sum and repay the loan with substantially equal periodic payments from her IRA. Because she is aged 50, she would need to make substantially equal payments for 9½ years.

12. It is important because the decision can affect whether or not the participant has enough funds throughout retirement.

13. At the participant's death, amounts in tax-sheltered plans are included in the taxable estate. If withdrawals are made from the plan at that time to pay estate taxes, income taxes also become due—and suddenly up to two thirds of the pension asset is used to pay taxes. The most common strategy to resolve this problem is to purchase life insurance to address the estate tax liquidity need so that the pension asset can stay in the plan as long as possible. In many cases, under the required minimum-distribution rules, distributions can continue for many years after the participant's death.

14. A Roth conversion can be an effective tool even for an older individual. The conversion results in income taxes, which reduce the taxable estate. After the participant dies, the Roth IRA can create a stream of tax-free income over the beneficiary's life expectancy.

APPENDIX A: POST-ERISA LEGISLATION

Below is description, law by law, of legislation affecting the pension field. Following that is a table identifying the laws for those interested in researching them further.

In 1981, the **Economic Recovery Tax Act (ERTA)** expanded the retirement market by breathing new life into old retirement products. ERTA lifted the prohibition against employees who were active participants in employer-sponsored plans having an individual retirement account (IRA) and opened the door for widespread sales of IRAs. The public response was tremendous as millions flocked to save for retirement. ERTA also contributed to the success of stock option plans by liberalizing the rules for deducting leveraged employee stock ownership plans (ESOPs) and creating payroll-based stock option plans (PAYSOPs). PAYSOPs, phased out in 1987, allowed for an income tax credit that benefited certain corporations. Finally, ERTA started the trend of making the rules for retirement plans for the self-employed (Keogh plans) similar to those for corporate plans.

The Tax Equity and Fiscal Responsibility Act of 1982 (TEFRA) created plan parity between Keogh plans and corporate plans, finishing the job started by ERTA. The major emphasis of TEFRA, however, was on stopping tax abuses, primarily loopholes used by small-employer plans. TEFRA created special rules for plans that unduly benefit key employees—if a plan inordinately favors the privileged few, restrictive "top-heavy" rules take effect. The top-heavy rules guarantee minimum benefits for rank-and-file employees and restrict benefits available for key employees. TEFRA also closed other loopholes: it stopped plan loan abuses, limited contributions to the plan and distributions from the plan by reducing the maximum contributions or distributions allowed, and forced plan distributions to be used for retirement purposes, as opposed to sheltering the money for the beneficiary.

The Retirement Equity Act of 1984 (REA) shifted Congress's focus from tax abuses by small employers to perceived mistreatment of women under pension rules. REA helps people (male or female) who do not fit the standard work pattern, especially those who interrupt or stop their career for children, by reducing the age required to participate in a retirement plan. REA makes it harder to lose pension benefits because of career interruptions. REA also protects the rights of a plan participant's spouse or ex-spouse by ensuring that the spouse has some say in how retirement money is distributed and by allowing retirement funds to be part of a divorce settlement.

The Tax Reform Act of 1986 (TRA '86) represented the biggest shake-up since ERISA. A need for revenue was the motivation for TRA '86 rules that cut back salary reduction contributions previously allowed under some types of plans [401(k)s, tax-sheltered annuities] and restricted the deductibility of contributions made to individual retirement accounts. A second target of TRA '86 was the discrimination in favor of officers and key employees. Existing discrimination restrictions were tightened, and some plans that had previously escaped nondiscrimination coverage were brought under a new, tougher nondiscrimination umbrella. Other tax reform changes were also included:

- modifications to the profit-sharing rules, which permit profit-sharing contributions when the employer has no profits (this was a response to the trend of using profit-sharing plans as a major source of pension benefits)
- amendments liberalizing ERISA's vesting schedules
- creation of a 10 percent premature distribution penalty tax for most plan distributions prior to age 59½
- minimum-distribution requirements and restrictive changes in the taxation of retirement distributions

The Omnibus Budget Reconciliation Act of 1987 (OBRA '87) focused on yet another legislative target—underfunded pension plans. OBRA '87 tightened ERISA's funding requirements in an effort to prevent plans from being inadequately funded and consequently reneging on the pension-benefit promises that they made. OBRA '87 took away some of the leeway actuaries had concerning the amount and timing of plan contributions and forced employers to meet stricter funding requirements. In addition to tightening funding standards, the Revenue Act of 1987 also increased insurance premiums that are owed the PBGC from $8.50 to $16 per participant per year. Under the higher premium schedules, underfunded plans were subject to a variable rate greater than $16, depending on the amount by which they were underfunded.

The Revenue Reconciliation Act of 1989 represented yet another legislative change to pension law. This act focused on, among other things, restructuring the rules governing employee stock ownership plans (ESOPs). Specifically, the act abolished many of the special tax advantages that an ESOP had, such as the estate tax reduction brought about by selling employer stock back to the ESOP after an employee's death.

The Revenue Reconciliation Act of 1990 dramatically changed the rules governing an employer's ability to acquire an asset reversion from a terminating defined-benefit plan. In addition, the new law enhanced an employer's ability to prefund retiree health benefits in a so-called 401(h) account by allowing excess pension assets to be transferred to the 401(h) account without the employer having to pay either regular income tax or a pension reversion excise tax on the amount transferred. Finally, the new law increased annual PBGC premiums for covered defined-benefit plans from $16 to $19 per participant.

The Emergency Unemployment Act of 1992 changed several of the rules governing distributions from qualified plans. Apparently the policy behind the changes was to encourage employees to save preretirement distributions for their retirement needs. These, effective for distributions after December 31, 1992, liberalize the rollover rules (allowing most preretirement distributions to be rolled into a tax-sheltered IRA or qualified plan); require mandatory 20 percent federal income tax withholding on most distributions made directly to participants; and require qualified plans to allow participants the option to have distributions transferred directly to another tax-sheltered vehicle. (Transferred amounts are not subject to the 20 percent withholding requirements.)

The Omnibus Budget Reconciliation Act of 1993 targeted the benefits of the highly compensated by capping the amount of compensation that could be taken into account for determining contributions or benefits to $150,000.

The Retirement Protection Act of 1994 (RPA '94) made significant changes in the funding rules for single-employer defined-benefit plans, the cash-out provisions for lump sums, and the PBGC premium structure for underfunded defined-benefit plans. The primary focus of the legislation was to give employers added incentive to fund underfunded defined-benefit plans and to put the PBGC in a better financial position.

The Small Business Job Opportunities Act of 1996 was the most sweeping legislation in the pension area in years. Believe it or not, the new law actually simplifies the pension rules. For example, the law creates a less complicated definition of highly compensated employees, simplifies the nondiscrimination testing in a 401(k) plan, and even eliminates nondiscrimination testing in 401(k) plans that comply with certain safe harbors. In the distribution area, the law simplifies the annuity taxation rules and eliminates special 5-year averaging. To provide a 401(k) look-alike savings plan for small employers, the law establishes a SIMPLE (savings incentive match plan for employees).

The Economic Growth and Tax Relief Reconciliation Act of 2001 (EGTRRA) is the most positive pension law in years. It increased many pension limits. For example, the $35,000 limit on annual additions in a defined-contribution plan for each participant increased to $40,000 and the defined-benefit annual benefit limit increased from $140,000 a year to $160,000. All maximum salary deferral limits increased as well. Limits for Sec. 401(k) plans and Sec. 403(b) plans will increase over the next several years to $15,000 (up from $10,500); the SIMPLE limit will increase from $6,500 to $10,000 over the next several years as well. Even IRA limits were increased, going from $2,000 in 2001 up to $5,000 in 2008. Participants over age 50 can also make additional catch-up contributions to 401(k), 403(b), and even to IRA plans.

Many other changes in the law were intended to encourage small business owners to establish plans. This was done in a number of ways, from eliminating IRS user fees for new plan sponsors to tax credit, to eliminating some of the complexity of maintaining a plan. For example, the top-heavy rules were simplified and the prohibition against certain owners borrowing from the plan was removed. Also, the maximum deductible contribution to a profit-sharing plan went up to 25 percent of compensation, so a sponsor can maximize contributions to a defined-contribution plan with just one plan. Other provisions provided simplification for both plan sponsors and plan participants. The most important change was allowing participants to roll over pension benefits between qualified plans, IRAs, 403(b) plans, and Sec. 457 plans.

The Katrina Emergency Tax Relief Act of 2005 (KETRA) was passed in response to the hurricane that devastated New Orleans and other Gulf Coast cities. This law provided for penalty-free withdrawals for people under age 59½ in the affected areas. It also provided for tax relief by taxing withdrawals using 3-year averaging and waiving income tax if withdrawals were returned within 3 years. Also it allowed for participant loans of up to $100,000.

The Deficit Reduction Act of 2005 made three important PBGC premium changes. First, it increased the PBGC's premiums from $19 to $30 per participant in single employer plans. Second, it increased the premiums from $2.60 to $8 per participant in multiemployer plans. Finally, it established an employer paid termination premium for companies that terminate their pension plans after 2005 and before 2011.

The Pension Protection Act of 2006 was a sweeping law that started as a plan funding statute and expanded into much more. Some of the key changes to the plan funding rules include:

- A complete revision of the minimum funding requirements for defined-benefit plans
- Changes in how lump-sum distributions are calculated (which will reduce the value of the lump-sum in many cases)
- Replaces the summary annual report with a notice to participants about plan funding
- Provides for additional consequences for severely underfunded plans referred to as "plans at risk"

Other changes in the Pension Protection Act included amending the fiduciary provisions of ERISA to allow more investment advice to participants, validation for cash balance plans, and strengthening of the automatic enrollment rules. In addition, it made permanent some EGTRRA provisions, liberalized payout and rollover rules, and allowed tax-free distributions from an IRA to a charity in certain situations.

The Tax Increase Prevention and Reconciliation Act of 2006 (TIPRA) included one important pension change. Beginning in 2010, the law eliminated the income limitations for individuals seeking to convert a traditional IRA into a Roth IRA.

The Worker, Retiree, and Employer Recovery Act of 2008 (WRERA) was passed in response to the financial crisis that occurred in 2008 and focused on providing funding relief to pension plans. In addition, it made nonspousal beneficiary rollovers a mandatory plan provision and suspended for the 2009 calendar year the required minimum-distribution requirements for participants in IRA, 401(k), 403(b), and other defined-contribution plans.

APPENDIX B: PENSION ACRONYMS

ADP test	actual deferral percentage test
AGI	adjusted gross income
AIR	assumed interest rate
Automatic J&S	automatic joint-and-survivor annuity
CODA	cash or deferred arrangement
COLA	cost-of-living adjustment
DA contract	deposit-administration contract
DB	defined benefit
DBO plan	death-benefit-only plan
DC	defined contribution
DOL	Department of Labor
ERIC	ERISA Industry Committee
ERISA	Employee Retirement Income Security Act of 1974
ESOP	employee stock ownership plan
FASB	Financial Accounting Standards Board
FSA	flexible spending account
GIC	guaranteed-investment contract
IG contract	investment-guarantee contract
IPG contract	immediate-participation-guarantee contract
IRA	individual retirement account
IRC	Internal Revenue Code
IRD	income in respect of a decedent
IRS	Internal Revenue Service
ISO	incentive stock option
LSD	lump-sum distribution
MPPAA	Multiemployer Pension Plan Amendments Act
NRA	normal retirement age
NRD	normal retirement date
PBGC	Pension Benefit Guaranty Corporation
PC	professional corporation
PLR	private-letter ruling
PTE	prohibited-transaction exemption

QDRO	qualified domestic relations order
QPAM	qualified professional asset manager
QPSA	qualified preretirement survivor annuity
QVEC	qualified voluntary employee contribution
SAR	summary of annual reports
SARSEP	salary reduction simplified employee pension
SEP	simplified employee pension plan
SERP	supplemental executive retirement plan
SIMPLE	savings incentive match plan for employees
SMM	summary of material modifications
SPAC	single-premium annuity contract
SPD	summary plan description
TDA	tax-deferred annuity
TPA	third-party administrator
TSA	tax-sheltered annuity
VDEC	voluntary deductible employee contribution
VEBA	Voluntary Employee's Beneficiary Association
401(a)(4)	discrimination rule
401(k) plan	cash or deferred arrangement
403(b) plan	tax-deferred annuity
410(b)(1)	discrimination rule
457 plan	state or local government plan
501(c)(3)	charitable organizations
5500s	pension forms filed with IRS

APPENDIX C: AVERAGE LIFE EXPECTANCIES

	\multicolumn{2}{c	}{1983 Individual Annuity Table (1971–1976)*}		
	Male		**Female**	
Age	**Deaths per 1,000**	**Expectation of Life (Years)**	**Deaths per 1,000**	**Expectation of Life (Years)**
30	.76	49.83	.44	54.75
31	.79	48.87	.46	53.77
32	.81	47.91	.48	52.80
33	.84	46.95	.50	51.82
34	.88	45.99	.52	50.85
35	.92	45.03	.55	49.87
36	.97	44.07	.57	48.90
37	1.03	43.11	.61	47.93
38	1.11	42.15	.65	46.96
39	1.22	41.20	.69	45.99
40	1.34	40.25	.74	45.02
41	1.49	39.30	.80	44.05
42	1.67	38.36	.87	43.09
43	1.89	37.43	.94	42.12
44	2.13	36.50	1.03	41.16
45	2.40	35.57	1.12	40.20
46	2.69	34.66	1.23	39.25
47	3.01	33.75	1.36	38.30
48	3.34	32.85	1.50	37.35
49	3.69	31.96	1.66	36.40
50	4.06	31.07	1.83	35.46
51	4.43	30.20	2.02	34.53
52	4.81	29.33	2.22	33.59
53	5.20	28.47	2.43	32.67
54	5.59	27.62	2.65	31.75
55	5.99	26.77	2.89	30.83
56	6.41	25.93	3.15	29.92
57	6.84	25.09	3.43	29.01
58	7.29	24.26	3.74	28.11

1983 Individual Annuity Table (1971–1976)*

Age	Male Deaths per 1,000	Male Expectation of Life (Years)	Female Deaths per 1,000	Female Expectation of Life (Years)
59	7.78	23.44	4.08	27.21
60	8.34	22.62	4.47	26.32
61	8.98	21.80	4.91	25.44
62	9.74	20.99	5.41	24.56
63	10.63	20.20	5.99	23.69
64	11.66	19.41	6.63	22.83
65	12.85	18.63	7.34	21.98
66	14.20	17.87	8.09	21.14
67	15.72	17.12	8.89	20.31
68	17.41	16.38	9.73	19.49
69	19.30	15.66	10.65	18.67
70	21.37	14.96	11.70	17.87
71	23.65	14.28	12.91	17.07
72	26.13	13.61	14.32	16.29
73	28.84	12.96	15.98	15.52
74	31.79	12.33	17.91	14.76
75	35.05	11.72	20.13	14.02
76	38.63	11.13	22.65	13.30
77	42.59	10.56	25.51	12.60
78	46.95	10.00	28.72	11.91
79	51.76	9.47	32.33	11.25
80	57.03	8.96	36.40	10.61
81	62.79	8.47	40.98	9.99
82	69.08	8.01	46.12	9.40
83	75.91	7.57	51.89	8.83
84	83.23	7.15	58.34	8.28
85	90.99	6.75	65.52	7.77
86	99.12	6.37	73.49	7.28
87	107.58	6.02	82.32	6.81
88	116.32	5.69	92.02	6.38
89	125.39	5.37	102.49	5.98

1983 Individual Annuity Table (1971–1976)*

Age	Male Deaths per 1,000	Male Expectation of Life (Years)	Female Deaths per 1,000	Female Expectation of Life (Years)
90	134.89	5.07	113.61	5.60
91	144.87	4.78	125.23	5.26
92	155.43	4.50	137.22	4.94
93	166.63	4.24	149.46	4.64
94	178.54	3.99	161.83	4.37
95	191.21	3.75	174.23	4.12
96	204.72	3.51	186.54	3.88
97	219.12	3.29	198.65	3.65
98	234.74	3.07	211.10	3.44
99	251.89	2.86	224.45	3.22
100	270.91	2.66	239.22	3.01
101	292.11	2.46	255.95	2.80
102	315.83	2.26	275.20	2.59
103	342.38	2.08	297.50	2.38
104	372.09	1.90	323.39	2.18
105	405.28	1.73	353.41	1.98
106	442.28	1.57	388.11	1.79
107	483.41	1.41	428.02	1.60
108	528.99	1.27	473.69	1.43
109	579.35	1.13	525.66	1.26
110	634.81	1.01	584.46	1.11
111	695.70	.89	650.65	.97
112	762.34	.78	724.75	.83
113	835.06	.70	807.32	.71
114	914.17	.67	898.89	.60
115	1000.00	.50	1000.00	.50

*These figures come from annuity tables which typically assume a longer life expectancy than other tables that can be used.

APPENDIX D: ANNUITY TABLES

Ages	0	1	2	3	4	5	6	7	8	9
0	90.0	89.5	89.0	88.6	88.2	87.8	87.4	87.1	86.8	86.5
1	89.5	89.0	88.5	88.1	87.6	87.2	86.8	86.5	86.1	85.8
2	89.0	88.5	88.0	87.5	87.1	86.6	86.2	85.8	85.5	85.1
3	88.6	88.1	87.5	87.0	86.5	86.1	85.6	85.2	84.8	84.5
4	88.2	87.6	87.1	86.5	86.0	85.5	85.1	84.6	84.2	83.8
5	87.8	87.2	86.6	86.1	85.5	85.0	84.5	84.1	83.6	83.2
6	87.4	86.8	86.2	85.6	85.1	84.5	84.0	83.5	83.1	82.6
7	87.1	86.5	85.8	85.2	84.6	84.1	83.5	83.0	82.5	82.1
8	86.8	86.1	85.5	84.8	84.2	83.6	83.1	82.5	82.0	81.6
9	86.5	85.8	85.1	84.5	83.8	83.2	82.6	82.1	81.6	81.0
10	86.2	85.5	84.8	84.1	83.5	82.8	82.2	81.6	81.1	80.6
11	85.9	85.2	84.5	83.8	83.1	82.5	81.8	81.2	80.7	80.1
12	85.7	84.9	84.2	83.5	82.8	82.1	81.5	80.8	80.2	79.7
13	85.4	84.7	84.0	83.2	82.5	81.8	81.1	80.5	79.9	79.2
14	85.2	84.5	83.7	83.0	82.2	81.5	80.8	80.1	79.5	78.9
15	85.0	84.3	83.5	82.7	82.0	81.2	80.5	79.8	79.1	78.5
16	84.9	84.1	83.3	82.5	81.7	81.0	80.2	79.5	78.8	78.1
17	84.7	83.9	83.1	82.3	81.5	80.7	80.0	79.2	78.5	77.8
18	84.5	83.7	82.9	82.1	81.3	80.5	79.7	79.0	78.2	77.5
19	84.4	83.6	82.7	81.9	81.1	80.3	79.5	78.7	78.0	77.3
20	84.3	83.4	82.6	81.8	80.9	80.1	79.3	78.5	77.7	77.0
21	84.1	83.3	82.4	81.6	80.8	79.9	79.1	78.3	77.5	76.8
22	84.0	83.2	82.3	81.5	80.6	79.8	78.9	78.1	77.3	76.5
23	83.9	83.1	82.2	81.3	80.5	79.6	78.8	77.9	77.1	76.3
24	83.8	83.0	82.1	81.2	80.3	79.5	78.6	77.8	76.9	76.1
25	83.7	82.9	82.0	81.1	80.2	79.3	78.5	77.6	76.8	75.9
26	83.6	82.8	81.9	81.0	80.1	79.2	78.3	77.5	76.6	75.8
27	83.6	82.7	81.8	80.9	80.0	79.1	78.2	77.4	76.5	75.6
28	83.5	82.6	81.7	80.8	79.9	79.0	78.1	77.2	76.4	75.5
29	83.4	82.6	81.6	80.7	79.8	78.9	78.0	77.1	76.2	75.4
30	83.4	82.5	81.6	80.7	79.7	78.8	77.9	77.0	76.1	75.2
31	83.3	82.4	81.5	80.6	79.7	78.8	77.8	76.9	76.0	75.1
32	83.3	82.4	81.5	80.5	79.6	78.7	77.8	76.8	75.9	75.0

Ages	0	1	2	3	4	5	6	7	8	9
33	83.2	82.3	81.4	80.5	79.5	78.6	77.7	76.8	75.9	74.9
34	83.2	82.3	81.3	80.4	79.5	78.5	77.6	76.7	75.8	74.9
35	83.1	82.2	81.3	80.4	79.4	78.5	77.6	76.6	75.7	74.8
36	83.1	82.2	81.3	80.3	79.4	78.4	77.5	76.6	75.6	74.7
37	83.0	82.2	81.2	80.3	79.3	78.4	77.4	76.5	75.6	74.6
38	83.0	82.1	81.2	80.2	79.3	78.3	77.4	76.4	75.5	74.6
39	83.0	82.1	81.1	80.2	79.2	78.3	77.3	76.4	75.5	74.5
40	82.9	82.1	81.1	80.2	79.2	78.3	77.3	76.4	75.4	74.5
41	82.9	82.0	81.1	80.1	79.2	78.2	77.3	76.3	75.4	74.4
42	82.9	82.0	81.1	80.1	79.1	78.2	77.2	76.3	75.3	74.4
43	82.9	82.0	81.0	80.1	79.1	78.2	77.2	76.2	75.3	74.3
44	82.8	81.9	81.0	80.0	79.1	78.1	77.2	76.2	75.2	74.3
45	82.8	81.9	81.0	80.0	79.1	78.1	77.1	76.2	75.2	74.3
46	82.8	81.9	81.0	80.0	79.0	78.1	77.1	76.1	75.2	74.2
47	82.8	81.9	80.9	80.0	79.0	78.0	77.1	76.1	75.2	74.2
48	82.8	81.9	80.9	80.0	79.0	78.0	77.1	76.1	75.1	74.2
49	82.7	81.8	80.9	79.9	79.0	78.0	77.0	76.1	75.1	74.1
50	82.7	81.8	80.9	79.9	79.0	78.0	77.0	76.0	75.1	74.1
51	82.7	81.8	80.9	79.9	78.9	78.0	77.0	76.0	75.1	74.1
52	82.7	81.8	80.9	79.9	78.9	78.0	77.0	76.0	75.0	74.1
53	82.7	81.8	80.8	79.9	78.9	77.9	77.0	76.0	75.0	74.0
54	82.7	81.8	80.8	79.9	78.9	77.9	76.9	76.0	75.0	74.0
55	82.6	81.8	80.8	79.8	78.9	77.9	76.9	76.0	75.0	74.0
56	82.6	81.7	80.8	79.8	78.9	77.9	76.9	75.9	75.0	74.0
57	82.6	81.7	80.8	79.8	78.9	77.9	76.9	75.9	75.0	74.0
58	82.6	81.7	80.8	79.8	78.8	77.9	76.9	75.9	74.9	74.0
59	82.6	81.7	80.8	79.8	78.8	77.9	76.9	75.9	74.9	74.0
60	82.6	81.7	80.8	79.8	78.8	77.8	76.9	75.9	74.9	73.9
61	82.6	81.7	80.8	79.8	78.8	77.8	76.9	75.9	74.9	73.9
62	82.6	81.7	80.7	79.8	78.8	77.8	76.9	75.9	74.9	73.9
63	82.6	81.7	80.7	79.8	78.8	77.8	76.8	75.9	74.9	73.9
64	82.5	81.7	80.7	79.8	78.8	77.8	76.8	75.9	74.9	73.9
65	82.5	81.7	80.7	79.8	78.8	77.8	76.8	75.8	74.9	73.9
66	82.5	81.7	80.7	79.7	78.8	77.8	76.8	75.8	74.9	73.9
67	82.5	81.7	80.7	79.7	78.8	77.8	76.8	75.8	74.9	73.9

Ages	0	1	2	3	4	5	6	7	8	9
68	82.5	81.6	80.7	79.7	78.8	77.8	76.8	75.8	74.8	73.9
69	82.5	81.6	80.7	79.7	78.8	77.8	76.8	75.8	74.8	73.9
70	82.5	81.6	80.7	79.7	78.8	77.8	76.8	75.8	74.8	73.9
71	82.5	81.6	80.7	79.7	78.7	77.8	76.8	75.8	74.8	73.8
72	82.5	81.6	80.7	79.7	78.7	77.8	76.8	75.8	74.8	73.8
73	82.5	81.6	80.7	79.7	78.7	77.8	76.8	75.8	74.8	73.8
74	82.5	81.6	80.7	79.7	78.7	77.8	76.8	75.8	74.8	73.8
75	82.5	81.6	80.7	79.7	78.7	77.8	76.8	75.8	74.8	73.8
76	82.5	81.6	80.7	79.7	78.7	77.8	76.8	75.8	74.8	73.8
77	82.5	81.6	80.7	79.7	78.7	77.7	76.8	75.8	74.8	73.8
78	82.5	81.6	80.7	79.7	78.7	77.7	76.8	75.8	74.8	73.8
79	82.5	81.6	80.7	79.7	78.7	77.7	76.8	75.8	74.8	73.8
80	82.5	81.6	80.7	79.7	78.7	77.7	76.8	75.8	74.8	73.8
81	82.4	81.6	80.7	79.7	78.7	77.7	76.8	75.8	74.8	73.8
82	82.4	81.6	80.7	79.7	78.7	77.7	76.8	75.8	74.8	73.8
83	82.4	81.6	80.7	79.7	78.7	77.7	76.8	75.8	74.8	73.8
84	82.4	81.6	80.7	79.7	78.7	77.7	76.8	75.8	74.8	73.8
85	82.4	81.6	80.6	79.7	78.7	77.7	76.8	75.8	74.8	73.8
86	82.4	81.6	80.6	79.7	78.7	77.7	76.7	75.8	74.8	73.8
87	82.4	81.6	80.6	79.7	78.7	77.7	76.7	75.8	74.8	73.8
88	82.4	81.6	80.6	79.7	78.7	77.7	76.7	75.8	74.8	73.8
89	82.4	81.6	80.6	79.7	78.7	77.7	76.7	75.8	74.8	73.8
90	82.4	81.6	80.6	79.7	78.7	77.7	76.7	75.8	74.8	73.8
91	82.4	81.6	80.6	79.7	78.7	77.7	76.7	75.8	74.8	73.8
92	82.4	81.6	80.6	79.7	78.7	77.7	76.7	75.8	74.8	73.8
93	82.4	81.6	80.6	79.7	78.7	77.7	76.7	75.8	74.8	73.8
94	82.4	81.6	80.6	79.7	78.7	77.7	76.7	75.8	74.8	73.8
95	82.4	81.6	80.6	79.7	78.7	77.7	76.7	75.8	74.8	73.8
96	82.4	81.6	80.6	79.7	78.7	77.7	76.7	75.8	74.8	73.8
97	82.4	81.6	80.6	79.7	78.7	77.7	76.7	75.8	74.8	73.8
98	82.4	81.6	80.6	79.7	78.7	77.7	76.7	75.8	74.8	73.8
99	82.4	81.6	80.6	79.7	78.7	77.7	76.7	75.8	74.8	73.8
100	82.4	81.6	80.6	79.7	78.7	77.7	76.7	75.8	74.8	73.8
101	82.4	81.6	80.6	79.7	78.7	77.7	76.7	75.8	74.8	73.8
102	82.4	81.6	80.6	79.7	78.7	77.7	76.7	75.8	74.8	73.8

Ages	0	1	2	3	4	5	6	7	8	9
103	82.4	81.6	80.6	79.7	78.7	77.7	76.7	75.8	74.8	73.8
104	82.4	81.6	80.6	79.7	78.7	77.7	76.7	75.8	74.8	73.8
105	82.4	81.6	80.6	79.7	78.7	77.7	76.7	75.8	74.8	73.8
106	82.4	81.6	80.6	79.7	78.7	77.7	76.7	75.8	74.8	73.8
107	82.4	81.6	80.6	79.7	78.7	77.7	76.7	75.8	74.8	73.8
108	82.4	81.6	80.6	79.7	78.7	77.7	76.7	75.8	74.8	73.8
109	82.4	81.6	80.6	79.7	78.7	77.7	76.7	75.8	74.8	73.8
110	82.4	81.6	80.6	79.7	78.7	77.7	76.7	75.8	74.8	73.8
111	82.4	81.6	80.6	79.7	78.7	77.7	76.7	75.8	74.8	73.8
112	82.4	81.6	80.6	79.7	78.7	77.7	76.7	75.8	74.8	73.8
113	82.4	81.6	80.6	79.7	78.7	77.7	76.7	75.8	74.8	73.8
114	82.4	81.6	80.6	79.7	78.7	77.7	76.7	75.8	74.8	73.8
115+	82.4	81.6	80.6	79.7	78.7	77.7	76.7	75.8	74.8	73.8

Ages	10	11	12	13	14	15	16	17	18	19
10	80.0	79.6	79.1	78.7	78.2	77.9	77.5	77.2	76.8	76.5
11	79.6	79.0	78.6	78.1	77.7	77.3	76.9	76.5	76.2	75.8
12	79.1	78.6	78.1	77.6	77.1	76.7	76.3	75.9	75.5	75.2
13	78.7	78.1	77.6	77.1	76.6	76.1	75.7	75.3	74.9	74.5
14	78.2	77.7	77.1	76.6	76.1	75.6	75.1	74.7	74.3	73.9
15	77.9	77.3	76.7	76.1	75.6	75.1	74.6	74.1	73.7	73.3
16	77.5	76.9	76.3	75.7	75.1	74.6	74.1	73.6	73.1	72.7
17	77.2	76.5	75.9	75.3	74.7	74.1	73.6	73.1	72.6	72.1
18	76.8	76.2	75.5	74.9	74.3	73.7	73.1	72.6	72.1	71.6
19	76.5	75.8	75.2	74.5	73.9	73.3	72.7	72.1	71.6	71.1
20	76.3	75.5	74.8	74.2	73.5	72.9	72.3	71.7	71.1	70.6
21	76.0	75.3	74.5	73.8	73.2	72.5	71.9	71.3	70.7	70.1
22	75.8	75.0	74.3	73.5	72.9	72.2	71.5	70.9	70.3	69.7
23	75.5	74.8	74.0	73.3	72.6	71.9	71.2	70.5	69.9	69.3
24	75.3	74.5	73.8	73.0	72.3	71.6	70.9	70.2	69.5	68.9
25	75.1	74.3	73.5	72.8	72.0	71.3	70.6	69.9	69.2	68.5
26	75.0	74.1	73.3	72.5	71.8	71.0	70.3	69.6	68.9	68.2
27	74.8	74.0	73.1	72.3	71.6	70.8	70.0	69.3	68.6	67.9
28	74.6	73.8	73.0	72.2	71.3	70.6	69.8	69.0	68.3	67.6
29	74.5	73.6	72.8	72.0	71.2	70.4	69.6	68.8	68.0	67.3

Appendix D: Annuity Tables

Ages	10	11	12	13	14	15	16	17	18	19
30	74.4	73.5	72.7	71.8	71.0	70.2	69.4	68.6	67.8	67.1
31	74.3	73.4	72.5	71.7	70.8	70.0	69.2	68.4	67.6	66.8
32	74.1	73.3	72.4	71.5	70.7	69.8	69.0	68.2	67.4	66.6
33	74.0	73.2	72.3	71.4	70.5	69.7	68.8	68.0	67.2	66.4
34	73.9	73.0	72.2	71.3	70.4	69.5	68.7	67.8	67.0	66.2
35	73.9	73.0	72.1	71.2	70.3	69.4	68.5	67.7	66.8	66.0
36	73.8	72.9	72.0	71.1	70.2	69.3	68.4	67.6	66.7	65.9
37	73.7	72.8	71.9	71.0	70.1	69.2	68.3	67.4	66.6	65.7
38	73.6	72.7	71.8	70.9	70.0	69.1	68.2	67.3	66.4	65.6
39	73.6	72.7	71.7	70.8	69.9	69.0	68.1	67.2	66.3	65.4
40	73.5	72.6	71.7	70.7	69.8	68.9	68.0	67.1	66.2	65.3
41	73.5	72.5	71.6	70.7	69.7	68.8	67.9	67.0	66.1	65.2
42	73.4	72.5	71.5	70.6	69.7	68.8	67.8	66.9	66.0	65.1
43	73.4	72.4	71.5	70.6	69.6	68.7	67.8	66.8	65.9	65.0
44	73.3	72.4	71.4	70.5	69.6	68.6	67.7	66.8	65.9	64.9
45	73.3	72.3	71.4	70.5	69.5	68.6	67.6	66.7	65.8	64.9
46	73.3	72.3	71.4	70.4	69.5	68.5	67.6	66.6	65.7	64.8
47	73.2	72.3	71.3	70.4	69.4	68.5	67.5	66.6	65.7	64.7
48	73.2	72.2	71.3	70.3	69.4	68.4	67.5	66.5	65.6	64.7
49	73.2	72.2	71.2	70.3	69.3	68.4	67.4	66.5	65.6	64.6
50	73.1	72.2	71.2	70.3	69.3	68.4	67.4	66.5	65.5	64.6
51	73.1	72.2	71.2	70.2	69.3	68.3	67.4	66.4	65.5	64.5
52	73.1	72.1	71.2	70.2	69.2	68.3	67.3	66.4	65.4	64.5
53	73.1	72.1	71.1	70.2	69.2	68.3	67.3	66.3	65.4	64.4
54	73.1	72.1	71.1	70.2	69.2	68.2	67.3	66.3	65.4	64.4
55	73.0	72.1	71.1	70.1	69.2	68.2	67.2	66.3	65.3	64.4
56	73.0	72.1	71.1	70.1	69.1	68.2	67.2	66.3	65.3	64.3
57	73.0	72.0	71.1	70.1	69.1	68.2	67.2	66.2	65.3	64.3
58	73.0	72.0	71.0	70.1	69.1	68.1	67.2	66.2	65.2	64.3
59	73.0	72.0	71.0	70.1	69.1	68.1	67.2	66.2	65.2	64.3
60	73.0	72.0	71.0	70.0	69.1	68.1	67.1	66.2	65.2	64.2
61	73.0	72.0	71.0	70.0	69.1	68.1	67.1	66.2	65.2	64.2
62	72.9	72.0	71.0	70.0	69.0	68.1	67.1	66.1	65.2	64.2
63	72.9	72.0	71.0	70.0	69.0	68.1	67.1	66.1	65.2	64.2
64	72.9	71.9	71.0	70.0	69.0	68.0	67.1	66.1	65.1	64.2

Ages	10	11	12	13	14	15	16	17	18	19
65	72.9	71.9	71.0	70.0	69.0	68.0	67.1	66.1	65.1	64.2
66	72.9	71.9	70.9	70.0	69.0	68.0	67.1	66.1	65.1	64.1
67	72.9	71.9	70.9	70.0	69.0	68.0	67.0	66.1	65.1	64.1
68	72.9	71.9	70.9	70.0	69.0	68.0	67.0	66.1	65.1	64.1
69	72.9	71.9	70.9	69.9	69.0	68.0	67.0	66.1	65.1	64.1
70	72.9	71.9	70.9	69.9	69.0	68.0	67.0	66.0	65.1	64.1
71	72.9	71.9	70.9	69.9	69.0	68.0	67.0	66.0	65.1	64.1
72	72.9	71.9	70.9	69.9	69.0	68.0	67.0	66.0	65.1	64.1
73	72.9	71.9	70.9	69.9	68.9	68.0	67.0	66.0	65.0	64.1
74	72.9	71.9	70.9	69.9	68.9	68.0	67.0	66.0	65.0	64.1
75	72.8	71.9	70.9	69.9	68.9	68.0	67.0	66.0	65.0	64.1
76	72.8	71.9	70.9	69.9	68.9	68.0	67.0	66.0	65.0	64.1
77	72.8	71.9	70.9	69.9	68.9	68.0	67.0	66.0	65.0	64.1
78	72.8	71.9	70.9	69.9	68.9	67.9	67.0	66.0	65.0	64.0
79	72.8	71.9	70.9	69.9	68.9	67.9	67.0	66.0	65.0	64.0
80	72.8	71.9	70.9	69.9	68.9	67.9	67.0	66.0	65.0	64.0
81	72.8	71.8	70.9	69.9	68.9	67.9	67.0	66.0	65.0	64.0
82	72.8	71.8	70.9	69.9	68.9	67.9	67.0	66.0	65.0	64.0
83	72.8	71.8	70.9	69.9	68.9	67.9	67.0	66.0	65.0	64.0
84	72.8	71.8	70.9	69.9	68.9	67.9	67.0	66.0	65.0	64.0
85	72.8	71.8	70.9	69.9	68.9	67.9	66.9	66.0	65.0	64.0
86	72.8	71.8	70.9	69.9	68.9	67.9	66.9	66.0	65.0	64.0
87	72.8	71.8	70.9	69.9	68.9	67.9	66.9	66.0	65.0	64.0
88	72.8	71.8	70.9	69.9	68.9	67.9	66.9	66.0	65.0	64.0
89	72.8	71.8	70.9	69.9	68.9	67.9	66.9	66.0	65.0	64.0
90	72.8	71.8	70.9	69.9	68.9	67.9	66.9	66.0	65.0	64.0
91	72.8	71.8	70.9	69.9	68.9	67.9	66.9	66.0	65.0	64.0
92	72.8	71.8	70.9	69.9	68.9	67.9	66.9	66.0	65.0	64.0
93	72.8	71.8	70.9	69.9	68.9	67.9	66.9	66.0	65.0	64.0
94	72.8	71.8	70.8	69.9	68.9	67.9	66.9	66.0	65.1	64.2
95	72.8	71.8	70.8	69.9	68.9	67.9	66.9	66.0	65.0	64.0
96	72.8	71.8	70.8	69.9	68.9	67.9	66.9	66.0	65.0	64.0
97	72.8	71.8	70.8	69.9	68.9	67.9	66.9	66.0	65.0	64.0
98	72.8	71.8	70.8	69.9	68.9	67.9	66.9	66.0	65.0	64.0
99	72.8	71.8	70.8	69.9	68.9	67.9	66.9	66.0	65.0	64.0

Ages	10	11	12	13	14	15	16	17	18	19
100	72.8	71.8	70.8	69.9	68.9	67.9	66.9	66.0	65.0	64.0
101	72.8	71.8	70.8	69.9	68.9	67.9	66.9	66.0	65.0	64.0
102	72.8	71.8	70.8	69.9	68.9	67.9	66.9	66.0	65.0	64.0
103	72.8	71.8	70.8	69.9	68.9	67.9	66.9	66.0	65.0	64.0
104	72.8	71.8	70.8	69.9	68.9	67.9	66.9	66.0	65.0	64.0
105	72.8	71.8	70.8	69.9	68.9	67.9	66.9	66.0	65.0	64.0
106	72.8	71.8	70.8	69.9	68.9	67.9	66.9	66.0	65.0	64.0
107	72.8	71.8	70.8	69.9	68.9	67.9	66.9	66.0	65.0	64.0
108	72.8	71.8	70.8	69.9	68.9	67.9	66.9	66.0	65.0	64.0
109	72.8	71.8	70.8	69.9	68.9	67.9	66.9	66.0	65.0	64.0
110	72.8	71.8	70.8	69.9	68.9	67.9	66.9	66.0	65.0	64.0
111	72.8	71.8	70.8	69.9	68.9	67.9	66.9	66.0	65.0	64.0
112	72.8	71.8	70.8	69.9	68.9	67.9	66.9	66.0	65.0	64.0
113	72.8	71.8	70.8	69.9	68.9	67.9	66.9	66.0	65.0	64.0
114	72.8	71.8	70.8	69.9	68.9	67.9	66.9	66.0	65.0	64.0
115+	72.8	71.8	70.8	69.9	68.9	67.9	66.9	66.0	65.0	64.0

Ages	20	21	22	23	24	25	26	27	28	29
20	70.1	69.6	69.1	68.7	68.3	67.9	67.5	67.2	66.9	66.6
21	69.6	69.1	68.6	68.2	67.7	67.3	66.9	66.6	66.2	65.9
22	69.1	68.6	68.1	67.6	67.2	66.7	66.3	65.9	65.6	65.2
23	68.7	68.2	67.6	67.1	66.6	66.2	65.7	65.3	64.9	64.6
24	68.3	67.7	67.2	66.6	66.1	65.6	65.2	64.7	64.3	63.9
25	67.9	67.3	66.7	66.2	65.6	65.1	64.6	64.2	63.7	63.3
26	67.5	66.9	66.3	65.7	65.2	64.6	64.1	63.6	63.2	62.8
27	67.2	66.6	65.9	65.3	64.7	64.2	63.6	63.1	62.7	62.2
28	66.9	66.2	65.6	64.9	64.3	63.7	63.2	62.7	62.1	61.7
29	66.6	65.9	65.2	64.6	63.9	63.3	62.8	62.2	61.7	61.2
30	66.3	65.6	64.9	64.2	63.6	62.9	62.3	61.8	61.2	60.7
31	66.1	65.3	64.6	63.9	63.2	62.6	62.0	61.4	60.8	60.2
32	65.8	65.1	64.3	63.6	62.9	62.2	61.6	61.0	60.4	59.8
33	65.6	64.8	64.1	63.3	62.6	61.9	61.3	60.6	60.0	59.4
34	65.4	64.6	63.8	63.1	62.3	61.6	60.9	60.3	59.6	59.0
35	65.2	64.4	63.6	62.8	62.1	61.4	60.6	59.9	59.3	58.6
36	65.0	64.2	63.4	62.6	61.9	61.1	60.4	59.6	59.0	58.3

Ages	20	21	22	23	24	25	26	27	28	29
37	64.9	64.0	63.2	62.4	61.6	60.9	60.1	59.4	58.7	58.0
38	64.7	63.9	63.0	62.2	61.4	60.6	59.9	59.1	58.4	57.7
39	64.6	63.7	62.9	62.1	61.2	60.4	59.6	58.9	58.1	57.4
40	64.4	63.6	62.7	61.9	61.1	60.2	59.4	58.7	57.9	57.1
41	64.3	63.5	62.6	61.7	60.9	60.1	59.3	58.5	57.7	56.9
42	64.2	63.3	62.5	61.6	60.8	59.9	59.1	58.3	57.5	56.7
43	64.1	63.2	62.4	61.5	60.6	59.8	58.9	58.1	57.3	56.5
44	64.0	63.1	62.2	61.4	60.5	59.6	58.8	57.9	57.1	56.3
45	64.0	63.0	62.2	61.3	60.4	59.5	58.6	57.8	56.9	56.1
46	63.9	63.0	62.1	61.2	60.3	59.4	58.5	57.7	56.8	56.0
47	63.8	62.9	62.0	61.1	60.2	59.3	58.4	57.5	56.7	55.8
48	63.7	62.8	61.9	61.0	60.1	59.2	58.3	57.4	56.5	55.7
49	63.7	62.8	61.8	60.9	60.0	59.1	58.2	57.3	56.4	55.6
50	63.6	62.7	61.8	60.8	59.9	59.0	58.1	57.2	56.3	55.4
51	63.6	62.6	61.7	60.8	59.9	58.9	58.0	57.1	56.2	55.3
52	63.5	62.6	61.7	60.7	59.8	58.9	58.0	57.1	56.1	55.2
53	63.5	62.5	61.6	60.7	59.7	58.8	57.9	57.0	56.1	55.2
54	63.5	62.5	61.6	60.6	59.7	58.8	57.8	56.9	56.0	55.1
55	63.4	62.5	61.5	60.6	59.6	58.7	57.8	56.8	55.9	55.0
56	63.4	62.4	61.5	60.5	59.6	58.7	57.7	56.8	55.9	54.9
57	63.4	62.4	61.5	60.5	59.6	58.6	57.7	56.7	55.8	54.9
58	63.3	62.4	61.4	60.5	59.5	58.6	57.6	56.7	55.8	54.8
59	63.3	62.3	61.4	60.4	59.5	58.5	57.6	56.7	55.7	54.8
60	63.3	62.3	61.4	60.4	59.5	58.5	57.6	56.6	55.7	54.7
61	63.3	62.3	61.3	60.4	59.4	58.5	57.5	56.6	55.6	54.7
62	63.2	62.3	61.3	60.4	59.4	58.4	57.5	56.5	55.6	54.7
63	63.2	62.3	61.3	60.3	59.4	58.4	57.5	56.5	55.6	54.6
64	63.2	62.2	61.3	60.3	59.4	58.4	57.4	56.5	55.5	54.6
65	63.2	62.2	61.3	60.3	59.3	58.4	57.4	56.5	55.5	54.6
66	63.2	62.2	61.2	60.3	59.3	58.4	57.4	56.4	55.5	54.5
67	63.2	62.2	61.2	60.3	59.3	58.3	57.4	56.4	55.5	54.5
68	63.1	62.2	61.2	60.2	59.3	58.3	57.4	56.4	55.4	54.5
69	63.1	62.2	61.2	60.2	59.3	58.3	57.3	56.4	55.4	54.5
70	63.1	62.2	61.2	60.2	59.3	58.3	57.3	56.4	55.4	54.4
71	63.1	62.1	61.2	60.2	59.2	58.3	57.3	56.4	55.4	54.4

Ages	20	21	22	23	24	25	26	27	28	29
72	63.1	62.1	61.2	60.2	59.2	58.3	57.3	56.3	55.4	54.4
73	63.1	62.1	61.2	60.2	59.2	58.3	57.3	56.3	55.4	54.4
74	63.1	62.1	61.2	60.2	59.2	58.2	57.3	56.3	55.4	54.4
75	63.1	62.1	61.1	60.2	59.2	58.2	57.3	56.3	55.3	54.4
76	63.1	62.1	61.1	60.2	59.2	58.2	57.3	56.3	55.3	54.4
77	63.1	62.1	61.1	60.2	59.2	58.2	57.3	56.3	55.3	54.4
78	63.1	62.1	61.1	60.2	59.2	58.2	57.3	56.3	55.3	54.4
79	63.1	62.1	61.1	60.2	59.2	58.2	57.2	56.3	55.3	54.3
80	63.1	62.1	61.1	60.1	59.2	58.2	57.2	56.3	55.3	54.3
81	63.1	62.1	61.1	60.1	59.2	58.2	57.2	56.3	55.3	54.3
82	63.1	62.1	61.1	60.1	59.2	58.2	57.2	56.3	55.3	54.3
83	63.1	62.1	61.1	60.1	59.2	58.2	57.2	56.3	55.3	54.3
84	63.0	62.1	61.1	60.1	59.2	58.2	57.2	56.3	55.3	54.3
85	63.0	62.1	61.1	60.1	59.2	58.2	57.2	56.3	55.3	54.3
86	63.0	62.1	61.1	60.1	59.2	58.2	57.2	56.2	55.3	54.3
87	63.0	62.1	61.1	60.1	59.2	58.2	57.2	56.2	55.3	54.3
88	63.0	62.1	61.1	60.1	59.2	58.2	57.2	56.2	55.3	54.3
89	63.0	62.1	61.1	60.1	59.1	58.2	57.2	56.2	55.3	54.3
90	63.0	62.1	61.1	60.1	59.1	58.2	57.2	56.2	55.3	54.3
91	63.0	62.1	61.1	60.1	59.1	58.2	57.2	56.2	55.3	54.3
92	63.0	62.1	61.1	60.1	59.1	58.2	57.2	56.2	55.3	54.3
93	63.0	62.1	61.1	60.1	59.1	58.2	57.2	56.2	55.3	54.3
94	63.0	62.1	61.1	60.1	59.1	58.2	57.2	56.2	55.3	54.3
95	63.0	62.1	61.1	60.1	59.1	58.2	57.2	56.2	55.3	54.3
96	63.0	62.1	61.1	60.1	59.1	58.2	57.2	56.2	55.3	54.3
97	63.0	62.1	61.1	60.1	59.1	58.2	57.2	56.2	55.3	54.3
98	63.0	62.1	61.1	60.1	59.1	58.2	57.2	56.2	55.3	54.3
99	63.0	62.1	61.1	60.1	59.1	58.2	57.2	56.2	55.3	54.3
100	63.0	62.1	61.1	60.1	59.1	58.2	57.2	56.2	55.3	54.3
101	63.0	62.1	61.1	60.1	59.1	58.2	57.2	56.2	55.3	54.3
102	63.0	62.1	61.1	60.1	59.1	58.2	57.2	56.2	55.3	54.3
103	63.0	62.1	61.1	60.1	59.1	58.2	57.2	56.2	55.3	54.3
104	63.0	62.1	61.1	60.1	59.1	58.2	57.2	56.2	55.3	54.3
105	63.0	62.1	61.1	60.1	59.1	58.2	57.2	56.2	55.3	54.3
106	63.0	62.1	61.1	60.1	59.1	58.2	57.2	56.2	55.3	54.3

Ages	20	21	22	23	24	25	26	27	28	29
107	63.0	62.1	61.1	60.1	59.1	58.2	57.2	56.2	55.3	54.3
108	63.0	62.1	61.1	60.1	59.1	58.2	57.2	56.2	55.3	54.3
109	63.0	62.1	61.1	60.1	59.1	58.2	57.2	56.2	55.3	54.3
110	63.0	62.1	61.1	60.1	59.1	58.2	57.2	56.2	55.3	54.3
111	63.0	62.1	61.1	60.1	59.1	58.2	57.2	56.2	55.3	54.3
112	63.0	62.1	61.1	60.1	59.1	58.2	57.2	56.2	55.3	54.3
113	63.0	62.1	61.1	60.1	59.1	58.2	57.2	56.2	55.3	54.3
114	63.0	62.1	61.1	60.1	59.1	58.2	57.2	56.2	55.3	54.3
115+	63.0	62.1	61.1	60.1	59.1	58.2	57.2	56.2	55.3	54.3

Ages	30	31	32	33	34	35	36	37	38	39
30	60.2	59.7	59.2	58.8	58.4	58.0	57.6	57.3	57.0	56.7
31	59.7	59.2	58.7	58.2	57.8	57.4	57.0	56.6	56.3	56.0
32	59.2	58.7	58.2	57.7	57.2	56.8	56.4	56.0	55.6	55.3
33	58.8	58.2	57.7	57.2	56.7	56.2	55.8	55.4	55.0	54.7
34	58.4	57.8	57.2	56.7	56.2	55.7	55.3	54.8	54.4	54.0
35	58.0	57.4	56.8	56.2	55.7	55.2	54.7	54.3	53.8	53.4
36	57.6	57.0	56.4	55.8	55.3	54.7	54.2	53.7	53.3	52.8
37	57.3	56.6	56.0	55.4	54.8	54.3	53.7	53.2	52.7	52.3
38	57.0	56.3	55.6	55.0	54.4	53.8	53.3	52.7	52.2	51.7
39	56.7	56.0	55.3	54.7	54.0	53.4	52.8	52.3	51.7	51.2
40	56.4	55.7	55.0	54.3	53.7	53.0	52.4	51.8	51.3	50.8
41	56.1	55.4	54.7	54.0	53.3	52.7	52.0	51.4	50.9	50.3
42	55.9	55.2	54.4	53.7	53.0	52.3	51.7	51.1	50.4	49.9
43	55.7	54.9	54.2	53.4	52.7	52.0	51.3	50.7	50.1	49.5
44	55.5	54.7	53.9	53.2	52.4	51.7	51.0	50.4	49.7	49.1
45	55.3	54.5	53.7	52.9	52.2	51.5	50.7	50.0	49.4	48.7
46	55.1	54.3	53.5	52.7	52.0	51.2	50.5	49.8	49.1	48.4
47	55.0	54.1	53.3	52.5	51.7	51.0	50.2	49.5	48.8	48.1
48	54.8	54.0	53.2	52.3	51.5	50.8	50.0	49.2	48.5	47.8
49	54.7	53.8	53.0	52.2	51.4	50.6	49.8	49.0	48.2	47.5
50	54.6	53.7	52.9	52.0	51.2	50.4	49.6	48.8	48.0	47.3
51	54.5	53.6	52.7	51.9	51.0	50.2	49.4	48.6	47.8	47.0
52	54.4	53.5	52.6	51.7	50.9	50.0	49.2	48.4	47.6	46.8
53	54.3	53.4	52.5	51.6	50.8	49.9	49.1	48.2	47.4	46.6

Ages	30	31	32	33	34	35	36	37	38	39
54	54.2	53.3	52.4	51.5	50.6	49.8	48.9	48.1	47.2	46.4
55	54.1	53.2	52.3	51.4	50.5	49.7	48.8	47.9	47.1	46.3
56	54.0	53.1	52.2	51.3	50.4	49.5	48.7	47.8	47.0	46.1
57	54.0	53.0	52.1	51.2	50.3	49.4	48.6	47.7	46.8	46.0
58	53.9	53.0	52.1	51.2	50.3	49.4	48.5	47.6	46.7	45.8
59	53.8	52.9	52.0	51.1	50.2	49.3	48.4	47.5	46.6	45.7
60	53.8	52.9	51.9	51.0	50.1	49.2	48.3	47.4	46.5	45.6
61	53.8	52.8	51.9	51.0	50.0	49.1	48.2	47.3	46.4	45.5
62	53.7	52.8	51.8	50.9	50.0	49.1	48.1	47.2	46.3	45.4
63	53.7	52.7	51.8	50.9	49.9	49.0	48.1	47.2	46.3	45.3
64	53.6	52.7	51.8	50.8	49.9	48.9	48.0	47.1	46.2	45.3
65	53.6	52.7	51.7	50.8	49.8	48.9	48.0	47.0	46.1	45.2
66	53.6	52.6	51.7	50.7	49.8	48.9	47.9	47.0	46.1	45.1
67	53.6	52.6	51.7	50.7	49.8	48.8	47.9	46.9	46.0	45.1
68	53.5	52.6	51.6	50.7	49.7	48.8	47.8	46.9	46.0	45.0
69	53.5	52.6	51.6	50.6	49.7	48.7	47.8	46.9	45.9	45.0
70	53.5	52.5	51.6	50.6	49.7	48.7	47.8	46.8	45.9	44.9
71	53.5	52.5	51.6	50.6	49.6	48.7	47.7	46.8	45.9	44.9
72	53.5	52.5	51.5	50.6	49.6	48.7	47.7	46.8	45.8	44.9
73	53.4	52.5	51.5	50.6	49.6	48.6	47.7	46.7	45.8	44.8
74	53.4	52.5	51.5	50.5	49.6	48.6	47.7	46.7	45.8	44.8
75	53.4	52.5	51.5	50.5	49.6	48.6	47.7	46.7	45.7	44.8
76	53.4	52.4	51.5	50.5	49.6	48.6	47.6	46.7	45.7	44.8
77	53.4	52.4	51.5	50.5	49.5	48.6	47.6	46.7	45.7	44.8
78	53.4	52.4	51.5	50.5	49.5	48.6	47.6	46.6	45.7	44.7
79	53.4	52.4	51.5	50.5	49.5	48.6	47.6	46.6	45.7	44.7
80	53.4	52.4	51.4	50.5	49.5	48.5	47.6	46.6	45.7	44.7
81	53.4	52.4	51.4	50.5	49.5	48.5	47.6	46.6	45.7	44.7
82	53.4	52.4	51.4	50.5	49.5	48.5	47.6	46.6	45.6	44.7
83	53.4	52.4	51.4	50.5	49.5	48.5	47.6	46.6	45.6	44.7
84	53.4	52.4	51.4	50.5	49.5	48.5	47.6	46.6	45.6	44.7
85	53.3	52.4	51.4	50.4	49.5	48.5	47.5	46.6	45.6	44.7
86	53.3	52.4	51.4	50.4	49.5	48.5	47.5	46.6	45.6	44.6
87	53.3	52.4	51.4	50.4	49.5	48.5	47.5	46.6	45.6	44.6
88	53.3	52.4	51.4	50.4	49.5	48.5	47.5	46.6	45.6	44.6

Ages	30	31	32	33	34	35	36	37	38	39
89	53.3	52.4	51.4	50.4	49.5	48.5	47.5	46.6	45.6	44.6
90	53.3	52.4	51.4	50.4	49.5	48.5	47.5	46.6	45.6	44.6
91	53.3	52.4	51.4	50.4	49.5	48.5	47.5	46.6	45.6	44.6
92	53.3	52.4	51.4	50.4	49.5	48.5	47.5	46.6	45.6	44.6
93	53.3	52.4	51.4	50.4	49.5	48.5	47.5	46.6	45.6	44.6
94	53.3	52.4	51.4	50.4	49.5	48.5	47.5	46.6	45.6	44.6
95	53.3	52.4	51.4	50.4	49.5	48.5	47.5	46.5	45.6	44.6
96	53.3	52.4	51.4	50.4	49.5	48.5	47.5	46.5	45.6	44.6
97	53.3	52.4	51.4	50.4	49.5	48.5	47.5	46.5	45.6	44.6
98	53.3	52.4	51.4	50.4	49.5	48.5	47.5	46.5	45.6	44.6
99	53.3	52.4	51.4	50.4	49.5	48.5	47.5	46.5	45.6	44.6
100	53.3	52.4	51.4	50.4	49.5	48.5	47.5	46.5	45.6	44.6
101	53.3	52.4	51.4	50.4	49.5	48.5	47.5	46.5	45.6	44.6
102	53.3	52.4	51.4	50.4	49.5	48.5	47.5	46.5	45.6	44.6
103	53.3	52.4	51.4	50.4	49.5	48.5	47.5	46.5	45.6	44.6
104	53.3	52.4	51.4	50.4	49.5	48.5	47.5	46.5	45.6	44.6
105	53.3	52.4	51.4	50.4	49.4	48.5	47.5	46.5	45.6	44.6
106	53.3	52.4	51.4	50.4	49.4	48.5	47.5	46.5	45.6	44.6
107	53.3	52.4	51.4	50.4	49.4	48.5	47.5	46.5	45.6	44.6
108	53.3	52.4	51.4	50.4	49.4	48.5	47.5	46.5	45.6	44.6
109	53.3	52.4	51.4	50.4	49.4	48.5	47.5	46.5	45.6	44.6
110	53.3	52.4	51.4	50.4	49.4	48.5	47.5	46.5	45.6	44.6
111	53.3	52.4	51.4	50.4	49.4	48.5	47.5	46.5	45.6	44.6
112	53.3	52.4	51.4	50.4	49.4	48.5	47.5	46.5	45.6	44.6
113	53.3	52.4	51.4	50.4	49.4	48.5	47.5	46.5	45.6	44.6
114	53.3	52.4	51.4	50.4	49.4	48.5	47.5	46.5	45.6	44.6
115+	53.3	52.4	51.4	50.4	49.4	48.5	47.5	46.5	45.6	44.6

Ages	40	41	42	43	44	45	46	47	48	49
40	50.2	49.8	49.3	48.9	48.5	48.1	47.7	47.4	47.1	46.8
41	49.8	49.3	48.8	48.3	47.9	47.5	47.1	46.7	46.4	46.1
42	49.3	48.8	48.3	47.8	47.3	46.9	46.5	46.1	45.8	45.4
43	48.9	48.3	47.8	47.3	46.8	46.3	45.9	45.5	45.1	44.8
44	48.5	47.9	47.3	46.8	46.3	45.8	45.4	44.9	44.5	44.2
45	48.1	47.5	46.9	46.3	45.8	45.3	44.8	44.4	44.0	43.6

Ages	40	41	42	43	44	45	46	47	48	49
46	47.7	47.1	46.5	45.9	45.4	44.8	44.3	43.9	43.4	43.0
47	47.4	46.7	46.1	45.5	44.9	44.4	43.9	43.4	42.9	42.4
48	47.1	46.4	45.8	45.1	44.5	44.0	43.4	42.9	42.4	41.9
49	46.8	46.1	45.4	44.8	44.2	43.6	43.0	42.4	41.9	41.4
50	46.5	45.8	45.1	44.4	43.8	43.2	42.6	42.0	41.5	40.9
51	46.3	45.5	44.8	44.1	43.5	42.8	42.2	41.6	41.0	40.5
52	46.0	45.3	44.6	43.8	43.2	42.5	41.8	41.2	40.6	40.1
53	45.8	45.1	44.3	43.6	42.9	42.2	41.5	40.9	40.3	39.7
54	45.6	44.8	44.1	43.3	42.6	41.9	41.2	40.5	39.9	39.3
55	45.5	44.7	43.9	43.1	42.4	41.6	40.9	40.2	39.6	38.9
56	45.3	44.5	43.7	42.9	42.1	41.4	40.7	40.0	39.3	38.6
57	45.1	44.3	43.5	42.7	41.9	41.2	40.4	39.7	39.0	38.3
58	45.0	44.2	43.3	42.5	41.7	40.9	40.2	39.4	38.7	38.0
59	44.9	44.0	43.2	42.4	41.5	40.7	40.0	39.2	38.5	37.8
60	44.7	43.9	43.0	42.2	41.4	40.6	39.8	39.0	38.2	37.5
61	44.6	43.8	42.9	42.1	41.2	40.4	39.6	38.8	38.0	37.3
62	44.5	43.7	42.8	41.9	41.1	40.3	39.4	38.6	37.8	37.1
63	44.5	43.6	42.7	41.8	41.0	40.1	39.3	38.5	37.7	36.9
64	44.4	43.5	42.6	41.7	40.8	40.0	39.2	38.3	37.5	36.7
65	44.3	43.4	42.5	41.6	40.7	39.9	39.0	38.2	37.4	36.6
66	44.2	43.3	42.4	41.5	40.6	39.8	38.9	38.1	37.2	36.4
67	44.2	43.3	42.3	41.4	40.6	39.7	38.8	38.0	37.1	36.3
68	44.1	43.2	42.3	41.4	40.5	39.6	38.7	37.9	37.0	36.2
69	44.1	43.1	42.2	41.3	40.4	39.5	38.6	37.8	36.9	36.0
70	44.0	43.1	42.2	41.3	40.3	39.4	38.6	37.7	36.8	35.9
71	44.0	43.0	42.1	41.2	40.3	39.4	38.5	37.6	36.7	35.9
72	43.9	43.0	42.1	41.1	40.2	39.3	38.4	37.5	36.6	35.8
73	43.9	43.0	42.0	41.1	40.2	39.3	38.4	37.5	36.6	35.7
74	43.9	42.9	42.0	41.1	40.1	39.2	38.3	37.4	36.5	35.6
75	43.8	42.9	42.0	41.0	40.1	39.2	38.3	37.4	36.5	35.6
76	43.8	42.9	41.9	41.0	40.1	39.1	38.2	37.3	36.4	35.5
77	43.8	42.9	41.9	41.0	40.0	39.1	38.2	37.3	36.4	35.5
78	43.8	42.8	41.9	40.9	40.0	39.1	38.2	37.2	36.3	35.4
79	43.8	42.8	41.9	40.9	40.0	39.1	38.1	37.2	36.3	35.4
80	43.7	42.8	41.8	40.9	40.0	39.0	38.1	37.2	36.3	35.4

Ages	40	41	42	43	44	45	46	47	48	49
81	43.7	42.8	41.8	40.9	39.9	39.0	38.1	37.2	36.2	35.3
82	43.7	42.8	41.8	40.9	39.9	39.0	38.1	37.1	36.2	35.3
83	43.7	42.8	41.8	40.9	39.9	39.0	38.0	37.1	36.2	35.3
84	43.7	42.7	41.8	40.8	39.9	39.0	38.0	37.1	36.2	35.3
85	43.7	42.7	41.8	40.8	39.9	38.9	38.0	37.1	36.2	35.2
86	43.7	42.7	41.8	40.8	39.9	38.9	38.0	37.1	36.1	35.2
87	43.7	42.7	41.8	40.8	39.9	38.9	38.0	37.0	36.1	35.2
88	43.7	42.7	41.8	40.8	39.9	38.9	38.0	37.0	36.1	35.2
89	43.7	42.7	41.7	40.8	39.8	38.9	38.0	37.0	36.1	35.2
90	43.7	42.7	41.7	40.8	39.8	38.9	38.0	37.0	36.1	35.2
91	43.7	42.7	41.7	40.8	39.8	38.9	37.9	37.0	36.1	35.2
92	43.7	42.7	41.7	40.8	39.8	38.9	37.9	37.0	36.1	35.1
93	43.7	42.7	41.7	40.8	39.8	38.9	37.9	37.0	36.1	35.1
94	43.7	42.7	41.7	40.8	39.8	38.9	37.9	37.0	36.1	35.1
95	43.6	42.7	41.7	40.8	39.8	38.9	37.9	37.0	36.1	35.1
96	43.6	42.7	41.7	40.8	39.8	38.9	37.9	37.0	36.1	35.1
97	43.6	42.7	41.7	40.8	39.8	38.9	37.9	37.0	36.1	35.1
98	43.6	42.7	41.7	40.8	39.8	38.9	37.9	37.0	36.0	35.1
99	43.6	42.7	41.7	40.8	39.8	38.9	37.9	37.0	36.0	35.1
100	43.6	42.7	41.7	40.8	39.8	38.9	37.9	37.0	36.0	35.1
101	43.6	42.7	41.7	40.8	39.8	38.9	37.9	37.0	36.0	35.1
102	43.6	42.7	41.7	40.8	39.8	38.9	37.9	37.0	36.0	35.1
103	43.6	42.7	41.7	40.8	39.8	38.9	37.9	37.0	36.0	35.1
104	43.6	42.7	41.7	40.8	39.8	38.8	37.9	37.0	36.0	35.1
105	43.6	42.7	41.7	40.8	39.8	38.8	37.9	37.0	36.0	35.1
106	43.6	42.7	41.7	40.8	39.8	38.8	37.9	37.0	36.0	35.1
107	43.6	42.7	41.7	40.8	39.8	38.8	37.9	37.0	36.0	35.1
108	43.6	42.7	41.7	40.8	39.8	38.8	37.9	37.0	36.0	35.1
109	43.6	42.7	41.7	40.7	39.8	38.8	37.9	37.0	36.0	35.1
110	43.6	42.7	41.7	40.7	39.8	38.8	37.9	37.0	36.0	35.1
111	43.6	42.7	41.7	40.7	39.8	38.8	37.9	37.0	36.0	35.1
112	43.6	42.7	41.7	40.7	39.8	38.8	37.9	37.0	36.0	35.1
113	43.6	42.7	41.7	40.7	39.8	38.8	37.9	37.0	36.0	35.1
114	43.6	42.7	41.7	40.7	39.8	38.8	37.9	37.0	36.0	35.1
115+	43.6	42.7	41.7	40.7	39.8	38.8	37.9	37.0	36.0	35.1

Ages	50	51	52	53	54	55	56	57	58	59
50	40.4	40.0	39.5	39.1	38.7	38.3	38.0	37.6	37.3	37.1
51	40.0	39.5	39.0	38.5	38.1	37.7	37.4	37.0	36.7	36.4
52	39.5	39.0	38.5	38.0	37.6	37.2	36.8	36.4	36.0	35.7
53	39.1	38.5	38.0	37.5	37.1	36.6	36.2	35.8	35.4	35.1
54	38.7	38.1	37.6	37.1	36.6	36.1	35.7	35.2	34.8	34.5
55	38.3	37.7	37.2	36.6	36.1	35.6	35.1	34.7	34.3	33.9
56	38.0	37.4	36.8	36.2	35.7	35.1	34.7	34.2	33.7	33.3
57	37.6	37.0	36.4	35.8	35.2	34.7	34.2	33.7	33.2	32.8
58	37.3	36.7	36.0	35.4	34.8	34.3	33.7	33.2	32.8	32.3
59	37.1	36.4	35.7	35.1	34.5	33.9	33.3	32.8	32.3	31.8
60	36.8	36.1	35.4	34.8	34.1	33.5	32.9	32.4	31.9	31.3
61	36.6	35.8	35.1	34.5	33.8	33.2	32.6	32.0	31.4	30.9
62	36.3	35.6	34.9	34.2	33.5	32.9	32.2	31.6	31.1	30.5
63	36.1	35.4	34.6	33.9	33.2	32.6	31.9	31.3	30.7	30.1
64	35.9	35.2	34.4	33.7	33.0	32.3	31.6	31.0	30.4	29.8
65	35.8	35.0	34.2	33.5	32.7	32.0	31.4	30.7	30.0	29.4
66	35.6	34.8	34.0	33.3	32.5	31.8	31.1	30.4	29.8	29.1
67	35.5	34.7	33.9	33.1	32.3	31.6	30.9	30.2	29.5	28.8
68	35.3	34.5	33.7	32.9	32.1	31.4	30.7	29.9	29.2	28.6
69	35.2	34.4	33.6	32.8	32.0	31.2	30.5	29.7	29.0	28.3
70	35.1	34.3	33.4	32.6	31.8	31.1	30.3	29.5	28.8	28.1
71	35.0	34.2	33.3	32.5	31.7	30.9	30.1	29.4	28.6	27.9
72	34.9	34.1	33.2	32.4	31.6	30.8	30.0	29.2	28.4	27.7
73	34.8	34.0	33.1	32.3	31.5	30.6	29.8	29.1	28.3	27.5
74	34.8	33.9	33.0	32.2	31.4	30.5	29.7	28.9	28.1	27.4
75	34.7	33.8	33.0	32.1	31.3	30.4	29.6	28.8	28.0	27.2
76	34.6	33.8	32.9	32.0	31.2	30.3	29.5	28.7	27.9	27.1
77	34.6	33.7	32.8	32.0	31.1	30.3	29.4	28.6	27.8	27.0
78	34.5	33.6	32.8	31.9	31.0	30.2	29.3	28.5	27.7	26.9
79	34.5	33.6	32.7	31.8	31.0	30.1	29.3	28.4	27.6	26.8
80	34.5	33.6	32.7	31.8	30.9	30.1	29.2	28.4	27.5	26.7
81	34.4	33.5	32.6	31.8	30.9	30.0	29.2	28.3	27.5	26.6
82	34.4	33.5	32.6	31.7	30.8	30.0	29.1	28.3	27.4	26.6
83	34.4	33.5	32.6	31.7	30.8	29.9	29.1	28.2	27.4	26.5
84	34.3	33.4	32.5	31.7	30.8	29.9	29.0	28.2	27.3	26.5

Ages	50	51	52	53	54	55	56	57	58	59
85	34.3	33.4	32.5	31.6	30.7	29.9	29.0	28.1	27.3	26.4
86	34.3	33.4	32.5	31.6	30.7	29.8	29.0	28.1	27.2	26.4
87	34.3	33.4	32.5	31.6	30.7	29.8	28.9	28.1	27.2	26.4
88	34.3	33.4	32.5	31.6	30.7	29.8	28.9	28.0	27.2	26.3
89	34.3	33.3	32.4	31.5	30.7	29.8	28.9	28.0	27.2	26.3
90	34.2	33.3	32.4	31.5	30.6	29.8	28.9	28.0	27.1	26.3
91	34.2	33.3	32.4	31.5	30.6	29.7	28.9	28.0	27.1	26.3
92	34.2	33.3	32.4	31.5	30.6	29.7	28.8	28.0	27.1	26.2
93	34.2	33.3	32.4	31.5	30.6	29.7	28.8	28.0	27.1	26.2
94	34.2	33.3	32.4	31.5	30.6	29.7	28.8	27.9	27.1	26.2
95	34.2	33.3	32.4	31.5	30.6	29.7	28.8	27.9	27.1	26.2
96	34.2	33.3	32.4	31.5	30.6	29.7	28.8	27.9	27.0	26.2
97	34.2	33.3	32.4	31.5	30.6	29.7	28.8	27.9	27.0	26.2
98	34.2	33.3	32.4	31.5	30.6	29.7	28.8	27.9	27.0	26.2
99	34.2	33.3	32.4	31.5	30.6	29.7	28.8	27.9	27.0	26.2
100	34.2	33.3	32.4	31.5	30.6	29.7	28.8	27.9	27.0	26.1
101	34.2	33.3	32.4	31.5	30.6	29.7	28.8	27.9	27.0	26.1
102	34.2	33.3	32.4	31.4	30.5	29.7	28.8	27.9	27.0	26.1
103	34.2	33.3	32.4	31.4	30.5	29.7	28.8	27.9	27.0	26.1
104	34.2	33.3	32.4	31.4	30.5	29.6	28.8	27.9	27.0	26.1
105	34.2	33.3	32.3	31.4	30.5	29.6	28.8	27.9	27.0	26.1
106	34.2	33.3	32.3	31.4	30.5	29.6	28.8	27.9	27.0	26.1
107	34.2	33.3	32.3	31.4	30.5	29.6	28.8	27.9	27.0	26.1
108	34.2	33.3	32.3	31.4	30.5	29.6	28.8	27.9	27.0	26.1
109	34.2	33.3	32.3	31.4	30.5	29.6	28.7	27.9	27.0	26.1
110	34.2	33.3	32.3	31.4	30.5	29.6	28.7	27.9	27.0	26.1
111	34.2	33.3	32.3	31.4	30.5	29.6	28.7	27.9	27.0	26.1
112	34.2	33.3	32.3	31.4	30.5	29.6	28.7	27.9	27.0	26.1
113	34.2	33.3	32.3	31.4	30.5	29.6	28.7	27.9	27.0	26.1
114	34.2	33.3	32.3	31.4	30.5	29.6	28.7	27.9	27.0	26.1
115+	34.2	33.3	32.3	31.4	30.5	29.6	28.7	27.9	27.0	26.1

Ages	60	61	62	63	64	65	66	67	68	69
60	30.9	30.4	30.0	29.6	29.2	28.8	28.5	28.2	27.9	27.6
61	30.4	29.9	29.5	29.0	28.6	28.3	27.9	27.6	27.3	27.0
62	30.0	29.5	29.0	28.5	28.1	27.7	27.3	27.0	26.7	26.4
63	29.6	29.0	28.5	28.1	27.6	27.2	26.8	26.4	26.1	25.7
64	29.2	28.6	28.1	27.6	27.1	26.7	26.3	25.9	25.5	25.2
65	28.8	28.3	27.7	27.2	26.7	26.2	25.8	25.4	25.0	24.6
66	28.5	27.9	27.3	26.8	26.3	25.8	25.3	24.9	24.5	24.1
67	28.2	27.6	27.0	26.4	25.9	25.4	24.9	24.4	24.0	23.6
68	27.9	27.3	26.7	26.1	25.5	25.0	24.5	24.0	23.5	23.1
69	27.6	27.0	26.4	25.7	25.2	24.6	24.1	23.6	23.1	22.6
70	27.4	26.7	26.1	25.4	24.8	24.3	23.7	23.2	22.7	22.2
71	27.2	26.5	25.8	25.2	24.5	23.9	23.4	22.8	22.3	21.8
72	27.0	26.3	25.6	24.9	24.3	23.7	23.1	22.5	22.0	21.4
73	26.8	26.1	25.4	24.7	24.0	23.4	22.8	22.2	21.6	21.1
74	26.6	25.9	25.2	24.5	23.8	23.1	22.5	21.9	21.3	20.8
75	26.5	25.7	25.0	24.3	23.6	22.9	22.3	21.6	21.0	20.5
76	26.3	25.6	24.8	24.1	23.4	22.7	22.0	21.4	20.8	20.2
77	26.2	25.4	24.7	23.9	23.2	22.5	21.8	21.2	20.6	19.9
78	26.1	25.3	24.6	23.8	23.1	22.4	21.7	21.0	20.3	19.7
79	26.0	25.2	24.4	23.7	22.9	22.2	21.5	20.8	20.1	19.5
80	25.9	25.1	24.3	23.6	22.8	22.1	21.3	20.6	20.0	19.3
81	25.8	25.0	24.2	23.4	22.7	21.9	21.2	20.5	19.8	19.1
82	25.8	24.9	24.1	23.4	22.6	21.8	21.1	20.4	19.7	19.0
83	25.7	24.9	24.1	23.3	22.5	21.7	21.0	20.2	19.5	18.8
84	25.6	24.8	24.0	23.2	22.4	21.6	20.9	20.1	19.4	18.7
85	25.6	24.8	23.9	23.1	22.3	21.6	20.8	20.1	19.3	18.6
86	25.5	24.7	23.9	23.1	22.3	21.5	20.7	20.0	19.2	18.5
87	25.5	24.7	23.8	23.0	22.2	21.4	20.7	19.9	19.2	18.4
88	25.5	24.6	23.8	23.0	22.2	21.4	20.6	19.8	19.1	18.3
89	25.4	24.6	23.8	22.9	22.1	21.3	20.5	19.8	19.0	18.3
90	25.4	24.6	23.7	22.9	22.1	21.3	20.5	19.7	19.0	18.2
91	25.4	24.5	23.7	22.9	22.1	21.3	20.5	19.7	18.9	18.2
92	25.4	24.5	23.7	22.9	22.0	21.2	20.4	19.6	18.9	18.1
93	25.4	24.5	23.7	22.8	22.0	21.2	20.4	19.6	18.8	18.1
94	25.3	24.5	23.6	22.8	22.0	21.2	20.4	19.6	18.8	18.0

Ages	60	61	62	63	64	65	66	67	68	69
95	25.3	24.5	23.6	22.8	22.0	21.1	20.3	19.6	18.8	18.0
96	25.3	24.5	23.6	22.8	21.9	21.1	20.3	19.5	18.8	18.0
97	25.3	24.5	23.6	22.8	21.9	21.1	20.3	19.5	18.7	18.0
98	25.3	24.4	23.6	22.8	21.9	21.1	20.3	19.5	18.7	17.9
99	25.3	24.4	23.6	22.7	21.9	21.1	20.3	19.5	18.7	17.9
100	25.3	24.4	23.6	22.7	21.9	21.1	20.3	19.5	18.7	17.9
101	25.3	24.4	23.6	22.7	21.9	21.1	20.2	19.4	18.7	17.9
102	25.3	24.4	23.6	22.7	21.9	21.1	20.2	19.4	18.6	17.9
103	25.3	24.4	23.6	22.7	21.9	21.0	20.2	19.4	18.6	17.9
104	25.3	24.4	23.5	22.7	21.9	21.0	20.2	19.4	18.6	17.8
105	25.3	24.4	23.5	22.7	21.9	21.0	20.2	19.4	18.6	17.8
106	25.3	24.4	23.5	22.7	21.9	21.0	20.2	19.4	18.6	17.8
107	25.2	24.4	23.5	22.7	21.8	21.0	20.2	19.4	18.6	17.8
108	25.2	24.4	23.5	22.7	21.8	21.0	20.2	19.4	18.6	17.8
109	25.2	24.4	23.5	22.7	21.8	21.0	20.2	19.4	18.6	17.8
110	25.2	24.4	23.5	22.7	21.8	21.0	20.2	19.4	18.6	17.8
111	25.2	24.4	23.5	22.7	21.8	21.0	20.2	19.4	18.6	17.8
112	25.2	24.4	23.5	22.7	21.8	21.0	20.2	19.4	18.6	17.8
113	25.2	24.4	23.5	22.7	21.8	21.0	20.2	19.4	18.6	17.8
114	25.2	24.4	23.5	22.7	21.8	21.0	20.2	19.4	18.6	17.8
115+	25.2	24.4	23.5	22.7	21.8	21.0	20.2	19.4	18.6	17.8

Ages	70	71	72	73	74	75	76	77	78	79
70	21.8	21.3	20.9	20.6	20.2	19.9	19.6	19.4	19.1	18.9
71	21.3	20.9	20.5	20.1	19.7	19.4	19.1	18.8	18.5	18.3
72	20.9	20.5	20.0	19.6	19.3	18.9	18.6	18.3	18.0	17.7
73	20.6	20.1	19.6	19.2	18.8	18.4	18.1	17.8	17.5	17.2
74	20.2	19.7	19.3	18.8	18.4	18.0	17.6	17.3	17.0	16.7
75	19.9	19.4	18.9	18.4	18.0	17.6	17.2	16.8	16.5	16.2
76	19.6	19.1	18.6	18.1	17.6	17.2	16.8	16.4	16.0	15.7
77	19.4	18.8	18.3	17.8	17.3	16.8	16.4	16.0	15.6	15.3
78	19.1	18.5	18.0	17.5	17.0	16.5	16.0	15.6	15.2	14.9
79	18.9	18.3	17.7	17.2	16.7	16.2	15.7	15.3	14.9	14.5
80	18.7	18.1	17.5	16.9	16.4	15.9	15.4	15.0	14.5	14.1
81	18.5	17.9	17.3	16.7	16.2	15.6	15.1	14.7	14.2	13.8

Ages	70	71	72	73	74	75	76	77	78	79
82	18.3	17.7	17.1	16.5	15.9	15.4	14.9	14.4	13.9	13.5
83	18.2	17.5	16.9	16.3	15.7	15.2	14.7	14.2	13.7	13.2
84	18.0	17.4	16.7	16.1	15.5	15.0	14.4	13.9	13.4	13.0
85	17.9	17.3	16.6	16.0	15.4	14.8	14.3	13.7	13.2	12.8
86	17.8	17.1	16.5	15.8	15.2	14.6	14.1	13.5	13.0	12.5
87	17.7	17.0	16.4	15.7	15.1	14.5	13.9	13.4	12.9	12.4
88	17.6	16.9	16.3	15.6	15.0	14.4	13.8	13.2	12.7	12.2
89	17.6	16.9	16.2	15.5	14.9	14.3	13.7	13.1	12.6	12.0
90	17.5	16.8	16.1	15.4	14.8	14.2	13.6	13.0	12.4	11.9
91	17.4	16.7	16.0	15.4	14.7	14.1	13.5	12.9	12.3	11.8
92	17.4	16.7	16.0	15.3	14.6	14.0	13.4	12.8	12.2	11.7
93	17.3	16.6	15.9	15.2	14.6	13.9	13.3	12.7	12.1	11.6
94	17.3	16.6	15.9	15.2	14.5	13.9	13.2	12.6	12.0	11.5
95	17.3	16.5	15.8	15.1	14.5	13.8	13.2	12.6	12.0	11.4
96	17.2	16.5	15.8	15.1	14.4	13.8	13.1	12.5	11.9	11.3
97	17.2	16.5	15.8	15.1	14.4	13.7	13.1	12.5	11.9	11.3
98	17.2	16.4	15.7	15.0	14.3	13.7	13.0	12.4	11.8	11.2
99	17.2	16.4	15.7	15.0	14.3	13.6	13.0	12.4	11.8	11.2
100	17.1	16.4	15.7	15.0	14.3	13.6	12.9	12.3	11.7	11.1
101	17.1	16.4	15.6	14.9	14.2	13.6	12.9	12.3	11.7	11.1
102	17.1	16.4	15.6	14.9	14.2	13.5	12.9	12.2	11.6	11.0
103	17.1	16.3	15.6	14.9	14.2	13.5	12.9	12.2	11.6	11.0
104	17.1	16.3	15.6	14.9	14.2	13.5	12.8	12.2	11.6	11.0
105	17.1	16.3	15.6	14.9	14.2	13.5	12.8	12.2	11.5	10.9
106	17.1	16.3	15.6	14.8	14.1	13.5	12.8	12.2	11.5	10.9
107	17.0	16.3	15.6	14.8	14.1	13.4	12.8	12.1	11.5	10.9
108	17.0	16.3	15.5	14.8	14.1	13.4	12.8	12.1	11.5	10.9
109	17.0	16.3	15.5	14.8	14.1	13.4	12.8	12.1	11.5	10.9
110	17.0	16.3	15.5	14.8	14.1	13.4	12.7	12.1	11.5	10.9
111	17.0	16.3	15.5	14.8	14.1	13.4	12.7	12.1	11.5	10.8
112	17.0	16.3	15.5	14.8	14.1	13.4	12.7	12.1	11.5	10.8
113	17.0	16.3	15.5	14.8	14.1	13.4	12.7	12.1	11.4	10.8
114	17.0	16.3	15.5	14.8	14.1	13.4	12.7	12.1	11.4	10.8
115+	17.0	16.3	15.5	14.8	14.1	13.4	12.7	12.1	11.4	10.8

Ages	80	81	82	83	84	85	86	87	88	89
80	13.8	13.4	13.1	12.8	12.6	12.3	12.1	11.9	11.7	11.5
81	13.4	13.1	12.7	12.4	12.2	11.9	11.7	11.4	11.3	11.1
82	13.1	12.7	12.4	12.1	11.8	11.5	11.3	11.0	10.8	10.6
83	12.8	12.4	12.1	11.7	11.4	11.1	10.9	10.6	10.4	10.2
84	12.6	12.2	11.8	11.4	11.1	10.8	10.5	10.3	10.1	9.9
85	12.3	11.9	11.5	11.1	10.8	10.5	10.2	9.9	9.7	9.5
86	12.1	11.7	11.3	10.9	10.5	10.2	9.9	9.6	9.4	9.2
87	11.9	11.4	11.0	10.6	10.3	9.9	9.6	9.4	9.1	8.9
88	11.7	11.3	10.8	10.4	10.1	9.7	9.4	9.1	8.8	8.6
89	11.5	11.1	10.6	10.2	9.9	9.5	9.2	8.9	8.6	8.3
90	11.4	10.9	10.5	10.1	9.7	9.3	9.0	8.6	8.3	8.1
91	11.3	10.8	10.3	9.9	9.5	9.1	8.8	8.4	8.1	7.9
92	11.2	10.7	10.2	9.8	9.3	9.0	8.6	8.3	8.0	7.7
93	11.1	10.6	10.1	9.6	9.2	8.8	8.5	8.1	7.8	7.5
94	11.0	10.5	10.0	9.5	9.1	8.7	8.3	8.0	7.6	7.3
95	10.9	10.4	9.9	9.4	9.0	8.6	8.2	7.8	7.5	7.2
96	10.8	10.3	9.8	9.3	8.9	8.5	8.1	7.7	7.4	7.1
97	10.7	10.2	9.7	9.2	8.8	8.4	8.0	7.6	7.3	6.9
98	10.7	10.1	9.6	9.2	8.7	8.3	7.9	7.5	7.1	6.8
99	10.6	10.1	9.6	9.1	8.6	8.2	7.8	7.4	7.0	6.7
100	10.6	10.0	9.5	9.0	8.5	8.1	7.7	7.3	6.9	6.6
101	10.5	10.0	9.4	9.0	8.5	8.0	7.6	7.2	6.9	6.5
102	10.5	9.9	9.4	8.9	8.4	8.0	7.5	7.1	6.8	6.4
103	10.4	9.9	9.4	8.8	8.4	7.9	7.5	7.1	6.7	6.3
104	10.4	9.8	9.3	8.8	8.3	7.9	7.4	7.0	6.6	6.3
105	10.4	9.8	9.3	8.8	8.3	7.8	7.4	7.0	6.6	6.2
106	10.3	9.8	9.2	8.7	8.2	7.8	7.3	6.9	6.5	6.2
107	10.3	9.8	9.2	8.7	8.2	7.7	7.3	6.9	6.5	6.1
108	10.3	9.7	9.2	8.7	8.2	7.7	7.3	6.8	6.4	6.1
109	10.3	9.7	9.2	8.7	8.2	7.7	7.2	6.8	6.4	6.0
110	10.3	9.7	9.2	8.6	8.1	7.7	7.2	6.8	6.4	6.0
111	10.3	9.7	9.1	8.6	8.1	7.6	7.2	6.8	6.3	6.0
112	10.2	9.7	9.1	8.6	8.1	7.6	7.2	6.7	6.3	5.9
113	10.2	9.7	9.1	8.6	8.1	7.6	7.2	6.7	6.3	5.9
114	10.2	9.7	9.1	8.6	8.1	7.6	7.1	6.7	6.3	5.9
115+	10.2	9.7	9.1	8.6	8.1	7.6	7.1	6.7	6.3	5.9

Ages	90	91	92	93	94	95	96	97	98	99
90	7.8	7.6	7.4	7.2	7.1	6.9	6.8	6.6	6.5	6.4
91	7.6	7.4	7.2	7.0	6.8	6.7	6.5	6.4	6.3	6.1
92	7.4	7.2	7.0	6.8	6.6	6.4	6.3	6.1	6.0	5.9
93	7.2	7.0	6.8	6.6	6.4	6.2	6.1	5.9	5.8	5.6
94	7.1	6.8	6.6	6.4	6.2	6.0	5.9	5.7	5.6	5.4
95	6.9	6.7	6.4	6.2	6.0	5.8	5.7	5.5	5.4	5.2
96	6.8	6.5	6.3	6.1	5.9	5.7	5.5	5.3	5.2	5.0
97	6.6	6.4	6.1	5.9	5.7	5.5	5.3	5.2	5.0	4.9
98	6.5	6.3	6.0	5.8	5.6	5.4	5.2	5.0	4.8	4.7
99	6.4	6.1	5.9	5.6	5.4	5.2	5.0	4.9	4.7	4.5
100	6.3	6.0	5.8	5.5	5.3	5.1	4.9	4.7	4.5	4.4
101	6.2	5.9	5.6	5.4	5.2	5.0	4.8	4.6	4.4	4.2
102	6.1	5.8	5.5	5.3	5.1	4.8	4.6	4.4	4.3	4.1
103	6.0	5.7	5.4	5.2	5.0	4.7	4.5	4.3	4.1	4.0
104	5.9	5.6	5.4	5.1	4.9	4.6	4.4	4.2	4.0	3.8
105	5.9	5.6	5.3	5.0	4.8	4.5	4.3	4.1	3.9	3.7
106	5.8	5.5	5.2	4.9	4.7	4.5	4.2	4.0	3.8	3.6
107	5.8	5.4	5.1	4.9	4.6	4.4	4.2	3.9	3.7	3.5
108	5.7	5.4	5.1	4.8	4.6	4.3	4.1	3.9	3.7	3.5
109	5.7	5.3	5.0	4.8	4.5	4.3	4.0	3.8	3.6	3.4
110	5.6	5.3	5.0	4.7	4.5	4.2	4.0	3.8	3.5	3.3
111	5.6	5.3	5.0	4.7	4.4	4.2	3.9	3.7	3.5	3.3
112	5.6	5.3	4.9	4.7	4.4	4.1	3.9	3.7	3.5	3.2
113	5.6	5.2	4.9	4.6	4.4	4.1	3.9	3.6	3.4	3.2
114	5.6	5.2	4.9	4.6	4.3	4.1	3.9	3.6	3.4	3.2
115+	5.5	5.2	4.9	4.6	4.3	4.1	3.8	3.6	3.4	3.1

Ages	100	101	102	103	104	105	106	107	108	109
100	4.2	4.1	3.9	3.8	3.7	3.5	3.4	3.3	3.3	3.2
101	4.1	3.9	3.7	3.6	3.5	3.4	3.2	3.1	3.1	3.0
102	3.9	3.7	3.6	3.4	3.3	3.2	3.1	3.0	2.9	2.8
103	3.8	3.6	3.4	3.3	3.2	3.0	2.9	2.8	2.7	2.6
104	3.7	3.5	3.3	3.2	3.0	2.9	2.7	2.6	2.5	2.4
105	3.5	3.4	3.2	3.0	2.9	2.7	2.6	2.5	2.4	2.3
106	3.4	3.2	3.1	2.9	2.7	2.6	2.4	2.3	2.2	2.1

Ages	100	101	102	103	104	105	106	107	108	109
107	3.3	3.1	3.0	2.8	2.6	2.5	2.3	2.2	2.1	2.0
108	3.3	3.1	2.9	2.7	2.5	2.4	2.2	2.1	1.9	1.8
109	3.2	3.0	2.8	2.6	2.4	2.3	2.1	2.0	1.8	1.7
110	3.1	2.9	2.7	2.5	2.3	2.2	2.0	1.9	1.7	1.6
111	3.1	2.9	2.7	2.5	2.3	2.1	1.9	1.8	1.6	1.5
112	3.0	2.8	2.6	2.4	2.2	2.0	1.9	1.7	1.5	1.4
113	3.0	2.8	2.6	2.4	2.2	2.0	1.8	1.6	1.5	1.3
114	3.0	2.7	2.5	2.3	2.1	1.9	1.8	1.6	1.4	1.3
115+	2.9	2.7	2.5	2.3	2.1	1.9	1.7	1.5	1.4	1.2

Ages	110	111	112	113	114	115+
110	1.5	1.4	1.3	1.2	1.1	1.1
111	1.4	1.2	1.1	1.1	1.0	1.0
112	1.3	1.1	1.0	1.0	1.0	1.0
113	1.2	1.1	1.0	1.0	1.0	1.0
114	1.1	1.0	1.0	1.0	1.0	1.0
115+	1.1	1.0	1.0	1.0	1.0	1.0

INDEX

Symbols

2-year/100 percent rule	7.12
21-and-one rule	7.12
401(a)(26) minimum-participation rule	7.8
403(b) plans	6.12

A

accrued benefit	8.4
accumulated earnings tax	1.20
active participant	17.7
activities of daily living (ADLs)	23.27
actual contribution percentage (ACP) test	5.16
actual deferral percentage (ADP)	5.13
actuarial assumptions	
actuarial cost method	11.3
actuarial equivalent	25.11
adoption agreement	7.3
adult day care	23.24
advance-determination letter	13.5
advance directive	23.30
affiliated service group	7.19
age-banded approach	22.20
age-restricted housing	23.5
age-weighted formula	8.12
assumed interest rate (AIR)	25.13
automatic enrollment	5.10
average-benefits percentage test	7.6
average indexed monthly earnings (AIME)	19.12

B

baby-boom generation	20.14
benefit period	23.14
break in service	9.12
bucket approach	22.20

C

cash-balance plan	4.12
cash equivalents	11.19
cash or deferred arrangement (CODA)	5.8
COLA	19.17
common trust funds	
contingency fund	22.10
controlled group	7.17
covered compensation	8.20
cross-testing	8.11
currently insured	19.8
custodial care	23.24

D

deemed IRA	18.17
deferred retirement	9.15
defined-benefit plan	3.7
defined-contribution plan,	3.7
designated Roth accounts	5.20
direct rollover	17.11, 24.21
disability insured	19.8

discretionary contributions	5.5
distress termination	14.8
diversification requirement	12.9
dollar cost averaging	21.21
domicile	23.6
do-not-resuscitate orders	23.30
double-bonus plans.	15.36
downsize	23.3

E

early-retirement provision	9.14
Earnings and Benefit Estimate Statement	19.18
earnings test	19.16
eligible rollover distribution	24.20
Employee Retirement Income Security Act (ERISA)	2.2
enrollment meeting	13.4
ERISA Sec. 404(c) (individual account plan exception)	12.12
ESPP	
essential-versus-discretionary approach	22.22
excess contribution	17.5
excess withdrawal risk	22.12
excludible employees	7.5
exclusive-benefit rule	12.6

F

family maximum	19.15
FICA tax	19.6
fiduciaries	12.4
fiduciary	2.11
final-average compensation	4.8
final regulations	2.9
financial hardship	5.11
first distribution year	24.30
fiscal welfare	20.17
flat-amount formula	4.6
flat-amount-per-year-of-service formula	4.6
flat-percentage-of-earnings formula	4.5
flooring approach	22.22
forfeiture	9.9
frailty risk	22.16
full retirement age	19.9
fully insured	11.6
fully insured status	19.8
funding instrument	11.9
funding policy	11.14
funding target	11.5

G

golden handcuffs	15.15
golden handshakes	15.15
golden parachutes	15.15
guaranteed investment contracts (GICs)	11.24
guaranteed renewable	23.28

H

health care and long-term care risks	22.15
health-care power of attorney (HCPOA)	23.30
highly compensated employees (HCEs)	5.13
home health care	23.24
human capital	22.7

I

incentive pay	15.15
incentive stock option (ISO)	
income-replacement ratio	4.4
individual retirement account (IRA)	1.8
inflation risk	22.11
integration with Social Security	8.8
intermediate care,	23.24
investment guidelines	11.13
investment policy	11.16
involuntary cash-out option	25.3
involuntary termination	14.14
IRA	17.3
IRC Sec. 121	23.3

K

Keogh plans	3.17
key employee	9.16

L

leased employee	7.21
leveraged ESOP	5.29
life-care communities	23.4
lifetime reserve days	23.14
living will	23.30
longevity risk	22.10
lump-sum distribution	24.26

M

master and prototype plans	2.16
Medicare Part A	23.12
Medicare Part B	23.12
Medigap insurance	23.17
minimum-participation rule	3.9
money-purchase pension plan	4.17

N

net unrealized appreciation (NUA)	24.26
new comparability	8.11
noncompete clause	
nonqualified plans	1.7
nonqualified stock options (NQSOs)	
normal form of payment	4.9
normal retirement age	9.13
notice to interested parties	13.6

P

partial termination	14.12
party in interest	12.16
past service	4.8
Pension Benefit Guaranty Corporation (PBGC)	2.12
pension plan category	3.15
percentage test	7.5
phantom stock	
primary insurance amount (PIA)	19.12
private letter rulings	2.10
profit-sharing plans	3.15
prohibited-transaction exemptions	12.17
prohibited transactions	12.15
projected benefit	8.4
proposed regulations	2.9
provisional income	19.20
prudent-fiduciary rule	12.8

Q

qualified default investment alternative	12.14

qualified domestic relations orders
    (QDROs)   13.17
qualified joint-and-survivor annuity
    (QJSA)   10.3
qualified plans   1.4
qualified preretirement survivor annuity
    (QPSA)   10.3
quarters of coverage   19.8

R

rabbi trust   15.26
ratio test   7.6
reallocated forfeitures   9.9
recharacterization   17.5
replacement-ratio method   21.10
required beginning date   24.30
restricted stock plan
revenue rulings   2.9
reverse mortgage   23.8
risk tolerance level   21.21
rollover   17.10, 24.20
Roth 401(k)   5.19
Roth IRA   17.3

S

safe savings rate   22.8
salary reduction plan   15.16
sale-leaseback arrangement   23.8
savings incentive match plan for
    employees (SIMPLE)   6.7
Sec. 72(t) penalty tax   24.4
Sec. 162 plan   15.35
Sec. 401(a)(4) nondiscrimination rule   8.2
Sec. 457 deferred compensation plans   15.32
Sec. 501(c)(3) organizations   6.12
SECA tax   19.6
secular trust   15.28
self-directed IRAs   18.3
separate account GIC   11.25
separate line of business   7.8
SEPs   7.22, 7.23
sequence of returns risk   22.13
simplified employee pension   6.2
single-premium group annuity contract
    (SPAC)   14.10
skilled-nursing care   23.24
social assistance   20.17
Social Security   19.2
split-funded plan   11.11
spousal IRAs   17.4
stable value funds   11.24
stand-alone plan   5.25
standard termination   14.8
stock appreciation right (SAR)
stock bonus plans   5.27
subsidized benefits   25.11
substantially equal periodic
    payments   24.4
summary of material modification
    (SMM)   13.12
summary of the annual report (SAR)   13.12
summary plan description (SPD)   13.6
superannuated employees   1.17
supplemental executive retirement plan
    (SERP)   15.17
Supplemental Security Income

(SSI)	20.17
surety bond	15.29
synthetic GIC	11.25
systematic withdrawal approach	22.17

T

Table 2001	10.6
target-benefit pension plan	4.19
taxable wage base	19.6
tax-advantaged retirement	1.4
tax-advantaged retirement plans	1.4
temporary regulations	2.9
terminal funding approach	11.3
third-party administrators (TPAs)	2.15
time-based segmentation approach	22.20
top-hat exemption	15.29
trustee-to-trustee transfers	17.11

U

unit-benefit formula	4.3

V

vesting schedules	9.6
voluntary after-tax employee contribution	8.22